Net income $'000	Return on Invested capital before tax %	Return on Shareholders equity after tax %	Five year profit growth %	Employees	Foreign ownership %	Major shareholders
880,764	73.4%	54.4%	256.8%	45,391	100	General Motors Corp., Detroit
376,903	11.5%	8.8%	−25.8%	120,000		Power Corp. of Canada 11%
299,500	49.3%	33.8%	14875.0%	35,600	90	Ford Motor Co., Dearborn, Mich.
940,300	17.0%	15.1%	117.4%	108,100		Wide distribution
533,000	34.2%	12.1%	13.2%	14,331	70	Exxon Corp., New York
88,800	14.8%	12.3%	34.7%	56,000		Wittington Investments Ltd. 57%
279,677	10.8%	7.6%	−43.9%	70,000	44	Wide distribution
176,600	63.1%	79.3%	n.a.	12,448	100	Chrysler Corp., Detroit
423,000	36.2%	21.6%	60.2%	3,635	90	Texaco Inc. 68%, Texaco International 22%, New York
158,000	12.7%	6.4%	−39.0%	7,136	72	Shell Investments Ltd., Netherlands/Britain
308,000	19.0%	12.6%	6.9%	8,982	70	Chevron Corp., San Francisco 60%
n.a.	n.a.	n.a.	n.a.	532		Federal government 100%
214,951	11.4%	6.7%	26.7%	66,234		Federal government 100%
251,532	7.9%	5.9%	99.6%	6,697		Federal government 100%
(107,434)	2.9%	n.a.	n.a.	42,500		Woodbridge Co. 73%
40,335	25.4%	20.5%	105.4%	11,157		Caisse de dépôt 26%, Sobeys Stores 17%
265,900	15.7%	16.8%	182.9%	1,915		Bell Canada Enterprises Inc. 47%
575,000	6.7%	15.1%	114.6%	29,613		Ontario government 100%
105,200	7.4%	7.9%	96.3%	24	16	Brascan Holdings Corp. 44%
81,100	8.7%	6.9%	n.a.	18,000		Federal government 47%
301,000	10.2%	4.6%	−59.7%	18,560		Quebec government 100%
155,268	13.1%	10.5%	33.4%	7,800		Wide distribution
229,000	16.3%	12.7%	n.a.	10,300	12	Interprovincial Pipe Lines Ltd. 16%, Olympia & York et al. 11%
66,219	16.1%	10.0%	20.5%	23,441	100	Safeway Stores Inc., Oakland, Ca.
15,021	9.4%	3.7%	−44.1%	31,000		Steinberg family trusts 97%
37,316	9.8%	6.0%	−44.9%	55,098	61	Sears, Roebuck & Co., Chicago, Royal Trust 15% (in escrow)
(4,451)	4.6%	n.a.	n.a.	50,000		Brascade Resources 37%, Kerr Addison 10%
25,275	13.2%	8.7%	20.9%	13,500		McCain Foods Ltd. 12%
316,000	51.6%	32.0%	n.a.	11,725	100	IBM Corp., Armonk N Y.
169,201	n.a.	n.a.	58.8%	22,500		Thomson family 74%
14,541	9.5%	4.0%	−58.3%	4,500	44	Compagnie française des pétroles, France
36,179	24.7%	17.2%	258.0%	6,998		Wolfe family 100%
162,799	25.0%	16.4%	38.7%	26,256	14	Wide distribution
499,240	n.a.	n.a.	154.5%	n.a.		Bronfman family trusts 41%
21,193	5.9%	4.2%	−61.7%	21,824		Federal government 100%
66,015	22.1%	22.9%	80.0%	4,027		Co-op members
(196,800)	8.9%	n.a.	n.a.	6,000		Dome Mines Ltd. 24%
48,280	4.3%	3.1%	−69.2%	20,612		Wide distribution
5,682	0.3%	0.3%	n.a.	61,486		Federal government 100%
27,053	7.6%	6.1%	12.4%	n.a.		Argus Corp. & associated companies 45%
194,172	24.8%	21.4%	244.2%	18,292	40	BAT Industries, Britain
72,326	10.0%	8.2%	−52.6%	14,793		Olympia & York Developments 93%
66,729	19.9%	16.0%	197.0%	10,500		Brascan Ltd. 37%, Caisse de dépôt 11%
19,300	6.2%	2.0%	87.5%	14,994		Noranda Group 48%
28,004	14.5%	4.8%	−23.3%	6,266		Billes family 61%
89,500	13.2%	12.8%	−7.7%	15,408		Dofor Inc. 30%, Caisse de dépôt 15%
2,770	9.4%	3.7%	n.a.	3,000		D.E. Gillespie 50%
180,605	17.5%	16.6%	31.9%	13,200		Ivaco Inc. 12%
131,800	10.7%	11.8%	4.2%	18,000	45	Société générale de Belgique 15%
9,370	6.7%	2.4%	n.a.	20,262	82	Wide distribution

[4] All figures converted from British pounds.

[5] After a corporate reorganization in July, 1984, shares in Dominion Stores were exchanged on a share-for-share basis for shares in Argcen Holdings, a new company.

n.a. Not available/not applicable.

AN INTRODUCTION TO
CANADIAN BUSINESS
FIFTH EDITION

AN INTRODUCTION TO
CANADIAN BUSINESS

FIFTH EDITION

Maurice Archer
Professor of Business Management
Ryerson Polytechnical Institute

McGRAW-HILL RYERSON LIMITED

Toronto Montreal New York Auckland Bogotá Cairo Guatemala
Hamburg Lisbon London Madrid Mexico New Delhi
Panama Paris San Juan São Paulo Singapore Sydney Tokyo

AN INTRODUCTION TO CANADIAN BUSINESS
FIFTH EDITION

First edition copyright © McGraw-Hill Company of Canada Limited, 1967. All rights reserved.
Copyright © McGraw-Hill Ryerson Limited, 1986, 1982, 1978, 1974. All rights reserved. No part of this publication may be reproduced, stored in a retrieval system, or transmitted, in any form or by any means, electronic, mechancial, photocopying, recording, or otherwise, without prior written permission of McGraw-Hill Ryerson Limited.

ISBN 0-07-549046-3

5 6 7 8 9 0 JD 5 4 3 2 1 0

Printed and bound in Canada by John Deyell Company

Care has been taken to trace ownership of copyright material contained in this text. The publishers will gladly take any information that will enable them to rectify any reference or credit in subsequent editions.

Canadian Cataloguing in Publication Data

Archer, Maurice, date-
  An introduction to Canadian business

Includes index.
ISBN 0-07-549046-3

1. Industrial management - Canada.   2. Business.
I. Title.

HF5351.A8 1986   658.4′00971   C85-099826-3

To
my
wife,
Odette

SUMMARY OF CONTENTS

PART A: CANADA'S BUSINESS SYSTEM — 1

Chapter 1: Canada's Mixed Economy — 2
1.1 Private Enterprise — 3
1.2 Social Responsibilities of the Business Firm — 18
1.3 Government Intervention — 36

PART B: FORMS OF BUSINESS OWNERSHIP — 49

Chapter 2: Sole Proprietorship and Partnership — 50
2.1 The Sole Proprietorship — 51
2.2 The Partnership — 64

Chapter 3: The Business Corporation — 81
3.1 The Corporate Form of Ownership — 82
3.2 Advantages and Disadvantages of Incorporation — 97
3.3 Big Business — 102
3.4 The Co-operative — 114

PART C: BUSINESS MANAGEMENT — 121

Chapter 4: The Nature of Business Management — 122
4.1 Levels and Functions of Management — 123
4.2 Planning — 135
4.3 Directing — 145
4.4 Controlling — 162
4.5 Staffing — 166

Chapter 5: Business Organization — 172
5.1 Designing an Effective Organization — 173
5.2 Basic Types of Organization — 185
5.3 Centralization and Decentralization of Authority — 192

Chapter 6: Management Theories — 205
6.1 The Scientific Approach to Management — 206
6.2 The Human Relations and the Systems Approaches to Management — 218

PART D: PRODUCTION MANAGEMENT — 237

Chapter 7: Modern Manufacturing — 238
7.1 Types of Manufacturing — 239
7.2 Plant Layout, Equipment, and Buildings — 252
7.3 Methods Analysis and Time Study — 266

Chapter 8: Production, Inventory, and Quality Control — 279
8.1 Product Planning and Development — 280
8.2 Production Control — 286
8.3 Inventory Control and Purchasing — 293
8.4 Quality Control — 304

PART E: MARKETING MANAGEMENT — 317

Chapter 9: Marketing and the Marketing Department — 318
9.1 Functions of Marketing — 319
9.2 The Marketing Department — 332
9.3 Types of Markets — 349

Chapter 10: Distribution — 358
10.1 Types of Goods and Services — 359
10.2 Distribution Channels — 367
10.3 Wholesaling — 386
10.4 Retailing — 392

Chapter 11: Sales Promotion — 412
11.1 The Promotional Program — 413
11.2 Advertising — 417
11.3 Selling — 430

PART F: FINANCIAL MANAGEMENT — 443

Chapter 12: Financial Planning and Control — 444
12.1 Budgeting — 445
12.2 Evaluating Profitability — 454

Chapter 13: Financial Solvency — 473
13.1 Cash Management — 474
13.2 Short-Term Financing — 483
13.3 Medium-Term Financing — 494
13.4 Business Insurance — 499

Chapter 14: Long-Term Financing — 508
14.1 Equity, Debt, and Financial Leverage — 509
14.2 Equity Financing — 518
14.3 Debt Financing — 527
14.4 The Securities Market — 535

PART G: HUMAN RESOURCES — 551

Chapter 15: Personnel Management — 552
15.1　Functions of Personnel Management — 553
15.2　Wage and Salary Administration — 573

Chapter 16: Labour Relations — 586
16.1　Labour Unions and Collective Bargaining — 587
16.2　Labour Legislation — 604

PART H: SMALL BUSINESS — 611

Chapter 17: Starting a Small Business — 612
17.1　Basic Requirements — 613
17.2　Preparing a Business Plan — 628
17.3　Government Assistance — 631
17.4　Basic Business Records — 634

PART I: INTERNATIONAL BUSINESS — 639

Chapter 18: Exporting — 640
18.1　Canada's International Trade — 641
18.2　Export Marketing — 653
18.3　Export Financing — 664

PART J: ELECTRONIC DATA PROCESSING — 669

Chapter 19: Computers in Business — 670
19.1　Computer Hardware — 671
19.1　Business Software — 684

TABLE OF CONTENTS

Preface xxiii
Plan of the Book xxvii

PART A: CANADA'S BUSINESS SYSTEM 1

Chapter 1: Canada's Mixed Economy 2

Unit 1.1: Private Enterprise 3
Private Enterprise Defined 3 Private Property 4 Pursuit of Profit 4 Competition 5 Right to Employ Productive Resources 8 Right to Choose One's Job 8 Consumer's Freedom of Choice 10
Reading: From Wrecks to Riches 12

Unit 1.2: Social Reponsibilities of the Business Firm 18
Business Awareness of Social Responsibilities 18 Responsibilities Towards Consumers 19 Responsibilities Towards Employees 22 Responsibilities Towards The Community 28 Business Ethics 30 Purpose and Use of Case Problems 32
Case Problems: Motor Specialty Manufacturers (Ont.) Ltd. 33 Snow White Ltd. 34 Redirack Industries Limited 34 Landing Rights 35 S.S. Britanis 36

Unit 1.3: Government Intervention 36
Historical Background 36 Government Regulation 37 Consumer Protection 37 Employee Protection 40 Community Protection 41 Shareholder Protection 41 Government Economic Policies 42
Case Problems: Cooper Metal Co. Ltd. 45 Complaints About a New Car 46 Scherbluk Manufacturing Industries Ltd. 47

PART B: FORMS OF BUSINESS OWNERSHIP 49

Chapter 2: Sole Proprietorship and Partnership 50

Unit 2.1: The Sole Proprietorship 51
Sole Proprietorship Defined 51 Advantages of the Sole Proprietorship 51 Disadvantages of the Sole Proprietorship 53

Case Problem: Vetch Office Furniture and Supplies 57
Reading: Newfoundland's Helicopter King 58

Unit 2.2: The Partnership —— 64
Partnership Defined 64 Formation of a Partnership 64 General versus Limited Partnership 64 Types of Partners 64 Eligibility 65 Partnership Name 65 Registration 65 Written Agreement 68 Settlement of Disputes 68 Dissolution of a Partnership 69 Advantages of a Partnership 71 Disadvantages of a Partnership 72
Case Problems: The Toy Shop 76 Alford and Wells, TV Repairs 76 Bolton's Photo Studio 77
Reading: Women: The Best Entrepreneurs 78

Chapter 3: The Business Corporation —— 81

Unit 3.1: The Corporate Form of Ownership —— 82
Business Corporation Defined 82 Public versus Private Business Corporations 82 Provincial versus Federal Business Corporations 82 Provincial Incorporation 82 Shareholders and their Rights 84 The Directors 85 Divorce between Ownership and Management 87 Auditing 88
Case Problem: Whitby Chemicals Inc. 90
Reading: The Aesthetic Entrepreneur 90

Unit 3.2: Advantages and Disadvantages of Incorporation —— 97
Advantages 97 Disadvantages 99
Case Problem: John Pieters, Builder 101

Unit 3.3: Big Business —— 102
Reasons for Growth of Big Business 102 Mergers, Takeovers and Conglomerates 104 Multinational Corporations 104 Cartels, Gentlemen's Agreements and Trusts 105
Readings: Swallowed Alive 107 Fast Footwork Wins Big Bouts for Jimmy Pattison 111

Unit 3.4: The Co-operative —— 114
Co-operative Defined 114 Types of Co-operatives 114 Characteristics 115 Advantages 115 Disadvantages 115
Case Problem: Hastings Lodge 116
Reading: Supermarket Socialism 117

PART C: BUSINESS MANAGEMENT —— 121

Chapter 4: The Nature of Business Management —— 122

Unit 4.1: Levels and Functions of Management —— 123
Business Management Defined 123 Levels of Management 124 Basic Functions

of Management 125 Managerial Method 125 Management Specialization 126 Non-Managerial Tasks 126 Entrepreneurship versus Administration 126
Case Problem: Jones Furniture Co. Ltd. (1) 128
Reading: Lord of the Rinks 130

Unit 4.2: Planning — 135
Planning Defined 135 Planning Process 135 Company Objectives 135 Sales Forecasting 137 Company Plans 138 Considerations in Planning 140
Case Problem: Fairview Stores Ltd. 142
Reading: Popcorn Explosion: Home Poppers Open Up the Market 143

Unit 4.3: Directing — 145
Principles of Direction 145 Board of Directors 146 Motivating 146 Discipline 147 Leadership 148 Co-ordinating 150
Case Problem: George Sharpe & Company Ltd. 151
Reading: The Rewards of Running Your Own Show 154

Unit 4.4: Controlling — 162
Controlling Defined 162 Standards 162 Financial Ratios 162 Inventory Turnover Ratios 163 Deviations 164

Unit 4.5: Staffing — 166
Recruitment of Managers 166 The Recruitment Program 166 The Management Trainee 167 Training of Managers 168 Management Training Techniques 168 Promotion 169 Transfers 170 Appraisal of Managers 170

Chapter 5: Business Organization — 172

Unit 5.1: Designing an Effective Organization — 173
Organizing Defined 173 Organization in the Small Business 173 Organization in the Medium or Large Business 175 Departmentation 175 Organization Charts and Manuals 176 Informal Organization 178 Organizational Design 178 Principles of Effective Organization 179
Case Problems: Miller Drugs Inc. 182 Campbell Stores Ltd. 183

Unit 5.2: Basic Types of Organization — 185
Line Organization 185 Line-and-Staff Organization 186 Functional Authority 188 Use of Committees 188 Matrix Organization 189 Project Management 190

Unit 5.3: Centralization and Decentralization of Authority — 192
Authority, Responsibility, and Accountability 192 Delegation of Authority 193 Centralized Management 193 Decentralized Management 194 Compromise between Centralization and Decentralization 196

Case Problem: Pohlmann Equipment Co. Ltd. 197
Reading: King of the Real Estate Jungle 199

Chapter 6: Management Theories — 205

Unit 6.1: The Scientific Approach to Management — 206
Management Studies 206 Classical Origins of Management Thought 206 Scientific Management 208 Management by Objectives 210
Reading: The Iron Will of Harry Steele 211

Unit 6.2: The Human Relations and the Systems Approaches to Management — 218
The Human Relations Approach 218 Elton Mayo 219 Maslow's Hierarchy of Needs 220 Socially Acquired Motives 220 Behaviour of Small Work Groups 221 Behaviour of Supervisors 222 Inter-Group Behaviour 222 Theory X and Theory Y 223 The Systems Approach 223
Reading: The Japanese Fix 225

PART D: PRODUCTION MANAGEMENT — 237

Chapter 7: Modern Manufacturing — 238

Unit 7.1: Types of Manufacturing — 239
Manufacturing Defined 239 Primary, Secondary and Tertiary Industries 239 Manufacturing Processes 239 Size of Production Run 240 Job-Order versus Standard Manufacturing 243 Characteristics of Modern Manufacturing 243 Manufacturing Productivity 245
Case Problem: Bentley Shoes Ltd. 248
Reading: David Confronts Goliath in Attempt to Win Piece of Glass Fibre Market 249

Unit 7.2: Plant Layout, Equipment, and Buildings — 252
Plant Layout Defined 252 Purposes of Plant Layout 252 Types of Plant Layout 252 Factors Influencing Plant Layout 256 Plant Layout Aids 258 Plant Equipment 259 Plant Buildings 260
Reading: Everything's Coming Up Blueberries 262

Unit 7.3: Methods Analysis and Time Study — 266
Methods Analysis 267 Process Analysis 267 Motion Study 269 Principles of Motion-Economy 272 Time Study 273 Purposes of Time Study 273 Equipment 273 Time Study Procedure 273 Production Studies 274 Predetermined Time Standards 275
Case Problems: Swansea Steel Products Ltd. 277 Brock Machine Works Ltd. 277

Chapter 8: Production, Inventory, and Quality Control — 279

Unit 8.1: Product Planning and Development — 280
Product Policy 280 Product Planning and Development 280 Product Design 283
Case Problem: Mallory Soups 284
Reading: Turfed Out? Why Not Try Nelson Adam's Fast-Growing Product: Instant Grass 285

Unit 8.2: Production Control — 286
Nature and Purpose of Production Control 286 Overall Production Control 286 Detailed Production Control 287 Organization for Production Control 288 Variations in Production Control Methods 288 Production Control Procedure in a Large Job-Order Firm 289 Production Control in a Large Standard-Manufacturing Firm 290
Case Problem: Anderson Lumber Co. Ltd. 292

Unit 8.3: Inventory Control and Purchasing — 293
Inventory Control Defined 293 How Much Stock to Carry? 293 ABC Inventory Classification 295 Industrial Purchasing 296 Purchasing Department 296 Centralized versus Decentralized Purchasing 296 Purchasing Policies 297 Purchasing Procedure 298
Case Problems: King Electric Ltd. 300 Save-More Ltd. 302 Finch Commercial Stationery Ltd. 304

Unit 8.4: Quality Control — 304
Quality Standards 305 Quality Circles 306 Inspection Department 306 Types of Inspection 307
Readings: There's Money in Boats 308 Why John Voortman's Muffins Sell Like Hot Cakes in the U.S. 315

PART E: MARKETING MANAGEMENT — 317

Chapter 9: Marketing and the Marketing Department — 318

Unit 9.1: Functions of Marketing — 319
Marketing Defined 319 The Marketing Concept 319 The Marketing Mix 319 The 4Ps of Marketing 319 Product 320 Price 322 Place 324 Promotion 325 The Need for Marketing 326
Case Problem: Weeks Farms Ltd. 329
Readings: Diners Cheer as a New PEI Industry Flexes Its Mussels 329 Cartons, Bubbles and Boxes: Just Promotional Tools? 331

Unit 9.2: The Marketing Department — 332
Organization 333 Sales Forecasts 335 Controllable and Uncontrollable Factors

336 Marketing Plan 337 Product Life-Cycle 338 Implementation 339 Control and Analysis 339
Case Problems: McCowan Bakeries 341 XYZ Consumer Products Ltd. 342 Long-Life Orange Juice 343 Dunn Products Inc. 343
Reading: Love for Sale 344

Unit 9.3: Types of Markets — 349
Domestic Consumer Market 349 Industrial User Market 352 Government Market 353 Export Market 353
Case Problem: Economy Diaper Service Ltd. 355

Chapter 10: Distribution — 358

Unit 10.1: Types of Goods and Services — 359
Consumer Goods 359 Industrial Goods 361
Reading: The Business That Beer Built 363

Unit 10.2: Distribution Channels — 367
Channel of Distribution Defined 367 Types of Marketing Intermediaries 368 Distribution to Domestic Consumers 368 Marketing Boards 370 Distribution to Industrial Users 371 Distribution to Government Users 371 Distribution to Export Markets 372
Case Problem: The Spee-Dee Fire Extinguisher 374
Reading: The Hidden Dollars in Distribution 375

Unit 10.3: Wholesaling — 386
Wholesaling Defined 386 Merchant Wholesalers 386 Marketing Agents 387 Why Use a Wholesaler? 388 Marketing Co-operatives 389
Case Problem: W. Harper & Son Ltd. 391

Unit 10.4: Retailing — 392
Retailing Defined 392 Types of Retailers 392 Retail Ownership 395 Services Provided by Retailers 396 Suggested Retail Prices 397 High Entry and Dropout Rates 397 Retailing Trends 398
Case Problems: Smith's Meat Market 400 George Andrews Ltd. 402
Readings: Crisis of Identity 405 The Deli Way 408 Pizza with Pizzazz 409

Chapter 11: Sales Promotion — 412

Unit 11.1: The Promotional Program — 413
Sales Promotion Defined 413 Promotional Blend 413 Pull and Push Promotional Strategies 414 Other Sales Promotion Activities 414
Project: Tropical Products Ltd. 417

Unit 11.2: Advertising — 417
Advertising Defined 417 Kinds of Advertising 417 Purposes of Advertising 418 Advertising Media 419 Choice of Advertising Media 422 Circulation 422 Preparing Advertisements 422 The Advertising Agency 423 The Advertising Department 425
Case Problem: Mercedes-Benz 426

Unit 11.3: Selling — 430
Three Main Types of Selling Activity 430 The Selling Process 430 Types of Selling Jobs 432 The Sales Manager 433
Case Problems: Jane Appleby 437 Cliff Reed Real Estate Ltd. 440

PART F: FINANCIAL MANAGEMENT — 443

Chapter 12: Financial Planning and Control — 444

Unit 12.1: Budgeting — 445
Tasks of Financial Management 445 The Finance Department 445 The Operating Budget 447 The Capital Budget 449 Zero-base Budgeting 450
Reading: Zero Base Budgeting Technique Seems Certain to Spread 451

Unit 12.2: Evaluating Profitability — 454
The Income Statement 454 Breakeven Analysis 454 Return on Capital 458 Payback Period 459 Non-Monetary Factors 460
Case Problems: Ace Record Company Inc. 460 Blake Uniform Rental Company Ltd. (1) 461
Reading: Attic's At the Top 463

Chapter 13: Financial Solvency — 473

Unit 13.1: Cash Management — 474
Importance of Monitoring the Cash Flow 474 The Bank Statement 474 The Cash-Flow Statement 474 The Cash Budget 475 Liquidity Ratios 477
Case Problems: ABC Enterprises Inc. 478 Blake Uniform Rental Company Ltd. (2) 478 William Spencer Ltd. 479
Reading: Entrepreneur Blames Investment Community for Company's Misfortune 480

Unit 13.2 Short-Term Financing — 483
Working Capital versus Fixed Capital 483 Working Capital Needs 483 Trade Credit 484 Bank Loans 488 Finance Company Loans 490 Factor Companies 491 Short-Term Money Market 491 Loans from Directors, Shareholders and Employees 491
Case Problem: J. Fox & Son Ltd. 493

Unit 13.3: Medium-Term Financing _____ **494**
Medium-Term Financing Defined 494 The Chartered Banks 494 Other Private Sources 494 Small Businesses Loans Act 495 Federal Business Development Bank (FBDB) 496 Collateral for Medium-Term Loans 496

Unit 13.4: Business Insurance _____ **499**
Types of Business Risk 499 The Nature of Insurance 499 Principal Elements of an Insurance Policy 500 Fire Insurance 500 Marine Insurance 502 Theft Insurance 502 Fidelity Bonding 503 Surety Bonding 503 Credit Insurance 503 Liability Insurance 503 Key-Personnel Insurance 503 Partnership Insurance 504 Business Interruption Insurance 504 Business Automobile Insurance 505

Chapter 14: Long-Term Financing _____ 508

Unit 14.1: Equity, Debt, and Financial Leverage _____ **509**
Equity versus Debt Financing 509 Equity-Debt Ratio 509 The Balance Sheet 510 Financial Leverage 512 Effects of the Form of Ownership 513 The Investment Dealer 513 Sources of Long-Term Funds 514 Reducing Fixed Capital Needs 514
Case Problems: Excelsior Products Ltd. 515 Maskow Enterprises Ltd. 517

Unit 14.2: Equity Financing _____ **518**
Capital Stock 518 Share Values 518 Common Shares 520 Preferred Shares 521 Prospectus 522 Retained Earnings 523 Depreciation Allowances 523
Case Problem: Mitchell Electrical Industries Limited 525

Unit 14.3: Debt Financing _____ **527**
Bonds Defined 527 Secured Bonds 528 Unsecured Bonds 530 Special Features in Bonds 530
Case Problem: Brown Manufacturing Industries Limited 532

Unit 14.4: The Securities Market _____ **535**
Securities Defined 535 Trading of Securities 535 Stock Exchanges 535 Stock Trading Process 538 Stockbroker's Office 539 Over-the-Counter Market 540 Securities Legislation 541 Buying Stocks and Bonds 541
Reading: The Little Pizza That Could 544

PART G: HUMAN RESOURCES _____ 551

Chapter 15: Personnel Management _____ 552

Unit 15.1: Functions of Personnel Management _____ **553**
Personnel Policy 553 Employment Planning 554 Recruitment 555 Induction, Training, and Follow-Up 557 Transfers, Promotions, Layoffs, and Dismissals 559 Personnel Services 563 Health and Safety 564 Employee Records and Statistics 564 The Personnel Manager 564 The Personnel Department 565

Case Problems: Jones Furniture Co. Ltd. (2) 567 The Security Finance Company Ltd. 568
Reading: Our Human Resources Plan Works 571

Unit 15.2: Wage and Salary Administration 573
Wages and Salaries Defined 573 Reasons for Differences in Pay 573 Purpose of a Firm's Pay Policy 574 Job Evaluation 574 Different Methods of Employee Remuneration 575 Different Types of Fringe Benefits 577
Reading: Distinctions Between Capitalist, Worker Blurred at Trent Rubber Services 581

Chapter 16: Labour Relations 586

Unit 16.1: Labour Unions and Collective Bargaining 587
Labour Relations Statutes 587 Labour Union Defined 588 Types of Labour Unions 588 Union Membership 589 Aims of Labour Unions 589 Why Workers Join a Labour Union 590 Organization of a Labour Union 591 Labour Councils 593 Labour Federations 593 Canadian Labour Congress 594 Certification of a Labour Union 594 Collective Bargaining 594 Conciliation 595 Union Finances 595 Union Security 595 Grievances 595 Arbitration 597 Labour's Methods 597 Management's Methods 599
Case Problem: Frost Electrical Co. Ltd. 601

Unit 16.2 Labour Legislation 604
Common Law Duties of the Employer 604 Common Law Duties of the Employee 604 Labour Jurisdiction 604 Canada Labour Code 605 Industries under Federal Contract 606 Unemployment Insurance 606 Canada Pension Plan 607 Provincial Labour Legislation 607

PART H: SMALL BUSINESS 611

Chapter 17: Starting a Small Business 612

Unit 17.1: Basic Requirements 613
Importance of Small Business 613 Pros and Cons of Small Business Ownership 613 Small Business Opportunities 614 Business Knowledge 615 A New Business Versus an Established One 616 Franchises 617 Guidelines for Small Business Success 618 Canadian Federation of Independent Business (CFIB) 619
Case Problems: Jack Stoddart 621 The Log Cabin 621
Project: Choosing a Business 623
Readings: Where There's Paint There's Profit for Students—and College Pro 623 Franchises Attracting Growing Numbers of Would-be Private Businessmen 625

Unit 17.2: Preparing a Business Plan — 628
Essentials of a Business Plan 628 Personal Background 628 Proposed Business 628 Physical Facilities 628 Profitability 628 Cash-Flow Forecast 629 Borrowing Proposal 629 Miscellaneous Documents 630

Unit 17.3: Government Assistance — 631
Federal Business Development Bank (FBDB) 631 Small Businesses Loans Act (SBLA) 632 Enterprise Development Program (EDP) 632 Income Tax Relief 632 Other Federal Government Assistance 633 Provincial Ministries 633 Provincial Development Corporations 633

Unit 17.4: Basic Business Records — 634
Balance Sheet 634 Income Statement 635 Ledger Accounts 635 Debit and Credit Entries 635 Journals 636 Statement Analysis 637

PART I: INTERNATIONAL BUSINESS — 639

Chapter 18: Exporting — 640

Unit 18.1: Canada's International Trade — 641
Why Firms Export 641 Reasons for Predominance of U.S. Market 641 Principal Exports 642 Principal Export Markets 642 Current Account Deficit 643 Canada's Need for More Exports 643 Principal Imports 645 Principal Foreign Suppliers 645 Pattern of Goods Traded 646
Readings: Aloro Foods 648 Electronics Put Small Nova Scotia Town on the Map 651

Unit 18.2: Export Marketing — 653
Direct versus Indirect Exporting 653 Export Organization 653 Export Research 653 Export Pricing 655 Export Barriers 655 Export Promotion 656 Selling 657
Case Problem: T. Jones & Co. Ltd. 659
Reading: Champion Launches Sales Offensive 662

Unit 18.3: Export Financing — 664
Methods of Payment 664 Open Account 664 Documentary Drafts 664 Discounting 665 Letters of Credit 665 EDC Insurance 667

PART J: ELECTRONIC DATA PROCESSING — 669

Chapter 19: Computers in Business — 670

Unit 19.1: Computer Hardware — 671
Characteristics of a Computer System 671 Basic Types of Computers 671 Benefits of Computerization 672 Computer Hardware 672 Computer Operation 673 Central Processing Unit 674 Keyboard with Video Display 675

Input Devices 675 Output Devices 680 Auxiliary Storage 682 Electronic Workstations 682

Unit 19.2: Business Software _____ **684**
Computer Programs 684 Program Preparation 684 Networks 685 Business Applications 685
Case Problem: Rayburn Industries Ltd. 689

Index of Case Problems _____ **691**
Index of Readings _____ **692**
Subject Index _____ **693**

PREFACE

CANADIAN BUSINESS is a broad term that refers to the many different types of enterprises operating in our country. These vary according to: (a) activity: manufacturing, mining, agriculture, services, export, import, etc; (b) size: small, medium, or large; (c) ownership: private or public; Canadian or foreign; independent, franchise, or corporate chain; and (d) location: urban, suburban, or rural; national or multinational.

In their many different forms, these businesses all help contribute, with varying efficiency and success, to the production and marketing of the goods and services that we tend to take for granted as part of our standard of living.

Nowadays, however, as firm after firm succumbs to foreign competition, and unemployment remains well over the one million mark, Canadians must strive more than ever to revitalize their industries. This is particularly necessary in the manufacturing sector—so that we create more jobs and income, rather than relying so heavily on the exports of foodstuffs, minerals, energy, and other raw and semi-processed materials to pay for the foreign goods and services that we buy.

Blessed with abundant natural resources, an educated population, and the richest market in the world on our doorstep, we have only ourselves to blame if, as a people, we waste our economic opportunities and continue to slip down the ranks of wealthy nations.

It is an undeniable fact that business makes possible all the finer things of life, as well as the bread and butter of existence. Without its wealth-creating activities, we would, for example, have to be a recipient rather than a donor of foreign aid. And our schools and hospitals, as another example, would be in much worse financial shape than they already are.

Business, as well as being vitally important to our livelihood and therefore well worthy of our study, offers an exciting, mentally and financially rewarding challenge to those who wish to make it their career. And this introductory study of Canadian business and its management points out the different paths that can be followed in such a pursuit and provides many examples of Canadians who have already found creative and financial success, as well as social prestige, in the Canadian business world.

One basic purpose of this book, now in it fifth edition, is to present the student with a clear but reasonably detailed picture of the environment, ownership, management, and operations of modern Canadian business. Another basic purpose, assisted by the use of many short case problems and selected readings about actual Canadian businesses, is to present the material in a manner that is stimulating as well as informative. Organized into self-contained units, within each of nineteen chapters, the book permits great flexibility in course design, either on a one-or two-semester basis, with a self-chosen blend of text material, review questions, case problems, and readings.

The plan of the book (illustrated by the chart at the end of this Preface) is to examine, first of all, Canada's business system and the basic types of business firms that operate within it. Next, we consider the levels and functions of business management, including basic management theories. Then we look at each of the three broad functional areas of business: production, marketing, and finance. Although each area is equally vital to the success of an enterprise, we examine production first. This is to stress that, however astute the marketing plan, only a well-designed and well-made product, offered at reasonable cost, can enable a firm to capture and keep a substantial market share. Of course, market research will be necessary in the early stages of product planning and development. After the operating functions, we consider personnel management and labour relations.

A new feature in this edition is the inclusion, at the end of the book, of three chapters entitled, respectively: Starting a Small Business, Exporting, and Computers in Business.

Each chapter begins with a list of Chapter Objectives and a Chapter Outline—the latter indicating the units into which the chapter is divided. Usually, each unit contains text material, explaining the topic and emphasizing the management principles and practices involved; Key Terms, to stress the business vocabulary covered in the text; Review Questions, to provoke thinking about the topics studied; Case Problems, to provide practice in critical analysis, problem-solving, decision-making, and co-operative effort; and Readings with Questions, to provide insight into the entrepreneurial mind and the business challenges that still abound in Canada.

For those who like facts and figures, there are in this fifth edition: 10 parts, 19 chapters, and 59 units. Scattered throughout, in reasonably logical sequence, are Case Problems and Readings. At the beginning of the book, there is a Summary of Contents, followed by a detailed Table of Contents. At the end of the book, there is an index of case problems; an index of readings; and a subject index.

My continued thanks to my colleagues in the School of Business Management at Ryerson, notably C. d'Arcy Dakin, Lee Maguire, Patrick Northey, George L. Parker, Joe Trubic, and Douglas Worrell for their steady advice and encouragement in trying to build a better book.

Maurice Archer

ACKNOWLEDGEMENTS

The cartoons in this book are the copyright of Mr. Trevor Hutchings and are reproduced with his permission.

The tables from The Financial Post 500 appearing on the inside covers and page 6 are used with the permission of *The Financial Post.*

PLAN OF THE BOOK

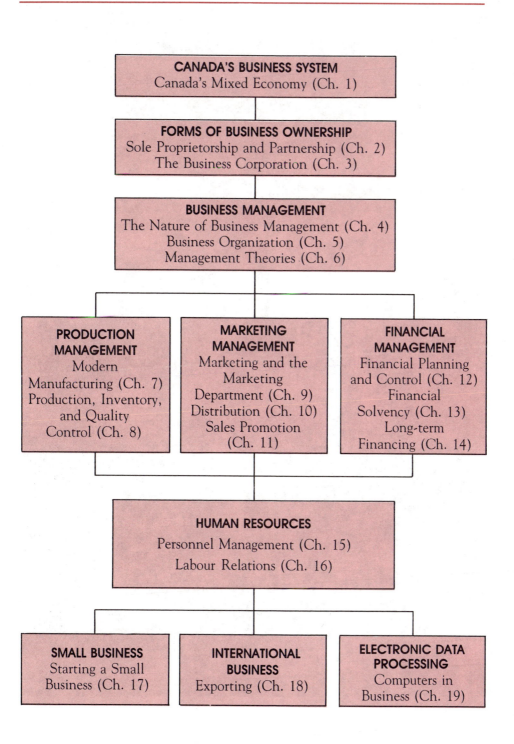

PART A
CANADA'S BUSINESS SYSTEM

CHAPTER 1
CANADA'S MIXED ECONOMY

CHAPTER OBJECTIVES

☐ To explain what is meant by private enterprise.

☐ To pinpoint the responsibilities that a private business firm has towards consumers, employees, and the community.

☐ To explain how and why our various levels of government intervene in the economy, mainly by statutes that restrict or encourage various types of business activity.

CHAPTER OUTLINE

1.1   Private Enterprise
1.2   Social Responsibilities of the Business Firm
1.3   Government Intervention

UNIT 1.1: PRIVATE ENTERPRISE

In Canada, most business activity is undertaken by private business firms. However, there are also many other business activities such as the supply of electricity and the provision of mail service that are carried on by government-owned enterprises. Because of the predominance of the private sector, we usually call our economic system one of *private enterprise*. Sometimes the terms *free enterprise, free market system*, and *capitalism* are also used.

The *private enterprise system* has a number of distinguishing characteristics, which include the individual's rights: (a) to own property; (b) to earn profit; (c) to compete in business; (d) as an employer, to hire labour and other productive resources; (e) as an employee, to choose one's job and negotiate the terms; and (f) as a consumer, to spend one's money as one sees fit.

Courtesy *Oakville Beaver*

Private Property

In Canada, a person's property rights are protected by common and statute law, and by the existence of an efficient police force and judiciary. Subject to payment of taxes, people are practically free, furthermore, to dispose of their property as they wish. Consequently, there is every incentive for a person to accumulate wealth.

For most people, the right to own property is an important incentive to work hard, improve knowledge and skills, to save money, and undertake business risks. This is because ownership of property (for example, a house, car, stocks, or bonds) can help provide a higher material standard of living and greater financial security, for the future as well as the present.

From the viewpoint of society as a whole, private ownership of property seems to have brought about a faster rate of economic growth and a higher material standard of living for everyone than in countries where property is owned mainly by the state.

The right to private ownership of property has been criticized on the grounds that it encourages a person's greed and selfishness and promotes economic and social inequality. However, there can be no doubt that the economic and social inequalities so characteristic of previous centuries are now greatly mitigated by progressive income taxation (which takes more from high- and middle-income earners than from low-income ones), by social security payments (which mainly benefit low-income families), and by other public welfare legislation.

Pursuit of Profit

Profit is the amount by which a business firm's revenue exceeds its expenses. It is the reward that the owners of a business firm receive for risking their capital in, and applying their efforts and ingenuity to, such an enterprise. Unless the opportunity to earn profit exists, few persons would be willing to invest their money in the ownership of a business. For it is much easier to incur a loss (an excess of expenses over revenue) than to earn a profit.

It is often argued that a business firm should earn only a "reasonable," or "fair" amount of profit. Certainly, a business firm should be prevented by government action from exploiting a monopoly situation—one in which a firm can charge what it likes because there are no other suppliers to whom the public can turn. However, a fair rate of return must obviously be greater than the current rate of interest on long-term loans. If this were not so, the rate of profit would not compensate for the risk involved. It must also be remembered that the profits of one year must be sufficient to offset the losses of another—for businesses have bad years as well as good. Also the profits on one of a firm's products must often help offset the losses on another. Undoubtedly, the public is not willing to subsidize a business if it makes a loss. Many large, stable business firms consider that a return (before income tax) of about 10 to 15 per cent per annum on the money invested in the business by the owners is a satisfactory rate. Other, riskier business enterprises aim for a return of 20 per cent or more, particularly if the cost of borrowing funds is high. The actual rates of return vary greatly, of course, from firm to firm, from industry to industry, and from year to year. The top 50 firms, in profitability, are shown in the table on page 6.

If the profit motive did not exist, business investment and operations would have to be undertaken or directed by the government. This is what occurs in the communist countries. The accompanying centralized government control, with its emphasis on production quantity rather than quality, and its apparent disregard of consumers' wishes, has not, however, brought good results. In other countries, certain key industries such as coal, steel, and railways, have been taken over by the government; profit has, however, been retained as a yardstick for measuring the efficiency of the government-appointed managers and as a source of funds for future investment. Many such industries, infortunately, are more prone to incur a loss than to earn a profit and the public, through taxation, must make up the deficit. Management, in these instances, tries to reconcile three aims: keeping the loss to a minimum; maintaining a reasonable output or standard of service to customers; and providing satisfactory pay and working conditions for the firm's employees.

In Canada, and in other private-enterprise countries where the profit motive still exists, most business firms try, in the long run, to maximize their profits. In the short run, however, they may be willing to forgo any profit to establish themselves in a market, to protect or enlarge their present market-share in the face of the efforts of rival firms, or to comply with government price controls.

Competition

If private business firms are to produce and market goods as efficiently as possible, and to pass on the benefits to consumers in the form of lower prices or better-quality products, there must be *price competition*—that is, a situation in which business firms try to promote the sale of their products by offering them at lower prices than those of their competitors. In this way, the public can share the benefit of the greater economic efficiency of such firms, who can still make a profit despite selling at a lower price.

Monopolies. One type of business firm that may operate against the public interest is the *monopoly*. This occurs when there is a sole supplier of a good or service for which there are no close substitutes. A monopoly can arise for various reasons. It may be because of the ownership by a firm of some key raw material such as bauxite, used to manufacture aluminium. It may be because the economies of scale have led to the survival of only one large firm in an industry. Or it may be because the government has given a firm the exclusive right to supply a product in a particular area, such as water, electricity, natural gas, telephone service, mail service or liquor. Whatever the origin, the monopoly firm is in a position, if left unregulated, to set the price or output that best suits its own interests. This is because no business rival exists to help ensure that the consumer obtains a good-quality product at the lowest possible price.

For many years governments have recognized the need to regulate such monopolies in the public interest. This has been done either by outright government ownership or by government control of the prices charged. Publicly owned monopolies

INDUSTRY'S 500
Profitability is what it's all about

Invested capital

Rank by return on invested capital	Pretax return on invested capital 1984	Company	Rank in FP500
1	193.0%	Toshiba of Canada	443
2	97.2%	JVC Canada Inc.	461
3	94.2%	Consolidated Gathering Systems	152
4	89.6%	Volkswagen Canada Inc.	162
5	88.2%	Epiciers Unis Métro-Richelieu	63
6	82.7%	OE Inc.	469
7	73.4%	General Motors of Canada Ltd.	1
8	73.1%	Royal Canadian Mint	127
9	67.3%	Volvo Canada Ltd.	315
10	66.5%	Donlee Manufacturing Industries	490
11	63.8%	Nissan Automobile Canada Ltd.	180
12	63.1%	Chrysler Canada Ltd.	8
13	58.0%	Hewlett Packard Canada Ltd.	266
14	54.9%	Tremco Ltd.	497
15	54.1%	Hoechst Canada Inc.	338
16	51.6%	IBM Canada Ltd.	29
17	49.3%	Ford Motor Co. of Canada	3
18	48.2%	Rockwell International Canada	190
19	48.1%	Clouston Foods Canada Ltd.	471
20	46.9%	Kraft Ltd.	108
21	45.5%	Digital Equipment of Canada Ltd.	183
22	45.3%	H.J. Heinz Co. of Canada	230
23	44.0%	Interprovincial Co-operative Ltd.	308
24	43.1%	Hitachi (HSC) Canada Ltd.	351
25	42.3%	Noma Industries Ltd	369
26	40.9%	Kelsey-Hayes Canada Ltd.	296
27	40.0%	Mobil Oil Canada Ltd.	60
28	37.4%	CAE Industries Ltd.	232
29	37.3%	PPG Canada Inc.	147
30	37.0%	Gillette Canada Inc.	430
31	36.2%	Texaco Canada Inc.	9
32	35.6%	3M Canada Inc.	201
33	35.3%	Gendis Inc.	167
34	35.2%	Boise Cascade Canada Ltd.	175
35	34.6%	Thomson Newspapers Ltd.	107
36	34.5%	Allied Canada Inc.	114
37	34.2%	Imperial Oil Ltd.	5
38	34.0%	Bristol-Meyers Canada Inc.	242
39	33.3%	Motorola Canada	273
40	33.1%	Dover Industries Ltd.	498
41	32.7%	American Motors (Canada) Inc.	111
42	32.4%	Canadian Salt Co.	460
43	32.1%	Lillydale Co-operative Ltd.	421
44	32.1%	Barbecon Inc.	306
45	32.0%	McDonald's of Canada	99
46	31.8%	Robin Hood Multifoods Inc.	204
47	31.6%	Cascades Inc.	343
48	31.5%	Cooper Canada Ltd.	495
49	31.5%	Drug Trading Co.	223
50	31.2%	Wirth Ltd.	499

Shareholders equity

Rank by return on shareholders' equity	After-tax return on shareholders' equity 1984	Company	Rank in FP500
1	101.8%	Toshiba of Canada	443
2	79.3%	Chrysler Canada Ltd.	8
3	63.1%	Nova Scotia Power Corp.	166
4	54.4%	General Motors of Canada Ltd.	1
5	50.8%	St. Lawrence Cement Inc.	206
6	48.8%	Volkswagen Canada Inc.	162
7	47.9%	Daon Development Corp.	98
8	47.9%	JVC Canada Inc.	461
9	47.3%	Donlee Manufacturing Industries	490
10	45.5%	Groupe Videotron Ltée	465
11	45.3%	Yamaha Motor Canada Ltd.	420
12	43.8%	Interprovincial Co-operative Ltd.	308
13	40.8%	Cascades Inc.	343
14	38.9%	OE Inc.	469
15	38.5%	Volvo Canada Ltd.	315
16	37.8%	Lillydale Co-operative Ltd.	421
17	36.8%	Hoechst Canada Inc.	338
18	36.0%	CAE Industries Ltd.	232
19	35.5%	Nissan Automobile Canada Ltd.	180
20	33.9%	Honda Canada Inc.	109
21	33.8%	Ford Motor Co. of Canada	3
22	32.0%	IBM Canada Ltd.	30
23	31.3%	Calgary Co-operative Association	212
24	30.1%	Dismat Inc.	383
25	29.9%	Rockwell International of Canada	190
26	29.7%	Tremco Ltd.	497
27	29.6%	Kraft Ltd.	108
28	29.4%	Boise Cascade Canada Ltd.	175
29	28.5%	Hewlett Packard Canada Ltd.	266
30	28.2%	Noma Industries Ltd	369
31	28.1%	Clouston Foods Canada Ltd.	471
32	28.0%	Canadian Oxygen Ltd.	446
33	28.0%	H.J. Heinz Co. of Canada	230
34	27.1%	ProGas Ltd.	239
35	26.7%	Magna International Inc.	160
36	26.3%	Digital Equipment of Canada Ltd.	183
37	25.9%	Saskatchewan Oil & Gas Corp.	364
38	25.8%	Unicorp Canada Corp.	438
39	25.7%	PPG Canada Inc.	147
40	25.0%	McDonald's of Canada	99
41	24.8%	Kelsey-Hayes Canada Ltd.	296
42	24.8%	Keycorp Industries Ltd.	221
43	24.4%	Canada Northwest Energy Ltd.	451
44	24.4%	Alberta Natural Gas Co.	234
45	24.2%	Computer Innovations	459
46	24.1%	Pratt & Whitney Canada Inc.	132
47	24.0%	Hayes-Dana Inc.	203
48	23.9%	Thomson Newspapers Ltd.	107
49	23.9%	Mercedes-Benz of Canada Ltd.	361
50	23.6%	Alberta Wheat Pool	61

are, indeed, quite widespread in Canada—for example, the provincial and municipal electricity commissions. Because such public monopolies often aim to break even rather than maximize profit, they are usually beneficial to society. However, some of them may be accused of inefficiency and may justify the claim that society might benefit more from a private firm even if it does make more profit. Also, if a government has to meet the operating losses of a government enterprise from its tax revenue, the public may well be paying more than for a privately-run service. Some privately-owned monopolies in Canada, such as the telephone service, must have any price increases first approved by the government.

In some cases, it should be noted, federal and provincial governments in Canada have themselves supported the elimination of competition in an industry. One example has been the establishment of agricultural marketing boards for eggs and other farm produce. Another is the imposition of import quotas, (e.g. clothing, footwear, beef) to help protect Canadian firms.

Imperfect Competition. Most businesses in Canada operate under conditions of what economists call *imperfect competition*. This may take the form of either monopolistic competition or oligopoly. *Monopolistic competition* means a market structure in which: (a) there are many firms each of which is responsible for only a relatively small part of the total supply; (b) each firm's product, although basically the same, is different in some way (for example, by brand name or package design) from that of competing firms; (c) each firm has only limited power to raise the price of its products without losing sales; and (d) new firms can still enter the market. This type of market structure is characteristic of retailing. *Oligopoly* is a market structure in which there are only a few firms in an industry and each firm is interdependent in its price and output policy on the others. This market structure characterizes such industries as steel, cars, oil, furniture, appliances, food and soap. We should note the significant difference between monopolistic competition and oligopoly. In the former, the individual firm is too small for its price and output behaviour to cause competing firms also to adjust their prices and output. In the latter, the individual firm is large enough to affect the actions of competitors.

Non-Price Competition. Firms operating under both types of imperfect competition, but particularly oligopoly, are characterized by a high degree of *non-price competition*. That is to say, these firms spend a great deal of money and effort in trying to persuade people to buy their products, by means other than a reduction in price. One form of non-price competition is *advertising*. Other forms of non-price competition include differences in product design, differences in packaging, differences in customer services, including credit and refunds, and the use of a distinctive name, symbol, or design (known as a *brand*). Most of this non-price competition is aimed at achieving *product differentiation*—that is, making a firm's product appear different from and superior to that of rival firms, even though the products are basically the same. The cost of this non-price competition, it should be noted, is passed on to the consumer, in the form of higher prices. A considerable part of this cost may be considered an unnecessary burden on society.

Non-price competition, including product differentiation, does, however, offer some benefits to society. There is a great variety of product styles and qualities from which the consumer can choose. And firms, although reluctant to reduce prices, try to outbid each other in customer services such as pleasant shopping surroundings, customer credit and easy availability of goods.

In the case of price competition, the cost is borne by the producer. The only one who can benefit is the consumer. As a result, most firms, but particularly those operating under conditions of oligopoly, avoid price-cutting whenever possible. For any initial increase in sales caused by a reduction in price will probably be lost as soon as other firms also cut their prices. As a result, the public often fails to receive the fruits of greater efficiency.

Right to Employ Productive Resources

In order to produce and market goods and services, a business firm must be able to call upon productive resources. These include (a) *labour*—that part of the population able and willing to work; (b) *land*—the various raw materials in and on the land, the land itself, power resources, and natural means of transportation and communication; (c) *capital*—the various man-made aids to production such as buildings and equipment; and (d) *technology*—the technical knowledge of how to produce and market goods and services.

In many communist countries these resources are allocated to factories and farms by the various planning commissions. If factory managers wish to increase their labour force or obtain more equipment, they must obtain permission from the government. Furthermore, the wage rates or equipment prices to be paid are prescribed by the authorities. In a private-enterprise economy, by contrast, a business firm hires its labour and other productive resources by bidding for them in the market in competition with other firms. If a resource is particularly valuable, the market price of that resource will rise relative to that of other resources. Thus, for example, a heavy demand for computer programmers, compared with a small supply, will be reflected in relatively high salaries for this job. As a result, more persons train for that career and so labour is directed, by the price mechanism, to a more productive use. The same applies to any other resource.

Right to Choose One's Job

Another characteristic of the private-enterprise economy is the individual's right to choose his or her job. Of course, this does not mean absolute freedom of choice. A person must choose from the range of jobs available for someone with his or her abilities and skills. Since people are free in Canada to train for any of a number of careers, there is always a surplus of qualified persons seeking one particular type of job and a shortage of qualified persons seeking another. It is impossible, without government control, to match the demand for each type of job with the supply. This imbalance is also caused by the fact that many people, sooner or later, switch careers. In most communist countries, this problem does

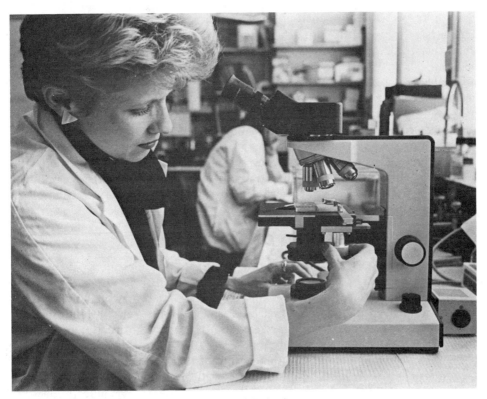
Courtesy The Ontario Ministry of Industry, Trade and Technology

not arise, for a person is assigned to a particular job and cannot leave it without government permission.

The freedom to choose one's job is attractive to most people—for it means that, given equality of opportunity, a person can, to a considerable extent, carve his or her own future. The most important constraint is the person's own ability. However, this freedom also has disadvantages. First of all, it has so far proved impossible in our private-enterprise economy to provide jobs for all. And, as industry continues to adopt more capital-intensive (and therefore, labour-saving) methods of production, the problem must inevitably become more acute. One solution is a very high rate of economic growth that will create more jobs. Such a rate of growth was once thought possible for Canada with its vast resources and enormous neighbouring market. Another possible solution to unemployment is the provision of government-paid community-improvement jobs. A second disadvantage of this freedom of choice is that the individual bears the responsibility for choosing his or her career. This responsibility imposes considerable mental and emotional strain. However, it is probably far less than the frustration that could arise if the government assigned a person to a job for which he or she has no liking and from which there is no escape.

In the private-enterprise economy, a person has another important freedom—that of negotiating with one's employer the terms of employment. One is not given a job by a government official, and told how much one will be paid. A person has the right to decline the salary or wage, and to ask for more. At one time, this freedom was not greatly esteemed by the individual. This was because he or she was the weaker party in any negotiations with an employer, and invariably got the worst of the bargain. However, now that individual workers are represented in many industries by strong labour unions, they are often very successful in their demands for better wages and fringe benefits. Consequently, this freedom to negotiate wages is now highly valued by the employee.

From the viewpoint of the economy as a whole, the individual's freedom to choose a job and negotiate wages is an essential part of the market system. For it means that industries whose products are more highly valued by consumers can attract workers away from less favoured industries or secure the best of the new entrants to the labour force, by offering them higher wages.

Consumer's Freedom of Choice

Another important characteristic of the private-enterprise economy is the consumer's freedom of choice. That is to say, a person can spend his or her money on the goods or services that he or she chooses. A person is not told what to buy, or rationed in the amounts that he or she can have—except by the size of one's purse. The only government restrictions in Canada on this freedom of choice relate to public health and morals.

Freedom of choice benefits consumers in that they can adjust their pattern of spending to suit their particular tastes. It also has the important effect, for the economy as a whole, of helping to allocate the use of available productive resources in accordance with consumer wishes. For an increase in demand for a particular good or service will, through the working of the price mechanism, eventually cause business firms to increase their production of it. And a decrease in demand will have the opposite effect.

The fact that the use of a country's productive resources is left mainly to consumers does have a disadvantage. For it cannot be said that the consumer always knows what is best either personally or for the country as a whole. However, the situation might be much worse if the government assumed control over the use of all the country's resources. Perhaps the most sensible situation is the one that now exists, whereby the government, by its own spending and by control over the sale of certain products, tries to ensure that the use of a country's resources, although left mainly up to consumers, is tempered by government "wisdom." Thus, if the public, left to its own devices, would spend much less on education than it would on entertainment, the government can adjust the use of the country's resources by its own educational expenditures.

Of course, there is always the danger of a serious difference of opinion between the public and the government as to what is best for the country and for the individual. However, the democratic election of governments in many private-enterprise economies helps ensure that the government is reasonably attuned to the wishes of the public and the mood of the times.

KEY TERMS

Private enterprise

Private property

Profit

Fair rate of return

Profit motive

Price competition

Monopoly

Oligopoly

Non-price competition

Product differentiation

Right to employ productive resources

Right to choose one's job

Consumer's freedom of choice

REVIEW QUESTIONS

1. What names are used to describe the system of business in Canada? How suitable are they?
2. Why is the right to own property an indispensable feature of our economic system? What are its advantages and disadvantages?
3. What is profit? What purpose does it serve? What is a "fair" rate of profit?
4. What is competition? Why is it essential in our economic system? To what extent is it absent?
5. What is a monopoly? Why are most monopolies government-owned or regulated? How desirable is this?
6. Distinguish between monopoly and oligopoly. Give examples of oligopolies in Canada. Are oligopolies necessarily harmful to the public?
7. Explain monopolistic competition. Where is it evident in Canada? What are its advantages and disadvantages (a) for the business firms involved and (b) the public?
8. What is product differentiation? Why do business firms consider it desirable? What are its advantages and disadvantages for the consumer?
9. How are resources allocated in a private-enterprise system? In a communist one?
10. The right to choose one's job and negotiate the terms of one's employment are accepted features of our economic system. What are the advantages and disadvantages of these features from the viewpoint of (a) the country and (b) the individual?
11. Why is freedom of consumer choice an important characteristic of the private-enterprise economy?
12. It can be argued that the main purpose of business is not to make a profit but to produce goods or services as efficiently as possible. And that profits can be considered the measure of such efficiency—just as marks at school are not the purpose of learning but an indication of performance. Discuss.

READING

From Wrecks to Riches

How Ed Alfke turned used cars into a thriving franchise business

BY PAUL GRESCOE

Source: *The Financial Post Magazine.*
©1983 Paul Grescoe.

Hell, all he wanted was a reliable car to get him to the beach where he could learn how to surf. Ed Alfke and his girlfriend were in Hawaii, on their first holiday together, that January, 1976. For the first time in his life, the 25-year-old Alfke had rented a U-Drive. But the new car from a local company kept stalling, and when he returned it in disgust, the advertised $9.95 daily rate—counting all the insurance and gas and mileage costs—proved to be about $30 a day. He exploded with anger. "Take your damn car back!" he told the owner. "To hell with you."

And Alfke went hunting for a cheap heap to tote his surfboard during his last week on the island. After three days, he spotted a rusting, old Buick Skylark on a service-station lot. A classic clunker, the Buick was waiting to be rejuvenated and sold for maybe $300. It took hours to persuade the Filipino garage owner to let this crazy Canadian rent it for $5 a day. His security was a $100 cash deposit, most of which would be refunded if Alfke brought the car back in a single piece. He did—and paid the owner a reasonable $20 for his improvised beach buggy.

It was on the Wardair charter back to Vancouver, when Ed Alfke told seatmates what a sweet deal he'd made and heard their encouraging responses, that rent-a-wreck was conceived.

By the end of 1982, Alfke had taken that desperate solution to his holiday predicament and turned the concept into a flourishing international franchise system, with at least 2,000 rental vehicles and more than $10 million in revenues a year. From Victoria to St. John's, 86 of his franchises offer well-used, yet clean, cars, vans and trucks—few, if any of them, wrecks—for $8.95 to $16.95 a day; plus $3.95 for $250 deductible insurance and five cents a kilometre. Or a customer can lease a car, with 1,600 free kilometres, for $299 to $499 a month.

Not only has the business been virtually recession-proof, it appears to have thrived in these thorny times. Twenty-five new Canadian locations opened this past year alone. In six years, Alfke claims, the turnover of franchise-holders has been about 10 percent; only one has gone bankrupt. He has already sold franchises in Tampa and Sarasota, Fla., and is negotiating with businessmen in five other states. Alfke is also involved in a joint venture with a European partner to export rent-a-wreck to London sometime this year. And Australia beckons enticingly.

Franchisees pay $10,000 to $25,000 to buy in and $20 a month per car in royalties to support the system. At 33, Ed Alfke is worth at least $2 million, but until recently he operated out of an ugly little office in his own rental agency in the blue-collar east end of Vancouver; now he's in a high-rise office near the downtown. "This place really cranks out a lot of money," he says of the east end location, which has a fleet of 120 vehicles. "I mean, this gives me

$100,000 cash a year after my wages, which are quite substantial. I feed all that into the systems company for its growth and development."

For a banker's son who grew up to be a businessman, Alfke has a shaky foundation in figures, having messed up in high school math and flunked economics in his half-year at a community college. His relentless sobriety of speech and manner—he cracks no jokes and rarely relaxes—belies his boyhood hell-raising and goofing-off, which became worrisome enough for his parents to board him in a punitive private school for a year. And as a specimen of the west-coast millionaire species—the hedonistic sort Peter C. Newman's *The Acquisitors* describes hyperbolically as "sungods living on the playing fields of the Lord"—Alfke is certainly letting down the side these days.

No playboy, he's well married to his second wife, Deborah, a woman of model-like beauty, who has china-doll black hair and an ivory complexion and who works with him daily as a company accountant. They live in a mock-Tudor house in Vancouver's unfashionably bourgeois suburb of Richmond, where their leisure is seldom more exciting than cycling and walking the English setter. "He's probably a tough guy to get to know really well," says a banker friend, Tom Sutton. "Certainly, he tries his darndest, running around in his yellow Corvette, to give the appearance of being a very outgoing, easy, carefree kind of guy." In fact, Alfke recently sold his sports-car collection: the '65 Corvette Stingray, '66 Thunderbird convertible, '71 Corvette modified, and the de Tomasa Pantera (an exotic Italian two-seater designed by an Argentine racing driver). Well, he did hang on to his '56 and '64 T-birds.

Perhaps his most unusual and endearing quality, one that scarcely ever surfaces in the newly rich entrepreneur, is his ability to criticize himself, to admit that he's been wrong. Real men don't eat crow, but Alfke has no qualms about castigating his teen-aged self. For instance: "I was an ass—." And, more to the point, he says of those so-recent years when he was creating rent-a-wreck, "We did everything wrong." At times, he confesses, "I've been totally depressed and scared to death."

There is only one subject about which he is sensitive: Just who *had* come up with the impudent idea of renting out '77 mud-brown Malibus with dented fenders and '78 Plymouth Volares with more thn 85,000 miles on the speedometer?

Alfke acknowledges that used cars were for hire in Florida as long ago as World War II, when new ones were not to be had. But he prefers to scoff at published reports that a Los Angeles car dealer named Dave Schwartz was renting old cars in an organized fashion in the early '70s. Alfke's touchiness may have something to do with the fact that by 1977, a year after rent-a-wreck's birth in Canada, Schwartz was publicizing his own franchise system in the U.S. It too is named Rent-A-Wreck, although the two companies have neither links with nor love for one another. Alfke still smarts, remembering the year it took his lawyers to trademark the name in this country. "We could have trademarked it in the U.S. too," he says ruefully, "but we weren't smart enough to do that."

No matter who came first, the reality is that the rivals now have scores of competitors in both countries, sporting such names as Rent-A-Dent, Oldies But Goodies, Ugly Duckling and Classic Car Rentals. And collectively, these used-car companies are beginning to erode the 80 percent of the market traditionally controlled by the major new-car companies, Tilden, Budget, Hertz and Avis.

Neilly Robertson, a rent-a-wreck franchise-holder in Thornhill, north of Toronto, says her clientele is changing. "We're getting doctors, lawyers, retired business people who can well afford to go to Hertz or Budget but have opted not to." Her first 26-car rental office was so successful that she is about to open a second, with a fleet of 70, in the Yonge-Lawrence area, bringing to 10 the number of rent-a-wrecks that now operate in Toronto.

"Is this your corporate office?" the middle-manager from IBM asks wonderingly. Tall, nicely tailored in a three-piece navy-blue suit, he looks around Ed Alfke's lilliputian office—with log-cabin siding painted a hideous yellow—located in his east-end rental outlet. The only adornments are ratty-looking rubber plants, a collage of articles about the company, and some badly hung magazine car-ads from the '40s and '50s.

Alfke is dressed in Lotusland Casual: French stretch cords, striped shirt open to the second button, exposing the inevitable gold chain, and an Ultrasuede jacket ("I buy these at cost from a friend who has a factory in Montreal: I don't pay retail for anything"). He has a surfer's blond hair, a full russet beard, and a plump nose with a Bob Hope ski jump. And on this day, an impacted wisdom tooth, a bad chest cold, and sundry aftereffects of a bout with laryngitis and the flu.

He speaks quietly as he explains the business to the IBM man, who is thinking of selling his house and buying a rent-a-wreck franchise to run with his wife. "The rule of thumb is that you're going to make about $1,000-a-car-per-year profit. That's after bank and wages. So if you run 50 cars, you make 50 grand, more or less."

A franchisee buys a car for between $2,000 and $3,000, which is the wholesaler's range of prices to a dealer. But not just any car. "For instance, a Pinto will last an awful lot longer on the fleet than a Maverick will, simply because Mavericks tend to loosen up a great deal quicker." Alfke says a vehicle should stand up for about a year. A middle-range car rents for $10.95 a day; a typical customer totes up about $3 in mileage charges and buys $3.95 worth of extra insurance to get $250 deductible on $1 million worth of collision and comprehensive. That adds up to $17.90 a day (about $20 less than a corresponding new car).

Each vehicle will likely sit idle one week out of four, he estimates, so the franchisee can expect an income of just over $400 per car per month. Direct monthly expenses are: $65 a car for insurance, $20 in systems royalties, and an average $60 in maintenance, which includes a thorough washing, vacuuming and vinyl cleaning after each rental, as well as mechanical servicing and road testing every 3,000 miles. This totals $145, leaving a margin of $255. Fixed costs—rent, wages, advertising—run from $175 to $200. The remaining $60 is gross profit: $750 per car per year.

After about a year's use, though, the car is sold to the public through signs on the lot or newspaper ads. If it costs $2,000 from the wholesaler, it was actually worth $3,000 retail. Take off $600—the standard, annual 30-percent depreciation for a car that's older than three years. The vehicle could still be sold for $2,400, making a further $400, and yielding a total gain of more than $1,000. "Roughly," Alfke adds. "Rule of thumb."

In a 12-hours-a-day, six-days-a-week, two-week session at his east-end Vancouver location, franchise-holders are trained by Mary Jane Hlynialuk, who used to be Vancouver city manager for Hertz. Among many other lessons, she teaches franchisees how to buy cars, and they attend a car auction with Alfke's head buyer. Afterward, his chief mechanic, who used to be Budget's maintenance supervisor in Vancouver, keeps franchise-holders current with a catalogue of vehicles to buy or avoid, based on in-house mechanics' reports of their durability. They learn the daily-accounting system, which usually takes a bookkeeper half a day a month to summarize, and receive an encyclopedic operations manual. Franchisees also get on-location training in qualifying customers—that is, deciding which ones you will trust your cars to.

Which is where the science ends and the art begins. Unlike Hertz or Tilden, where a valid credit card guarantees virtually anyone a vehicle, rent-a-wreck must screen its customers. Used cars simply can't take the beating that new cars can. "First impressions of the customer are the biggest factor in qualifying," says Hlynialuk. "Appearance, his dress, his attitude."

A driver must be 21, and if he's paying with cash instead of a card—and about one fifth of Alfke's clients do—he must have a job. The rental clerk will verify his employment and perhaps pose other questions: "How long have you been living at your present address?" "Do you own that house?" Then the cardless customer has to leave a deposit of between $100 and $300. No one can buy zero-deductible insurance, as at the new-car companies. "If you're going to drive my car," Ed Alfke argues, "you should invest a little bit in my fenders." And if a customer has three problems in a row with a car, rent-a-wreck asks him politely to take his business elsewhere.

Even people on Alfke's Vancouver staff make bad judgment calls. The day the IBM manager is visiting, a clerk sets off to confront a delinquent customer at his home about an overdue $92 bill. "I should be taking my cane," he mutters. A young man in jeans and T-shirt comes in to complain about the brakes on his Nova. A clerk gives him another car and remarks after the customer leaves: "That's the same guy who's rented five different cars from us. I think he's planning to buy a used car and this is one long test drive."

Meanwhile, in his office, Alfke is questioning whether the IBM manager is making a mistake by being there. "When I look at you," he says, "when I see a sophisticated blue suit, expensive shirt and silk tie, it's got to make me wonder: Do you want a rent-a-wreck?"

"I grew up in the North: I'm most comfortable with unsophisticated, earthy people," Ed Alfke says later, over lunch. His father was a manager for the Canadian Imperial Bank of Commerce during the boom years in Peace River and Dawson Creek. In his teens, Alfke was a top competitive ski racer in the B.C. interior and played on the province's championship water-polo team.

"But I was not your nice, calm, quiet banker's son. I was lousy in school. I gave my teachers a hard time. I was competitive, egotistical. I was into motorcycles and raising hell." Nothing too serious—speeding tickets, Saturday-night high jinks—but his father thought that he needed straightening out. Grade 11 at University School in Victoria helped with its weekend detentions and bamboo canings. Says Alfke, "I was forced to study."

Still, he just squeaked through Grade 12 back home, and his six months at a new regional college were illuminated only by his presidency of the student council; he was elected simply by being the most outspoken candidate. He got 38 percent in economics and left to work in the laboratory of a pulp mill in Prince George, B.C., 798 kilometres north of Vancouver, where he lost respect for unions, like many entrepreneurs.

Another half-year, and he quit again—this time to work for his older brother, who ran a steakhouse in town. Alfke, deciding he wanted a piece of the place, sold his Harley-Davidson motorcycle for straight cash and did some fast creative financing. "I went to a finance company, borrowed money ostensibly for another Harley and I also gave them mine as security [neglecting to tell them that he'd already sold it]. "Then I went to another finance company, borrowed some more and took all that money to the bank and borrowed the balance to buy 50 percent of my brother's restaurant for 15,000 bucks. All within 48 hours. That way I got away with it all, you see. Anyway, financial institutions weren't that careful in those days." Alfke's later deals would be far more conventional.

For three years, he put in 120 hours a week in the restaurant, washing dishes, cleaning up and cooking. He was married at 19 and his wife worked as a waitress with him. "It just killed the relationship," he says now. (He separated from his wife in 1975; she has raised their daughter, Lisa, now 13.) The brothers sold out in 1972; Alfke realized only $10,000 after he'd paid back a second $15,000 loan.

With another $12,000 from his father-in-law and a loan from the Royal Bank, he opened a clothing store called Jean Jungle in the south-central B.C. interior city of Kamloops. Later, Alfke entered into a sort of franchise agreement with a couple in Prince George, to create a chain of these profitable basic-jean shops across the province. Recalling that time, he says: "I made a lot of money in the retail store business [In 1979, he sold his interest for a six-figure profit]. I bought a 450SL [a Mercedes-Benz sports car] and I went crazy for a couple of years, spent a lot of money, lived very high and damn near died of ulcers."

At the height of his craziness in January 1976, he decided to decelerate for three weeks and took his new girlfriend, Deborah, on their first holiday. In Hawaii. Where he hired his first U-Drive.

When he came home to Kamloops with the concept of renting used cars, Alfke was as excited as a 16-year-old learning to drive. Yet car-dealer friends did their damndest to get him off the track, saying: "The maintenance will kill ya, Ed." At a bar in Prince George one night, a beery Australian who heard about the idea stood up and toasted him: "The birth of a new company, rent-a-wreck. Alfke, King of the Wrecks."

He had a name. Now, he needed money. At first, his banker, Tom Sutton of the Royal's main branch in Kamloops, laughed. "First of all," Sutton remembers, "the name turned me right off. And I didn't think it was all that good an idea." As Alfke recalls their meeting, the banker told him, "This is a Looney Tunes idea. But you're good for $15,000. On a personal note."

It was the autumn of 1976. Alfke was ripe for an adventure. With Dale Granger, a partner, who had owned several Hertz franchises, he launched rent-a-wreck in the corner of a used-car lot on the outskirts of Prince George. They had five cars, worth $300 or less, all of them old crocks with more than 100,000 miles. Ten dollars a day and 10 cents a mile. "Dale had a lot of borderline customers at Hertz and they were perfect candidates for rent-a-wreck then. Guys known around town, a little iffy, but basically okay people as long as they weren't drinking," says Alfke. "And merely on word of mouth, business went wild from the beginning."

However, there were a few dents in their rental system that needed hammering out. "We were under-maintaining badly and buying the wrong cars in the first place," he says. "We were qualifying our customers along the Hertz way, which was totally wrong. We had a lot of problems with breakdowns. The gross was just pouring in the door. But the bookkeeping system wasn't set up. Hell, it was six months before we realized we'd lost a whole bunch of money"—about $20,000.

Still, they were starting to attract a more

stable, blue-collar customer who was fascinated enough with the craziness of the concept to come in with his broken-down, rented junker on the back of a tow truck and be willing to wait a day, if necessary, to pick up a replacement.

The Prince George location grew to 40 cars (Dale Granger sold his 10-percent share of it in 1978) and a manager with a Datsun dealership paid Alfke, the sole owner of the rent-a-wreck franchise system, $3,500 for rights to open in Kamloops. Encouraged, Alfke decided to expand to Vancouver the same year. Without even a sign in place, he rented out his entire fleet of 26 cars the day he opened on well-travelled West Broadway.

Yet problems continued to dog him. Although he was now paying $500 to $700 a car, the big-city wholesalers sold the boy from the sticks a crop of lemons. The first Vancouver banker that he dealt with, in a branch office of the Royal, had no confidence in rent-a-wreck. "I tell you," says Alfke, "in '77 I was very close to giving it up, I just couldn't make it work right."

He squeezed through his first year in Vancouver. He even sold three franchises in other areas of B.C. And when he finally transferred to the Royal's main branch, he was again dealing with Tom Sutton, who showed him how to draft an impressive borrowing proposal to keep rent-a-wreck afloat. Alfke brought in an accounting firm to help design a financial-reporting system that would grow with the company. Robert Harris and Associates of Toronto offered solid franchising advice, such as: Don't grow so fast that the system's infrastructure collapses.

New franchise-holders themselves added their expertise. One who'd acquired administrative experience in the air force further streamlined the accounting system; another who was a car dealer shared his knowledge of buying and selling used vehicles. Cars were costing more, but lasting longer. The franchisee-training program moved into the classroom with a proper operations manual. Alfke was feeling confident enough to cancel agreements with two operators who failed to meet his maintenance standards.

By 1980, rent-a-wreck was running smoothly. By the end of 1982, it was speeding along at a 100-percent annual growth rate, and its president was planning to move to Toronto and set up a head office there—it has since opened—to steer his company's expansion overseas and into the U.S., where the system is called Practical rent-a-car.

Ed Alfke is still learning, still making mistakes. He backed down when his Toronto owners argued that they didn't care what he did in Vancouver, they had to offer 50 kilometres a day free to *their* customers (however, they have since decided to drop the free mileage). And until last year, he was adamant about national advertising: rent-a-wreck simply didn't need it. His franchisees disagreed and insisted, at one of their two annual owners' meetings, that the company launch an ad campaign ("Good Cars . . . Cheap") in the fall of '82, on radio, billboards and in newspapers. Then, they opposed his decision to handle the campaign in Vancouver. Neilly Robertson of Toronto was one of his critics. "What the hell do they know about our advertising problems here?" But she adds, to Alfke's credit, that he has since admitted, "I'm wrong. I tried to do it all and obviously, I made a mistake."

Neilly Robertson is no longer as concerned as she once was that Alfke attempts too much on his own. This past winter she had said, "Ed has to learn to let go a little bit and let other people assume some responsibility . . . He's going to be his own worst enemy. He can't work 20 hours a day, seven days a week." She now thinks he is learning to delegate. Banker Tom Sutton says: "He works harder and puts in longer hours and does his homework better than 99 percent of the business people that I've ever dealt with. And I've been in banking for 17 years now. Ed's a very serious man . . . Maybe too serious at times."

Ed Alfke is 33. "You gotta remember," he says, "that rent-a-wreck's only seven years old—but seven of *my* years. You put 110 hours a week in for seven years, you've all of a sudden got 10 or 12 or 14 years in experience."

For all his ferocious energy, he has a burgeoning, international franchise company. And for all that, he no longer has time to fool around in one of his sports cars, mess about on his dirt bike, or even rent a heap to get to the beach and learn to surf.

Assignment
1. What was the origin of the Rent-a-Wreck concept?
2. What exactly does this business offer the customer?
3. Why has the business proven to be "recession-proof"?
4. How and why has the business been franchised?
5. How did Ed Alfke's educational background help him to become a business tycoon?
6. What kind of a person does Ed seem to be?
7. How important is trademark registration?
8. Why might a Rent-a-Wreck franchise be a good investment?
9. Explain, on a per car basis, the investment and rate of return in a Rent-a-Wreck venture.
10. What training does a franchisee receive?
11. Who is allowed to rent cars from Rent-a-Wreck? What must the staff try to avoid?
12. What business experience did Ed acquire prior to Rent-a-Wreck?
13. How did Ed arrange the initial financing for Rent-a-Wreck?
14. What mistakes did the business make in the beginning?
15. What is Rent-a-Wreck's advertising strategy?

UNIT 1.2: SOCIAL RESPONSIBILITIES OF THE BUSINESS FIRM

Because private business firms are allowed to flourish within society and to make use of the various natural and human resources available, as well as public services such as roads, bridges, and schools, most people believe that such firms have a considerable obligation to society. Some employers and other business people would argue that the creation of income and employment and the payment of taxes to government fulfil this obligation. Others believe that a private business firm has additional social responsibilities: to its consumers, to its employees, and to the community. Many firms have started to recognize these responsibilities and act accordingly. This positive attitude has been encouraged by three factors:

(a) a more enlightened and socially conscious outlook on the part of professional managers; (b) growing pressure by organized labour, consumer groups, and governments; and (c) the realization that it is in the self-interest of business to help eliminate the defects of the private-enterprise system. For such defects can, if politically exploited, cause the overthrow of an economic system that, on the whole, does much more good than harm; a system which has, in fact, proved far superior in raising a country's average standard of living than its main alternative, socialism.

Responsibilities Towards Consumers

The private business firm is entrusted, in our type of economy, with the task of producing and marketing goods as efficiently as possible. If it fails to pass on the fruits of this efficiency to consumers in the form of lower prices, it is not living up to its social responsibility. Also, if it persuades the public to buy goods that do not match the firm's claims, or that are mechanically unsafe or otherwise harmful to human beings and the environment, it is not fulfilling its obligations to society.

A Fair Price. Theoretically, the most efficient type of market structure for a country is one in which there is a high degree of price competition. Thus, if a firm can produce and market, at lower cost, the same good or service that other firms supply, consumers will benefit from being able to buy the good or service at a lower price. The consumer's money will therefore go further and his or her standard of living will rise.

In practice, most firms are reluctant to engage in price-cutting. They fear the retaliation of other firms that may well culminate in a price war by which all firms stand to lose. Instead, to promote sales, they prefer to undertake non-price competition in such areas as advertising, credit, and packaging. This means that consumers, instead of benefiting from lower prices, are saddled with the cost of expensive non-price competition. In an attempt to promote price competition at the retail level, the Canadian government has made resale price maintenance illegal. In other words, a manufacturer in Canada cannot legally force retailers to sell his or her goods at a fixed price. If one retailer is more efficient than others, he or she may pass on some of the benefits to consumers in the form of lower prices and at the same time help expand sales.

Where there are only a few large firms in an industry, it is relatively easy for these firms to agree to minimize price competition. And even if formal price and output collusion is prohibited by law (as it is in Canada under the Combines Investigation Act), informal arrangements do continue to exist. Furthermore, informal, "follow-my-leader" price policies ensure that stable price structures are the rule rather than the exception. As a result, the consumer obtains the benefit of greater productivity in an industry (for example, from technological innovation) mainly, if at all, in the form of a better-quality product or prices that increase slowly compared to the general price level. Sometimes, if there is a strong labour union in the industry, many of the benefits of increased productivity will be appropriated by the work force before they can reach the consumer. Also, it is likely that the owner will take a share. However, we must remember that the employees and shareholders are also part of the public—so, for some consumers, what is not available in the form of lower prices is available in the form of higher wages and dividends. Nevertheless, competition has been successful in a number of instances in causing the benefit of improved technology to be passed to the customer in the form of a lower price for the good or service—for example, ball-point pens, electronic calculators and digital watches.

Finally, we must not forget the role of government in helping to ensure a maximum amount of business competition. If a government does not set and enforce reasonable minimum standards, can private business firms be held entirely to blame if they take advantage of any opportunity to evade competition? That is why the Canadian Combines Investigation Act, with its limited enforcement staff and small fines, has for many years been considered unsatisfactory.

A Good Quality Product. A business firm knows that the best way to secure a large market for its goods or services is to offer them for sale at a reasonable price. To be able to do this, and also to obtain a satisfactory profit, the business firm is under constant pressure to reduce, or at least hold down, production and

Courtesy *Oakville Beaver*

marketing costs. A business firm has, therefore, a difficult and delicate task. It must, on the one hand, keep the price within the consumer's reach; and on the other, try to give as great a value as possible for the price.

Since labour costs are steadily rising, most business firms try to substitute cheaper materials in the production process, employ more capital-intensive methods of production, and generally use labour more sparingly. One of the effects of these economies is to reduce the quality of the product and the amount of testing and inspection that it undergoes. Also, since a rival firm may be working on a similar product, there is pressure to get the good quickly on the market. Furthermore, boredom and frustration on an assembly line can sometimes mean that a product incorporates shoddy work, and despite testing and inspection, this product may still reach the customer. Examples of poor-quality products are not hard to find—indeed all kinds of articles of daily household use, ranging from toys to stoves, are subject to early malfunction; and every year, thousands of cars are recalled because of defects. An example of an inadequately tested product is the thalidomide drug that had such tragic consequences for so many children.

The situation is bad enough, from the consumer's point of view, if a product breaks down or in some other way fails to live up to reasonable expectations. It is worse, however, if the manufacturer refuses to accept responsibility for the product or charges an exorbitant amount for its repair. Many firms issue warranties with durable consumer goods such as cars and household appliances; but these vary greatly, from firm to firm, in their coverage and duration.

The thalidomide drug was withdrawn from the market because its harmful effects were only too apparent. But there are other products still sold that are believed to endanger human health, such as tobacco and alcohol. What should the manufacturer's social responsibility be in such cases? There are also many foodstuffs sold (for example, refined white sugar) that promote malnutrition; yet the consumer is led to believe, by the manufacturer's claim, that the product is good for him or her. Also, the consumer is often given no indication in the label of a product of its nutritional content, if any. Does this problem of malnutrition fall within the social responsibility of the business firm? Or is it solely the responsibility of the government, particularly the health and education authorities?

Better Advertising. There is no doubt that a business firm fulfils a socially useful purpose in advertising the nature and virtues of its products. As is often said, a better mousetrap is of little use if its existence is practically unknown. However, consumers do question the extent and nature of today's advertising. Does it have to be so repetitive and so often inane? Does it have to spoil the streets and countryside and interrupt the enjoyment of television shows? Can it not be cheaper and less obtrusive? Must consumers continue to pay so much for advertising—both in the private cost of higher prices and in the social cost of unsightly landscapes?

So far, the only area in which the advertising industry feels that it may be accused of being socially irresponsible is that of misleading advertising. This occurs when a firm claims that its product has specific qualities that it does not in fact possess. It goes beyond the claim that the product is superior to anything else. Because a consumer believes that a specific claim must be truthfully made, he or she is persuaded to purchase the product. If the claim had not been made, the sale would not have taken place. Misleading advertising is, in fact, illegal in Canada. Also, self-policing by the communications media and by advertising agencies and departments helps greatly to eliminate it.

Responsibilities Towards Employees

It is perhaps inevitable, given the profit motive, that the owners and managers of a business firm tend to regard the firm's employees in a predominantly economic light, carefully monitoring the services performed by such employees and comparing them against the cost in wages and fringe benefits. If workers in a private business firm are not earning their keep, they can soon expect to be dismissed. Furthermore, if the managers of a firm can find a machine to perform a job more accurately, reliably, or cheaply than human labour, they will install it, for one of the tasks of the business firm, spurred by competition and the profit motive, is to find the cheapest, most efficient production and marketing methods. This is not to say, of course, that human warmth and sentiment are absent in the modern business firm. In fact, many business firms do much to make life better for their employees.

Wages. Every employee would like to earn good wages to be able to buy the goods and services that he or she would like to have. However, the employer cannot be expected to pay exactly what the employee, rather than the firm, thinks he or she is worth. The employer must compare the benefits to the firm of hiring the person with the cost incurred. There is, consequently, a limit to what the employer can afford to pay. If the wage-rate required by an employee exceeds this limit, the employer is better off not to hire him or her. The greater the output, or productivity, of the worker, the more the employer can afford to pay.

Looking at its total operation, rather than just the additional or marginal worker's efforts, a firm may find that the productivity of land, labour, capital, entrepreneurship, and technology combined enables it to produce and sell goods and services at considerable profit. The question then arises: to whom should this profit belong? Traditionally, in a private-enterprise society, the owners of a business firm have been entitled to the profits—for they have risked their capital and efforts in establishing and operating the enterprise. However, many workers, particularly when their point of view is formulated by a labour union, argue that large profits mean that a firm has been underpaying its employees. Consequently, the amount of these profits is used by labour unions in contract negotiations to support claims for higher wages and more generous fringe benefits. If the amount of the firm's profit is not made public (the case with most private business corporations), labour unions make their own estimates. At the extreme, the claim is sometimes made that all the profit belongs to the workers, on the grounds that they have earned it with their toil. But this Marxist point of view overlooks the contribution made to profits by the other factors of production.

To help reduce the tension and ill-will that may exist in a firm over the level of wages and the distribution of profits, a number of firms have introduced profit-sharing plans. In most of these, a substantial percentage of each year's total profits is shared amongst a firm's employees according to job position and years of service. It can be argued that the spread of profit-sharing in Canada may be a valuable way both to reduce industrial unrest and to give an employee greater involvement and satisfaction in his or her work. So also may be the opportunity for worker representatives to participate, at the board of directors level, in top management policy-making as is now done, for example, in West Germany and other countries.

It is considered to be a firm's responsibility to pay "fair wages." However, wage-rates for each type of labour in a particular area are determined, in practice, mainly by the interaction of the forces of demand and supply. Thus, for example, if the demand for coal miners increases in British Columbia, while the supply of workers remains unchanged, the wage-rate will rise. For any type of labour in a given area, there is, consequently, a "going rate." To prevent the going rate from settling at a level that would not afford a worker a decent standard of living, provincial governments have set minimum wage rates. While these rates have caused firms to dismiss those workers whose cost exceeded the value of their services, they have meant a reasonable basic wage for the workers who have remained employed.

Fringe Benefits. Business firms make payments to their workers in money or kind over and above the regular wage or salary. These fringe benefits, varying from firm to firm, include paid annual vacations, paid public holidays, reductions in the length of the workweek, subsidized meals, time off for special occasions, paid sick leave, extra payment for overtime work, a share of the firm's profits, and company contributions to employee pension and insurance plans and to Workers' Compensation. Some of these fringe benefits were once a novelty, but are now taken for granted. Thus, for example, few people remember that sixty hours was the standard workweek at the turn of the century. Over the years the number and variety of fringe benefits have increased—as the result of government legislation, labour union action, or employers' initiative.

What should be the business firm's social responsibility with regard to fringe benefits? Undoubtedly, society must welcome any steps that a firm can afford to take to improve the lot of its employees. However, history has shown that the main impetus for improvements must come from labour and government. For a firm, in increasing the fringe benefits of its employees on its own, is adding to its costs and weakening its competitive position, and experience shows that only the very wealthy firms can afford to do this. Government legislation, on the other hand, makes some fringe benefits, such as the employer's contribution to the Canada Pension Plan, mandatory for all firms; and no firm, except perhaps a labour-intensive firm, is unfairly penalized. Labour union action, if taken on an industry-wide scale, can also have a uniform effect on the amount of fringe benefits offered by business firms.

Job Security. To most workers, the assurance that their firm will continue to employ them in the months and years ahead is just as important as good wages and fringe benefits. However, from the firm's point of view, it seems unreasonable to have to pay workers if their output cannot be sold profitably, if at all.

One of the desirable characteristics of the private-enterprise economy is the competition that takes place between different firms. Competition encourages firms to introduce new goods and to produce and market them as cheaply as possible, to the benefit of the consumer. However, as time goes by, competition inevitably results in some firms having to discontinue certain product lines or even close whole plants. And this, of course, means a loss of jobs. Some firms are faced also with fluctuations in sales for seasonal or other reasons; and others with interruptions in supplies of materials and parts, often due to strike action in other plants or in transportation facilities. As a result, they must temporarily discontinue the employment of some part of their work force. Most firms would consider as essential this right to "lay off" workers when there is no work for them to do.

Just what is a firm's social responsibility regarding job security? First of all, there can be no doubt that a firm must retain the right to dismiss workers if it is to remain profitable and efficient.

"I'm reasonably confident your job will be waiting for you, should you return."

However, although retaining the right to dismiss employees, many firms in Canada mitigate the effects of such dismissal by cash settlements and retraining allowances. Furthermore, while it is in the interests of a firm to dismiss its inefficient employees, many firms have agreed in labour contracts to go by seniority—in other words, to dismiss first of all those persons with least service, even though they may be more efficient than other workers who have been at the plant longer. Also, of course, business firms (as well as employees) contribute to the federal government's unemployment insurance program, which provides benefits to those who become unemployed. Furthermore, business income taxes help finance government-administered manpower retraining programs and the federal Employment Centres, which help to find new job opportunities for the unemployed. Business firms could help further in mitigating the effects of dismissal by providing more advance warning, so that the employee involved would have more time to seek alternative employment. Current practice in this regard varies greatly. A middle manager in one firm may be given several months to find a new position, while a similar employee in another firm may arrive one day to find his or her office locked or desk or secretary removed. In countries such as Japan, business firms appear to make a greater effort to ensure that an employee, once he or she joins the firm and works loyally for it, has life-time employment.

Layoffs. As regards layoffs, many labour spokespersons take the view that a business firm has a social responsibility to employ a person on a regular basis. To this end, sales fluctuations can be partly offset by seasonally complementary product-lines, and by production for inventory. If production cannot be spread out by these means, labour spokespersons feel that a firm should still continue to pay the employee a regular wage. For, so the argument goes, a firm should provide in its good months for the losses suffered in its bad months. If a firm can treat its directors, managers, security and maintenance staff, land, buildings, and equipment as a fixed expense throughout the year, why not also the plant labour force? Some firms have, in fact, accepted this point of view and pay all their employees a guaranteed annual wage. This is a guaranteed minimum wage payment for each week of the year regardless of the amount of work to be done. Others guarantee a minimum total number of hours of work for each year.

Labour-Saving Equipment. Throughout history, agricultural and other workers have deeply resented being replaced by machines; and this has led to sporadic machine-smashing riots. Today, in Canada, labour unions recognize the need for technological progress, since it is one of the keys to higher labour productivity and better wages. However, they are deeply concerned with the lot of the workers who must inevitably be displaced. Unions have insisted, in many labour contracts, on financial and other assistance for workers affected in this way. Along these lines, the federal and provincial governments have introduced "technological" clauses in their Labour Relations Acts. These give a labour union the right to renegotiate the terms of an existing labour contract should a firm make changes in its production technology that affect the jobs of a significant number of employees. This change has been hotly opposed by many business firms on the grounds that it will discourage technological improvements. Just what a firm's social responsibility is with regard to technological unemployment is still a matter of dispute.

Plant Closings. A practice (involving another conflict between private and social costs of production), that has caused great public indignation in recent years has been the sudden closing of a whole plant. On some occasions, such as a prolonged strike for excessively high wages, this may be justifiable. But on others, when considerable prior notice could have been given to the employees, it would seem socially and morally indefensible. In some cases, as a last resort, the federal or provincial government may hurriedly step in to keep a plant operating, even at a loss. But this kind of scrambled action hardly seems the desirable solution. It would seem reasonable to expect that a business firm's social responsibility should include giving substantial prior notice of plant closures. In this way, a government or private individual would have time to investigate the possibility of making the plant profitable. Also, if it could not be saved, the employees would have more time to find other jobs. In some provinces, for example, Ontario, substantial prior notice of plant closure is now required by law. Whether a firm's responsibility should extend beyond the giving of prior notice to cash for retraining and resettlement is controversial.

Job Satisfaction.
Men and women, unlike buildings or machines, expect to draw some personal satisfaction from their jobs, however lowly they may be. For human beings are creative creatures with minds and ambitions of their own; and if their minds are not challenged and their ambitions are not given scope, they can soon become frustrated and dissatisfied. Of course, humans vary greatly in their needs: and some can find satisfaction in jobs that would drive others berserk. Unfortunately, the high degree of specialization of labour required for modern, low-cost mass production means that a large portion of the labour force, particularly factory workers, must perform repetitive, routine tasks that prove monotonous for even the dullest mind. And when we consider that, in every weekday, the average worker spends half of his or her non-sleeping hours at a job, we can appreciate how easily he or she can become frustrated. Although a person can try to achieve satisfaction from hobbies and other creative activities in non-working hours, he or she would still usually prefer to find satisfaction in his or her work. Many people will, in fact, switch to a lower-paid job if it offers interest and challenge. Only the payment of high wage-rates and generous fringe benefits can ensure a sufficient supply of workers at car and other assembly-line plants; and despite good financial treatment, the workers in these plants are ever eager for a break in their monotonous daily routines.

There is no doubt that manufacturers of cars and other mass-produced goods have successfully fulfilled their economic role of producing goods at the lowest cost. As a result, the consumer can now buy a whole range of goods that formerly did not exist or were financially out of reach. But do business firms also have a social responsibility to make work reasonably interesting for their employees? Obviously, a balance must be maintained between productive efficiency on the one hand and job satisfaction on the other. Experiments in Canada and abroad have shown that some progress towards alleviation of job boredom and frustration can be achieved—for example, by rotating workers from job to job. From the employer's point of view, efforts to increase job satisfaction are not just a one-way street. Better worker morale can improve productivity and labour relations, and reduce stoppages and sabotage.

To be satisfied with his or her job, a worker must feel that it is in some way important. And when a worker is taken on, the importance of the job to the efficient operation of the firm should be pointed out. Periodically the value of his or her efforts should be explicitly recognized. Furthermore, every worker, however lowly his or her position, should be treated with dignity.

Another responsibility of the employer in helping to provide job satisfaction is to treat employees fairly. Nothing can be more demoralizing in a factory or office than to feel that promotion or special benefits are based on favouritism.

Equal Opportunity. For many years, women have been discriminated against in the workplace, missing out on promotion opportunities and usually being paid less for the same work performed by men. Nevertheless, in the public sector, the position of women has improved considerably from what it used to be. However, in private business firms, the situation is only now beginning to change — as more and more women, with higher education and ambitious career plans, push their way up the management ladder. In many cases, women have found the route to the top more quickly, by starting and operating their own business firms.

Employee's Responsibilities. So far we have spoken only of the employer's social responsibilities. We should also take a few paragraphs to remind

"This *is* the president speaking!"

ourselves that employees, as well as being the recipients of wages and a variety of fringe benefits, have social responsibilities too. Thus, having entered into a contract of employment, a worker should perform the job loyally and energetically. He or she should not, for example, waste time, demoralize fellow-workers, be careless, steal materials or finished goods, or indulge in unofficial strikes. The more inefficient and dishonest a worker, the larger the price that the consumer will have to pay for the final goods or services. Also, the more carelessly the work is performed, the greater the chance of poor-quality and even dangerous products reaching the consumer. And, in the plant, a careless worker may endanger the lives of his or her colleagues.

An extremely important social responsibility that is shared by employers and employees alike is to develop some way of resolving their differences without hardship to the public. In a private-enterprise economy such as Canada's, employees of business firms have the right, once a labour contract has expired, to withdraw their services if dissatisfied with their pay and fringe benefits. This right is also enjoyed by many government employees, including, for example, post office and railway workers. Employers also have the right, although they seldom use it, to lock out workers if a new labour contract cannot be agreed upon. In Canada in recent years, labour strikes have caused considerable hardship to the public, increasing ill-will between management and labour, and a great deal of lost production. In some countries, such as those ruled by communist governments that set the wage-rates, strikes are illegal and persons participating in them are liable to arrest and imprisonment. However, in exchange for apparent industrial harmony, motivated mainly by fear, shoddy work and drunkenness on the job are commonplace. Canada's system of setting wage-rates in different industries based on freedom of negotiation is undoubtedly more attractive to the worker. Nevertheless, much improvement is necessary.

Responsibilities Towards The Community

Many business firms have long taken an interest in the community in which they produce or sell their goods. And with the growth of large firms, this interest is often on a nation-wide or regional scale. It covers not only the basic institutions of our society, but also such matters as education, health and social welfare, entertainment and the arts, and the environment. This interest is now generally considered to be part of a business firm's social responsibility—just as the storekeepers in the frontier towns were expected to join the posse when somebody was murdered or when bandits robbed the bank. Of course, not all firms have lived up to this obligation. Indeed, some firms are only beginning to recognize it as such. However, public pressure, government action, and publicity by the communications media have all helped to bring this matter to the attention of business. Let us now consider just how business firms have helped the community.

Basic Institutions. Business firms have always felt themselves responsible for helping to safeguard the private-enterprise system in which they operate. This interest, often expressed in the form of financial contributions to the political party best representing their outlook, has naturally been engendered by self-interest. However, it also reflects the firm belief of businesspeople that this system is the one most beneficial for society as a whole. Business firms can be expected, therefore, to support actively any measures, government or private, to protect such essential features of the private-enterprise system as private ownership of property, enforcement of private contractual obligations, freedom of consumer choice, and the right to make profit.

Education. Apart from their contribution in taxes, firms have made direct donations to schools, colleges and universities. They have also helped to finance the cost of university research for professors and students alike. Furthermore, they have contributed prizes and scholarships for students in all fields. Perhaps the greatest scope for usefully extending business firms' interest in education, particularly in such areas as business and engineering, is in collaboration with universities and colleges in planning courses, arranging plant visits, and offering students actual job experience that may eventually lead to career placement. Although difficult to arrange, "sandwich" courses that combine classroom academic training with on-the-job plant experience have proven, in engineering, for example, to be an extremely fruitful form of undergraduate education. Business firms have also, as mentioned earlier in this chapter, established and helped finance educational programs for persons working in their own profession or industry.

Health and Social Welfare. Many business firms pay more than half the cost of monthly medical plan contributions made on behalf of an employee and his or her family. They play an important role in raising money for a new hospital or for an addition to an existing one. They also spearhead fund-raising drives (for example, the United Way) for a variety of charitable organizations. Of course, some firms are more public-spirited than others. And it is easier for a large, prosperous firm to lend top executives and donate money than it is for a small or even medium-size business which is on the way up or struggling to survive. Nevertheless, business firms, as a whole, do make an important contribution in this area. And clubs such as the Lions and Rotary Club enable the small-businessperson to participate in charitable, community-oriented works.

Entertainment and the Arts. Business firms have helped to establish community centres in many towns in Canada and have sponsored sports ranging from ice hockey to lacrosse. They have also made possible, by their advertising, the showing of many sports events on television. Until recently, it can be said that they did more to foster sport in Canada than did the government. In addition, business firms have been patrons of the arts; and, although it is sometimes said that they could do a lot more, their purchases of paintings and other works of art and of tickets for concerts have certainly helped many artists and artistic organizations. The action of one businessman even saved a theatre, the Royal Alexandra in Toronto, from closing.

The Environment. One area of social responsibility that is now attracting the attention of many business firms is the protection of the environment. A business firm, in its desire to reduce costs and increase profits, tends to seek the cheapest way of disposing of its waste products. This may be up the chimney into the surrounding air; or down the drain into the nearest stream, river, lake, or ocean. These methods of waste disposal, with their resultant pollution, have rapidly been contaminating the air that we breathe, the water we drink, and the rivers and lakes in which we bathe. Up to a certain point, the air and water can absorb and satisfactorily dispose of pollutants. But, as the population grows, industrial pollution (in addition to household pollution) becomes unbearable in many areas.

In recent years in Canada, the federal, provincial and municipal governments have started to spend more money on the treatment of industrial and household wastes. Also, they have overhauled anti-pollution legislation, imposing stiffer penalties and establishing better means of enforcement. However, there is no doubt that business firms have a major social responsibility for pollution control and should be expected to take more initiative in this matter. Unfortunately, too many firms in the past have not lived up to the letter of the law, let alone its spirit. Of course, the public must recognize that effective pollution control is expensive and will eventually be reflected in higher prices for goods and services—as buyers of new anti-pollution-equipped cars have discovered. However, the public is much more pollution conscious today than ever before and should be willing to accept this additional cost. Certainly, they would get far better value for their money than they do from the brand advertising and other forms of non-price competition for which they are now paying.

Business Ethics

In fulfilling the social responsibilities discussed in this chapter, it is not considered sufficient that a business firm merely adhere to the letter of the law. For, although laws are generally made for the good of the public, they often lag behind the needs of the times. Furthermore, they are usually unable to cope with every situation. Thus, for example, a firm may be legally able to dismiss an employee who has been made redundant by the installation of new machinery in a plant. However, if the employee has spent most of his or her working life with the firm and is now too old to be retrained or find employment elsewhere, the firm is considered to have a moral responsibility to help the employee. This responsibility may call for more than just a small redundancy payment that will be used up in a few months. Similarly, a firm may be legally entitled to charge whatever it likes for a product; but if it costs only twenty cents to make and market, is the firm morally justified in charging five dollars for it, even to help offset losses on the firm's other products?

In business, there is, as in other areas of human activity, a recurring conflict between legal and moral requirements. The guide to resolving such conflicts in business must be the businessperson's ethical code or standard of moral behaviour. This ethical code, influenced by religion, custom, reason, and sentiment, changes as the years go by. Thus, few people in North America today would contemplate using slave labour, even if it were legal, whereas it was commonplace only two centuries ago. The moral guidelines for business behaviour have become a special subject of study called *business ethics*.

One important area involving business ethics is the use of bribes by business firms to secure orders from customers in the face of competition from other suppliers. Many employees do in fact accept gifts at Christmas and on other occasions from suppliers. Government officials, particularly in certain foreign countries, have been known to accept "gifts" in return for contracts, licences, and other favours.

KEY TERMS

Fair price for product
Good quality product
Better advertising
Economic view of employee
Wages
Fringe Benefits
Right of dismissal
Unemployment insurance
Layoffs
Labour-saving equipment
Plant closures

Job satisfaction
Job security
Employees' responsibilities
Basic institutions
Education
Health and social welfare
Entertainment and the arts
Environment
Energy
Business ethics

REVIEW QUESTIONS

1. Why is a business firm considered to have social responsibilities as well as an economic role in our society? What factors have encouraged a positive social attitude among business firms?
2. What are the most important social responsibilities to its customers that a firm should fulfil?
3. How socially useful is advertising?
4. Most business firms have a very limited concept of their social responsibility towards their employees. Comment.
5. How are wage-rates determined? What constitutes a "fair wage"?
6. What are fringe benefits? What should be a firm's social responsibility in this regard?
7. Ideally, a worker should have complete job security. Comment.
8. Workers have every right to oppose technological innovation if it threatens their jobs. Comment.

9. Business firms have a social responsibility to make jobs more personally satisfying. Comment.
10. Who is now mainly responsible for job training in our society? Why is this so?
11. How essential is a college or university education for an aspiring business manager?
12. What responsibilities should an employee have to his or her employer?
13. What should be a firm's responsibilities to the community with regard to (a) basic institutions, (b) education, (c) health and social welfare, and (d) entertainment and the arts?
14. What are the various types of industrial pollution? Who has the responsibility for preventing it? Who should bear the cost?
15. Why has so little been done up to now to protect the environment? What are the best methods of control?
16. The elimination of industrial pollution is only a matter of priorities. Comment.
17. What are business ethics? Illustrate your answer with three examples.

Purpose and Use of Case Problems

Just below in this Unit, there are several short case problems—the first of many scattered throughout the book. Now seems an appropriate time, therefore, to say something about the purpose and use of these problems.

Ideally, their purpose is: (a) to improve a student's ability to think logically and imaginatively; (b) to improve his or her ability to communicate orally and in writing; (c) to provide experience of teamwork—that is to say, getting along with other people (even when they hold different views) and making the best use of a group containing a mixture of energies, knowledge, and talents; (d) to stimulate a student's interest in the subject matter by personal involvement in problem-solving; (e) to reinforce a student's previous reading of the text material; and (f) to provide him or her with new insights into the subject matter. How successful a case problem is in achieving these goals will depend on two things: the quality of the problem and the effort that the student makes.

Case problems can be short, medium or long in length. In this book, most of the problems are short. The rest are medium-length—for example, Jones Furniture Co. Ltd. and Blake Uniform Rental Company. In later, more specialized courses, the student will probably encounter the long, "Harvard-style" case problem where the student is expected to sift through a great mass of detail just to identify the various problems as well as to solve them.

At the end of each case problem in this book, we ask a number of questions. The student's major task is to answer these questions. However, he or she may also be asked to identify and solve additional problems. In many instances, there is no single, correct answer to a problem. This corresponds to the situation in business.

In his or her study of the case, and in the subsequent group discussion, a student should try to determine exactly what the problems are; use his or her imagination and logic to see the alternative possible solutions, and the advantages and disadvantages of each; and finally make a decision supported by logical reasoning. The development of these abilities is essential to any business management career.

CASE PROBLEMS

MOTOR SPECIALTY MANUFACTURERS (ONT.) LTD.
Punch machine operator loses four fingers
Source: *The Mississauga News*

A Mississauga industrial firm has been convicted of failing to provide adequate protection on one of their punch presses and as a result, has been hit with a $2,000 fine in provincial court.

Motor Specialty Manufacturers (Ont.) Ltd., was charged under the Industrial Safety Act after an operator of a punch machine lost four fingers last August as a result of inadequate safety precautions on the machine itself.

The facts of the accident, as related to Judge Donald August by Crown Attorney Eric Scott, were that on Aug. 14, Giovanni Chiafari, an employee with the defendant company, was told to operate a punch press.

Mr. Chiafari took the stand and said he had only been told how to turn the machine on and off but not the intricacies of the device.

The result of this situation was that Chiafari left his operator's seat and moved to the side of the machine in order to remove some material that was jamming it. He opened the guard, which should have kicked out the circuit but the press came down, cleanly amputating four of the man's fingers on his right hand.

Chiafari had been holding down two full time jobs at the time but stated he had been off the day previous to the accident and therefore wasn't tired.

A spokesman for the company said a safety guard had been placed on the machine but someone had cut out a portion of it, enabling the operator to get his fingers under it in the path of the punch.

Mr. Scott said the company had a terrible record for industrial accidents previous to the August 14 amputations but he admitted that after prosecution proceedings had commenced, there had been a definite improvement in conditions at the plant.

Defence counsel argued that the company had done everything it could to stop accidents on the machine but they still persisted.

Judge August accepted Mr. Chiafari's evidence and found that no inspection of the machine had taken place on anything but an irregular basis, and found the company guilty as charged.

After condemning Motor Specialty's horrible safety record, Mr. Scott said the accident had resulted in dire consequences to Mr. Chiafari and called for a substantial fine to show firms they can't get away with installing inadequate safety precautions on their machines.

He then suggested a fine of $2,000, which is still $8,000 less than the maximum penalty as set out by the Industrial Safety Act.

Following the registering of a conviction against the company, Judge August imposed the $2,000 fine and said the Ministry of Labour must think the offence was serious if it made provision for a $10,000 penalty.

Assignment
1. What other types of industrial accidents can occur? Do you have any personal experiences?
2. What are a business firm's moral and legal responsibilities for the safety of its employees?
3. How can safety on the job be improved?
4. What does your provincial government do to improve job safety?
5. What compensation does an employee receive if injured on the job? What happens if the employee is killed?

SNOW WHITE LTD.
Facing up to ethics in business

1. How would you judge the following situations? Indicate any extra information you would need.
   An employee:
   1. Uses the office telephone for a non-business call.
   2. Uses the office photocopying machine to copy a personal document.
   3. Mails a private letter through the office mailing system.
   4. Pads an expense account.
   5. Uses company time to do shopping.
   6. Reveals company business to friends.
   7. Takes company supplies home for personal use.
   8. Accepts gifts from company suppliers.
   9. Lingers over lunch.
   10. Spends too long on a job.
   11. Hides mistakes.
   12. Shifts blame onto others.
   13. Falsifies reports.
   14. Stays away from work, pretending to be sick.
   15. Fails to report on the misdoings of other employees.
   16. Types her own, or others' personal work for remuneration, during slack periods.
2. Give examples of other situations that might be considered to be unethical business practices.

REDIRACK INDUSTRIES LIMITED
Boredom on the job

Courtesy F.W. Reilly and Redirack Industries Ltd.

Mr. Fred W. Reilly, president of Redirack Industries, said in one of the firm's recent newsletters: "Years back, I conducted a factory survey on the theme:

what would make you happier in your work? At that time our management was bent on moulding an outstanding work staff. The surprise was that, although the workers were surrounded by repetitive processes, boredom was scarcely mentioned. Anger at a supervisor? Yes. Frustration at material hold-ups? Yes. Boredom with many other things. Yes. But seldom was the mindlessness of the task mentioned. Maybe a closer look should be taken at the problem of boredom in workshops. Conceivably, plant workers could tell us more than professional writers. In my daily tour of the plant, I see that some of the happiest faces belong to the men operating punch presses and press brakes, or to others proudly watching the cascading sparks of fusing metals. They seek sympathy from no one, and if they are justifiably demanding, their demands centre on the degree of overcrowding that occurs. Most of them appear to have no particular envy of teachers or disc jockeys or even front-office staff. Some time back a press operator put it this way: 'Mustn't salesmanship be a boring occupation, making eight calls daily? I'd die at such work!' If temporary boredom does occur, our plant workers don't tell me about it, nor do their actions or speed of work suggest they are suffering from it. I suspect that they are smart enough to realize that repetitive work provides an opportunity to think and plan for tomorrow. In such situations, we may either stay bored to death or go forward with great expectations for the future."

Assignment
1. How widespread is boredom at work? What are its advantages and disadvantages?
2. What causes boredom? How can it be reduced?
3. How do you plan to avoid boredom in your future career?
4. "Too much formal education usually results in a person's being bored with his job and consequently dissatisfied." Discuss.

LANDING RIGHTS
Buying influence abroad

"An inquiry revealed last summer that a major airline had agreed to make confidential payments to a Mid-East tourism minister. The proposed payments—up to $5 000 annually—were to cover his expenses in trying to obtain landing rights for the airline in that country.

The airline's vice-president testified at the inquiry that the tourism minister was never actually paid any sums, though he did receive a free pass on the airline.

"I don't understand the mores and morals of the Middle East," the Vice-President said, 'but when in Rome . . .'."

Assignment
1. Why is it necessary to make such proposed payments? How are landing rights obtained elsewhere?
2. What would you have done in the vice-president's position?
3. What steps are being taken to outlaw such practices? What are the possible effects?

S.S. BRITANIS
Disposing garbage from a cruise ship

Source: *The Globe and Mail*, Toronto.

Recently our family enjoyed a trip visiting a number of islands in the Caribbean Sea, aboard the very nice *S.S. Britanis*. The eight-day cruise from Dec. 20 to Dec. 28, was one of the most exciting travels we have experienced. Everything connected with the tour was thoroughly organized and the service, as well as the food, on board was just marvellous.

With all the thoughtfulness, organization and preparation for these cruises, why then does no one connected with management think of pollution? How is it possible that all garbage is simply thrown overboard? I am referring to crates, old chairs, bottles, cans, boxes, kitchen refuse, oil pails and hundreds of filled plastic bags. Is there really no one who cares about such a beautiful area like the Caribbean Sea? Do all ships use this method for discarding their refuse? Is it not entirely against their own interest for cruise operators to spoil these areas? Can the sea, especially close to harbors and shallow areas, clean itself of all this pollution? How can a ship as large as the *S.S. Britanis* with passengers numbering approximately 1,300, possibly justify leaving a trail of garbage, thrown from both sides of the ship for miles and miles, as was the case in Venezuela? How many tons of garbage would there be daily from all ships combined? What happens to raw sewage?
Fred Zander
Kettleby

Assignment
1. How would you answer the questions posed in this letter?
2. What can be done to prevent this type of pollution? Whose responsibility is it?
3. How is Canada ensuring, if at all, that its inland waterways and lakes remain clean?

UNIT 1.3: GOVERNMENT INTERVENTION

At one time, many influential people believed that a country would be better off if the government refrained from interfering with business. Adam Smith, the great Scottish economist, was a major proponent of this economic philosophy. Thus, he wrote in 1776 in his famous book, *An Inquiry into the Nature and Causes of the Wealth of Nations*, that the individual, by pursuing his own self-interest, would (as if led by an "invisible hand") unwittingly promote the public interest. And he used the term *laissez-faire* to describe this situation of free enterprise.

Although favoured by many early industrialists, the doctrine of laissez-faire in its extreme form never gained complete political acceptance. For, with the development of the factory system in nineteenth-century Britain, examples of labour mistreatment multiplied overnight. And it soon became clear that business firms ought not to be left alone to pursue profit regardless of all other considerations. It was realized also that government intervention was needed not only to protect the interests of the employee; it was also necessary to protect the interests of the consumer. In fact, examples of such intervention go back to mediaeval times and earlier.

Government Regulation

Over the years, governments, while recognizing the vital importance of private business enterprise, have passed laws to regulate the activities of business firms so that they coincide better with the public interest. Also, through taxation, business firms are required to help pay for government-provided services, such as roads, police and fire protection, and unemployment insurance. This type of contribution to society has now generally been accepted by business—though there is, of course, controversy concerning the level of such taxation and the government's share of the gross national product. In monopoly situations, our governments have either established their own firms (e.g. Canada Post and local electricity commissions) or closely regulated the private ones (e.g. Bell Canada) that have been given exclusive authority to offer a service.

In the following pages, we briefly review the main types of government intervention in business as they affect (a) consumers, (b) employees, (c) the community, and (d) shareholders. We should remember that, under Canada's constitution, the federal Parliament is given the sole right to legislate in certain matters—for example, trade and commerce. In others, such as labour practices, which fall under provincial jurisdiction, the federal Parliament has only the right to pass laws that apply to federal government employees, employees of banks, airlines and various other industries of an interprovincial nature, and employees of firms working under federal government contract.

Consumer Protection

To help protect consumers, whose aim is to obtain good quality products at reasonable prices, various federal and provincial laws have been passed.

Restrictive Trade Practices. A federal statute, the *Combines Investigation Act*, authorizes the government to investigate and prosecute firms which combine to "restrain trade"—that is, to lessen competition.

The most important practice outlawed by the Act is the formation of mergers or monopolies. A *merger* occurs when one firm gains control of a competitor and thereby reduces competition. A *monopoly* is obtained when a firm gains complete or almost complete control of a certain type of business in a particular area and thereby reduces competition. Such a monopoly is legal only if the monopoly right is conferred by the Patent Act or by any other Act of the federal Parliament.

Pricing practices outlawed by the Act are: (a) *price fixing*—an agreement by business firms, often unwritten, to charge the same price for similar products; (b) *price discrimination*—the practice of selling goods more cheaply to one firm than to another; (c) *predatory pricing*—the practice of charging abnormally low prices in order to reduce or eliminate competition; (d) *price misrepresentation*—the practice by a firm of misrepresenting the price at which it sells its goods; and (e) *resale price maintenance*—the practice by a manufacturer of setting the price at which wholesalers and retailers may sell the product and ensuring that these prices are observed by the actual or threatened cutting off of supplies. All these practices limit competition and prevent the public from being able to buy goods at the lowest price. Such practices interfere, in other words, with the free play of the market forces of supply and demand. The prevention of such practices has, therefore, long been considered to be in the public interest.

Under the terms of the Act, a Director of Investigation and Research is responsible for investigating alleged offences and a Restrictive Trade Practices Commission is responsible for reviewing the evidence and recommending action by the Registrar General of Canada. An inquiry into alleged offences can be held following an application by six adult Canadian citizens, on the initiative of the Director, or at the direction of the Registrar General of Canada.

Although the Act seems positive enough, particularly with the various amendments made in 1949, 1952, and 1960, its enforcement has suffered from lack of staff. Various ways have also been devised—for example, consignment selling by oil companies—to avoid prosecution under the Act. In addition, any fines imposed under the Act have been considered too low to have any real deterrent effect.

Because of the inadequacies of the Combines Investigation Act, in 1971 the federal government proposed new legislation in this area. However, Bill C-256, as it was called, provoked a great deal of criticism, particularly from business, and was subsequently withdrawn.

In 1973, it was decided to implement changes in competition policy in two stages. The first stage, Bill C-2, was passed by Parliament in October 1975 and came into force on January 1, 1976. Stage I greatly increased the powers of the present Restrictive Trade Practices Commission, giving it review power over such trade arrangements as refusal to sell, consignment selling, exclusive dealing, tied sales, market restriction, and trade practices detrimental to small business firms and the public at large. In this respect, the Commission can now hold hearings and issue remedial orders including the prohibition of the offending trade practice. It would not be necessary to use the criminal or civil courts. A second major change is the extension of the coverage of the Combines Investigation Act to all service industries except electric power, rail transportation, telephone service, and bona fide trade union activities. Previously, only industries producing, transporting, storing, distributing, or selling physical goods were included. A third important change is that it is no longer necessary to prove "complete or virtual elimination" of competition, but only a sufficient reduction in competition to cause harm to the public.

In November 1977, new competition legislation (Bill C-13) was introduced by the federal government to replace Bill C-42. However, the legislation was not passed. In the 1980s, a new attempt to reform Canada's competition policy can be expected.

False or Misleading Advertising. Under common law, the system of law used throughout Canada, except in Quebec, consumers had some protection from false or misleading advertising. However, such protection has been strengthened by Sections 36 and 37 of the Combines Investigation Act, which provide for fines and/or imprisonment as penalties for persons who misrepresent the goods they sell—for example, claiming that goods are being sold below cost, making claims about the product that are not supported by tests, or misrepresenting the country of origin of a product.

Canada's *Criminal Code* also has several provisions dealing with false or misleading advertising. Thus Section 338(1) makes it an offence for a person "by deceit, falsehood or other fraudulent means" to defraud the public or any person "of any property, money, or valuable security." Section 339 makes it an offence to use the mails to advertise schemes intended to deceive or defraud the public. And Section 366 includes the offence of passing off wares or services as those ordered when they are not, or making false assertions regarding the kind, composition, origin or manufacture of such wares or services.

The federal *Consumer Packaging and Labelling Act* imposes labelling standards on goods imported into Canada and minimum information requirements on all "purchased" goods. The *Textile Labelling Act* requires that a label be attached to clothing and other textile products giving the generic name of each textile fibre comprising 5% or more of the total fibre weight of the article, and the identity of the manufacturer.

Other federal statutes that contain provisions relating to false or misleading advertising include the Bank Act, the Broadcasting Act, the Food and Drugs Act, the Hazardous Products Act, the National Trade Mark and True Labelling Act, the Precious Metals Marking Act, and the Trade Marks Act.

Safety Standards Act. To ensure that products meet certain minimum safety standards, the Standards branch of the federal Ministry of Consumer and Corporate Affairs conducts research and tests in its Standards laboratory. The Standards branch also administers the *Weights and Measures Act* (to ensure that weighing and measuring devices used for selling goods to the public are accurate); the *Electrical Inspection Act;* and the *National Trade Mark and True Labelling Act.*

Provincial Statutes. At the provincial level, there are many statutes that attempt to protect consumers. These statutes, administered by a provincial Ministry (the Ministry of Consumer and Commercial Relations in Ontario), provide for registration of firms (e.g. car dealers, travel agents) selling goods or services to the public; licensing of salespersons; bonding of persons handling funds; supervision of trust funds; and mediation on behalf of dissatisfied customers. The statutes include, in Ontario: the Bailiffs Act, Business Practices Act, Caisses Populaires Act, Cemeteries Act, Collection Agencies Act, Consumer Protection Act, Consumer Reporting Act, Mortgage Brokers Act, Motor Vehicle Dealers Act, Real Estate and Business Brokers Act, Sale of Goods Act, Travel Industry Act, Trust Companies Act, and Upholstered and Stuffed Articles Act.

In Ontario, the *Business Practices Act* prohibits a firm from making false, misleading or deceptive representations in any offer, statement, or proposal related to supplying goods or services. The Act gives the consumer the right to void any contract involving such an unfair practice, requires the supplier to return any money, and authorizes the courts to impose exemplary and punitive damages.

The *Sale of Goods Act* requires any contract of sale above $40 to be evidenced in writing and provides for implied conditions of marketability and fitness of the goods sold.

The *Consumer Protection Act* requires disclosure of actual borrowing costs in credit transactions.

The *Consumer Reporting Act* limits the categories of persons who may obtain personal information from credit reporting agencies, specifies the types of information that should be excluded from credit reports and gives the consumer the right to see and, if necessary, correct his or her credit file.

Under common law, a manufacturer or retailer can be held liable for injury caused to a consumer by the goods sold. Basically, for a consumer to obtain damages, he or she must show that the seller failed to observe the "duty of care." The classic common law case is *Donoghue v. Stevenson* [1932 A.C. 562], in which a girl, invited to a restaurant by a friend and treated to a bottle of ginger beer, discovered, after drinking half the contents, that a decomposed snail was inside. With regard to inherently dangerous products, a manufacturer has a common law duty to warn the consumer of inherent dangers (for example, inflammability).

Employee Protection

The following is a brief review of labour legislation in Canada. A more detailed treatment is provided in Unit 16.2 of this book.

The *Canada Labour Code*, which came into force in 1971, regulates conditions of employment in most industries under federal jurisdiction. Originally, the Code consisted of five parts: fair employment practices; female employees' equal pay; labour standards; safety of employees; and industrial relations. However, Parts 1 and 2 have since been repealed and replaced, in effect, by the *Canadian Human Rights Act*. Under this Act, it is illegal to discriminate in employment against any person on grounds of race, national or ethnic origin, colour, religion, age, sex, marital status, conviction for which a pardon has been given, and physical handicap. Exceptions are permitted for bona fide occupational requirements and for termination of employment at normal retirement age (although the latter is now being challenged under the Canadian Charter of Rights and Freedoms).

Under labour standards, the Canada Labour Code specifies minimum wages to be paid, limits the hours of work of employees to eight per day and 40 per week, provides for minimum paid vacations and holidays, and requires employers to provide written notice of termination of employment once a person has been employed for three months.

In the field of labour relations, Part 5 of the Canada Labour Code gives workers falling under federal jurisdiction (e.g. banks and airlines), the right to join trade unions and bargain collectively with employers. Most persons employed directly by the federal government (e.g. federal ministry employees) are governed by the *Public Service Staff Relations Act*.

Also at the federal level, the government operates an *unemployment insurance program*. This program, compulsory for most employees, provides for benefits to persons who lose their jobs. The government also administers the *Canada Pension Plan* which provides for retirement benefits and supplementary benefits to the retired, disabled, surviving spouses and children, and orphans. Contributions are made by both employers and employees.

Provincial Legislation. In Ontario, an *Employment Standards Act* sets out minimum labour standards for employed persons, covering minimum wage rates, minimum age for employment, limited working hours, annual vacation with pay, public holidays with pay, equal pay for women, maternity leave, and minimum notice requirements. The *Ontario Human Rights Code* prohibits discrimination, or intention to discriminate, against a person in employment practices (such as job advertisements and interviews). A *Labour Relations Act* sets out the procedure by which a trade union can become the certified bargaining agent for a group of employees and bargain collectively with the employer for a labour agreement, covering pay and other conditions of work. A *Workers' Compensation Act* provides financial compensation, as well as medical treatment, for workers who are injured or disabled at work. Benefits are paid from an employer-financed Workers' Compensation Fund. And an *Occupational Health and Safety Act* gives a worker the right to refuse unhealthy or unsafe work; makes joint labour-management health and safety committees mandatory in many industries; and tries to control toxic substances in the workplace.

Community Protection

Business firms have a moral obligation to act as good citizens in the community in which they operate. However, various municipal bylaws have been passed to make such obligations both legal and specific. Thus business firms are required to pay local property taxes, as well as federal and provincial income taxes and sales taxes. Also, within the local community, most types of business firms are restricted geographically, by zoning bylaws, to specific areas—commercial, light industrial, heavy industrial, etc.

An important area of possible community abuse is pollution. This may take the form of air contamination (e.g. smells from an oil refinery or failure to control ragweed), water contamination (e.g. discharge of untreated industrial wastes into the nearest stream), noise pollution (e.g. shunting of freight trains at all hours of the night), and even visual pollution (unsightly displays, derelict buildings). In an effort to prevent this, provincial legislatures have passed Pollution Acts that impose penalties for various types of offences and municipal governments have added their own bylaws.

Shareholder Protection

There are many examples, current and past, of people who have purchased shares of what later turn out to be worthless companies. To help protect investors, provincial legislatures have passed Securities Acts that require, amongst other things, that corporations wishing to sell shares to the public first submit a *prospectus* to a provincial Securities Commission for approval. The prospectus must contain specified information about the directors, capitalization, and purpose of the corporation.

The federal and provincial *Business Corporations Acts* (see Unit 3.1) specify the rights of corporation shareholders and the duties of the directors elected at the annual shareholders' meetings to run the company on the shareholders' behalf. Sometimes, when there are too many "inside" appointments of directors (i.e. appointments of employees to the board), the best interests of the shareholders may be disregarded. Sometimes, also, majority shareholders may act in a manner that is detrimental to the minority shareholders. The Corporations Acts try to afford protection to the weaker parties.

Government Economic Policies

As we have just seen, a large amount of government intervention in Canada is designed to protect people from economic exploitation: in the marketplace, in the workplace, and in the community. However, our governments also intervene in the economy to help make things happen.

"The Prime Minister has asked me to assure you that by working together, government and business, we can build a better Canada ...."

Fiscal Policy. This is the use by a government of its powers of taxation, expenditure, and borrowing to stimulate or dampen economic activity. By spending more than it receives, the government causes economic activity to increase. Conversely, by spending less than it receives, the government causes economic activity to decline. At the present time, our federal and provincial governments would like to reduce the large public debt since the interest payments are so great. However, they can only do so at the risk of less economic activity.

Monetary Policy. This is the alteration of a country's level of interest rates and money supply to achieve various economic goals. The "Bank Rate" is the rate of interest charged by the Bank of Canada, Canada's central bank, and the one on which all other interest rates are based. By lowering this rate, the government can encourage business investment and thereby economic growth. Also, by increasing the money supply, the government can make loans easier to obtain.

International Trade Policy. The federal and provincial governments (see Chapter 19) are deeply involved in the promotion of Canada's exports, so that there will be more jobs and income for Canadians. As a member of GATT (the General Agreement on Tariffs and Trade), Canada is committed, on a reciprocal basis with other member countries, to a gradual reduction in import duties (or "tariffs"). The Autopact between Canada and the U.S., a direct result of government intervention, has permitted free trade (and an expansion in production) in auto vehicles and parts between the two countries since 1965. Nevertheless, the federal government also makes use of "non-tariff barriers," particularly import quotas (which restrict imports of a good to a certain amount per year), to protect certain Canadian industries such as textiles, footwear, and beef.

Employment Policy. To reduce unemployment, Canada's most pressing economic and social problem, our governments rely heavily on the fiscal, monetary, and trade policies just mentioned. In fact, Canada's rate of job creation has been one of the highest in the Western World. It is only the heavy influx of new job seekers, because of the "baby boom" generation and the higher labour force *participation rate* (a larger percentage of each age group seeking work in recent years, particularly females), that has kept the unemployment rate so high.

To combat unemployment, our governments also have other more selective tools. One of these is income tax investment incentives—for example the R & D investment tax credit and the limited lifetime capital gains exemption. Another tool is job retraining. A third type of selective tool is government grants and loans to industry through, for example, the federal Department of Regional Industrial Expansion, the Federal Business Development Bank, and the provincial development corporations.

KEY TERMS

- Laissez-faire
- Adam Smith
- Government regulation
- Consumer protection
- Restrictive trade practices
- Combines Investigation Act
- Merger
- Monopoly
- Price fixing
- Price discrimination
- Predatory pricing
- Price misrepresentation
- Resale price maintenance
- False or misleading advertising
- Criminal Code
- Consumer Packaging and Labelling Act
- Textile Labelling Act
- Safety Standards Act
- Weights and Measures Act
- Business Practices Act
- Sale of Goods Act
- Consumer Protection Act
- Consumer Reporting Act
- Employee protection
- Canada Labour Code
- Canadian Human Rights Act
- Public Service Staff Relations Act
- Unemployment Insurance Plan
- Canada Pension Plan
- Employment Standards Act
- Ontario Human Rights Code
- Labour Relations Act
- Workers' Compensation Act
- Occupational Health and Safety Act
- Zoning bylaws
- Pollution control
- Fiscal policy
- Monetary policy
- Bank rate
- International trade policy
- GATT
- Tariff
- Autopact
- Import quotas
- Employment policy
- Investment incentives
- Job retraining
- Grants and loans

REVIEW QUESTIONS

1. Explain the concept of "laissez-faire." What, in practice, are its good points and bad points?
2. Why have our governments passed laws regulating the activities of private business firms?

3. What are the various types of restrictive trade practices prohibited by the Combines Investigation Act? Why are they considered detrimental to the public?
4. Who enforces the Combines Investigation Act? How effective has such enforcement been?
5. Give three examples of misleading advertising.
6. What statutory requirements exist with regard to the labelling of goods for sale to the public in Canada?
7. Explain the consumer protection role of the Safety Standards Branch of the federal Ministry of Consumer and Corporate Affairs.
8. How have provincial governments tried to protect consumers from unscrupulous business firms?
9. What is the Canada Labour Code? To whom does it apply?
10. Explain the nature and purpose of the Canadian Human Rights Act.
11. What are the key features of the federal Unemployment Insurance Program?
12. Explain the key provisions of the Canada Pension Plan.
13. What is the Employment Standards Act?
14. Explain the nature, scope and purpose of the provincial Labour Relations Act.
15. What is the purpose of the Workers' Compensation Fund? Who pays for it? What benefits are available and to whom?
16. How are business firms encouraged to be good members of their community?
17. How are shareholders protected from unscrupulous promoters and directors?
18. Explain the nature and purpose of "fiscal policy."
19. What is monetary policy? How can it affect business activity?
20. What is Canada's international trade policy?
21. How do our governments try to reduce unemployment? Why have they been relatively unsuccessful in this decade?

CASE PROBLEMS

COOPER METAL CO. LTD.
Allegations of air pollution

Cooper Metal Co. Ltd. is a medium-size industrial firm producing lead for batteries and paints. Located in the older section of Winnipeg, the plant employs 250 workers and has been in operation for over forty-five years. Most of the land surrounding the plant is covered by warehouses. However, immediately to the south of the plant there is a small neighbourhood of older-type residential houses, with a population of some 600 persons.

Over the past few years, the nearby residents have begun to complain about emissions from the firm's alloying and refining furnaces. They have claimed that the plant has contaminated local children as well as adults. A health survey ordered by the local medical officer has, in fact, revealed that four out of the approximately five hundred adults and children surveyed have an unusually high level of lead in their blood. One of the adults, however, works in the lead plant.

The Air Management Branch of the provincial government's Ministry of Environment is now considering the issue of a stop-work order that would close down the offending plant. If the firm fails to comply, a fine could be levied of $5,000 a day for the first offence and $10,000 a day for the second offence.

The firm's president claims that there is insufficient evidence of the plant's harmful effects. He asserts that even if the allegations were true, it would make more sense to move the residents out of what is a predominantly industrial district.

Assignment

1. What responsibilities does a firm have for ensuring clean air?
2. What should the government do?

Complaints about a new car

Source: *The Toronto Star*, Toronto. Reprinted with permission—The Toronto Star Syndicate.

With my first $6,000 I went with my dad to an auto dealer on Aug. 13, to buy a new sports car. Delivery was to be in a week. I picked the car up; it had two kilometres on it.

Two days later I drove it to work. It hesitated and backfired, but I made it. That afternoon it rained. When I turned the wipers on, the left one flew off and landed three cars away. I got a local dealer to fit it. At the same time I told them about the backfiring so they opened the hood and found two spark plugs just hanging by the wires. They fixed that, too.

That was just the beginning. Through last fall I was back at the dealer's every two or three weeks. The brakes pulled, the steering was off, there was a terrible noise in the dash. About a year ago, I was told it was in the best condition it could be.

In January the power steering went. When I braked, the car turned half-way around. I asked for a tow into the dealer's but was told to leave the car where it was. So I got another dealer to fix it. Three days later it broke down again. The back end, brakes and differential were gone. That was a $600 job and the dealer was very reluctant to pay. Finally it was done, plus front shocks, the whole steering mechanism and both front and rear ends. This was at 4800 km and I only got the service because I hired a lawyer.

The topper was on May 7 at 2 a.m. in the middle of nowhere: The car just died.

I had to push it off the road and have it towed the next day. This time it was the alternator and a dead battery. When I complain to the dealer they only say they can't guarantee a car will be trouble-free.

I could have been killed in a brand new car and it seems I have no recourse against the manufacturer.

There are still a lot of faults unfixed—it would take another four pages to write them down. Can you persuade the manufacturer to help me?

*The response we got from the manufacturer surprised even us. The firm's attitude is that the problem has gone away. "We have been advised," the manufacturer wrote us, "that the person has sold this vehicle and purchased another car. For this reason we are closing our file on this matter." We wonder who's got the car now.

Assignment
1. What responsibility *should* a firm have for defective products?
2. What legal responsibility does it actually have?
3. If you were the manufacturer, how would you have handled this complaint?

"Watch your P's and Q's — on the left are the shareholders and on your right their lawyers."

SCHERBLUK MANUFACTURING INDUSTRIES LTD.
A shareholder challenges a firm's policy on charitable donations

At the annual shareholders' meeting of Scherbluk Manufacturing Industries Ltd., Connie Harris, a shareholder, has submitted a proposal to amend the company's bylaws. This proposal, which has already been circulated to all other shareholders, would, if approved, prevent the firm from making any further donations to charities, educational establishments, or similar organizations unless some direct benefit were received in return.

Ms. Harris argues that the firm is supposed to be run for the benefit of the shareholders and that if a shareholder wants to give money away it should come from his or her own private purse.

The president of the company, Mr. Kenneth Clark, has pointed out that it has always been company policy to make such donations on the behalf of the firm and its shareholders. These have cost about one cent per share of company stock and have been given mainly to universities located in the province. Furthermore, he emphasized that private business firms, as good corporate citizens, have a responsibility to provide such funds.

Assignment
1. What are the arguments against such donations?
2. What are the arguments for?
3. As a shareholder, how would you vote on the proposal?

PART B
FORMS OF BUSINESS OWNERSHIP

In this second part of the book, we examine the various forms of business ownership—sole proprietorship, partnership, corporation, and co-operative. As a result, we should be in a position not only to understand what these different legal forms of business ownership mean but also to appreciate their relative merits for different types and sizes of business enterprise. To facilitate our task, we set out for each form of business ownership, first, the main characteristics; second, the principal advantages that it offers to the business person; and, third, the principal disadvantages.

CHAPTER 2
SOLE PROPRIETORSHIP AND PARTNERSHIP

CHAPTER OBJECTIVES

☐ To explain the legal form of ownership used by a person operating a business on his or her own.

☐ To discuss the advantages and disadvantages of using this form of ownership.

☐ To describe the forms of ownership that can be used by persons who wish to operate a business together.

☐ To explain how such partnerships can be set up.

☐ To discuss the advantages and disadvantages of the partnership forms of ownership compared with other forms of business ownership.

CHAPTER OUTLINE

2.1 The Sole Proprietorship

2.2 The Partnership

UNIT 2.1: THE SOLE PROPRIETORSHIP

A sole proprietorship is a business owned by only one person who alone is legally responsible for all its debts and other legal obligations. Usually the business is managed by the owner, but sometimes a paid manager is employed. In the latter case, it is legally possible, if the owner so wishes, to arrange for a share of the profits to be paid to the manager. The owner cannot, however, make any legally binding agreement to share losses. Otherwise, the business may be held in court to be a partnership.

The sole proprietorship is the form of ownership used by many small businesses including manufacturers, retailers, wholesalers, professional firms and tradespersons. Sometimes, instead of sole proprietorship, the term *individual ownership* is used—for example, by Statistics Canada.

To start a business as a sole proprietor, it is usually necessary to obtain a municipal licence. The cost of such a licence will vary according to the type and size of the business and the municipality in which it is to be operated.

Name. If one wishes to use a name or designation other than one's own or to use the words "and Company," the name must be registered at a central provincial registry office. If the name chosen conflicts with one already registered, another must be chosen. A person may always use his or her own name, even though it is the same as that of a competitor, so long as it is not used in a manner intended to deceive the public. As a sole proprietor, a person may not, however, use the term "Limited," "Incorporated" or "Corporation" or their abbreviations "Ltd.," "Inc.," or "Corp." with the business name, as they imply limited liability.

Advantages of the Sole Proprietorship

These include: ease and low cost of establishment; high personal incentive; freedom and speed of action; privacy; possible income tax savings; and ease of dissolution.

Ease and Low Cost of Establishment. Compared with a partnership or corporation, it is quite easy and cheap to establish a business, using the sole proprietorship form of ownership. Only if some other name is used, does the owner need to register the business. Unlike a partnership, there is no agreement to be drawn up. And, unlike a corporation, there are no "articles" to be obtained or government and lawyer's fees to be paid.

High Personal Incentive. The sole proprietor, being entitled to all the profits of the business after tax, has the highest possible incentive to make the business a success. To many persons, a business of one's own offers great challenge and personal satisfaction. Many sole proprietors willingly work fifty, sixty, or more hours per week in their own businesses, sometimes with little or no annual vacation. Also, owning one's own business may provide greater economic security than being an employee of someone else.

Courtesy *Oakville Beaver*

Freedom and Speed of Action. The sole proprietor shares the ownership of the business with no one. He or she is, therefore, completely free to make whatever decisions seem fit, without waiting to consult others and obtain their approval. The proprietor can decide to hire or fire employees, open or close shop, add new lines of goods or discontinue old ones, promptly and without discussion.

Like all businesspeople, the sole proprietor is subject to government control and must, for example, observe tax requirements, local closing hours, labour laws, and fire and sanitary regulations. If the proprietor wishes to provide certain products or services, for example, alcoholic drinks, he or she must obtain a special licence. Nevertheless, the sole proprietorship has fewer government restrictions than the other forms of business ownership.

Privacy. Unlike a public business corporation, a sole proprietor need not publish a financial statement. The financial condition of business is known only to the proprietor, his or her accountant, and Revenue Canada. Where secret processes, formulae, recipes, contacts, or other confidential information are involved, the best solution, whatever the form of ownership, is to restrict the number of people with access to the information and try to ensure that they are trustworthy.

Possible Income Tax Savings. A sole proprietor must include the gross and net income from the business in his (or her) personal income tax return, in the section "Income from Self-Employment." He or she must also file with the return a Statement of Income and Expenses and a Balance Sheet. Unlike the corporation, the sole proprietor is not subject to a specific tax levied on the income of the business. Up to certain levels of business income, and depending on how much income the sole proprietor receives from other sources, there are income tax advantages in being a sole proprietor. Until recently, a sole proprietor was not permitted for tax purposes to include a salary paid to a spouse among expenses. Now he or she is permitted to do so as long as the amount is reasonable for the work done.

Ease of Dissolution. If a sole proprietor wishes to cease business, he (or she) does not have to ask permission, but merely stops doing business. If there are outstanding debts, he may go into voluntary bankruptcy. In this case, the local bankruptcy official, the Official Receiver, will then administer his financial affairs and attempt to settle any claims. If the sole proprietor has been using a designation other than his own name, a signed declaration of dissolution must be filed with the local or central registry.

Disadvantages of the Sole Proprietorship

The sole proprietorship form of business ownership does have a number of disadvantages: unlimited personal liability; limited capital; limited talent; lack of continuity; and possibly heavier income taxation.

Unlimited Personal Liability. A serious disadvantage is the unlimited personal liability of the sole proprietor for all debts of the business. This means that if the liabilities of the business exceed the assets, the owner can be required by law to pay the difference from his or her own personal assets. If the business has incurred a serious financial loss, the sole proprietor may have to sell his or her house, car, furniture, summer cottage, stocks, and anything else owned.

The risk that comes from unlimited personal liability varies with the type of business. Statistics of business failures indicate, for example, a high mortality rate among restaurants, retail stores and house builders. Other businesses, such as doctors' and dentists' practices, as long as they have adequate liability insurance, face relatively little risk.

Often a sole proprietor, if male, will reduce the risk of financial loss from business failure by giving part of his personal assets to his wife. Since a wife is an independent legal person and can hold assets in her own name, the unsatisfied creditors of the husband's business cannot touch her property. An exception occurs when the gift was made recently with the intention of defrauding the creditors. There is a limit, however, beyond which a businessman will not want to go in giving his personal assets to his wife. This will occur when he begins to worry about the loss of his wife rather than the business. The same applies with regard to a husband, if a woman is in business on her own account.

The desire for the greater financial security offered by limited liability is often the most important reason for a sole proprietor's changing the legal form of business to that of a corporation.

Limited Capital. A business set up as a sole proprietorship is usually limited in the amount of funds it can obtain. The equity capital (that is, the owner's investment) is restricted to the owner's personal savings; the borrowed capital, to the amount he or she can convince friends, relatives and the bank to lend.

"A moment, sir. We of Revenue Canada wish to share your ... uh ... joy."

From the lenders' viewpoint, there is only one person who is pledged to repay the loan. This means greater risk and therefore less willingness to lend. If the business proves successful, expansion may be financed partly from internally-generated funds as well as from bank loans. Often, however, a change in the form of ownership may become necessary. Thus, for example, a person with money to invest may be taken in as a partner.

Limited Talent. In a sole proprietorship, the owner is responsible for every phase of the business—research, buying, selling, manufacturing, financing, accounting, advertising, and personnel. He or she may employ other people to help, on either a full-time or a part-time basis. Part-time employees for a store might include Saturday help, the weekly window-dresser, and the accountant. However, the sole proprietor cannot usually afford to employ top-flight full-time people to help run the business. Even when this is possible, the chances of retaining them for long are not very great. Usually, an employee with ability and initiative will soon establish a business of his or her own. Sometimes, to prevent this and to reward loyalty, the sole proprietor will offer the outstanding employee a share of the business. This means, of course, that the form of the ownership of the business will have to change to that of a partnership.

Another disadvantage of being a sole proprietor is that the owner has no partner who can be trusted to run the business in his or her absence, for example, when on holiday or sick in bed. Again this is a motive for changing to a partnership, if a suitable partner can be found.

Lack of Continuity. The fact that the sole proprietor is the sole owner and manager of the business means that his or her permanent absence through illness or death can quickly throw the business into confusion. This lack of continuity can, to some extent, be overcome by developing trusted employees. In the case of death, the administrators of the estate can continue the business under letters of administration. If they are not knowledgeable about the business, or cannot spare adequate time, the business may lose customers before it can be sold or the title transferred to the deceased owner's heirs.

Possibly Heavier Income Taxation. When a sole proprietor reaches a certain level of taxable personal income from all sources (the business and elsewhere), it may be financially more advantageous for him or her to incorporate the business—especially if the business is eligible for the special low rate of corporation income tax available to Canadian-controlled small businesses. Otherwise, the sole proprietor may soon pay a top marginal tax rate of about 50 per cent, depending on the province, on any additional business income.

KEY TERMS

Sole proprietorship

Unlimited personal liability

REVIEW QUESTIONS

1. What are the essential characteristics of the sole proprietorship form of business ownership?
2. If the owner finds a good manager, can that person be given a share of the profits as a management incentive without altering the form of business ownership? Can the owner also provide for the manager to share losses to ensure that he or she does a conscientious job? Explain.
3. What types of business firms use this form of business ownership?
4. Does the owner of a sole proprietorship business need to register the name and address of the business? In what circumstances? What information is required? What is the cost?
5. Are there any restrictions on the name that a sole proprietor may use for his or her business? Explain.
6. "After I left my job and opened my own business, I found that I had swapped one boss for several hundred." Discuss.
7. "Although it's not been easy running my own business, I felt good when I saw all those guys being laid off at my old firm." Discuss.
8. "I used to have a lot more freedom in running my business than I do now." Discuss.
9. "Privacy is becoming more and more difficult to maintain in business regardless of the form of ownership." Discuss.
10. Explain how the income of a sole proprietor is taxed. What information does Revenue Canada require? What expenses are deductible from the gross revenue of the business?
11. Explain how the rates of personal income tax will increase as a sole proprietor becomes more successful in his or her business. What is the maximum rate?
12. How can a sole proprietor minimize income tax? Explain, as part of your answer, the difference between tax minimization and tax avoidance. What are the penalties for tax avoidance?
13. Suppose that you are a sole proprietor operating a sports store in a suburban shopping mall, but decide to move to another part of the country. Unfortunately you are unable to find a buyer for the business. How would you go about closing it? What obligations, if any, would you have? How would you settle them? What legal requirements, if any, must you meet?
14. Suppose your sports store really "bombed" and you have a pile of debts for inventory, rent, utilities, wages, advertising, etc. that you just cannot meet from your business bank account. What can your creditors do? What kind of liability do you have?
15. Different types of business are riskier than others. Explain with examples. How can a sole proprietor reduce the risk involved in operating a business? What risks cannot be reduced?
16. "A sole proprietor's capital is limited only by his imagination." Discuss.
17. "Limited ability is one of the most serious disadvantages of operating a business as a sole proprietor." Discuss.

18. How can a sole proprietor (a) arrange and (b) afford to take a holiday from the business? What happens in practice?
19. What happens to a sole proprietorship business when the owner dies or becomes permanently disabled?
20. When does it become advantageous from the income tax point of view for a sole proprietor to incorporate his or her business?

CASE PROBLEM

VETCH OFFICE FURNITURE AND SUPPLIES
Legal position of the sole proprietor

Arthur Vetch, after losing his job as regional sales manager for a large Canadian printing firm, decided to become self-employed. After careful market research, he rented a vacant store on the main street of a medium-sized town, and went into business selling office furniture and supplies. For working capital, he used his savings and a credit union loan secured by a mortgage on his house. After a shaky start, the business prospered, due in large measure to Arthur's warm personality and sales expertise and the help received from his wife and daughter who "minded the shop" while he was out drumming up business and arranging various types of sales promotion. Soon the store was overcrowded and it became necessary to rent warehouse space in a nearby industrial park.

At a local Chamber of Commerce lunch one day, he overheard that a hardware store, just down the street, was coming on the market. As it was a much larger store than his present one, with access and parking at the rear, he reckoned that he could use the second floor (which was quite open) of the store for storage and conduct a successful hardware business below. However, he would have to hire a store manager. After consulting his wife and accountant, and carefully examining the financial statements of the hardware store, he went ahead and, after some negotiating, purchased the hardware business—paying for it with money earned in his existing business as down payment and a promissory note for the balance.

Assignment:
1. Is Arthur still a sole proprietor?
2. How should he go about hiring a hardware store manager?
3. What financial and other arrangements should he make with the new manager?
4. How should he ensure adequate direction and control of the new store?
5. What would happen if the hardware store lost money?
6. What would happen if the hardware store became unable to pay its creditors? Who would be liable?

READING

Newfoundland's Helicopter King

Craig Dobbin's boundless energy has helped to make him more than $40 million

BY STEPHEN KIMBER
(Stephen Kimber is a Halifax-based freelance writer and editor.)

Source: *The Financial Post Magazine.* Used by permission of Stephen Kimber.

"When I'm up in a helicopter, you know, I feel just like a bird," Craig Dobbin was explaining. "That's how I felt the first time I went up in one and that's still the way I feel today. For me, there's just a real joy in flying in a helicopter."

I'd been trying to find out what in the world had possessed Dobbin, a flashily successful Newfoundland real estate developer, to jump into the helicopter business four years ago after just one flight—a decision which, at the time, seemed impetuous and perhaps even foolhardy but which, today, puts him in a perfect position to cash in handsomely on Newfoundland's anticipated offshore oil wealth—and Dobbin was obliging with a little philosophizing on the run. Everything he does, he does on the run. He was still in mid-reverie, in fact, when the hostess at the Halifax International Airport's VIP lounge interrupted for the second time to caution that his flight to St. John's was about to take off. "I've got to go, but listen, if you have any more questions, you just call me. We'll get together. Okay?"

It's not that simple. I'd already been to his St. John's headquarters once to interview him. "No problem," he'd said on the phone, "I'll be here." He was in Montreal. "An interview?" said the startled secretary. "Oh my, he didn't say anything about an interview. But then, he doesn't usually tell me too much." We tried again a month after our brief airport encounter. "I'll be in London this week, but I'll be back the week after that. Let's see, why don't you come and see me that Tuesday. I'll be here this time. I promise." He was in Saint John, N.B. "He has some meetings there today," explained an associate, "and then I think he's going to Montreal. I'm not sure when he'll be back."

Dobbin isn't trying to avoid the press and he doesn't have anything to hide. It's just that there are people to be seen and deals to be done and fun to be had. Craig Dobbin wants to be in on all of it. Interviews? Well, he says, he's never been much on details.

Craig Dobbin, as he himself is the first to admit, isn't one of your average "vested, pinstriped-suit style" businessmen. He's a street-smart, boardroom-cocky corporate hustler who started with nothing, played his hunches and indulged his fancies, and ended up, at 44, with assets of more than $40 million. "The world," he allows, "is a bottomless pit of opportunity." Craig Dobbin is still digging. The third child of a middle-class, St. John's family of 11 kids, he was born, as he puts it now, "with a basic sense of insecurity. I had an urgent desire to make money and I was willing to work twice as hard as anybody else to do it." After graduating from high school in 1951, he took a job in his father's lumber yard while at the same time running a short-haul trucking firm on one side and dabbling in underwater salvage work on the other. "It was frustrating," he says, "I couldn't seem to get the kind of return I was looking for."

His break came in 1963. With a downpayment scraped together by his wife Penney, a registered nurse, he built their growing family its first house on Sussex Pl. in a suburban development on the edge of St. John's. Almost before they'd settled in, however, Dobbin sold the house for a $3,000 profit. He quickly concluded that he would become a real estate developer and, over the next two years, the family moved five more times as Dobbin built and sold, built and sold, and each time walked away with a bigger profit.

Soon, he was plowing his earnings into duplexes, and then apartment buildings and row houses. "The whole thing was as simple as that," Dobbin says today.

In his first decade in business for himself, Dobbin threw up more than 2,500 houses, duplexes, row houses, apartment buildings, and office towers in Newfoundland, New Brunswick and Quebec. Today, he won't deny that many of them were what one critic has described as "CMHC-tacky," but almost all of them, he points out, made him money. His various enterprises are now estimated to be worth $40 million. (His failures, however, were spectacular: he took a million-dollar bath on a badly located apartment building in New Brunswick and got burned for another million in 1970 when he touched off a violent, eight-day wildcat walkout by Cape Breton construction workers by trying to import non-union Newfoundland labour to work on one of his projects in the cradle of Canadian trade unionism.) In the early '70s, when "the juice began to go out of the housing market"—when larger competitors squeezed into his market and municipalities tightened up their zoning requirements—Dobbin switched to shopping centres and quickly built a dozen small, "K-Mart-style" plazas in Ontario and Quebec as well as four more in the United States. But that, too, began to pale after his merchant-tenants, who had once willingly shouldered much of the cost, "began to get more and more demanding." They began to ask for lower cost leases and more tailored outlets. Dobbin decided it was time to move on.

He was casting about for new opportunities four years ago when he seemingly accidentally stumbled into the helicopter business. (His friends will tell you it was no accident. "Craig has an intuitive sense about these things," says one.) Frank Moores, the then-Newfoundland premier and a close friend, had invited Dobbin to join him for a fishing weekend. Because the salmon river was in a remote part of the province, Moores borrowed a provincial helicopter to ferry them to their destination. For Craig Dobbin, it was love at first flight. He purchased his first helicopter shortly afterwards "as a toy" but then quickly realized the enormous commercial possibilities. Today his company, Sealand Helicopters Ltd., owns a fleet of three dozen machines and already has about one-third of Newfoundland's light helicopter business (where the vehicles are used for firefighting, rescue, and surveying). Now he is buying larger helicopters to challenge Universal Helicopters, an Okanagan subsidiary, in the lucrative and growing offshore oil market. And last year Sealands revenues were estimated at close to $7 million. "Craig is one of those people who sees an opportunity and goes after it," says Moores, who is now a St. John's investment dealer. "I think he looked at Newfoundland and realized that because of our geography, a helicopter was often the most efficient way to get from Point A to Point B. Newfoundland is potentially the richest province in the country, but to exploit that potential—whether you're talking about forestry, or minerals, or hydro, or offshore oil and gas—you have to have a convenient way of getting people and things from place to place. Once he realized all of that, Craig didn't have to call a board meeting. He just got going."

Dobbin's business philosophy is simple: "Get in fast, do whatever it is you want to do, and then get out." He considers himself an idea man and he cheerfully admits he gets bored with the details of running his various enterprises. He prides himself instead on hiring the best managers he can find—"I'm not proud, I look for people who are smarter than I am"—and then letting them handle day-to-day matters. "I'm not like old man Kresge," he says without argument. "I can't take an idea and work on it and refine it and spend my whole life creating the perfect department store. I have to always be trying something new."

For Dobbin, it's an approach that works splendidly, thank you very much. Manulife recently bought a one-third interest in Sealand. Furthermore, two of his St. John's office buildings are now rented out to companies engaged in the offshore oil search.

But Craig Dobbin is more than just smart and rich. He's also a fun-loving, high-living Newfoundland good-old-boy who plays at least as hard as he works. His passion for salmon fishing is just one case in point. "Four years ago," suggests Les Thoms, a St. John's lawyer and a long-time friend, "Craig wouldn't have known a salmon from a trout." But after that first fateful fishing trip with Frank Moores, Dobbin hopped on a plane and flew to London for a week's crash course in casting at the world-renowned Hardy Fishing Rod Co. These days, whenever he gets the urge, Dobbin rounds up some friends, piles them into one of his helicopters, and heads off into the Newfoundland interior for a day or a weekend of salmon fishing and fun.

Dobbin, you see, is obsessive about his pursuits. "Before fishing," says his wife, "it was golf." He'd think nothing of flitting off to Bermuda or California for a few rounds of golf. Now, in the winters, he's an equally devoted cross-country skier. "Craig is one of those rare people who has the ability to be anything he wants to be," adds Bob Cole, the hockey commentator who grew up with Dobbin. "Right now he wants to be an outdoorsman. Everything he does, he does full hog."

Cole still remembers with awe a day the two spent together several years ago in Montreal. "I'd gone up to do a Montreal-Chicago game and Craig happened to be in town so he called and suggested we get together for breakfast." Fifteen whirlwind hours later—during which time Dobbin befriended a number of hockey players he'd never even met before ("He strikes just the right chord with people," marvels Cole), inspected a couple of his shopping centre developments, checked out a few new investment possibilities, took in the hockey game, and ingratiated himself with most of Cole's sportswriting colleagues—Dobbin was still flying and anxious to make a night of it. "I told him, 'Never again.' " Cole recalls. "I was wiped out. But for him, that was just a normal day."

His friends—a tight group of a dozen or so successful Newfoundland businessmen, lawyers, doctors, and academics, many of whom he grew up with—delight in recounting their favourite Craig Dobbin stories. They'll tell you, for example, about the day that Dobbin bundled a group of cronies into his helicopter and flew 250 miles just so they could all share a gourmet lunch on the French island of St. Pierre. Or about the time, two years ago, when he brought his helicopter down at the St. John's golf club and stepped out with both Premier

Moores and country singing star Charlie Pride in tow.

Dobbin's flashy style and his political connections have inevitably won him as many enemies as friends. "He's one of those people who can't seem to have a low profile," says Frank Moores, "and so he's controversial and people don't tend to understand him very well." Moores admits that their personal friendship may have actually hurt the developer's public image. "He'd bid on a government contract and he'd have the lowest tender but people would inevitably say, 'Well, you know, he's a friend of the premier.' I'm sure that our friendship has worked to his detriment."

These days, Dobbin would also prefer to play down his "Rowdyman" image. "I think it is a little unfair," he says seriously. "I do like to have fun and that, but I work hard at my business. I just try to make an honest living." His wife Penney agrees that her husband's image is overblown . . . slightly. "I think it's somewhat exaggerated. But he *is* impulsive and he *is* impatient. He's always wanting to be doing something, he can't sit still, and everything always has to be done yesterday."

But there is something else about Craig Dobbin that is often overlooked by outsiders. "There's a quality to the man that's hard to put your finger on," explains one friend, "but it has to do with loyalty and kindness. He cares, he really does, and he'll do anything for a friend. There's real character in the man."

There is indeed.

It was Friday, August 10, 1979—just three days after Craig Dobbin had been trying to explain, between planes in the Halifax airport, just what it was that had first attracted him to helicopters—and now he was going to use one of those helicopters both to get in a little fishing and also to transact some business. He had invited Jim Walsh, a Royal Bank branch manager in St. John's, and Robert "Red" Everett, the bank's regional manager to join him so that they could discuss some deals he was cooking up for the helicopter company as well as Moses Morgan, the president of Memorial University, so that he could iron out some details about a building Dobbin was planning to erect on the campus. The plan was that they would all fly to St. Alban's at the head of Bay D'Espoir on the province's south coast, fish and talk the day away, and then return to St. John's that night.

Timothy Neuss, Dobbin's pilot, eased the seven-passenger, Bell Long Ranger helicopter up and away from St. John's airstrip shortly after seven that morning. After one brief stop to take on fuel at Clarenville, a community near the Terra Nova National Park, they began what was supposed to be the final leg of their journey to St. Alban's, 175 kilometres to the west, at around 9 a.m.

But they were barely back in the air when the machine suddenly sputtered and lost power. Instinctively pilot Neuss went into an autorotation manoeuvre that, under normal circumstances, should have allowed the helicopter to float gently back to earth. But the circumstances were far from normal. They were flying over rugged, hilly, and bushy terrain and Neuss realized almost as soon as he started that manoeuvre that it would bring them down into hydro lines that would inevitably reduce both the helicopter and its occupants to cinders. In an act that Dobbin was later to describe as "heroism," the pilot switched off the autorotation at the last possible moment and allowed the helicopter to free-fall the final 150 feet—roughly equivalent to dropping off the top of a 10-story building.

The machine, a mess of broken and twisted metal no longer even recognizable as a helicopter, came to rest on its side on a hill in woods so thick that the crash site could not be seen from a distance of 25 feet away. Jim Walsh was dead, Tim Neuss was unconscious and breathing heavily, and Red Everett and Moses Morgan—though conscious—were both in great pain and barely able to move. So was Craig Dobbin. He was bleeding profusely from the head and he felt a dull aching somewhere in his body that he could not place. Still, he managed to free himself from the wreckage and, after briefly examining his companions, ripped off his shirt and wrapped it around his head to staunch the flow of blood. Then, using the sun to orient himself, he picked his way through the dense bush to the railway tracks he had glimpsed briefly from the air just before the crash. He marked the spot on the track with a log and then walked, stumbled and crawled toward what he thought was Clarenville, five kilometres away. He was, he learned later, going in the wrong direction but, luckily, he came across a maintenance crew which put in an urgent call for help to Clarenville and then rushed back to the scene ahead of the hobbled Dobbin.

"If he hadn't had the presence of mind to find those tracks and go for help," Bob Cole says today, "they probably wouldn't have been discovered for some time. It could have been much, much worse."

As it was, two men—Neuss succumbed several days later in hospital—died as a result of the crash, and Morgan and Everett required nearly four months convalescence to recover from their injuries. Craig Dobbin? When he finally allowed himself to be treated, after his companions had been tended to, it was discovered that he had a split sternum and required nearly 50 stitches to close the gash in his head. "I went to see him two days after he went into the hospital," Cole remembers, "and he couldn't move. Forty-eight hours later, he was out of the hospital and back to work. I tell you, there aren't many in the world like him."

The roots of what Craig Dobbin's friends like to call his "special personality"—that alluring mixture of personal charm and business savvy that is given substance and depth by his intense sense of loyalty to friends—can be found in his childhood. "When you're one of 11 in a family," suggests his wife, "you have to work that much harder just to make a mark in your own family."

Although the Dobbins, originally from Ireland, had been in Newfoundland for generations, it wasn't until Craig's father Paddy went into business for himself in 1950 that the family finally escaped from fishing, traditionally the lowest rung of Newfoundland society. P.J. Dobbin Lumber and Building Supplies Ltd. was the kind of place "where you bought lumber in the morning and sold it in the afternoon," Craig Dobbin remembers with admiration. "My father was one of those one-armed paperhanger types who worked extremely hard all his life just to get by. He pulled every string in the book to make a living but, in all his dealings, he was still always the essence of honesty."

The Dobbin family was well-known in the east end of St. John's and not just because of its numbers. "They had a real willingness to share their home with people," says Bob Cole, "and it was common when we were growing up for people just to drop in on them because you knew that the hospitality mat would always be out. You know, I think it says something for Paddy Dobbin and his wife," he adds, "that all of their children turned out so well." They did. Dobbin's five sisters all became nurses or teachers (one sister was killed in a car accident). Of his brothers, one is now an engineer, another is a doctor, a third is a contractor, and a fourth is a union negotiator (the fifth brother was paralyzed as the result of a diving accident in his youth).

Ironically, the most successful of all the

Dobbin children—Craig—is the one who didn't make it to university. He was too busy trying to figure out how to make his first million to have time for the relaxed life of a university student. "I think that he always wanted to be in business for himself," Penney Dobbin says. "Even when we met in 1955 and he was collecting accounts for his father's business (she was then a nursing student in the same class with one of Dobbin's sisters and was a frequent visitor to the house), you could see right away that he was very ambitious."

They were married in 1958 and, while he chased his still-elusive fortune, she continued to work as a nurse. "I was making more than Craig was then and so we lived very frugally on his salary and banked everything I made so that someday we'd be able to afford a house of our own."

That first house, of course, was the turning point and the Dobbins have never looked back. Today, they live in a comfortable but not ostentatious St. John's house and have a cottage on Sandy Lake in central Newfoundland. "Craig doesn't go there too often though," sighs his wife. "He finds it too quiet for his tastes."

Dobbin himself admits that he has, until recently, spent far too little time with his growing children but he adds that that is changing now. "He's a very good father when he's around," admits his wife but she will also suggest that she's just as happy that all of their children—four of them, Joan, 20, Mark and David both 19, and Carolyn 17, are studying at university, while 15-year-old Craig goes to high school in St. John's—have different temperaments than their father. "They have at least a little bit of patience with the world."

Craig Dobbin's well-known impatience—he's been known to toss the telephone receiver at the wall in his office whenever a conversation doesn't please him—and his equally famous impulsiveness are enough to convince most of his friends that even the helicopter business cannot hold him for long. "He is a man," sums up Cole, "who can't accept being ordinary and that makes him always want to find that something different that he can do before anyone else gets involved." But neither Cole nor any of Dobbin's other friends will hazard a guess at what might come next for Craig Dobbin.

For his part, Dobbin would rather talk about the helicopter business; about the work the company has been doing off Newfoundland and Labrador and in the north for oil exploration companies, and about lucrative contracts just around the corner. "I like the feeling of being in on something at the beginning. When there gets to be too much competition in the helicopter business I suppose I'll start to look around for something else. I can't tell you what it would be right now because I don't have a clue. But I'm not worried. Something always comes along."

Craig Dobbin still believes that opportunity is a bottomless pit.

Assignment
1. How did Craig Dobbin get started on his road to riches?
2. What made him change his area of business activity?
3. How did he get into the helicopter business? What has kept him there?
4. What is Dobbin's business management philosophy?
5. How do you assess Dobbin's "special personality"? What were its roots? How has it benefitted him in his business career?
6. Would you agree that in Canada today opportunity is still "a bottomless pit"?

UNIT 2.2: THE PARTNERSHIP

A *business partnership* exists when two or more persons join together to carry on a business for profit without becoming incorporated. The partners' individual contributions to the partnership business may include name, reputation, time, experience, skill, ideas, personal contacts, and/or capital.

This form of business ownership, like that of the sole proprietorship, is to be found in large numbers in manufacturing, the wholesale and retail trade, in the professions (where incorporation is sometimes specifically forbidden) and in the carpentry, painting, plumbing and other trades.

Formation of a Partnership

A partnership may be formed by express agreement or by implication. *Express agreement* means that the parties agree verbally or in writing to establish a partnership. Partnership by *implication* arises when a court holds that two or more parties intended to act as partners—for example, to share the losses of a business venture—even though no express agreement was made. The Partnerships Act in each province sets out certain rules for determining whether or not a partnership exists.

General versus Limited Partnership

There are two main kinds of partnership: general and limited. In a *general partnership*, all the partners, known as *general partners*, share in management of the business and have unlimited personal liability for any losses incurred. This liability is both joint and several. Joint liability means that all the partners are together liable for the debts of the firm. Several liability means that any one partner may be required to pay all the debts if the other partners are unable to pay their proportionate shares. Of course, such a partner will have a claim against the other partners. But this will be of little comfort if they are penniless or have conveniently disappeared.

A *limited partnership* is a partnership consisting of both general and limited partners in which the personal liability of the limited partners for business debts is limited to their investment in the partnership. There is no limit on the number of these limited partners. There must, however, be at least one general partner who has unlimited personal liability.

Types of Partners

Partners may be divided, first of all, into two basic categories: general or limited. A *general partner* is one who has unlimited personal liability for the debts of the business. A *limited partner* is one whose personal liability for debts incurred by the partnership is limited to the amount he or she has invested in the business. This kind of partner is found only in a limited partnership.

Another basis of distinction is whether the partners are actively engaged or not in the operation of the business. An *active partner* is one who is so engaged.

A *dormant*, *silent*, or *sleeping partner* is one who does not take an active part. Limited partners automatically fall into this last category.

If a general or limited partner conceals from the public his or her participation in the partnership, he or she may be termed a *secret partner*.

If a partner has a position of considerable authority in the partnership business because of the amount of his or her investment, the breadth of his or her experience, or the management role that he or she plays, that individual may be known as a *senior partner*. The other partners would be known as *junior partners*. This terminology is used in, for example, law and accounting firms.

Eligibility

Any person who is legally competent may enter into a partnership agreement and thereby acquire the full legal rights and duties of a partner.

In the case of minors (persons under 18 or 19 years of age, depending on the province), although they may become partners, they are not liable for the debts of the partnership unless guilty of fraud. If, however, they repudiate the liabilities of the partnership, they disqualify themselves from sharing in the profits. A minor may repudiate the contract of partnership at any time before reaching 18 years or within a reasonable time thereafter. If a minor fails to do so, he or she will be considered a full partner and liable with the other partners for debts incurred by the business after his or her majority.

A married person may enter into a contract of business partnership with his or her spouse.

Partnership Name

A general partnership may use as the firm's name the actual names of some or all of its partners. If it wishes to use another name, it must not be that of any other previously registered firm, or sufficiently similar to create confusion. Also, it must not use the words "Limited," "Incorporated," or "Corporation," or their abbreviations, "Ltd.," "Inc.," or "Corp."

A limited partnership business may also use as its name the names of one or more of its general partners. However, it may not include the surname or a distinctive part of the corporate name of a limited partner. Otherwise, the limited partner is liable as a general partner to any creditor of the limited partnership who is unaware that the limited partner is not a general partner.

Registration

Every province requires that a general partnership for trading, manufacturing, or mining purposes be registered within a certain period after its formation. This registration consists of filing with a local or central registry office a declaration (Figure 2.1) giving full particulars of the partners, including: the name and address of the business; the business activity carried on; the date when the partnership was started; the full name and address of each partner; the birthdate if a minor; the capital contribution, if a limited partner; and the partners' signatures.

Ministry of Consumer and Commercial Relations — Ontario
Ministère de la Consommation et du Commerce

DECLARATION Under the Partnerships Registration Act and the Limited Partnerships Act

DÉCLARATION Aux termes de la Loi sur l'enregistrement des sociétés en nom collectif et de la Loi sur les sociétés en commandite

Form/Formulaire CD-375

07219 12/85

1. Name of partnership, sole proprietorship / Nom de la raison sociale de la société, entreprise individuelle: **Alford and Wells**

2. Mailing address (see instruction 3 & 4) / Adresse postale (voir instruction 3 & 4): **1024 Earl Road, Oakville, Ontario** — Postal Code/Code postal: **L6J 2L1**

3. Business address (if different than mailing address) (see instruction 3) / Adresse de l'entreprise (si elle est différente de l'adresse postale) (voir instruction 3): Postal Code/Code postal:

4. Date of establishing partnership, sole proprietorship (month, day, year) / Date de la fondation de l'entreprise ou de la société (mois, jour, année): **June 1, 198—**
   ☐ Check if renewal or change / Cocher s'il s'agit d'un renouvellement ou d'un changement

5. Business activity carried on / Activités de l'entreprise: **Television Sales and Service**

6. Jurisdiction in which formed if other than Ontario / Autorité compétente sous laquelle l'entreprise a été fondée (si ce n'est pas l'Ontario):

MINISTRY USE ONLY / RÉSERVÉ AU MINISTÈRE
Registration Date / Date d'enregistrement:
Expiry Date / Date d'expiration:

CARD / CARTE OF / DE

| 1978/87 | 1979/88 | 1980/89 | 1981/90 | 1982/91 | 1983/92 | 1984/93 | 1985/94 | 1986/95 |
| 1 2 3 4 | 1 2 3 4 | 1 2 3 4 | 1 2 3 4 | 1 2 3 4 | 1 2 3 4 | 1 2 3 4 | 1 2 3 4 | 1 2 3 4 |

This registration expires in five years but may be renewed. Renewal is your responsibility. The registration expiry date will be shown in your Certificate of Registration. The registration does not confer on the partnership or proprietorship any right to the name or style that it does not otherwise have.

Cet enregistrement expirera dans cinq ans mais pourra être renouvelé. C'est à vous que revient la responsabilité de faire le renouvellement. La date d'expiration sera inscrite sur votre certificat d'enregistrement. La demande d'enregistrement ne confère à la société ou à l'entreprise aucun droit en ce qui concerne sa raison sociale ou son nom commercial qui ne lui serait pas à priori conféré.

The registration has not been accepted for the following reasons:
L'enregistrement n'a pas été effectué pour les raisons suivantes:

☐ The fee of $10.50 was not enclosed. / Les frais de 10.50$ n'étaient pas inclus.
☐ The cheque is post-dated, stale dated, not dated, not signed. / Le chèque est post-daté, périmé, n'est pas daté, n'est pas signé.
☐ The cheque must be certified and payable to the Treasurer of Ontario. / Le chèque doit être certifié et payable à l'ordre du Trésorier de l'Ontario.
☐ Late registration - over 60 days - affidavit required. / La demande d'enregistrement est en retard de plus de 60 jours - déclaration sous serment requise.
☐ The form has not been fully completed in Item Number _____. / La section _____ du formulaire n'a pas été remplie complètement.
☐ See instruction Number _____. / Voir le paragraphe _____ des instructions.
☐ The information is not legible or not suitable for microfilming. / Les renseignements donnés ne sont pas lisibles ou ne peuvent pas être photographiés sur microfilm.
☐ This form has been folded or damaged. / Le formulaire a été plié ou abîmé.
☐

Complete questions on the reverse / **Répondez aux questions au verso** ▼

7. All members of the partnership/the proprietor where natural persons are 18 years of age or over, except those whose birthdate appears in column 'A' of item 8.
   Le propriétaire ou tous les associés sont des personnes physiques ayant 18 ans ou plus à l'exception de ceux dont la date de naissance est inscrite dans la colonne 'A' du paragraphe 8.
8. The names and particulars of all partnership members/or the proprietor. (All first, middle names for partners or proprietors - first, middle name, initials and last names for limited partners).
   Noms de tous les associés ou du propriétaire (le propriétaire et les associés doivent donner tous leurs prénoms - les commanditaires doivent donner leur prénom, leurs initiales et leur nom).
   REMARQUE: *Tous les masculins et féminins se rapportent également aux hommes et aux femmes.*

A. Name in full (including all first names) Nom au complet (y compris tous les prénoms)	B. Residence address or address for service (see instruction 3) Adresse de la résidence ou adresse pour signification (voir instruction 3)	C. Type of partnership Genre de société		D. Signature
		General on nom collectif ☐	Limited en commandite ☐	
James F. Alford	683 Hidden Valley Trail Mississauga, Ont. L5K 1T5	If limited partner, contribution to capital *Commanditaire contribution au fonds commun* $		*James F. Alford*
Peter T. Wells	847 Chartwell Road Oakville, Ont. L6J 2L1	If limited partner, contribution to capital *Commanditaire contribution au fonds commun* $		*Peter T. Wells*
		If limited partner, contribution to capital *Commanditaire contribution au fonds commun* $		
		If limited partner, contribution to capital *Commanditaire contribution au fonds commun* $		
		If limited partner, contribution to capital *Commanditaire contribution au fonds commun* $		
		If limited partner, contribution to capital *Commanditaire contribution au fonds commun* $		

Figure 2.1 Partnership Registration Form

Written Agreement

The existence of a partnership is easier to prove in court when it is in writing. Consequently, a prudent person when entering into such an arrangement will require: first, that there is a written contract (Figure 2.2); and second, that a lawyer examines, or helps draw up, the contract to ensure that the client's interests are protected. The contract should contain at least:

1. The name, address, and purpose of the firm.
2. The names and addresses of the partners.
3. The amount of each partner's investment.
4. The manner in which profits and losses are to be shared.
5. The drawing privileges, if any, of the partners (for example, $500 per week for each partner).
6. The authority and duties of each partner.
7. Limits to a partner's right to individual action (for example, a stipulation that he or she may not enter into a financial commitment for over $1,000 without the other partner's consent).
8. The life of the partnership (for example, for a stated number of years, with an automatic renewal).
9. The manner in which a retired, deceased, or expelled partner's share of the partnership is to be settled.
10. The way in which disputes between partners are to be resolved (for example, by arbitration or by court action).
11. The way in which the partnership may be dissolved in case of disagreement.

Settlement of Disputes

If a dispute arises between the partners—for example, as to the sharing of profits—and no express or implied agreement relating to the matter can be proven, the dispute would be resolved in court by reference to the Partnerships Act for the province. In Ontario, some of the most important rules that would apply in the absence of a partnership agreement covering the matter are:

1. All the partners are entitled to share equally in the capital and profits of the business, and must contribute equally towards the losses, whether of capital or otherwise. (This is so, even though the partners may not have invested equally in the partnership.)
2. The firm must indemnify every partner in respect of payments made and personal liabilities incurred by him or her in the ordinary and proper conduct of the business of the firm, or in or about anything necessarily done for the preservation of the business or property of the firm.
3. Every partner may take part in the management of the partnership business.
4. No partner is entitled to remuneration for acting in the partnership business. (However, he or she may draw so much per week or month against expected profits.)

5. No person may be introduced as a partner without the consent of all existing partners.
6. Any difference arising as to ordinary matters connected with the partnership business may be decided by a majority of the partners, but no change may be made in the nature of the partnership business without the consent of all existing partners.
7. No majority of the partners can expel any partner unless power to do so has been conferred by express agreement between the partners.
8. Subject to any agreement between the partners, a partnership is dissolved: (a) if entered into for a fixed term, by the expiration of that term; (b) if entered into for a single adventure or undertaking, by the termination of that adventure or undertaking; or (c) if entered into for an undefined time, by a partner giving notice to the other or others of his or her intention to dissolve the partnership.
9. Subject to any agreement between the partners, every partnership is dissolved as regards all the partners by the death or insolvency of a partner.
10. If a partner, without the consent of the other partners, carries on a business of the same nature as and competing with that of the firm, he or she must account for and pay over to the firm all profits made in that business.

Most of the above rules apply, it must be remembered, only if there is no partnership agreement, express or implied, or if the partnership agreement makes no provision for the particular point of dispute.

Dissolution of a Partnership

Many business partnerships are terminated each year for a variety of reasons, such as: the death of a partner; the completion of the purpose for which the partnership was formed; the failure of the partners to maintain amicable relations with each other; the failure of the partnership to fulfil the profit expectations of the partners; or, at worst, the financial insolvency of the business.

According to the Partnerships Registration Act, when dissolution occurs, any or all of the persons who composed the partnership may sign a declaration certifying the dissolution of the partnership. Until such a declaration is made, a person may still be held in law to be a partner and therefore liable for debts incurred by the business after as well as before the date that he or she effectively ceased to be a partner. On application by a partner, the court may, in certain circumstances, order a dissolution of a partnership—for example, when a partner, other than the partner suing, becomes in any other way permanently incapable of performing his or her part of the partnership contract.

AGREEMENT OF PARTNERSHIP

AGREEMENT made this 1st day of September, 198-,

BETWEEN Ray Lund, of 10 Northill Crescent, Don Mills, Ontario, and John Ballard, of 53 Brownridge Drive, Don Mills, Ontario.

WITNESSETH:

1. That the said parties will, as partners, engage in and conduct the business of a sporting goods store.
2. That the name of the firm shall be John-Ray Sporting Goods.
3. (a) That the term of the partnership shall commence on the 1st day of September, 198-, and shall end on the 31st day of August, 198-.

    (b) That the partnership shall be renewed automatically for further 12-month periods, subject to 3 months' written notice being given by one partner to the other of his wish to terminate the partnership.
4. That the place of business shall be The Seven Points Plaza, Don Mills, Ontario.
5. (a) That the capital of the firm shall be $20 000, to be contributed in equal cash amounts of $10 000 each on the signing of the Agreement.

    (b) That neither party's contribution to the partnership capital shall bear him interest.
6. That the partnership capital and all other partnership moneys shall be deposited in the Don Mills branch of the Royal Bank of Canada, from which all withdrawals shall be only by cheque signed jointly by both partners.
7. (a) That books of accounts shall be kept in accordance with standard accounting procedures.

    (b) That these books shall be kept on the premises and open to the inspection of either partner.
8. That each partner shall be entitled to draw 500 dollars per week from the funds of the partnership on account of his profits.
9. (a) That at the end of August of every year, an inventory shall be taken and the assets, liabilities, and gross and net income of the business ascertained.

    (b) That the net profit or net loss shall be divided equally between the partners, and the account of each shall be credited or debited accordingly.
10. That neither partner shall, without the written consent of the other, draw, accept, sign, or endorse, any bill of exchange, promissory note or cheque, or contract any debt on account of or in the name of the partnership, except in the normal course of business and up to the amount of $1 000.
11. That each partner shall devote his whole time and attention to the partnership business, and shall not, during the term of the partnership, engage in any other business.
12. That should one of the partners die, his executors shall be entitled to receive the value of his share of the partnership property at the time of his death, together with 9 per cent interest in lieu of profit from that day on until final settlement of the property.
13. That on termination or dissolution of the partnership, other than by the death of a partner, an audit shall immediately be made of the firm's assets and liabilities and the balance be divided equally between the partners.

14. (a) That in the event of a disagreement between the partners as to the conduct of the business, as to its dissolution, or as to any other matter concerning the business, the same shall be referred to arbitration within 10 days of written notice being served by one partner on the other.

    (b) That each partner shall appoint one arbitrator, who shall in turn appoint a third arbitrator.

    (c) That the matter referred to arbitration shall be decided by simple majority of the arbitrators.

IN WITNESS WHEREOF, the parties hereto set their hands and seals, the day and year first above written.

Witnesses:
Frank Smyth   *Frank Smyth*   Ray Lund   *Ray Lund*
Murray Paulis   *Murray Paulis*   John Ballard *John Ballard*

Figure 2.2 Example of a Partnership Agreement (no set form prescribed by law)

Advantages of a Partnership

These include: more capital; better credit standing; more owner talent; keeping valuable employees; personal incentive; and few legal restrictions.

More Capital. Whereas a sole proprietorship must rely on the savings and borrowings of one person, the general partnership combines the financial resources of two or more persons. Also, a person with a good business idea or with good business ability may be able to set up in business only by finding a partner who has money to invest. Many sole proprietorships, faced with a growing demand for their products or services, have changed their form of ownership to that of a partnership for the specific purpose of obtaining additional financing.

Better Credit Standing. A partnership usually finds it easier to obtain credit from suppliers and loans from banks or finance companies than does a sole proprietorship. This is because the lender has several persons, rather than just one, to whom it may look for repayment. As in the sole proprietorship, the personal assets of the partners are additional security for repayment of the money borrowed or credit obtained.

More Owner Talent. A partnership provides the opportunity for two or more persons, each with a specific talent—for example, vehicle maintenance and repairs, and car and truck selling—to join in business together. Where the talents are complementary, each partner can benefit from the association. On his or her own in a sole proprietorship, the same person, with limited knowledge and ability, might not be able to build a profitable business. Although persons with other talents may be hired, this is usually too expensive, particularly in the early stages of a business.

The combined judgment of the partners may also be beneficial for the business. Snap decisions will be less likely to take place in matters of policy. On the other hand, decisions may be made too slowly. Much will depend on the personalities of the partners.

Keeping Valuable Employees. Even if a sole proprietor can hire or develop an outstanding employee, he or she may not find it easy to keep the person. An employee's demands for ownership status and a share in profits are usually met by leaving his or her present employer to start a firm of his or her own. If the present employer believes that an individual is too valuable to lose—for example, the loss of a good restaurant manager may cause clientele to go elsewhere—the employer may offer higher wages and/or a partner's share of the business. The new partner's contribution may be only in small part financial. His/her entitlement to a share in the profits may be based mainly on the service that he/she performs in attracting customers.

Personal Incentive. Even if a sole proprietor can afford to hire and is able to retain talented employees, such employees will still not have the personal incentive that comes from ownership. This incentive induces people to work hard and for long hours, often with little immediate financial reward. It often makes the difference between success and failure in the business. A partnership allows a number of individuals to have the strong personal incentive that comes from ownership of a business.

Few Legal Restrictions. It is more complicated and expensive to start a partnership than it is a sole proprietorship. Because more than one person is involved, each with unlimited liability for partnership debts, the rights and duties of each partner must be carefully spelled out. This is normally done by means of a written agreement, for which legal expenses will usually be incurred. Also, the partnership must be registered, and a small fee is charged for registration. Once the partnership is established, no other formalities are required, except registration of a change in the membership or name of the partnership or of dissolution if and when the partnership is terminated.

However, compared with the establishment and operation of a corporation, the partnership form of business ownership is relatively simple. No charter is required, nor is a written partnership agreement legally necessary.

Disadvantages of a Partnership

The possible disadvantages include: unlimited personal liability; possibly heavier income taxation; possible management disagreement; limited capital; possible lack of continuity; and a relatively frozen investment.

Unlimited Personal Liability. Each general partner in a general or limited partnership has unlimited personal liability for the debts of the business. If the partnership becomes insolvent, the partners will be required by law to pay from their personal funds the debts which are outstanding. This liability is the same as that of the sole proprietor.

The partners' unlimited personal liability is both joint and several. In other words, all the partners are together liable for the debts of the business, and yet, at the same time, each one has the liability to pay all the partnership debts if the others cannot or do not pay their share. The only remedy for the partner or partners saddled with the other partners' share of the debts is to sue them for breach of the partnership contract. However, this can be of little comfort if the other partners have absconded or disposed of their assets.

The combination of unlimited personal liability and joint and several liability often deters people from entering a partnership. In some cases, where the partner wishes only to make a financial investment and not to participate actively in management, a limited partnership may be suitable. A limited partner's liability is limited to his or her business investment.

A general partner can by law enter into a binding agreement on behalf of the partnership. Thus a partner may make an unwise decision—for example, buying goods which can be resold only at a loss—which may result in loss to all the partners. If sufficiently great, this loss may wipe out the business and personal assets of all the partners. Many partnership agreements therefore restrict the right of a partner to enter into commitments above a certain sum without approval of the other partner or partners. Such an agreement does not, however, prevent the partner from legally committing the firm. It merely provides the other partners with the right to sue the delinquent partner for breach of the partnership contract. However, this may be meaningless if such a partner has few assets left or is no longer around.

In the case of a married person, the creditors cannot normally touch the personal assets of the spouse, if he or she is not a partner in the business.

Possibly Heavier Income Taxation. A partner in a business must include his or her share of the net partnership income in a personal income tax return under "Income from Self-Employment." Like the sole proprietor, a partner will find that once the business starts to prosper the marginal personal income tax rate is very high. However, by becoming instead the part owner of a Canadian-controlled small business, he or she may be eligible for a much lower flat rate of corporation income tax, as explained in the next chapter.

Possible Management Disagreement. Usually, one of the strengths of a partnership is the pooling of knowledge and experience. Sometimes, however, the personalities of the partners prove incompatible. The resultant discord among partners can create confusion and dismay among employees, with a consequent lowering of morale. This situation can soon paralyze action throughout the firm, causing customers to be lost, and profits to be whittled away.

Limited Capital. Compared with a sole proprietorship, a partnership is abundantly supplied with capital. Compared with a business corporation, particularly a public one, the partnership is supplied with very little. Few people possess the large sums of money that are now required to establish and successfully operate many modern businesses, such as steel plants and supermarkets. Much of the required capital must come, in fact, from a multiplicity of investors, large and small. Also, even if those relatively few persons with extremely large sums were desirous of investing their money in business, the drawbacks of the partnership, even in its limited form, would dissuade them. These drawbacks are: unlimited and several liability as a general partner; restricted control over one's investment as a limited partner; the relatively frozen nature of the investment for general and limited partners alike; and the high rate of personal income tax that would have to be paid on any profit.

Possible Lack of Continuity.
Unless suitable provision is made in the partnership agreement, a partnership will legally terminate if one of the partners dies, becomes insolvent, incapacitated, or insane, commits a breach of the partnership agreement, conducts himself to the prejudice of the business—for example, by persistent drinking—or, if the partnership is for an indefinite period, gives notice of intention to dissolve the partnership.

Where provision has been made in the agreement to buy out the share of a partner who dies or retires, continuity of the business is normally assured. The problem of finding cash to buy the share is frequently met by taking out term insurance on the life of each partner with the other partners as beneficiaries.

Relatively Frozen Investment.
Compared with the shareholder of a business corporation, a partner cannot easily liquidate his/her investment by selling it to someone else should a sudden need for funds arise. Even though the partnership agreement may give a partner the right to sell his/her share of the business, the remaining partners must normally approve of any new partner. If they do not approve, they will have to buy the share themselves or see the partnership dissolved. But even so, considerable time will elapse before the former partner can withdraw his/her funds.

KEY TERMS

Partnership	Dormant, or silent partner
Express agreement	Senior partner
Partnership by implication	Junior partner
Partnerships Act	Eligibility
General partnership	Partnership name
Limited partnership	Partnership registration
General partner	Unlimited personal liability
Limited partner	Joint liability
Active partner	Several liability

REVIEW QUESTIONS

1. How would you define a business partnership?
2. What are the various types of contributions that a partner may make to a business partnership?
3. Which types of business make use of this form of business ownership?
4. "A partnership may be formed by express agreement or by implication." Explain.
5. Distinguish between a general partnership and a limited partnership.
6. Limited partnerships are being used more and more for real estate and movie investment ventures. Why?
7. Distinguish between:
   (a) a general and a limited partner
   (b) an active and a dormant partner
   (c) a senior and a junior partner.
8. Can anyone become a partner in a business? Explain.
9. Which types of business partnership need to be registered? Why? How and where does this registration take place? What is the cost?
10. What special requirements exist for the registration of limited partnerships?
11. Is it necessary to draw up a written partnership agreement? If so, what items should be included in it?
12. How can partners in a business resolve any disputes that may arise? What can they do beforehand? What does the law have to say on this matter?
13. What is the procedure for dissolving a business partnership?
14. Must all partners agree upon dissolution of their partnership? If not, what are the circumstances in which one partner can bring about dissolution?
15. One of the main advantages of the partnership form of business ownership is its suitability for obtaining more capital than a sole proprietorship can. Explain, with particular reference to the role of the limited partnership.
16. What assets of a partnership and of its owners are available to meet the claims of creditors of the business? Explain in your answer the difference between the liability of general and limited partners.
17. "Two heads are better than one." Does this always apply to a business venture?
18. What are the advantages and disadvantages of giving a valuable employee a share of your business? What else could you do to keep him or her motivated? If you do decide to give him or her a partnership share, what would be the best arrangement to make?
19. Does the partnership business have more legal restrictions than the sole proprietorship? Explain.
20. A general partner's unlimited personal liability for the debts of the business is both joint and several. Explain.
21. So long as the partnership agreement specifically states that a partner may not sign cheques for more than a certain amount without the agreement

of the other partners, there is little risk of loss for the other partners. Comment.
22. The creditors of a partnership business have the right to claim the personal assets of a partner's spouse if the partner's assets are insufficient to meet any outstanding debts. Is this true? Discuss.
23. How is the income that a partner receives from his or her business taxed? In what way, if at all, does it differ from the way that a sole proprietor's income is taxed? Does the partner pay tax on the money that he or she might take out of the business as a weekly wage? Explain.
24. Why does a partner in a business soon start worrying about income tax and the possible tax advantage of incorporating the business once it starts to become successful?
25. Is a partnership a suitable vehicle for raising large sums of money for business ventures? What are its major drawbacks?
26. What happens when a partner in a business dies? What practical problems can arise? How are these usually taken care of?
27. How easy is it to get one's money out of a partnership? What is the usual procedure?

CASE PROBLEMS

THE TOY SHOP

Six women in a small town have decided to start their own toy shop and share the responsibility of operating it.
1. What form of business ownership should they use? Why?
2. One of the women has suggested using the name "Educational Toys Unlimited." Is this a good business idea? What restrictions are there, if any, on the name they might use?
3. One of the women's husbands, who is a lawyer, has offered to prepare an agreement for the business ownership. What should it cover?
4. Another husband has expressed the concern to his wife that they might lose their home if something goes wrong in the business. How can this be prevented?
5. One woman has stated that they should share the profits according to the hours worked. Another said that that is impossible as the law states that all profit must be shared equally. Who is right?

ALFORD AND WELLS, TV REPAIRS
Resolving a dispute in a business partnership

Jim Alford and Pete Wells had worked together for several years in a locally well-known TV and appliance repair business. They had often discussed the possibility of a business of their own, particularly after some minor disagreement with their boss. Finally, after some years of saving money, they were ready to begin their own business. As good friends, they felt no need to go to the trouble and expense of drawing up a formal partnership agreement. It was understood that each would contribute $10,000 to the business, each put in the same amount of hours, and each share equally in the profits. They did, however, register the partnership, as required by law.

By the end of their first six months of business together, relations between the two men had become very strained. Basically, Jim felt that Pete was not pulling his weight. Whereas Jim would go out on evening and weekend calls in order to build up the business, Pete would spend his spare time either with his family or helping his brother to establish a similar TV repair business on the other side of town. Jim made a careful note of how much extra time he was devoting to the business and how much extra money he was earning for it. Although both he and Pete were drawing the same weekly wage of $500 from the business, Jim determined that at the end of the year he would insist that the profits be shared in proportion to the amount of work that each had put in. However, when the end of the year arrived and Jim brought up the matter, Pete disagreed violently and insisted on receiving half the profit.

Assignment
1. Is Jim legally entitled to a larger share of the profit?
2. How would Pete's legal position have been affected if the partnership had not been registered? Explain.
3. How could the partnership agreement be altered to enable Jim to obtain an extra share of the profits for his extra work?
4. Can Jim prevent his partner from helping his brother to establish a similar TV repair business?

BOLTON'S PHOTO STUDIO
The role of the limited partner

Janice Bolton, a graduate of a photo-arts course, has decided to start her own photo studio. Her father, a keen amateur photographer and the instigator of Janice's interest in photography, has offered to lend her $10 000. With this money, together with a loan from the bank, Janice Bolton plans to rent and equip a small store in her home town.

Mr. Bolton thinks it advisable to get the advice of his solicitor and friend, Jim Andrews, about the legal form that his participation in the business should take, before he gives the $10 000 to his daughter.

Assignment
1. Explain the various ways (other than as a corporation shareholder) in which Mr. Bolton could help his daughter and yet safeguard his own money.
2. Discuss the pros and cons for each way.
3. Recommend what you consider to be the most suitable way.

READING

Women: The Best Entrepreneurs

Why are so many women succeeding in business? Turns out it's because they know they can't do it without really trying

BY JANE T. COOK

Source: *Canadian Business Magazine*, June 1982, p. 69

Despite the economic deep freeze, there's a group of entrepreneurs out there that is not only lining up to jump aboard the small business bandwagon, it's raking in the big bucks as well.

It's a group that keeps its expectations to realistic size, its debt ratio low and its collective attention alert to advice from anywhere it can be bought, borrowed or burgled. It's a group that admits to an ignorance of high finance and megabusiness techniques, a group that prefers to move cautiously, scouting the land mines as it goes. It's a group that plays the waiting game for personal cash rewards, one that unhesitatingly elects to plow back profits into a fledgling enterprise.

It's also a group that is now employing a large number of Canadians that have been given the heave-ho by other groups out there, and there is evidence that these numbers of employed will continue to grow. It is the group that has been working its way through the nation's kitchens, factories, typing pools and middle-management offices to a point where the upwardly mobile route to independence seems the only way left to travel. It is, of course, the entrepreneurial group made up of women of all ages, the group that could well be the nucleus of a new female capitalism.

The phenomenon is already sparking unusual interest in government, academic and big business circles. These days, the US and Canada are awash with surveys that not only agree women are currently taking the entrepreneurial plunge at a far faster clip than men are doing, they also seem to be following the yellow brick road to sole proprietorship for different reasons.

A study of women owner/managers presented at a 1980 University of Washington Entrepreneurial Research Conference showed, for example, that a lust for loot is not necessarily the prime motivation for women going into business for themselves. Women quizzed for the survey admitted that money was marvelous ("I want to buy the same toys that men enjoy," said one interviewee, "a boat, an airplane") but that job satisfaction was even more important a goal and so was the need to achieve.

When a team from Queen's University questioned 275 Ontario women proprietors for a paper called *Canadian Women Owner/Managers* that was released last January by the Department of Industry, Trade and Commerce's Small Business Secretariat, "challenge" was ranked as the most significant reason for striking out on one's own. The next most important was "being one's own boss" and there were only scattered votes for "monetary reward."

But even if the prospect of fat profits is not a potent lure, a recently released study of sole proprietorship by the chartered accountancy firm of Thorne Riddell shows that women entrepreneurs are likely to end up with healthier bank accounts than their male counterparts anyway. Thorne Riddell began its research in 1978 with a random sampling of new business starts, and 1,989 companies were then picked for the survey. It was found that 486 of the firms were led by male owner/managers, 1,364 were headed by women and 139 were rejected as "not determined." The same sample was reviewed in 1981 to see how the budding entrepreneurs had fared.

The result was startling. Of the 486 firms with male owners, just 123 or approximately 25% had survived the three-year period. Of the 1,364 led by women, 644 or around 47% were still in business. But why? In search of answers, Thorne Riddell sent questionnaires to 100 of the women owner/managers whose companies were now grossing more than $100,000 a year and an equal number of queries to proprietors (both men and women) whose firms had failed. Four factors emerged that seemed to separate the winners from the losers.

• Questionnaires returned to Thorne Riddell showed that the owners of the surviving companies had taken between six and 10 months to research and prepare for their new business ventures. In contrast, an analysis of answers to the same question indicated that, on average, owners of the failed firms took less than four months to prepare for startup.

• Close to 90% of the successful proprietors replied that they had used professional advisers such as lawyers and accountants in setting up their enterprises. Conversely, just 25% of those whose companies were no longer operating reported they had sought professional help in the early stages of the business.

• Almost 70% of the successful respondents said they had taken business-related courses before launching their enterprises and that they also regularly read books and magazines dealing with business management, finance and marketing. Most felt that this kind of ongoing study was crucial to their survival. But polls of the failed proprietors showed that only 10% had attended courses or now took time to read business material.

• More than half of the surviving owner/managers said they had started their enterprises with modest expectations of income (an expected annual salary of $12,000 was most often mentioned), and that they were prepared to be patient for signs of business success. In contrast, 36% of the failed owner/managers admitted they fully expected the enterprise to make barrels of cash within three years. The anticipated annual salary most often quoted was $40,000.

Thorne Riddell researchers concluded from all of this that the tendency of women to seek help without choking up with embarrassment and to make realistic projections without sounding apologetic is working in their favour in small business. Other characteristics that have surfaced in surveys also seem to show that women entrepreneurs could indeed have an edge on their male counterparts, particularly in today's hostile economic climate.

The Small Business Secretariat's study found, for example, that women owner/managers generally use their own personal savings as startup capital (a 1978 US President's Interagency Task Force on Women Business Owners reported the same thing) and that they also tend to meet operational financing needs from income, with suppliers and banks playing an auxiliary role. This could mean that women continue to be wary of discrimination from financial institutions and big business. Or it could even mean that a woman in business will likely try to find ways of making do on a modest cushion of capital. Whatever the reason, the fact is that women entrepreneurs seem to be keeping their debt loads to reasonable size, thus avoiding the scourge of high interest payments.

Women owner/managers will also likely exhibit a sense of independence and staying power that could be to their advantage in discouraging times. More than two-thirds of the women interviewed for the Secretariat's study (a figure substantiated by the Interagency Task Force report) said they had made their own way into business, quashing the notion that most enterprises run by women have been handed over by a father or spouse.

Four out of five of the Canadian women surveyed for the Secretariat also reported they had never before owned a business, while the Thorne Riddell research flushed out the information that men are somewhat more restless—the majority of male interviewees admitted they had jumped in and out of more than one entrepreneurial situation. Many said they had already owned more than seven businesses.

The figures show, too, that even in the face of economic slowdown, women are showing a spunky penchant for risk. The Interagency Task force analyzed US census data for as long ago as 1972-1977 and concluded that the growth rate for self-employed women as a group was then three times that of self-employed men. The later Secretariat study agreed with this. When Revenue Canada's *Taxation Statistics* for 1969 through 1979 were examined, it was seen that women were not only becoming owner/managers at three times the rate of men, but the proportion of female to male proprietors in Canada had more than doubled during the decade—to 36% from 16%. And the kinds of businesses run by women were changing. Of the 1,364 female-owned enterprises studied by Thorne Riddell, 614 were retail operations, 382 services and 172 craft or cottage industries. But then, 94 owner/managers were in manufacturing and 102 had bought franchises.

Checked against other statistics, these numbers begin to look even more interesting. According to Secretariat forecasters, close to 60,000 new businesses will be incorporated in Canada in the next 12 months and, if the trends hold, women will be running the majority of them.

Larry Grossman, Ontario's former minister of Industry and Tourism, has said, for example, that there were 100,000 new jobs created in that province during the past three years. So, if the Canadian Federation of Independent Business' reckoning is correct that 70,000 of these jobs were created by small business, and if three times as many women as men are launching these businesses, close to 52,000 Ontarians since 1979 may have found employment because of women's enterprise.

If it is also true that small businesses owned and operated by women are relatively large employers (the Secretariat study estimated the average full- and part-time employment figure for these firms at 5.57 with a median of 4), then women proprietors could soon be making a significant dent in the unemployment statistics.

Fun with figures, perhaps. But the basic statistics are firm. It's clear that there is, indeed, a new female capitalism and that women are savouring it.

As one respondent told interviewers working for the study presented at the University of Washington: "When people ask me if I like being in business, I say that on days when there are more sales than problems, I love it. On days when there are more problems than sales, I wonder why I do it. But basically, I do it because it gives me a good feeling about myself.

"You learn a lot about your capabilities by putting yourself on the line. Running a successful business isn't only a financial risk. It's an emotional risk as well. I get a lot of satisfaction from having dared, done it and been successful."

Assignment
1. Why are more and more women becoming entrepreneurs?
2. Why do women entrepreneurs seem to have an edge over male entrepreneurs?

CHAPTER 3
THE BUSINESS CORPORATION

CHAPTER OBJECTIVES

☐ To explain what a business corporation is and how it may be federal or provincial, public or private.

☐ To examine the rights of shareholders in a corporation.

☐ To describe the duties and powers of the directors of a corporation.

☐ To discuss the advantages and disadvantages of the corporate form of ownership as compared with the sole proprietorship and the partnership.

☐ To discuss the reasons for the emergence of big business firms.

☐ To explain what a co-operative is and the advantages and disadvantages of this form of business ownership.

CHAPTER OUTLINE

3.1 The Corporate Form of Ownership

3.2 Advantages and Disadvantages of Incorporation

3.3 Big Business

3.4 The Co-operative

Unit 3.1: THE CORPORATE FORM OF OWNERSHIP

The term *business corporation* is used to describe a business that has a legal existence of its own. Unlike a sole proprietorship or partnership, the owners of which are legally responsible for all acts performed or obligations incurred by the business, the corporation is itself the responsible legal entity. As an "artificial person," created by statutory authority, the corporation is distinct from its owners—the shareholders. It has its own name, its own address, its own capital, its own life, and its own right to sue and be sued.

Public versus Private Business Corporations

A distinction is made between business corporations that "offer their securities to the public" and those that do not. In other words, between corporations whose shares are widely held and corporations whose shares are closely held. The former are called *public business corporations* and the latter *private business corporations*. In order to safeguard the public interest, the federal and provincial Business Corporations Acts set out much stricter rules for the operation of public business corporations—for example, with regard to the duties of directors—than for private ones.

Provincial versus Federal Business Corporations

Business corporations may be either provincially or federally incorporated. If the persons establishing a corporation expect to do business in only one province, then provincial incorporation is sufficient and cheaper. If business is expected in more than one province, federal incorporation, which gives a corporation the right to operate throughout Canada free from discriminatory provincial legislation, may be more appropriate. All corporations, whether federally or provincially incorporated, are subject to provincial laws of general application such as taxation, land, licences, returns, contracts and so on.

About 10 per cent of all business corporations in Canada are federally incorporated and include most of the largest ones.

Provincial Incorporation

Each province has its own Act permitting the establishment of business corporations. Depending on the province, applicants must use one of three systems of incorporation: the registration or memorandum system; the letters patent system; or incorporation by articles.

Registration System. This system, based on the English Companies Act, enables a corporation to be established by authority of parliament rather than by royal prerogative. Persons wishing to set up a corporation must register a document called a *memorandum of association* with the Registrar of Joint Stock Companies for the particular province, and pay the required fee. The memorandum of association contains the names of the applicants, the amount of share capital, and so on, as specified. Alberta, British Columbia, Newfoundland, Nova Scotia, Saskatchewan, the Northwest Territories, and the Yukon use this system.

Letters Patent System. Under this system, a corporation is established by the issuance by the Provincial Secretary (under the authority of the Crown's representative, the Lieutenant-Governor of the province) of an incorporating document, called the *letters patent*. This document, sometimes called the charter, is similar to the royal charters formerly issued directly by the Crown and based on royal prerogative. It is the system used in Manitoba, New Brunswick, Prince Edward Island, and Quebec.

Incorporation by Articles. This system, used in Ontario, is basically the same as the registration system.

Requirements for Incorporation. These vary from province to province. Typically, the applicants or applicant must file with the provincial government an application showing:

(a) The name in full, the place of residence, and the occupation of each of the applicants. These may be unlimited in number; they must all be 18 or more years of age.
(b) The name of the company to be incorporated. This must not be the same as or similar to the name of a known corporation, association, partnership, individual, or business, if its use would be likely to deceive, except where consent has been given by the party concerned. Nor must the name be publicly objectionable. Also, the company must use the word "Limited" or "Incorporated" or "Corporation," or its corresponding abbreviation "Ltd.," "Inc.," or "Corp." as the last word of its name. The name should be prominently displayed at head office and on letterheads.
(c) The purpose for which the company is to be incorporated.
(d) The place where the head office of the company is to be situated.
(e) The authorized capital; the classes of shares, if any, into which it is to be divided; the number of shares of each class; and the par value of each share, or, if the shares are to be without par value, their maximum issue price, if any.
(f) Where there are to be preference shares, the preferences, rights, conditions, restrictions, limitations, or prohibitions attaching to them, or to each class of them.
(g) If the company is to be a private company, a statement to that effect and the restrictions to be placed on the transfer of its shares.
(h) The names of the applicants who are to be the first directors of the company.
(i) The class and number of shares to be taken by each applicant, and the amount to be paid for them.
(j) Any other matters that the applicants desire to have included in the letters patent.

Shareholders and Their Rights

The owners of a business corporation are called the *shareholders* or *stockholders*. According to the *Canada Business Corporations Act*:

1. A business corporation must have at least one shareholder. There is no maximum.
2. Each shareholder has limited liability. The shareholders of a corporation are not, as shareholders, liable for any liability, act, or default of the corporation.
3. Each shareholder is entitled to attend an annual shareholders meeting. The directors of a corporation shall call an annual meeting of shareholders

---

HEATH MANUFACTURING INDUSTRIES LIMITED
348 ALBERT DRIVE
TORONTO, ONTARIO

*Proxy for Annual and Special Meeting of Shareholders
Solicited on Behalf of Management*

The undersigned Shareholder of Heath Manufacturing Industries Limited hereby appoints J.F. Heath, President, whom failing, R.T. Smith, Vice-President, whom failing, L.M. Jones, Vice-President, or .... as nominee of the undersigned, to attend and act for and on behalf of the undersigned, at the annual and special meeting of shareholders of Heath Manufacturing Industries Limited to be held May 19, 198-, and at any adjournment or adjournments thereof in the same manner, to the same extent and with the same powers as if the undersigned were present at the said meeting or such adjournment or adjournments thereof, and, without limiting the general authority and power hereby given to such nominee, the shares represented by this proxy are specifically directed to be voted as indicated below:

FOR ☐ 1. Approval of the report of the directors containing the Financial Statements of the Cor-
AGAINST ☐ poration for the year ended December 31, 198- together with the auditors' report thereon.

FOR ☐ 2. Approval, with or without variation, of By-Law Number 8 of the By-Laws of the Corpo-
AGAINST ☐ ration, being a By-Law providing for increasing the Board of Directors from seven (7) to nine (9).

This proxy revokes any other proxy heretofore given by the undersigned for the annual and special meeting of shareholders to which this proxy relates.

This proxy will be voted and where a choice is specified, will be voted as directed. Where no choice is specified this Proxy will confer discretionary authority and will be voted in favour of the matters referred to above.

This Proxy also confers discretionary authority to vote in respect of any other matter which may properly come before the meeting and in such manner as such nominee in his judgment may determine.

The shareholder has the right to appoint a person to attend and act for him and on his behalf at the meeting other than the persons designated in this form of Proxy. Such right may be exercised by filling in the name of such person in the blank space provided and striking out the names of Management's nominees.

Dated the .... day of ...., A.D. 198-.

....
(Signature of Shareholder)

Note:
1. A person appointed as a nominee to represent shareholder need not be a shareholder.
2. Where the instrument is signed by a Corporation, its corporate seal must be affixed.

Figure 3.1 Example of a Proxy

not later than eighteen months after the corporation comes into existence and subsequently not later than fifteen months after holding the last preceding annual meeting. The directors may also at any time call a special meeting of shareholders. Notice of the time and place of a shareholders meeting must be sent to each shareholder and director and to the auditor not less than 21 days and not more than 50 days before the meeting.
4. At shareholders meetings, each shareholder is entitled to cast one vote for each share held by him or her, unless the articles otherwise provide.
5. A shareholder's vote may be given in person or by proxy. A *proxy* (Figure 3.1) is a written statement, signed by a shareholder, authorizing another person to vote on his or her behalf at a meeting of the shareholders.
6. At every annual shareholders meeting, the directors must place before the shareholders comparative financial statements for the last financial year and for the previous one; the report of the auditor, if any; and any other required financial information. Copies of these documents must be sent to each shareholder not less than 21 days before the annual meeting.
7. Unless otherwise provided for in the articles of incorporation, all questions considered at the shareholders meetings are determined by a simple majority of votes, with the chairman holding the deciding vote in the event of an equality of votes. The business transacted at the annual meeting normally includes: the president's report; the auditor's report (Figure 3.2); confirmation of bylaws passed by the directors since the previous meeting; election of the directors for the next year; appointment of the company auditors; and any other business. More serious matters, such as a proposal to reorganize the company's share capital, require more than a simple majority.
8. A shareholder is entitled to receive the dividends that the directors declare payable.
9. A shareholder of a business corporation is free to transfer his or her fully paid shares of ownership to anyone else, so long as there are no restrictions stated in the articles of incorporation.

The Directors

These are the persons elected by the shareholders to be responsible for the management of the corporation. The role of the directors has, however, been the subject of controversy for many years. It is sometimes argued that the directors' first responsibility, morally and legally, is to the corporation itself rather than to its shareholders.

The Canada Business Corporations Act stipulates that a corporation shall have one or more directors. However, if shares in a corporation are to be sold to the public, there must be at least three directors, two of whom are not officers or employees of the company or of its affiliates.

After the certificate of incorporation has been issued, the first directors have the power to meet to make bylaws, authorize the issue of shares, appoint officers, appoint an auditor, make banking arrangements, and transact other business.

The shareholders, at their first meeting and at subsequent meetings, elect the directors for a term of not more than three years. Directors' terms may be staggered.

Persons disqualified from being a director include: anyone less than 18 years of age; anyone found by a court in Canada or elsewhere to be of unsound mind; a person who has the status of a bankrupt; or a corporation. The majority of the first directors and a majority of the subsequent directors must be resident Canadians.

Powers. The directors are given the power to manage the business and have authority to make *bylaws* (legally enforceable rules governing the conduct of the business) covering such matters as:
1. The allotment of shares; the making of calls thereon; the payment thereof; the issuance and registration of certificates for shares; the forfeiture of shares for non-payment; the disposal of forfeited shares and of the proceeds thereof; and the transfer of shares.
2. The declaration and payment of dividends.
3. The amount of the share qualifications of the directors and the remuneration of the directors.
4. The appointment, functions, duties, and removal of all agents, officers, and servants of the company; the security, if any, to be given by them to the company; and their remuneration.
5. The time and place for the holding of meetings of the shareholders; the calling of meetings of the shareholders and of the board of directors; the quorum at such meetings; the requirements as to proxies; and the procedure in all things at such meetings.
6. The conduct in all other particulars of the affairs of the company not otherwise provided for.

Any new bylaws passed by the directors are effective only until the next annual shareholders meeting, when they must be approved or rejected. Certain bylaws must be approved by more than a simple majority.

Restrictions. To protect the shareholders and the creditors of the company, various restrictions are placed on the powers of the directors by the Canada Business Corporations Act. For example, if the directors pay a dividend out of the capital fund of the company, they then become jointly and severally liable to the company and its creditors for the amount.

Also, at each annual shareholders meeting, the directors are required to present: an income statement for the specified period; a statement of surplus for that period; a statement of source and application of funds for that period; a balance sheet for the end of the period; the report of the auditor to the shareholders; and any other financial information required by the articles of incorporation or bylaws.

Furthermore, every director and officer of a corporation has a "duty of care" in exercising his or her powers and discharging his or her duties (a) to act honestly and in good faith with a view to the best interests of the corporation; and (b) to exercise the care, diligence, and skill that a reasonably prudent person would exercise in comparable circumstances.

Divorce Between Ownership and Management

One of the most important changes brought about by the growth in the number of business corporations in Canada has been the divorce between business ownership and management. One of the great advantages of the public business corporation is that capital can be raised in large and small amounts from a large number and variety of people. Limited liability encourages such people to invest their surplus funds in various business ventures—for, at worst, they could only lose their investment. Also, the easy transferability of share ownership means that they can sell their shares quickly if, for some reason, they need the cash.

The creators of many of these businesses have retained control of the board of directors (set up to represent the shareholders' interests). However, there has also gradually emerged a new breed of professional managers with little or no shareholding in the companies for which they worked. Their incentive to work hard on the shareholders' behalf is secured by their interest in the job, their innate energy and ambition, good salaries, bonuses, promotions, and the threat of dismissal for poor performance. The appointment of the president by the board of directors usually ensures the shareholders' control over the professional management. And if the management of a business is unsuccessful in earning profits,

---

CHARTERED ACCOUNTANTS

Auditor's Report

To the Shareholders of

Armstrong Enterprises Limited

We have examined the consolidated balance sheet of Armstrong Enterprises Limited and subsidiaries as at December 31, 198- and the statements of consolidated earnings, retained earnings and source and application of funds for the year then ended. Our examination included a general review of the accounting procedures and such tests of accounting records and other supporting evidence as we considered necessary in the circumstances.

In our opinion these consolidated financial statements present fairly the financial position of the companies as at December 31, 198- and the results of their operations and the source and application of their funds for the year then ended, in accordance with generally accepted accounting principles applied on a basis consistent with that of the preceding year.

Chase, Smith, Wagner & Stewart
Chartered Accountants

Halifax, Canada
February 18, 198-

Figure 3.2 Example of an Auditor's Report

the board of directors can appoint a new president who then builds his or her own new management team.

This divorce between ownership and management occurs mainly in the large public business corporations. In the case of the many small and medium-sized incorporated businesses in Canada, the managers are usually the principal shareholders.

Auditing

Auditing is the task of inspecting accounting records to determine whether they have been properly kept. This involves the periodic checking of journals, ledgers, and such accounts as cash, securities, inventories, and receivables. *Internal auditing*, that is, auditing by a member of the firm itself, is carried out almost constantly throughout the year. It helps ensure that the company's accounting system is being properly used; that accuracy is being maintained; and, very importantly, that company funds, inventory, and other assets are not being stolen or misused. In the case of public business corporations, management must arrange for a firm of public accountants to conduct an annual audit of the firm's financial statements and records. (Figure 3.2). This is called *external auditing*. Although it does not guarantee that all is financially well, it does serve as an outside safeguard of the shareholders' interests. The accountant who does this auditing is called an *auditor*.

KEY TERMS

Business corporation	Shareholders
Public business corporation	Limited liability
Private business corporation	Annual shareholders meeting
Provincial incorporation	Voting by proxy
Federal incorporation	Directors
Registration system	Eligibility
Letters patent system	Disqualification
Incorporation by articles	Auditing

REVIEW QUESTIONS

1. How would you explain to a friend what a business corporation is and how it differs from a sole proprietorship and a partnership?
2. Why are the sole proprietorship and partnership unsatisfactory forms of business ownership for large-scale manufacturing enterprises?
3. Business corporations may be public or private. Explain the difference and the reasons for preferring one type of incorporation rather than the other.

4. Business corporations may also be either provincially or federally incorporated. Explain why this is so and the reasons for choosing one manner of incorporation rather than the other.
5. There are three different ways of incorporating a business firm provincially. What are they? What system is in use in your province?
6. What information is required when incorporating a business in your province?
7. What is the procedure for incorporating a business in your province? What does it cost?
8. What restrictions are placed on the name that a corporation may use?
9. Does a corporation have complete freedom to undertake any types of business activities?
10. Suppose that you buy some shares in Happy Valley Enterprises Ltd. which subsequently goes bankrupt with large unsatisfied debts. What is your liability as a shareholder?
11. You find out that you did not receive an invitation to the annual shareholders meeting at which the existing board of directors was re-elected. Do you have cause for complaint?
12. Another shareholder did receive an invitation to the meeting but was ill in bed and so could not attend. He sent his friend with a written statement authorizing him to cast the shareholder's votes against the re-election of the present board of directors. However, the votes were rejected on the grounds that the friend was not himself a shareholder. Is this legally correct? What can the shareholder do?
13. Suppose that the shareholder held 100 common shares. How many votes should he or she have?
14. What matters are normally discussed and voted upon at the annual shareholders meeting? How are the resolutions approved?
15. Suppose that the corporation in which you have invested some of your savings never pays dividends on your shares even though the corporation has a good net income. Are you legally entitled to sue the company? Explain and discuss.
16. Having become disenchanted with the economy, you decide to get rid of your shares and find a willing buyer. Do you need to use the services of a stockbroker? Can the corporation deny you permission to sell your shares?
17. What is the board of directors of a business corporation? To whom is it responsible? And for what?
18. "It is sometimes argued that the directors' first responsibility, morally and legally, is to the corporation rather than to its shareholders." Explain and discuss.
19. What restrictions, if any, exist on the persons eligible to become directors?
20. What are usually the first duties of the persons appointed as directors of a business corporation?
21. What other powers do the directors of a business corporation possess?
22. Explain, with examples, how a director may abuse his or her "duty of care." What action can the shareholders take?

23. How did a divorce come about between the ownership and management of many large business enterprises?
24. What is professional management? To what extent can management without ownership provide a rewarding career?
25. Explain the nature and purpose of auditing. Who carries it out?

CASE PROBLEM

WHITBY CHEMICALS INC.

Role of corporation directors

At the annual shareholders meeting of Whitby Chemicals Inc., Rosalie Evans, a shareholder, stood up to speak in support of a resolution calling for the company to add four "outside" members to the firm's present board of directors. She argued that the present lack of outside members meant that the shareholders' interests were not properly protected. However, the Chairman of the Board vehemently recommended rejection of the resolution, stating that it was a tradition at Whitby Chemicals to have directors who "knew what they were talking about."

Assignment:
1. Explain the distinction between an "inside" and an "outside" board of directors.
2. What are the arguments in favour of an outside board?
3. What are the arguments in favour of an inside board?
4. What other protection do the shareholders have?
5. What would you recommend?

READING

The Aesthetic Entrepreneur

Stockbroker Christopher Ondaatje also turns a nice dollar in Canadian publishing and art

BY WILLIAM STEPHENSON

Source: *The Financial Post Magazine.* Used by permission of William Stephenson.

As the publisher of more than 600 books, many of them now perennial favourites in Canada and the U.S., Philip Christopher Ondaatje, 50, of Toronto, rates a niche in the Canadian literary firmament beside the Hurtigs and the McClellands. But because publishing has been only a larky, ego-stroking sideline to his main profession of founding partner in the stock brokerage firm of Loewen, Ondaatje, McCutcheon & Co. Ltd., Ondaatje has neither sought nor received the literary acclaim that is his due.

His third, equally major profession, as the brain and moving spirit behind one of Canada's largest private art galleries, is so profitable and time-consuming that it has often threatened to overwhelm the other two. But despite the gallery's estimated $6-million worth of art—including the major works of several pioneer Canadian artists—Ondaatje is almost unknown in the Canadian art world at large.

What is surprising about these anomalies, however, is that in the context of Ondaatje's career, they're *not* surprising. Ever since he landed in Canada from Ceylon (now Sri Lanka) in 1955, penniless and friendless at 21, Ondaatje (who pronounces his name On-dah-chay) has operated simultaneously on a multitude of planes and maintained a low, almost imperceptible profile, even in highly public positions. So cleverly has he camouflaged his own business personality that even knowledgeable financial associates are often at a loss as to how to regard him.

"I'd heard so many conflicting stories about him," recalls John Mahoney, a Toronto investment analyst whose book Ondaatje published, "that when I first shook his hand I wasn't sure whether I should count my fingers afterward or ask for his autograph."

The financier-publisher-art dealer's somewhat blurred public image is distinctly coloured, however, by his zestful enthusiasms, the boyish candour with which he answers the most pointed financial or personal questions and his utter lack of fear when charging into areas about which he knows less than nothing.

His first book, *The Prime Ministers of Canada 1867-1968*, came about in 1967 only because he couldn't find any other readable volume on the subject. But where others might have simply shrugged and gone off muttering about Canadians' notorious lack of interest in their antecedents, he set about correcting it. Though he knew nothing about publishing, he got a group of people he knew to write the prime ministerial biographies and do pen-and-ink sketches. Then, with $3,000 put up by friends, Ondaatje put out the book as *his* Centennial contribution to his adopted country.

When *The Prime Ministers* made a net profit of $2,686, Ondaatje was intrigued enough to start thinking of other possible volumes to inform poorly served Canadians about each other. Ten years and at least 600 books later, his Pagurian Press was doing almost $1-million worth of business a year, not one cent of it as a subsidy or grant from the public purse.

"If I have any skill at all," Ondaatje says, "it's in controlling and profiting from cash flow. At any time of the day, I know almost to the dollar how much I am worth and what parts of it are in cash, stocks or other assets."

Ondaatje's choice of name for his publishing firm is itself an indication of the puckish way his mind works. A pagurian is a hermit crab; indigenous to the waters around Britain, it commonly makes its home in larger mollusks' shells. The connection is that for years Ondaatje's books were put together and distributed by other Canadian publishers, including Macmillan and General Publishing. Unlike the hermit crab, however, Ondaatje professes warm gratitude toward these accommodating hosts, and they speak highly of him.

Ondaatje is also deeply, emotionally grateful for the chance that came his way in 1960, even before he was officially a Canadian citizen, to do something tangible for Canada. He was working in Montreal at the time, and he and eight others who skied and socialized together conceived the notion of trying to regain Canada's once-undisputed supremacy in bobsledding. They went at this dream with such fervour that they captured the top award: the coveted gold medal at the Winter Olympics of 1964 in Innsbruck, Austria.

"*I* didn't win anything. My sled came in 14th," Ondaatje hastens to assure anyone who mentions this exploit. "It was the other sled, captained by Vic Emery, that won glory for Canada and us."

Just being part of this blithe romp, however, undoubtedly made Ondaatje and his teammates the envy of their generation of sports-oriented businessmen. It helps explain Ondaatje's subsequent easy entry into boardrooms and corporations that otherwise might have been difficult to penetrate.

Another possible explanation is that Ondaatje has the *aura* of wealth about him, even if in the early days he was short of the green stuff itself. For he is a member of a Ceylonese family, which, for a period of 300 years ending in 1948, had enjoyed wealth and social position. Its doings are loosely chronicled in *Running In The Family*, a recent novel by brother Michael Ondaatje, an award-winning Canadian poet.

"There were always doctors, writers and other professional people, but it was my Dutch grandfather, a lawyer, who made the most money," Ondaatje explains. "He used to buy property that had conflicting British, Dutch or even Portuguese claims clogging the title, clear these away and sell at big profits. My father, Mervyn Ondaatje, was running the family tea and rubber plantations when the blow fell."

The "blow," of course, was Ceylon's winning of independence from Britain and the rise to power of a rabidly Socialist government. One sunny day the Ondaatjes were worth millions. The next, with the confiscation by the state of all their assets—and the concurrent collapse of markets for tea and rubber—they were paupers. Ondaatje, eldest of four children, was at boarding school in England at the time. He didn't have to leave immediately, but the following year, when he was 16, he found work with a London bank, National & Grindlays, whose proudest boast was that it had helped finance the early oil boom in Texas.

In 1955, just after turning 21, Ondaatje immigrated to Canada. It was the least socialistic country he knew of that was still developing and might provide the opportunities to recoup the family fortunes.

Landing in Toronto, he used his banking background to land himself a job "in the cage" (checking stock certificates) for brokers Burns Bros. & Denton Ltd. Shortly afterward, he moved to Montreal as an advertising salesman and general dogsbody, first for *The Montrealer* magazine, then for Maclean Hunter publications, including *The Financial Post*. In 1963, he moved to the Toronto office of *The Financial Post*.

Connections established in those early jobs led in 1965 to a position on the institutional sales team of Pitfield Mackay Ross. A year later, he became vice-president and manager of the institutional division. "Chris was a marvellous salesman," says Douglas Mackay, one of the partners, "and he thrived on work."

Ondaatje left this post five years later, taking with him another Pitfield stalwart, Charles "Chuck" Loewen. With $400,000 and a third partner, Fred McCutcheon (son of Wallace McCutcheon, finance minister in the Diefenbaker cabinet), they incorporated their new brokerage house of Loewen, Ondaatje, McCutcheon & Co. Ltd. (LOM) on January 1, 1970. Their forte, of course, was sales to institutions.

LOM was soon one of the top institutional trading firms on the Toronto Stock Exchange, dealing at the international level with banks, trust companies, mutual funds, insurance firms and foundations. It was so successful that in 1976, the TSE named Fred McCutcheon as its own chairman. His explanation of LOM's success is a simple one: "Chuck was the organizational genius, and I had the contacts and know-how to stick-handle through corporate mazes. Chris was the guy who could sell anything to anybody. We worked well as a team."

One of LOM's earliest and biggest coups was arranging the financing in 1970 for the newly formed Harlequin Enterprises Ltd., the Toronto publisher that each month turns out half a dozen lightweight romances. For well over a century, the British publishing firm of Mills & Boon had been churning out these love stories in paperback at prices even scullery maids could afford. Toronto entrepreneur Richard Bonnycastle (now better known as a Calgary-based oil magnate) was sure that modern packaging and supermarket-oriented sales techniques could make Harlequin the publishing sensation of North America.

He was as correct in his thinking as he was in choosing LOM to raise the $4 million required to get the project off the ground. So well did LOM know its institutional clients that in less than a month, the convertible debentures were subscribed. Ondaatje not only steered LOM to this early triumph (and the subsequent sale of Harlequin to the *Toronto Star*), but also invested heavily in Harlequin shares for his own Pagurian Press. Within a couple of years, those shares would earn more than $1 million in profit, thus saving Pagurian from having to borrow money and suffer the loss of freedom which, financier J.P. Morgan used to claim, always ensues. "I have no intention of losing my freedom," declares Ondaatje. "So I never borrow."

Pagurian's first book, *The Prime Ministers of Canada 1867–1968*, printed by McCorquodale & Blades and distributed by General Publishing in 1967, had been followed the same year by two more books, both on Canadian sports. One, *Olympic Victory*, a joint effort by Ondaatje and fellow bobsledder Gordon Currie, detailed the strenuous trek to their 1964 triumph. The other, *50 Years of Hockey*, was by professional broadcaster and writer, Brian McFarlane.

Victory sold a modest 3,500 copies. But *Hockey* racked up sales of 30,000 in hardcover alone and, when issued in paperback, another 200,000. Ondaatje estimates he has made between $40,000 and $50,000 on it over the years.

Electrified with the idea that these sincere attempts to tell Canadians about each other could pay off, Ondaatje was soon producing as many as 60 new titles each year. Among these were *The Black Donnellys*—published in paperback only, it sold over 1,600,000 copies—and *Vengeance of the Black Donnellys*, both by the late Thomas Kelley; *The Grey Cup Story*, by Jack Sullivan; *The Best of Mme. Jehane Benoit*, by Mme. Benoit herself; and *The Best of Trudeau* and *Dining Out in Toronto*, by Jeremy Brown.

Pagurian also published books covering every recreation known to Canadians, from baseball, football, canoeing and golf to kung fu, painting, winemaking, playing the guitar (an Ondaatje skill) and theatre. The authors of the recreation volumes were usually big names connected with the activity—including Gordie Howe and Nancy Greene—but many were comparative unknowns.

Then Ondaatje discovered America. "Canadians had always been chary about the huge U.S. market," he says, explaining his 1973 expansion. "But I figured that Americans were just as nuts about nature as we were becoming, and I convinced Scribner's, for example, that Canadian outdoor books were the world's best. My first co-publishing efforts were such successes that I've seldom put out an all-Canadian book since then."

Ondaatje's most popular works were *The Edible Wild* and *Wilderness Survival*, both by Berndt Berglund, a former survival instructor with the RCAF. Each sold 60,000 copies in the U.S. alone.

All was not always harmony in the ranks of Pagurian authors, however. A Writers'

Union of Canada spokesman recalls that it had several complaints about Ondaatje in the mid-'70s. But he claims to no longer remember the details of these beefs and concludes that its protests led Pagurian "to clean up its act." Brian McFarlane, the voice and face of *Hockey Night in Canada*, has a better memory. Ondaatje's first commissioned author, who wrote not only *50 Years of Hockey* but many other hockey books, McFarlane feels he may be speaking for other Ondaatje authors when he describes his own experiences with Pagurian.

"My contract with Chris didn't specify any definite royalty on book sales, only a 'share of the profits,' " he explains. "This seemed reasonable at the time, since Pagurian was working on a shoestring and had no printing or distribution setup of its own. But though I used to deliver finished books, including not only photographs of my own but often free prefaces by such personalities as, say, Jean Beliveau, my share of the profits was always disappointingly small. When I mentioned this to Chris, he suggested I bring my accountant along to look at the books. I did so once, and my accountant said everything was in order. I don't blame Chris," McFarlane concludes. "But these days, I only sign contracts that detail specific payments and royalties."

Shortly after his epochal discovery of America, Ondaatje discovered Art. While publishing books on things Canadian, he had become aware of an artist named William Kurelek, who brought to painting a perspective on Canada that was akin to Ondaatje's: He chose subjects illustrating the immigrant's way of life. About 1975, immigrant financier Ondaatje concluded that general book publishing would soon be facing economic disaster. With paper prices and interest rates rising rapidly, why would publishers risk issuing new books when they could get 14-percent interest or more on money they already had?

But, he concluded, if one owned certain paintings and published books about those works and the artists who had done them, art and literature could help each other to boost sales of both. With these twin goals in mind, Ondaatje asked Kurelek to go to the Arctic on his behalf. He caught the artist completely by surprise.

"I was only halfway through . . . the series of paintings reproduced in this book . . . when it dawned on me: These, too, belonged with the series I'd been doing on the various ethnic groups that make up Canada," Kurelek confessed in his foreword to *The Last of the Arctic*, published in 1976. "I'd probably not have done them at all, had not Christopher Ondaatje approached me. He asked me to record the story of the Eskimos in 30 paintings before their identity was completely swamped by our southern white civilization. . . . I simply hadn't thought of the Eskimo as immigrant. . . ."

The Last of the Arctic was a best-seller. Not only that, its 30 paintings, augmented by line drawings of animal traps, snowfjgoggles and other native artifacts, and with Kurelek's comments, added up to more than a book: It was a vital record of a rapidly disappearing culture, seen through the eyes of a man uniquely endowed to interpret it. And Ondaatje had options on all parts of the enterprise.

"Our first hardcover run of 10,000 was soon sold out at $19.95, and when we ran off 250 prints of four of the paintings at $150 apiece, they vanished almost totally overnight," he recalls. "I wish we had more left. I hear they're trading for as high as $1,500."

The previous year, Pagurian had published *Kurelek's Canada*, a charming cross-country tour through 31 previously painted works, with Kurelek's wry text on each province. To prove he was as much concerned with the artist's and Canada's welfare as with profits, Ondaatje included none of his own Kurelek paintings, though there is one owned by his friend, Richard Bonnycastle. Both volumes were later reissued in soft cover for around $10. It's tragic that Kurelek, bursting with plans for more paintings and books, didn't have much longer to undertake them, or to bask in his newly won acclaim. He died at 50 in Toronto in November, 1977.

Instead of trying to repeat the Kurelek successes with other contemporary painters, Ondaatje turned to an already abundant source: pioneer Canadian art, including the thousands of maps and prints produced since the 17th century. There was peril in this approach. Early Canadian art had excited relatively few collectors and even fewer dealers. It might not catch on, no matter how clever or abundant the publicity it received. Take, for instance, a painter such as Frederick Arthur Verner, born in Upper Canada in 1836 and a prolific recorder of the Canadian West. Ask 100 average Canadians about Verner and chances are that two might recognize the name, another might connect him with the West and a fourth would figure you really meant Vermeer. To Ondaatje's despair, most Canadian educators have overlooked Verner and other pioneer artists out of sheer lack of knowledge.

But Ondaatje had another of his hunches, the kind that had often made him money as a stock-broker. In 1969, for example, he had converted to cash every stock he and Pagurian owned, a month before a major market slump. Again, in early August, 1981, he cannily liquidated $40-million worth of Pagurian securities, a few weeks before the decline.

In 1978, however, he was certain that historical Canadian art was ready for its deserved, if belated, recognition. So, putting his money where his desire dictated, Ondaatje began buying pioneer art, both in Canada and anywhere in the world it was for sale.

He soon realized that to take a commanding lead in the Canadiana boom he was helping to create, he needed much more cash. So, in 1979, he transformed the 12-year-old Pagurian Press into a holding company called Pagurian Corp. Listed as a public company on the Toronto and Vancouver stock exchanges, Pagurian—through its president and controlling shareholder, Christopher Ondaatje—was now ready to begin buying and selling for some 700 shareholders, instead of just Ondaatje and a few friends.

The results were spectacular. Though publishing and fine art revenues sagged from a 1978 high of $838,000 to a 1980 low of $225,000, net earnings from other areas zoomed from $1 million to $4.5 million over the same period. "I try to double assets and after-tax profits each year," Ondaatje told a *Canadian Business* writer last year. "It's almost impossible, but I've managed it so far."

To earn more money, he began branching out into other fields. He believed that colour photography was a bullish hobby all over North America, and thought that the retail and processing approaches of Black's, Canada's most profitable photographic firm, were sound ones. When he saw that shares in Toronto-based Black's were selling well below the firm's break-up share value, he bought 31.3 percent of them, with the blessings of Pagurian Corp.'s directors.

Then, turning to the energy field, he gained control of 50 percent of the shares of Vancouver-based Westdale Oil & Gas Ltd. A third acquisition was 50 percent of the shares of a U.S. firm called American Resources Corporation, which is a financial services and resource-management company.

The results were all that Ondaatje-backers had come to expect from their leader:

1981's net earnings were $8.9 million, only a whisker away from double the previous year's profits.

"Next to Harlequin, we are probably the most successful publishing company in Canada," says Ondaatje with satisfaction. "Many Canadian firms have absorbed publishing houses, but we must be the only publisher which has parlayed profits of $3,000 into control of a variety of other industries worth well over $100 million."

In 1981, for a modest $650,000, Pagurian bought a house in Toronto's fashionable Yorkville district as both its corporate headquarters and the display gallery for what is now known as "The Pagurian Collection." Here reside paintings representing a substantial share of the $1.6 million that Ondaatje originally invested in art and publishing, together now assessed at approximately $8 million.

Over the fireplace in the boardroom is a Verner for which Ondaatje paid $100,000 last year. At the time, he confided to a reporter that he wouldn't sell it for twice that amount. "Unfortunately, she implied to everyone that I had doubled the sale price overnight, which gave the entirely wrong impression. We are collectors of and investors in early Canadian art, not sellers. I would never sell it or any of the other 69 Verners for any amount. They are far too valuable an asset for Pagurian."

To the 52 Verners he owned at the end of 1981 he has added 18 more, 11 of which he bought at a Toronto auction in March. The main one cost him $34,000, but as the capacity crowd realized that he was set on acquiring them all, they relented and let him buy the other 10 for a total of $129,000.

To affirm that an artist doesn't have to be dead to earn acclaim, Ondaatje is sponsoring a French-Canadian painter named René Marcil. Though ill and unable to leave his home in the south of France, Marcil is, in Ondaatje's opinion, "our only true Impressionist, as good, I believe, as some of the original French Impressionists, say, the early Matisse." A book on Marcil is in the works.

At the same time as winning acclaim for others, Ondaatje has realized his own successes, and they have altered him. At one time, he put up with bad lunches just to belong to men's clubs that served no liquor. But his resolve has softened. He now enjoys wine or spirits with gourmet repasts served either in the LOM offices or at Winston's, the exclusive Toronto restaurant of which Pagurian owns one percent.

His family, starting with his wife, Valda, is intensely supportive. "For the first few years, Valda edited nearly all the books Pagurian published," he says. Son David, 22, is at Harvard and daughter Janet, 18, is at Bishop's College School in Lennoxville, Que. Sarah, now 20, is at Middlebury College in Vermont, taking fine-art and English courses. She also works at Paguarian during holidays.

Ondaatje insists he'll never leave LOM, even though he is directing passionate energy toward promoting native art and the Pagurian Collection. He sees no conflict of interest whatever in being both a director of a TSE member brokerage house and of a TSE client firm as well. "I keep them strictly separate," he says.

The den in his sprawling, comfortable home in Rosedale, the wealthy, wooded heart of Toronto, is all bookcases from floor to ceiling. He once vowed that when they were full of books, he would stop publishing. And he has, except for the hardy perennials. But with a many-roomed, four-storey house as his headquarters and a board of directors that seems ready to back him to $1 billion and beyond, setting limits on his art collection still leaves him vast amounts of scope.

"Speculators gamble on the weather,"

he's been known to say, paraphrasing J. Paul Getty to potential clients. "Investors bank on the climate." When you can toss off such cryptic remarks and make them sound quite profound, the world can't help but be your oyster—or your hermit crab.

Assignment
1. What kind of business does Christopher Ondaatje operate?
2. How did he get started as a Canadian entrepreneur?
3. What was his early family and business background?
4. Who and what was LOM? What was Ondaatje's involvement?
5. How did Pagurian Press make its mark as a Canadian book publishing house?
6. Explain the business logic behind Pagurian's interest in historical Canadian art.
7. Why did Pagurian go public? What was the result?
8. "Speculators gamble on the weather, investors bank on the climate." Explain and discuss.

UNIT 3.2: ADVANTAGES AND DISADVANTAGES OF INCORPORATION

Advantages

The following are usually considered to be the possible advantages of incorporation: lower income tax; limited liability for the owners; greater ease of raising capital; greater continuity of the business; ability to sell one's shares should the need arise; and professional management.

Possibly Lower Income Tax. A corporation must pay corporate income tax on its taxable income. Also, when profits after tax are paid out to shareholders in the form of dividends, these are subject to another tax—the personal income tax. This is known as "double taxation." However, because of the "dividend tax credit," the extra tax is relatively small. If a salary is paid to a shareholder for management duties, this will reduce the taxable income of the corporation. But the shareholder will then be liable for personal income tax on that salary.

Whether the taxation of a corporation is disadvantageous for its shareholders compared with that of other forms of business ownership will depend on a number of factors. These include the amount of taxable corporate income; the corporation income tax rate applicable; the company's dividend policy; and the shareholders' personal income from all other sources.

Usually, the corporate form of ownership offers substantial tax savings for the shareholders. This is because the corporate tax rate is a flat one, whereas personal marginal income tax rates increase progressively, to just over 50 per cent. In the case of a Canadian-controlled, private business corporation, which is eligible for the special "small business deduction," the effective corporate rate of tax may be reduced to about 25 per cent. Furthermore, the corporate rate may be reduced if a firm is engaged in manufacturing or processing, or qualifies as a Canadian-controlled "small business." For business corporations not eligible for the small business deduction, the flat rate is 46 per cent. However, this rate may also be reduced by the "manufacturing or processing deduction."

Limited Liability. The shareholders of a corporation risk only the money that they have paid for their shares. If the business becomes financially insolvent, the creditors cannot compel the shareholders to sell their personal assets to pay off the outstanding debts of the corporation. Usually, however, a bank or other lender will require personal guarantees of repayment from principal shareholders, particularly in the case of a small private business corporation.

More Capital. A corporation is usually able to raise larger amounts of investment funds than a sole proprietorship or partnership. There is no limit on the number of shareholders, and in the case of a public business corporation, the public may be openly encouraged to buy shares. Investors who purchase such shares know that their liability is limited to their investment; that they can quickly liquidate their investment by selling their shares; that the continuity of the firm in which they have invested is practically assured; and that professional management will enable them to be part owners of a business without having to devote much, if any, time to it.

Continuity. A corporation is a legal person in its own right. Unlike a sole proprietorship or partnership, the death or insanity of one of the shareholders does not affect the life of the corporation. The only way in which its life can be terminated is by the expiry of its charter, by vote of its shareholders to surrender its charter, or by bankruptcy.

Transferability of Ownership. If a sole proprietor wishes to sell his or her business, the only problem is finding a buyer. He or she needs no one's permission to transfer ownership to someone else. When the business is sold, the existing sole proprietorship ceases and a new one (that of the purchaser) comes into existence.

If a partner wishes to sell his or her shares of a partnership, the other partners must agree to accept the new partner or buy the shares themselves. The transfer of ownership is, therefore, slow and possibly controversial.

In a business corporation, there may or may not be restrictions on the transfer of shares. If there are no restrictions, a shareholder may sell his or her shares of ownership without permission from anyone. He may sell them himself or with the assistance of a stockbroker. Once a buyer has been found, the transfer of ownership can take place very quickly.

Professional Management. Because of their financial resources, many public and even private business corporations obtain able and well-trained managers to operate the business. Also, because of their size, many corporations can afford to allow line management to specialize, as well as to use staff specialists for advice. The form of ownership facilitates employee stock ownership, often encouraged by the board of directors, particularly for top managers, as an additional means of motivation and as a way of keeping good employees. By comparison, a sole proprietorship usually must rely solely on the capabilities of its owner. Little money is available to hire outstanding employees, and specialization is often uneconomical. A partnership does make more managerial talent available than in a sole proprietorship, however, and new partners can be admitted as the business grows. Also, specialization among partners often takes place. In most cases, the private business corporation does not employ professional managers; management is provided by the owner or owners.

More Prestige. The incorporated business seems to confer more prestige on the owner than does the sole proprietorship or partnership. Banks and other lenders view the enterprise more favourably, assuming that the owner is more serious in his or her business endeavours. One must, however, be alert to the fact that the unscrupulous business operator may incorporate mainly to help limit his or her personal liability in case of bankruptcy, perhaps deliberately contrived.

Disadvantages

The most important possible disadvantages of the corporate form of ownership include: cost to establish and operate; government restrictions; some lack of personal incentive; and lack of privacy.

Cost to Establish and Operate. It is more expensive to establish a corporation than a sole proprietorship or partnership. Charter fees will depend on whether the company is to be provincially or federally incorporated, and on the amount of capital stock to be authorized. Lawyer's fees will also be incurred for advice as to the objectives, capital structure, and name of the corporation, and for the handling of the application. Also, once the corporation has been established, there will normally be a recurring legal fee for handling minutes of shareholders meetings, dividend declarations, appointment of auditors, and other matters. Another cost is the accountant's fee for preparing the financial statements and corporate income tax returns and providing tax planning advice.

Government Restrictions. Under the federal and provincial Business Corporations Acts, a corporation must: keep a set of books detailing shareholders, directors, capital, and so on; keep specified books of account; hold annual shareholders meetings; appoint an auditor; file annual returns covering share capital, and so on, with the government. The corporation is also restricted by its charter as to the transactions in which it may engage. Any enlargement of powers, including the amount of authorized capital, requires the issue of supplementary letters patent.

Possible Lack of Personal Incentive. In most small business corporations, the major shareholders are also the managers of the business, and will therefore be highly motivated. In large business corporations, with management undertaken by corporation employees, personal incentive is not always as strong. Motivation is provided to some extent, however, by genuine interest and ambition, good salaries, profit-sharing plans, ownership of shares, and the threat of dismissal or loss of promotion.

Possible Lack of Privacy. A public business corporation must provide each shareholder with an annual report in which the firm's income and expenditures, assets and liabilities are set out in some detail. This information can sometimes be of advantage to competitors, and for this reason, among others, many firms try to reveal as little as possible in their annual statements. Many corporations consider it disadvantageous to have to reveal anything at all. This disadvantage does not apply to the private business corporation.

REVIEW QUESTIONS

1. What is the present corporate income tax rate in your province? How is this divided between the federal and the provincial governments?
2. What is the "dividend tax credit"? How is it calculated?
3. Why is income from a corporation sometimes said to be subject to double taxation?
4. What factors will help determine whether the owners of a business will be better off, from the income tax point of view, by incorporating their business?
5. What special tax deductions are available to a business corporation that may significantly reduce the actual rate of income tax paid on taxable corporate income?
6. Explain how the liability of the shareholders of a business corporation for business debts differs from that of a general partner in a partnership business.
7. Why is the corporate form of ownership usually a better financial vehicle for raising funds from investors than is the sole proprietorship or partnership?
8. Compared with a partnership, a business corporation has much greater legal continuity. Explain and discuss.
9. Transferability of ownership is much easier in a corporation than in a partnership. Is this true?
10. The advantage of professional management relates more to the size of the business than to the form of ownership. Discuss.
11. "If it is not paying for a lawyer's services, the business is probably not worth incorporating in the first place." Discuss.
12. What legal and accounting services are required in establishing and operating a private business corporation? What do they cost?

13. What new types of government regulations must a business owner comply with once he or she incorporates the business?
14. Is lack of incentive really a disadvantage of the corporate form of ownership? How do many firms successfully overcome it?
15. What information, if any, must a business corporation reveal about its financial affairs and to whom?

CASE PROBLEM

JOHN PIETERS, BUILDER (A)

The benefits of the corporate form of business ownership

Some years ago, John Pieters, a master housepainter, came to Canada from Holland and settled in the suburbs of a medium-sized Canadian city. After working for a painting contractor for a year and a half, he used his savings to buy a second-hand truck, ladders, and brushes, and started to work on his own account. Before long, he was getting enough work, except in January and February, to keep himself and three men fully employed.

After some years, Pieters bought a house with a store front and began to sell paint, brushes, wallpaper, and other house-decorating items. While he was out on jobs, his wife would look after the store.

Two years later, Pieters decided to build a new house for himself and family on a lot that he had bought adjoining his present house. Prior to this he had learnt as much as he could about house construction, and was confident that he could arrange for the concrete work, bricklaying, carpentry, plumbing, and electrical work to be done efficiently on a contract basis. In this way, he believed that he could have a new house built to his own design, at a cost much below market price. Pieters was in fact correct in his belief, and paid only $99,000 (including the cost of the land) for a house worth an estimated $114,000.

Emboldened by his experience in building his new house, Pieters decided to engage in some speculative housebuilding in addition to his housepainting activities. As before, he continued to operate as a sole proprietor. With his own funds, together with financial help from the bank, Pieters bought several ravine lots and began the construction of five houses in the $157,000 range, using variations of the plan which he had designed for his own house. Pieters intended, once the basements were constructed, to arrange mortgage financing on the houses.

Unfortunately, Pieters was unaware of two facts: mortgage funds were becoming scarce and lenders were becoming wary of lending on the security of houses built on ravine lots, following several well-publicized landslides. As a result, before Pieters was able to arrange satisfactory financing or sell his now half-completed houses, his creditors (the suppliers of building materials and firms which had contracted to do work for him) successfully petitioned for him to be declared a compulsory bankrupt.

Assignment

1. What liability does Pieters have to his creditors?
2. Can the creditors touch the assets of the painting business for which Pieters has kept a separate bank account?
3. Can the creditors cause the new house in which Pieters lives and which has always been owned by Pieters' wife to be sold to help to pay Pieters' debts?
4. How much would it have cost Pieters to set up a private corporation at present fees? What disadvantages, in addition to cost, would incorporation have brought?
5. How could Pieters legally have prevented the creditors of his building business from obtaining the assets of his paint store and painting business?
6. What do the facts indicate about Pieters' abilities as a businessman?

JOHN PIETERS, BUILDER (B)

John Pieters, now discharged from bankruptcy, plans to get back into the building business. Specifically, he wants to build a 50-unit townhouse complex on land that belongs to Peter Wells, who used to be in a TV repair business. However, Pieters' wife, who burned her fingers in a toy shop venture, advises caution. The two men, Pieters and Wells, who met at Hastings lodge, a Muskoka resort, do not have sufficient funds of their own, nor can they borrow enough to finance the townhouse project. However, they have the land and believe they have the real estate know-how.

Assignment

1. What form of business ownership would you recommend for their building venture? And why?

UNIT 3.3: BIG BUSINESS

In this century, we have seen not only a rapid growth in the number of business corporations, but also a rapid increase in the size of many of them. This has been true in most industries, notably manufacturing, mining, and finance. Only in agriculture, retailing, and the service industries generally has small business been able to hold its ground—owing mainly to the willingness of the proprietor to work long hours, often for low pay, and of the consumer to pay extra for personal service.

Reasons for Growth of Big Business

Practically every large business firm has had humble beginnings. But, whereas many small business firms have remained small or disappeared altogether, today's large firms have been successful in establishing and maintaining a momentum of growth. They have been able to do this for a variety of reasons, as set out below.

Consumer Satisfaction. One key ingredient of business growth is being able to produce and market goods or services that meet a real consumer need.

Efficient Management. Another key ingredient to growth is the ambition and managerial competence of a firm's owners and/or managers.

Economies of Scale. In certain types of production, notably manufacturing and assembly, substantial reductions in cost per unit of output can be obtained by large-scale production. These reductions (or *economies of scale*) stem from: (a) the spreading of fixed costs, such as plant, equipment, and office overheads, over a larger volume of production; (b) the ability to use special-purpose equipment that requires a minimum production run to be worthwhile; (c) the ability to use highly mechanized means of handling materials, parts, and finished products; and (d) the ability to obtain significant price discounts on materials and parts, as well as prompt delivery, through purchase in bulk.

Market Power. One way a firm can enlarge its share of the market and improve its control over it, is to buy out some, most, or all of its competitors. Once this has been done, a firm is better able to retain not only its customers, but also any desired price level. It can then spend less on advertising and other forms of non-price competition without fear of losing its customers to rival firms. In some cases (for example, the cigarette industry), heavy advertising costs will continue—not only to increase the number of customers but to make it almost impossible for a new firm to enter the industry.

Production Technology. Certain products, such as airliners, ocean-going ships, pulp and paper, require expensive plant and equipment for their manufacture. Consequently, only a large business firm can afford the heavy capital investment that is required.

Product Development. Firms in certain industries—for example, pharmaceuticals and computers—must undertake expensive research and development if they are to bring out new products and thereby remain competitive. Without this research and development capability, a firm cannot survive. As a result, small firms in such industries tend inevitably to disappear, either through bankruptcy or through sales to a more powerful rival.

Securing Materials and Markets. Another reason for business growth is a firm's desire to own sources of raw materials and established wholesale and retail outlets for the final products. By doing so, a firm reduces the risk of financial loss that might arise from an interruption in material supplies or exclusion from a market. The term *vertical integration* is used to describe the combination of business firms engaged in successive phases of production and marketing. More specifically, the term *backward integration* is used for the acquisition of sources of supply; and the term *forward integration* for the acquisition of sales outlets for the final product. Steel producers are good examples of vertical integration, both backward and forward.

Government Policy. Governments in Canada often prefer to deal with large companies. Thus, for example, timber rights may be assigned to a few forest product giants rather than made available to independent loggers. As another example, government transportation subsidies help large-scale manufacturers in Ontario to sell their products in all parts of Canada, often to the detriment of local small business. Also, very importantly, government conferred monopolies (such as telephone service) restrict certain fields to one firm. The federal and provincial governments have also set up many large businesses of their own.

Mergers, Takeovers, and Conglomerates

Many firms have grown to large size purely by expanding the organization with which they began. As sales volume has increased, more people have been hired, new departments and branches created, and more activities, such as marketing research, undertaken. To finance this enlargement of the firm, profits and the money represented by capital cost and depletion allowances are reinvested, and new funds obtained from investors by the sale of stocks and bonds.

However, this method of growth has been supplemented in many cases by mergers. A *merger* occurs when two firms join together to form one new firm. This is achieved by one firm's purchasing most of the voting capital stock of the other. Where the merger is opposed unsuccessfully by the board of directors of the corporation being acquired, the term *takeover* is frequently used. Some firms have used the merger technique as their principal means of rapid growth.

The types of firms that have been merged vary greatly in their nature. In many cases, a manufacturer has purchased control of firms supplying its raw materials or of firms distributing its products. The term *vertical merger* is sometimes used to describe this method of integration. In other cases, a firm has purchased control of other firms producing similar goods or services—a form of integration known as *horizontal merger*. In yet other cases, a firm has acquired control of other firms producing quite dissimilar products. Such a merger is sometimes undertaken to spread investment risk; but more often it is to acquire any potentially profitable enterprise that is undervalued in the market. The resultant collection of firms is called a corporate *conglomerate* or *group* of companies. The corporation that acts as the parent company, through its ownership of controlling amounts of the voting stock of the other corporations in the conglomerate, is known as a *holding company*.

Multinational Corporations

There are some large business firms in Canada whose overseas involvement has gone far beyond just exporting. As well as producing at home, they manufacture goods and provide marketing and financial services in other countries of the world. In such cases, a firm's international involvement may eventually become so large that its marketing, production, financial, investment, and other major decisions are taken on a predominantly world-wide rather than national basis. As a result, such firms are now usually called *multinational corporations, transnational companies,* or *multinational enterprises*. As with most definitions, the borderline between a national company with international connections (for example, export sales and overseas licensing agreements) and a multinational company with interests restricted to just a few countries is somewhat hazy. Nevertheless, the rapid growth in the number and size of these global enterprises, particularly since the 1950s, has made "big business" not just a national phenomenon, but an international one.

Such expansion abroad has taken place for a variety of reasons: for example, to hold on to an export market threatened by higher tariffs or competitors' products, to establish control over a source of raw materials, or to take advantage of a market opportunity.

Canada, although it is the parent country of a few large Canadian multinational corporations, is better known as the host country for a vast number of manufacturing, mining, and other subsidiaries of U.S. multinational corporations. This situation has arisen because of various factors: Canada's tariff policy, which at one time discouraged imports of manufactured goods and, at the same time, encouraged local production; a relatively friendly government policy towards foreign investment in Canada; good markets in certain areas of Canada, particularly southern Ontario and southern Quebec; abundant natural resources; an adequate labour supply; political stability; a common language; geographical closeness to the United States; and U.S. military protection.

The growth of multinational corporations has undoubtedly brought economic and social benefits to the various host countries in which their subsidiaries are located. North American managerial ability, technological know-how, and financial resources have all been made available to help produce jobs and income in the host country. Obviously, however, these benefits have not been given away for nothing—a steady stream of income has flowed from the subsidiary to its parent corporation (usually U.S.) in the form of dividend remittances, low-priced materials, and management and licence fees. Furthermore, there is always the danger that the foreign-owned subsidiary will take actions (for example, under-pricing components exported to sister plants in other countries or closing down a plant) that will not be in the best interests of the host country. In some host countries, including Canada, the situation has arisen where the managerial ability is now supplied predominantly by natives of the host country and most of the additional financing required for growth is obtained locally. Thus, the current benefits to the host country are not as great as they are supposed to be.

Cartels, Gentlemen's Agreements, and Trusts

For most business firms, competition of any kind is costly and dangerous. It means that a firm may, at any time, lose all or part of its share of a market—with a consequent decline in revenue and profits. The loss may even be so severe that it jeopardizes the continued existence of the firm. A much safer and more profitable situation exists when the industry as a whole regulates total output and market price. In this way, output and price can be set at a level that is most beneficial for the industry rather than for the consumer.

The existence of only a few firms in an industry, as under oligopoly, makes it relatively easy for such firms (unless restricted by law) to enter into agreements to restrict competition. There have, in fact, been various types of price and output collusion throughout the world. They have included: (a) *cartels*—formal, written agreements between independent firms, often in different countries, to restrict output, fix prices, and allocate markets; (b) *gentlemen's agreements*—oral agreements between different firms, usually with regard only to the price to be charged; and (c) *trusts*—the amalgamation of a number of different firms into one by the exchange of trust certificates for shares.

At one time, cartels and gentlemen's agreements were accepted as one of the facts of business life, particularly in Europe. Even today in countries such as Japan, West Germany, and Britain, the merger of medium-sized firms into large ones receives government approval—for this "rationalization" of industry is considered to help make an industry more efficient (through economies of large-scale production, research, and marketing) and better able to compete with foreign firms.

The United States, by contrast, has a long history of "trust-busting" dating from the second half of the nineteenth century. In Canada, any agreement to fix prices or otherwise reduce or eliminate competition is illegal under the terms of the Combines Investigation Act. However, because many agreements of this nature are oral rather than written, they are not easy to detect. Even when the firms involved have been successfully prosecuted, the fines imposed have not been considered to be sufficiently high to act as a deterrent. However, changes in the Combines Investigation Act are expected to correct this. There can be no doubt that business firms, because of the profit motive, have a constant temptation to reduce competition. Therefore, governments have a responsibility for ensuring that competition by firms operating under conditions of monopolistic competition and oligopoly is kept at a maximum and society's interests thereby protected.

KEY TERMS

Big business

Economies of scale

Market power

Production technology

Product development

Vertical integration

Merger

Takeover

Vertical merger

Horizontal merger

Conglomerate

Holding company

Multinational corporation

Cartel

Gentlemen's agreement

Trust

REVIEW QUESTIONS

1. What is meant by the economies of scale?

2. What is product development? In which industries is it particularly important? Why?
3. What other reasons exist for the growth of large business firms?
4. What is meant by the term "vertical integration"? Distinguish, with examples, between backward integration and forward integration.
5. Distinguish between a merger and a takeover as a means of business growth. Explain, with examples, the difference between a vertical merger and a horizontal merger.
6. What is a corporate conglomerate? Why has this type of business firm grown increasingly popular in recent years? What special management problems does it pose?
7. What is a multinational corporation? Why has Canada become a host country for many such corporations? What particular problems do they present for Canada?

READINGS

Swallowed Alive

The top business story was the one that won't go away: the nation's wealth is becoming concentrated in fewer and fewer hands. But is all this merging good for business?

BY DIANE FRANCIS

Source: *Canadian Business Magazine*. Used by permission of Diane Francis.

Calgary entrepreneur Rob Vanderham can tell you what it's like to be on the wrong side in a takeover game. As president of Peyto Oils Ltd. of Calgary, an oil and gas exploration company, he felt more personally than most about his job—after all, he'd helped found the company in 1970 and had built it into an enterprise with sales of some $10 million and assets of more than $70 million. Then, in January 1980, while sunning himself in the Caribbean, he got a call from the office. Someone was snapping up the stock, trading had been suspended and he and his company were no longer players, but pucks. Only a few days earlier an eastern broker had rounded up 38% of Peyto's float from its nine or 10 largest institutional shareholders and peddled them to Westburne International Industries Ltd., a Calgary-based conglomerate, for $31.8 million. Vanderham, a 53-year-old Dutch immigrant who owned about 10% of the company, recalls, "As soon as that first call came, I knew it was all over. I put the phone down and felt as though somebody had just stolen my baby."

Takeovers—Canada's most popular corporate sport—continued unabated in 1980. Fifteen of the Toronto Stock Exchange 300 corporations were taken over or merged, and a total of about $1.6 billion (or almost 4.5% of the TSE 300's total 1978 value) in seasoned securities disappeared, perhaps forever, into the exceedingly deep pockets of a handful of the country's larger holders of capital. (Since Jan. 1, 1978, 51 firms have disappeared or soon will from the TSE 300). Despite alarms about the economic and social dangers of allowing power to concentrate in fewer and fewer hands, and the calls for a referee, the free-for-all continues.

Economists measure two types of concentration: the accumulation of assets in industries that may not be related (by conglomerates or passive holding companies), and the increase of market share within a sector by a few firms. Both types have relentlessly accelerated in Canada, particularly during the 1970s. And both can be economically harmful. In 1965 our 25 largest non-financial enterprises controlled 23.8% of private-sector assets and 10.4% of sales; by 1978 their slice had jumped to 31.1% of assets and 21.6% of sales. (The rest of the corporate pie was divided up among some 264,915 enterprises.) To measure market share, economists use "four-firm concentration ratios"—the share enjoyed by the four dominant firms in an industry. Like any economic matter, the optimum levels are debatable. Some economists think that if four firms control 60% of a market, competition can still thrive. Others believe that if they get any more than that, the temptation to act as a cartel is too great for them to resist setting prices or bullying suppliers. No matter the viewpoint, market share for the four dominant firms in most of Canada's major sectors has increased dramatically. Between 1948 and 1978, the four largest breweries, leather tanneries, shoe manufacturers, fish processors and biscuit manufacturers enlarged their stakes collectively by 20% or more. (By 1978 some four-firm groups already enjoyed as much as 60% of the market; any merger or takeover in industries with this degree of concentration automatically triggers an antitrust investigation in the US.) Between 1965 and 1978, four-firm groups increased their market share by more than 10% in 21 industries. And there were other dramatic jumps. The four largest manufacturers of shoes, iron and steel, concrete and soap increased their share by between 10% and 19.9%.

The US has traditionally fostered greater competition through tough antitrust laws. Any merger resulting in a significant increase in market share automatically spurs Federal Trade Commission investigators into action. Their job is to determine whether such concentration is economically desirable for both competitors and consumers. The result of such vigilance is notable. By 1978 Canada's 100 largest enterprises controlled 48.6% of all corporate assets. In the US, latest available data shows that in 1975 the top 100 giants controlled 30.6%. Of course, competition also thrives in the US because of the sheer size of its economy. After all, even after its largest enterprise, American Telephone and Telegraph Co. (with $125 billion in assets) has carved out its massive share of the market, there's still room for other players. But it can also be argued that without regulation, AT&T would probably be larger than it already is. In fact, the Justice Department has waged a monumental antitrust suit against the utility for six years, and 40 private lawsuits are also pending against it and its subsidiaries. Such comparisons show that vigorous competition policies and laws protect US capitalism, while here in Canada, the absence of deterrents protects upper crust capitalists.

Figures on aggregate market share alone don't tell the whole story. Canada Safeway Stores Ltd. of Winnipeg, for instance, accounts for less than 10% of Canada's grocery retailing market, but it controls more than 50% of Alberta's. The K.C. Irving interests own an insignificant portion of this nation's newspapers, but they own all five English-language dailies in New Brunswick. Even when Ottawa's combines officials suspect abuses by monopolies, they are powerless to prosecute. In November 1976, the Supreme Court of Canada ruled that the Irvings hadn't violated combines laws by acquiring the papers. Using the court's logic, a single firm could conceivably acquire all of Canada's newspapers, providing none were in direct competition.

In 1980 FP Publications Ltd., Toronto (bought out by Thomson interests), and Southam Inc., Toronto, carved up several newspaper markets. Virtual monopolies were created overnight in Ottawa (for Southam) and Winnipeg (for Thomson), and control of more than 80% of British Columbia's daily newspaper circulation passed to Thomson. (Thomson's share of the BC market has since declined with the sale of its 50% interest in Pacific Press Ltd., publisher of Vancouver's *Sun* and *Province*, to Southam.) Ottawa's response was to create the Royal Commission on Newspapers. The Royal Commission would have been unnecessary had Ottawa enacted Consumer and Corporate Affairs Canada policy calling for a specialized competition tribunal to deal with all mergers. Thanks to business lobbying, the proposed legislation died soon after it was introduced in the House of Commons in November 1977. The government opted instead for the recommendations of the Royal Commission on Corporate Concentration (chairman Robert Bryce)—which was established in 1975 and released its report in 1978—that Cabinet evaluate mergers to determine whether Parliament should intervene. But Parliament wasn't in session during the FP merger or during 1980's most spectacular merger, the $1.3-billion marriage of Hiram Walker-Gooderham & Worts Ltd., Windsor, Ont., and Consumers' Gas Co., Toronto (now Hiram Walker Resources Ltd.).

The Canadian attitude so far presents a stark contrast to that of the British government. The UK's Monopolies and Mergers Commission puts at least six weeks' worth of investigative work into major takeover applications—this despite the avowed non-interventionist stance of Margaret Thatcher and her Tory government. In the US, victims of unwelcome takeover attempts can resort to several federal and state regulatory agencies for help—or get it involuntarily. US newspaper owners are afforded an extra measure of protection by the Newspaper Preservation Act of 1970. The act exempts purchases from antitrust laws only if one of the newspapers in a city can demonstrate it is in danger of imminent financial failure.

In the past two years, the Canadian government has been less concerned about being a referee than becoming an aggressive player in its own right. Petro-Canada paid $1.4 billion in February of this year for Petrofina Canada Inc. of Montreal and anounced its intention to make some more billion-dollar acquisitions. And the provincial-government spawned British Columbia Resource Investment Corp. (BCRIC), Vancouver, gobbled up Kaiser Resources Ltd., Vancouver, for $664 million in September, though it failed in its bid for control of locally based MacMillan Bloedel Ltd., Canada's largest forestry firm. Private-sector firms, without the benefit of bottomless budgets, have been no less active. Many are cash-rich, and assets remain cheaper to buy than build. Top scorers last year included Noranda Mines Ltd. of Toronto, which bought MacLaren Power and Paper Co. of Buckingham, Que., for $240 million and put in a successful $600-million bid against BCRIC to buy 49% of MacMillan Bloedel; and the Reichmann brothers of Toronto, who picked up Vancouver's Cassiar Asbestos Corp. for $88 million, obtained Abitibi-Price Inc. of Toronto for $560 million and became the largest shareholder in Royal Trustco Ltd. of Toronto with more than 23% of the float, worth about $100 million.

In 1980 the only whistles blown during

play were by businessmen themselves. The shrillest were the managements of Royal Trustco and Calgary Power Ltd., which repelled takeovers by those upstart outsiders Robert Campeau of Ottawa and Ron Southern of Calgary's Atco Ltd. (At this writing, Nu-West Group Ltd. of Calgary is bidding $517 million for 49% of Calgary Power, now renamed Transalta Utilities Corp.) Royal Trustco management took out large newspaper ads, echoing the sentiments of many who fear the consequences of economic concentration: "No single person should be entrusted with [Royal's] $26 billion in assets." (The $26-billion figure included assets managed by the firm for its clients; its own assets are $8.2 billion.) And Calgary Power harped publicly about the hazards of allowing Southern to gain control over 80% of Alberta's utilities (he had just bought 58% of Canadian Utilities Ltd.).

The huge deals get the headlines, but activity has been no less frenzied among smaller, private firms. Of an estimated $5 billion in merger transactions in 1979, some $2 billion involved small or medium-sized firms with $10 million in sales or less. Such firms create most new jobs (about 60%), provide much innovation and prod competitors into efficient ways of doing business. Their rapid disappearance is a danger sign, cautions economist Patricia Johnston, vice-president for legislative affairs of the 59,000-member Canadian Federation of Independent Business. "Too often mergers have become the only way a young company can survive because of the lack of other equity capital markets," she says. "And post-acquisition studies in the US point out that once they are absorbed, their steam and entrepreneurial drive disappear."

Even so, many business people agree with Pierre Nadeau, one of the Bryce Commission's three commissioners, who believes in leaving these matters up to the marketplace. Competitive forces will weed out the weak, and rationalization will result in efficient world-scale industry. Mergers aren't bad things if they don't lessen competition and do result in efficiencies. It may be ironic that Nadeau himself has fallen victim to the game rules he upholds: as chairman of the board of Petrofina Canada Inc., he found his own corporation swallowed by the voracious Petro-Canada. He promptly announced he would resign once the reins were handed over, explaining: "I favor takeovers as a way to improve the economy, but not by Crown corporations."

Consumer and Corporate Affairs has once more begun rumbling about new combines legislation. But if Ottawa continues to pussyfoot, it may find itself in the same kind of predicament it inherited in 1870. Until then, the Hudson's Bay Co. owned 38% of the entire country. When it wanted to have an east-west railway built, Ottawa had to buy back a portion of Hudson's Bay's lands at a king's ransom of £300,000 (worth billions of today's dollars) to pay the railroad company. As the players grow more aggressive, it's hard not to think of The Bay.

Assignment
1. What is a "takeover"? How does it occur?
2. What makes a takeover possible?
3. What are two basic types of business concentration that have been taking place in Canada?
4. What are the effects of this increasing business concentration? Are they harmful or beneficial to the consumer?
5. What steps has the Canadian government taken to discourage business concentration? How effective have they been?

6. What is being done in the United States?
7. How are takeovers treated in the United Kingdom?
8. Should takeovers be encouraged or discouraged?

Fast Footwork Wins Big Bouts for Jimmy Pattison

Maple Leaf Mills fight unlikely to be his last challenge

BY ALEXANDER ROSS
Source: *The Financial Post.*

He'd taken his jacket off hours ago and now he was pacing around the ninth-floor suite in the Royal York Hotel in a shirt and vest, barking orders, listening hard, grabbing telephones, huddling with lawyers and brokers, yelling in that urgent, high-pitched voice. It was nearly noon, and for the past few hours Jimmy Pattison had known he was involved in the biggest fight of his incredible career.

The room fairly crackled with urgency. The day before, Pattison had told the world that his company, *Neonex International Ltd.*, had acquired 38% of the shares of *Maple Leaf Mills Ltd.* Now he was buying on the open market towards that magic 51% mark—and only a few hours ago he'd learned that *Molson Industries Ltd.* was in the bidding too.

Jimmy Pattison vs Molson's! This is not to be believed! It's like the Bowery Boys vs the Chase Manhattan Bank. *Jimmy Pattison?* Two years ago, yes, two years ago, he was the hotshot little car salesman in Vancouver, the sort of man you gladly bought your Buick from but definitely didn't expect to see much of in the quiet watering places of the cautious and conservative Establishment.

And now here he was in his ninth-floor command post, his shiny tie loosened and the top button of his shirt undone, battling for control of a company that would make Neonex, on the basis of sales, the second largest public company in British Columbia.

Standing there, watching Jimmy pacing around the room like an aroused terrier, I couldn't help inventing my own 1930s movie, the kind of thing you sometimes catch on the Late Late show:

It's Mickey Rooney, or Jimmy Pattison himself, slumped in his corner between rounds, chest heaving, badly cut above the eye, all guts and gumption, fighting for the bantamweight championship of the entire world. His manager whispers in his ear: "Sure he's big Jimmy, but he's SOFT. He's got the reach, but you've got the speed. Now go in there and get him . . ."

There are about five other people in the suite with Jimmy, prudent-looking bluesuit types. Mrs. Maureen Chant, Jimmy's secretary, is hammering away on a typewriter she's set up on a card table in one corner. In a tiny bedroom next door, Wilf Ray, Jimmy's PR man, is on the phone to somebody from Dow-Jones. There are three telephone lines in constant use. Trading in Maple Leaf Mills had been suspended at 10:40 that morning, after the Molson-Pattison bidding contest drove the price from $18 to $30. Now it's lunchtime, although nobody has thought of eating, and trading is scheduled to resume any minute now. The Molson name is one of the oldest and haughtiest in Canada, a power in this country since the eighteenth century. The Pattison name is . . . well, two years ago, who'd ever even *heard* of him?

Can you blame me for viewing this corporate takeover battle as some kind of stylized prize-fight? And will you forgive me and my West Coast upbringing if I admit that right then, just before the market opened for the second round of the day, I found myself rooting like mad for Jimmy Pattison?

It pains Jimmy when you refer to Neonex as a conglomerate. He prefers to call it a company with a "consumer-oriented pattern of diversification" or something. The distinction is pretty fine, since Neonex, in the past two years, has been doing precisely what conglomerates do: acquiring other companies, usually in exchange for Neonex shares, that are showing good profits by making things that people buy. These acquired profits improve the earnings picture of the parent company, become an even more attractive currency for financing further acquisitions, which drive the price of Neonex shares even higher, which in turn . . .

Well, you get the idea. In the past two years, since Pattison took over *Neon Products of Canada Ltd.*, Neonex has acquired 15 companies (16, if you count Maple Leaf Mills), most of them in growth industries such as transportation, mobile homes or carpets. Total annual sales are now more than $150 million.

But not all of the company's growth has been through acquisition. Of Neonex's 16 components, three showed reduced earnings in 1969, one was the same as in 1968, and all the rest earned more. The recent appointment of Ross Turner as president is indicative of Jimmy's emphasis on internal growth. As the division of labour now stands, Turner stays home and minds the store; Pattison, as chairman, races around the continent in a Lear Jet, acquiring more companies.

With the Maple Leaf acquisition in the bag, Neonex revenues next year will be in the $300-million range. There is only one public company in British Columbia that pulls in more dollars than that: MacMillan Bloedel. To anyone who knows the Vancouver Establishment, it is a startling thought, the idea of Jimmy Pattison as the corporate peer of J.V. Clyne.

Out on West Broadway in Vancouver, in an area of pizza parlours and car lots, there stands an immense electric sign which, until he started building Neonex, was the nearest thing there was to a personal monument to James Pattison.

The sign says BOW MAC, in electric letters eighteen feet high. Prior to setting up his own Pontiac-Buick dealership in 1961, Pattison was general manager of *Bowell-Maclean Ltd.*, one of the city's biggest GM dealers. And it was in that capacity that he erected the tallest, most monstrous, most garish electric sign west of the Rockies.

"Jim spent six months on that sign," says Wilf Ray, then and now his executive assistant, photographer and PR man. "We looked at all kinds of designs—cascading waterfalls, showers of neon, you name it. But Jim picked this design. He knew he had to put up something bigger than the opposition's, and this was the result."

The thing is as tall as a 10-storey-building, and Pattison can still quote the wondrous statistics: total cost, $120,000; enough concrete to build 60 driveways; 10 miles of wiring; two little elevators built in, so the light bulbs can be changed.

When it was finished in 1959, Pattison staged a sort of plastic-and-neon festival.

He had disc jockeys racing each other up and down in the elevators. He painted a huge checkerboard on the parking lot, and used B.C. Lions football players and cheerleaders as the pieces. That month, he also sold more than 1,000 cars, which in 1959 was some kind of a record.

Jimmy's experience in selecting that sign, along with a number of others he erected during his career as a car dealer, was one of the reasons he chose Neon Products as the target of his first takeover, and the vehicle for his expansion plans. "There was a strong cash flow and no control block of shares. But Neon Products was also in the advertising business, which is something I have a feel for," he says.

Everyone acknowledges that Jimmy Pattison is a great little businessman. Even before he started Neonex, his personal empire included the Pontiac-Buick dealership he'd started in 1961 and built into the biggest west of Toronto; radio station CJOR (where his friend, Wilf Ray, still hosts a Sunday-night religious program as "CJOR Radio's Man of God"); the local Muzak franchise; and a car and truck leasing business, which Pattison has merged, along with some of his other non-Neonex interests, into *Great Pacific Industries Ltd.*

So far, so good. In 1967, this mini-empire was grossing $16 million a year. For a man not yet 40, who'd started his business career as a car-washer, this would seem like a perfectly respectable plateau. For Pattison, it was only a start. He staked everything he had, and a lot of money he didn't have, on buying Neon Products. Working in deepest secrecy with a New York investment house, he picked up between 10%-15% of the company's shares at an average pre-split price of about $9 per share. Then, for $1.88 million, he bought Neon President Art Christopher's 175,000 shares to clinch control of the company.

Since then, he's developed his talent for grabbing off unsuspecting companies into something approaching a fine art.

"The most important thing in this business," he says, "is to keep your mouth shut. Acquisitions are made in dark rooms and strange places. Even my wife doesn't know what I'm doing. When you're ready to move, you move fast, and with courage."

Pattison's father was a down-and-outer in the 1930s. Jimmy can still remember the winter of 1934 in Saskatchewan, when there was no coal for the stove. Later the family moved to Vancouver, where Pattison Sr. worked as a door-to-door piano tuner before acquiring a Packard dealership.

Jimmy's father was a religious man. Every year he'd bring home bums and rubby-dubs, the wretched of the earth, for Christmas dinner. Jimmy grew up religious too. Today, wherever he is, no matter how urgent the deal he's working on, he drops everything on Friday afternoons and grabs the Lear Jet back home to Vancouver—to spend the weekend with his family. Twice every Sunday, unfailingly, he attends the Glad Tidings Temple on Fraser St., a Pentecostal church in a blue-collar district. He and his son both play trumpet in the church's band. Jimmy is very matter-of-fact about his religion; it is simply something he does, a fact of life to be accepted, not questioned.

Sociologically, this is several light years away from the life style of the Canadian Establishment with which Jimmy deals every weekday of his life. He has no illusions about his status, or how success is changing it. "These days my mantle-piece is loaded with invitations to cocktail parties. And there's a bank that invited me—just me and about 10 Canadian business leaders—to a seminar in the Laurentians."

We are sitting in the den of Jimmy's big house at the top of the hill in West Vancouver as he tells me this. It is Saturday morning, and you can see half of Greater Vancouver out the picture window. The house used to belong to the mayor.

Jimmy is wearing a knitted polo shirt and alligator shoes. He is relaxing. On Monday he will fly back to Toronto to resume his secret raid on Maple Leaf Mills. "All the players are coming to the table," he tells me, "but some of them don't know it yet."

I reflect that this small, sincere, urgently ambitious car salesman has done more in two years to combat foreign ownership than Walter Gordon achieved in two decades.

I ask Jimmy a question. I am not completely serious. "Jimmy," I say, "how would you like to take over the CPR?"

Jimmy Pattison doesn't laugh. He just sits there, and the most astonishing look comes over his face. I can't describe how he looked at that moment. But his eyes sort of glazed over, and you could almost see the dreams and deals chasing themselves through his head.

He didn't say anything for almost a minute. Then he looked at me, a funny hardness in his face, and said:

"You know, there's a funny thing about that company. I've heard that Queen Juliana owns 7% of the CPR."

Assignment
1. What exactly was Jimmy Pattison's big fight?
2. Who or what is Neonex? Why has it been called a "conglomerate"? Explain.
3. How has Neonex grown so quickly?
4. How did Jimmy Pattison come to be President of Neonex?
5. What is his corporate acquisitions philosophy?
6. Contrast Jimmy Pattison's business and personal lives.

UNIT 3.4: THE CO-OPERATIVE

A *co-operative* is a business set up by a number of persons who wish to supply themselves with commodities or services at a lower cost than would otherwise be possible. Most co-operatives are incorporated either federally or provincially, and thus enjoy the benefits of limited liability and continuity of existence. They differ from business corporations because they are not established for a speculative purpose; they are democratically controlled (one member, one vote); and they share any surplus on operations among their members in proportion to the amount of business done with them by each member.

Types of Co-operatives

The principal types of co-operative enterprise in Canada are:
1. *Consumers' co-operatives*—which retail goods to members and others.
2. *Marketing co-operatives*—which market milk, fruit, and other produce for their members, and buy seed and fertilizer for them.

3. *Financial co-operatives* (known as Credit Unions or Caisses Populaires)—which accept savings deposits from members and make loans to them.
4. *Insurance co-operatives*—which provide life, fire, hail, and liability insurance to members.
5. *Service co-operatives*—which provide members with services such as housing, rural electrification, medical insurance, transportation, recreation facilities, machinery rental, and funerals.

Characteristics

The main characteristics of the co-operative business are:
1. Capital funds are obtained by the sale of shares to members.
2. Each member, whatever his or her capital contribution, is entitled to only one vote.
3. No voting by proxy is permitted.
4. A board of directors, elected annually by the members, is responsible for the management of the co-operative. Usually a paid manager is appointed by them.
5. That part of the profit which is not retained is paid out as interest on capital or as patronage return.
6. The patronage return, or share of surplus, which a member receives is in proportion to the amount of business which the member has done with the co-operative. For example, if he or she has bought one-twentieth of the goods sold, he or she is entitled to one-twentieth of the patronage returns.
7. Shares may not be transferred without the approval of the board of directors.
8. By registering as a corporation in the province in which it is situated, the co-operative obtains limited liability for its members and continuity for the business.

Advantages

The advantages of the co-operative form of ownership, from the members' point of view, are: members can save money on purchases, and obtain more on sales; the one-vote-per-member stipulation helps prevent control of the business by a few members; members have limited liability when the co-operative is incorporated; and the co-operative enjoys continuity of existence when incorporated.

Disadvantages

The disadvantages of this form of ownership are that control is not proportional to ownership, and the need for good management is not always met. Few persons are willing to invest large sums of money under such conditions. Furthermore, this form of ownership cannot be used to raise money from the general public.

KEY TERMS

Co-operative

Consumers' co-operative

Marketing co-operative

Financial co-operative

Insurance co-operative

Service co-operative

REVIEW QUESTIONS

1. What is a co-operative? What are its origins?
2. Can a co-operative be incorporated? If so, how does it still differ from any other business corporation?
3. What are the main types of co-operative enterprise in Canada? Explain the purpose of each.
4. What are the main characteristics of the co-operative form of business ownership?
5. What are the principal advantages of this form of business ownership compared with the partnership form? And with the corporate form?
6. What are the principal disadvantages?

CASE PROBLEM

HASTINGS LODGE

The benefits of the co-operative form of business ownership

The staff association of a large manufacturing firm is considering the purchase of a lodge and 406 acres of land. It will be used by its members, their families and friends for fishing, hunting, swimming, and other forms of recreation. The lodge consists of a main building containing 16 guest bedrooms, a dining hall capable of seating 55 persons, and 12 small cabins. During the winter, a local farmer will take care of the property. During the summer, a paid manager, together with a kitchen, table, and cleaning staff will be required to run the place.

The staff association will charge its members rates slightly below normal for the use of the facilities, and will share any profits among them at the end of each year. Jennifer Foster, the secretary of the association, has suggested that the enterprise be set up as a co-operative.

Assignment

1. Could the co-operative form of business ownership be used for this enterprise?
2. What advantages would the co-operative form bring?
3. What would the disadvantages be?
4. What form of ownership would you recommend, and why?

READING

Supermarket Socialism

Nanaimo's no-frills Hub Co-op works mainly because of the cheap prices

BY FRANK APPLETON

(Frank Appleton is a freelance writer living in Edgewood, British Columbia.)

Source: *The Financial Post Magazine*. Used by permission of Frank Appleton.

Last February, an abandoned cart of groceries was found outside Hub Co-op's Bowen Rd. store, on the outskirts of Nanaimo, B.C. Unusual enough, but particularly at Hub, where members are highly cost-conscious, and dutifully return carts to the store. Days later, a puzzled Hub store manager traced the missing buyer's membership number and name. The name seemed oddly familiar, and turned out to be that of the manager of a newly-opened Safeway superstore in Nanaimo—Hub's chief competition. In disbelief, the Hub manager phoned his opposite number and asked if he would care to come and claim his purchases. The Safeway manager at first denied everything, but finally confessed when confronted with a membership card (later revoked) with his signature.

Why the Safeway manager joined Hub is obvious—you can't shop there unless you are a member, and he was ordered by senior management to find out Hub's prices. Abandoning the groceries was more curious: presumably he couldn't tolerate co-op products in his cupboards, and possibly thought the cart would be quickly emptied by passers-by. But he reckoned without the loyalty and unity of Hub shoppers—key factors in the amazing growth of North America's largest direct-charge cooperative. Hub began its grocery store operation in 1971 and since then yearly sales have soared from $711,000 to over $26 million; it's obviously an organization that has the competition scared.

Nanaimo has always had a strong trade-union tradition, dating back to the miners who came to work the coal seams early in the century. Their successors, like retired civil servant Owen Morgan and schoolteacher Ieuan Williamson, are key directors of Hub. So are pulp-mill workers Reg Briginshaw and Art Sunnus. NDP MLA Dave Stupich was on the board but is now a charter member of the co-op. All directors are unpaid, and from the start were dedicated to the idea that workers' collectives were not only for wage-bargaining, but also to ensure distribution and sale of goods at reasonable mark-ups. From the start, a Hub director was not a remote name in a boardroom, but someone residents rubbed shoulders with in the plant. This had tremendous appeal in a town dominated by blue-collar pulp-mill workers and fishermen. And this appeal is in a town that has been growing at almost twice the B.C. average for the past 20 years, ballooning from slightly more than 14,000 people in 1961 to about 44,000 today.

Hub grew out of the Nanaimo & District Credit Union, which gave it office space in which to operate, voluntary directors with financial experience and a tailor-made membership. In 1962 Hub itself began by borrowing credit union money to build a plant to handle bulk gas, heating oil and propane sales and created a gas co-op. Then in 1964 it embarked on a six-year expansion into the grocery business. Hub's directors didn't like the example of other co-ops, with a "sell-to-anyone" policy which diluted membership feeling and reduced the co-op to another cut-price supermarket. Instead, board chairman Rod Glen looked elsewhere for a model and found it in Ottawa in 1966. The Ottawa co-op store Dr. Ralph Staples had established in that year paid the overhead by charging its members a weekly service fee. (Hub now charges a $2.50 service fee and a two-percent levy on all purchases.)

This concept was so successful that when Glen died last April, he left behind Vancouver Island's second-largest credit union and two 34,000-square-foot supermarkets. Hub's membership is now made up of 10,000 families, of which 7,200 families take advantage of grocery and hardware specials, while the others only belong to the gas co-op.

And the savings are still considerable. For instance, compared with competing supermarkets, Hub's prices on 30 common grocery items are 14.7 percent lower, while hardware, including "big ticket" items like TVs, stereos and camping supplies, is 23.5 percent less expensive. Hub's average mark-up on food is a tiny $3^1/_2$ percent, compared with the standard five to 40 percent supermarkets charge.

That two-percent surcharge which is added to every co-op bill is really not an outright charge, but a loan to the co-op on which members receive 10-percent interest. When the surcharge reaches $30, members receive a certificate redeemable for $39 in three years. Thus Hub is able to finance its rapid growth and large amounts of ready cash are available to spend on additions to buildings and to pick up "buys," such as carloads of frozen turkeys, factory clearouts of Hush Puppy shoes and five-ton lots of bacon.

Hub's original membership of 100 co-op idealists has been swelled by many more pragmatists who know a bargain. And low prices—not doctrine—are responsible for Hub's fantastic recent growth. Take Rose Drixler for instance, a woman I spoke with who had driven 12 miles from Ladysmith to the Harewood store. Were the savings worth it? "Oh, for sure," she said. "The prices here are much lower, and besides, I buy my gas here and save on that." Roberta Webster has three teenagers and spends an average of $90 weekly at Hub. "I like to go to other stores because they have things (brand names) you can't get here," she says. "But then I see the prices and figure I'll go back to the co-op." Eileen Patterson shops at the co-op because at Safeway it takes too long to get served. If it takes you too long at Hub, it's probably your own fault, since shoppers have to do their own price-marking, bagging and cart-returning. "Serving yourself is not that great, but the prices are," she told me.

Hub is still very much a "no-frills" operation. The buildings are galvanized-steel warehouses with no elaborate displays or hidden lighting. Concrete floors are left bare, while some of the coolers and freezers are second-hand. Cases of goods are not unpacked but simply cut open and placed on the shelves. Prices are marked on the cases and buyers copy these prices onto each item with a marking-pencil. Special checkouts with double ramps enable a cashier to check out a customer while the previous customer is doing his or her own bagging. The stores are run by regular paid staff with the store managers answerable to the voluntary, elected board of directors.

Managers of local retail stores don't hate

Hub as much as fear it, since it's operating in a way they don't understand. As Art Heppner, manager of a nearby Rutherford Village Overwaitea store, says: "We're a full-service store and they're a 'you-mark-it' operation. Of course their prices are lower: you put a case on the shelf and slit the side open, there's no overhead in that. It (Hub) is doing a lot of business and that's a concern of ours. But you can't get in there unless you're a member and there will always be people who don't like being tied to a membership in a particular store. The only thing we can do is run a tight operation, advertise and work on those people."

But Hub works on other ways to keep its membership loyal. Each time a flyer announcing specials goes out to the membership it arrives with an inspirational newsletter from president Hume Compton, a former newspaperman, who reminds members that the only way to enjoy such low prices is to shop co-op. Last year Hub even started a member benefit plan which gives a household groceries worth 50 percent of the family's purchases during the previous year if a family breadwinner dies. Since the average member spends about $70 a week at Hub, the plan usually awards the survivors about $1,100 worth of food.

Hub shoppers even get some perks. While it's part of the co-op's philosophy to avoid "patronage refunds" from manufacturers, if those manufacturers want to refund the thousands of "cents off" coupons, the store shoppers get annually, the store staff will turn those into free coffee for its shoppers. Furthermore, if appliance manufacturers want to offer free trips to store managers who sell many of their products (as Hub managers obviously do), then Hub staff will raffle these trips off to the membership.

One sometimes wonders what socialism would be like if applied to North America. The answer is Hub. An ex-member says, "Oh, it's great so long as you're a large family and *prices* are your only consideration. But there's only two of us, and I go shopping for *stimulation* as much as savings." There's nothing very stimulating about Hub. It's so practical and plain, it's almost dull. Hub is not the American Dream. It is not the supermarkets of the '60s and '70s opened with great fanfare by celebrities, titillating us with cubes of free cheese. But when a new shopping centre opened a half-mile down the road from the Bowen Rd. store last October, and its bright new supermarket offered litre bottles of soft drinks below Hub's price, Hub manager Stan Glydon put up signs in his store, telling members they could save money by buying their pop from the competition. "What this business is about is maintaining your customers' confidence in your prices," says Glydon. Hub might not have much charisma, but it's got plenty of confidence.

Assignment
1. Just what is the Hub Co-op?
2. What were the reasons for its "amazing growth"?
3. Why did the Safeway manager join the Hub? What else could he have done? Did he do anything wrong?
4. Explain the philosophy of the Hub's founders.
5. Describe the history of the Hub.
6. Explain how the Hub operates. How does it differ, if at all, from other retail co-operatives in its methods?
7. How does a person benefit from membership in the Hub?
8. From the consumer's point of view, how does the Hub compare with other food stores?

9. How are the Hub stores managed? Does being a co-operative create any problems?
10. What advertising and other sales promotion does the Hub undertake? How effective does it seem to be?
11. "Hub is not the American dream." Discuss.

PART C
BUSINESS MANAGEMENT

This part of the book consists of three chapters. In the first we consider the levels and functions of business management. In the second chapter, we consider how a business firm is organized for maximum efficiency. Finally, in the third chapter, we review the different theories of business management.

CHAPTER 4
THE NATURE OF BUSINESS MANAGEMENT

CHAPTER OBJECTIVES

☐ To describe the different levels of business management.

☐ To explain and discuss the basic functions of business management.

☐ To distinguish between entrepreneurship and administration.

☐ To identify and discuss the goals of the business firm.

☐ To review the different kinds of plans that business firms use.

☐ To discuss how orders should be given to obtain the best results.

☐ To identify the attributes of a business leader.

☐ To show how management attempts to ensure that its orders are properly carried out.

☐ To detail the various financial ratios used to assess current operations.

CHAPTER OUTLINE

4.1 Levels and Functions of Management
4.2 Planning
4.3 Directing
4.4 Controlling
4.5 Staffing

UNIT 4.1: LEVELS AND FUNCTIONS OF MANAGEMENT

Business management is the art of using human and material resources to produce and market goods and services. These goods and services must, of course, be ones that consumers, governments, and other business firms want and are willing to pay for. Otherwise, the business firms producing and marketing them will make a loss on their activities and will eventually have to close down. Also, unless there is a monopoly situation, firms that produce inefficiently will be forced out of an industry.

What is particularly significant about business management is that it is a wealth-creating activity. Without it, the various human and material resources in our society would be producing far less than they currently do. And the high material standard of living that the average Canadian now enjoys would no longer be possible. Business management is, in other words, the art by which the output of our various resources (or *factors of production*), when combined in a business firm, is made vastly greater than if each individual factor were used on its own.

Courtesy *Oakville Beaver*

Of course, business management can vary in quality. Thus, one firm, although manufacturing products for which there is a strong demand, may, because of high operating costs, make a financial loss. Whereas another, more efficiently managed firm, manufacturing the same product, may make a substantial profit. However, bad management can only last so long. Soon it must be replaced or the firm will run out of funds and no longer be able to operate.

Levels of Management

In the small business, there is only one level of management—the owner-manager. But one person can manage effectively only a limited number of subordinates, and handle only a certain number of tasks. Thus, in the medium- or large-size business, there are many different levels of management, each with varying amounts of authority and responsibility. The different levels of management found in the large firm are sometimes classified into three groups: top management, middle management, and supervisory management.

Top Management. The *top management team* normally includes the president; the executive vice-president (or general manager); and the vice-presidents in charge of marketing, production, finance, personnel, and other departments. As well as a vice-president, finance, there may be a comptroller and a treasurer. In the large firm, there may also be a company secretary. In the smaller firm, the finance function may be the responsibility of only one person—either a comptroller or treasurer. Sometimes, this officer will also discharge the duties of company secretary—hence the term secretary-treasurer.

The *president*, as the chief executive officer, has complete authority for the day-to-day management of the business. He or she is appointed by, and is responsible to, the board of directors; is often a member of the board of directors; and, in the case of a private corporation, may also be the chairman. In the large firm, the *chairman of the board* is likely to be a different person, sometimes a major stockholder, responsible for setting long-term policies.

The *executive vice-president*, or *general manager*, is the second-in-command of the corporation and is responsible to the president for the efficient running of the business. The executive vice-president usually assumes full command in the absence of the president. Some firms do not have such a position; others do, especially those where the president may spend considerable time away from the firm on plant visits, meetings at home and abroad, and charitable work. The executive vice-president position is also used to ensure that an immediate successor to the president is always available. Some firms, instead of relying on a president alone, use an executive committee, comprising a president and two or three executive or senior vice-presidents, to manage the firm. The president delegates authority and responsibility in varying degree to the vice-presidents for the management of their respective divisions, departments, or functions. The *company secretary* (or *secretary-treasurer* in the smaller firm) is responsible for the formal records of the corporation, including minutes of directors' meetings and company bylaws. He or she is also responsible for representing the corporation in court or at government hearings.

Middle Management. Also known as *executive management*, this consists of department managers, branch office managers, plant managers, and production superintendents. In the large firm each of these persons will be responsible to a vice-president for his or her particular management task. In the smaller firm the department managers may report directly to the president (or executive vice-president) and may themselves be called vice-presidents.

Supervisory Management. Also known as *first-line management*, these are the persons directly supervising the work of the bulk of the corporation's employees. These managers include supervisors, foremen, and section heads.

Basic Functions of Management

All managers, whatever their position in the organizational hierarchy or whatever their specialization, will have one thing in common. They must "manage" other people and resources. Each manager will have responsibility for one or more tasks and will have the authority to command subordinate employees to work in various ways for the completion of these tasks.

The basic management functions which managers perform in varying degree are:
1. *Planning*—establishing objectives for the firm;
2. *Organizing*—deciding on the various positions to be held in the firm, the duties of each, and the relationships between positions;
3. *Directing*—giving orders to subordinates;
4. *Controlling*—checking, by means of budgets, reports, and visits, that orders are being carried out and objectives met.
5. *Staffing*—recruiting and training personnel for each position.

Other functions of management that may be important, depending on the circumstances, include *co-ordinating*, getting the employees to work harmoniously together; *innovating*, developing new profit opportunities for the firm; *motivating*, persuading people to work enthusiastically; and *representing*, acting as the firm's representative in its dealings with the public, other businesses and government.

Managerial Method

Another approach to the study of management stresses the *managerial method*. In this approach, the essential functions of management are considered to be:
1. *Problem analysis*—analyzing a problem in all its aspects and setting out all the possible solutions;
2. *Decision making*—evaluating and comparing the possible solutions and deciding on the best.
3. *Solution implementation*—making sure that the chosen solution is carried out as quickly and efficiently as possible.

Management Specialization

The various management functions, it should be noted, do not absorb equal amounts of each manager's time. Thus, top management is greatly concerned with planning, while middle, or executive, management may be more concerned with control. In addition to this vertical specialization, the large firm usually divides each level of management horizontally into various departments (such as finance, production, and marketing) so that each manager can become an expert in a particular field.

In the small business, the manager is more likely to perform all the management functions. In starting the business, he (or she) will be preoccupied with planning, organizing, and staffing; later, he will be more concerned with direction and control. Then, to remain successful, he must plan ahead for new products, new markets, and new methods; he must adapt the organization to the growth of the firm; he must seek and train new employees; he must try to give orders that leave no confusion or resentment; and he must carefully watch the sales, purchases, inventory, cash, and overall finances of the business.

Non-Managerial Tasks

A manager may also devote part of his or her time to work that is not strictly managerial. An example of this would be the lending activities of the branch manager of a bank. Or the office manager who helps out with the clerical work when staff are away sick.

Entrepreneurship versus Administration

Business management can be divided into two main aspects: entrepreneurship and administration. By *entrepreneurship* we mean several things. First, there is the creative ability to anticipate consumer demand—for example, in clothing fashions. Second, there is the ability to make ideas conceived in pure research, often at a university or government laboratory, turn into actual marketable products. For example, the rapid commercial development of jet aircraft, since the discovery of jet propulsion just before World War II, has made possible fast, cheap air travel for millions of people. Indeed, one of the great triumphs of North American business management in the twentieth century is the great reduction in the time required between a new scientific discovery and its emergence as a new product or service in the everyday world. A third aspect of entrepreneurship is the ability to develop and apply new ways of producing existing goods. Thus, new methods of car manufacture have meant that a car, instead of being the luxury item that it was early in this century, is now within almost everyone's financial reach. A fourth aspect of entrepreneurship is the ability to choose, motivate, and, if necessary, train a management team. For, as a business grows, no one person, however able, can manage it alone. Indeed, the success of many a business entrepreneur has rested to a large extent on his or her ability to find, keep, and motivate outstanding associates and subordinates.

There is no doubt that entrepreneurship is very much alive today, particularly among small business firms. And there are many examples in Canada of new industrial successes. Also, many older well-established firms are constantly seeking new, more efficient ways to satisfy the customer. However, there are many business managers whose jobs offer little opportunity to exercise entrepreneurship talents. Many business managers are, in fact, concerned only or primarily with *administration*. This is the important, but different task of ensuring that a business firm continues to operate smoothly along well-defined lines. As a private business firm or government enterprise increases in size, the scope for waste and efficiency grows accordingly. Administering an enterprise employing thousands of persons and millions of dollars' worth of buildings, equipment, and materials, becomes consequently a valuable, but highly demanding task.

Entrepreneurial and administrative duties are quite different in nature and consequently call for different qualities in the business managers who perform them. Often, particularly in the smaller firm, the business manager may have to be both a good entrepreneur and a good administrator. However, the qualities that make a person a good entrepreneur (for example, willingness to take chances) may make him or her a poor administrator, and vice versa.

Business management of both kinds is carried out in firms of all sizes—but the larger the firm, the more difficult and complex the task. In the small firm the business manager must be able to cope with management problems of all types, while in the larger firm there is scope for management specialization. Nevertheless, managers in large firms must also be versatile, for experience in different departments and different plants is often considered essential to a middle and top management career. Even within one department the range and depth of management and other problems can be quite immense.

KEY TERMS

Business management

Top management

President

Executive vice-president

Company secretary

Secretary-treasurer

Middle management

Supervisory management

Planning

Organizing

Directing

Controlling

Staffing

Co-ordinating

Innovating

Motivating

Representing

Entrepreneurship

Administration

REVIEW QUESTIONS

1. How would you explain the meaning of the term "business management"? How might management differ between the private and the public sectors of the economy? What is so special about the task of management?
2. Give some current examples of business firms that are being managed well and others that are being managed badly. What seem to be the basic reasons for the difference?
3. The larger firm will usually have more levels of management than the smaller one. Why? Illustrate your answer with examples of large and small business firms.
4. What person in the top management of a business corporation has the ultimate decision-making authority? Distinguish in your answer between the role of the chairman of the board and the company president.
5. Explain the role of the executive vice-president, or general manager, in the corporate hierarchy.
6. Explain these positions: vice-president, finance; comptroller; treasurer; company secretary; secretary-treasurer; and controller.
7. Distinguish between the tasks of middle and supervisory management. Do both types of managers require the same educational background and work experience?
8. What are the various management functions that a business manager may be called upon to perform? Are these all equally important?
9. What is meant by the "managerial method"? How useful does it seem to be?
10. "Very few managers spend all their business time managing." Discuss, with examples.
11. "The small business offers a person better management experience than a large firm." Discuss.
12. "There is no basic difference between the roles of the entrepreneur and the administrator." Discuss, with examples. Explain also what makes a good entrepreneur.
13. "A badly managed firm is soon out of business." Discuss, with reference to the contemporary business scene.

CASE PROBLEM

JONES FURNITURE CO. LTD. (1)

Managing a furniture business

The Jones Furniture Co. Ltd. was started in 1947 by David Jones, a former furniture salesman. The original place of business was a small store of 1300 m² in size at the end of a busy shopping street. The most important lines sold were bedroom furniture and chesterfields. Staff in the early days comprised Jones as manager and two salesmen. In 1960 the adjoining store was leased to provide an additional 1000 m² of space, and the business converted from a sole proprietorship to a private corporation.

By 1980, the volume of business had increased so much that Jones felt justified in moving his business to a large new store further up the street. The new store possessed over 5000 m² and made it possible for Jones to carry a much larger variety and stock of furniture and related merchandise. Notable among new lines were hi-fi, stereo, and television sets. Jones also purchased, on the outskirts of town, a one-storey steel warehouse to house part of his stock. To handle the larger sales volume, Jones hired another five salesmen, raising his total sales staff to eleven including himself. He also had a secretary to handle the bookkeeping and mail.

One business fact that had impressed Jones was the much lower price that he had to pay for his merchandise by buying in bulk directly from manufacturers. This was one of the reasons behind his present expansion. However, for a number of lines, even with his present turnover, he could not always take advantage of such quantity discounts. As a result, Jones felt justified in expanding even further by acquiring branch stores in several growing and prosperous nearby towns.

The goods offered in the various stores were advertised by insertions in the local newspapers, by direct mail pamphlets, and by attractive window displays. Sales were made mainly on credit, with a 10 per cent down payment required and the balance payable with interest over 1 to 2 years. The salesmen were paid on a commission basis. Goods were delivered free of charge.

After a few years of experience with the new store and the branch stores, Jones had noted the following facts: he was under considerable nervous strain and continually exhausted by trying to keep control of everything; he was less happy about his sales staff than he used to be, even though he did all the hiring (customers had complained that they were being talked into buying items they did not really want); the net profit on sales had dropped from 11 per cent to 4 per cent; there had been great trouble in collecting the balance on many customers' accounts and the percentage of bad debts had risen; two branch store managers had complained that they were being forced to stock goods they could not sell; and the firm's financial position was not as solid as it used to be—current assets exceeded current liabilities by a much smaller margin than before.

Assignment
1. What management duties does Jones perform? How can he exercise control over his business, and yet prevent himself from being over-worked?
2. How can Jones best prepare his daughter, who is now finishing Grade 12, to take over management of the business when Jones retires in a few years' time?
3. How, and in what degree, should Jones let his branch store managers decide what to buy and sell?
4. Is Jones' dissatisfaction with his staff justified, considering that each salesman is now selling more than before?
5. How can Jones improve (a) the net profit on sales, and (b) the company's financial solvency?

READING

Lord of the Rinks

How Marc Ruel spun a multimillion-dollar hockey stick business from a few strands of fibreglass

BY WAYNE LILLEY

Source: *The Financial Post Magazine*. Used by permission of Wayne Lilley.

When Marc Ruel tentatively set out nine years ago to seek his fortune, he wanted to do it with his own company, preferably by exercising manufacturing ingenuity. By the fall of 1978, the 42-year-old, salt-and-pepper-haired engineer had achieved his objective. Canadian Hockey Industries Inc. (CHI), the Drummondville, Quebec firm he'd hitched his career to in 1969 with a few strands of fibreglass, had become the industry leader in technology and by the end of 1978 it had become a business success as well. Sales of about $5 million make the firm the largest Canadian-owned hockey stick manufacturer, and the third largest in the world. Ruel, in fact, has been responsible for redefining the hockey stick and in the process he may have done more than anyone else to protect a piece of the world hockey stick business for Canadian companies.

If Ruel has been satisfied with the way his life has gone, however, along the way he has discovered that being an entrepreneur has become more intriguing than being a manager. So one day last fall, following his unvarying breakfast—cereal with milk and fresh fruit—the shy, disciplined Ruel left home to close the deal that would result in the sale of CHI to Action Traders Inc., a Toronto-based sporting goods marketing company.

Ruel, as proud of CHI's five patents for hockey stick construction as he is of its sales record, liked the financial details of the sale. Though he would stay on for six years under a management contract with Action, he could conceivably retire at 48, two years ahead of the schedule he once set.

Had he then become a success? "I think the business has," he acknowledges as though considering the idea for the first time. "But I think my personal definition of success has changed." Indeed, instead of suffering the twinges of post-partum depression at the sale of CHI, Ruel, who one senior Quebec government official calls the province's most dynamic businessman, has become the consummate entrepreneur. CHI was the model for an education in entrepreneurship.

By most standards of the day, Marc Ruel had already become successful by the mid-'60s. After graduating from the University of Montreal, he went to work for Eagle Pencil Co. Ltd., in Drummondville in Quebec's Eastern Townships where he had grown up. By 1967, he had risen to general manager of the plant, a division of an American-owned company, and he and his wife settled down to raise two sons and a daughter.

Ruel also joined an investment club, one of the symbols of Canadian optimism in the '60s. The reasoning behind such clubs was that a group could make intelligent investment decisions using members' modest monthly contributions and by reinvesting gains, the members might eventually have a piece of a healthy portfolio.

Trouble was, it became increasingly apparent to the members of Ruel's club that not only were they not getting rich making their own investment decisions, but they didn't have much control over their money either. "Owners of companies we were investing in were making the decisions that counted," says Ruel. "We started talking amongst ourselves of actually being in a business that we controlled."

The idea especially intrigued Ruel. Soon he began doodling ideal management structures on paper, but he still had no business in mind. "About the only thing I was sure of was that it would be in Drummondville. I wasn't ready to give up my job."

That entire project remained a back-of-an-envelope fantasy until he was on holidays in July 1969 and stopped at Sherbrooke to see his brother who worked for Sherwood-Drolet, the biggest manufacturer of hockey sticks in Canada. "He told me that Sherwood was on fire and that he didn't know if he would have a job by the end of the day," says Ruel. "But all I could think of was the hole of about one million hockey sticks there would be in the market if Sherwood couldn't meet its fall deliveries. It was the opportunity I'd been waiting for."

There were a few hurdles to overcome, however, not the least of which was that he knew nothing about the hockey stick industry and had no start-up capital. Furthermore, besides his brother Gaston, he knew only three people in the business. Nevertheless, one of them, chemical engineer Leo Tessier, had come up with a five-piece stick design that relied heavily on fibreglass in its construction. Though the design was potentially superior to conventional three-piece sticks, the cost of retooling made it too expensive for big companies. Ruel had no such reservations since he had not yet done any tooling. He and Tessier recruited Marcel Goupil, a machine designer, to create the required production equipment, and went into business.

Time had become important. To meet industry delivery dates by the middle of August, the partners had only 30 days, yet the five-piece stick they pinned their hopes on had never been mass produced and they had no production facilities.

"I spent the first week of the 30 days driving around Drummondville looking at possible sites," remembers Ruel. "Finally I found a farmer who was trying to sublease some farmland and we took it so we could get his barn for $300 a month." While Goupil built machines from scratch, Ruel and Tessier started cranking out sticks practically by hand. Finally when the 30 days were up, Ruel bundled the first seven dozen sticks into his station wagon and took them off to distributors.

By the end of July, Ruel's brother from Sherbrooke and Jean-Louis Gatien, a production expert with experience in the industry, were brought into the company. But capital was still needed. Ruel had applied for a federal Department of Regional and Economic Expansion (DREE) [now Department of Regional Industrial Expansion (DRIE)] grant and was told he had to own his own production facilities to qualify. So each partner put up $5,000 to buy the farm and Canadian Hockey Industries was born. "We got the grant and we were on our way," says Ruel. "In our first year we managed to sell $250,000 worth of sticks."

It was an auspicious start. From nothing, CHI had broken even and become a factor—albeit a small one—in the Canadian hockey stick market. But to become profitable, the business was facing long odds.

With the possible exception of maple syrup, there is no more uniquely Canadian product than hockey. Thus when the game enjoyed phenomenal growth around the world in the early '60s, Canada was, as they say in baseball, in the catbird seat: virtually all the world's production of hockey sticks was Canadian. By 1970, sales of Canadian-made sticks reached unit volumes of 637,731 dozen with a wholesale value of $9.2 million, about one-third of which came from exports.

In the late '60s, though, Canada was becoming as well known for selling its profitable industries to foreigners as it was for hockey prowess; and as the stick business became profitable, it proved no exception. In 1970, 80 percent of Sherwood-Drolet Corp. Ltd. was bought by ATO Inc. of Cleveland, manufacturers of Rawlings sports equipment; Victoriaville Hockey Sticks Ltd. of Victoriaville, Quebec, had been sold to a subsidiary of Colgate Palmolive of New York while in 1968 the Wally Hockey Stick Co. of Wallaceburg, Ontario had been bought by Hillerich and Bradsby Co. Ltd., the Missouri-based maker of Louisville Slugger baseball bats.

Of course, there were Canadian firms still making sticks. CCM Ltd. of Toronto had a name renowned around the world and Cooper Canada Ltd. was making sticks in Hespeler, Ontario.

At the same time, dents were appearing in Canadian export markets, mainly in the United States, where the biggest challenge came from the Finnish firms Karhu Titan Oy and Koho Tuote Oy and from Sweden's Jofa AB, a subsidiary of Volvo. Yet not until Canada's hockey reputation took a pummeling in 1972 did stick manufacturers realize their business was being threatened. Although the team of professionals from the National Hockey League didn't lose the tournament to the Russians, it needed a last minute goal to win. The Russians proved their hockey skills were almost the equal of Canadian pros', and they did so using Koho, Titan and Jofa sticks. Furthermore while Canadian hockey stick production hit a high of 683,321 dozen that year, a more significant fact emerged: sales of imported sticks which had been $583,000 in 1971 jumped to $1.1 million in 1972. Even worse, the Scandinavian sticks cut the lucrative Canadian share of the U.S. market in half.

But while all this was going on Ruel and his partners were building CHI, of which Ruel was now full-time president. To raise capital new shareholders were added: businessmen and three members of the Montreal Canadiens. Although pros aren't a major market, hockey stick firms have found that minor league and recreational players who are, like to spend their $3 to $15 on sticks used by their heroes.

So it's common practice for firms to offer pros cash payments to endorse their sticks. But Ruel, who couldn't compete in that way anyway, offered the three—team captain Yvon Cournoyer and stars Serge Savard and Guy Lapointe—shares instead. He did get an unexpected bonus, though, with the business experience of Savard. "He owns race horses, a Loto Quebec concession and a Montreal weekly newspaper," says Ruel. "He can look at a financial statement and understand it right away so when he accepted our offer, it gave us much more confidence." (However, none of the three is still associated with CHI.)

In the market conditions of 1972, the young firm needed every advantage it could get. Instead of going out of business following its fire, Sherwood-Drolet was back the same year when president Leon Drolet sold 80 percent of his equity to get rebuilding capital; Victoriaville was able to increase production with new equipment; and CCM spent lavishly on advertising to keep its name before the buying public.

In the meantime, Koho upset the whole market with uniquely Finnish veneer technology. While most Canadian producers stuck with traditional white ash for handles, the Finns cornered the market on equipment that could produce plywood with as many as 60 laminations. The result was a lighter stick that had the same strength and "feel" as wood. "Koho achieved a kind of breakthrough when it got its sticks under 20 ounces," says Ruel. "The average weight had been 23 ounces and that would appear heavy to most players now."

The course was clear as far as Ruel was concerned: CHI would use research and development to beat the Finns at the weight-reducing game. He applied for and got the first National Research Council grant in the sporting goods industry, began working on a synthetic hockey stick and, by 1973, had four patents on the first manufactured fibreglass stick. These sticks sold so well that now he notes: "Every company has a fibreglass stick or is working on one."

CHI had hardly been welcomed to the market in 1969, and now competitors began to complain that the company was using federal and provincial funds to steal a share of the market. Indeed Ruel has become adept at stickhandling through red tape to snare financial and technical help. He has had three additional DREE grants since the original one, two NRC grants and a $300,000 grant from the federal Program for the Advancement of Industrial Technology (PAIT). When Ottawa formed the Export Development Program in 1976, CHI got in on that too as well as numerous support programs and forgivable loans made by the Quebec government.

Typically Ruel refuses to apologize: "Governments give grants to General Motors and Ford, too, and they need it less than we do. We've proved we can make the grants pay and we've provided employment for 125 people in Drummondville."

Federal and provincial officials tend to support his view. "We were impressed with Ruel and with the management team he put together," says an official with the ITC. "Other companies who complained because they didn't get money," he adds, "simply didn't have the grounds Ruel did.

He was the only one who had good concepts and knew where he wanted to go. Nobody else was doing anything substantial to combat imports."

Claude Desjardins, a senior official with the Quebec ministry of commerce, is even more impressed with CHI precisely *because* it takes advantage of government help. "One of the biggest problems we have is making businessmen aware of the programs that are available to help them," he says. "But Marc Ruel makes maximum use of all the tools available to him, he finds good people, is able to identify his markets and goes after them."

Whether verbally or by imitation, Ruel's competition has shown grudging respect for what he has accomplished. For instance, for a couple of years now Sherwood-Drolet has been experimenting with graphite as a strengthening agent in hockey sticks. Cooper developed, and has since ceased trying to market, a stick so durable it cost $44.95 and came with a season's guarantee, while CCM commissioned Dalhousie University's physical education department to test a stick matched to a player's strength.

Ruel, perhaps because of his good record, is also one of the few executives willing to discuss market share. Right now, he reckons, of the approximately 14.4 million sticks produced in the West, Sherwood-Drolet is the leading Canadian producer with unit sales of about 90,000 dozen; CHI is second with about 75,000 dozen and Victoriaville third with about 50,000 dozen. Hillerich and Bradsby produce about 60,000 dozen Louisville sticks, while Cooper and CCM make about 25,000 dozen each. Koho is the undisputed leader among foreign firms, though, with about 125,000 dozen unit sales, about 45 percent of which goes to Canada and 30 percent to the U.S., according to an Industry, Trade and Commerce report.

The year before he concluded his deal with

Ruel, Don Swift, head of Action Traders Inc., a marketing company, already had a lesson in the recreation industry. In 1977, his company, then called Capital Diversified Industries Ltd., decided to concentrate on sporting goods and so it bought Action Sports Ltd., a Montreal importer of Salomon bindings and Nordica boots and distributor of Koho hockey sticks.

But Action did its job too well. After establishing distribution and the name of Salomon and Nordica, the manufacturers decided to take over marketing—and the commission—themselves. Then last year, when Koho cancelled its contract and began negotiating with Ruel, Swift countered with his own offer.

The situation posed a dilemma for Ruel. On one hand Koho would make a formidable partner, on the other he wasn't sure it was wise to deepen his commitment to the still risky hockey stick business. Finally, despite the fact that the two offers were almost financially identical, he settled on Swift's almost instant diversification.

At that point he had to deal with the 11 shareholders who were not members of the five-man management group and who were asked to sell their shares as part of the Action offer. He had tried to buy them out in the past, but the price they had set was too high. Now, though, with the money Action was providing (he refuses to say how much) he could afford to meet their price before turning over 75 percent of the shares to Action.

By last October it was decided that the Drummondville manufacturing plant would house the complete line of Action products while the original barn was soon jammed to capacity with ski manufacturing equipment. In 1979, according to Swift, the combined sales of Action and CHI should reach $35 million, and at that rate, notes an official from Industry, Trade and Commerce, "Action will be going toe to toe with companies like CCM in the Canadian sporting goods market."

Ruel, a skier who recently exchanged his Drummondville house for an apartment and a weekend retreat at nearby Mount Orford, seems to enjoy the prospect of the ski business and the challenge of bringing efficiency to the manufacture of bicycles and other sporting goods equipment. Outmanoeuvring the competition with innovative technology has always had more appeal than outmuscling competitors with marketing and sales hype.

As a shareholder in Action, Ruel also has some control over the value of his stock—one of the things that he and his colleagues in the investment club had wanted back in the '60s. But the money he received for CHI's shares, the money that would make retirement possible, has now been redesignated as venture capital. "I'm involved in a couple of groups now and I'm sure there will be more," he says. "I still think if the right people are brought together, good ideas can be turned into sound businesses and I know it's enjoyable to build a business from nothing. The difference now is that I have the money to make it happen."

Marc Ruel has no intention of waiting for a chance fire to launch the next stage of his life, not now that he knows he can control his own destiny. For the true entrepreneur, everything else is just a garnish, like fruit on cereal that you add for variety and flavor.

Assignment
1. How did Marc Ruel come to start a business of his own?
2. What was his business background?

3. How did he arrange for the necessary capital?
4. Describe the Canadian hockey stick market at that time.
5. What competition did CHI face?
6. What type of sales promotion did CHI undertake? What novel twists were involved?
7. How did the Finns "upset" the hockey stick market? How did CHI respond?
8. What government assistance did Ruel receive? Why? Was it a good use of the taxpayers' money?
9. Explain and discuss Marc Ruel's product development efforts. How successful was he? How pertinent, in this case, was the old adage: "necessity is the mother of invention"?
10. What is CHI's share of the Canadian hockey stick market? Who are its main competitors?
11. How did the firm come to locate in Drummondville?
12. Why do you think Ruel decided to sell his controlling interest in CHI to Action Traders Inc.?
13. "If Ruel has been satisfied with the way his life has gone, however, along the way he has discovered that being an entrepreneur has become more intriguing than being a manager." Discuss.

UNIT 4.2: PLANNING

Planning is the management function of: (a) determining objectives for the firm as a whole and for each of its divisions, branches, departments, and sections; and (b) deciding how these objectives are to be achieved. Planning inspires a sense of purpose and motivation in a firm, provides goals towards which employees can strive, helps promote a sense of unity, and thereby enables the firm to compete more effectively against its business rivals.

Planning Process

A well-designed and properly implemented planning process can be an important motivating factor for managers at all levels of a business enterprise. This is because it: (a) gives managers a strong feeling of participation in the running of the firm; (b) removes their uncertainty as to the future actions of the firm; (c) helps them to appreciate better their role in the firm and their relationships with other managers and departments; and (d) provides a strong sense of purpose.

The planning process is illustrated in Figure 4.1.

Company Objectives

The overriding objective of any business firm is to make a profit—subject, of course, to observance of legal and social responsibilities.

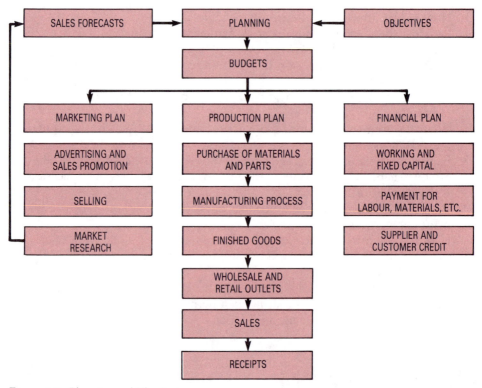

Figure 4.1 Planning and The Business

This pursuit of profit is a perfectly legitimate aim, for without this incentive few people would be willing to risk their capital and time in business ventures. The government instead would have to undertake the production and marketing of all goods and services. And, at least by the record of governments in most communist countries, it would not do a very efficient job.

For most companies, an equally important goal is financial stability. This means that the firm will be careful not to take undue risks, particularly in the development and marketing of new products or in the choice of major investment projects, that might impair its cash flow and threaten its financial liquidity. Because of this concern for financial stability, many firms will be content with a profit goal such as a certain *target return on investment*, rather than a headlong rush to maximize profit. The target return on investment may be what is "fair and reasonable"; what is traditional in the industry; what is an improvement over the previous rate of return; or what the firm feels it could earn in the long run.

An important objective for many companies is to maintain or enlarge their *share of the market*. In some industries, the market is viewed in terms of the total number of units of output, such as automobiles. In others, it is viewed in terms of total sales revenue—often from a multiplicity of products. By maintaining or expanding its market share, a firm has the assurance that it is competing efficiently against other firms.

Subordinate to a firm's main objectives are such goals as improving customer satisfaction (sometimes considered a primary objective), maintaining stability, developing new products, building more modern production facilities, acquiring new markets, establishing a good public image, developing good labour relations, and improving production and marketing methods.

In practice, it has been found that it pays to establish objectives for each key area of an enterprise, not just for the firm as a whole. Thus, objectives might be set, for example, for sales, output, solvency, profits, innovation (in products and techniques), plant efficiency, labour productivity, labour relations, management performance, and community work. Also, whenever possible, it pays management to express objectives in quantitative terms. This is because a quantitative objective is much more precise and meaningful to the people who have to work for its achievement. Thus, it is better to state that the firm's objective is "to increase sales next year by 10 per cent" than "to increase sales next year by as much as possible."

Sales Forecasting

Before a firm can set its sales objectives and begin its detailed marketing, production, and financial planning, it must make a reasonable estimate of how the demand for its products is likely to change during the years ahead. Usually a firm will try to forecast sales on both a long-term and short-term basis. Thus, it will try to look at sales prospects over, say, the next five or even ten years, as well as over the coming year. Naturally, the further ahead the firm looks, the more uncertain its forecasts become.

Sales forecasts are usually based on such factors as: past sales figures; the anticipated future size of the market and the firm's expected share of it; market research as to future demand for existing or new products; anticipated new product development within the company; a study of the actions and plans (if known) of competitive firms; and assessment of the expected economic growth and political and social stability of the country or countries in which the firm's products are sold; trends in market prices of similar products; and anticipated tax changes and other proposed legislation—for example, customs duties and other import restrictions in foreign markets.

In obtaining such information, the opinions of a great number of people are often solicited, including the company's own sales force, customers, managers, and market research agencies. The overall sales forecast, built up from individual estimates for each region or territory, is sometimes called a *composite sales estimate*. *Secondary data* (that is, data that has already been printed) is obtained from a variety of sources including the company's own files, public libraries, trade publications, economic and financial newspapers and periodicals, the Bank of Canada, the provincial governments, and Statistics Canada. *Primary data* (that is, data not previously available, but prepared specially for the purpose) is obtained from market research agencies and private economic consultants.

*"Boys, it would appear that perhaps **now** is the time for us to take a long, hard look at our objectives."*

Company Plans

Once a firm's primary and secondary objectives have been clearly specified, they must be translated into actual plans. Only in this way can "management by objectives" become a profitable reality.

A *plan* is a detailed course of action, covering a particular activity of the firm, specifying the goals to be achieved, the human and material resources to be employed, the methods to be used, and the time period involved. Such plans should cover the long term as well as the immediate future. A firm, when faced with such problems as acquiring additional funds, investing in research, or building an additional plant, must often look several years ahead and prepare a *long-range plan* (or L.R.P.). If it does not, it may find that it is unnecessarily saddled with debt, that its research money has been frittered away, or that its new plant has become obsolete. A firm must also prepare an *operational* or *short-range plan* (or S.R.P.); it must know what it must produce this week, this month, and this year, if its employees are to be given direction and its long-run objectives are to be met. Plans should also be both *general* and *specific*. Goals must be set for the firm as a whole (profits, sales, output, and so on), but each department or section of the firm must have its own specific targets. If they do not, the general plan will have little meaning for most employees. The most important types of company plans are its *budgets*. Other company plans include policies, procedures, rules, and single-use plans.

Budgets. The *operating budget* is a plan of financial action for the coming year involving the marketing, production, and all other departments of the firm. It is based on the sales forecast for the firm's various products and services over a future period of time, usually a year. This sales forecast, as we have seen, is generally based on past experience, intelligent guesswork as to the future, and market research. The forecast may originate with the sales or marketing manager, but will be thoroughly discussed and probably modified by top management before being adopted as one of the firm's primary goals. The firm will next draw up a production plan, based on the sales forecast, to ensure that output will meet expected sales. This will, in turn, be broken down into department and section plans, with detailed forecasts of spending on manpower, material, overhead, supplies, and so on. The operating budget consists, therefore, of a detailed weekly or monthly sales and production plan for the firm as a whole.

To supplement the marketing effort, an *advertising budget* will be set. Often, for lack of any better rule, this will be a percentage of the value of anticipated sales.

To help ensure financial solvency, a *cash budget* will be drawn up based on the operating and capital budgets. This is a forecast, usually month by month, of the flow of cash into and out of the firm.

For major investment expenditures, a *capital budget* can be prepared. This is a plan for purchasing additional fixed assets, notably plant and machinery, over the next few years. The plan also pinpoints the expected sources of the necessary funds. The various types of budgets that a business firm may use are discussed in more detail later in the book: in Unit 12.1 (Budgeting) and Unit 13.1 (Cash Management).

Policies, Procedures, and Rules. The policies, procedures, and rules of a company set out a firm's traditional practice in a variety of fields and circumstances. These are often called *standing plans*.

A *policy* is a statement of a firm's attitude on a particular point—for example, "the customer is always right." It is a guide to action, rather than an explicit instruction of what to do in a particular situation. It could be consulted, for example, when a customer insists that he or she has been shortchanged. Policies enable subordinates to know what the firm expects without having to consult a superior whenever a problem arises. To be effective, a policy should be clearly stated (preferably in writing), be reasonable, be consistent with other policies, and be familiar to all employees.

There are, of course, many types of business policies, covering the whole range of a firm's business activities. Some of these are as follows:
1. *Product policy* involves a decision as to the types of products to produce and market.
2. *Marketing policy* involves such matters as the prices to be charged, the

amount and type of advertising and other sales promotion, the credit to be given, the after-sales service, the allocation of sales territories, and the remuneration of the sales force.
3. *Production policy* involves such matters as the amount of each good to be produced, the timing of production, the use of shifts, the parts and materials to be purchased, and the most economic production quantity.
4. *Purchasing policy* involves the choice of suppliers and the cost and timing of deliveries.
5. *Personnel policy* involves such matters as recruitment and training of the labour force, improvements of employee morale, determination of wages and fringe benefits, and relations with the labour union.

A *procedure* is the sequence of steps that must be followed in a particular task, such as the hiring of a new employee, or the taking and filling of a customer's order. This sequence is the plan devised by the company (often after hard experience) to handle a task most efficiently. For example, in completing a customer's order, various members of the firm must be advised: the production foreman, the shipping clerk, the billing clerk, and the stock clerk. Without a standard procedure, confusion can easily arise. The order can be lost or delayed, a bad credit risk accepted, or no payment asked—all of which can cost the firm money.

Rules are strict instructions as to what an employee should or should not do. Unlike policies, they are not meant to be used with discretion. "No smoking on the shop floor" is one example; "no credit" is another.

Single-Use Plans. One other type of plan which a company employs is a single-use plan. This, as the name implies, is a plan drawn up to achieve a single, temporary goal. Once this goal is achieved, the plan is terminated. Establishing a new office or plant, researching a new product, or taking over a competitor—any one of these might be the subject of a single-use plan.

Considerations in Planning

There are a number of factors to take into consideration in order to make a firm's planning more effective. These are:

Strengths and Weaknesses. A firm should carefully assess its strengths and weaknesses before choosing a course of action. Thus a firm with an established reputation for fine custom-made furniture might destroy its name and profit position by diversifying into the cheaper, mass-production field.

External Factors. A company must be aware of what is happening to the demand for its products, including the actions of its competitors, before it completes its plans. Although this may appear obvious, many firms have lost money by failing in this area. An example is the storekeeper who invests heavily in traditional food shopping facilities, without properly realizing the effect that chain supermarket competition will have on him or her.

Timing. Circumstances change quickly, and a firm that has drawn up a good plan for one set of circumstances may find that the timing for its execution is no longer appropriate. For example, a plan to raise funds by a corporate mortgage bond issue may be swiftly rendered unsatisfactory because of a general tightening of the money market, making funds scarcer and interest rates higher.

Flexibility. A plan should always be capable of adjustment in the face of unforeseen events, such as unexpected competition. On the other hand, a plan that is too flexible is no longer a plan, since its goals are not considered mandatory for the employees.

Participation. Since all members of a firm contribute in various degrees to the attainment of the firm's objectives, it is psychologically good to have as many employees as possible help draw up the plan. It is important that department and section heads should help set targets, since they will then be more inspired to fulfil them.

Simplicity. The planning process should be kept as simple and practical as possible so that the average manager, along with his or her regular day-to-day activities, can participate intelligently and enthusiastically.

Responsibility. There should be someone appointed, on a full-time basis, to make sure that a firm's planning works smoothly and, if possible, with the minimum of paperwork.

Control. There should be provision for control to ensure that the plan is being carried out as intended.

KEY TERMS

Planning	General and specific plans
Profit maximization	Budgets
Financial stability	Standing plans
Target return on investment	Policies
Share of the market	Procedures
Company plans	Rules
Long-range and short-range plans	Single-use plans

REVIEW QUESTIONS

1. What is involved in the management function of planning?
2. What are its purposes?
3. A good planning process can be an important motivational tool. Explain and discuss.
4. Do business firms try to maximize profits? Discuss.
5. What other primary goals may a business firm have?
6. What might be a business firm's secondary goals?
7. Why does planning begin with a sales forecast?
8. How is a sales forecast prepared?
9. What is a composite sales estimate?

10. Distinguish between primary and secondary market data.
11. Company plans should be both short-term and long-term, general and specific. Explain.
12. Distinguish between an operating budget and a capital budget.
13. What other types of budget are often used?
14. What are the major types of company policies?
15. Distinguish between company procedures and company rules.
16. Give three examples of single-use plans.
17. One of the factors that should be taken into account when planning is a firm's strengths and weaknesses. Illustrate with examples.
18. What external factors may affect a firm's planning, particularly for the long-term?
19. Explain, with examples of your own, why timing and flexibility are important in company planning.
20. What other factors should a company take into account when drawing up its plans?

CASE PROBLEM

FAIRVIEW STORES LTD.

Improving the profitability of a chain variety store operation

The firm of Fairview Stores Ltd. was founded in Halifax in 1903 by James Fairview, an immigrant from Bristol, England. Starting originally as a variety dime store located in what was then a prosperous shopping area near the heart of the city, the firm grew rapidly in size as its price-cutting policy met a warm response from consumers. Along with Woolworth's, Kresge's, and Sherman's, Fairview was, by the 1930s, known throughout Eastern and Central Canada as a low-cost, mass distributor of inexpensive goods.

After World War II, however, the firm's prosperity began to suffer from the effects of three new trends in retailing. First of all, department store basements, supermarkets, and drug stores began rapidly to take away a large share of the variety store market. Second, shopping centres springing up in the suburbs of most large cities began to draw away a large number of customers from the downtown shopping areas. And, third, most people now used a car to go shopping.

Fairview Stores, in an attempt to adjust to the new situation, did two things: first, it attempted to increase the quality and variety of its merchandise. This was not altogether successful, however, because many of the stores' customers were unwilling to pay higher prices for higher quality merchandise and many of the stores were too small to accommodate a larger inventory. Also, the firm could do little to increase parking facilities, and in most instances, parking space was available only on the street.

The second step Fairview Stores took was to move with the tide and establish stores in the new shopping centres. As a result, the firm now has 103 shopping centre stores in operation throughout Canada. In most cases, however, these new stores are competing with other Fairview stores that were previously built in downtown locations. Consequently, although sales volume for the Fairview stores as a whole continued to increase, the total net profit has become less. Also, of course, with the new stores, the firm's investment has increased. An example of this situation is provided by the firm's three stores in Ottawa, Ontario. Ten years ago, the firm had only one large downtown store in the city. Since then, the firm has opened two suburban stores. The overall financial results of these stores are as follows:

	Sales volume	Net Profit Before Tax	Return on Investment (before tax)
Ten years ago (1 store)	$2,126 million	$437 million	23%
This year (3 stores)	$3,354 million	$421 million	12%

Although Fairview had foreseen that the total net profit might be less with the additional stores, if felt that the reduction in profit would have been even greater if it had let its competitors move into these suburban shopping centres instead. The continued expansion of suburban shopping facilities in most of the towns and cities where Fairview operated indicated that the net profit from the firm's new suburban stores might soon begin to decline and that the net profit of the downtown store might even turn into a net loss.

The president of Fairview Stores, Mr. James Lundy, was not disposed to let the profitability of the company gradually decline without doing everything in his power to prevent it. Consequently, he appointed a firm of management consultants to study the company's situation and recommend ways of improving the company's profitability. He also appointed a four-person committee, headed by himself, to meet each week to discuss and possibly implement recommendations made by the firm's own staff.

Assignment
1. What can Fairview Stores Ltd. do to improve its profitability?

READING

Popcorn Explosion: Home Poppers Open Up the Market

BY MIKE MACBETH

Source: Mike Macbeth, *Canadian Business Magazine*, February 1983

Profits from popcorn are traditionally prodigious. "It's corny, but the joke goes that businessmen used to buy themselves a popcorn machine, then build a theatre around it," laughs Sydney Spiegel, vice-president of Super Pufft Popcorn Ltd. of Scarborough, Ont., a man who really knows what's popping in the popcorn industry.

Spiegel, whose firm is Canada's major independent theatre popcorn supplier, stresses, however, that the key words here are "used to." Ten years ago, a box of movie popcorn was made up of 20% product and 80% profit. Now, skyrocketing costs in packaging materials and butter have evened up the figures. Today's 75¢ serving of munchies will return just 45¢ in gross profit to the businessman who's running the operation.

But after 36 years of responding to change in the popcorn market, Spiegel is ready to tackle the problem of softening theatre receipts by introducing a butter substitute that will sell for about half the price of a $72 tub of the real thing. And, with more and more movie buffs buying or renting their own video equipment, Spiegel is now moving into the only popcorn market he doesn't already dominate in Canada: the sale of commercial quality kernel corn for popping in the home.

New wrinkles in the popcorn industry began to show up two years ago when sales of electric corn poppers began to take off in the US and Canada. Ironically, 1980 was a poor year for corn crops, and Spiegel found he had to ration his regular customers. But bountiful harvests in all 2,000 varieties of US corn in 1981 and 1982 (Spiegel buys carloads of kernels from Indiana), plus an increase in quality Canadian corn (grown primarily near Chatham, Ont.), have given him the incentive to make the big push into the home popping field. To supply it, he expects to boost his purchases to 4 million lbs. of raw corn in 1983 from 3 million lbs. in 1982.

Unlike many other sectors of the economy, the popcorn industry has been steadily increasing its sales volume by $6\frac{1}{2}$% annually during the past five years. "People don't consider popcorn a junk food," says Spiegel when he's asked why popcorn continues to rack up big sales. "They know it's a natural, inexpensive food item and that they get quite a lot of it for their money. And our company is still doing well because a big percentage of Canada's adult population was weaned on Super Pufft popcorn."

Super Pufft was founded in January, 1946, by the proprietors (Spiegel among them) of the now-defunct Dairy Maid Chocolate Products company of Toronto. "We did it because of postwar sugar rationing," Spiegel remembers. "Popcorn was a snack food that didn't utilize sugar, so we began popping it in a room on King Street. We then sold it to confectionery jobbers."

When rationing was abolished later that year, Spiegel approached Famous Players and suggested the installation of popcorn warmer machines in their theatres (yes, Virginia, there was a time when you couldn't buy hot-buttered popcorn in movie houses). The ingenious idea immediately caught on with customers at the foyer refreshment counters and, by 1948, Super Pufft was doing enough business with theatres, variety stores and sporting-event organizers to build a new plant on Princess Street in Toronto. The following year, the company also acquired a 5,500-sq.ft. factory and distribution centre in Winnipeg to supply its western clients. Although Spiegel today supplies approximately half of Canada's 1,200 movie houses with unpopped kernels, Famous Players, his first major customer, now does its own purchasing and distributing.

Super Pufft outgrew the Princess Street plant and has moved twice in the past three decades, finally renting a 30,000-sq.-ft. factory in Scarborough, where 18 employees produce 45 lbs. of seasoned and 360 lbs. of caramel popcorn per hour for the "prepackaged" trade. Although Spiegel has spent $250,000 in leasehold improvements and another $250,000 in new equipment for the plant, he's quick to point out that his raw corn is still popped in the old-fashioned way—just 32 oz. at a time, in a battery of copper kettles primed with coconut oil.

And profits have continued to explode, along with the size of the Super Pufft company. The enterprise is projecting gross sales of $3.5 million this year on boxed popcorn, butter and seasonings, commercial popping equipment and the expected upswing in demand for raw kernels. "We've always made a profit," says the small, bespectacled Spiegel. "But we're still looking for our best year. As a matter of fact, we've yet to hit our prime."

Assignment
1. How profitable is popcorn?
2. How are Sydney Spiegel and Superpufft keeping up with the times?
3. Why is popcorn a growing industry?
4. How did Sydney get started in the industry?
5. What was Sydney's greatest popcorn idea?
6. How has Superpufft met its production needs?
7. Where does Superpufft's product fit in the "product life cycle?"

UNIT 4.3 DIRECTING

A manager is responsible to his or her superior or superiors for a number of tasks. He or she also has authority to command the help of subordinates and other resources in carrying out these tasks. The orders given should be designed to make the best use of employees, equipment, and materials. Good orders, therefore, require careful thought.

Principles of Direction

Some principles that help make direction more effective are:
1. *Orders should be clear and definite.* If they are not, they may be accidentally (or even deliberately) misunderstood.
2. *They should be in harmony with the firm's overall objectives.* If they are not, managers will be working at cross purposes and the morale and profits of the firm will suffer.
3. *Responsibility for carrying out the orders should be pinpointed.* If it is not, the order may not be carried out; each subordinate may leave the work up to another and "pass the buck" if things go wrong.
4. *Sufficient authority should be delegated to enable the subordinate to carry out the order.* For example, authority may be needed to obtain funds or assistance of other employees.
5. *Orders should be given to a subordinate by only one superior.* This is the "unity of command" principle discussed earlier in this book, which aims at preventing conflicting demands on the employee's time and efforts.
6. *Orders should be given with enthusiasm and tact.* Enthusiasm is infectious. If the manager lacks enthusiasm, so will his or her subordinates. Also, if

orders are given in a tactless manner, a subordinate's feelings may be hurt, and his or her cooperation in carrying out duties will be less than 100 per cent.

Board of Directors

The most important directing body in a business corporation is the board of directors. These persons, as we saw earlier in this book, are elected by the shareholders to be responsible for the efficient management of the business. Their most important duties are: (a) approving and helping to formulate long- and short-term goals and plans for the company; (b) appointing the company president and other chief executives; (c) ensuring sufficient funds and approving capital and other important budgetary expenditures; (d) approving the method of distribution of profits; (e) keeping shareholders informed of the progess of their company; and (f) ensuring that all other legal requirements are met. By law, there must be at least three directors in a public business corporation, and in practice there may be as many as twenty or thirty. They may be chosen from the firm's own senior managers, from important suppliers, customers, and banks, and from persons eminent in other walks of life. Whatever their background, their chief task is to give direction to the enterprise on whose board they sit.

Motivating

An order can be carried out badly, or it can be carried out well. Often the difference lies in the ability of the manager to motivate subordinates. The ultimate power of the manager to enforce commands is his or her ability to reward or punish, either directly or by recommendation. An employee may be praised or reprimanded, salary increases and promotions may be given or withheld, or a person may be dismissed. The use, or threatened use, of this power of dismissal should be used only as a last resort. Most employees respect the authority of their superior and will work better if they are led rather than threatened.

Every human being has a variety of needs and wants. These have been ranked in order of priority as: *physical needs*, such as food, drink, and shelter; *safety needs*, such as elimination of danger and availability of medical care; *social needs*, such as love, care, and a sense of belonging; and *self-fulfilment needs*, such as creativity, responsibility, self-improvement, wealth, power, and prestige. At one time, people were concerned mainly with physical and safety needs. However, as the average standard of living has risen, attention is being directed more and more to social and self-fulfilment needs.

The key to successful employee motivation lies in an understanding of the needs described above. Good pay and reasonable job security are necessary to satisfy physical needs, but it is the social and self-fulfilment needs that are more difficult to meet—particularly as factory and office jobs become more specialized and routine. However, promotion opportunities, canteen and recreation facilities that permit the development of social relationships, house magazines, more dignified job titles, special fringe benefits, suggestion boxes, and so on, have helped meet these very real needs. By doing so, management is usually able to bring about a state of *high morale*—that is, a positive attitude by all or most employees towards the firm, their jobs, and each other. The achievement of good morale, based upon satisfaction of the various human needs, means that management's orders will be carried out willingly and cheerfully.

Discipline

In a business enterprise, *discipline* is the observance by each employee of the policies, procedures, and rules that have been set by top management for the efficient conduct of the firm's activities. Good discipline is usually obtained by proper motivation of the work force. Unlike the situation in many armed forces, fear is usually a secondary factor. Nevertheless, a firm does have the power, if it wishes to use it, to penalize the employee who fails to toe the line. In labour agreements, the penalties that may be imposed for various offences are usually set out in a special appendix. Thus, for example, a worker who is found drunk or asleep on duty may be laid off for one day for the first offence, a week for the

"You're maybe reading too much into it, Howard. When he said 'Don't rush back,' he probably meant have a nice vacation."

second, and dismissed altogether for the third. For management personnel, the penalties for lack of discipline may be loss of promotion, loss of salary increment, demotion, or even dismissal.

In practice, the more valuable an employee is to the company, the greater the likelihood that management will overlook temporary lapses in discipline. For, after all, it is the continued well-being of the firm that is the ultimate aim. However, persistent flouting of company rules can only lead to a breakdown of both employee morale and confidence in management. For its part, management must always be sure that rules are necessary, reasonable, and fair; that they do not become an end in themselves; that persons breaching discipline are punished fairly; and that management observes the rules itself.

Leadership

Leadership, in business, is a manager's ability to persuade subordinates to work enthusiastically at their jobs and thereby help the firm achieve its goals. To be a leader, a manager must command the respect of those who work for him or her. This respect is based on such things as the manager's ability to manage, mastery of the tasks that the subordinates themselves perform, fairness and courtesy towards them, and praise for work well done. A leader must also be able to make good decisions under pressure, communicate ideas and orders clearly, and enlist and train good subordinates.

Sometimes, in trying to analyze the nature of leadership, a contrast is made between two extremes. A manager who uses *authoritarian leadership* tries to persuade subordinates to work hard by use of fear, threats, and a dominant personality. A manager who uses *democratic leadership* tries to influence subordinates to work hard by setting a good example, by discussing aims with subordinates, and by personal persuasion untinged with threats. Most leadership in business falls somewhere between these two extremes. Another type, *laissez-faire leadership*, is also sometimes to be found. Here, the leader assumes a back-stage position and encourages subordinates to formulate their own goals and plan the ways in which they will achieve them. The leader, in such a situation, plays a consulting role but may nevertheless intervene should the subordinates head off in the wrong direction.

Confidence in Leader.
Factors that affect the esteem in which subordinates hold their supervisor, or "boss," include:

1. *The supervisor's relationship with his or her own superior*. If the leader has a good relationship and a secure position in the firm's organizational hierarchy, this will give confidence to subordinates and help inspire better performance by them.
2. *The supervisor's technical ability and experience*. If the leader "knows what he or she is doing," subordinates are much more likely to follow his or her lead.
3. *The type of leadership used—autocratic or otherwise*. An overly autocratic approach may be resented, whereas an overly democratic one may be

considered a sign of weakness. Factors that will influence a manager's leadership style include: (a) his or her value system, including religious beliefs and cultural background; (b) his or her own leadership inclinations—for example, desire to have responsibility for others, to succeed socially, to have power; (c) confidence in subordinates—can he or she trust them, do they need close supervision?; and (d) mental and emotional stability—does he or she feel secure when new problems arise and uncertainty prevails?
4. *The personality of the supervisor.* The attitude, manners, dress, communicativeness, all reflect the leader's personality and will hinder or help him or her in the job.

Courtesy *Oakville Beaver*

Co-ordinating

If orders are to be carried out efficiently, management must try to achieve good *co-ordination*. This is the management function of ensuring that the many different people, sections, and departments involved in the various facets of the firm's activities work harmoniously together. Nothing is more likely to raise costs and delay fulfilment of orders than to have a firm whose managers, departments, or sister plants are at loggerheads with each other. Good planning, organizing, staffing, directing, and controlling will do much to eliminate this danger. But the larger the firm, the greater this hazard becomes.

Principles of Co-ordination. Some principles to promote better co-ordination within a firm are:
1. The members of each department should be given the opportunity to understand (a) how every department contributes, in its own way, to the firm's common goals, and (b) how each department's activities interact with those of others.
2. The managers of each department, division, or plant should be given the opportunity, through joint committees, meetings, or conferences to meet periodically with their opposite numbers to discuss common problems.
3. Whenever a new project involving various departments is begun, co-ordination should commence as early as possible and be on a continuing basis.
4. Top management should endeavour, by means of good pay, good working conditions, reasonable job security, social facilities, a staff canteen, a house magazine, and other methods, to promote high employee morale.
5. Whenever possible, a written program should be used to set out clearly the activities to be co-ordinated and the timetable to be observed.

KEY TERMS

Principles of direction	Leadership
Board of directors	Authoritarian leadership
Motivation	Democratic leadership
Human needs and wants	Laissez-faire leadership
Morale	Confidence in leader
Discipline	Co-ordination

REVIEW QUESTIONS

1. How can the management function of directing be made more effective?
2. What is the board of directors of a business firm? What are its principal duties?

3. What do you consider to be the key to successful motivation of a firm's employees?
4. What is discipline? How necessary is it in a business firm? How can it best be enforced?
5. What are the two extremes of business leadership? What do you consider to be the attributes of a good business leader?
6. Why is co-ordination considered to be an important management function? How can the performance of this function be improved?

CASE PROBLEM

GEORGE SHARPE & COMPANY LTD.

Getting ahead as a management trainee

Arthur Blackmore had decided, in his final year of college, to make his career in marketing. His aim was to obtain a job that would eventually lead to a sales management position—one that would be interesting and financially rewarding.

Many companies—large, medium, and small—recruited potential management personnel from the graduates of his college. For several years, there had been more job opportunities than eligible candidates.

Arthur planned to have interviews with representatives of several of the larger merchandising companies, such as Eaton's and The Bay. He hoped, however, that an opening might turn up in a smaller company, where he believed his abilities and energy would be more quickly recognized and rewarded.

The letter on the following page, which was posted on the placement board, caught Arthur's attention.

The next day, Arthur telephoned Mrs. Ralph and arranged for an interview.

At the interview, Mr. Blake, a short, serious man, asked Arthur a number of questions about himself and explained in some detail what the job involved. He then took Arthur to meet Frank Sharpe, the president, and Alex McLeod, the secretary-treasurer. Mr. Blake promised to let Arthur know as soon as possible whether he had been accepted for the job.

On the following Monday, Arthur received a message via the placement office to call Mrs. Ralph. When he called he was told that he had been chosen from three candidates. Arrangements were made for him to start work on June 1.

The firm in which Arthur Blackmore was to work was started by George Sharpe in 1936. In that year, Sharpe secured the sales agency for all Canada of dinnerware, teaware, and various gift items of fine-quality bone china manufactured by Wedge Potteries Ltd. and George Ramsbottom and Son of Staffordshire, England. To these lines he later added a fine semi-porcelain dinnerware by R.S. Peebles Ltd., a high quality earthen dinnerware by Strange Potteries, an inexpensive kitchenware by Regal China, plaster plaques by Richard Addison, and a medium-priced lead crystal by Dartford Crystal Ltd. These items are sold by George Sharpe & Co. Ltd. to retailers across Canada.

The head office and main warehouse of the firm is in Toronto at 6 South Service Road, Etobicoke. Other warehouses are located in Vancouver, Winnipeg,

GEORGE SHARPE & COMPANY LTD.
Importers and Distributors of Fine English China
6 South Service Road, Etobicoke, Ontario
Telephone 251-7565
March 6, 198-

Mr. J. Harrison
Placement Officer,
Kent College,
Ontario

Dear Mr. Harrison:

I am looking for a young person of character and ability to act as my assistant.

We are a leading importer and distributor of fine English china and crystal with an enviable record of recent growth.

The young man or woman chosen would, after adequate training, perform the following main functions: (a) handle most of my routine and semi-routine correspondence and paper work; (b) prepare, under my general direction, instructions and news bulletins for our salespeople; (c) prepare annual and quarterly sales expense budgets; (d) draw my attention to significant deviations of actual revenues and expenditures from the budgets; (e) make arrangements, including agenda, for sales meetings; and (f) carry out research on particular sales and other topics.

The salary for this position is extremely attractive and subject to periodic review. The company also has a generous pension scheme and other fringe benefits.

Would you ask any candidates to contact my secretary, Mrs. Ralph, for an appointment.
Yours very truly,

Arthur Blake

Arthur Blake,
Sales Manager.
AB/mr

Montreal, and Halifax. In the warehouses, the china, crystal, and porcelain are unpacked, made up into individual orders, repacked, and then shipped out by road and rail to the various retailers. Sales are divided geographically as follows: Ontario 55 per cent, West Coast 18 per cent, Quebec 12 per cent, Prairies 10 per cent, Maritimes 5 per cent. Approximately 32 per cent of the goods are sold to the large department stores such as Eaton's, Simpsons, The Bay, and Woodward's; 25 per cent to chain stores such as Kresge's, Woolworth's, Stedman's and Zeller's; and 40 per cent to small retailers such as gift shops.

The organization of the sales force is shown in Figure 4.2.

At each location, one of the salespeople acts as an "inside" salesperson. He receives customers' orders over the telephone, helps to unpack deliveries, and makes up individual orders, using temporary help when required. The inside salesperson receives a salary of $25,000 per annum. The other salespeople work strictly on commission—last year the highest income was $47,500, and the lowest $23,500.

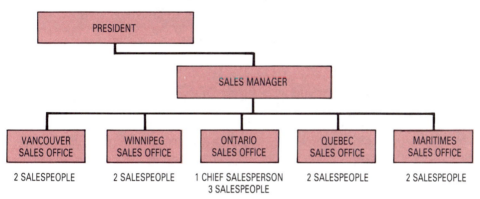

Figure 4.2 Sales Organization Chart for George Sharpe & Co. Ltd.

During the first year, Arthur worked hard to make a success of his job and felt some satisfaction when Mr. Blake, at the end of that year, praised his efforts and raised his salary to $22,000.

One fact, however, was causing Arthur some disquiet. Mr. Blake, now relieved of much of his paperwork, was using his newly found time not to expand the sales force or improve their efforts, but to undertake selling himself. Mr. Blake, who was a first-class salesman, would visit the department stores and other large customers, together with the regular salesperson, and later split the commissions. One of the salespeople had protested this policy, but when the matter was brought to the president's attention, Blake secured his agreement by pointing out the greatly increased level of sales.

Blackmore felt that this policy was not a good one for the company from the long-run point of view and said so to Mr. Blake. From this point on, Blake became more and more critical of Blackmore's work and relations between the two men gradually deteriorated.

Finally Blackmore felt that there was no future for both him and Mr. Blake in the company and decided to look for another job. With his educational background and one year's experience of the chinaware business, Blackmore felt that he could successfully hold down a management position in that field. He also remembered, however, what several of the salespeople had told him: "You'll never make any money while you're young on the salaries they pay at head office.

Get out and sell on commission. Stop patsying around with the sales manager and be your own boss!"

Blackmore, who is 24 years old, married, with an 8-month-old daughter, must now decide what to do.

Assignment

1. Discuss Blackmore's belief that a smaller company, rather than a large department store, would be quicker to recognize and reward his abilities.
2. How could Blackmore, during his time at college, have improved his chances of finding the right career for himself?
3. Was Blackmore correct in telling Blake that he disagreed with the way he spent his time?
4. How could Blake's active participation in selling act against the long-run interests of the firm?
5. What are the duties of a sales manager?
6. What would you do if you were Blackmore?
7. How could Blake have used his extra time to increase company sales without himself taking part in selling?
8. Might a different form of salespeople's compensation help this firm to increase its sales?

READING

The Rewards of Running Your Own Show

Worker-run plants are catching on as a result of bailouts of near-bankrupt firms and takeovers of formerly U.S.-owned operations. Still, despite their grave-to-cradle origins, enthusiasm for the idea is by no means universal and the union movement is hostile.

BY JUDY STEED

Source: *The Globe and Mail*, Toronto.

Chris Romas sharpens his knife, a 15-centimetre stainless-steel blade set in a heavy black handle. At his station on the hamboning line, in the chill of Swift Eastern's Toronto meat-packing plant, Romas is a happy man—and very surprised to find himself part-owner of a company with sales in excess of $150 million a year.

"Did I buy shares?" He laughs. "Sure I buy. Keep the job, eh." By participating in the employee buyout of his company, which would otherwise have shut down, Romas became part of a burgeoning trend that variously exhilarates and dismays a wide variety of observers. Employee-management buyouts, accompanied by assorted versions of profit-sharing schemes, are occurring at an ever-increasing pace in North America. The name of the game is increasing productivity and profits. In fact the process is notable for its ability to resurrect dying companies. The evidence is impressive, from the high-profile rescue of Weirton Steel Works in 1983 by more than 7,000 U.S. employees to the takeover 12 years ago by Quebec workers of a dead Canadian International Paper Co. mill (now known as Tembec) in Temiscaming. South of the border, entrepreneurs have been quick to transform the traditional image of corporate organization. There are more than 440,000 U.S. companies with 20 million workers involved in some form of profit sharing and/or employee stock ownership, according to the Profit Sharing Research Foundation of Evanston, Ill. In Canada, the evidence is less dramatic but the opportunities are more widespread.

The Profit Sharing Council of Canada estimates there are as many as 25,000 companies operating in similar fashion across the country, with the prospect of many more joining them. Management consultants expect to see an increase of buyouts by managers and/or employees, particularly in the so-called branch-plant sector of the economy, where subsidiaries are susceptible to withering on the multinational vine as parent companies retrench. Says Phill Doherty, partner in charge of mergers and acquisitions for management consultants Ernst & Whinney of Toronto: "Branch plants get the least amount of attention but probably offer the most potential." Corporate lawyer Walter Bowen of Toronto, who has specialized in acquisitions and mergers for 20 years, says it is only recently that he has seen a stream of employee-management buyouts. The reason for the change, he says, is that in the past, "Canadians didn't have the moxie or the money. Now they've got both."

Swift Eastern, for one, is still on the same block in a dingy industrial section of midtown Toronto. What has changed is the atmosphere, profitability, and ownership. It has been a dizzying transformation in a few short years from a money-losing subsidiary of Esmark Inc. of Chicago to a division of Pocklington Financial Corp. of Edmonton—under the western Gainers label—to Maybank Foods Inc. of Toronto, which is wholly owned by its employees and is the proprietor of Swift Eastern.

In 1981, Peter Pocklington, millionaire empire builder and owner of the Edmonton Oilers hockey team, bought the Swift Canadian division from Esmark and incorporated it into his smaller Gainers meatpacking company. The timing was bad, the marriage did not work and two years later Pocklington sent word to the Toronto plant that he was going to close the place. Consumer demand for meat was steadily declining and the meat industry—the fourth-largest manufacturing sector in Canada, with sales of about $7 billion in 1980—had lost 30 plants and more than 5,000 jobs in a decade. Swift Eastern almost swelled those grim ranks.

But Fred Russell, now Maybank's chairman of the board and then vice-president of Gainers' eastern meat division, refused to say die. Horrified at the prospect of shutting down the company, which had 482 employees and plants in Quebec and the Maritimes, Russell mobilized the workers. Together they raised more than $1 million, found a bank prepared to lend up to $12.5 million in a leveraged deal where debt loomed over equity, and negotiated a new union contract cutting wages by 16 to 21% at the Toronto plant. After a year of operation, the new company is showing a profit in which workers will eventually share.

Union leaders across the country—most notably Robert White, Canadian director of the 120,000-member United Auto Workers—have decried employee buyouts and profit-sharing schemes as regressive, anti-union tactics that make workers pay the price of bad management through lower wages. White says that workers should get their fair share of the economic pie through negotiated wage increases and any profit sharing should be on top of that. Critics such as White suggest employees can receive little benefit from their ownership stake when they have no real power in running the company. They warn that, without access to financial records and top-level management meetings, workers cannot know whether the books are being manipulated to hide profits. The net result, White has argued, is that workers' wages go down over the long term.

Indeed, there are schemes that are scams, according to Bert Metzger, president of the Profit Sharing Research Foundation. Said Metzger: "We see a lot of plans for employee ownership or profit sharing that aren't worth the paper they're written on. If management uses these ideas as gimmicks, if it exploits the rhetoric but doesn't really do anything by way of sharing power, information or money, then it doesn't work."

When the rhetoric is matched by reality, the results can be impressive. A recently completed study by the New York Stock Exchange shows a positive correlation between superior corporate performance and a sharing of profits or ownership. Titled *People and Productivity: A Challenge to Corporate America*, the study notes, for instance, that employee-participation committees, often known as quality circles, exist in only 14% of traditional U.S. corporations with more than 500 employees, but in 49% of profit-sharing companies and in 56% of firms with employee stock purchase plans.

A study by business professors Donald Nightingale of Queen's University in Kingston, Ont. and Richard Long of the University of Saskatchewan found a direct relationship between the amount of employee-held equity and the success of a firm. The more real involvement of workers in corporate activity, they concluded, the more effective the company.

Nightingale, author of a 1982 book *Workplace Democracy*, notes that Marc Lalonde's last budget while the Liberals held power in Ottawa included proposals to support profit sharing. As part of a finance department team that met corporate heads to explain and win backing for the idea, Nightingale was struck by the overwhelmingly negative reaction from people he describes as "conventional managers." The Bay Streeters were interested only in whatever tax incentives Lalonde could offer; as it was, they felt he was not offering enough.

The Entrepreneurs at Swift Eastern

Organizing Swift Eastern's survival was an arduous experience for Fred Russell, but he brought to the task a very old-fashioned spirit of dedication. Russell, 59, joined the company as a salesman in 1947. Now the company chairman, he doesn't hide his affection for the old Swift plant on Maybank Avenue near Keele Street and St. Clair Avenue in the stockyard district of Toronto. He leads a tour past enormous steel-lined smokehouses and computerized assembly lines that each year slice 4.5 million kilograms of bacon and pack 3.2 million kilograms of wieners.

Rod Middleton, a 39-year-old Canadian and a vice-president of Citibank Canada, voted to finance the 1983 employee buyout because prospects were good and it had "leadership, a good game plan and grassroots support." As well, the bank was able to secure its current $7-million loan against $7 million worth of accounts receivable and inventory

Russell and his cohorts reported a quarterly profit last fall. The key, he says, is employee dedication. Last spring, fighting closure, Russell met every company unit from Toronto to St. John's. He asked for money as well as moral support. Would they buy shares? He got a 94% positive response to a survey that, he says, "gave me courage." His optimism was borne out when 400 employees raised $1 million. Some of them, like executive secretary Kimberley Swift (no relation to the company), took a bank loan to buy in at the minimum level of $1,500. "I can tell you it has changed the atmosphere around here," she says. "People take more care in what they do." They also give a lot more: last June, the Toronto plant employees voluntarily accepted a 16 to 21% salary rollback, saving the company $1 million a year.

Local union president Joseph Micallef, who has worked at the Maybank plant for 41 years, is extremely relieved that Swift did not follow a Burns Foods plant in Kitchener into extinction. Last October, more than 600 Burns workers refused wage concessions averaging $1.14 an hour. "The union fought for what it believed in but the company shut the place down," Micallef says. "We lost $2 an hour but we've got our jobs. The average age of our workers is between 50 and 55, and where would these people get another job? We've doubled our benefits and we've got profit sharing. I admit there's no profits yet, but maybe soon. . . . And we're owners." What does that mean in practical terms? Not much, he says, when it comes to the day-to-day running of the business. "But we (union members) own majority control, we've got two people on the board of directors and we go to shareholders' meetings."

President Alan Beswick, 59, has gone out of his way to ensure that employee-owners feel their importance. "This is an unusual takeover," he says. "More typically you find five or six senior managers have bought up a company. Here, 400 people did it and the managers don't own a controlling interest." Beswick roams the plant constantly asking one question: "What's wrong?" Worker-owners were a little alarmed by his blunt pursuit of imperfection but they are beginning to appreciate his motives—especially since the balance sheet has started to improve. Says Beswick: "It doesn't matter how hard we go at it, if we're not efficient we're going to close down."

Every second Tuesday at 8:30 a.m., Beswick meets an employee monitoring committee for what he calls "a bitching session." He says ideas on how to improve quality and productivity "pour out." Follow-up procedures ensure that good ideas are implemented, boosting employee self-esteem.

The company's sales last year amounted to $151 million, and no one was surprised when there was no profit. The turnaround in the first quarter (with an enlarged sales force and more than 500 employees) was anticipated and welcomed, particularly by the bank. "Most bankers would never have touched that deal," says Middleton. In the spring of 1983, the group working to save the Swift plant made presentations to four different banks in four days. Three were Canadian and one was American—Citibank. The Canadian banks were not encouraging. By the time they got around to asking for more information, Russell and John Patterson, vice-president of finance, had signed letters of intent with Citibank.

Middleton is proud of his judgment on Swift Eastern's prospects. "They've had a tough time, no question," he says. "It took them a year to bring costs down, but progress is significant." He attends management meetings, keeping abreast of all details of business. Notes the banker: "You can't go to sleep on a customer who is highly leveraged."

According to Nightingale, what the managers were really saying "was that they're not interested in the underlying philosophy." He defines that philosophy as a belief that "making workers partners will improve our economic performance." Nightingale says that traditional managers and unions object equally vociferously to "innovative arrangements." But he believes their objections do not matter, because "innovation is coming. More worker control is inevitable."

Nor does the presence of unions automatically hamper the process. Swift Eastern's Russell says he was warned that "I'd never get the union members onside, but I had no trouble at all." Ross Eaket, president of Northern Breweries Ltd. of Sault Ste. Marie, had a similar experience. He led an employee buyout of the firm from Carling O'Keefe in 1977—and he is quick to note that Northern's achievements were won without wage cuts.

In a frantic bid to keep the operation alive in four Northern Ontario locations—the Sault, Thunder Bay, Timmins and Sudbury—Eaket sought to raise $700,000 from 137 employees, most of whom were members of the Canadian Union of United Brewery, Flour, Cereal, Soft Drink and Distillery Workers. In only three months, he exceeded his goal by more than 100%, putting together $1.5 million from 100 employees at $1,000 per unit. Employees paid cash and received 50 shares plus a company promissory note for $950 bearing interest. Each $1 share now is worth $40. If a worker decides to leave the firm with, say, 50 shares, he must sell them to the company, or to another employee who will pay cash for the accumulated $900 value.

Northern's profit-sharing plan has not yet paid dividends because of the company's determination to put profits back into plant modernization. More than $4.5 million has been spent on new equipment, and sales have more than doubled in the past six years to $25 million in 1984. At the same time, wage increases have kept pace with industry rates while the payroll has grown by 40 jobs. Worker-management committees meet in each plant at least once a month, and corporate planning is approved by a board of directors weighted so that management does not have formal control. The result, says Eaket, is a corporate camaraderie that pays off in more ways than one. Workers act as unpaid salesmen for Northern beer in their communities, and their pride in that product has won the company international awards.

At Epton Industries Inc. in Kitchener, Ont., employees are less engaged in corporate activity because they were not invited to participate in the management buyout. Epton was a multinational subsidiary facing a grim future of being sold (maybe) or being shut down (more likely). At stake were 500 jobs at B.F. Goodrich's money-losing engineered products division (Epton stands for engineered products to optimal needs.)

On Feb. 9, 1983, the company's U.S. parent announced it wanted to sell the division so it could concentrate on more profitable products—tires and chemicals. Goodrich appointed two Kitchener managers, Michael Weedon and Jim Aylward, to prepare a marketing document for Ernst & Whinney which would try to find a buyer.

Weedon and Aylward knew the Kitchener plant was failing for lack of adequate attention, but they were impressed with the possibilities. Certainly there was a healthy list of purchasers (Syncrude, Noranda, Kimberly-Clark, the Toronto Transit Commission) for Goodrich's custom-engineered rubber and vinyl hose. The two men decided that the company could be a moneymaker, and they believed they knew how to make it happen.

On March 16, 1983, having recruited a

third partner, plant production manager Laurence Belanger, they announced their intention to buy. With the help of a $4-million federal interest-free loan under the Industry Labor Adjustment Program, and what they call "a superb performance" from the Bank of Montreal, they flew to Goodrich headquarters in Ohio six months later and made a deal.

The Epton name replaced B.F. Goodrich on the plant water tower in October and the new owners took over. Instead of bringing in workers as shareholders, the trio chose to retain control and devised group incentives with cash bonuses for departments with low wastage, high output and few returns of faulty goods. As well, Weedon, the new president, instituted a profit-sharing plan tied to corporate performance. At quarterly meetings, Epton distributes 20% of pretax income to employees. (One key factor is whether a company is labour intensive or capital intensive. Percentages tend to be higher when labour costs are lower, as at Epton.)

The most ardent advocates of profit sharing see it as just a stop on the way to the ultimate goal: employee stock ownership. David Knowland, president of Rumble Equipment Ltd. of Toronto, says that full employee ownership of his company serves to attract the best people, increase motivation, and decrease turnover. It has also revolutionized an operation in which control used to be held by the Rumble estate and was administered by a trust company. In 1962, Rumble was primarily a distributor of U.S.-manufactured equipment, with sales of about $980,000. That year, 16 employees (including Knowland, then a sales representative) bought the firm and expanded it to the point where it became an innovative, high-technology designer and manufacturer of electronic equipment for industrial uses. The company, now wholly owned by its 100 workers, had sales last year of more than $14 million.

Knowland says most people do not understand what employee ownership or profit sharing involves. Such schemes are no substitute for good wages, he says, yet he finds many executives interested in the concepts only as ways to institute flexible wage packages. He disagrees vehemently with such an approach, saying: "To make this work, you *really* have to treat your employees as partners. You have to continuously talk to them and exchange ideas. If you don't want this sort of participatory management, don't bother with employee ownership or profit sharing. It won't work."

At Supreme Aluminum Industries Ltd., in Toronto, board chairman Sheldon Lush makes the same point. The largest cookware manufacturer in Canada, with sales of about $30 million in 1984, Supreme employees, by the end of 1986, will own 38% with the balance held by the Lush family and retired employees. Pioneers in profit sharing going back to the 1940s, the Lushes have for decades made a big, public celebration out of sharing company profits. In 1974, Lush gave out $980,000 or $3,100 to each of 316 workers; in 1983 there was no big party when the cheques amounted to $1,927 for each of 240 workers, for a total of $462,000.

In a recession the profit share may not be as great, but Lush says that the benefits continue over time. Every year, 30% of Supreme's pretax profits are split three ways: one-third cash, one-third company shares and one-third deferred (in a retirement fund). The company provides interest-free loans of up to $20,000 to enable employees to buy shares.

Still, Supreme is not universally admired. It operates in a non-union environment and its employee association is headed by the company's industrial relations manager. Yet Lush rejects any suggestion that management is autocratic. He points to a host of committees designed to promote productivity and employee involvement in the company. SAFER (Supreme Association for Effective Results) and PROFIT (People Reaching Out For Improved Techniques) are typical of the snappy acronyms applied to the so-called "quality and productivity circles." According to Lush, the reason they work is that they provide a reason for management and workers to get together and talk. Said Lush: "The most important thing is to make sure people hear things from the top of the house. If you're not always telling them what's going on, they won't trust you."

Nothing endures but change, is a quote from the ancient Greek philosopher Heraclitus framed on Lush's office wall. The Supreme chairman is worried about recovering from the recession, about competition from the Third World, about the Conservative Government's decision to weaken foreign investment controls. And he believes that Canadian workers and managers now more than ever need to find ways to band together if Canada is to build its manufacturing base. Next to Heraclitus is a framed quote from S. Lush offering his prescription: *Do Something! Either lead or follow or get the hell out of the way.*

Taking Control at Epton

What is so different about working for a company owned by its management? "Before, it was just a job," says Epton's controller, Ron Woelk. "Now, the really exciting thing is the decision-making process. We're a close-knit team. We can meet on a moment's notice. We don't get bogged down in 14 levels of approval and then have to send off to the U.S. for the *Good Housekeeping* seal of approval. It gives us a competitive advantage. We can move fast."

But taking control is harder than it looks. Brass bands played and 1,000 people celebrated the plant's new incarnation on Oct. 1, 1983, but Weedon and his partners—Laurence Belanger, vice-president of manufacturing, and Jim Aylward, vice-president of marketing—could not enjoy the party. "We were basket cases," Aylward says.

The first initiative that would transform B.F. Goodrich's engineered products division into Epton Industries came innocently enough in March, 1983. The bid to purchase set off a nonstop rush of exhilarating highs and crushing lows that included the threat of another bidder. As well, Weedon's wife gave birth to twins (their third and fourth children) in June at the height of the deal-making. Said their lawyer, Walter Bowen: "It was an exhausting process." Known to his clients as Uncle Walter, he held their hands, told them when to shut up and went out on a limb for them because, he says, "I like seeing these guys succeed." Bowen had his hands full: when it came down to the crucial point, it was just Weedon and Bowen against a battery of B.F. Goodrich lawyers in the boardroom of corporate headquarters in Akron, Ohio.

An economic nationalist, Bowen is pleased by the trend of "Americans selling out and Canadians buying up." He attributes it in part to a resurgence of Canadian gutsiness and to the high cost of U.S. takeovers. Says Bowen: "They've paid whopping prices for companies in the States and they've got to sell off assets to come up with the purchase price."

It is a situation that provides opportunities for those prepared to take a chance. Weedon, 31, believes that "this generation has the tools to make a difference." He joined B.F. Goodrich eight years ago fresh from the MBA program at the University of Western Ontario in London, Ont. The first Canadian sent to head office to learn Goodrich management techniques, he was only 28 when he was appointed vice-president of finance for the engineered products division. Little did the company know it was training an heir.

After leading the company to independent status, Weedon spent the first year extricating it from systems that had tied it to the U.S. parent: accounting and computer systems, phones and payroll. That meant "a highly internal focus," Weedon says, but now that Epton is standing on its own feet it is looking at how it can better serve its customers. Epton recently bought a Uniroyal line (a type of engineered hose) that was being taken out of production in Montreal. Weedon talks enthusiastically about team play and co-operative effort. Still, not everyone at Epton is happy with the bosses. Said one worker: "They want to portray a nice image, but I'm not sure it's real." Weedon writes a chatty newsletter, but is seldom seen around the plant, and there is no regular contact with employees through management-worker committees. As a result, communication is spotty—unlike Swift Eastern, where management virtually harasses workers to say what is on their minds at meetings held at least every few weeks.

Some Epton workers feel the profit-sharing scheme is inequitable, favouring managers over workers; others say that "we took too big a pay cut." Last August, 300 members of the United Rubber Workers voted to accept a three-year contract calling for a 23% wage cut—between $2 and $2.50 an hour on the existing wage of about $10.50 an hour. The vote was close, with a margin of victory for concessions of only 28.

Union president Ed Devlin, who has worked at the plant for 23 years, acknowledges that there remains considerable resentment and distrust among unionized workers. At the same time, he notes the trauma among Kitchener workers caused by the closing of the city's Burns Foods plant last fall. It is not a good time for workers, he says, when they are given the choice of plant closing or wage concessions. "That's no choice at all." For himself, Devlin is taking a wait-and-see attitude, hoping the company comes up with a sweeter deal when the current contract expires in 1986.

Assignment

1. Who is Chris Romas? What is keeping him so happy?
2. Why do worker-run plants often fail to survive?
3. Why are Canadian union leaders opposed to employee buyouts and profit-sharing schemes?
4. Explain how Swift Eastern became an employee-owned business.
5. What has been the profit-sharing experience of Ross Eaket, president of Northern Breweries?
6. How did Epton Industries turn to profit-sharing? With what result?
7. What has been the experience with profit-sharing of Rumble Equipment Ltd. of Toronto?
8. Is Supreme Aluminum Industries Ltd. an example of successful profit-sharing? Discuss.

UNIT 4.4: CONTROLLING

Controlling is the management function of ensuring that company plans and orders are properly carried out and company goals thereby achieved. The manager, in checking on performance, tries to spot any divergence from the accepted plans, so that he or she can then take remedial action to bring performance back into line. Effective controls must quickly reveal deviations and corrective measures must be immediately undertaken. Controlling involves, therefore, (a) the measuring of performance against approved standards; (b) the automatic reporting of any deviations; and (c) the taking of rapid remedial action.

Standards

There are many different standards against which business performance is measured. On the revenue side, a key standard is *projected sales*. If actual sales start to drop below the standard, a firm's production and profit plans can be thrown completely out of order unless remedial action (for example, a special sales campaign or a cut in prices) is quickly taken. From the point of view of a firm's liquidity, an important standard is the *cash budget* (see Unit 13.1) against which the actual flow of cash in and out of a business is compared, to monitor any increase or decrease in the firm's cash balance. From the shareholders' and directors' point of view, two vital standards are the rates of expected profits and dividends.

On the cost side, one very important standard is the *operating budget* (see Unit 12.1) for the firm as a whole and for each department. Thus, for example, the cost of materials actually used by the production department is compared with the amount budgeted for the particular week or month. If the actual cost deviates from the budgeted amount (the standard) something is wrong and must be investigated and corrected.

To control costs, management makes great use of pre-determined *standard costs*. These are estimates of what it should reasonably cost to produce a unit of a good. *Cost accounting* is the name given to the work of determining standard costs per unit of output, apportioning this cost to different sources (such as materials, labour, and overhead), and measuring and comparing actual costs with standard costs.

Financial Ratios

To simplify the detection of deviations, standards are often expressed in the form of *ratios*. These ratios describe numerically the relationship normally expected between two significant variables, such as production costs and sales. These ratios include:

Cost Ratios. These express the expected relationship between different types of costs, on the one hand, and other factors, such as volume of output or value of sales, on the other. Thus, we have standard ratios for: plant costs/sales;

administration costs/sales; selling costs/sales; advertising costs/sales; distribution costs/sales; and research and development costs/sales.

Stock Ratios. These are standards used to judge the efficiency of a firm's inventory control. They include value of inventory compared with sales; and work-in-progress compared with sales.

Sales Ratios. These serve as a measure for sales efficiency. They include sales compared with total assets, with fixed assets, and with working capital. Also, to judge the efficiency of credit sales, a standard ratio can be set for sales compared with total customer credit and with bad debt.

Solvency Ratios. To help ensure that a company's financial solvency (that is, its ability to meet its financial obligations) is not being impaired, standard ratios are set, for example, between current assets and current liabilities (the *current ratio*); and between highly liquid current assets and current liabilities (the *quick-asset ratio*).

Profitability Ratios. As a means for measuring profitability, standard ratios are set, for example, between net profit and total assets; and between net profit and equity capital.

Not all standards, we should note, are quantitative in nature. Thus, a high state of employee morale can be a very real standard for a firm's personnel department—even though it may be difficult to quantify except in terms of absenteeism and labour turnover. A satisfactory public image is another desirable standard which cannot be expressed in figures.

Inventory Turnover Ratio

This is the relationship between the amount of goods sold and the inventory carried. It is calculated by dividing the value of goods sold during, say, a year, by the average inventory for the same period. Both sales and inventory must be valued at the same prices—either sales or cost. Average inventory can be estimated by adding the inventory at the beginning of the year to the inventory at the end of the year and dividing by two.

The purpose of the inventory turnover ratio is to show how much sales revenue is being earned with a given amount of capital invested in stocks, or, in other words, how fast the inventory is being "turned over." Thus, if $1,000 worth of stock is sold every two months, then the business is more profitable than one which requires six months to "move" the same amount of goods. This assumes, of course, that both businesses have the same merchandising costs. The ratio is a useful indicator of business efficiency that a firm can use to compare present performance with past performance, or with the average for firms engaged in the same line of business.

In a wholesale or retail business, which usually has limited space available, the turnover ratio is one important factor influencing the choice of items to stock. The other key factor is the *profit margin* on each item. Ideally, a firm will choose products to stock which have both a high turnover and a high profit margin. In practice, high turnover goods usually have relatively low profit margins, and vice versa. Only in a monopoly situation (for example, liquor sales) do both high turnover and high profit margin exist together. Nevertheless, every business will strive for both.

Deviations

The second main step in controlling is the rapid detection and correction of deviations from the various standards established. Detection is facilitated by the preparation and careful scrutiny of statistical and written reports on the various activities of the firm. These include summaries of all actual expenditures, income statements, balance sheets, actual ratios, sales reports, inspection reports, stock counts, special and routine production and marketing reports and analyses. Personal visits to branch plants can also be very helpful.

Courtesy The Ontario Ministry of Industry, Trade and Technology

Management by Exception. Because there is so much data involved, most firms, in their controlling function, operate on the basis of *management by exception*. This means that, apart from highly summarized data such as the income statement and balance sheet, the manager has his or her attention called only to deviations (or exceptions) from standards. He or she does not waste time studying what is going right. He or she is concerned primarily with what is going wrong, the reasons for it, and the necessary corrective measures.

Management Information Systems. The development of the electronic computer has greatly facilitated the rapid, detailed monitoring of actual business performance, the comparison of it with the standards set, and the reporting of any deviations. The spread of computer-based *management information systems* that provide this type of reporting has, in fact, greatly improved the efficiency of business managers in the last few decades. The business manager can now spot emerging trouble spots much more quickly, and be much better informed before making decisions, and can be much faster in reacting to business problems.

PERT. For special projects, one highly sophisticated method of control is known as PERT (Program Evaluation Review Technique). This technique (also known as CPM, or Critical Path Method) was first successfully used by the United States Navy in 1958 in its Polaris submarine program, which involved 250 main contractors and 9,000 sub-contractors. The use of PERT requires: that every important event that must take place before a project is complete be listed in detail; that the sequence of these events and their relationships be shown on a PERT diagram; and that a specific time be set for the start and completion of each event (usually three times are given: an "optimistic" time, a "most likely" time, and a "pessimistic" time). Once these steps have been taken, the sequence of events that takes the longest time, the "critical path," is identified. This critical path is then subjected to careful attention while the project is being carried out, to make sure that no time-lag develops. If it does, then the completion of the whole project will be delayed.

KEY TERMS

Controlling

Standards

Projected sales

Cash budget

Operating budget

Standard costs

Solvency ratios

Profitability ratios

Inventory turnover ratio

Non-quantitative standards

Detecting and correcting deviations

Management by exception

Cost accounting

Ratios

Cost ratios

Stock ratios

Sales ratios

Management information systems

Program Evaluation Review Technique (PERT)

Critical Path Method (CPM)

REVIEW QUESTIONS

1. What is the controlling function of management?
2. Explain the nature and purpose of business standards.
3. What are standard costs? What is cost accounting?
4. What are the various types of financial ratios used to measure business performance?
5. Explain the nature and purpose of the inventory turnover ratio.
6. What is management by exception?
7. How has the development of electronic computers affected the controlling function of management?
8. Explain the nature and purpose of PERT, or CPM, by using the example of the preparation of a cooked dinner in the family kitchen.

UNIT 4.5: STAFFING

The staffing function of management includes the hiring, training, promotion, transfer, layoff, and dismissal of employees. Every manager, by the nature of his or her position, will devote part of the time to this task. A personnel department can (for example, by screening applicants for jobs) help to reduce the manager's load, but it cannot remove it.

In this unit, we confine ourselves to the staffing function of management as it applies to management personnel. In Unit 15.1, where we consider the work of the personnel department, we look at the staffing function with regard to other employees.

Recruitment of Managers

Business managers reach their positions in a variety of ways: by ownership (particularly the managers of small businesses); by nepotism (being hired by a relative who owns or manages a business); by entering a business from high school or trade school and later being promoted (the usual source of supervisory management and, to a lesser extent, of middle and top management); and by entering a business from college or university as a management trainee.

The Recruitment Program

As the success of a business depends largely on the quality of its managers, the need for a well-thought-out recruitment program is obvious. Some firms, particularly the smaller ones, rely on recruiting as the need occurs, either from within the firm or without. Recruiting from without has the advantage that training expenses are minimized when a person has already been trained by another firm. However, such a person will still need to learn about the company. Recruiting from within may produce good managers even without any conscious management training program, but many prospective managers will probably have failed to join the firm or will have left in frustration before opportunities for promotion occurred.

The larger firms, partly because of greater management personnel needs, usually have a well-thought-out management recruitment program. Such a program consists of:

1. *A decision as to the average number of prospective managers to recruit each year.* This decision is based on an analysis of the number and career stage of the firm's present managers; the expected growth of the firm; the annual turnover of managerial personnel (from retirement, resignation, and dismissal); and the expected dropout rate of the management trainees. Often, to improve its chances of obtaining good managers, a firm will select more trainees than needed to fill the probable number of future managerial openings.
2. *The development of sources for obtaining prospective managers.* These include colleges and universities, other employees within the firm, and other firms.
3. *A selection process.* This usually comprises: a preliminary personnel screening plus a written application from the candidate; persuasion of the candidate, if necessary, that the firm is a good one to work for; aptitude tests; and interviews with managers as a basis for the final evaluation.

The Management Trainee

It is common practice today for business firms to send members of their staffs to the campuses of Canadian colleges and universities to interview and recruit prospective managers. The students interviewed include those with an education in the liberal arts, as well as those with specific training in finance, marketing, engineering, and other specialized fields.

The following list, based on discussions with business interviewers, shows what attributes the ideal candidate should have.

A good general or specialized education
The ability to learn and to think logically and imaginatively
Ambition
A good character
The ability to make decisions
Self-confidence
A good appearance
The ability to communicate and to get along with people
Good physical and mental health.

It is not easy to determine, even in a series of interviews, whether a candidate possesses most of these attributes and will eventually make a good manager. Each interviewer has his or her own technique and ready stock of questions, ranging from "What can I do for you?" to "What do you expect to be doing five years from now?" The interview does, however, provide him or her with the opportunity for a personal judgment of the candidate which, with his or her background and experience in interviewing other candidates, is likely to be reliable. In appraising a candidate, many persons share the attitude expressed by one campus interviewer: "The best indication of what a person will do in the future is what he or she has done in the past." In other words, the prospective management trainee is judged to a considerable extent on what he or she has already done academically, in extra-curricular activities, and in summer or other employment.

Training of Managers

The training that a prospective manager will undergo, once hired, naturally varies from firm to firm. The possibilities are:
1. He or she is assigned various tasks (sometimes managerial) and left to learn on his or her own. This is the "sink or swim" theory of management training.
2. He or she is appointed *assistant to a manager* (a staff function) or *assistant manager* (a line function). The manager then guides and gradually trains him or her.
3. He or she is included in a definite management training program, to obtain experience in several departments by means of job rotation, will be given individual and group projects on which to work, and will receive classroom instruction within the firm in addition to normal on-the-job training. Gradually he or she is given more authority and responsibility, and his or her performance is methodically evaluated.

Many firms, to help broaden and deepen the education and training of their management personnel, arrange for their participation in selected courses. These courses, often lasting several days, are arranged by colleges, universities, and professional associations.

Management Training Techniques

Management training techniques used in the classroom include lectures, case problems, seminars, films, role-playing, group dynamics, and "in-basket" exercises.

Group Dynamics.
With this technique, participants form into small discussion groups that are usually *unstructured*—that is, they are without a definite purpose, plan, or agenda. During the ensuing discussion, a person observes how other members of the group behave, particularly when under stress, and by so doing obtains a better understanding of his or her own feelings and motivations and how he or she interacts with other members of a group. Since getting along with other people is an important requirement in a successful manager, it is

believed that the study of group dynamics (or how people interact with each other) may be helpful for the prospective manager.

In-basket Exercise. This is an on-the-job learning experience. As the manager or management trainee handles the problems that arrive in the in-basket or in-tray, he or she is observed closely by a superior and his or her decisions are evaluated. The exercise also includes an analysis of the results obtained from the decisions. Unlike other training methods, the in-basket exercise involves real problems and the manager being evaluated makes the analysis and decisions in his or her natural office environment.

Promotion

Once a person has started on the management ladder, the most important force that will push him or her upward is his or her merit in the jobs to which he or she has been assigned. Merit, from the business point of view, is "the ability to get things done." This includes not only the ability to do things oneself, but also the ability to get work done by others. Merit also includes the ability to accept orders from, and to communicate with, superiors. In firms where several promising candidates are suitable for a vacant position, seniority (length of service with the company) may be used as the ultimate criterion.

When the young manager's path upward is blocked—for example, by lack of company growth, by nepotism, or by few retirements—he or she must remain frustrated or look elsewhere. Some advice to ambitious management trainees is:

1. *Work hard.* Try to do every task well. This may mean that you have to take work home with you. Learn as much about your business as possible; continually try to broaden your mind by reading widely, listening to others, and taking courses; try to improve your ability to communicate.
2. *Be responsible.* When given a task, see it through to the end. Do not put off what is difficult. Also, do not run for help at the first obstacle you encounter—you are paid to think a problem through yourself.
3. *Be constructive.* Suggest in detail how to resolve a problem—for example, a misunderstanding with a customer; do not simply inform your boss that a problem exists.
4. *Be cheerful.*

The promotion of the experienced manager will also depend mainly on merit. However, because he or she is older, more experienced, and more highly paid, more will be expected of him or her. In making decisions which involve large sums of the company's money, he or she will be expected to have weighed carefully all the pros and cons—even if all the pertinent information is not available and the time in which to make the decision is uncomfortably short. In handling all the facets of the job, he or she will be expected to keep his or her head, even when under considerable nervous pressure. In working with colleagues (superiors as well as subordinates), he or she will be expected to communicate ideas, explanations and orders easily, both orally and in writing. And, in getting the firm's business done, he or she must be able to inspire confidence among those who work with and for him or her and be able to motivate them to give their best. In addition, the experienced manager must be willing, patiently and kindly, to train younger staff members, even though one of them may replace him or her at some time in the future. He or she must also be willing to read and to attend courses to keep his or her knowledge up to date.

Transfers

Many large companies believe that a manager should, during the course of a career, have work experience in various types of management jobs and in different work locations, sometimes even abroad. The potential manager should be prepared, therefore, to be periodically involved in new tasks, often in different geographical locations. Usually, this requirement is made clear to the potential manager before joining the company. For many persons, the prospect of new tasks and new locations offers excitement and challenge; many young college and university graduates are seeking to avoid the humdrum in their business careers. However, as a manager grows older, and he and his family develop community ties, the need to relocate may become onerous and result in resignation from a long-held job.

Appraisal of Managers

In order to determine whether a manager (or management trainee) should be promoted to a higher level within the organization, some method of appraising his or her performance must be used. Such an appraisal also help top management to decide what annual salary increases, if any, the manager should receive. It helps, furthermore, to identify the types of additional experience and training the managers should receive.

Sometimes, particularly in the smaller firms, the appraisal will be a continuous one, recorded only in the mind of the manager's superior, often the company president. However, in the medium- and large-size firm, *written appraisals* made on a periodic basis (for example, every three months) or on completion of a particular assignment are most common. Such written appraisals may be unstructured or structured. In the *unstructured*, or *free*, *report* the person doing the appraising indicates what appear to be the manager's good points and bad points. In the *structured*, or *controlled*, *report* the appraiser has to rate the manager according to a prescribed checklist of performance and ability—for example, knowledge of the job, reliability, judgment, ability to communicate, willingness to cooperate, leadership, and organizing ability. The manager is then given a rating for each of these areas—for example, A for outstanding; B for good; C for average; D for fair; and E for poor. Usually these reports are kept confidential. Sometimes, however, the manager is invited to discuss the report with an immediate superior or even to prepare a written evaluation of himself or herself as a basis for a joint review of performance.

KEY TERMS

Staffing

Recruitment of managers

Recruitment program

Management trainee

Management training techniques

Group dynamics

In-basket exercise

Promotion

Transfers

Appraisal of managers

REVIEW QUESTIONS

1. How are managers recruited? What is the best way?
2. What elements are to be found in the recruitment program of most large firms?
3. If you were looking for a management trainee, what would you seek in the candidates?
4. What kinds of questions can you expect to be asked at a job interview? What is the purpose of such questions?
5. How are managers trained? Can you suggest any better ways?
6. How does a person improve his or her chances of promotion?
7. Is it reasonable to expect a manager to accept transfers as a normal part of his or her business life? What complicating factors exist?
8. How are managers appraised? What do you consider to be the best approach?

CHAPTER 5
EFFECTIVE BUSINESS ORGANIZATION

CHAPTER OBJECTIVES

☐ To explain the need for effective organization in a business.

☐ To emphasize that, as a firm grows in size, the organization must change accordingly.

☐ To distinguish between line and staff personnel in a business organization.

☐ To show how departmentation serves the organizational needs of most large business firms.

☐ To demonstrate the use of organization charts and manuals.

☐ To indicate the role of a firm's informal organization in the daily operation of a business.

☐ To discuss the factors involved in designing an effective business organization.

☐ To distinguish between the basic types of business organization.

☐ To discuss the advantages and disadvantages of centralized or decentralized authority.

CHAPTER OUTLINE

5.1 Designing an Effective Organization

5.2 Basic Types of Organization

5.3 Centralization and Decentralization of Authority

UNIT 5.1: DESIGNING AN EFFECTIVE ORGANIZATION

Organizing is the management function of deciding for a business firm what departments and sections are to be established, the positions to be held, the duties of each position, and the authority and reporting relationship between the various positions, sections, departments, and branches. The overriding consideration in this task is how the organization will help the firm or department to achieve its plans and objectives. In practice, a manager's personal goals, such as increasing his or her importance in the organization, may lead to unnecessary creation of tasks and positions, popularly termed "empire-building."

Organization in the Small Business

In a one-person firm, the proprietor must take personal responsibility for every aspect of the business. Even with several employees, the organizational structure is simple. The proprietor makes all the main decisions on purchasing, production, personnel, finance, and sales, and there is *one line of command* as follows:

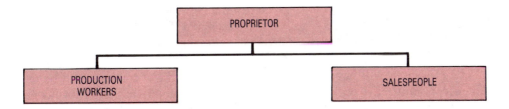

As the business grows, the owner finds it increasingly difficult to make all the decisions and to control all the employees. The finances may become neglected, and the employees may be left too much on their own. To resolve this problem, the proprietor will normally delegate authority, for example, by putting one employee in charge of production and another in charge of sales. Thus a *second level of management* is created with the bulk of employees no longer directly responsible to the owner. The organization structure has changed to the following:

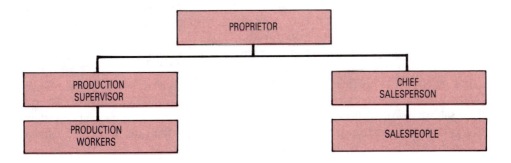

The structure in both cases is called a *line organization*, with authority and responsibility for performing the various tasks flowing directly from top to bottom, and each employee having only one immediate superior.

As the firm continues to grow, the proprietor may find that too much of his or her time, as well as that of the senior employees, is being taken up with such matters as finance. To permit himself or herself to devote more time to other matters such as developing new business contacts, and to let the key employees get on with their main functions of production and sales, the proprietor may hire a part-time accountant. This *specialist* or *staff* person would be included in the organization structure as follows:

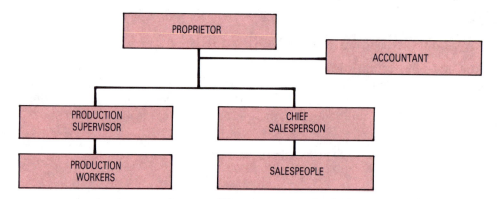

The proprietor will have to decide what authority the accountant will have. The accountant may, on the one hand, be given complete authority for his or her particular function of finance, over the production supervisor and chief salesperson. Under these conditions, he or she may give them orders as to the records they should keep. We then have what is known as *a functional organization* with each expert having authority for his or her special function and the employees having several bosses—one for each specialty. The accountant may, on the other hand, be allowed to give only advice. In such a case, we would have what is known as a *line-and-staff organization*, with staff specialists employed to advise the line managers.

Staff specialists are persons such as personnel managers, corporation lawyers, tax accountants, and systems analysts who are recruited by a firm on a full-time or part-time basis to provide specialized know-how and advice. The larger the firm, the more economical it is to employ such specialists so their cost can be spread over a larger volume of output and sales. In theory, their role is purely advisory; in practice, they may give orders as well as advice, depending on the firm, their position in it, and their personal authority.

For particular problems, such as planning for the coming year, the proprietor may feel the need to call in his or her accountant, production supervisor, and chief salesperson for discussion. This, in effect, is the use of a *committee system* as a part of the organization. Where this is a regular feature, it may be shown in the organization structure as follows:

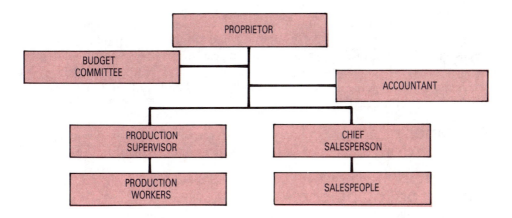

Organization in the Medium or Large Business

In the medium or large business, the various employees are grouped into departments and there is considerable use of staff specialists to supplement the efforts of these employees.

Departmentation

In our previous example of a small business firm, the two main activities were production and sales. However, in a medium- or large-size firm, many different types of business activity will be performed and on a much larger scale. Consequently, one of the first steps in organizing such a business is to decide how to group the firm's various business activities. This task is known as *departmentation*.

Function. The most usual form of departmentation is by function. Thus, departments may be established for such activities as marketing, production, finance, research and development, personnel, advertising, purchasing, and methods. This type of grouping is simple to understand and, more important, offers the firm the benefits of specialization of personnel and equipment. However, such functional specialization has the disadvantage that it encourages narrowness of outlook among employees and encourages them to put their own department's interests before those of the firm as a whole. Also, such departmentation may not be suitable if the firm's activities are spread over a wide geographical area.

Location. If a firm's marketing, production, and other activities are widely dispersed geographically, it may be more efficient to group them into regional branches than into centralized departments. Each branch will then have its own specialized functional departments. The advantages and disadvantages of decentralization of authority are discussed later in this chapter.

Product. Sometimes it is considered desirable to group a firm's activities according to the type of product manufactured. The use of product divisions is common among very large firms because of the desirability of decentralizing management authority in order to achieve best results. Each product division, in such an organization, serves as a separate profit centre and has a high degree of authority and responsibility for the marketing and production of its own products. Usually, some activities such as finance, industrial relations, and advertising are centralized at head office.

Customer. Occasionally, a firm will group certain of its activities by type of customer. Such specialization usually results in an improvement in the standard of service.

Process or Equipment. A firm may group all or part of its activities around a number of specialized manufacturing processes or types of equipment. Thus, for example, a manufacturing plant may be divided into a press shop, paint shop, and other such units.

Purpose. Employees may be grouped together for a particular purpose, such as developing a new product or opening a new branch.

Organization Charts and Manuals

The *organization structure* of a business is the way in which a firm's employees are arranged in relationship to each other to enable the firm to do business as efficiently as possible. This structure is sometimes set out diagrammatically in the form of an *organization chart*. Such a chart permits, at a glance, a basic understanding of the positions and relationships of the different persons and departments of the firm. It also helps to pinpoint any weaknesses in an organization. The usual chart is a *vertical chart*, comprising a number of rectangular boxes joined by unbroken lines and arranged in vertical or "pyramid" order. *Horizontal charts* contain the same basic information, the only difference being that the relationships are set out horizontally rather than vertically. This has the virtue (to some people) of downplaying the idea of superior-subordinate relationships and of different management levels. Another way to de-emphasize superior-subordinate relationships is by the use of *concentric charts*, with the top manager in the centre. All three types of organization chart are shown in Figure 5.1.

Organization charts do not tell a complete story. They do not spell out the duties which accompany each position. This is done in an *organization manual*, which states the duties of each position and the relationship, or line of command, between the different positions.

Each manager has control not only over various other persons within the firm, but also over various non-human resources such as funds, materials, and equipment. How the latter are organized comprises several topics (plant layout, materials control, methods analysis, and budgeting) which are not covered, except very indirectly, by the organization structure.

5.1 DESIGNING AN EFFECTIVE ORGANIZATION 177

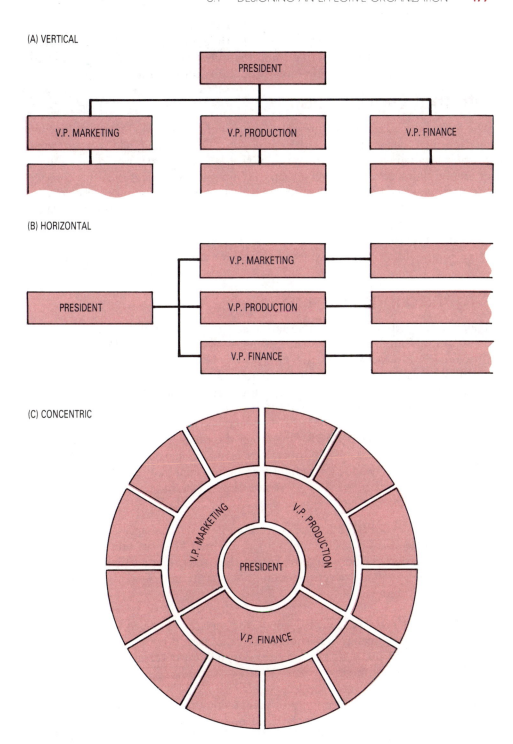

Figure 5.1 Types of Organization Chart

Organization charts and manuals are sometimes criticized, it should be noted, on the grounds that they (a) stifle employee initiative; (b) are quickly outdated; and (c) rarely present the real power structure within a firm.

Informal Organization

The formal organization of a firm does not completely describe the positions and relationships that exist among the employees. There are, in addition, informal relationships which develop among employees for various reasons: social contact, as among members of a bowling team; communication of information through the traditional grapevine; discussion of a real or imagined grievance; or participation in a common job, as by workers in the same office. Leaders emerge from these informal groups because of age, personality, knowledge, and/or experience. For a manager to be more effective, he or she should recognize the existence of these informal groups and, wherever possible, enlist the cooperation of their leaders.

Organizational Design

There is no single organization structure suited to the needs of every firm. An organization structure must be custom-made, and once established, cannot be permanently satisfactory. As the firm grows, alters, or declines, so must the organization structure change shape. If not, the organization can hamper efficiency rather than help it. The following factors should be considered when designing or redesigning the organization structure of a firm.

Number of Employees. The larger the number of employees, the more necessary it becomes to establish various levels of management in order that effective control may be exercised. The grouping of employees into departments and sections should be such as to ensure that all managers have a reasonable span of control.

Variety of Activities. The more complex the business, the greater the need to divide the line personnel into specialized fields in order to reap the benefits of division of labour; and the greater the need to employ highly specialized staff personnel, such as lawyers, accountants, statisticians, systems analysts, and computer programmers.

Variety of Products. If the goods and services produced by the firm vary considerably, the organization should take this into account. If, for example, there are different methods of production or marketing techniques, product divisions can be established.

Equipment Used. Grouping of equipment (for example, production machinery and computer equipment) would require separate organizational units. Thus, the manufacturing plant of a firm is often quite separate from the head office and sales branches.

Ease of Communication. The organization must take into acco[unt] required communication flows, including person-to-person encounters.

Geographical Distribution. If the manufacturing or marketing a[ctiv]ities of a firm are scattered geographically, this should also be reflected in the organization structure. Branch plants, each with a manager reporting to the appropriate vice-president at head office, would be a logical solution to such an organizational problem.

Principles of Effective Organization

Experience has proven that the following principles are conducive to effective organization.

1. *There should be clearly stated and non-conflicting objectives.* Each part of the firm should work towards a common goal, for example, maximizing profits. The individual departments' aims and the individual employees' aims should be in harmony with this overall objective. This is called the "unity of objective" principle. The grouping of employees into departments and sections should be planned so as to promote such cooperation.
2. *The duties of each position should be clearly defined.* Every person in the firm should know what tasks he or she is responsible for, and what authority he or she has to make decisions and give orders. However, some critics argue that too strict a job definition saps a manager's initiative.
3. *The relationship of each person to the rest of the organization should be clearly defined.* Each person should know who is his or her superior and who are his or her subordinates. In other words, each employee should know from whom to receive orders and to whom to give orders. He or she should also know of any lateral relationships, for example, a foreman's cooperative relationship with members of the industrial engineering department for the satisfactory completion of time studies, or with members of the inspection department for efficient inspection of production.
4. *Wherever possible, an employee should have no more than one immediate superior.* This is called the "unity of command" principle. If an employee has more than one boss, there is likely to be misunderstanding and resentment because of conflicting orders and possible excessive demands on the employee's time.
5. *The number of immediate subordinates to each manager should be kept within reasonable limits.* No hard-and-fast rule can be laid down as to how many immediate subordinates a manager can handle effectively. Much will depend on the complexity of the business, the amount of other, non-supervisory work the manager must perform, the occurrence of new problems, the experience and ability of the subordinates, the amount of guidance they require, and the amount of authority delegated to them. This principle is known as the "optimum span of control" or, in the case of shop-floor employees, the "effective unit of supervision."
6. *The number of levels of management should be kept to a minimum.* Every time

another level of management is added to an organization, the chain of command from top to bottom of the firm is lengthened. This can mean slower decisions, poorer communications and lower morale. The number of levels of management that a firm should have must be kept to a minimum consistent with the principle of optimum span of control. The larger the number of employees, the larger, inevitably, must be the number of levels of management.

7. *An organization should be adaptable to change.* The market does not remain static; neither should a firm and its organization. New departments should be added and old ones scrapped, as necessary. And more levels of management should be created when a growing number of employees overstrain the existing ones.

8. *Where one person in the organization is meant to be a check on another, he or she should not be subordinate to the other.* Thus, for example, plant inspectors should be independent of the foremen; the credit manager independent of the sales manager; and the auditor independent of the accountant.

9. *No one should, within reason, fail to make proper delegation of authority to his or her subordinates.* On paper, a firm may appear to be efficiently organized with various levels of management and reasonable spans of control. If, however, the president insists on deciding almost every problem, regardless of the level at which it occurs, the firm will be slow-moving and its managers nothing more than communications people. Such a centralization of authority can, of course, occur at other points within the firm, for example, the head of a division or department. If, on the other hand, the head of the firm or one of its departments delegates too much authority, the firm may lose leadership and cohesion. This can be equally bad.

10. *The activities of a firm should be grouped in such a way as to take advantage of any possible economies of scale.* By grouping similar activities (sometimes called *grouping by process*), five types of savings are possible: (a) technical economies, such as ability to use highly specialized equipment that would otherwise be unprofitable; (b) managerial economies, such as a specialized advertising department or personnel manager that would be unprofitable for, say, a string of independently operated retail stores or branch plants; (c) financial economies, such as cheaper borrowing; (d) purchasing economies, such as discounts on bulk purchases; and (e) workload economies, such as lower typing costs by use of a typing pool instead of typists for each section.

11. *A firm's organization structure should facilitate the communication of information required for managerial decision making and the communication of decisions and orders to subordinates.* In other words, a firm's organization structure and its communications network should be in harmony rather than conflict.

KEY TERMS

Organizing

Empire-building

Organization structure

Organization chart

Line of command
Delegation of authority
Line organization
Staff specialist
Functional organization
Line-and-staff organization
Committee system
Departmentation

Vertical chart
Horizontal chart
Concentric chart
Organization manual
Informal organization
Unity of command
Optimum span of control

REVIEW QUESTIONS

1. What does the management function of organizing involve? What should be the criterion for organizational changes? What can easily happen in practice? Refer in your answer to the phenomenon of "empire-building."
2. How would the organization of a typical small business change as the firm starts to grow and prosper?
3. What is meant by the term "line organization"? What modification usually soon takes place even in the small business? Why?
4. What are committees? Why are they popular even in a small organization? What purposes are they used for? What form do they take?
5. What is meant by the term "departmentation"? How soon does this usually occur in an organization? Why does it take place?
6. What are the various types of departmentation?
7. Explain the following terms: (a) organization structure, (b) organization chart, and (c) organization manual. What is the relationship among them?
8. What are the various basic types of organization charts? What is the most common type? What are the reasons for this? When would the other types be more appropriate?
9. What do an organization chart and an organization manual not reveal? Answer with actual or hypothetical examples.
10. Is an organization better off without organization charts and manuals? Discuss.
11. Ideally the informal organization should complement the formal one. In practice it is impossible. Discuss.
12. What factors must be taken into account in designing or redesigning a firm's organization? Give an example of an organization affected by any three factors.
13. What is a "reasonable span of control" for a manager? Why might it vary from one organization to another?
14. What would be the typical organization of a large manufacturing firm with production in one province and sales elsewhere in Canada and abroad?

15. What is meant by the "unity of objective" principle of organizational design? Explain with a real or hypothetical example. What might happen in a firm if this principle is not observed?
16. "Too strict a job definition tends to sap a manager's initiative." Does this argument outweigh the advantages of clear definition of each person's duties? Discuss.
17. "The relationship of each person to the rest of the organization should be clearly defined." Why? What can happen if it is not? Give examples.
18. What is meant by the "unity of command" principle of organizational design? Is it (a) desirable and (b) feasible? Discuss with examples.
19. "Increasing the number of levels of management in an organization is an effective way of improving morale as it increases the opportunities for promotion." Discuss.
20. "An organization should be adaptable to change." Why? Answer with examples.
21. Why in a business organization should the credit manager not be a subordinate of the sales manager? Would not the firm's sales efforts be more successful if he or she were?
22. When should a manager delegate authority for certain of his or her tasks to subordinates?
23. What economies of scale can a firm obtain by grouping many of its activities?
24. How is the need for information for decision making reflected in a firm's organization structure?

CASE PROBLEMS

MILLER DRUGS INC.

Preparing an organization chart

Miller Drugs Inc. is a large Canadian manufacturer of patent medicines and prescription drugs. Its manufacturing plant is divided into the following departments:
1. *Production*—a production manager, a secretary, a compounding supervisor, 4 compounders, a production supervisor, a production clerk, 2 material handlers, 3 foreladies, 32 female workers, and 2 janitors.
2. *Engineering*—a plant engineer, an assistant plant engineer, a head line mechanic, 5 line mechanics, a utilities mechanic, a utility serviceman, a machine shop mechanic, and 2 equipment mechanics.
3. *Quality control*—a chief analyst, an assistant analyst, a technician, and a sample-inspector.
4. *Purchasing*—a purchasing agent, a secretary, a buyer, a steno-clerk, a purchasing trainee, and a clerk-typist.
5. *Traffic*—a traffic manager, a secretary, a traffic supervisor, a warehouse supervisor, a shipper/receiver, and 5 stockmen.

6. *Accounting*—an accounting manager, a secretary, an accountant, 2 junior accountants, a ledger clerk, 2 cash clerks, a payroll clerk, and a receptionist.
7. *Personnel*—a personnel manager, a secretary, a senior office services clerk, an office services clerk, a junior offset machine operator, and a nurse.

The heads of the various departments are responsible to the plant manager, who in turn is responsible to the company president.

Assignment
1. Draw an organization chart for this manufacturing plant.
2. Explain briefly what you consider to be the duties of each department.
3. What type of organization structure does this plant have?
4. Why is the personnel manager responsible for office services? Who else might be responsible for these in other firms?

CAMPBELL STORES LTD.
Improving the organization of a chain of clothing stores

Campbell Stores Ltd. is a chain of 23 small stores spread throughout Ontario, specializing in the sale of medium-to-high-price clothing for men, women, and children. The chain was founded in London, Ontario, in 1892 by Ian Campbell, an importer and wholesaler of British woollen goods. The firm's new head ofice is still located in London, a short distance from the original offices and warehouse. The firm's main warehouse is now, however, situated on the outskirts of the city.

Campbell Stores Ltd., after many years of steady growth, is at present organized as shown in Figure 5.2.

In accordance with normal practice, the president of the firm is responsible to the board of directors for the day-to-day management of Campbell Stores Ltd. Mr. Francis Bush, the President, is also a director of the firm and takes part in a small directors' committee that determines basic operating policies and long-range plans. Major decisions made by this executive committee include approving the establishment of new branch stores and raising money for expansion by debenture issues.

The Vice-President, Finance, Mr. Harold Peabody, is responsible for preparing the firm's overall operating and capital budgets for each six-month period. These are reviewed by the directors' executive committee and then submitted in their amended form to the board of directors for approval. At the executive committee meeting, the president sees the budget for the first time and often persuades other members to make substantial changes. Mr. Peabody is also responsible for all accounting activities, including the preparation of income statements and balance sheets; for the auditing of branch store accounts; for customer credit and collection; and for all real estate operations. The last activity has become more important in recent years as the firm is now embarked on an expansion program which involves the acquisition of three additional branch stores each year.

Jack Foster, the Vice-President, Operations, and possibly the busiest man in

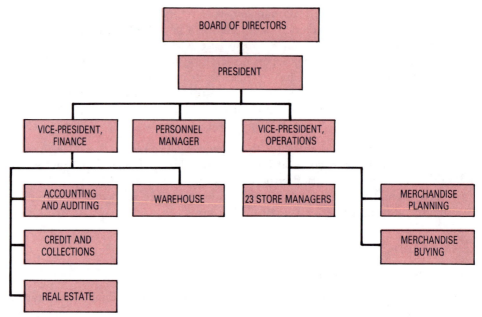

Figure 5.2 Organization Chart of Campbell Stores Ltd.

the firm, is in charge of all store managers. His task is to see that each store carries out the various plans and policies decided at head office. In particular, he must watch that budgeted expenditures are not exceeded, that store sales are conducted as arranged, that goods are not marked down more than permitted, and that the monthly advertising and display allowance given to each store manager is effectively utilized. He is also responsible to the president for merchandise planning, merchandise buying, and the warehouse.

Under merchandise planning, Mr. Foster draws up, with the aid of his staff, merchandising plans for the chain as a whole, for each store of the chain, and for each department within each store. These plans cover sales, purchases, markdowns, turnover, and gross profit.

With regard to merchandise buying, Mr. Foster makes sure that the monthly amounts budgeted for each store are not exceeded but entrusts much of the actual day-to-day buying supervision to Susan Schafer, the chain's head buyer. Ms. Schafer oversees nine buyers, one for each of the following types of goods: ladies' coats and dresses; ladies' sportswear; men's and boys' wear; girls' and children's wear; ladies' gloves and hosiery; ladies' accessories; piece goods; linens and domestics; and gift wear and house furnishings. Each good purchased is shipped by the Canadian and U.S. manufacturer to the firm's warehouse where it is then divided and sent out to the branch stores on the basis of last year's sales of this or a similar item. The Warehouse Superintendent, Mr. Fred Lipski, who is responsible to Mr. Peabody, is extremely proud of the efficient way in which the various goods are controlled and handled.

The manager of each branch store is also responsible to Mr. Jack Foster, the Vice-President, Operations, for the efficient running of his store. This includes the recruitment, training, and supervision of staff; maintenance of fixtures; the receipt and marking of new merchandise; the processing of invoices; the development of customer charge accounts; participation in meetings of local businessmen; and other public relations work.

In each store, the various department heads are responsible for: displaying merchandise; receiving new merchandise from the marking room; taking monthly counts of the various items of merchandise; supervising counter staff; serving customers; handling complaints; and writing up orders which, after the approval and signature of the store manager, are forwarded to the appropriate head-buyer.

Each month, after stock has been physically counted, a sales forecast is made for the next month. Orders for additional merchandise are then sent to head office, which arranges for the goods to be shipped from the warehouse to the branch store concerned.

Assignment
1. How is this retail firm organized? Draw an organization chart.
2. How might the firm's organization be improved?

UNIT 5.2: BASIC TYPES OF ORGANIZATION

In this unit, we look more closely at the characteristics, advantages, and disadvantages of the basic types of business organization.

Line Organization

This is an organization in which there is a direct (sometimes called *scalar*) chain of command from top to bottom of the firm, with each employee (including managers) having only one immediate superior; and in which there are no staff specialists to give advice or orders to persons working in the main activities of the business such as production and sales. Such an organization is usually found only in the small firm which does not find it worthwhile to employ staff specialists (Figure 5.3).

The *advantages* of the line plan of organization are:
1. The authority and responsibility of each person in the firm are clearly defined, thus helping to eliminate the evasion of responsibility for a task poorly done.
2. The relationships between employees are easily understood, thus reducing possible confusion.
3. The simple lines of communication facilitate quick decisions and the flow of information up and down the organization structure.
4. With only one immediate superior for each employee discipline is improved.
5. A certain degree of specialization is possible.

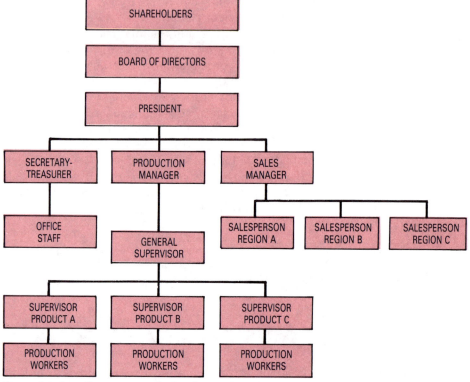

Figure 5.3 Line Organization of a Small Manufacturing Firm

The *disadvantages* of the line plan of organization are:
1. Each department is a specialized, self-contained unit, with no provision for assistance or advice from outside. Thus, the sales manager must do all the personnel work for his or her department.
2. As business becomes more complex, highly trained and specialized staff personnel are needed to research and solve business problems. The line plan makes no allowance for this.
3. As a firm grows, too many duties tend to be thrust upon each line manager. Many of these duties—for example, wage calculations and payments—could be more efficiently done by one person or department for the whole firm. This would give the line manager more time for his or her main duties.

Line-and-Staff Organization

This type of organization is the one most commonly used in business. Personnel are divided into line and staff positions.

Line personnel are those employees engaged in the primary activities of the firm, such as manufacturing refrigerators, lending money, or serving food.

Staff personnel are those employed to enable the line personnel to carry out their tasks more efficiently—by providing engineering, financial, legal, and personnel services. Strictly speaking, staff personnel may give only advice; they have no authority to give orders, except to their own staff subordinates. In practice, many staff departments are also given functional authority for certain matters.

An example of a line-and-staff organization is shown in Figure 5.4. In this organization, all the operating and staff departments are responsible directly to an executive vice-president. Sometime the advisory role of the staff departments with respect to the line departments is shown by a broken line. However, most firms omit this from their organization charts to avoid overcomplicating them.

Line and staff personnel, we should emphasize, have horizontal as well as vertical relationships with other members of the organization. These can be called *colleague relationships*—between different members of the same department; or *collateral relationships*—between members of different departments. Without such co-operation, the efficiency of a firm would be drastically reduced.

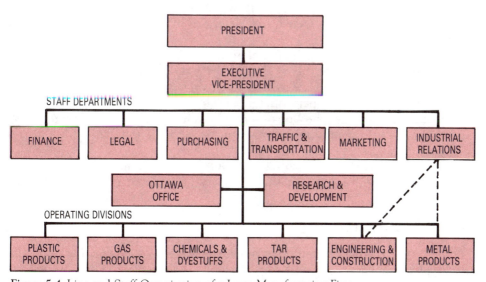

Figure 5.4 Line-and-Staff Organization of a Large Manufacturing Firm

The *advantages* of the line-and-staff plan of organization are:
1. More specialization of duties is possible than in the line structure. Thus there may be a legal department to handle all legal matters.
2. The chain of command remains direct, and each employee continues to have only one immediate superior. There is no overlapping of authority.
3. The line personnel can obtain specialized advice and other help, such as hiring a new employee, as and when required. Such advice should ensure sounder decisions.

The *disadvantages* of the line-and-staff plan of organization are:

1. Possible friction between the line and the staff personnel. This may arise because: the staff personnel may try to give orders instead of advice; the line personnel may arbitrarily try to shift some of their work onto the staff personnel; or educational differences between the two groups may cause conflict.
2. The cost to the firm of having staff specialists on its payroll.
3. A possible slowing-up of the decision-making process through the necessity of waiting for staff studies.
4. The danger of undermining the authority of the line managers.

Functional Authority

A staff specialist may, in some business firms, be given a dual role: to provide advice on some matters and to give orders on others. The authority of a staff specialist to give orders concerning his or her particular specialization, such as finance, to line personnel, is called *functional authority*. A personnel manager may be permitted not only to advise the line organization on how to handle employees' grievances, but also to issue definite orders as to the procedure. This functional authority is considered to be delegated by the line superior of the staff specialist.

The *advantages* of giving functional authority to staff personnel are that the line superior is relieved of this work; and the staff specialist is best qualified by his or her specialist knowledge to give orders on matters in his or her particular field—such as financial or personnel procedures.

The *disadvantages* are: the line subordinate now has more than one superior, and this can cause confusion and resentment, and friction can easily develop between line and staff persons.

Very occasionally, a firm will adopt a full-blown functional plan of organization. In Figure 5.5 for example, each supervisor reports to five superiors, one for each function.

Use of Committees

A committee is a group of employees (usually managers) called together to discuss and resolve problems; to report to a superior on work being accomplished; to enable a superior to give orders and motivate subordinates (sometimes called a "briefing session"); or to foster good employee morale by allowing representatives of the rank-and-file employees to meet with top or middle management to discuss problems.

The committee is superimposed on the line or line-and-staff organization. It is not an alternative to them. Examples of committees are: the board of directors of a corporation; an executive committee to make top management decisions; and a budget committee to approve the sales forecast and planned expenditures for the coming year.

The *advantages* of using a committee are:
1. It may be used as a co-ordinating device to help management carry out its tasks.

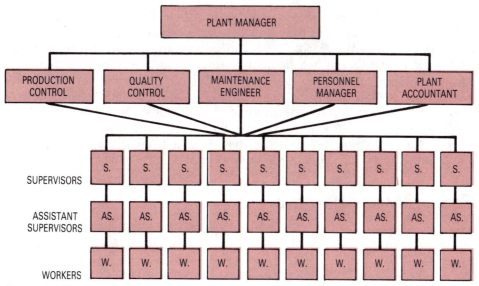

Figure 5.5 Functional Plan of Organization for a Manufacturing Plant

2. Several minds may be better than one in solving a problem or recommending a course of action. Also, specialist knowledge can be drawn upon.
3. Allowing persons who must carry out orders to participate in making them may be a good means of motivation.
4. The committee can serve as an informal means of controlling the work of subordinates.
5. It can be a useful means of transmitting information.
6. Responsibility for decisions is shared.

The *disadvantages* of using a committee are:
1. Too many minds may slow the decision-making process.
2. An original idea or recommendation may easily become distorted by compromise in the process of gaining acceptance.
3. Responsibility for a decision is not so easily pinpointed.
4. The cost in time and money may be high.

Matrix Organization

Usually, a firm's employees are grouped into major functional areas such as marketing, production, and finance. However, if the firm undertakes large, technically complex projects such as ship, aircraft, or power dam construction, it will need to co-ordinate the activities of many specialists and other employees drawn from the various functional departments. To do this, the firm will usually appoint a project co-ordinator. For the duration of the project, the employees chosen from the various departments will be working for both the project co-ordinator and their usual department heads. When the project is completed, they will resume, full-time, their previous departmental duties.

The type of organization that exists during the project, with many of the firm's employees responsible to two different bosses, is known as a *matrix organization*, because the lines of authority and responsibility run horizontally as well as vertically. An example of such an organization is shown in Figure 5.6. As long as there is good co-operation between project co-ordinator and the functional department heads, and as long as competing demands are not placed on the employee's time, this type of organization may serve well—particularly for relatively minor projects such as the removal of a department to new quarters.

Project Management

Although, with the matrix organization, a project may be given official priority in the employee's time over departmental duties, conflicts inevitably arise between the demands of the project coordinator and those of the department heads. As a result, the employee, torn between two loyalties, often does not give of his or her best. Also, the project co-ordinator, working with employees whose first loyalty may still lie elsewhere, may not be able to obtain the degree of control over operations that he or she would like. As a result of these two factors, the project, instead of being completed on time, may be subject to confusion, substandard work, extra costs, and delay. Furthermore, the firm may lose money through penalties for failure to deliver on the agreed completion date.

To reduce the risk of such a fiasco, many firms avoid the matrix organization and use instead what is called *project management*. In this type of organization, the employees chosen from the functional departments (or newly recruited from outside for the particular project) are placed at the full-time disposal of the project manager and are answerable to no one but him or her for the duration of the project. Such an organization eliminates the possibility of conflict between the project manager and the functional department heads. In fact, in some industries, such as construction, where projects are the main activity, there may be very few functional departments. However, most project-type firms find that it pays to retain some functional areas (for example, accounting, legal, and office services) on a company-wide basis to avoid duplication of work.

KEY TERMS

Line organization

Direct chain of command

Line-and-staff organization

Line personnel

Staff personnel

Colleague relationships

Collateral relationships

Functional authority

Use of committees

Matrix organization

Project management

Project-type firm

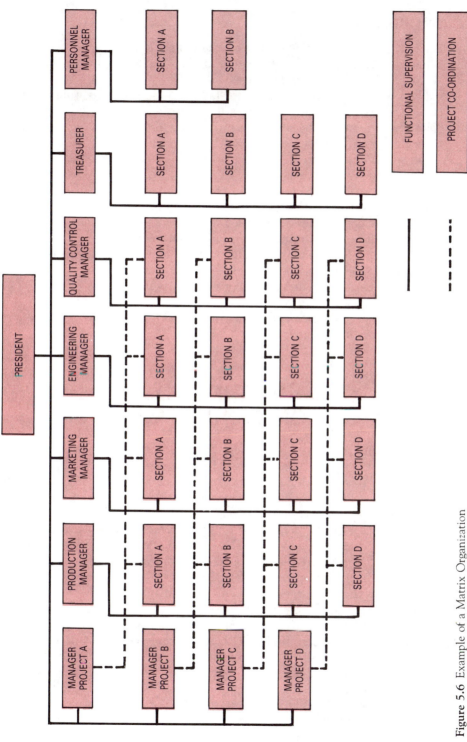

Figure 5.6 Example of a Matrix Organization

REVIEW QUESTIONS

1. What are the basic characteristics of a line organization?
2. What are the possible advantages to a firm of such an organization?
3. What are the possible disadvantages?
4. Explain what is meant by a line-and-staff organization. Why would a firm change from a line organization to a line-and-staff one?
5. "Horizontal relationships are usually just as important in an organization as vertical ones." Explain and discuss.
6. "Staff specialists can create just as many problems as they solve." Explain and discuss.
7. What is meant by a functional plan or organization? Why is this type of organization rarely used? When is it most appropriate?
8. Explain how committees can be used to improve the organizational efficiency of a firm. Give examples of such committees.
9. Compare the advantages and disadvantages of using a committee rather than a president for the management of a business enterprise.
10. What is a "matrix organization"? For what purposes is it used? Give examples.
11. What is project management? How does it differ from matrix organization? When is it used and why?

UNIT 5.3: CENTRALIZATION AND DECENTRALIZATION OF AUTHORITY

A manager has the right to make business decisions and to command reasonable obedience from his or her subordinates. This *authority*, in the case of a corporation, is vested by the shareholders in the board of directors. The board then delegates authority for the day-to-day management of the business to a president, who, in turn, delegates part of his or her authority to subordinates, and so on down the chain of command. The sanctions to enforce obedience include transfer, dismissal, and loss of promotion. However, the good manager will employ these only as a last resort. Usually his or her own personality and abilities will ensure the respect and co-operation of subordinates.

Responsibility is the obligation of each employee (manager or other) to perform, to the best of that person's ability, the duties assigned to him or her. The higher the level of management, the greater is the degree of responsibility, because the decisions affect more persons and more material resources. A manager cannot properly accept responsibility for a task unless he or she has the authority to carry it out. Authority and responsibility must therefore accompany each other if the organization is to be effective. Sometimes the term *accountability* is used to denote a person's responsibility to a superior for the performance of his or her duties. Accountability also implies that the subordinate must be willing to accept reward or rebuke for his or her actions.

Delegation of Authority

We have said previously that no one in an organization should, within reason, fail to make proper delegation of authority to subordinates. *Delegation*, or the transfer to a subordinate of the authority for carrying out a task, means that the manager who does that delegating is removing some of the firm's work from his or her own shoulders to those of a subordinate. However, the delegating manager retains the ultimate responsibility for satisfactory completion of the task. Thus, he or she cannot delegate a task and promptly forget about it. There must be some method—for example, a reporting system—to ensure that he or she is informed as to the satisfactory completion of the delegated work.

Reasons for Delegating Authority. Delegation is not just a matter of pushing one's own work onto someone else. It is, rather, a matter of priorities. The company president is not paid to clean the offices—his or her time is far too valuable. He or she must delegate authority for completion of this task to someone else. A person can only do so much without suffering a nervous breakdown or heart attack. Consequently, a manager must constantly adjust priorities and ration his or her efforts. As he or she rises higher in the organization, the decisions and other managerial tasks become more and more critical. Unless the various tasks in the enterprise are assessed as to their relative importance, and authority and responsibility for their completion delegated to the various levels of management, a firm cannot operate properly. Sometimes the owner-manager of a once-small business will try to continue to make all the decisions—even though the firm may have grown a hundred-fold since its inception. And, because of the lack of delegation, the business can slowly grind to a halt.

Another reason for delegating authority is the high degree of technical knowledge or specialized skill required for certain tasks. Thus, for example, the company president (who may be a marketing expert) may be unable to run the company's finance department. And the production manager may be a hopeless marketing head.

A third reason for delegating authority is the need for managerial development. Only if lower-level managers are given experience in decision making will they ever become suitable replacements for higher-level managers. Such experience can be obtained only if real authority and responsibility for important tasks are given to them.

Managers may, however, be reluctant to delegate authority because they believe that only they can make the correct decisions or do the job properly or, conversely, that the subordinate may do a better job and so threaten the superior's position.

Centralized Management

Centralization is the term used to describe the retention of most of the decision-making authority of a firm in the hands of top management at head office.

In a firm with *centralized management*, the most important marketing, production, and other business decisions are made by the vice-presidents or other top managers at head office. The managers of the various departments and branch plants, although consulted, must abide by the top management decisions—for example, sales and production targets, new investment expenditure, and advertising campaigns. However, the plant managers still have the responsibility for operating their plants efficiently and achieving the various sales, production, cost and profit goals set by head office. Subject to these goals, they possess, therefore, considerable decision-making authority with regard to plant operation. They also have an important role in carrying out such other management functions as directing, controlling, communicating, and motivating—without which the head office goals could never be achieved.

Improvements in Transportation and Communications.

In recent years, improved air travel facilities and cheaper, faster communications have meant that head office managers can exercise much closer personal control over branches—thus facilitating greater centralization of authority. By frequent visits, head office personnel can also obtain a much better understanding of local conditions, local problems, and the local manager's point of view. Of course, the question of the degree of decentralization of authority is vital for a firm with many plants and branches scattered geographically. However, it can be equally vital for a large firm located in only one place.

In Figure 5.7 we show the organization chart of a business firm with centralized management.

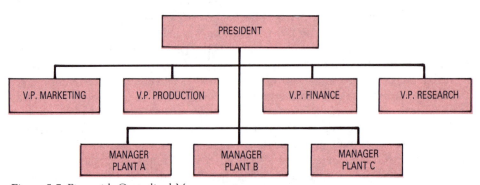

Figure 5.7 Firm with Centralized Management

Decentralized Management

Decentralization is the systematic delegation of a large amount of authority by the president and other chief officers of a company to the middle- and lower-level managers of a company's various departments, divisions, or branches.

In a firm with *decentralized management*, the managers of the various departments and branch plants (or retail stores) are given a great deal of decision-making authority in all the major functional areas. The only activity retained by top management is overall co-ordination and control. Such a high degree of decentralization is found, first of all, in many multinational corporations which have branch plants scattered overseas—where local conditions and problems differ greatly from one country to another. Decentralized management is also used in many modern business *conglomerates*—firms which control, through majority share ownership, a large number of very different types of manufacturing plants or other business enterprises, mainly within the home country.

The board of directors of the typical multinational corporation or conglomerate usually tries to keep a top-notch president and troubleshooting team at head office and lets the president of each subsidiary enterprise get on, in his or her own way, with the running of the firm. However, each branch or subsidiary is viewed by head office as an individual *profit centre* and its president must render regular, frequent financial statements to head office and be prepared to explain in detail what has transpired. As long as a good earnings record and cash flow are maintained, the president of the subsidiary remains otherwise free from head office interference. However, if profits start to decline, or solvency becomes impaired, head office will not only want to know why, but will proffer advice as to what remedial action to take. If necessary, the president may even be replaced.

In Figure 5.8 we show a firm which has practically all its management activities decentralized.

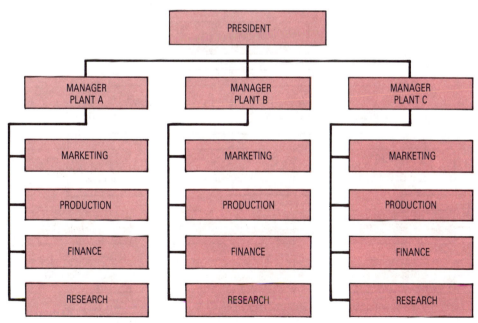

Figure 5.8 Firm with Decentralized Management

The *advantages* of decentralization, in the case of a branch manager, are: it provides an incentive for him or her to do a good management job; problems concerning the branch can be decided more quickly; and local and branch conditions can be better taken into account. Possible *disadvantages* are: duplication in each branch of such facilities as advertising and research; and costly mistakes which could be made by branch managers who exercise too much initiative.

Compromise between Centralization and Decentralization

In practice, most firms are neither highly centralized nor highly decentralized—they are somewhere in between. Some activities (not necessarily management ones), such as research and development, are better performed on a centralized basis; others, such as recruitment of clerical and secretarial staff, are better performed in a decentralized way. Thus, to avoid duplication of facilities, many firms with branch plants carry out a number of staff functions at head office, such as recruitment of management personnel, advertising, engineering, and marketing research, and delegate a large amount of authority for the operating functions to the branch manager. This is a compromise between centralization and decentralization.

In Figure 5.9, we show a firm which has decentralized only some of its management activities.

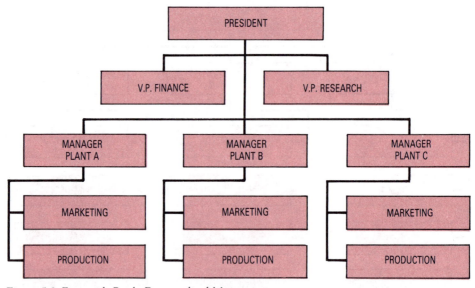

Figure 5.9 Firm with Partly Decentralized Management

KEY TERMS

Authority   Decentralization

Responsibility   Profit centres

Accountability

Delegation of authority

Centralization

Advantages of decentralization

Disadvantages

REVIEW QUESTIONS

1. What is "authority"? Compare the authority of a parent, a teacher, and a business manager. How necessary is authority?
2. Distinguish between responsibility and accountability. Give examples.
3. What is meant by the delegation of authority in a business firm? Why is it necessary? Are responsibility and accountability delegated at the same time?
4. Why are managers sometimes reluctant to delegate authority? Are their reasons valid?
5. Prepare two diagrams showing the difference between a centralized and a decentralized organization.
6. Why is it easier nowadays for a firm to operate with a highly centralized management even though many parts of the organization are geographically dispersed?
7. The profit-centre approach is a highly successful form of decentralized management. Explain and discuss.
8. Contrast the advantages and disadvantages of decentralized management.

CASE PROBLEM

POHLMANN EQUIPMENT CO. LTD.

The need for decentralization in management

The Pohlmann Equipment Co. Ltd., a manufacturer of electrical and electronic assemblies for military and civilian aircraft, was founded in Toronto in 1948 by Kurt Pohlmann, an immigrant originally from Dresden, East Germany. Since that time, the firm has grown from 12 employees to 250, and from a plant of 325 m^2 to one of 4700 m^2. By ensuring careful quality control from the very beginning of his firm, Pohlmann has built up a reputation as a supplier of excellent-quality, reliable products. Customers now include such firms as Avro, Canadair, DeHavilland, and Orenda Engines. Kurt Pohlmann is the major shareholder, the chairman of the board of directors, and the president of the firm.

Because much of the company work is done under federal government contract, Kurt Pohlmann makes frequent visits to Ottawa. He handles all contract negotiations in Ottawa on behalf of the firm and has established good relations with the government officials involved in purchasing. Other sales are developed by three regional salesmen, Jim Edwards in Toronto, Mike Rademacher in Vancouver, and Fred Kutz in Halifax. Rademacher and Kutz report to Edwards who in turn is responsible to Pohlmann. Each regional salesman has an assistant salesman.

Edwards also has responsibility for advising Pohlmann on the amount and use of the firm's advertising budget. The firm's advertising usually takes the form of direct mailing of brochures to prospective customers and insertions in trade magazines. Advertising has become particularly important in recent years as efforts have been made by the firm to develop a new product line: fuel oil filters of better than normal quality, for industrial as well as military use.

On the production side of the business, Kurt Pohlmann acts as plant manager. When he is in Toronto he meets every afternoon with the supervisor of each of the seven production departments and two service and overhaul departments to discuss plans and performance. In his absence the supervisors (who have been with the firm for many years) carry on by themselves. For important decisions, Pohlmann is contacted in Ottawa or wherever he may be. Very occasionally, a delay or even the loss of an order occurs because Pohlmann cannot be reached in time.

Pohlmann has strong views about labour. His firm pays a wage that is slightly above average for the types of workers that he employs; pays fully, or in part, the employees' contributions to unemployment insurance, hospitalization and medical insurance, Canada Pension Plan, and a private employee retirement pension plan; and provides the statutory vacations and holidays. In return, Pohlmann expects from his workers a high degree of personal loyalty. Once a week, Kurt Pohlmann makes a point of walking around the plant and meeting and talking to employees. Some weeks ago, a few of his most trusted employees reported to him that efforts were being made to unionize the firm. So far, no appeal has been made by the union concerned to the Ontario Labour Relations Board for certification as the employees' bargaining agent. The hiring and training of workers is entrusted by Pohlmann to his supervisors. However, if a worker has a grievance, he must bring it directly to Pohlmann the first thing in the morning. Sometimes, Pohlmann in settling grievances will overrule earlier decisions by his supervisors.

In addition to sales and production, the firm has departments for purchasing, accounting, production control, engineering and research, inspection and quality control (including two RCAF inspectors) methods, and for receiving, storage, and shipping combined. The heads of these departments (except sales and production) report to the executive vice-president. The chief storekeeper (responsible for receiving, storage, and shipping) and the chief plant engineer (responsible for engineering and research) also take orders from Kurt Pohlmann.

The executive vice-president of the company, appointed last year, is Hans Pohlmann, the 26-year-old son of the founder. Hans, after completing a business program at college, has worked in practically all departments of the business to obtain training and experience. Sometimes his attempts to prove his worth by outperforming everyone else have aroused considerable enmity. In fact, several promising young men have left the company after only a few months' stay partly because of this. There has also been a lot of muttering among the older men, both in the office and in the plant.

Assignment

1. Draw an organization chart of the company, showing each position and department and (where indicated in the case description) the person occupying it.
2. Explain the strengths and weaknesses of this organization, noting any principles of organization that appear to have been violated.

READING

King of the Real Estate Jungle

A.E. LePage [now Royal LePage] is now a giant in a field dominated by voracious pygmies. Can it still act lean and hungry when it's so fat and successful?

BY GARY WEISS

Source: *Canadian Business Magazine*. Used by permission of Gary Weiss.

The setting is functional modern—all whites and greys and hard edges. At the centre of attention a slim, well-dressed young man is proclaiming the fundamentals. He's polished, professional, sincere—his hands moving just so, eye contact perfect, voice well modulated. No fanatic he; his sermon is in the bright, up-tempo mode of the talk-show evangelists. But rather than a new faith, he's preaching the joys of a much more secular pursuit. The speaker is Roy St. John, manager of residential training in Ontario for real estate broker A.E. LePage Ltd. And the setting is the company's new $100,000 training centre in the basement of one of its suburban Toronto sales offices.

Every new member of LePage's Ontario sales staff undergoes an intensive four days of such sessions, which include role playing, using instant playback videotape equipment—and sermons. Agents outside Ontario get the same message in local offices. Refreshers are suggested for those with lagging quotas or sagging egos. According to LePage, this inspirational training has kept turnover to a minimum and commissions to a maximum.

Such modern management practices as formal sales training are an innovation in the brokerage business. Not so long ago the point was to sell anything you could, any way you could. Management wasn't complicated, since few brokers had more than a handful of agents. Typical real estate agents (at least, in the public perception) were first cousins to hawkers of snake-oil. But in the past decade the business has changed. Though the independents are still a strong force in the non-residential end of brokerage business, the residential sector is increasingly dominated by national and international firms, especially the trust companies and, increasingly, the franchise operations such as Century 21 Real Estate Corp. and Realty World Ltd. Those giant concerns practise the same technique that's made the chain restaurants and hotels so successful: aggressive advertising and careful training to build up a reputation for dependable, trustworthy service.

That technique is working spectacularly well for LePage. The company was founded by Albert Edward LePage in 1913 after he quit his father's mail-order business in a huff. One of his less successful properties was Toronto's celebrated white elephant, Casa Loma: the city expropriated it for back taxes before he was able to complete a deal. His other transactions fared better; his company is today the largest diversified real estate business in Canada, and perhaps the third-largest brokerage firm in the world. It's exceeded in size by California-based Coldwell, Banker & Co. of which it owns 21%. In Canada, only Royal Trust Co. is bigger, with $126 million in real estate fees and commissions on $2.8 billion in brokerage business last year [1979]. LePage's revenues last year [1979] were $104 million: $77 million on residential brokerage of $2 billion and $27 million on commercial transactions totalling $600 million. Measured by dollar volume, LePage handles roughly one-tenth of all the real estate transactions in the country.

Besides its brokerage revenues, LePage collects fees for services as diverse as property development and management, appraisals, research and planning, consulting, shopping centre development and management, interim financing, asset management and land assemblies (including the Toronto-Dominion Centre, the Eaton Centre and the Royal Bank Plaza). Its investment in Coldwell, Banker added $2.5 million in earnings (before carrying costs) last year. Other revenue derives from Canlea Ltd., a real estate partnership with the Canadian Imperial Bank of Commerce, and its subsidiary Amlea Inc. in the US; from a share in Toronto College Street Centre Ltd., the $45 million redevelopment of the former Eaton's College Street store which LePage manages; and from several smaller properties. Profits last year were $4.2 million, excluding earnings from Coldwell, Banker and its other equity interests. The company doesn't make public formal reports yet, though it admits it has an increasing responsibility to do so.

"I never cease to be amazed at the breadth of our activities," says president and chief operating officer William Dimma. Dimma's presence at LePage is another sign of changing times in the brokerage business: the mild-mannered Bill Dimma never sold anything in his life. But he has a formidable reputation as a manager—a skill that chairman and CEO Gordon Gray, 52, was astute enough to realize the company badly needed in order to weld its 3,500 entrepreneurial agents to a common cause. Gray chose the 52-year-old Dimma over such hopeful LePage executives as David Colville-Reeves, senior vice-president for commercial development and a whiz at downtown acquisitions; David Crawford, national director for investments; and shopping centre expert Geoffrey Still, president of A.E. LePage Western Ltd.

Why did Gray pick Dimma? "The company is just too big for one person to run the real estate aspects, marketing and employee philosophy, plus administration on a day-to-day basis as well," says Gray. "There aren't many businesses where the administrative component is as big as this. Yet real estate brokerage isn't a particularly good training ground for the classical type of administrator."

Dimma joined the company after three years as president and chief operating officer of Torstar Ltd. and Toronto Star Newspapers Ltd. For two years before that, he was dean of the Faculty of Administrative Studies, York University, a post he took after a year as an associate at Woods Gordon and Co. and three years earning a business doctorate at Harvard. But he's offended at the suggestion that he's an academic: he spent 21 years at Union Carbide Canada Ltd., including three as executive vice-president. At LePage, he's responsible for the administration of the company, and all senior line managers report directly to him.

Keeping his army of agents revved up and on the move is a job that Dimma regards as top priority. And that creates something of a paradox. Real estate brokerage is an industry in which every company has the same product; the only difference is the people. But in spite of the inspirational seminars, successful real estate sales-people can't be mass-produced. They are inevitably independent-minded and entrepreneurial. They like being their own bosses and, in effect, setting their own incomes. LePage management must balance the need to keep personal initiative high with the corporate need for a systematic approach.

Even the traditional carrots of promotion don't apply in brokerage. "There are no levels in this business," Dimma points out. Since income is based on commissions, salesmen may make more than managers, and administration is a promotion they can often do without. On the other side, income in most sales jobs is set by performance. If somebody doesn't perform, he drops out without being told. "There is a kind of Darwinian aspect to it," says Dimma.

"The most important part of my job," he maintains, "is to preserve the entrepreneurial thrust, this sense of it as a partnership, a family—not a stultifying bureaucracy." The company's ownership structure makes it easier. With the exception of 15% held by the Toronto Dominion Bank and the Toronto Dominion Bank Pension Fund, ownership is restricted to company employees; when they leave they must sell their shares. Gray owns about 15%, and Dimma a much smaller percentage, "not even in the top 10," he says. The rest of the shares are spread among 1,100 employees, from switchboard operators to vice-presidents.

One of the lucky shareholders is Joyce Rea, manager of office staff services, who started her career at the company as a switchboard operator. She bought her first shares 17 years ago at 50¢ apiece. "I have thousands of them," she says. "I'd buy them even if it means borrowing the money from the bank. They're too good an offer to pass up." The most recent price was $5.20, more than 20 times their original value when they were first offered back in 1955. But Gray stresses that there are no plans to go public. "It would go against our concept," he says. "It's the retention of those chips of ownership that's the largest single element in our success."

Ambitious acquisition had a lot to do with it too. The push began in 1952 when A.E. sold his controlling interest to a group of three employees headed by Brian Magee, who had joined the firm four years earlier. The change prompted mass resignations, including those of A.E.'s brother Harry and his sons. But through bank loans and recruiting, Magee managed to right the ship. He had a little help from one E.P. Taylor. Two weeks after Magee took control of the company, Taylor offered him the job of planning Don Mills, a "new town" in suburban Metro Toronto. Magee said no, but was retained by Taylor to assemble the land for the project. The company later assembled land for the new towns of Erin Mills and Meadowvale. The latter was a project of Markborough Properties Ltd., which Magee founded in 1965. LePage also put together the sites for the O'Keefe Centre, Woodbine Raceway and the Toronto-Dominion Centre. Magee retired in 1978, but still bears the title of honorary chairman.

Gray, an accountant who handled Taylor's real estate investment at Price Waterhouse, joined LePage as controller in 1955, when the firm had fewer than 35 employees. He and Magee made an impressive duo, recalls a former colleague admiringly. Magee put together the team and the money needed for growth. Gray set up the property management and commercial departments. But his big contribution was to create an information retrieval system containing lease information on every Toronto office building of more than 20,000 sq. ft. Now computerized, the system lets the company know when vacancies are coming up and when to check with potential clients as their leases run out, and it has contributed to LePage's long-time domination of the Toronto office market.

The acquisition spree started in 1970, when LePage bought the 90-person Toronto firm, W.B. Shorthill & Co. Then it expanded outside of Ontario by acquiring, in regular order, Boultbee Sweet Ltd. and the 100-year-old Bell-Irving Ltd., Vancouver (1972), Westmount Realties Co., Montreal (1973), Gibson-Willoughby Ltd., Toronto (1975), Melton Real Estate Ltd., Edmonton (1976), Young & Biggin Ltd., then in receivership, Toronto (1978) and Oldfield, Kirby & Gardiner Real Estate Ltd., a 90-year-old Winnipeg firm (1979).

Other companies came into the fold, including shopping centre consultants Geoffrey Still & Associates (1976). Services such as property management and development were added and expanded. Says Gray, "We try to merge with the most successful and best-established firms in each province. And it's not always easy. It took us four years to acquire Melton." At times the reputation as an eager shopper can be a nuisance. LePage must often rebuff local brokers eager to make a bundle by dumping marginal businesses.

Crucial to LePage's success as a national company is the "referral aspect, the ability to serve clients wherever they are and in whatever business they're in," says Gray. And diversification spreads the risk, so that, for example, if the commercial business slumps, residential may perk up and vice versa. Fee-for-service business, which has been stressed in recent years, helps provide a stable base. Finally, geographical expansion entices repeat business and national accounts.

If recent trends are any indication, bigness may be the only way to survive in the real estate business. The first of the big players were the trust companies, which moved into real estate with a vengeance in the late 1960s. Thus they had direct access to quality mortgage investments, and at the same time the brokerage side could make use of the in-house financing expertise. The trust companies and corporate brokers also began acquiring small independent firms. Simultaneously, the largest brokers, such as Vancouver-based Block Bros. Industries Ltd., hit the acquisition trail.

Then, in the 1970s, came the franchise companies. They played on the independent brokers' fears of trust company competition. The most prominent in Canada are: Century 21, with 410 affiliated brokers here and 4,000 in the U.S., which brokered an estimated $2.1 billion last year; North-Vancouver-based Realty World, with 140 Canadian affiliates and brokerage valued at $1 billion; and Peterborough-based Gallery of Homes Canada Ltd., which brokered $275 million of Canadian real estate in 1979. A Quebec government survey, the only one of its kind done in Canada, suggests how concentrated the industry has become. In 1976, eight of the 739 real estate companies in the province accounted for 58% of sales. Two-thirds of the companies had revenues of less than $50,000.

Keeping track of growth—and keeping the growth on track—has become a prime concern for LePage's management. Two years before Dimma was hired, the company began tackling that problem systematically with the aid of management consultant Charles St. Thomas, now vice-president of corporate services. The biggest change he recommended was the move from a geographic to a specialty orientation. Sales agents used to report to sales managers in their territory, whether they dealt in commercial or residential; now the reporting is functional. St. Thomas also called for further specialization within the broad categories of commercial and residential real estate. Since then, special divisions for starter homes, carriage-trade homes, condominium marketing, mortgage financing, town and country properties, farms, corporate relocation and a coast-to-coast referral have been developed or expanded. St. Thomas has also helped implement systematic planning and better management communication.

But can modern management methods keep the entrepreneurial spirit alive? The answer is: not entirely.

No matter to what extent LePage executives may deny it, organization and hierarchies have grated on a number of senior sales staff, mostly in the non-residential field. Many have left, and several have set up successful rival firms. "It's a super company, a successful company," says one defector. "But at some point in time, the huge company comes into conflict with the entrepreneurial thrust."

Adds another former LePage salesman: "There was always a feeling you didn't mess in the other guy's thing." For instance, he says, if he was selling an office building and the purchaser or vendor happened to be interested in an industrial building, he couldn't work both deals at once or integrate them in a trade. He had to involve other people as well. Because managers receive overrides on any commissions, he was sure to catch hell if he didn't involve the other department. In consequence, departmental rivalries—and battles—have been frequent and vigorous.

"Because of its size it requires specialization," says a former LePager. "But at the same time these rules box in and frustrate the best agents. To be really successful in real estate, you have to be creative. In LePage, though, you tend to get tunnel vision; you fail to see the opportunities."

LePage's entry into office development has also turned off some major building-owner clients who don't like the idea of competing for tenants with their own broker. Other property owners have been turned off by LePage's practice of selling space in directly competing buildings—say, on opposite corners of an intersection. Not surprisingly, commercial brokerage accounts for a declining percentage of the company's revenues, down from 50% four years ago to less than 30% today [1980], even though the dollar volume is up.

On the residential side, though, bigness is an advantage across the board. This year [1980] alone, 40 new offices are being opened, to bring the total to 170. The goal is [was] to reach 218 by 1983. More acquisitions, especially in Atlantic Canada, are on the horizon. And the specialized fee business is still growing; since last October, for example, LePage services have been promoted at Eaton-Bay financial centres in Toronto. The idea is more to spread the LePage name than to list or sell properties; the centres refer people to the regular offices. In fact, the company is spending a lot of money to make the name as well known as McDonald's. In addition to the $9 million it spends in advertising each year, mostly on classifieds, it's launched a $1.5 million national TV campaign designed to promote a greater awareness of the company name in residential brokerage.

That campaign, however, has created some dissension in the ranks. Most of the agents at the Westmount, Que., branch resigned last spring in protest when LePage started docking residential commissions by 1% to help pay for it. They joined a rival firm.

But that's a minor setback. Gray says the company has only begun to tap some of the more promising aspects of the real estate business. One area with enormous potential is direct real estate investment by the pension funds. Under the direction of G.E.A. Pacaud, formerly of Morguard Properties Ltd., the company is setting up pooled funds in the hope of luring some of that $40 billion in Canadian pension assets. Further down the road, Gray foresees a move into mortgage banking, and ultimately, perhaps, a merger with an insurance broker.

For all that, LePage firmly intends to maintain a close eye on its core residential business. The more agents it can inspire, the more commissions they'll bring in: as at McDonald's, the key is in the volume of business. It may not attract the supersalesmen who don't want to be part of the crowd. For the majority, though, the system pays off. Explains one new agent, discouraged by two months of no sales after a good start: "You really start feeling down, thinking you're alone and the only one with the problem. But with training meetings, you realize you're not alone, and that there are things that can be done, skills you can learn, that'll help you start selling again. And that you're part of a big team with a lot of things going for it."

Assignment

1. How big a business firm is A.E. LePage Ltd.?
2. How did it start? What made it grow?
3. Why was William Dimma chosen as president? What are his most important management functions?
4. How does A.E. LePage Ltd. try to motivate its employees?
5. How are the salespeople trained?
6. "Ambitious acquisition" has had a lot to do with the success of A.E. LePage Ltd. Explain.
7. What is the information retrieval system? Why is it such an effective marketing tool?
8. What was Gordon Gray's role in the development of the company?
9. What competition has the company had to face in the real estate market?
10. Explain the company's move from a geographic to a specialty orientation. Does it make good marketing sense? What problems has it caused?
11. Have modern management methods been able to keep the entrepreneurial spirit alive in this company? Discuss.
12. How does the company make use of advertising?

CHAPTER 6
MANAGEMENT THEORIES

CHAPTER OBJECTIVES

- To show how thinking about business management evolved.
- To describe the scientific approach to management thought.
- To introduce the concept of management by objectives.
- To explain and discuss the human relations approach to management thought.
- To describe the systems approach to management thought.

CHAPTER OUTLINE

6.1 The Scientific Approach to Management

6.2 The Human Relations and the Systems Approaches to Management

UNIT 6.1: THE SCIENTIFIC APPROACH TO MANAGEMENT

During the last century and a half, many countries of the world have been transformed from predominantly agricultural to predominantly industrial ones. Manufacturing and service industries have replaced agriculture as the main source of a country's income and employment. And the flow of technological innovation that made possible the industrial revolution of nineteenth-century Britain has been succeeded in the twentieth century by a veritable flood. Thus, in contrast with the situation 150 years ago, many countries throughout the world now have vast numbers of business firms which are active in industries of every sort. These firms, some of huge proportions, together provide their country's population with an average material standard of living far superior to that enjoyed by previous generations.

Because of their vital economic importance, business firms and their methods of operation have over the years been the object of increasing scrutiny. As the principal aim of such firms is to produce and market goods and services that consumers want, at a price they can afford, it is not surprising that this scrutiny has been directed mainly towards improving the efficiency of these firms. Many studies of business management and operation have been undertaken by business managers, by management consultants (a whole new profession that has emerged to diagnose the ills of unprofitable firms and to prescribe suitable remedies), and by professors of the departments and schools of business that have sprung up at many colleges and universities. As a result, there is now a vast library of books, journals, and magazines about the art, practice, and concepts of business management.

Classical Origins of Management Thought

When we look back in history, we see that every major civilization has at one time or another been greatly concerned with the management of people and materials. The Great Wall of China, the pyramids of Egypt, the temples of Greece, the roads of the Roman Empire, the castles of the Normans, and the cathedrals of Christendom are all examples of the endeavours of our ancestors. Also, the wars that have been fought through the ages testify to our ancestors' skills in amassing, feeding, transporting, arming, directing, and controlling large numbers of people. For countless centuries the tasks of secular and ecclesiastical government have also challenged our management ability. In the business field, the medieval craft guilds in Europe stand out as an early example of business organization. We can also be impressed by the management of the European trading companies that ranged throughout the world as early as the seventeenth century.

In our present-day practice of business management, we have inherited many attitudes and concepts from the past. Some examples are: that a person works, not because of any innate desire, but because he or she has to (after all, Adam and Eve were cast out of the Garden of Eden); that fear is the best taskmaster, whether it be of losing a job, a raise, or a promotion; that a firm, like an army, should have a hierarchy of positions and a definite chain of command; that orders should be obeyed loyally and without question; that all employees should conform in appearance and behaviour to given standards; and that almost everyone in a firm should work similar hours. As society's outlook changes, some of these old beliefs will continue to be preserved. But others will doubtless change. Thus, slavery, once highly respectable in business, is now a thing of the past; while lending money at interest, once good reason for public execution, is now a virtuous act.

Perhaps our biggest inheritance from the past, insofar as business management is concerned, is the organizational methods and concept of discipline of the military. However, as we shall see later, motivation by fear alone has not proved very successful in modern business.

Henri Fayol. One of the first important thinkers about business management was the Frenchman, Henri Fayol (1841–1925). Appointed engineer to the Commentry-Fourchambault group of coal mines and steel mills in France in 1861, he became the company's managing director (or president) in 1888, and succeeded in making the almost bankrupt firm a highly profitable one. As managing director he had the opportunity not only to theorize on business management, but also to test his ideas in practice. In 1916, his work, *Administration Industrielle et Générale*, was published in Paris; it contained his views, based on 30 years' experience as company president, on (a) the necessity and possibility of teaching management and (b) the principles and elements of management.[1] This second part is the forerunner of much of our present management theory and practice.

Specifically, Fayol stated that *management* comprised the following activities: (a) *forecasting* and *planning*—examining the future and drawing up a plan of action; (b) *organizing*—building up the structure of the enterprise; (c) *directing*—maintaining activity among the personnel; (d) *coordinating*—unifying and harmonizing all activity and effort; and (e) *controlling*—ensuring that everything done conforms with the established plan. Fayol also stated that these activities could be performed better by the observance of certain rules, or principles. These principles include the need in a business for "unity of command"—whereby an employee receives orders from only one superior; the need for "unity of direction"—whereby everyone works towards a common goal; the need for a reasonable "span of control," whereby the number of persons reporting to each manager is kept to the most efficient maximum; and the need for placing authority and responsibility together in a manager's job.

Many of the principles enunciated by Fayol are commonly applied in business today, although in modified form. And in our discussion of management in the following chapters of this book we use Fayol's methodical, function-by-function

---

[1] Henri Fayol, *Industrial and General Administration* (English translation), London: Pitman & Sons, 1930. A new translation, entitled *General and Industrial Management*, was published by Pitman in 1949.

approach. However, although Fayol was a pioneer in business management thinking, his work was not available in North America until the 1930s. As a result his influence was not as great as that of Frederick Taylor, referred to below, whose studies were far more widely published.

Scientific Management

As early as 1776, the Scottish economist, Adam Smith, in his book *An Inquiry into the Nature and Causes of the Wealth of Nations*, was pointing out the advantages of organizing factory production along scientific lines. In his example of a nail factory, he showed how specialization (or *division of labour*) among workers substantially increased output. And in 1835, Charles Babbage, in his book *On the Economy of Machinery and Manufacturers*, recommended that manufacturers use a scientific approach in organizing their factories to produce goods at the lowest cost.

Frederick W. Taylor. The term *scientific management* began to be widely used with regard to business management only from the early twentieth century, after an American, Frederick W. Taylor (1856–1915), used it in the title of his book.[2] Although recognizing that business management could never be a science in the physical sense, Taylor, an engineer by profession, believed that a scientific approach could help solve management problems. His studies focused on two main areas: (a) industrial engineering and (b) lower levels of management (foreman and supervisor). Some of his ideas are as follows:

1. *A science for each element of a man's task, instead of the old rule-of-thumb.* Taylor demonstrated his belief in the value of the scientific approach by a systematic analysis of a number of manual factory jobs. In one example he showed how, by use of this approach, the output of a worker loading pig iron could be increased from $12\frac{1}{2}$ tons per man per day to 47! What Taylor did was to break each job down into its various component elements; study and redesign each element; choose, with the aid of a stopwatch, the most efficient method of performance of each one; arrange the elements in the most efficient sequence; and then train the worker how to perform the job in this way. Since at the beginning of this century large numbers of manual labourers were employed in North American industry, with relatively little management direction as to work methods, Taylor's findings had considerable beneficial impact on production costs.

2. *Scientific selection, training, and placement of workers.* Taylor also believed that the scientific approach could profitably be used in the recruitment and placement of personnel. At that time, hiring and allocating workers on a first-come, first-served basis was the prevailing practice for many jobs. Taylor believed that much better results could be obtained by first analyzing the requirements of the job and then trying to match the qualities and abilities of the applicant to it. Although an accepted principle of

---

[2] Frederick W. Taylor, *The Principles of Scientific Management*, New York: Harper and Brothers, 1911.

personnel management today, such a procedure was often neglected in the past—with the result that a firm's efficiency suffered much more than today from an abundance of square pegs in round holes. Taylor also recommended the scientific training and development of a firm's employees.

3. *Greater management involvement.* Taylor also stressed that, if the benefits of the scientific approach were to be obtained, managers should not (as was often the case) remain aloof from the factory floor. As well as developing a "science" for each element of a person's work, they should, in Taylor's words, "heartily cooperate" with the workers to ensure that the most desirable methods were in fact used. Managers should also be willing to work harder and assume more responsibility than they had previously.

Henry L. Gantt. Another important member of the scientific management school was Henry L. Gantt (1861–1919), also an American, and a colleague of Frederick Taylor. Gantt emphasized the importance of the human factor in work and stressed the responsibility of management for training its workers. He also recommended that management adopt proper methods of planning and control. To help with this task, he used graphical recording systems and machine and man record-charts, the most notable being the Gantt production control charts, on which the progress of a job is continuously recorded.

Frank and Lillian Gilbreth. Other notable contributors to the scientific management approach in the early twentieth century were Frank Gilbreth (1868-1924), an American engineer, and his wife, Dr. Lillian Gilbreth. Whereas Taylor introduced the technique of *time study* for each particular job, the Gilbreths concentrated on human motions in general, systematically analyzing each human work motion to discover the most efficient way of performing it, whatever the task. The result of the Gilbreths' *motion study* was (a) the identification of seventeen elementary movements or groups of movements into which all types of human activity can be divided and (b) the setting out of a series of motion-economy principles that could be applied to any job—for example, that both hands should never be idle at the same time. The Gilbreths developed a process (flow) chart which facilitates the study of a complete operation rather than a single task. They also studied the problem of industrial fatigue and suggested how needless fatigue might be eliminated.

Scientific Management Today. Although Taylor and his contemporaries were active many years ago, we should not think that scientific management was in vogue only in the early decades of this century. In fact, scientific management, in the sense of the *systematic analysis of work*, is considered by some modern management thinkers to be the management concept most widely used today—and indeed the one American concept that has penetrated the entire world. When we think of the present widespread use of time and motion studies, process charts, and job instruction sheets; of the high degree of specialization of labour and equipment; of the use of standardized materials and parts; and, above all, of the scientific approach that many business managers apply to their problems (carefully analyzing them and dispassionately weighing alternatives, particularly in terms of dollars and cents, before choosing a solution), we can apreciate the reasons for this belief.

Management by Objectives

Another important expression of the scientific approach in modern business is the philosophy of "management by objectives." This philosophy, adopted by many business firms, involves: (a) the clear statement of a firm's objectives, and (b) the evaluation of each management decision in the light of these objectives. Although making profit for the shareholders is the chief goal of most business firms, there are many other objectives as well. They include customer satisfaction, continued financial solvency, good employee morale, continuous product development, steady sales growth, and modernization of plant and equipment.

The importance of clearly defining management's objectives and then organizing the firm's resources and activities so as to achieve them has been recognized by most management writers. However, many managers, caught up in the daily bustle, find it easy to overlook.

The term "Management by Objectives" (or MBO for short) was first coined in 1954 by Peter Drucker, the well-known management consultant, in his book *The Practice of Management*. It was first formally described as a system of management by George S. Odiorne in his book, *Management by Objectives: A System of Leadership* in 1965. However, many firms had already been using this approach for many years.

According to Odiorne, MBO is a process whereby the superior and subordinate managers of an organization jointly identify its common goals, define each individual's major areas of responsibility in terms of the results expected of him or her, and use these measures as guides for operating the unit and assessing the contribution of each of its members.

KEY TERMS

Management studies

Henri Fayol

Functions of management

Principles of management

Scientific management

Adam Smith

Charles Babbage

Frederick W. Taylor

Henry L. Gantt

Gantt production control charts

Frank and Lillian Gilbreth

Motion studies

Management by objectives

Peter Drucker

George S. Odiorne

REVIEW QUESTIONS

1. Explain the nature and purpose of management studies. In what publications are they to be found?
2. What are the classical origins of modern management thinking?
3. Explain the contribution made by Henri Fayol to the development of management techniques.
4. Explain the scientific approach to management. When and how did it originate?
5. What contribution did Henry L. Gantt make to modern management techniques?
6. What was the contribution to management techniques of the Gilbreths?
7. To what extent is scientific management employed in business today? Include in your answer a brief explanation of "management by objectives."

READING

The Iron Will of Harry Steele

The head of Eastern Provincial Airways can make any business fly—even in a stormy economy

BY STEPHEN KIMBER

(Stephen Kimber is a freelance journalist based in Halifax.)
Source: *The Financial Post Magazine.* Used by permission of Stephen Kimber.

To say Harry Steele is pleased with himself this morning is like suggesting the fox doesn't mind being locked in a hen house with a flock of slow-moving, ripe-for-plucking chickens.

Harry Steele, 53, is the president, chief executive officer and major shareholder of Newfoundland Capital Corporation, a holding company he formed two years ago. NCC, in turn, owns Eastern Provincial Airways, one of the few airlines anywhere turning a profit these days, as well as Clarke Transport Canada Inc., a $75-million-a-year group of companies involved in almost everything that moves, from steamships to tractor-trailer trucks. NCC reported profits in 1981 of $9.2 million—up from $1.4 million the year before—on revenues of $104 million.

Harry Steele, as might be expected, smiles grandly as he offers a copy of NCC's latest annual report, but NCC's lush profit picture doesn't begin to explain why he is so absolutely, totally, positively delighted with himself this morning. The reason for that, quite simply, is that he is about to eat his pilots' union solidarity for breakfast.

"Here, have a look at this," he says, pushing a piece of paper across his wing-shaped desk. It's a letter to the pilots signed by Steele's director of flight operations, Captain Rod MacKay. Negotiations for a new contract between the pilots' union, the Canadian Airline Pilots Association and

Eastern Provincial have broken down. The company says it will accept—"with misgivings"—a conciliator's recommendations to settle the dispute, but the union has rejected that report outright. It is scheduled to take a strike vote tonight.

"Let there be no misunderstanding," MacKay's letter tells the pilots. "If you vote to reject the offer and the strike vote is successful, the pilots will be considered on strike as of the date the vote count is confirmed."

"Did MacKay really write this?" the visitor asks. "Or did you?" Harry Steele smiles mysteriously. He smiles a lot these days. Even when he complains that Ottawa mollycoddles Air Canada, his bitter rival, or fulminates that Canadian National is using its access to federal funds to undercut his own container-shipping business, the hint of a smile still plays at the corner of his mouth. "Did I write that? Or did MacKay?" Steele repeats the questions thoughtfully, as if trying to understand them. He brushes back a stringy lock of hair that refuses to stay put on the top of his balding head. The smile becomes a broad, boyish grin. "Does it matter?"

It doesn't. Whoever wrote the actual words, the message is pure Harry Steele. Blunt and bloody-minded. "We simply cannot allow negotiations to drag on indefinitely," it says flatly. "[The conciliator's report] is as far as we can go and any settlement, whenever it comes, will be within this framework."

Harry Steele leans forward in his chair and freezes his visitor with a stare from his basset-hound eyes. "It's got to stop somewhere," he earnestly insists. "Hell, the conciliator's report still gives them $80,000 a year. That's enough. Everyone talks about safety this and safety that," he says, "but what's the difference between a pilot and a poor, old CN bus driver? They're both responsible for the lives of a lot of people. Nobody is saying the bus driver is worth $80,000 a year. The problem is . . ."—Harry Steele smiles even more broadly—"no one has ever stood up and said so."

Harry Steele will. Today. "Let's see how we're doing," he commands. A rumpled, shambling, six-foot bear of a man, Steele leads the way through a labyrinth of hallways in Eastern Provincial's converted-hangar head office at the Gander International Airport. Whenever he's in Gander—Steele still lives in a fashionable but unspectacular modern house in this small, unremarkable northeastern Newfoundland airport town of 12,000, but now spends more than half his time on the road keeping tabs on his growing empire—he checks in at the airline's operations centre first thing.

"Jesus," he says softly, scanning a computer printout. Only seven people flew on one of EPA's regular Halifax-to-Toronto flights yesterday. "We'll have to see about that," he says to no one in particular.

The computer printouts—updated daily—tell Steele not only how many people flew on each leg of each flight the day before, but also how much they paid for their seats and how much EPA is making—or losing—today as compared with yesterday and how that will ultimately translate into month-end and year-end statistics.

Steele, a straightforward dollars-and-sense administrator, insists that each NCC division boss defend his profit performance during monthly grillings. Any NCC subsidiary needing cash from the holding company, Steele notes proudly, pays "well above market" for the privilege.

"We're doing a bigger volume of business," Steele says, running a finger over the numbers on the computer paper, "but we're making fewer dollars." He pauses, stares at the numbers. "Discounting," he says, spitting out the word. "If the marketing people had their way, everyone would fly free."

There are no free rides on Harry Steele's

airline anymore. Since he bought government-supported, perennially money-losing EPA in 1978 for $5 million, Steele has worked assiduously to, as he puts it, "stop the bleed." Steele has not only paid off the company's government loans, but has also transformed its $815,000 operating loss in 1977 into a $4.4-million profit last year.

"I think of him as one of the last of the pioneers," Steele's brother-in-law, Nova Scotia Development Minister Roland Thornhill, says. "He's of the same ilk as [the late Nova Scotia pulp and power magnate] Roy Jodrey, the kind of person who is willing to take risks to develop something worthwhile." Adds Ivan Kilpatrick, NCC's senior vice-president of finance: "Steele is the only guy I know with the guts to take a pilots' strike, if necessary, just to show who's really in charge."

"What's the story on the strike?" Harry Steele demands, poking his head into Rod MacKay's office in the operations centre. "Looks good," MacKay answers. "Just got a call from one of the pilots. Third one so far today. Says he'll fly if we want him to. No matter how the vote goes."

"Good, good," Steele says, already hurrying down the corridor to his office. "I don't think," he calls over his shoulder to the visitor, "we have anything to worry about now."

"Somehow we have to instill in all our people—management as well as the hourly rated—the belief that hard work, long hours and open minds will crack time away below decks. You'll have more sea sickness with your crew in their hammocks smelling the bilge than on deck where the wind is free."

—Harry Steele
Chamber of Commerce speech
Dartmouth, N.S.
June 15, 1982

For Harry Raymond Steele, the strange truth is that our worst of times is his best of times. It's not just that his is the ultimate poor-boy-makes-very-very-good story. In actual physical distance, he has travelled only 50 miles from tiny Musgrave Harbour to small Gander; in psychic terms, he has covered an immeasurable distance, from tending to his father's homemade cod traps as a child to ministering to his $86,000 Ferrari as a man. And it isn't simply that his late-blossoming success has brought him out of almost total obscurity—shortly after he bought EPA, *Maclean's* referred to him as "Barry Steele"—and made him a public figure, either. It's not even the reality that he's now running a successful, still expanding corporate empire while most of his competitors are shrivelling like so many dried-up pieces of fruit.

What makes this Harry Steele's best of times is that governments and the public are finally humming the back-to-basics, cut-the-fat, chop-the-lean business tune he's been singing for years. Now Steele can get a respectful hearing, even when he's saying—as he did this past summer in Halifax—that businessmen should fire accountants who have more than two friends, because any accountant who isn't a mean, friendless son of a bitch obviously isn't tough enough to pass corporate muster in this cruel economy. "There's going to be some bad times," Steele says, sounding unperturbed by the prospect. "Businessmen are going to have to be tough to survive."

Steele knows all about survival and about being tough. He has called Musgrave Harbour, the outport on Newfoundland's northeast coast where he grew up, "a place of seagulls and seals and human tragedy." One hundred kilometres by boat from Lewisporte, the nearest larger centre, Steele's family struggled just to survive, eking a bare but mostly self-sufficient living out of fishing, tending their small garden, keeping a few animals and gathering firewood from the forest. After getting his high-school diploma in Musgrave Harbour's two-room, two-teacher schoolhouse, Steele tried his hand on his father's fishing boat and as a Department of Highways ditch digger.

He might never have escaped, except for his own stubborn determination and Joey Smallwood's equally stubborn vision. Having dragged Newfoundland into Confederation in 1949, Smallwood knew he had to quickly improve the province's public education system, so he offered $300 to any prospective teacher enrolling at Memorial University in St. John's.

Steele wasn't sure that he wanted to be a teacher, but he knew he didn't want to get up at three in the morning to go fishing or spend his days digging ditches. Smallwood's $300, plus the tuition and living allowance he earned as a member of the navy's University Naval Training Division (UNTD), financed his studies at Memorial, where he enrolled in 1949.

While there, Steele not only earned his B.Ed., but he also courted and married Catherine Thornhill, a St. John's music teacher. They now have three children: Peter, 25, with Quebec Road Transport; Rob, 21, taking arts at Memorial; and John, 16, also in arts at Memorial.

Steele joined the regular navy in 1953 merely to fulfill his UNTD obligations, but after a couple of years he was seduced by the military life. A communications and electronics specialist, he worked his way up to lieutenant-commander, earned prestigious postings—including a four-year hitch as military attaché to the Canadian Embassy in Washington—and even quietly nursed ambitions to become an admiral, until Paul Hellyer, then defence minister, announced his controversial plans to unify the armed forces in the mid-'60s.

Steele, a supporter of William Landymore, the renegade admiral who publicly attacked unification, brooded for several years before finally abandoning the navy. Even then, in order to ease his transition back to civilian life in his native Newfoundland, Steele took one last posting in Gander in 1970 as head of a new $17-million military communications research centre.

Until he retired in 1974 at 45, Steele still wore his traditional blue uniform rather than the newly minted bottle-green outfits Ottawa issued after unification. "I was probably the last holdout in the country," he says proudly.

He was also one of the few servicemen who could claim to be a millionaire. During the '50s and '60s, while serving as an instructor at the navy's Maritime Warfare School in Halifax, he began dabbling in the stock market. Roland Thornhill, then a stockbroker, recalls that he and Steele spent hours talking about the market. Steele even took a career aptitude test offered by Richardson Securities. "He had one of the highest scores ever on the test," Thornhill says today. Through Thornhill, Steele also met Seymour Schulich, then research director of Eastern Securities and now vice-president of Beutel, Goodman & Company Ltd., the Toronto investment company. Schulich gave the neophyte Steele useful oil-stock pointers; 15 years later, Steele named Schulich chairman of NCC's board.

Although Steele lost the first $500 of his savings that he invested—he keeps framed copies of the worthless Canamera Oilsands and Hardee Farms stock certificates that he bought on his wall—he turned out to be right far more often than he was wrong. He used some of his profits to buy Halifax apartment buildings. Then, in 1970, he edged into the hotel business by purchasing the bankrupt 48-room Albatross Motel in Gander for $30,000 and assuming its $250,000 debts. The Albatross began to prosper and, eventually, Steele invested in two more hotels in nearby Grand Falls.

Although he could have settled comfortably into a postmilitary life of calling his broker, clipping his coupons, and counting his hotel profits, Steele concedes he had already become intrigued with the turnaround prospects of money-losing, Gander-based Eastern Provincial. A bush-plane operation when it was founded by legendary Newfoundland wheeler-dealer Chesley Crosbie in 1949, EPA had become a major regional carrier—and equally major money-loser—by the early '70s.

Besides the simple and direct challenge of making the airline make money, Steele's interest in EPA—the only carrier serving Labrador—was piqued by the potential windfall he believed would follow from provincial government plans to develop $3 billion worth of hydroelectric projects there.

Steele bought shares in the airline as soon as they were publicly offered in 1971, then joined the company full-time as vice-president of traffic and sales in 1976. He quit 13 months later, complaining that the airline was badly managed.

Eighteen months later, though, EPA's major stockholders gave Steele the chance to put his money where his mouth was. Offering eight dollars a share for stock then trading at five dollars, Steele quickly acquired 67 percent and effective control of the airline and began recasting it in his own image.

He eased out almost all the top executives he inherited and recruited his own hands-on management team. Ivan Kilpatrick, who had spent most of his 25-year business career breathing life into such moribund companies as Warnock-Hersey, TIW Industries and Bombardier, was comfortably ensconced in semi-retirement at the University of Prince Edward Island's business school when Steele approached him to come to EPA. Now a director of NCC as well as its vice-president of finance, Kilpatrick makes no bones about his role. "I'm here to let the operating people know that the NCC guys are bastards. We look only at results, and they'd better be good." Bill Verrier, EPA's vice-president of marketing, is as silky smooth as Kilpatrick is blunt. Enticed away from a secure, high-profile job as Air Canada's director of operations for the United Kingdom and Ireland, Verrier dramatically increased EPA's passenger load by offering enticements ranging from cheap one-way fares to free wine with meals.

Even as he was rearranging top management, Steele sent unmistakable messages to the rest of the airline's 900 employees as well. While he made it a point to get to know personally as many workers as possible, he also eliminated the jobs of one-third of the airline's 175 flight attendants and prodded pilots to operate their planes on more efficient flight patterns, thus saving $1.5 million in fuel alone last year. Steele coupled his tight fist with an open palm and offered a generous employee profit-sharing scheme to keep remaining employees happy.

But Larry Wark, a business agent for the Canadian Airline Employees' Association, argues that EPA "seems to believe you can buy an employee's dignity for a couple of bucks in a profit-sharing scheme." He calls the company's labor relations "extremely harsh and unenlightened. It's incredible, but we've had cases where they tried to fire employees with 10 years' experience and good records just because they made one little mistake writing out a ticket." Surprisingly, however, Wark doesn't blame Steele personally for the problems. "Steele himself is the most intelligent, enlightened guy in the operation," Wark says. "I don't have problems when I talk to him. It's his middle management. They're always trying to do things to win points with him."

That, suggests one middle manager, may

be because Steele himself always talks about the bottom line. "He's always talking about profits here and profits there. But it's working. All you have to do is look at EPA today."

Steele himself says the key to charting the airline's profitable course was simply its success in escaping the undependable Atlantic economy. After the Canadian Transport Commission awarded a plum Halifax-to-Toronto direct route to CP Air instead of EPA in 1980, Steele orchestrated a massive "Atlantic First" coalition of key politicians—including such unlikely bedfellows as former federal secretary of state Gerald Regan, Nova Scotia Premier John Buchanan and Newfoundland Premier Brian Peckford—and powerful eastern businessmen to convince the federal government to overturn the CTC decision. That, along with Steele's threat to liquidate EPA—then Newfoundland's second-largest private employer—and simply sell off its $29 million in assets, finally persuaded Ottawa to give him the route. "It was a great morale-booster for us," Steele says now. Today, Steele hopes to stretch EPA's horizon still more by seeking direct St. John's-Toronto and Maritimes-Boston routes, while trying to spin off EPA's less profitable short-haul flights—"We've lost millions in the New Brunswick triangle [Moncton, Fredericton, and Saint John]," he complains—into a new company called Air Maritime that will use only more efficient, propeller-driven planes.

But Steele admits the airline business—even in the best of times—is chancy. (His original dream of a bonanza from massive hydro projects in Labrador remains in limbo because Newfoundland and Quebec can't agree on power-transmission rights.) That's why he created Newfoundland Capital Corporation in 1980.

Thanks to Steele's record at EPA—not to mention the then-searingly-hot Newfoundland oil and gas boom, freshly minted Newfoundland government regulations encouraging oil companies to buy from firms that are at least 51-percent owned by Newfoundlanders, and Steele's own decision to appoint such oil-smart directors as Seymour Schulich and John Fleming, the chairman of Bonanza Oil & Gas Ltd. of Calgary, to NCC's board—NCC's initial private share placement of $10 million was oversubscribed. Today, Steele owns 47 percent of NCC's shares, while Schulich and Fleming hold seven percent each. A group of life insurance companies, pension plans and Ontario-based financial institutions own another 10 percent, while the remainder is split among hundreds of small investors, easily giving Steele effective personal control of the company.

But the offshore ownership squabble between Ottawa and St. John's—now apparently headed for the Supreme Court—has slowed NCC's planned major thrust into offshore oil and gas, so Steele is pushing NCC down new avenues.

In October, 1981, the company paid $18.5 million for Clarke Transport Canada Inc., a 60-year-old, Montreal-based company with 1,500 employees and a mixed bag of Canada-wide transportation interests, including ferries, trucking companies, coastal trading ships, railway pool cars, auto dealerships and even a one-third interest in a Halifax container terminal.

Eight months later, he married Clarke's Newfoundland Steamships Ltd. to a competing operation, Atlantic Freight Lines, in a new company called Atlantic Container Express. That merger, Steele explains, will enable the new company to compete head-to-head with Terratransport, a federal Crown corporation Steele accuses of using its access to the public purse to undercut private Newfoundland firms.

But if NCC is doing quite well, thank you very much, the airline business generally is in a frightful nosedive: Internationally, Braniff and Laker airlines have gone bust; at home, CP Air lost four times as much in the first nine months of 1982 as it did last year, and Air Canada, by the end of the year, was predicting its first loss since 1976. Even at Eastern Provincial, where the news is the best in the country, Harry Steele claims his profit so far this year has been much too low and he, too, has had to cut back on routes and lay off staff.

EPA pilots didn't need much more than the nudge of Steele's tough talk; after receiving Rod MacKay's letter, they abandoned even the pretense of a strike vote and agreed to accept the company's last offer. "I knew there wouldn't be a problem," Steele says simply.

Although he admits NCC is still attempting to fully digest its Clarke takeover and the creation of Atlantic Container, Steele insists he's still looking for companies to buy. He recently tried to gobble up a network of five Newfoundland radio stations owned by Don Jamieson, Canada's newly appointed high commissioner to the U.K., for example, but they were sold to Toronto's CHUM Ltd. instead. In retaliation, Steele has hired Kenner Arnell, one of Canada's top radio consultants, to fight the sale before the CRTC. As in his battle for the Halifax-Toronto route, Steele is cloaking himself in the robes of regional patriotism and orchestrating a letter lobby to the CRTC, opposing any sale to outsiders.

The CRTC is still considering his complaint in the case of the radio-stations sale. "We're going to go as far as we have to on this one," Steele says. "We're going to win." But he adds quickly that his appetite for investing is far from sated. "We're always looking!"

Harry Steele leans forward into a snake pit of radio and television microphones. By the magic of modern technology, Ian Gray, the president of CP Air, appears on a huge television screen above his left shoulder, staring fixedly into the middle distance. Steele smiles, as if at a great private joke; Gray seems glum, as if at a funeral. Gray is actually in a hotel room in Vancouver, listening as Steele begins to answer a question at the Halifax end of their joint press conference.

It is three months later, and Steele has come to Halifax on this late September afternoon to announce that tiny Eastern Provincial—profits of $750,000 on revenues of $55 million during the first seven months of 1982—and huge CP Air—with a loss of $30 million on revenues of $405 million for the first half of the year—are about to enter into an operational marriage of convenience.

Under the terms of the agreement, a year in the dickering, CP Air will abandon its Halifax-Ottawa and Halifax-Montreal flights to Eastern Provincial, leaving EPA as Air Canada's only major competitor in Atlantic Canada. At the same time, the two airlines will mesh their separate scheduled flights into Toronto from the west and east coasts, thus giving Eastern Provincial its long-sought opening to provide a truly national service. Eastern Provincial is the clear winner in this marriage contract. CP Air has merely been permitted to cut its losses and slink back to the west coast.

"Does Eastern Provincial want to swallow CP Air?" someone asks jokingly after the press conference. Steele laughs, too, but he doesn't answer. He simply says he believes the ultimate loser will be Air Canada. Forgetting his old animosities with CP Air over the Halifax-Toronto route, Steele calls the deal an example of "free enterprises getting together" to tackle the government monster. "Will this deal with CP Air finally satisfy Steele's need to keep pushing at the edges of his corporate horizons?" someone else wants to know.

"How's the fishing industry?" Steele asks out of nowhere. The smile is huge. The non sequitur is gaping. "The secret of Steele's success," Ivan Kilpatrick explains, "is that he's always asking questions, always inquisitive. He likes to look into queer things no one else sees any sense in." Few things these days seem queerer than Canada's eastcoast fishing industry. Steele, who spent part of his early life escaping the life of a fisherman and who later suggested he didn't think there was any money to be made in fishing, is suddenly sizing the business up anew.

"What are you hearing over in Nova Scotia?" Steele demands. "Is it getting better?" The answer, of course, is that it is not. The region's four biggest processing companies are all on the edge of ruin, in desperate need of government financial help and unlikely to be able to turn that dismal situation around anytime in the next couple of years.

"Perhaps this is the time to invest in fishing," Harry Steele muses aloud. He pauses, offers his best enigmatic smile. "Everything has its season," he says.

This is, without question, Harry Steele's season.

Assignment
1. Who is Harry Steele?
2. What type of manager is he?
3. What is Harry's business philosophy?
4. What was his social and educational background?
5. Why did Harry and the military decide to part ways? What does it say about Harry?
6. How did Harry become one of the few servicemen who could claim to be a millionaire?
7. Why didn't Harry just retire gracefully, clipping his coupons and counting his hotel profits?
8. How did Harry come to run EPA?
9. As President of EPA, Harry had to be a politician as well as a businessman. Explain.
10. How were Harry's labour relations problems at EPA finally resolved?
11. What was the conglomerate that Harry began to build? What was its objective?
12. Explain EPA's relationship with CP Air.
13. Should Harry get into the fishing business?

UNIT 6.2: THE HUMAN RELATIONS AND THE SYSTEMS APPROACHES TO MANAGEMENT

Although the scientific management approach (in its broadest sense) has helped business firms all over the world to achieve a vast increase in production, it is open to a very serious complaint: that it treats employees more like machines than live human beings. The *human relations approach* to management emerged in response to this complaint.

Elton Mayo

During the 1920s and early 1930s, a team of researchers led by Professor Elton Mayo of Harvard University conducted a series of experiments at the Hawthorne (Chicago) plant of the Western Electric Company. The Hawthorne experiments, as they came to be known, were initially designed to assess the effect on worker productivity of such physical factors as lighting, temperature, and work schedules. However, they showed quite dramatically that human motivation was a far more important determinant of labour productivity than the physical work environment. Although many firms were already well aware of the benefits of worker motivation, the publication of the results of the Hawthorne experiments helped give human relations much wider recognition as an important and valuable approach to management. Indeed, the whole field of personnel management, with its emphasis on human needs, is considered to date from that time.

The conclusions reached by Mayo during twenty years of research beginning in 1927 were that (a) emotion is more important than logic in determining a worker's productivity; (b) a person's work should satisfy his or her own goals as well as those of the firm; (c) management-labour cooperation is more productive than management insistence on strict employee obedience; (d) group effort is more productive per person than individual effort; and (e) "social skills," or "the ability to secure cooperation between people," are very important for everyone in a firm, but particularly for managers and supervisors.

"I don't understand it. We've raised their pay and given them flexible hours, but production keeps going down."

In subsequent years, many other people conducted research into different types of human motivation and behaviour. In the following pages, we outline the most important areas of research and the conclusions reached.

Maslow's Hierarchy of Needs

Professor A.H. Maslow, in an article entitled "A Theory of Human Motivation," published in the United States in 1943, in the *Psychological Review*, stated that a person has at least five sets of basic needs:
1. *physiological*—a person's need for food, shelter, clothing, etc.
2. *safety*—a person's desire for security.
3. *love or social*—a person's need to belong to a group, to interact with other people.
4. *esteem*—a person's desire for recognition and respect from others.
5. *self-actualization*—a person's need to satisfy his or her creative ability and to be mentally challenged.

According to Maslow, these needs can be ranked in order of priority, with the physiological needs first and the self-actualization ones last. Once one set of needs is satisfied, the next ranking one becomes the most urgent.

The significance of this concept for management is simple: reasonable pay is not usually sufficient to motivate an employee. Since physical needs (such as food and shelter) and safety needs (such as protection from physical aggression or unsafe machinery) are usually met, a worker's other three needs now tend to be paramount. Thus, only if a worker has an opportunity in his or her job to realize full human potential is he or she likely to be satisfied. And only if management can provide this opportunity will individual productivity be very high.

The types of barriers that prevent the fulfilment of individual needs and wants have been carefully studied. They include, for example, an excessive degree of routine in a job (usually the result of labour specialization), an unsuitable formal organization for a department or section, unreasonable work demands, and poor treatment by managers. Such barriers give rise, of course, to worker frustration. This, in turn, causes various sorts of worker reaction: (a) *aggression*—for example, striking the foreman or smashing a piece of equipment; (b) *apathy*—the apathetic acceptance of, for example, a demotion; (c) *rationalization*—the invention of a plausible explanation for a frustrating event, such as being passed over for a promotion or raise; and (d) *regression*—the reversion to such childish behaviour as name-calling.

Socially Acquired Motives

David C. McClelland, in an article, *The Two Faces of Power*, in the *Journal of International Affairs* in 1970, drew attention to what he called "socially-acquired motives."
1. The *achievement motive*—a person's desire to achieve success (which is in-

fluenced to some extent by the type of society in which that person lives).
2. The *affiliative motive*—a person's desire to have good interpersonal relationships.
3. The *power motive*—a person's desire to have authority over others; to be a leader rather than a follower.

According to McClelland, these motives are also extremely important for many employees. Therefore, management should watch out for them and try to satisfy them, if the firm's operations are to be performed more harmoniously and efficiently.

A person who aspires to be a manager would need to have all three motives.

Courtesy The Ontario Ministry of Industry, Trade and Technology

Behaviour of Small Work Groups

A "group" exists in a firm when employees join together for some common purpose. This may be a formal grouping (for example, a number of employees manning a workshop, or the members of an executive committee) or an informal one (for example, a number of employees making a complaint, or making up a plant sports team). The significance of the work group is that the individual, when a member of a group, often does not act as he or she would alone. He or she is, in other words, influenced in his or her behaviour by the attitude of the group as a whole or by that of certain of its members. Thus, on joining a group a worker will usually have to adjust his or her own work speed to that of the group. The study of the behaviour of small groups is known as *group dynamics*.

In order to predict future behaviour of work groups, researchers have designed questionnaires to help identify the characteristics of such groups. These characteristics include: *autonomy*—independence of other groups; *cohesiveness*—extent to which the group functions as a unit; *control*—extent to which the group regulates its members' behaviour; *hedonic tone*—extent to which members enjoy belonging to the group; *homogeneity*—similarity in age, sex, and outlook; *intimacy*—familiarity of members with each other; *permeability*—ease of entry of new members; *polarization*—extent to which members agree on common goals; and *stratification*—existence of status levels within the group.

Another method of determining the internal relationship of groups of workers is by use of a *sociogram*. This is a diagram that shows, with arrowed lines, various types of relationship—for example, the person with whom each member of the group would most like to work, the person who commands most respect, or the person with whom each member has most contact.

Considerable research has also been made into the role and characteristics of the *group leader*—defined as the one who exerts more influence over his or her colleagues than they do over him or her. Such leadership, it has been observed, depends as much on the work situation as on the personal characteristics of the person. Different situations, in fact, usually call for different types of leaders. Also, a leader cannot afford to diverge too greatly in his or her thinking from that of the group, otherwise he or she will lose their support. That is why efforts by management or a particular person to "win over" the leader of a group, even though successful, may prove to be fruitless.

Behaviour of Supervisors

Most members of the human relations school of management thought attach great importance to the role of the plant supervisor. This is because, first, it is the level of manager who is in direct contact with the bulk of the firm's work force and with the work groups into which it is formally and informally divided. And secondly, because the way in which the supervisor behaves can greatly influence worker productivity. At one extreme, the supervisor can be autocratic in the way he or she treats the people under his or her charge. At the other, the supervisor can be unduly free and easy. The ideal behaviour lies somewhere in between.

Another distinction that has been made is between (a) the *employee-centred supervisor*—one who has great interest and confidence in his or her subordinates and does not interfere unduly in their work, and (b) the *job-centred supervisor*—one who is concerned mainly with completing the job and regards his or her subordinates (who, in his or her opinion, require close supervision and little discretion) purely as means to this end. According to most researchers, the employee-centred supervisor is the one who achieves the best results.

Inter-Group Behaviour

The efficiency of a firm is affected not only by the relationships within a group, but also by the relationships among the various groups. Researchers have found, not surprisingly, that the higher the degree of co-operation between groups, the higher usually is the level of their output. Various suggestions have been made on how to obtain this co-operation. One is that groups which may be in conflict (for example, a firm's production and marketing departments) should be given a sense of common purpose by careful "brainwashing" or by creation of a joint committee to help each department appreciate the other's point of view. Another suggestion to reduce inter-group conflict is to ensure that the normal flow of demands should proceed from higher status groups to lower status ones, rather than vice versa. Thus, in a business office, the clerks should not be given orders by the boss's secretary. Or, in a restaurant, the cooks should not be given orders by the waitresses.

Theory X and Theory Y

One of our inheritances from the past has been a pessimistic view of the nature of the average worker. This view, called Theory X by Professor Douglas McGregor,[3] holds that the average person is basically lazy, lacks ambition, dislikes responsibility, likes to be told what to do, likes security, is self-centred, dislikes change, has to be driven, is not very bright, is gullible and consequently can easily be led astray. Strict adherence to this view has led, in the past, particularly in military organizations but also in many factories, to extremely close supervision and strict discipline of subordinates—backed up by the threat of harsh punishment, such as immediate dismissal, for failure to obey orders or work sufficiently hard.

This view was challenged by McGregor, who argued that people are not basically lazy, unwilling to accept responsibility, and so on, but are made to become that way by the firm's organization and management. Given the right organization and treatment, particularly motivation, the workers in a firm can change completely. The increase in their productivity will be greatest if, in achieving the firm's goals, they are also achieving their own. This optimistic view of human nature was called, by McGregor, Theory Y, and it has already had considerable impact in modern business.

The Systems Approach

The newest approach to business management is the systems approach. A *system* is a set of interrelated elements (such as the various departments of a firm) which together form a complete unit that performs a particular function. Each of these elements (for example, the finance department) may in turn comprise a *sub-system*, with its own network of interrelated elements (the various sections and job positions).

A useful way of looking at a business organization, using the systems approach, is to consider the firm (the system) as comprising (a) a *technical sub-system*—the plant, equipment, layout, and technology required to produce the firm's goods;

---

[3] Douglas McGregor, *The Human Side of Enterprise*, New York: McGraw-Hill, 1960.

(b) a *human sub-system*—the persons employed and their attitudes; and (c) an *organizational sub-system*—the way in which the firm's material and human resources are used by management. At any time, changes can occur in one or more of these sub-systems (for example, introduction of new machinery or an increase in wage rates) that will affect the others, as well as the firm (or system) as a whole.

So far, we have considered the firm to be the system. But, in practice, a system must embrace all the various elements, external as well as internal, that are likely to affect a business management decision. Thus, any marketing decision by a firm must be based partly on information about the action of consumers, who form one of many external elements that affect marketing decisions.

The advocates of the systems approach conceive of business management primarily as a decision-making activity. Consequently, for a firm to achieve maximum efficiency, it should be organized so as to facilitate and improve this decision making. Each main decision-making area (for example, marketing management) has its own appropriate system and sub-systems through which information and communication should flow. In applying the systems approach, management, so it is argued, should identify the appropriate system for each particular decision-making centre and arrange information and communication flows accordingly. In fact more and more systems analysts are now being employed in business both to improve existing systems and procedures and to prepare for a conversion from manual to computerized information processing.

The systems approach has, in fact, been broken down into the following steps: (a) *determining goals*—unless these are correctly determined, an inappropriate system may be chosen; (b) *determining the main decision-making centres*—for example, production planning; (c) *determining information needs*—the information for decision making should be both timely and pertinent; (d) *determining communication channels*—the relevant information must be communicated from its various sources to the decision maker, whose decisions are communicated to subordinates; and (e) *grouping decision-making areas to reduce the burden of communications*—by grouping, say, all production planning and control staff physically close to each other, delays in communicating information and orders between them are reduced and co-ordination consequently improved.

KEY TERMS

Elton Mayo

Hawthorne experiments

Group dynamics

Sociogram

Group leader

Employee-centred supervisor

Job-centred supervisor

Inter-group behaviour

Theory X

Theory Y

Systems approach

Sub-system

REVIEW QUESTIONS

1. What is meant by the human relations approach to management?
2. Explain and discuss the significance of the Hawthorne experiments conducted by Elton Mayo.
3. What do most persons seek in their jobs? Why are they not always able to obtain what they want? What are the possible effects?
4. "People act differently when in a group than when on their own." Discuss with examples.
5. Explain the nature and purpose of a sociogram.
6. What makes a "group leader"? What types exist in business? How influential are they?
7. Productivity and inter-group behaviour are closely linked. Explain with reference to the modern business firm.
8. What is McGregor's "Theory X and Theory Y" concept? What possible uses can be made of this concept?
9. Explain what is meant by the systems approach to management. How does it affect a firm's organization? What technological developments have encouraged such an approach?

READING

The Japanese Fix

Theory is all very fine, but what really happens when eastern managers meet western workers?

BY ROBERT COLLISON

Source: *Canadian Business Magazine.* Use by permission of Robert Collison.

As opposed to such monikers as Ted Rogers and Conrad Black, the name Masaru Okumura doesn't quite have the ring appropriate for a man who could become a role model for Canadian business in the 1980s. Nevertheless, Okumura, the 44-year-old executive vice-president of Sony of Canada Ltd., symbolizes a revolution that is transforming the managerial culture of Canada. If it succeeds in its aims, this revolution will replace the traditional adversarial relationship between management and labor with one that stresses collaborative rather than competitive values. And it might also turn a man like Okumura into a more fitting symbol of the times than, say, a man like Conrad Black, whose high-octane ego and blustering style seem more reminiscent of the 1920s, when his mentor Bud McDougald began his career, than the 1980s, when such great corporations as Chrysler Corp. and Massey-Ferguson Ltd. are falling like dominoes in the face of cutthroat competition from the soft-spoken managers of the Orient.

Although there are many labels attached to the various forms of participatory management now being retailed in North America, all owe a debt to Japan for creating a more benign corporate culture.

In the last few years, as the Japanese industrial juggernaut has sent US and Canadian car makers scurrying to Ottawa and Washington for relief from Japanese imports—Ottawa has exacted from Tokyo a "voluntary" quota of 174,000 cars this year—numerous books have attempted to explain "How the Japanese Do It." [See p. 233.]

How has an impoverished group of islands about the size of the state of Montana managed in 30 years to recover from the radioactive rubble of Hiroshima and build the world's second-largest economy—a trillion-dollar economy, which, it should be noted, imports 100% of its aluminum, 99.8% of its oil and 66% of its wood? How has this resource-poor island been able to create certainly the most competitive and probably the most sophisticated industrial establishment in the world?

For many years, observers of the Japanese phenomenon attributed its success to such factors as a different work ethic, low defence expenditures, highly aggressive trade practices and the so-called advantages of having to rebuild after World War Two. But, as US consultant and Japan watcher William Givens notes, this explanation not only ignores the incredible competitive advantages enjoyed by North Americans, but also fails to grasp the real reason: superior economic policies. And the men who created and executed the policies that have made Japan Number One (to use Harvard sociologist Ezra Vogel's graphic term) are the super-managers in government—the Ministry of International Trade and Industry, the External Trade Department—and the big trading companies such as Mitsui & Co. Ltd. and Mitsubishi Corp.

Among the most important books recently published on the Japanese model is William Ouchi's *Theory Z: How American Business Can Meet the Japanese Challenge*. In this book, Ouchi, who is a management theorist at the University of California, tells about the day he brought the vice-president of one of the US's largest companies to meet two of his PhD students at UCLA. When he was asked what he considered the principal issue confronting American business in the 1980s, the executive replied without hesitation. It wasn't technology or investment, regulation or inflation. "The key issue will be the way in which we respond to the fact that the Japanese know how to manage better than we do."

Inherent in Japanese corporate culture is a variety of institutionalized managerial practices that nourish trust and cooperativeness—the qualities that even the most skeptical observers admit characterize Japanese industry. Possibly the most important is the practice of lifetime employment that covers about 35% of the work force and provides Japanese workers with the security so notably lacking in the West. And lifetime employment, according to many experts, explains why Japanese industry can more easily incorporate new technologies in the production process. If a robot makes a man on the assembly line redundant, he is retrained for another job. Because of the long-term commitment of workers to a company, management can justify the large investment in continuous employee training. (Job rotation is another spinoff of lifetime employment.) And during periods of recession, a worker will often be reassigned. "My brother-in-law works at Mazda headquarters," says Mamoru Iwamoto, deputy executive director of the Japan Trade Centre in Toronto. "After the oil shock, when there was a slump in car production, he was sent to a Mazda dealership in Tokyo to help with their marketing."

But lifetime employment is just the most dramatic demonstration of a totally different attitude of management toward workers. According to Yoshihiro Tsurumi, an international business professor at Baruch College in New York, "Many perceive our system as paternalistic, but in fact any well-managed company operates the same way. Look at Michelin & Company in France."

In a lecture in Toronto recently, Tsurumi, an expert on Japanese productivity, accused North American business of "scapegoating" workers. When business is good, management pays out big dividends to shareholders and fat bonuses to itself. "When business slumps, often because of poor management decisions, workers are laid off."

To managers like Okumura of Sony, or Neil Nagano, vice-president and general manager of Matsushita Industrial Canada Ltd. in Toronto, this cavalier attitude is incomprehensible. "The basic difference between Japan and Canada," according to Okumura, "is that you can't fire workers there." Unless, he says, laughing, "they're criminals."

"When we hire a worker at Sony, Mr. Akio Morita [Sony's chairman and cofounder] believes he becomes a member of the Sony family. You can't lay off a member of your family."

Some Japanese corporations have successfully imported the practice of long-term (as opposed to lifetime) employment to North America. Sony, for instance, has never laid off a worker at its huge television factory in San Diego. But it doesn't necessarily work here. At his 10-year-old Panasonic assembly plant in Toronto, Nagano laid off his first workers last year, because of "poor market conditions," although he remains committed to the idea of giving workers "security."

If the payoffs for both workers and managers of a practice like lifetime employment are quickly grasped by most westerners, Japan's consensus decision-making mystifies most non-Japanese.

Following a bottom-up decision-making process, Japan's senior executives expect that problems will be identified and policies initially suggested by their middle managers, who, in turn, have similar expectations of their subordinates. And by employing the *ringi* system—a *ringi* is a policy document that circulates to all the "appropriate people" involved in making a decision—responsibility for the decision is shared jointly by senior management.

"Our decision-making system seems very slow to many outsiders," says Tatsuo Fujimura, the executive director of the Japan Trade Centre, "but once a decision is made, it's implemented very quickly." Unlike North American CEOs, Japanese senior managers are spared the resistance of colleagues who've been uninformed about major new initiatives.

The effect of Japan's consensual style is to involve as many people as possible in the decision-making process and distribute responsibility evenly. Quality-control circles, another innovation crucial to the Japanese model, achieve similar effects on the shop floor. More than 10 million Japanese workers are organized in a million quality control circles throughout the country. The problem-solving worker groups meet regularly to monitor the quality standards of the goods they produce. They employ statistical quality-control methods perfected by the US industrial statistician W. Edwards Deming, who brought his ideas to Japan in the 1950s. (Today, the Deming Prize, awarded for meeting the highest quality standards, is the most coveted award in Japanese industry.)

The *ringi* system, quality-control groups and small work groups, which are the basic building blocks of Japanese industry, all serve to increase the sense of personal responsibility of workers and managers.

In Toronto recently, University of Michigan sociologist Robert Cole, the author of a major comparative study on Japanese and American industry, noted that Japan's participatory management model depends for its success on the willingness of managers to share information and power with workers. Because of the hierarchical nature of our industrial system, North American managers jealously hoard their power and perks. And this, more than any other factor, Cole believes, will make it difficult to transfer the Japanese system here.

Curiously, it's Japan's relative egalitarianism that most Japanese managers regard as central to the success of their industrial relations. "I don't think we have any more managerial skill than Canadians," says Tsutomu Iwasaki, a Toronto-based economic consultant. "Whatever genius our system possesses can be condensed to one point: equality. Equality between people in business, equality in pay, equality between workers and managers."

Iwasaki adds, "Compared with the case in North America and Europe, the difference in pay between senior executives and middle managers and workers in Japan is trifling. The president of a major company makes about $100,000. A middle manager will earn about $45,000."

According to Tatsuo Fujimura of the Japan Trade Centre, "A recent poll showed that 90% of Japanese consider themselves middle class." "Japan is a classless society," adds his colleague Mamoru Iwamoto.

"Ask a Japanese manager about blue-collar workers and he may tell you there are no blue-collar workers in his company," says Robert Cole. "In many companies people all wear the same uniform as a way of eliminating class distinctions. US managers would find that threatening."

"When Mr. Morita visits a Sony factory," says Masaru Okumura, "he always wears a light blue smock like all the other workers."

"When a visitor comes into my boss's office," says Mildred Setterington, a secretary at Toyota Canada Inc., "Mr. Sakai always introduces me. Most Canadian executives treat you as though you're invisible. Here, everyone is treated the same. Everyone's opinion is considered."

According to audit partner Michael Howard, of Peat, Marwick, Mitchell & Co. in Toronto, the Japanese managerial culture "blurs the distinction between workers and bosses." And if the testimony of Canadian workers such as Setterington is indicative, the common touch practised by such Japanese managers as Toyota Canada's president, Yukiyasu Togo, works miracles. Many of the books recently published on Japan argue that the West can learn a few lessons from the Japanese experience. This, in itself, is an about-face. Until recently, even such shrewd Japan watchers as management theorist Peter Drucker doubted that Japan's business techniques were exportable. In a 1971 essay, Drucker argued that it would be folly for managers in the West to imitate them. In fact, he claimed, "it would be impossible. Each of them is deeply rooted in Japanese traditions and culture." Quality-control work circles, consensus decision-making, lifetime employment, semi-autonomous worker groups, job rotation, and worker bonuses tied to the profitability of the company are great ideas, the theorists admitted. But like company songs and calisthenics before the morning shift, they're inappropriate for the free-wheeling individualists who man the assembly lines in Windsor and Detroit. Employing a "history-is-destiny" argument, these critics suggested that only in a "group-oriented" society like Japan's could such novel innovations work. Even the Japanese government contributes to this bias; a recent government-sponsored film attributes Japan's unique form of corporate decision-making, and the supposed predisposition of the Japanese to working harmoniously in groups, to social skills acquired after centuries of cultivating wet rice.

But in a recent book, Peter Drucker says that Japan's present system of industrial relations emerged from the fact that Japan "so far, alone among major industrial countries, has asked the right questions" about how to run complex industrial organizations.

Drucker provides no conclusive answer as to how the Japanese arrived at their present wisdom—except to suggest that it probably emerged as a result of the national "rethink" the country engaged in after its devastating defeat in World War Two. But he does debunk the myth that it's their culture that makes the masses work industriously together like a human ant colony. Granted the Japanese prize loyalty and cooperativeness as civic virtues. And the quest for social harmony—what the Japanese call the spirit of *wa*—is an obvious advantage for any society wishing to create a more fraternal system of industrial relations. But the fact remains that Japan's history of labor relations has been, until recent times, abysmal. As Drucker writes, "As late as the 1920s, that is through the formative stage of modern Japanese industry, Japan had the worst, most disruptive, and most violent labor relations of any industrial country in the world."

If Japan's relatively peaceful system of worker/management relations owes less to the peculiarity of Japanese society, and more to conscious decisions made after the last war, then Japan as a model for the West takes on much more credibility.

The present interest in the Japanese model infuriates many business and labor leaders in both North America and Europe. Over the past 30 years men and women on both sides of the Atlantic have been tinkering with our system. Experiments in worker participation in ownership, profit sharing and decision-making at both the corporate level—what the Germans call "co-determination"—and in the workplace—what the British call "industrial democ-racy"—have been common. In the past few years a movement called the Quality of Working Life (QWL) has gained momentum, especially in an auto industry that is desperately trying to improve productivity and the quality of its products to check Japanese competition. (Japan has captured 24% of the North American car market.)

In fact, since the 1960s many of these alternate-management models have already transformed the corporate personalities of firms in both the US and Canada. According to William Ouchi, numerous corporations—IBM Corp., Hewlett-Packard Co. and Procter & Gamble Inc.—demonstrate qualities similar to those thought to be uniquely "Japanese." He might have mentioned Dofasco Inc. of Hamilton, too. These Type Z organizations practise many of the same techniques as similar Japanese corporations: long-term employment, a heavy investment in worker training, worker self-management, slow evaluation and promotion and the conscious cultivation of a strong corporate persona.

What distinguishes a company like an IBM from a Sony isn't so much its managerial culture as the national environment in which it does business. Sony functions in a culture where its business practices are more or less the norm; North America's Type Z corporations are wildly idiosyncratic.

Nevertheless, Type Z companies represent the fruition of ideas advanced by management theorists such as Douglas McGregor. His famous formulation about the differences between Theory X and Theory Y managers, advanced in 1960, anticipated much of the contemporary debate. And McGregor's Theory Y managers possess a distinctly Japanese hue.

Old-line Theory X managers believe that people are inherently lazy, dislike work, and require strict supervision. Big telephone companies are a good example of Theory

X organizations. Theory Y managers believe that people like to work and do well. An effective Theory Y manager encourages his staff to perform by cultivating an atmosphere of trust and cooperation. And Abraham Maslow's ideas about humanistic psychology, which gained currency in the 1960s, reinforced McGregor. According to Maslow, once an employee is making enough to satisfy his primary needs, such desires as the respect of his peers and self-esteem become more important than a higher pay packet. Theory Y was a radical repudiation of the "scientific management" approach of theorists such as Frederick Taylor, who attempted to reduce workers to adjuncts of machines.

Although McGregor's ideas influenced Type Z corporate managers, most American industries continued to operate on the premise that management buys "hired hands" for eight hours a day. And management prefers, according to Yoshihiro Tsurumi of Baruch College, that "workers keep their heads, their screwed-up heads, at home." The separation of work life from private life is the aspect of North American business culture that most puzzles Japanese managers. According to Yukiyasu Togo of Toyota, "In Japan we spend so much time at work we want to be as happy there as at home."

If the Japanese model and the new western movements in industrial relations spring from different environments, they have reached many similar conclusions, although QWL gurus such as York University's Eric Trist are infuriated when too close a parallel is drawn. According to Trist, "QWL is much wider and deeper than the Japanese system. We're attempting to redesign work to optimize both its social and technical requirements." And to Harvey Kolodny, a management studies professor at the University of Toronto, "QWL is about changing values." But in attempting to restore "dignity" to the workplace and to give workers genuine participation in the work process, QWL may be asking Canadian society to buy into a set of values already in place in Japan.

Among the most zealous converts to QWL is Roy Bennett, the president of Ford Motor Co. of Canada Ltd. Last year, Bennett bluntly stated that North American industry is at a "fork in the road. It will tend to follow either the English or the Japanese examples. In the English example, there has been a continuous increase in the adversarial relationship between management and employees: more friction, more hostility, and probably less satisfaction. In the Japanese example, there is a more harmonious relationship and more interaction between workers and management. I'm not suggesting that North America should, or will, adopt the model of Japanese industrial society . . . but it is the principle and the philosophy of employee-management relations that is the issue. . . . QWL reflects a fundamental change in [our] management style from the authoritative approach to the participative approach. In effect, it's saying to [our] employees, 'We need your help'."

If QWL ideas are developing *in utero* at such places as Ford's Oakville, Ont., plant, Japanese managers are introducing the same ideas in their Canadian and US subsidiaries. In theory, they provide an environment in which to test these new ideas about the worker/boss relationship.

Partly motivated by the increasingly protectionist policies of government, business, and labor in North America, Japanese companies are opening up more factories overseas. Such businessmen as Okumura of Sony of Canada (1980 sales $106 million; net income $4.4 million) and Nagano of Matsushita Industrial Canada (1980 sales $50 million) are the bridgehead of a growing legion of corporate managers crossing the Pacific to run "Canadian" companies. A few months ago, Nissan Motor Co. broke good Tennessee topsoil for a half-billion-dollar truck plant; it's the largest industrial investment in the state's history. Toyota is currently negotiating with the BC government about establishing a parts plant on the West Coast. Panasonic Industries Canada Ltd., Sanyo Electric Trading Co. Ltd., and Hitachi Sales Corp. of Canada Ltd. assemble televisions in plants in Toronto, and YKK, the world's largest zipper company, runs a Japanese-style plant in Montréal.

Is it, then, only a matter of time before Japanese miracles erase all our industrial woes? If the meteoric rise of US-style business management ideology in the 1960s and its precipitous fall in the 1980s provide any clues, a certain skepticism is in order. This isn't to say that the Japanese model or Type Z corporations are a mere fad. But as any great economic empire emerges, a certain fascination with its folkways ensues. In the early 1960s, when the American empire was at its zenith and US multinationals were setting up shop around the globe, the French journalist Jean-Jacques Servan-Schreiber wrote a celebrated book called *Le défi américain (The American Challenge)*, in which he said that Americans were superior not because of their money, resources, or technology, but because of their management skills. And, over the next 20 years, the world's best and brightest flocked to Harvard or Stanford to pick up the tricks necessary to turn a company around in a quarter, and pump up bottom lines through the artful manipulation of numbers.

In contrast to the marketing and financial wizards that American business schools graduate, Japanese industry hires generalists fresh out of school and apprentices them in the company's business. Okumura, for example, says "I was interested in marketing, but I worked in a factory when I began at Sony."

If American management techniques look shopworn a generation after Servan-Schreiber's warning, Type Z management appears freshly minted and squeaky clean. But how well *does* it work here?

If the experiences of Japanese corporations in Canada are any evidence, the results to date are contradictory. Like the enthusiastic secretaries at Toyota, most Canadian employees give their Japanese bosses high marks in human relations. But even the most successful expatriate managers have, so far, only played with Japanese techniques. And this "timidity" reflects the tact that the Japanese bring to their dealings with foreigners. As Togo of Toyota says laughingly, "We have a semi-Japanese system here. We are interested to know the Canadian way."

But then Toyota, like most Japanese corporations in Canada, remains essentially a small (150 employees at head office) marketing arm of the parent company. Neil Nagano, on the other hand, runs a factory making TV sets. He supervises a staff of 220, organizes a complex manufacturing system and deals with a union.

When the Panasonic plant opened in 1972 it became the 10th television manufacturer in Canada. "At the time we weren't manufacturing color televisions in Japan and there was a market for them in Canada. So we decided to open a plant here." Eight years later, five other companies have closed down, and Panasonic has becomes the second-largest producer in the country.

Yoshihiro Tsurumi has noted that both Matsushita and Sanyo took over rundown US factories and turned them around in six months. "In other words, by employing only Japanese management techniques they made a profit." It took Nagano, who began from scratch, three years. But Japanese managers take a long-term view, and Nagano didn't complain. "Initially we produced 20-25 sets a day, 500 units a month. Today we assemble more than 10,000 units a month. Seventy thousand are sold in Canada yearly, and 60,000 are exported to the US." On the business side, Panasonic appears a success.

Konosuke Matsushita, the founder of the Matsushita Electrical Co., is one of the great management innovators of postwar industrial Japan. Committed to producing high-quality consumer goods at a reasonable price, Matsushita developed his company as a corporate city state by being a combination of Machiavelli, Henry Ford, and Rev. Moon. At Matsushita in Japan, all employees receive two types of training. One is basic skills training, but the second, more fundamental one is training in Matsushita values. The Employee's Creed, which workers recite each day, goes as follows: "Progress and development can be realized through the combined efforts of our company. Each of us, therefore, shall keep this idea constantly in mind as we devote ourselves to the continuous improvement of the company."

Reciting the company creed has never been attempted in the Panasonic plant on the Queensway, although a few years back they tried a morning exercise call. It fizzled out.

At the Panasonic plant all the workers are organized into groups that elect their own leader, who reports to a supervisor. Although there are no quality-control circles as such, each morning the group meets to discuss the day's work. Nagano hopes to set up QC circles, although unlike Japan, they will meet on the company's time, not the employee's. As well, Nagano trains his workers in a variety of jobs both to avoid tedium and to make the work arrangements more flexible. Last year he laid off workers for the first time in eight years, but he remains committed to the idea that "the employees should feel they have a job here as long as they want." In an industry with an annual turnover of 100%, Panasonic's 30%-40% looks good.

"When I first came to Canada, I thought workers were lazy and lacked initiative," he says. "But later I came to realize it was because of the way they were treated by management. At first we had only 10 Canadian employees, and it was easy to maintain a family atmosphere. Today we have 220 employees. It isn't as easy." Still, the company provides an impeccably clean factory, an airy cafeteria and spacious washrooms. ("You won't see lavatories like this at most factories," says Nagano.)

But if the palatial WCs symbolize the spirit of Konosuke Matsushita's paternalism, a recent contretemps between Nagano and the union fingers some of the problems Japanese managers are likely to encounter in the rough-and-tumble of Canadian labor relations. In Japan, most unions are company unions; all Matsushita employees belong to a Matsushita union, not one representing workers in the electrical industry. And most company unions "cooperate" closely with management. Last year, Panasonic was organized by the United Electrical, Radio and Machine Workers of America. In Japan, Mr. Matsushita may expect the dutiful devotion of his loyal employees, but Nagano is unlikely to be able to perch comfortably on a pedestal in his Queensway plant. In an interview with the *Toronto Star* this spring, Nagano made some unflattering remarks about Canadian workers that riled the shop steward. As a result, both Nagano and production head Dominic Spina suggested it would be best "not to mention the union at all." But the union is unlikely to play dead for any management, no matter how benign. And Neil Nagano's little misunderstanding with his shop steward may be a sign that Japanese ways won't root effortlessly in Canada.

Read How the Japanese Do It

As Japanese cars pile up in Yokohama harbor because of the "voluntary" export restraints imposed by the West, another Japanese-inspired product has been doing a booming business. Japanese "how-to" books have suddenly become the hottest item in publishing, as numerous academics, management consultants and Japan watchers rush to offer us advice on how we can emulate the world's great emulators.

Among the most popular of these books are William Ouchi's **Theory Z: How American Business Can Meet the Japanese Challenge** (Addison-Wesley, $16.25) and Richard Pascale and Anthony Atho's **The Art of Japanese Management** (Simon & Schuster, $15.95). Riding the crest of a trend, both books have catapulted into the *New York Times* bestseller list, which is a distinction rarely enjoyed by books on business management theory. Ouchi and Pascale, in fact, originally collaborated back in 1973 on a study about management practices in the US and Japan, when they both were on the Stanford University faculty.

Ouchi's book is breezier and less academic. *Theory Z* is very much the "how-to" guide for North American managers interested in transforming themselves into benign rather than belligerent bosses. *The Art of Japanese Management* provides a considerably more sophisticated analysis of the various qualities that distinguish Japanese business organization. As well, it includes two fascinating chapters comparing the management styles of Harold Geneen, the tyrannical head of International Telephone and Telegraph Corp., with Konosuke Matsushita, the legendary and benevolent founder of Matsushita Electric Co.

Ezra Vogel's **Japan As Number One: Lessons for America** (Harper & Row, $6.75) is a detailed analysis of contemporary Japanese society. Vogel suggests Japan is even further advanced as a superbly functioning postindustrial society than we care to admit. He concludes with these bracing words: "Unless America's competitiveness is improved, short-range palliatives are likely to have little effect and the imbalance may well increase."

In his new book of essays, **Toward the Next Economics** (Harper & Row, $15.95), Peter Drucker includes two essays on Japan. Drucker has always been in the forefront on the subject of "Japan Inc." One of these new essays is an interesting explanation of Japan's success through an analysis of Japanese art, in which he writes, "Central to Japan is constant and continuing polarity between tight, enveloping community—supportive, but demanding subordination to its rules—and competitive individualism demanding spontaneity."

Robert Cole's **Work, Mobility & Participation** (University of California Press, $8) is a useful comparative study of the differences between Japanese and American industry. It joins a growing list of such books, including Ronald Dore's **British Factory—Japanese Factory** (Allen & Unwin, $61.60).

In a recent speech, Bob White, Canadian president of the United Automobile, Aerospace and Agricultural Implement Workers of America, criticized those individuals who seek "superficial solutions" to Canada's labor problems by looking to a "Japanese model." Although White acknowledged the strengths of the Japanese system, he suggested that Japanese productivity owes more to the longer hours that

Japanese workers put in (the 5½ day week is common) than management fixes. He advised the Japanese to "move toward European and North American standards."

Is the Japanese model an excuse for labor-bashing? Bob White thinks that those who push the Japanese model are "essentially company men." And certainly Sony's Morita has made every effort to keep unions from organizing his American plant. "We want to keep the union out to maintain our philosophy. We want to keep our family whole and not have a third party interfering."

Ultimately, the debate about whether the Japanese model, or any of the other new movements in participatory labor relations, can effect a major change in our economy inevitably leads to a few tough questions. Can the Japanese system coexist with independent unions? Will the likes of Ford's Roy Bennett really give workers some role in decision making? (QWL, he has noted, "is not a substitute for the managerial decision-making process.") But equally important, can Canadians begin to regard their work as a function of social life? To William Ouchi, Japan's work culture has three essential ingredients—intimacy, trust, caring. "The essential thread in Japanese life is intimacy—the caring, support, and disciplined unselfishness that make life possible come through close relations. In work terms this translates into three qualities that distinguish the Japanese company—trust, loyalty to the firm, and commitment to a job through one's working life.

If these attitudes can't be assimilated into Canada's economic culture, it's unlikely that quality-control circles will magically transform ours into a Type Z economy like Japan's.

And the big hurdle blocking such a transformation of attitudes is skepticism among both workers and managers. As one young auto parts worker observed at a QWL conference in June, "These things are management cons."

Maybe Canada will require a shock similar to the one Japan experienced in 1945. After the war, the ownership of Japanese industry moved from a few large supercompanies, the *zaibatsu*, to a much wider group of banks and insurance companies. After the war no one owned Japan, and management took over. As a result, according to Japan expert Robert Ballon, the companies don't belong to the shareholders. Business really belongs to the people who work there. And the object of business isn't usually or primarily to make money, but to provide jobs.

If Roy Bennett can convince the young auto parts worker that this is true in Canada as well, then Japan's other management techniques may survive the transplant. If not, labor will likely rouse its immunological defences and reject them as soon as Canada leaves surgery.

Assignment

1. Who is Masaru Okumura? What does he symbolize?
2. How has Japan been able to build the world's second-largest economy, despite all the odds stacked against it?
3. What is "Theory Z"?
4. Explain the accusation that North American business firms "scapegoat" their workers.
5. What is probably the biggest difference between the Japanese and North American styles of business management?

6. What is meant by the Japanese "ringi" system of management decision-making? What are its strengths and weaknesses?
7. What role do "quality circles" play in Japanese industry?
8. What is Ford Motor Co.'s QWL program? What is its long-term goal? What have been its effects so far?
9. Why may it be difficult to adopt the Japanese style of management in North America?
10. To what extent do cultural factors account for the difference in management approach between North American and Japanese business firms?
11. Contrast labour relations in North America and Japan.
12. What is YKK's "Cycle of Goodness"? How has it worked out in YKK's zipper plant in Montreal?
13. "North America's Type Z Corporations are wildly idiosyncratic." Explain.
14. Distinguish between Theory X and Theory Y managers.
15. The aspect of North American business culture most puzzling to Japanese managers is the separation of work life from private life. Discuss.
16. How do the Japanese train their business managers?
17. What are some of the problems that Japanese managers have encountered in Canadian labour relations?
18. Compare Japanese with Canadian labour unions.
19. Is the Japanese model an excuse for "labour-bashing"? Explain and discuss.
20. According to William Ouchi, Japan's work culture has three essential ingredients. Explain.

PART D
PRODUCTION MANAGEMENT

This is the first of the major functional areas of business that we examine. Only if goods can be manufactured of good quality, and at a competitive cost, can they be sold within Canada and abroad. Whatever the marketing effort (discussed in the next part), the ultimate success or failure of the enterprise, if a manufacturing one, is usually decided on the factory floor.

CHAPTER 7
MODERN MANUFACTURING

CHAPTER OBJECTIVES

☐ To describe the various types of manufacturing processes.

☐ To explain and discuss the characteristics of modern manufacturing.

☐ To indicate how a manufacturing plant is laid out and the factors involved.

☐ To describe the basic types of equipment and buildings used in manufacturing.

☐ To explain how methods analysis is used to improve production efficiency.

CHAPTER OUTLINE

7.1 Types of Manufacturing
7.2 Plant Layout, Equipment, and Buildings
7.3 Methods Analysis and Time Study

UNIT 7.1: TYPES OF MANUFACTURING

Manufacturing is the process of making goods with the assistance of power-driven machines, involving varying levels of worker skill and technological know-how. Originally, the term was used to describe the process of making goods by hand using relatively simple tools. Nowadays the term "handicraft" is applied to such work.

Today, in Canada, relatively few products are handmade. Modern manufacturing, by employing a high degree of mechanization, and in some cases automation, by using electric rather than human power, by specializing the work of each employee, and by using mass production techniques and standardization where appropriate, is able to produce goods much more abundantly and much more cheaply than any handicraft system.

Primary, Secondary, and Tertiary Industries

Business firms that produce similar goods or services are known collectively as an *industry*.

Canadian industry is sometimes classified into three broad groups—primary, secondary, and tertiary. Manufacturing falls mainly into the second category.

Primary industries. These industries are concerned with the extraction and initial or "primary" processing of raw materials from the land and sea—for example, milling wheat into flour. They include: agriculture, mining, forestry, fishing, oil and natural gas.

Secondary industries. These industries convert the processed raw materials into finished goods by various manufacturing or refining operations. Thus, for example, flour is made into bread and other bakery products; crude oil is refined into gasoline, lubricating oil, etc; and lumber turned into home and office furniture.

Tertiary industries. These are the industries that provide services to the public. They include government, tourism, hotels, restaurants, insurance, hospital care, education, entertainment, communications, transportation, and financial services.

Manufacturing Processes

There are many different manufacturing processes used to convert raw materials and parts into semi-finished or finished products. One simple classification of these processes is into: extractive; conditioning; analytical; synthetic; and assembly.

Extractive. In the manufacturing sense, this is the removal of raw materials from land, sea, and air. The mining of gold, silver, copper, and other minerals is an example of extraction from the land. The removal of salt, chlorine, and sodium from the sea and oxygen from the air are examples of extraction from other sources.

Conditioning (or fabricating). This is the process of changing a raw material into a more valuable form. Examples of conditioning are the conversion of wheat into flour, hides into leather, cotton into cloth, and sheet metal into bathtubs.

Analytical. These are processes in which a raw material is broken down into several different products. Thus, in a meat packing plant, a pig can be cut up into various meat products, such as hams, chops, sausage meat, and bacon, as well as into lard, fertilizer, and shoe leather. Similarly, petroleum can be broken down into such products as gasoline, lubricating oils, fuel oils, and paraffin.

Synthetic. These are processes in which two or more raw materials are combined (that is, synthesized) to form a finished product. Examples are the production of bread and cement.

Assembly. This is the process of putting together a number of component parts and materials to form a finished product—for example, cars, radios, and refrigerators. *Sub-assembly* is the same process, except that the product—for example, a carburetor—will be used as a component part of the finished product, the car.

Size of Production Run

In this classification, manufacturing is divided into three basic types: custom manufacturing, batch manufacturing, and mass production.

Custom manufacturing. Here one or a few items are made to the customer's particular specifications—for example, a tailored suit or several pairs of hand-made boots or shoes. This is the most expensive type of production per unit of output.

Batch manufacturing. In this type of manufacturing, the product is manufactured in batch lots of varying amounts, depending on the product. Because of the longer production run, per unit production costs are much lower than in custom manufacturing, nevertheless they are still much greater than that of a mass-produced item. However, costs of batch production can be significantly lowered by use of automation, involving numerically-controlled machine tools, and by computerized scheduling of raw material requirements. In fact, computer-assisted design and manufacture is already significantly lowering the cost of batch production.

Mass production. As the name suggests, this is the production of goods in great quantity. Where the demand for a product is large, and where the product can be satisfactorily manufactured or assembled with the use of machines, production tends to be concentrated in one or a few large manufacturing plants rather than in many small ones. This is because of the savings to be made (the

How newsprint is produced

Mechanical pulp, the chief ingredient of newsprint, may be made either by shredding logs on a grindstone (1); or by feeding chips to refiners (2) where they are defibrated between two circular blades. The first method gives groundwood pulp, the second either refiner mechanical pulp, or thermomechanical pulp. The difference is that for thermomechanical pulp the refiner is kept under pressure at temperatures up to 250°F. The pulp is then screened and thickened and blended with a chemical pulp (4), either sulphite or kraft, before moving on to the paper machine.

The chemical pulp accounts for about 25 per cent of the pulp mixture used in newsprint manufacture. It is produced (3) by reducing the wood to chips and then cooking the chips in chemicals. The pulp is blown through a pipe into a blow pit, and then washed and screened.

The stock, composed of one part pulp to about 200 parts water, flows onto the paper machine. There gravity, suction, pressure, and heat remove the water, and the paper receives its finish on the calender stack (5), before emerging as a continuous strip.

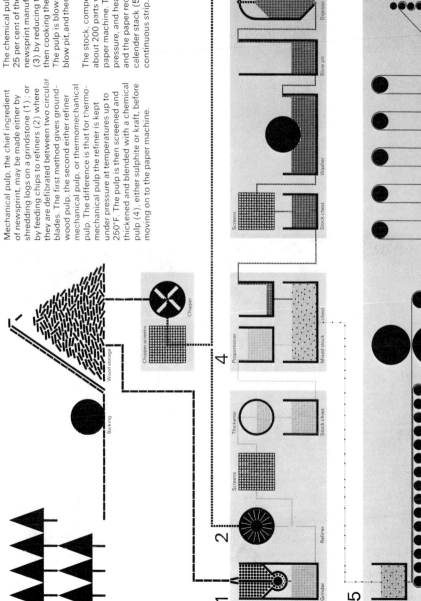

Figure 7.1 How Newsprint Is Produced.
Courtesy Canadian Pulp and Paper Association

"economies of scale") by long production runs. Fixed costs (such as rent, maintenance, office salaries, research, and advertising) per unit of output fall as production increases, and large quantities of materials and parts can be bought at a discount. This is the least expensive type of production per unit of output. However, such a manufacturing plant involves an extremely large initial capital investment.

In this type of production, identical or closely similar products are manufactured for long periods of time. Because all orders follow an identical sequence of manufacturing operations and involve relatively long production runs, machines and sub-assembly areas can be economically laid out in a continuous line and highly-mechanized materials handling methods can be employed. This is why the term *continuous-line manufacturing* is also sometimes used to describe this type of manufacturing production. An example of mass production is the manufacture of automobiles.

To avoid confusion, it should be mentioned that the term *continuous-flow manufacturing* is used to describe a manufacturing process that is continued on a 24-hour basis. One of the few examples of this type of manufacturing process is oil refining.

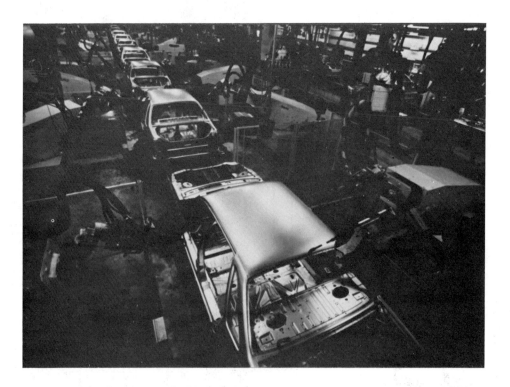

Courtesy of Ford of Canada

Job-Order versus Standard Manufacturing

Job-order manufacturing occurs in a plant that has a variety of relatively small orders, each having its own particular specifications. It is also known as *intermittent* or *custom manufacturing*. Examples of this type of manufacturing range from made-to-measure clothing to small orders for a particular line of machine components. With job-order manufacturing, the variety of orders means a variety of manufacturing operations and sequences, and this prevents the use of a continuous production line. In terms of quantity produced, a job-order may range from one or two of the same item to several thousand.

Standard manufacturing, by contrast, is production of standard items for stock—for example, most automobiles, kitchen appliances, and clothing. This type of production is also known as continuous-line manufacturing, repetitive manufacturing, and mass production.

Characteristics of Modern Manufacturing

Modern manufacturing has various distinctive features that we now consider in turn.

Mechanization.
This term means using machines to perform work formerly done by hand. Most industries are highly mechanized, for it has not been difficult over the course of years to devise machines that can perform most routine tasks more efficiently than human beings can. Thus, as one of innumerable examples, bread can be prepared, baked, sliced, and packaged by machines. Employees, instead of making the goods themselves, are used in smaller numbers to operate the machines.

Automation.
This is, in essence, the control of machines by machines. Whereas mechanization economized on human labour (by having machines do most of the work, but with people operating and controlling them), automation does without people almost completely by having other machines do the operating and controlling. In the car industry, for example, engine blocks can be moved, positioned, drilled, and inspected automatically.

A distinguishing feature of an automated system is what is termed *feed-back*. This is the ability of the controlling machine to detect and rectify errors as they occur. A simple example is the home thermostat, which starts the furnace operating when the temperature falls below a certain level. Another example is the system of elevators in a high-rise office building, which can be programmed to take account of traffic patterns.

Electric Power.
Electricity is used by manufacturing industry to drive machinery and equipment. The importance to industry of this relatively recent invention cannot be too highly stressed. Without it, manufacturing would have to fall back on the types of power commonly used in previous generations—steampower, water power, animal power, and human power. As most parts of

Canada are rich in water power, hydro-electricity has been the main type of electricity generated. The other type (one-third of the total generating capacity) is thermal electricity from coal, oil, or nuclear power stations.

Specialization. This means, in the case of labour, that a worker specializes in one or a few aspects of the production of a good rather than making the complete good himself or herself. By specialization, each worker can perform a specific task more skilfully and more quickly. Together, a group of workers, each specializing in a different aspect of the production process, can produce far more than if each produced the complete article individually. Today, of course, with the technical complexity of so many products, a person would often find it impossible to make the complete product. The principle of specialization is applied not only to labour, but also to machines and to manufacturing plants. For specialization to be economically feasible, the volume of output required must be sufficient to keep the specialized labour, machines, or plants fully employed.

Standardization. This is the adoption of standards for each material, part, machine, tool, product, process, or work method used in the manufacturing firm. A *standard* indicates exactly what characteristics a material, part, etc., should have, covering such items as performance, composition, colour, shape, size, weight, and finish. Standardization of materials and parts is essential if machines are to be used in the manufacturing process, as machines can be designed to handle efficiently only fixed sizes and shapes. Standardized machines offer the advantage that spare parts can be stocked in smaller quantities, and maintenance and repair (through specialized knowledge) done more quickly. Standard work methods mean that the best method (as identifed by time and motion studies) for each task is adopted for use in the plant. Standard materials are essential if a firm is to live up to its claims about the life expectancy and efficient performance of its products.

Synchronization. Modern manufacturing operations are usually quite complex, involving large numbers of workers, a vast array of machines, and a continuous inflow of materials and component parts to be assembled or otherwise made into finished goods. Therefore, precise timing of the various manufacturing and assembly operations is critical. Nowadays, in many manufacturing plants, a delay in a sub-assembly or other manufacturing operation, or in delivery of materials or parts, can easily hold up a whole production line. Because of this need for synchronization, each worker must keep up a certain pace in his or her work or else delay the work of many others. And "just in time" inventory control (with low safety stocks of materials and parts and exact timing of deliveries from locally situated suppliers) is becoming more and more widespread.

Technology. The technical knowledge employed to produce and market goods has increased at a fantastic rate in the twentieth century. In fact, most of the goods purchased today were not available two or three generations ago. Compared with the nineteenth century, it takes a much shorter time between the invention of a new material, product, machine, or method and its commercial application.

CAD/CAM. With the lower price and increased sophistication of modern electronic computers, more and more firms in Canada and elsewhere are turning to computer-assisted design and computer-assisted manufacturing, or CAD/CAM for short. Experience so far shows that the use of computers in designing products and manufacturing processes, as well as in planning and controlling production, can greatly improve productivity—that is, a greater value of output per person employed. Until recently, computers were applied to separate tasks such as inventory control, accounting, production control, etc. Nowadays, because of the enormous improvements in computer hardware and software, the thrust is towards computer integrated manufacturing (or CIM). This involves running many different operations within the manufacturing firm on an integrated basis.

Robotics. Already in Canadian auto plants, industrial robots are busy welding and painting cars. These robots operate under the instructions of built-in microcomputers. And the whole process, involving the use of robots on an assembly line, is known as "automated assembly." However, the more modern robots can be programmed for a variety of repetitive manufacturing tasks instead of just one. This process is called "automated flexible assembly." An example is the use of robots to put the trim on cars or seals on car doors. (The word "robot," incidentally, is derived from the Czech word *robota*, meaning worker. It was first used by Karel Capek in a 1921 play called R.U.R.—Rossum's Universal Robots—in which robots destroy the human race.)

Manufacturing Productivity

The term *productivity* is normally used in the sense of *labour productivity*—meaning the value of the average output per person employed over a given period of time such as an hour, a week, or a year.

Importance of High Productivity. The more goods a person can produce in a given amount of time, the lower is the per unit labour cost of such goods. The actual cost will also depend on the wage structure—how much the company has to pay in wages and fringe benefits for the employee's time. Thus, if wages and fringe benefits are higher in Canadian manufacturing than in, say, South Korea, then, for Canadian goods to be competitive in price with the Korean ones, the productivity of the Canadian worker must be relatively much higher in order to offset the wage differential.

For many years, unfortunately, the rate of increase in Canadian manufacturing productivity has lagged well behind that of most other industrial nations, particularly those of southeast Asia. As a result, many Canadian manufacturers have gone out of business or now buy all or part of their products from abroad, with a consequent reduction in income and employment in Canada. On the bright side, many Canadian manufactured goods are sold in Canada and others exported to the U.S., where industrial productivity is very similar to that of Canada. Also, a weak Canadian dollar, compared with the U.S. one, has reduced the U.S. dollar cost of Canadian goods and, therefore, made them more competitive in the United States.

Price is, of course, only one key factor that makes a product competitive in world markets. Another is quality. Other key factors are the advertising, selling, delivery, credit, product warranty, and after-sales service. However, if Canadians can increase their productivity, this will be an important step in (a) making Canadian goods more competitive in price, and thereby helping to keep existing jobs in Canada as well as creating new ones, and (b) improving present wage and salary scales.

Factors Affecting Productivity. There are many reasons why manufacturing productivity varies from one country to another. The following would seem to be the most important.

1. Research and Development. One way of increasing manufacturing productivity in Canada is to develop new products that can be readily sold at home and abroad. And this has happened, for example, with telecommunications

Courtesy The Ontario Ministry of Industry, Trade and Technology

equipment. It requires, however, a substantial and sustained research and development program, involving both the private and public sectors.

2. Attitude. Perhaps the master key to Japan's industrial success in modern times has been the attitude of its people. Only dedicated commitment by both management and labour, and a supportive government, can explain how a string of relatively small islands, with few raw materials or fuels, could have become the world's manufacturing powerhouse. Restoration of the "work ethic" in Canada, wherever it is lacking, would seem to be another critical requirement of higher productivity. Already, many Canadian firms have experimented with profit sharing, stock ownership and other plans as a way of securing more meaningful employee involvement. Also, with a "Theory Y" approach, managements in many companies have set up "quality circles" and other programs ("Quality is Job 1") to raise productivity, with the cooperation of the employees and their labour unions.

3. Capital Investment. Another path to higher manufacturing productivity is the installation of the most up-to-date equipment, and even a move to newer, better designed premises. More and more firms have automated their manufacturing processes and many more are now using computers to assist in both product design and manufacture. In the mass-production industries, such as automobiles, industrial robots are already carrying out repetitive tasks such as spot welding.

4. Government Support. In today's fiercely competitive world, Canadian manufacturing firms, if they are to create more jobs and income, need all the support they can get from government. Most other countries of the world have already recognized this need for a government-industry partnership. Research assistance, technological education, investment incentives, low-interest financing, export promotion, are all areas in which government can create a better environment for manufacturing. In Canada, the federal and provincial governments are already doing much in this regard.

KEY TERMS

Manufacturing	Continuous-line manufacturing
Primary manufacturing	Continuous-flow manufacturing
Secondary manufacturing	Job-order manufacturing
Manufacturing processes	Standard manufacturing
Extraction	Mechanization
Conditioning	Automation
Analytical processes	Specialization
Synthetic processes	Standardization
Assembly	Synchronization
Size of production run	CAD/CAM

Custom manufacturing
Batch manufacturing
Mass production
CIM
Robotics
Productivity

REVIEW QUESTIONS

1. Distinguish between primary and secondary manufacturing.
2. Explain, with examples, the five basic manufacturing processes.
3. Distinguish between custom manufacturing, batch manufacturing, and mass production. Why do all three types of manufacturing exist at the same time?
4. Distinguish between continuous-line manufacturing and continuous-flow manufacturing.
5. Distinguish between job-order and standard manufacturing.
6. Distinguish between mechanization and automation.
7. What are the various types of power used in industry? Why is electric power the most popular? What are its disadvantages, if any?
8. Why is specialization an essential characteristic of modern manufacturing production? What are its disadvantages?
9. Why is standardization necessary in manufacturing? What forms does it take?
10. Explain the concept of "synchronization" and its importance for manufacturing.
11. What is CAD/CAM? How will it affect Canadian manufacturing?
12. What is "automated flexible assembly"? Why is it being introduced?
13. What is "productivity"? Why is it so important? What factors cause it to be higher in (a) different industries and (b) different countries?

CASE PROBLEM

BENTLEY SHOES LTD.
An example of a manufacturing process

Bentley Shoes Ltd. manufactures men's work boots and shoes of various styles and qualities, men's everyday shoes, and men's and boys' "desert" suede boots. Production varies from about 10,000 pairs of footwear in June to 4,000 pairs in December. Average production is about 7,000 pairs per month.

The materials used in manufacturing include lace and lace eyelets, thread, welting (a leather or plastic stripping), tacks and nails, cork, fabric and paper liners, glue, waxes, dyes, and many different leathers such as calfskin, kip, side leather, kidskin, and suede (the flesh side of kid or calf).

During the course of its manufacture, each pair of footwear passes through four different work areas. These are the cutting room, the fitting and lasting room, the making room, and the finishing room.

In the cutting room, four men using hand knives and cutting machines cut shoe uppers, tongues, toe boxing (the leather or fabric used to hold the toe in shape), linings, and counters. In the fitting and lasting room, seven men are employed placing shoe uppers on foot dies of various shapes and sizes and tacking them to bottoms. In the making room, eleven female employees sew in the linings of the shoes and sew the ankles and the uppers to the bottoms. Six men then sew or glue the soles on boots and shoes. These soles are stamped out with hand dies in the soling room of the plant. Finally, in the finishing department, three men and two women are employed in such tasks as cutting off excess leather or thread, grinding down rough leather edges, dyeing scuff marks, and waxing and polishing the footwear ready for sale to the customers. The finished shoes are then brought to the packing room where each pair is wrapped in paper, and placed in a box which is then labelled and numbered.

It is the practice in the plant to manufacture each type of shoe in lots of 40 pairs and to ship them out in lots of 20 pairs. At any one time, lots for stock and lots for particular customer orders are being produced. The shoes are moved from one work area to another by means of push carts. The finished shoes are stored in the warehouse section of the plant to await shipment.

Assignment

1. How would you characterize the production of this firm?
   (a) Conditioning, analytical, synthetic, or assembly? Explain.
   (b) Custom, batch, or mass? Explain.
   (c) Job-order or standard? Explain.
   (d) Manual, mechanized, or automated? Explain.
2. To what extent is there specialization of labour in this plant? What purpose does it achieve? What are its disadvantages, if any?
3. Would you consider this to be an example of mass production? If not, why not?
4. To what extent is standardization employed in this manufacturing process?
5. Why would each type of shoe be manufactured in lots of 40 pairs? Why would they be shipped out in lots of 20 pairs?

READING

David Confronts Goliath in Attempt To Win Piece of Glass Fibre Market

BY EDWARD CLIFFORD
Source: *The Globe and Mail*, Toronto

David Graham used to read his letterhead to remind himself what business he was in, an exercise in self-discipline intended as a discouragement to venturing into new and unfamiliar territory.

Now he is a David taking on Goliath for a piece of the glass fibre insulation market shared by two foreign-owned companies. It is a market growing so fast that a newcomer who captures 10 per cent of it probably will not be denting the sales of his competitors.

Mr. Graham already owns one small but respected firm in glass fibre building products, Graham Products Ltd. of Inglewood, Ont. His decision to enter the insulation field was prompted by the success in Spain of an independent company operating in a market previously dominated by one of the three multinational firms that produce glass fibre wool insulation products.

The rationale behind his decision goes like this:

—Glass fibre wool products are bulky but lightweight. Building a small plant to serve a local market saves transportation costs. These savings offset manufacturing efficiencies that might be realized by building a huge central plant.

—New technology developed by the Spanish firm does not infringe on patents held by the giants, yet is efficient in a small-scale operation.

—By aiming at a small market share in several product categories, and having machinery that can switch quickly from one product to another depending on demand, a new entry avoids stepping on the toes of its giant competitors.

—Building material dealers, who have a choice of only two suppliers for fast-moving glass fibre insulation products, would welcome a third manufacturer.

The Caledon hills, 35 miles northwest of Toronto, seem an unlikely place to embark on breaking the stranglehold that two industrial giants have on a national market.

But that is where Mr. Graham, a confirmed exurbanite, started scouting for a location that offered high-voltage power, natural gas, rail transportation, proximity to a labour pool and easy access to highways.

He found it in the village of Erin, an easy 20-minute Mercedes-Benz ride from his home and plant at Inglewood. Starting with an unused building, he built a 110,000-square-foot plant and warehouse. Startup began early in September, barely a year after ground was broken.

The $10-million project was financed by loans from the Royal Bank of Canada, the Federal Business Development Bank, and the Ontario Development Corp., plus equity capital from Graham Products and Poliglas SA of Spain.

Mr. Graham said the strong support of federal and provincial governments was based on three factors. First, Graham Fiber Glass Ltd. would be a Canadian-controlled company, able to follow an independent marketing strategy that would include exporting to the United States.

Second, the plant would be transforming domestic raw materials into high-technology manufactured products. Third, the end use of the insulating products would be a factor in conserving energy.

Mr. Graham's competitors are Johns-Manville Canada Inc. of Toronto and Fiberglas Canada Ltd. of Oakville, Ont., both companies wholly owned by U.S. parents. His marketing strategy is based on pursuing a small piece of a lot of different product areas within a 300-mile radius of Toronto, including adjacent U.S. states.

He feels he will have a much better chance of avoiding a confrontation with his competitors than if he concentrated on just one product—say, insulation batts—in the lucrative Toronto market.

Mr. Graham has not asked for any government handouts or gifts in building his plant. "I was more interested in getting their moral support as a protection against encountering restrictive trade practices."

Mr. Graham's assessment of how the building supply industry would greet a new entry has been right so far. His first four months of production were sold to the trade before the plant was even running.

The original Graham firm, Graham

Products, is located on a family property nestled in a picturesque valley at Inglewood. The plant is housed in a century-old mill, producing glass fibre-reinforced panels, cladding, glazing panels, bubble skylights, and fascia panels with a pebble finish for decorative exterior use.

The company has been operating since 1954 when Mr. Graham, an engineer, decided to find a use for the mill, which had been operated before by family members, first as a lumber mill, later as a brick business.

There have been good years and bad, and a few false starts in other product categories. After one unsuccessful venture, Mr. Graham included on his company letterhead the words Continuous Process Manufacturers of Reinforced Plastics Composites, "to remind me of what business I was in."

It now employs about 50—inarguably, the largest (and perhaps sole) industry in Inglewood. More than two-thirds of the personnel have been with the company five years or more, quite an achievement for a company that offers jobs that require few skills.

One incentive is a profit-sharing plan, which he prefers to describe as a "wage dividend" program. This entitles employees to a bonus of up to 20 percent of salary a year, paid quarterly. The dividend has been missed only once since 1974, he said, and a similar plan will be put into effect at his Erin plant.

Much of the technology used at Inglewood originated with a West German company that sells its technical know-how around the world. The buyers in a dozen other countries are also independent operators, and get together every few months to talk shop and share experiences.

It was through such exchanges that Mr. Graham became interested in the glass fibre insulation business. Although there are lots of competing products on the insulation market, including plastic panels and cellulose fill, he is convinced that none offers the effectiveness or flexibility of glass wool.

"When we turned the machines on, we produced a product in the first shot that was better than the existing industry standards," he said.

He invited the Spanish firm that developed the technology to take a 15 percent equity position in Graham Fiber Glass, an assurance that he will continue to share in its technical advances. As well, "we will put as much back into research and development as possible."

His devotion to research and development is well illustrated by his description of the plant laboratory—not the production line—as the "heart" of the operation.

Although retrofitted home insulation is where the action is in the business today, Mr. Graham is convinced that industrial applications will account for an increasing share of business. "There's a huge market out there. As energy costs continue to rise, companies will be insulating things they never insulated before. It's a simple equation; when it costs less to insulate than the cost of waste energy, companies will insulate. The higher costs go, the more opportunities to save energy will be found."

Mr. Graham is hopeful that he will carve out a niche in the U.S. markets bordering Canada—highly populous centres in New York State, Pennsylvania, Ohio, and Michigan. It is a market untouched by other Canadian companies, since their parent U.S. corporations are also in the insulation business.

There are tariffs of between 8 and 11 percent on such products entering the U.S. market, but Mr. Graham said the value of the Canadian dollar more than offsets these. The company's initial overtures have been well-received among U.S. buyers, he said, and he hopes that as much as one-third of the 10,000 metric tonnes of insulation he

will produce annually will be exported to
the United States . . . enough to give all
Canadians a warm feeling.

Assignment
1. What made David Graham decide to enter the glass fibre insulation market?
2. Why did he decide to locate his production plant in the Caledon Hills? What were the key factors?
3. How did he finance his new venture?
4. Why did he receive government assistance?
5. What is his marketing strategy?

UNIT 7.2: PLANT LAYOUT, EQUIPMENT, AND BUILDINGS

The term *plant layout* is used to describe the arrangement of a plant's production facilities. These include manufacturing equipment, materials handling equipment, aisles, storage places, receiving and shipping areas, service equipment, changing rooms, and even the employees. Plant layout is one of the initial phases in establishing a manufacturing plant. It is also a continuing activity, for new product lines are taken on while others are discarded, and new, more efficient layouts are constantly required.

Purposes of Plant Layout

The two main purposes of plant layout are to reduce manufacturing costs and to improve working conditions. Manufacturing costs are reduced by making the most economical use of floor space; by keeping the handling of materials, parts, and finished products to a minimum; by reducing the number of stoppages and delays (which keep workers and machinery idle); by making supervision easier; and by facilitating maintenance. Working conditions are improved by better-spaced work areas and greater safety on the job.

Types of Plant Layout

There are three basic types of plant layout; continuous-line layout, shop layout, and stationary product layout. In practice, many firms find it convenient to use some combination of these, rather than one type alone.

Continuous-Line Layout. With this layout, machines are arranged in a continuous line according to the sequence of manufacturing operations required to produce a good. Some examples of continuous-line layouts are shown in Figures 7.2 and 7.3.

Continuous-line layout has the following advantages: materials handling costs can be reduced by mechanization; semi-skilled labour can be used for repetitive

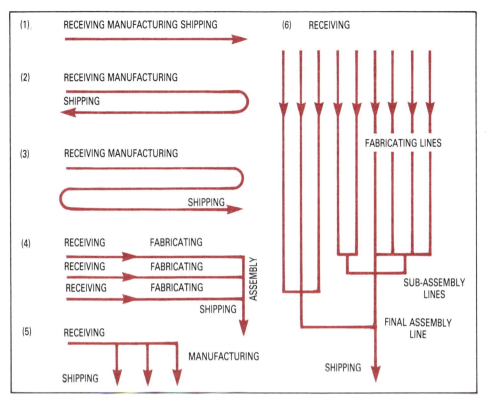

Figure 7.2 Continuous-Line Layouts

operations; labour productivity can be increased by a high degree of specialization; the amount of goods in process can be reduced by a shorter manufacturing time; and production control is made much easier. Disadvantages include: the large initial capital cost of a production line equipped with special-purpose machinery; and the relative inflexibility of the layout, which is designed to manufacture only one type of product.

Continuous-line layout is to be found in all mass-production industries such as cars, refrigerators, and other appliances. This is because these industries manufacture in large volume only one or a very few basic products.

Shop Layout. This is a layout in which similar machines are grouped together in shops or departments, such as the lathe shop, welding shop, and paint shop. The materials move from shop to shop according to the sequence of manufacturing operations required for each product. The shops themselves may be arranged so as to keep materials movement to a minimum (Figure 7.4).

Compared with a continuous-line layout, the shop layout offers these advantages: the initial capital cost is lower; the production facilities can be used for the manufacture of more than one type of product; and machinery breakdowns do not cause so much interruption to production. The disadvantages are: it costs

254 CHAPTER 7 MODERN MANUFACTURING

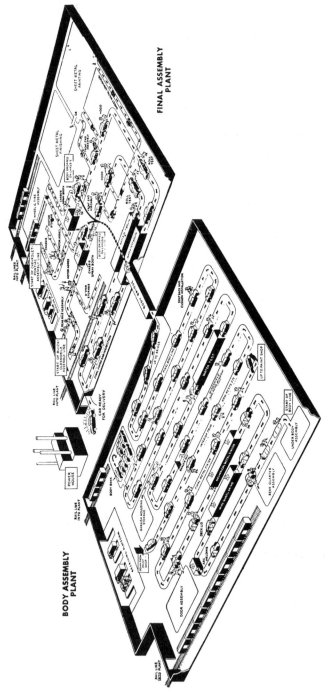

Figure 7.3 Continuous-Line Layout of Car Assembly Operations at the South Plant of General Motors of Canada, Limited at Oshawa, Ontario.

Courtesy General Motors of Canada, Limited

more to move materials; more highly skilled labour must be employed to use general-purpose machinery; the manufacturing process takes longer and therefore ties up more capital in the form of work-in-progress; and production control is more difficult because of the variety in manufacturing orders.

Stationary Product Layout. In the case of unusually large or heavy products that cannot be transported once made, without destroying them, it is necessary to build the product at the final place of use. Examples of products

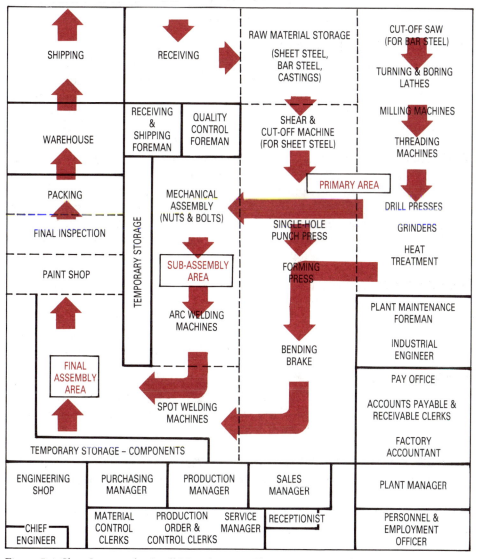

Figure 7.4 Shop Layout of a Small Manufacturing Plant

that cannot be moved when finished include most residential, industrial, and commercial buildings; dams; highways; and bridges. Products that must be built almost at the point of launch because of the high cost of moving them, include large ships and space rockets. Products that can be moved more easily but which are still cheaper to build mainly in one spot include large aircraft.

Factors Influencing Plant Layout

Many different factors influence the choice of a plant layout. These include: the manufacturing processes involved; the materials to be handled; the types of equipment; balance in production; minimum movement of workers and materials; service areas; utilities; and outside transportation.

Manufacturing Process. Every product must pass through a certain sequence of manufacturing operations. If all or most of a plant's output is to follow the same sequence of operations, as in repetitive manufacture, then a continuous-line layout is usually the most suitable. If each sequence of operations is different, then a shop layout may be best. This is the case with job-order manufacturing.

Materials Handling. If the materials and parts are extremely heavy or awkward to handle, it becomes very important to keep materials handling to a minimum. Thus a stationary product layout or a continuous-line layout is usually more suitable for heavy materials than a shop layout. Light materials, on the other hand, can be moved easily from department to department, as required by a shop layout. Sufficiently wide aisles and enough overhead clearance must be provided for materials handling equipment.

Types of Equipment. Attention must be given in the plant layout to the floor space to be occupied by each machine and its operator; to the weight and operating characteristics of each machine (to ensure that it is placed on a suitable floor and, if necessary because of excessive noise or smells, is enclosed or isolated); and to the accessibility of the machine for maintenance and replacement.

Avoidance of Bottlenecks. If bottlenecks in production are to be avoided, the plant layout should ensure that machine capacity for each operation is in balance with all the rest. This can be done by employing more or fewer machines at each stage or by using special-purpose equipment.

Avoidance of Unnecessary Movement. The layout should be such that the movement of workers and materials is kept to the minimum required.

Service Areas. The layout must include space for service areas, such as storage rooms, inspection areas, tool cribs, changing rooms, and eating rooms.

Light, Power, and Water. The need for these services in different locations must be allowed for, either overhead or underground.

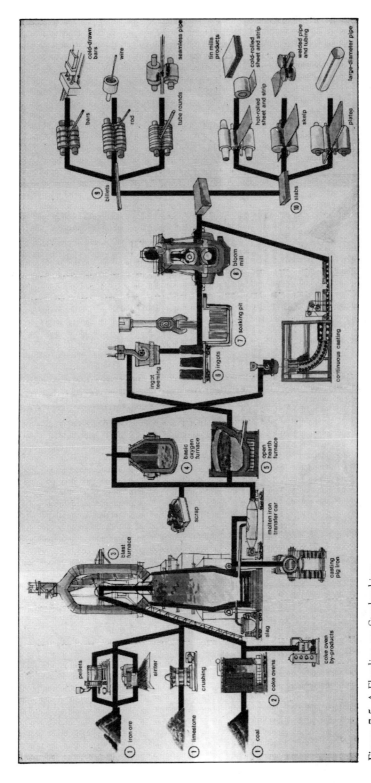

Figure 7.5 A Flowline on Steelmaking
Artwork courtesy of Stelco Inc.

Outside Access. Access to the plant should be predetermined, and the plant layout should take this fact into account, particularly in the location of receiving and shipping areas.

Flexibility. The need for changes in the plant layout is bound to occur sooner or later. Consequently, flexibility should be built into the original layout. For example, electrical outlets should be suspended overhead rather than embedded in a concrete floor.

Local Regulations. Compliance must be made with local fire and safety regulations.

Plant Layout Aids

There are various technical aids for preparing or revising plant layouts. These include process charts, flow diagrams, machine-data cards, template layouts, and scale-model layouts.

Process Chart. This is a written summary of the various production operations, storages, and inspections which take place in a manufacturing cycle. This summary enables a person to see more readily any weaknesses in the present system, such as unnecessary movement of materials and unnecessary storage.

Flow Diagram. This is a floor-plan sketch of all or part of a plant. It shows the location of the different machine areas, storage places, and corridors, and the path or paths that materials take during the manufacturing process. A flow diagram enables a person engaged in plant layout to visualize an actual or intended layout and to pinpoint any weaknesses, such as the back-tracking of materials.

Machine-Data Cards. These are cards on which is recorded data about a machine such as productive capacity and requirements for floor-space, power, and foundations. These cards provide a convenient source of information for people preparing plant layouts.

Template Layouts. A proposed plant layout may be visualized by the use of templates laid on a miniature floor-plan. *Templates* are heavy paper cutouts of the floor space occupied by a machine, drawn usually to a scale of $1/4$ inch to a foot. A great advantage of a template layout is that the templates can be moved around until the most suitable layout is agreed upon. The final template layout can be made into a drawing, photostated as is, or (if prepared on a plastic grid sheet) reproduced photographically.

Scale-Model Layouts. A more realistic, but also more expensive, aid than templates are models built to scale. In a *scale-model layout*, each machine, handling device, and fixture is shown in its planned position as a scaled three-dimensional model. Such a layout is particularly useful in visualizing the use of overhead space, as in the arrangement of pipelines in an oil refinery, or in visualizing the final appearance of a major construction project.

Plant Equipment

There are three main types of equipment in a manufacturing plant: production equipment, materials handling equipment, and service equipment.

Production Equipment.
This consists of tools, jigs, and fixtures. *Tools* are appliances used in working on materials, parts, or products. They include small hand-driven instruments, such as hammers, chisels, and screw-drivers; the cutting or shaping instruments used in various machines and power-operated machine tools, such as broaching and grinding machines. *Jigs* are devices used to guide tools during production and also sometimes to hold the material or part during the work operation. *Fixtures* are devices for holding materials or parts so that work can be carried out on them.

General-Purpose and Special-Purpose Machines.
Machines can be specialized to a greater or lesser degree. Machines that are designed to perform a variety of operations are called *general-purpose machines*. Those designed to perform one or a very few extremely similar operations are called *special-purpose machines*. An example of a general-purpose machine is a lathe which can be adapted for drilling, milling, and threading operations. An example of a special-purpose machine is a multiple-spindle drilling machine.

Special-purpose machines are to be found in mass-production industries, such as cars and household appliances, where the large volume of production keeps such machines fully employed. Although their purchase price is much higher than that of general-purpose machines, their greater efficiency results in lower costs per unit of output.

Materials Handling Equipment.
In a manufacturing plant, materials and parts have to be unloaded; transported to the various stock rooms; stored; moved as required to the different shops and departments; moved from machine to machine; stored temporarily at different intervals in the manufacturing process; stored as a finished product; and then finally shipped out. The task of handling these parts and materials is a considerable one and accounts for a substantial part of the final cost of a manufactured product.

To keep materials handling costs to a minimum, various types of equipment are used; some operating on the factory floor, and some suspended overhead. Floor-type materials handling includes hand trucks, truck tractors, power-lift trucks, gravity-roll conveyors, and power conveyors. Overhead-type equipment includes chain conveyors, cranes, tram-rail and monorail hoists.

Service Equipment.
Two important types of service equipment are those used for power and heating.

Power. Electric power is required by the manufacturing industry to operate machines to supply heat, steam, hot water, and compressed air, and to provide light, ventilation, and air conditioning. Most manufacturing firms rely for all or part of their electricity requirements on the local power utility because such power is relatively cheap and regular. Sometimes, however, a firm will find it advantageous to install its own generating equipment, either for regular use or for an emergency.

It is often economical for a firm to produce its own electricity if one or more of the following conditions is present: it regularly uses a large quantity of electricity; it requires steam for its manufacturing processes; it has waste materials that can be burned; and it can sell any surplus electricity.

The most common types of power-generating equipment used in industry are: a water boiler with a steam turbine or steam engine; internal combustion engines; and water turbines (in the case of large firms with hydro-electric resources).

Heating. Heat is required for use in many manufacturing processes and to provide a satisfactory working temperature throughout the plant. Heating can be provided in various ways: by hot water (heated by various fuels, including gas), by steam, by forced air, or by electricity. The heat from hot water and steam is released into the air from radiators placed in strategic positions and connected by pipe to the source of supply. Electrical heating is usually provided by individual heaters equipped with fans.

Plant Buildings

Factory buildings are designed to suit the requirements of the manufacturing firm that is to occupy them. As a result, buildings vary in size, shape, height, type of roof, strength of floor, and so on, depending on such factors as the manufacturing process to be used; the materials to be handled; the machinery to be employed; the volume of production; and the storage requirements.

Two extremely important considerations in modern industrial building design are flexibility and ease of expansion. *Flexibility* is the ability to use the building for a variety of layouts and manufacturing processes, either by the first owner or tenant, or by whoever should later occupy the premises. One way of achieving flexibility is to use large roof spans so that the number of columns is reduced. Other ways are by placing heating, power, and plumbing lines overhead, and by having moveable walls.

Ease of expansion is a necessary precaution for any manufacturing firm. This can be achieved by ensuring that the site is large enough for additional buildings and by planning how and where they should be constructed. Thus, for example, the walls facing the area where expansion will take place can be made non-load bearing. Or, if the expansion is to be upward, the foundations can be made stronger than required for the present building.

Single-Storey Buildings.
Most new plant buildings are of the single-storey type. The shape may be a simple rectangle or in the form of one of the following letters: L, T, U, H, F, or E. Often a plant will start with a rectangular building, then gradually grow, with additions, into a more sophisticated shape.

The roof can be one of several different kinds, of which the most common are the flat, saw-tooth and monitor (Figure 7.6).

The flat roof is the most economical type to build and is quite satisfactory if artificial lighting and ventilation are to be used. The saw-tooth roof, with glass in the shorter sloping surface, is designed to provide natural lighting throughout the plant area. The monitor-type roof, with its two levels, permits the use of travelling cranes to move heavy materials and parts across the factory floor.

Some of the advantages of single-storey buildings (compared with multi-storey buildings) are: lower construction costs per square foot of usable space; greater flexibility in plant layout; unrestricted floor load capacities; floors free from vibration; ease of expansion; and easier supervision of workers.

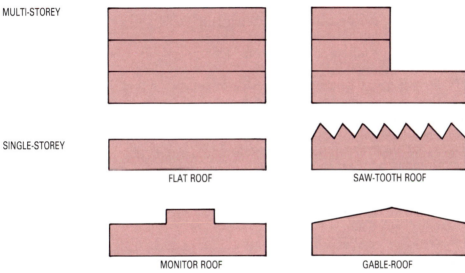

Figure 7.6 Some Types of Industrial Buildings

KEY TERMS

Plant layout

Continuous-line layout

Shop layout

Stationary product layout

Process chart

Flow diagram

Machine-data card

Template layout

Jigs

Fixtures

General-purpose machines

Special-purpose machines

Materials-handling equipment

Service equipment

Plant buildings

Flexibility

Scale-model layout

Tools

Ease of expansion

Single-storey buildings

REVIEW QUESTIONS

1. What is plant layout? What are its purposes?
2. Explain (a) continuous-line layout and (b) shop layout. Compare their merits.
3. Give three examples of stationary product layout.
4. Explain what you consider to be the three most important factors influencing plant layout.
5. Explain the nature and purpose of (a) a process chart and (b) a flow diagram.
6. What is a machine-data card? What purpose does it serve?
7. Discuss the usefulness of scale-model layouts.
8. Explain the following types of production equipment: (a) tools, (b) jigs, and (c) fixtures.
9. For what reasons may a firm decide to use special-purpose machines rather than general-purpose machines?
10. What are the basic types of materials handling equipment used on the plant floor?
11. What are the main types of overhead materials handling equipment used in industry?
12. For what reasons may a firm generate part or all of the electric power it needs?
13. Compare the merits of the following means of plant heating: (a) hot water, (b) steam, (c) forced air, and (d) electricity.
14. "Flexibility and ease of expansion are two extremely important considerations in modern industrial building design." Explain.
15. Compare the merits of the single-storey building with those of the multi-storey building.

READING

Everything's Coming Up Blueberries
BY ROGER WORTH
Source: *The Financial Post*

Oxford, N.S.

"Business is a game and it's supposed to be fun," says entrepreneur John Bragg as he bites into a home-cooked meal at this sleepy little town's tiniest restaurant. "It's also nice to win."

Bragg has been having a great deal of fun since he left university with a master's degree in business administration 11 years ago—he's been doing a lot more winning than losing.

"I guess it's fair to say we've been reasonably successful," he says, understating the case. "Opportunities arise and the business seems to have a momentum all its own."

From a standing start in 1967, Bragg has moved from picking blueberries, to food processing, to cable television, as well as dabbling in real estate along the way. But the basis of the 37-year-old businessman's mini-empire is the wild blueberries that grow in abundance in this part of the Maritimes near the Nova Scotia-New Brunswick border.

Bragg's family had been harvesting the berries for years, but it was John who spotted the need for a processing plant when he arrived home from university.

"Most of the farmers were shipping their blueberries to the nearest processing plant in Maine," he says. "I didn't know much about the processing business, but decided to research the subject."

His investigation led him to a firm in Pennsylvania that designed such facilities. So, armed with a financial proposal and a tentative plant design, he approached the Nova Scotia government and the Department of Regional Economic Expansion [now the Department of Regional Industrial Expansion (DRIE)], seeking financing for the project. That was 10 years ago.

DREE eventually loaned 25% of the $600,000 cost of a 20,000-square-foot plant and the province provided the remainder, taking the family's blueberry acreage as security. Bragg also negotiated a favourable tax deal with the province that ends in 1981.

"Perhaps we were naive," Bragg now admits. "We had virtually no working capital that first year, but it has worked out well, both for the governments and ourselves."

His Oxford Frozen Foods Ltd. has turned a profit every year but one. The original plant has expanded to 80,000 square feet.

"I'm a firm supporter of DREE and the provincial development agencies," says Bragg. "Certainly there have been a lot of disasters, but they took a chance on me and it's paid off handsomely."

The payoff for the governments, of course, is the 100 full-time and 220 seasonal jobs created in this high unemployment area as the company has grown. And those jobs are a source of stability for the town of 1,200.

"There's a certain sense of accomplishment just knowing we've been able to help," he says. "The people in the area—particularly the blueberry farmers and our employees—are really responsible for our success."

But success is a story of growing pains, overcome by long hours of hard work plus liberal doses of imagination and innovation. Still, Bragg's efforts have produced a prize company where sales should surpass $5 million this year. It's also a profitable firm, where income is continually plowed back into the operation.

"You can't stand still," says Bragg. "You have to keep expanding."

Total investment in the operation since 1967 has now reached about $2.5 million. As well as the $600,000 government financing, Bragg has tapped the federal and provincial lending agencies for $1.3 million more, reinvesting at least $500,000 of earnings.

But the blueberry processing plant is only part of the tale. As important, perhaps, is the entrepreneur's fine sense of salesmanship that has allowed him to develop solid markets for his product, not only in North America, but in Europe and Japan as well.

"More than 25% of our sales are offshore, particularly European countries," he says. "What's important is that these markets are continuing to grow."

The firm's customers read like a Who's Who of the food world: Sarah Lee, Duncan Hines, E.D. Smith, and McCain Foods, another Maritime firm that has achieved phenomenal success with frozen foods.

It was the McCain connection that allowed Bragg to expand the blueberry plant into other foods. After a major expansion in 1970, the firm started processing carrots, then onion rings for the McCain group, as well as other customers.

"The key to success in this business is quality," says Bragg. "Once you've developed a good customer, it's generally a matter of service. But in the food game, the quality must always be letter perfect."

Maintaining those high standards can sometimes be expensive. There was the time, for example, when the company had to recall a shipment. "Eating that loss was an expensive lesson, but worth the price," says Bragg. "Naturally, we changed our production system to eliminate the likelihood of a recurrence."

To offset high Maritime transportation and energy costs, Bragg runs a tight operation. "That's one of the keys to our success," he says. "We keep administration costs to a minimum."

But the management load is heavy, particularly with Bragg spending about 25% of his time on business travel in Europe, Japan, the U.S., and the rest of Canada. "During the peak blueberry season I work flat out, 16 hours a day, seven days a week," he says. "It's mandatory."

Which is one reason he's seriously considering hiring a senior executive to reduce the work load. "I know we need more management expertise, I'm pulled two ways. I've built the business and I'll find it difficult to hand it to someone else to run. But I'm going to make the change soon."

Not that Bragg is about to give up his creation. He'll certainly continue to be closely involved with the endeavour, but believes he has expanded the operation as much as possible.

"There's a healthy future for blueberries, but food processing in Nova Scotia is becoming extremely difficult," he says.

One reason: high power costs in an energy- and capital-intensive business. Since 1973, for example, Bragg's energy bill has quadrupled to about $200,000 a year, which he says is twice as high as a competitive plant in Maine.

"We won't be expanding the processing plant. There are too many things building up against us in Nova Scotia," he says.

Breaking Even

Still, there are other fields to be conquered. Bragg's latest endeavour is the cable television licence he was awarded for Amherst, Springhill, and Sackville, all within 50 miles of his home base in Oxford. "It's coming along nicely and we should be breaking even within a year or so," he says.

Refuting statements by some Maritime businessmen that Canada's major banks are backward in supporting local projects, Bragg is downright enthusiastic about his relationship with the Bank of Nova Scotia.

"Since the day we started business they've been helpful," he says. "But I was amazed at how quickly they accepted our entry into the cable television business, financing the $1-million-plus project."

While the money is being drawn down over an extended period of time, Bragg estimates he put up about $100,000 cash to get the project off the ground. Part of the reason for the bank's largesse is undoubtedly Bragg's capacity for dealing in large numbers, as well as the favourable business experience it has had with him.

For example, at the height of the blueberry season when Bragg is financing the inventory he will process and sell during the next year, Scotiabank provides an unconventional loan of up to $3.5 million, which is paid down over the next 12 months.

Bragg has also been dabbling in real estate, constructing several small apartment blocks in nearby Sackville.

"It's more a hobby than anything else," he says. "The opportunity existed, so we filled the void."

Not everything Bragg touches, of course, turns to gold. There was the attempt several years ago to set up a blueberry processing plant in Newfoundland. While Bragg says he simply backed away from the proposal, industry insiders suggest he dropped a hefty amount of cash on the scheme.

Still, the example perhaps indicates Bragg's ability to make tough decisions, cutting his losses to a minimum. The fact that he considered starting an operation in another province, far removed from his home base, also suggests he may be interested in moving farther afield.

Outspoken

But there is no question that Bragg's home turf matters. Along with a heavy business workload, he finds time to devote to Industrial Estates Ltd., Nova Scotia's business development organization. He's also an outspoken critic on matters he believes are creating problems for businessmen in Atlantic Canada.

Take transportation policy. It was Bragg, for example, who underscored one of the hundreds of ridiculous regulations included in Canadian National's freight rate schedules.

The firm had a shipment of 80,000 pounds to be moved to Chicago. Bragg approached CN, seeking a break on the price if he could get the shipment into one rail car, rather than using a second unit.

CN wouldn't discuss the issue, pointing out that its rate system is based on cost per pound. So Bragg ordered two rail cars, placing 40,000 pounds of goods in each, publicly making his point that the system is ridiculous.

"It didn't faze CN at all," he says. "Their people just pointed to the book on tariffs. The lack of flexibility makes no common sense at all."

Besides, Bragg finds it cheaper to ship by truck than by rail.

Considering the mind-boggling amount of time Bragg spends on business, he's still able to find time for relaxation. He's an avid curler at a club near the village of Collingwood (population, 300) where he lives with his wife and four children, ages four to 11.

In summer, he also spends time at a cottage at nearby Northumberland Strait, and manages a couple of southern vacation trips every year.

In a tiny denlike room at the plant where he does much of his heavy thinking, the balding businessman, who admits to being a trifle overweight, considers the reason for his success: "I get bored if I'm not on the go, doing things," he says. "I like to be involved, and I am."

So where does family man, entrepreneur, hard working John Bragg go from here? "Well, my family has always been involved in politics, on the Liberal side . . . "

Assignment

1. What was John Bragg's key business venture?
2. What financing was required?
3. How did he obtain it?
4. Explain how the investment was a success for:
    (a) the entrepreneur;
    (b) the federal and provincial governments; and
    (c) the local community.

5. Was the financing the principal reason for the success of this business? Discuss.
6. What management problems has John Bragg encountered?
7. What new fields of business activity is John Bragg considering? How promising do you think they are?
8. What business crises (as shown by the Reading) has John Bragg had to contend with during his business career? How did he handle them?

UNIT 7.3: METHODS ANALYSIS AND TIME STUDY

In its quest for profit, a business firm will attempt to reduce costs by simplifying

Courtesy The Ontario Ministry of Industry, Trade and Technology

and otherwise improving its methods of production. The systematic study of present methods of production to determine more efficient ones is known as *methods analysis*.

METHODS ANALYSIS

Methods analysis can be divided into two areas: process analysis and motion study.

Process analysis is the study of the whole production process or one complete phase of it. It includes the examination of each step in production (manufacture, assembly, transportation, storage, and inspection); the sequence of these steps; and the layout of the equipment, storage areas, tool cribs, work locations, and inspection points on the plant floor. The same techniques of analysis can also be used in a study of a firm's paper work.

Motion study is the study of various motions that an employee makes in performing his or her job. Its purpose is to alter or eliminate some of these motions so that the employee can perform the task more quickly and with less fatigue.

In the small firm, the manager or a supervisor is the one who occasionally undertakes methods analysis. However, the interest of all employees in methods improvement may be aroused by use of a suggestion box with cash bonuses for accepted ideas.

In the medium- or large-size firm, a specific department, called the *industrial engineering* or *methods department*, is usually responsible for investigating, on a systematic basis, possible improvements in a production method. The head of this department, usually an industrial engineer, normally reports to the plant manager. In more forward-looking firms, "quality circles," consisting of line employees and supervisory managers, may meet on a weekly basis to pinpoint opportunities for improved efficiency.

Process Analysis

The first task in process analysis is to record on a process chart (see Figure 7.7) all the different steps in production in the sequence in which they occur. These steps are: operations, transportations, delays, storages, and inspections.

An *operation* is one step in the manufacture or assembly of a part or product, taking place in one location—for example, the drilling of a hole in a part, or in the case of paperwork, the filling out of a form.

A *transportation* is a movement of materials or parts from one place to another—for example, from the welding shop to the grinding shop.

A *delay* is any abnormal interruption of the production process—for example, materials waiting to be moved or a form held awaiting a signature.

A *storage* is the retention of materials or parts in a particular area to await authorized use.

An *inspection* is the process of identifying materials, parts, or products, and verifying that they are in the required quantity and of the correct quality.

To facilitate analysis, a diagram may also be drawn showing the path that the materials or parts follow from the beginning of the production process to the

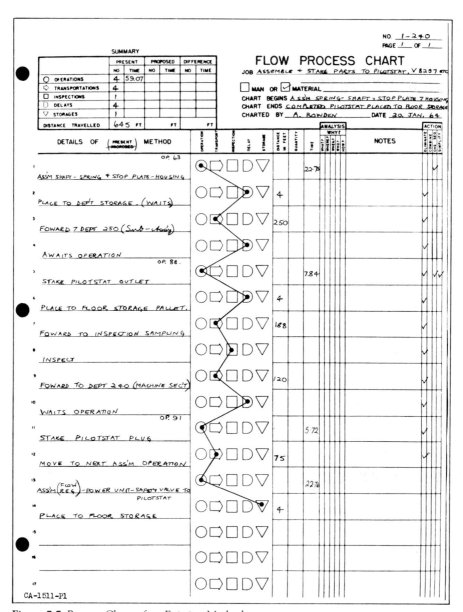

Figure 7.7 Process Chart of an Existing Method

end. This diagram is variously known as a *flow diagram*, a *layout*, a *flow layout*, or a *process layout*.

In examining each of the steps shown in the process chart and flow diagram, the methods analyst will try to establish whether the step can be eliminated, simplified, combined with some other step, or performed more efficiently elsewhere in the production process.

A process chart (see Figure 7.8) and flow diagram are then prepared, showing the improved production process.

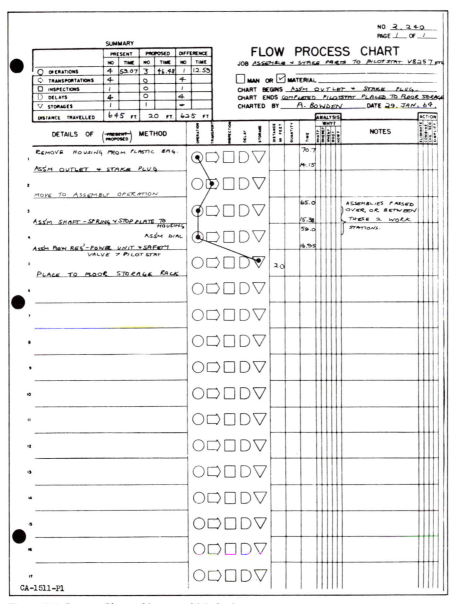

Figure 7.8 Process Chart of Improved Method

Motion Study

Whereas process analysis is concerned with the production process as a whole, motion study is directed at the individual job. By careful study of the various motions that an employee now uses to perform a task, the methods analyst tries to devise a quicker and possibly less fatiguing work method. This method is then adopted as the standard work method (Figure 7.9), and new and existing employees are trained and otherwise encouraged to use it.

Motion study can be applied to three different basic situations: where em-

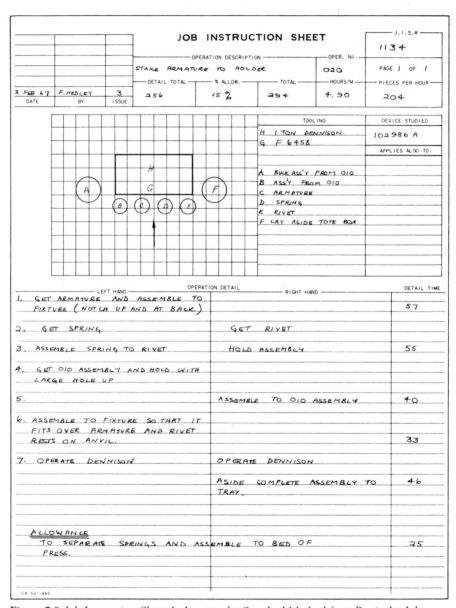

Figure 7.9 Job Instruction Sheet Indicating the Standard Method for a Particular Job

ployees work together in groups; where an employee works with a machine; and where an employee works alone, without a machine.

Multiple-Activity Analysis. Where several persons work together to perform a common task, such as loading or unloading stores, there is possible scope for improvement in the way that their individual efforts are combined.

To visualize what is taking place, a multiple-activity chart can be filled out. This chart shows, in a separate column for each member of the work team, what each person is doing at each particular time. The need for the various tasks and the logic of their present distribution among the members of the group can then be questioned, and a new improved arrangement may then be devised for trial.

Operator-Machine Analysis. There are many moments in a manufacturing plant when a machine, its operator, or both, are temporarily idle. These moments can be caused by the operator's obtaining new materials, removing the finished product, stopping and starting the machine, making adjustments to it, or watching while it performs its work. As each idle moment costs the firm money, either in wages or in overhead, it is to the firm's advantage to keep the number and length of such periods to a minimum.

An operator-machine chart is used to show, in respective columns, what the operator and the machine are doing simultaneously throughout the work cycle. This chart provides a visual basis for the methods analyst to pinpoint and query the need for idle moments, by either operator or machine.

Operation Analysis. This is the study of the movements that an employee makes when working without a machine. This type of analysis is applicable to most assembly jobs.

The first step in an operation analysis is to summarize, in an operation chart, the movements performed simultaneously by each of the worker's hands.

The next step in operation analysis is to examine the present method to determine whether any improvements can be made—for example, by sharing the work more evenly between the two hands.

A more efficient, but also more expensive, technique of studying a worker's movements is by first recording them on film. This method, called *micromotion analysis*, is particularly useful for analyzing relatively fast movements. With this technique, each hand motion is classified into one of seventeen basic types called *therbligs*. The motions recorded, together with the time (as shown on the film by a microchronometer placed at one side of the worker), are then entered on a *simo chart* (or simultaneous-motion-cycle chart) for analysis and possible improvement.

The symbols for each therblig are:

G — grasp
P — position
PP — pre-position
U — use
A — assemble

DA — disassemble
RL — release load
TE — transport empty
TL — transport loaded
SH — search
ST — select
H — hold
UD — unavoidable delay
AD — avoidable delay
R — rest for overcoming fatigue
PN — plan
I — inspect

Principles of Motion-Economy

The methods analyst, in looking for improvements, can attempt to apply the principles of motion economy pioneered in the 19th century by Frederick W. Taylor, and Frank and Dr. Lillian Gilbreth. The most important of these principles are the following:

CONCERNING THE WORKER
1. Work should be evenly balanced between the two hands so that both start and finish their work at the same time.
2. Both hands should never be idle at the same time.
3. The two hands should move in opposite and symmetrical patterns.
4. A smooth-flowing, rhythmic action is preferable to one which includes many stops and changes in direction.

CONCERNING THE WORKPLACE
5. Tools and materials should be placed in a definite and convenient location.
6. Gravity feed bins should be used whenever possible to supply parts to the workers.
7. Drop deliveries (either chute or conveyor) should be used wherever possible to take the assembled part or product away from the worker.
8. Tools and materials should be arranged for each hand in a way that allows the worker to use the most efficient sequence of movements.
9. Good lighting should be provided.
10. The workbench and chair should be at such a height that the worker can obtain relief by varying from a standing to a sitting position.
11. Chairs should be of a design that will permit good posture.

CONCERNING TOOLS AND MACHINERY
12. The hands should be released for more productive work by the use of a machine or a foot-operated device.
13. Two or more tools should be combined whenever possible to reduce the number of movements by the worker in reaching for tools.

14. Tools and materials should be pre-positioned close to the workplace whenever possible—for example, by suspension over the workbench.
15. Tool handles should allow maximum contact with the hand, especially if force is to be used—for example, a screwdriver.

Time Study

This is a study or analysis to determine how long it should take an average worker, operating under normal work conditions, to complete a job. This period of time is then known as a *time standard*. Time study is one of the functions performed by the methods or industrial engineering department of the larger firm, or by a supervisor or other responsible person in the smaller firm.

Not all tasks, it should be noted, can be the subject of a meaningful time study. This is the case with many office jobs. Answering a telephone in a certain length of time, for example, is not necessarily an indication of efficiency. Many manufacturing and assembly tasks can, however, be usefully time studied. This is particularly so where the task performed is a repetitive one and where the quality of the output remains constant.

Purposes of Time Study

By means of time study, management can obtain a valid measurement of the time reasonably required to perform many jobs. These time standards are then used by various departments of the firm as a basis for planning production; determining wage-incentive plans; evaluating employee performance; determining production costs; allocating work; measuring improvements in present work methods; and machine loading.

Equipment

The equipment used in a time study consists of a stop-watch, a time study observation sheet, a clipboard, and pencils.

The most commonly used type of stop-watch in industry is the decimal minute stop-watch. This watch has a large dial divided into 100 parts, each part representing 0.01 minute. Every revolution of the main hand, therefore, represents 1 minute. A smaller dial is divided into 30 parts, each representing 1 minute. The small hand moves forward one space on every complete revolution of the large hand, up to a total of 30 minutes. The watch can be stopped and started instantly by moving the control slide located at the left of the crown or stem of the watch. Both arms are returned to zero as soon as the crown is depressed.

Time Study Procedure

The following is the procedure commonly used in making a time study:
1. The cooperation of the supervisor is obtained.
2. An average operator, who is willing to cooperate, is selected as the person who will perform the job to be observed; the supervisor may help in the selection of this person.

3. Working conditions are checked to ensure that they are standard; the person observed should be using the standard work method, with standard materials, parts, and tools, standard lighting, and a standard workplace.
4. The task performed by the operator is studied and divided into individual movements, or *elements*. These elements—for example, picking up materials—are then written, together with other particulars of the study, down the side of the time study sheet.
5. Each element is timed several times by the analyst (either by continuous or snap-back techniques), who then records the results in the appropriate column of the observation sheet. The number of time study observations should be sufficient to ensure that an adequate and representative sample is obtained. Any abnormal actions, such as stopping to look around, are known as *foreign elements*. The times taken for these are excluded from the study, and a clear explanation is recorded of why they were not used.
6. After each element has been timed several times, an average time is calculated for each element. To allow for the fact that an element may not occur in every work cycle, each element is multiplied by the number of its occurrences per cycle. Thus an element performed once every two cycles would be multiplied by 1/2.
7. The time study analyst then determines a *levelling factor* for each manual element of the job. Under the overall 100 per cent rating factor system, normal pace is rated at 100 per cent, a slower-than-average pace at 90 per cent, and a faster-than-average pace at 110 per cent.
8. The time study analyst then calculates the *normal time* for the job. This is the time that an average trained worker would take, working at normal speed, to complete the task. Normal time is calculated by multiplying the average time for each element by the levelling factor—for example, 0.90 for a slow worker. The normal times for each of the elements are then added to get the normal time for the operation as a whole.
9. The next step, in order to arrive at a fair time standard for the job, is to add to the normal time a certain percentage of time for *allowances*. Time allowances (often 5 per cent each) are normally made for personal needs, fatigue, and preparation.

In summary, the formula for calculating standard time is:

Selected (or Average) Time × Levelling Factor = Normal Time
Normal Time + Allowance = Standard Time

A simplified example of a time study is shown in Figure 7.10.

Production Studies

In order to establish the personal allowances for a time study (if they are not already set down in a labour contract), a production study may be undertaken. It may also be undertaken if present allowances are held to be unjust.

A *production study* is the making of a detailed record, minute by minute, of what a worker does throughout the day. It can reveal whether the worker is in fact overworked—for example, by additional jobs—or whether the allowances made in calculating the time standard are insufficient. It may also reveal that the worker is not working hard enough.

Predetermined Time Standards

Time standards based on time studies are often criticized by employees and labour unions on the grounds that the rating or levelling factor used is arbitrary.

To overcome this objection, many firms use predetermined time standards. These indicate, based on widespread study, how long it should take a normal, trained worker to perform each of a variety of motions, under varying conditions.

Element	1 2 3 4 5 6 7 8 9 10	Average Time (hours)	Rating %	Normal Time (hours)
1. Pick up 12 pieces from tote and place on machine bed.	40	.0040 / 12	120	.00040
2. P/U single piece, place and position in die, operate press (hand buttons), pierce one hole and 1 slot.	19 22 20 19 30*20 22 22 23 22	.0189 / 9	105	.00165
3. Grasp piece and lay aside to tote.	9 11 9 9 9 9 11 11 11 11	.0100 / 10	110	.00110
4. Check piece with sample (1 in 50).	— — — — — — — 20 —	.0020 / 50	100	.00004
5. Straighten stacked pieces in tote (1 in 20).	— — — — — — — — 33	.0033 / 20	110	.00018

*Fumbled piece—disallowed.

Total Normal Time .00337

Allowances
    Fatigue   5%
    Personal   5%
    Preparation   5%
    Unavoidable delay   5%
                        20% × .00337 = .000674

Standard time per piece .00337 + .000674 = .00404 decimal hours = 14.54 sec.
Figure 7.10 Time Study of a Piercing Operation

These normal times are added together to get the normal time for the complete job. The various allowances are then added to this normal time to obtain the standard time for the job.

The use of predetermined time standards also has the benefit that it enables management to establish labour costs for a production order *before* manufacturing actually begins.

The predetermined time system that is most commonly used is called *Methods-Time Measurement*, or MTM for short. This system provides a detailed breakdown of the manual motions involved in a job and indicates the time required for each motion. Each manual motion is classified as one of the following: reach, move, turn, apply pressure, grasp, position, release, disengage, eye travel, eye focus, body motion, leg motion, or foot motion. Each motion is assigned one of several time standards depending on the variations in the motion and on the differences in the conditions under which it takes place.

The MTM system has the advantage over time study of permitting a proposed job method to be compared with the current method. It also allows accurate time standards to be obtained for a job without having the job actually performed. Many firms use a modified form of MTM. This is because MTM is considered by some managers to go into too much detail.

KEY TERMS

Methods analysis	Micromotion analysis
Process analysis	Therblig
Motion study	Simo chart
Operation	Time study
Transportation	Elements
Delay	Foreign elements
Storage	Levelling factor
Inspection	Normal time
Process chart	Allowances
Flow diagram	Time standard
Multiple-activity analysis	Production study
Man-machine analysis	Predetermined time standard
Operation analysis	MTM

REVIEW QUESTIONS

1. Explain briefly the nature and purpose of (a) process analysis and (b) motion study.

2. Explain the various symbols used in a process chart to indicate the different steps in production.
3. What is multiple-activity analysis? How is it carried out?
4. What is operator-machine analysis?
5. What is operation analysis?
6. Explain the nature and purpose of a simo chart.
7. Give an example of a motion-economy principle with regard to (a) the worker, (b) the workplace, and (c) the design of tools and machinery.
8. What is time study? Why cannot all jobs be meaningfully time studied?
9. What are the purposes of time study?
10. Outline the procedure commonly used in making a time study.
11. What is a production study? What purpose does it serve?
12. What is a time standard? What is it used for?
13. What is MTM? Why is it used by industrial management?

CASE PROBLEMS

SWANSEA STEEL PRODUCTS LTD.
Improving office efficiency

Mrs. Fraser, secretary to the personnel manager of Swansea Steel Products Ltd., is required every month to duplicate and staple together the pages of the S.S.P. Newsletter. This newsletter may contain from 5 to 8 pages, and is given to each of the firm's 110 employees to promote their interest in the firm.

To do this work, Mrs. Fraser arranges the various pages in separate piles along the top of a long table in the order in which they are to be picked up and stapled. She then picks up each sheet with her right hand and transfers it to her left hand. Finally she uses both hands to staple the collected pages together. This job has proven both time-consuming and tedious.

Assignment
1. Would the firm be justified in purchasing a mechanical collator to do this work? Discuss.
2. Which, if any, motion-economy principles are violated by the present method?
3. Devise a more efficient method, possibly involving a small capital investment.

BROCK MACHINE WORKS LTD.
Making a time study

At the Brock Machine Works Ltd., one of the operations involved in the production of a customer's order is the drilling of two 5/8-inch holes in a metal part by means of a hand-feed drill press. As the work is to be paid on a piecework basis, the plant manager wishes to know how many parts can be drilled in an hour by the average drill-press operator. It is the practice in this firm for the senior foreman, who has taken a course in time and motion study, to make any time studies required. Accordingly, he has chosen an operator he judges to be slightly above average and has observed the operation ten times. The information he has recorded is as follows:

ELEMENT	TIME (hundredths of a minute)
	1 2 3 4 5 6 7 8 9 10
1. Pick up part from box, and bring to vise.	9 11 12 10 8 12 13 11 12 10
2. Position part in vise, and tighten vise by hand.	18 12 15 14 17 12 19 13 14 17
3. Start drill-press.	6 7 5 6 3 4 6 5 6 7
4. Drill two 5/8-inch holes in part, hand-feed.	35 30 32 37 45 36 33 36 40 35
5. Stop drill-press.	5 6 8 4 7 5 4 6 7 6
6. Open vise, remove part, place in box.	17 20 23 22 25 16 18 17 20 21

The foreman has rated the operator at 110 per cent. He has also made a 3 per cent allowance for an operator's needs, a 7 per cent allowance for fatigue, and a 5 per cent allowance for unavoidable delays.

Assignment
1. What is the *normal time* for this operation? What is the *standard time?*
2. How many parts can a normal trained operator drill in an hour? What piece-rate should be paid to provide a basic wage of about $10 per hour?
3. Explain why the operator has been rated at 110 per cent.
4. Why must allowances be made for personal needs, fatigue, and unavoidable delays? Give examples of each.
5. Why would the senior foreman, rather than a time study analyst, be the person to carry out time studies in this firm? What possible advantages and disadvantages might the present arrangement have?
6. What preparations should the foreman have made before beginning his time study?

CHAPTER 8
PRODUCTION, INVENTORY, AND QUALITY CONTROL

CHAPTER OBJECTIVES

☐ To explain how a manufacturing firm plans and controls its production.

☐ To indicate the differences in production control between job-order manufacturing and standard manufacturing.

☐ To show how a firm decides how much inventory of materials and parts to carry.

☐ To describe the ways in which a firm goes about purchasing the materials and parts required for production.

☐ To show how a firm tries to ensure that its product meets minimum quality standards.

☐ To emphasize how a business firm needs constantly to review its present products and develop new ones in order to remain competitive.

CHAPTER OUTLINE

8.1 Product Planning and Development
8.2 Production Control
8.3 Inventory Control and Purchasing
8.4 Quality Control

UNIT 8.1: PRODUCT PLANNING AND DEVELOPMENT

Few business firms can afford to stand still: they must constantly evaluate the marketability of their products—adapting existing products and introducing new ones in the face of changing consumer tastes, demographic shifts, competitive pressures, and so on, in order to maintain and perhaps enlarge their "market share." Each year, for example, the North American auto makers bring out their new models, taking into account a variety of factors: a renewed emphasis on quality, prevailing world oil prices, government pollution regulations, the continued onslaught of Japanese and other foreign-made cars, and anticipated consumer reaction. Even Coke, a tradition in itself, has succumbed to the need for a "new taste" to compete with aggressively-promoted Pepsi.

Product Policy

Each firm has one or more products or product lines. A *product line* is a group of related products—for example, a range of office machines, kitchen utensils, soups, etc. Usually, a firm will have a "product image"—in other words, the public's general conception of the types of products that the firm sells. Therefore, in its product policy, it will try to maintain or enhance this image so that sales will be sustained, if not improved. Thus, if a firm has a reputation for supplying, for example, top-quality watches, it would normally be detrimental for it to start producing and selling bottom-quality items. In other words, a firm must have a well-defined and consistent "product policy"—an ongoing plan as to the types of products that it will sell. A firm must also have a mechanism for reviewing, on a regular basis, the products it already sells. This review mechanism should be designed to:
(a) check whether the firm's existing products are properly satisfying customers' needs and, if necessary, redesign or discontinue the unsatisfactory ones;
(b) develop new products that are consistent with the firm's "product image"; will meet new or changing consumer needs; and will help the firm maintain or enlarge its sales volume and market share. This activity, known as "product planning and development," is considered next.

Product Planning and Development

A firm's product planning and development process (or PPD for short) is a good example of a business activity that requires the cooperation of several major departments. Certainly it is not a matter for the production or marketing department alone. That is why some firms appoint a *product manager* to oversee all the different activities involved in the development of each new product.

Production Department. The Production Department will be involved with research and development, involving the search for new products, product design and modification, the manufacture and mechanical testing of prototypes, and the possible development of new production methods. This activity may be so large in scope that the persons involved will be grouped in a special R & D Section or Department. This is particularly true of the so-called "high-tech" industries such as aircraft, computers, telecommunications, and biotechnology, where "pure research," as well as applied research, is usually undertaken. *Pure research* is research of a fundamental nature in, for example, physics and chemistry, without direct regard for commercial applications. *Applied research*, as the name indicates, is research that is conducted with a view to commercial applications. Often, a considerable part of product research and testing is contracted out to specialized research firms and to university laboratories. However, many firms also have their own product design groups. These consist of engineers, design draftspersons, technicians, and machinists, skilled in the development of engineering designs and samples, often utilizing computer-assisted design (CAD). A *product designer*, in such a group, might be responsible for the development of a product from initial concept to release for production. And he or she would probably have to interface, in the case of manufactured industrial goods, with sales engineers, designers, development technicians, and production managers.

Marketing Department. This Department can also be an important source of new product ideas. (See, for example, Fig. 8.1.) In fact some large firms have groups of people who do nothing else but scan trade literature, newspapers, magazines, etc. looking for new product ideas, often on an international scale. The Marketing Department will also be responsible for conducting market research once a new product idea is obtained, either from inside or outside the firm. This market research can involve product assessment by the sales force, customer interviews, and product testing, perhaps in a sample or test area. Careful thought must also be given to the packaging, advertising, and distribution to be undertaken when the new product will be ready.

Finance Department. This Department will be involved in the pricing of the product, taking into account: (a) administrative, sales and factory "overhead," including development costs, as well as the direct cost of materials and parts; (b) prices of competitive products; and (c) an analysis of consumer demand. It will also be involved in establishing profitability guidelines for product development and in "costing out" each proposed new product so that management may decide, on a more informed basis, which new products merit actual development. Such financial analysis of new product proposals may take into account: estimated profit, degree of marketing risk involved, funding requirements, and the way in which the new product would complement existing products or fit into an existing product line. Break-even analysis and "pay-back period," explained later in this book, are two of the financial techniques that are often used. Obviously, there is a lot of guesswork involved. In fact, because of the difficulty of gauging customer reaction, actions of competitors, and other external or "uncontrollable" factors, many new products, however carefully researched, just fizzle out.

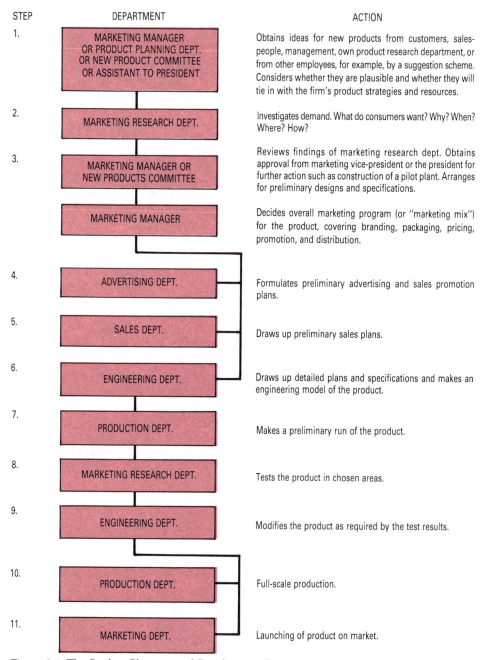

Figure 8.1 The Product Planning and Development Process

Need For Co-operation.
The Marketing Department is normally very keen to have new products to market and to have existing ones redesigned, if necessary, to meet customer requests. However, the Product Development section

or department may not be able to respond quickly enough to satisfy the Marketing Department. And this can lead to conflict and ill-will. Also, the Production Department may not be keen to add new products or replace existing ones, for it can mean delays and headaches in sorting out the inevitable production "bugs". The Finance Department too may be concerned about the costs of new product development. Therefore, top management must play a key role in ensuring proper co-ordination if the good of the firm as a whole is not to be sacrificed to departmental rivalry and resistance to change.

Product Design

In many firms (for example, fashion clothing, office furniture, automobiles, and aircraft), the product designer, or product design department, plays an extremely critical role. Usually, the persons responsible for the design of new manufactured products are engineers—however, creative artists of different kinds are also often involved—for example, in the styling of cars.

The factors commonly taken into account in product design include:
(a) *performance*—does the product do what it is supposed to do, e.g. a toaster?
(b) *appearance*—does the product please the eye?
(c) *durability*—will the product last?
(d) *safety*—is the product hazardous to use?
(e) *repairability*—can the product be easily repaired, if necessary? Are spare parts available?
(f) *cost*—is the cost of manufacture reasonable for the type of product?

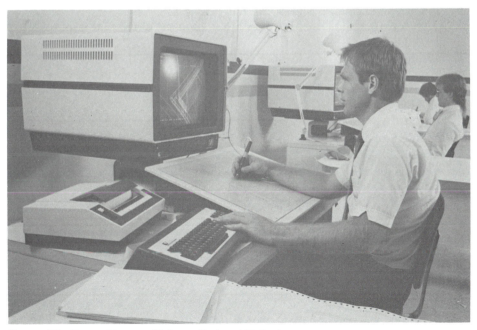

Courtesy The Ontario Ministry of Industry, Trade and Technology

The design for a product may start as a series of sketches. The draftspersons then convert them into detailed drawings and specifications which the production people can use to build a prototype or test version, for testing and subsequent modification.

Some firms do little product design of their own. Their business may be supplying materials and parts, on a contract basis, to a firm engaged in the assembly of a final product. In such a case, the specifications are supplied by the assembly firm and all the supplier firm has to do is to work to those specifications.

KEY TERMS

Product line

Product policy

Product image

Product planning and development

Pure research

Applied research

New product proposal

Product design

Prototype

REVIEW QUESTIONS

1. "Few business firms can afford to stand still." Discuss, with examples.
2. What is a "product line"? Provide three examples of your own.
3. What is meant by a firm's "product policy"? What factors influence it?
4. List the steps involved in the product planning and development process.
5. How does the small business firm handle the PPD process?
6. "The importance of R & D varies according to the types of business firm." Discuss.
7. Distinguish, with examples, between pure and applied research.
8. Which department in a firm is most heavily involved in PPD? Why?
9. What functions can the Finance Department of a large firm perform in the PPD process?
10. Why is the PPD process a potential source of conflict within a firm?
11. In which types of firm is product design critical for market success? Give examples of your own.
12. What factors should be taken into account in new product design?
13. What steps are involved in new product design? Illustrate your answer with reference to an actual product.

CASE PROBLEM

MALLORY SOUPS
Keeping ahead of the competition

Mallory Soups is one of Canada's leading food companies, supplying chain supermarkets and other retail stores with a variety of canned soups, TV dinners, tomato and other vegetable juices. However, over the last five years, the company has seen its market share steadily declining—in fact, sales have become almost static, and a steady profit has turned into a steady loss. To try to bring the company back to profitability, the board of directors have appointed a new president and given him full authority to make whatever changes he sees fit, the idea being to rejuvenate a company that has gradually grown old in both products and ideas.

Assignment
1. What could have gone wrong with this company?
2. How should the new president go about his task?
3. What changes should he consider?

READING

Turfed Out? Why Not Try Nelson Adams's Fast-Growing Product: Instant Grass

BY MIKE MACBETH

Source: Mike Macbeth, *Canadian Business Magazine*, March 1983.

Quick! What's green, weighs a ton and costs more than $100? Answer: enough sod to cover the average suburban lawn. Now then, what's brown, weighs 16 kg and costs less than $75? Answer: enough seeded matting to do the same job, thanks to Nelson Adams of Fredericton, NB, the inventor of the first lawn-making machine.

Adams, 66, retired seven years ago when he sold his lumber company. But something worried him. "I'd chopped down so many trees during the time I was in business that I wondered what I could do to replace them," he says. He began tinkering with ideas and came up with what he called a "goofball," a compressed ball of fertilized peat with a single tree seed embedded in the material. Adams imagined his goofballs being dropped from aircraft to reforest large tracts of land. "But the only people really interested in the product were in Afghanistan," he chuckles. "International Paper Co. and a few other companies ordered a million balls, but I would have had to produce 10 million before coffee break each morning for the idea to become a commercial success."

Adams then became interested in the way local farmers scattered chaff from their barns onto the soil to provide shade for seedlings. He began tinkering again and came up with the concept of "instant grass," a thin sheet or mat of compressed straw, peat and wood pulp that's implanted with goofballs of fertilized grass seed and is light enough to be carried home from a store. Nine days after being unrolled over the area to be made into a lawn and thoroughly watered, the grass begins to sprout. The lawn is long enough to cut within three weeks. The biodegradable fibrous matting eventually disintegrates.

Assignment
1. What was Adams' "goofball?" Why was it not a commercial success?
2. What is Adams' "instant grass?" How successful do you think it will be? Explain and discuss the commercial pros and cons.
3. What other new product, along these lines, has already become a commercial success in Canada and abroad?

UNIT 8.2: PRODUCTION CONTROL

The term *production control* refers to the task of planning and controlling the use of employees, machines, materials and parts in a manufacturing plant.

Purpose. The main purpose of production control is to ensure that the desired goods are produced as efficiently as possible—that is, in the right quantity, of the right quality, at the time required, and at the lowest cost. By careful co-ordination, production control helps to ensure that the manufacturing process takes place quickly and smoothly, and that customers' orders are filled on time.

Overall Production Control

Production control is normally carried on at two levels: the overall level and the detailed level.

The overall level is planning the total plant output for the coming month,

quarter, or longer period, so that arrangements can be made well in advance for obtaining additional equipment, if necessary; financing production; hiring and training workers; and procuring raw materials and parts. The aim is to balance the plant's manufacturing capacity with the marketing department's sales requirements. This overall production planning is usually done by a planning committee of top management.

Detailed Production Control

Detailed production control consists of the following activities: routing, scheduling, dispatching, and follow-up. Routing and scheduling are the planning functions; dispatching and follow-up (which includes corrective action) are the control ones. In the large firm, routing is usually performed by the engineering department or its equivalent. Scheduling, dispatching, and follow-up are usually the responsibility of the production control department.

Routing. This is deciding how a product is to be manufactured. It can involve the following tasks:
1. Determining which parts of the product to manufacture and which to buy.
2. Deciding on the manufacturing and assembly operations required.
3. Determining the proper sequence of these operations.
4. Deciding the type of equipment and personnel required to perform these operations.
5. Determining the materials needed to manufacture the various parts.
6. Deciding on the most efficient quantity to be manufactured (the *economic-lot quantity*), if production is for stock rather than for a customer's order.
7. Determining the amount of scrap to be allowed for (the *scrap factor*).

Scheduling. There are two types of scheduling. *Factory* (or *shop*) *scheduling* involves deciding, for each order, when each manufacturing or assembly operation should begin and finish. *Material scheduling* involves timing the purchase of materials.

Dispatching. This is the issuing of written orders for each manufacturing or assembly operation. The work of the dispatch clerk (or dispatcher) may also include preparing the manufacturing orders, guiding and controlling work in progress from one operation to another, keeping production records, and checking that production is being carried out as planned.

Follow-Up. This involves checking to see that production is on schedule and taking corrective action where necessary. This work is performed by the dispatch clerk or by a person called an expediter.

Organization for Production Control

In the small firm, the manager, supervisor, or a clerk may perform the production control functions. In the large firm, it is usually a specialized production control section or department that performs this important task. Where a production control department has been established, the person in charge is usually directly responsible to the plant manager.

An organization chart for a production control department is shown in Figure 8.2.

Variations in Production Control Methods

Methods of production control vary considerably from industry to industry and from plant to plant, depending on whether:
1. Production is of a single standardized product, or of a series of custom orders, or some combination of both.
2. Production is organized on a continuous-line basis, or on a shop basis, or on some combination of both.
3. There are few or many parts to the product.
4. There are few or many operations required for each part.
5. Few or many processes are dependent on each other.
6. Machines have fixed or varying capacities.
7. Few or many sub-assembly operations are required.
8. Manufacturing is for order, for stock, or for some combination of both.
9. The volume of production is large or small.

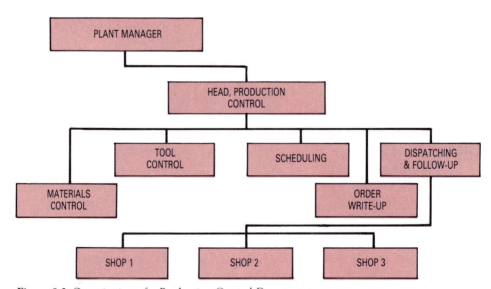

Figure 8.2 Organization of a Production Control Department

Production Control Procedure in a Large Job-Order Firm

A typical production planning and control procedure for a large job-order manufacturing firm is outlined on the following pages. A job-order firm is one in which most production is undertaken to fill specific customer orders that differ somewhat from each other (i.e., are not for standard products).

Routing. The production control department, on receipt of a customer's order, sends a copy to the engineering department for analysis.

The engineering department then does the routing and furnishes the production control department with the following documents:

1. A *route sheet* (or *operations sheet*). This sheet indicates how the parts are to be manufactured and assembled, the materials to be used, the machines to be used, the order in which the various operations are to be performed, and the time required for each operation.
2. *Blueprints*. These are copies of the engineering drawings of the product and its component parts.
3. *Specifications*. These are the measurements, strengths, and tolerances to which the product must conform. These are often shown on the blueprints rather than on a separate document.
4. A *bill of materials*. This is a list showing the name, quantity, and source of each material or part required.
5. A *tool analysis*. This is a list of any special tools which must be bought or made. This information is often shown on the route sheet.

A copy of the route sheet and other engineering data for each product is kept not only in the engineering department but also on file in the shop supervisor's office. These can be referred to when repeat orders come through.

Scheduling. This phase of production control consists of setting the starting and finishing dates for manufacturing and assembly operations.

For scheduling job-order work, the first step is to calculate the time required for each operation. This is done by multiplying the standard time per piece (as supplied by the engineering department) by the number of pieces in the order.

The second step is to check the availability of the materials to see whether manufacture of the goods will have to await the delivery of certain materials.

Third, machine-load charts must be examined to ascertain which machines will be free and at what times.

Fourth, starting and finishing dates are set for each operation, taking into account the time required for each operation, the sequence of operations, and the availability of machines and operators.

To ensure that the order is produced on time, scheduling is carried out backwards from the completion date for the final product. Thus, if the final assembly takes four days, then the completion date for the various sub-assemblies must be the final completion date less four working days.

Each order, as it is scheduled, is entered on a *master schedule*, for that particular part. The schedule shows, in chart form, all the orders already scheduled for each of the forthcoming weeks. The cumulative total can be easily compared with maximum and minimum weekly production capacity to see whether too much or too little work has been planned.

Dispatching. Dispatch clerks are members of the production control department who are located in the various shops. They receive from their department manufacturing orders for each job.

The *manufacturing order* (which may in some firms be the original route sheet) contains the routing and scheduling data for the job and is the written authorization for work to be undertaken. This document is accompanied by:
1. A *materials requisition form,* authorizing the withdrawal of materials from the storeroom.
2. A *tool requisition,* authorizing the withdrawal of tools.
3. *Time tickets,* for operators to record time taken on the job.
4. *Inspection forms,* for inspectors to record the amount of work accepted or rejected.
5. *Move orders,* authorizing the transportation of materials from storeroom to machine and from one machine to another.

The dispatch clerks issue the manufacturing orders to the various machine operators. This is not as simple as it sounds, as the dispatchers may be left to establish priorities and sort out delays.

In some firms, dispatch clerks are not used. Instead, the manufacturing orders are given ahead of time to the shop supervisor, who then allocates them to the machine operator.

Follow-Up. The task of following up an order to see that it is being produced according to schedule is done by the dispatchers or by special follow-up people called *expediters*. If there are no dispatchers, the follow-up work is done by the shop supervisor.

The work of follow-up involves not only uncovering delays—for example, due to machine breakdowns or absenteeism—but also taking steps to correct them—for example, by hastening the delivery of the materials.

Production Control Procedure in a Large Standard-Manufacturing Firm

Routing. Because the same products are being manufactured for long periods of time, the routing instructions, once established, remain standard. Authorizations for the withdrawal of materials must, however, be constantly prepared.

Scheduling. This involves drawing up a master schedule showing the amount of each product to be manufactured each week. The schedule takes into account expected sales and plant production capacity. The master schedule also serves as the basis for scheduling purchases of parts and materials. In some large firms, the timing and amount to be purchased or manufactured of each of the many different materials and parts are worked out for each production order by electronic computer.

The master schedule is then broken down into production schedules for each component part and assembly. These production schedules indicate for each part when production should take place and in what quantity. The rate of production of each part must be: in proportion to its use in the sub-assemblies and final assemblies; and in harmony with the rate of sub-assembly or assembly for which it is required. Copies of the production schedule are sent to the supervisor of each production department and serve as a manufacturing order in authorizing production.

Dispatching. When only one product is manufactured, dispatching consists merely of sending copies of the production schedule to the various departments. When there are several products or various assembly operations, manufacturing orders must be issued for the start of each manufacturing and assembly process.

Follow-Up. Dispatch clerks, expediters, and supervisors are required to check on the progress of production and to arrange for the correction of any bottlenecks or other problems.

KEY TERMS

Production control	Bill of materials
Overall production control	Tool analysis
Detailed production control	Master schedule
Routing	Manufacturing order
Scheduling	Materials requisition
Dispatching	Tool requisition
Follow-up	Time ticket
Route sheet	Inspection form
Blueprints	Move order
Specifications	Expediter

REVIEW QUESTIONS

1. What is the purpose of production control?
2. Distinguish between overall and detailed production control.
3. Explain the routing function of production planning.
4. What are (a) scheduling, (b) dispatching, and (c) follow-up?

5. Why do production control methods vary from plant to plant?
6. Explain the nature and purpose of (a) a route sheet, (b) blueprints, (c) specifications, (d) a bill of materials, and (e) a tool analysis.
7. How is scheduling typically performed in job-order manufacturing?
8. What is a manufacturing order? What documents normally accompany it?
9. Explain the work of the dispatch clerk.
10. How does production control in standard manufacturing differ from that in job-order manufacturing?

CASE PROBLEM

ANDERSON LUMBER CO. LTD.
Production control in a lumber firm

The Anderson Lumber Co. Ltd. sells a complete range of building supplies to builders and homeowners. These supplies include standard and custom-sized doors, windows, and trim, manufactured in the firm's own custom millwork shop.

Bob Anderson is the president and manager of the firm and Gail Anderson, his wife, the secretary-treasurer. These two persons share the overall management of the firm; Bob looks after purchasing and millwork, and Gail handles sales, deliveries, and accounts. The remainder of the personnel comprises a mill foreman, a yard foreman, a senior salesperson, three junior salespeople, an office secretary, a yard worker, four truck drivers, a lift-truck operator, and eight mill workers. The yard foreman is responsible to Bob for inventory control.

Production control in the mill is handled in the following manner: when an order for custom millwork is received, the salesperson concerned files one copy of the order in the office order book and gives another copy to the mill foreman. The foreman then states whether the item can be made, how much it will cost, and when it will be ready. If the foreman has any problems, he consults with the manager. Once the foreman has given a commitment, this is relayed by the salesperson to the customer.

The mill foreman records in a pocket notebook the work to be done and the promised delivery dates. He then allocates the work among the workers and machines so as to make the best use of their time. During any slack periods, the mill workers manufacture standard items for stock.

When any custom work has been completed, the mill foreman gives his copy of the order to the yard foreman, who then arranges for delivery. After delivery has been made, the delivery slip signed by the customer is given to the salesperson to arrange for payment. Until recently, the yard foreman was employed as a yard worker.

This system has worked satisfactorily for many years. However, an increasing volume of business has had the following results:
1. Many formerly acceptable orders are being turned away.
2. Longer delivery times are being quoted.
3. More overtime is being worked.
4. More orders are getting "lost."

5. Mill workmen are being interrupted by salespeople who are trying to find out the progress of customer orders.
6. Completed orders are being left in the yard for some time awaiting delivery.
7. More orders are overdue.

Assignment
1. Draw a chart showing the present organization of this firm.
2. What type of production is custom millwork? Continuous or intermittent? Job-order or repetitive? Explain.
3. What type of production is production of standard items for stock? Explain.
4. Explain the various production control functions performed by the mill foreman.
5. To what extent are the firm's present problems caused by inadequate production control?
6. What production control procedure would you recommend for a firm similar to Anderson Lumber but with a much larger number of employees and a much larger volume of business?

UNIT 8.3: INVENTORY CONTROL AND PURCHASING

Inventory control is the task, in a manufacturing plant, of ensuring (a) that production is not interrupted through lack of raw materials or parts; and (b) that no more of the firm's capital than is absolutely necessary is tied up in inventories of materials, parts, or finished products.

How Much Stock to Carry?

In determining how much stock to carry of each item, management must consider: the rate of usage; the reliability of deliveries; the storage facilities available; and the economic ordering quantity.

Rate of Usage. Each product to be manufactured will usually require a fixed quantity of materials or parts. If, therefore, the same goods are produced at a constant rate, the amount of stock required of each item is relatively simple to determine. Thus, at the beginning of each production period, say each month, the stock of any item would have to equal the amount to be used for production during that month. By sending a replacement order with adequate leadtime, a new supply would arrive just before the present stock runs out. This is shown in Figure 8.3.

However, the rate of usage of an item is seldom constant throughout the year. Thus, if the amount of stock to be kept is set at a level equivalent to peak monthly usage, an unnecessary amount of capital would be left tied up in unused stock during months of low usage.

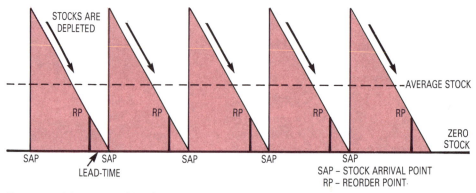

Figure 8.3 Movement of Stock

Whenever production is planned well in advance, however, changes in the type of products to be manufactured and in the rates of production can quickly be reflected in the levels of inventory. This is done by varying the amount of materials and parts to be purchased outside or made in the plant. Thus, in most large repetitive and job-order manufacturing operations, replenishment of stock is linked directly to production plans. In many large firms an electronic computer specifies the materials and parts required for each production order and prepares the purchase orders ready for mailing to suppliers.

In smaller job-order manufacturing operations, it is difficult, if not impossible,

to plan production very far in advance. In such firms, a wide variety of materials and parts must be stocked ready for any one of several possible production orders. In other cases, work on a production order is delayed until a purchase order has been placed and the necessary materials and parts received.

Deliveries. If stocks are to be kept to the minimum level possible, it is vital that replenishment orders be received on time. However, to provide for unexpected delays in deliveries of materials and parts or for unexpected increases in their rate of usage, many firms keep their levels of stock somewhat higher than those suggested by the expected rates of usage alone. This extra amount is sometimes called the *safety stock*; and the normal amount, the *working stock*. When the unit value of the item is small, the safety stock can be relatively large.

Storage Facilities. Lack of storage space will cause some firms to carry abnormally low stocks. This will, of course, hamper production and the service provided to customers. Usually it is a temporary situation.

Interest Cost. Most firms finance a large part of their inventory of materials and parts with a loan from the bank. The higher the interest rate being charged, the greater the cost of carrying the inventory. This is therefore an important incentive for keeping stocks as low as possible.

Economic Ordering Quantity. The *economic ordering quantity* or *E.O.Q.* for a material or part is the amount that is most economical for a firm to order at one time. It can be expressed either in dollars or units.

This amount is usually determined on the basis of experience and common sense, with an attempt to balance the savings from large-quantity purchase orders against the increased costs of carrying large inventories. Some firms use an algebraic formula to help determine the E.O.Q.

ABC Inventory Classification

In most manufacturing firms, a relatively small percentage of the items stocked accounts for the major part of total annual usage value (the unit cost of all the items times the frequency of their use). In order to make best use of the time and resources available for inventory control, many firms classify the various items stocked into high cost/usage items, intermediate cost/usage items, and low cost/usage items. The first group of these items, designated by the letter A, is subject to detailed control procedures to ensure that a fine balance is kept between sufficiency of supply and minimum investment. For the other groups, particularly C items, the control procedures are less detailed, and larger safety stocks are carried.

There are some items having a low cost/usage value that require more attention than is usual for that classification. These will be items which are critically important for production and which cannot be quickly obtained if a shortage should occur.

Industrial Purchasing

Industrial purchasing is the name given to all the activities involved in buying raw materials, parts, supplies, equipment, and specialized services for a manufacturing firm. These activities include: finding suitable suppliers; obtaining quotations; negotiating terms; placing orders; checking delivery; keeping informed on market trends and new materials; and keeping records.

Importance. This is underlined by the fact that, for many firms, the cost of materials, parts, and supplies accounts for more than half their total manufacturing expense. Careful purchasing can greatly help to hold down or reduce production costs and thereby increase profits.

Purpose. This is not just to obtain the required materials at the lowest cost. Equally important is the need to obtain the correct quality of materials and to know that the supplier is a reputable one who will actually deliver the goods promised by the agreed date.

Purchasing Department

In most medium- to large-size firms, purchasing is the responsibility of a *purchasing manager*, or *director of purchasing*. This executive is responsible either to the vice-president, production, or to the company president for the efficient purchasing of the materials, parts, and supplies required for the firm's operations. In the large firm, the purchasing manager or director will be assisted by a number of persons (for example, buyers, expediters, and clerical staff) who together comprise a purchasing department. This department is often treated by top management as a separate profit centre in the firm's organization.

The organization of the purchasing department of a large-size firm is shown in Figure 8.4.

Centralized Versus Decentralized Purchasing

Where a manufacturing firm has more than one plant, purchasing may be centralized, decentralized, or a mixture of both.

Centralized purchasing is the system in which materials and parts are bought by head office on behalf of the local plants. It enables the firm to use more highly specialized buyers and to benefit from quantity price discounts. It has the disadvantage that it may take more time for the local plant to get what it needs.

Decentralized purchasing means that each local plant is left to purchase its own needs. This system has the advantage that the local purchasing agent may be better and more quickly acquainted with his or her plant's requirements. The disadvantages include the extra purchasing staff required (one group for each local plant) and the possible loss of quantity price discounts.

A number of firms use a system of purchasing that is a compromise between centralized and decentralized purchasing, sometimes known as *co-ordinated local purchasing*. This sytem permits the purchasing manager for each local plant to

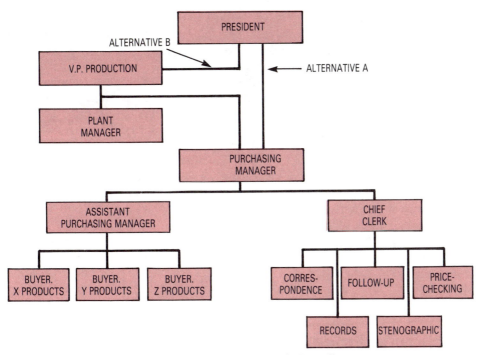

Figure 8.4 Organization of the Purchasing Department of a Large Firm

buy materials and parts up to certain limits. The purchasing department at head office exercises a general control over the local departments and may retain purchasing authority for certain materials. The latter would be the case where all plants use a particular material for which a significant discount is to be obtained by bulk purchase. Thus the head office may place an order for sheet steel for all its plants, leaving it to the discretion of the individual plants to advise the steel mill when and in what quantities they wish to receive it.

Purchasing Policies

The different types of industrial purchasing policy include:

Purchasing for the immediate future. Materials and parts are bought now to provide for the firm's needs a few days or weeks hence.

Purchasing as the need arises. This relates to goods which are required only in an emergency or to goods which are used so rarely that they are not kept in stock.

Purchasing for longer term. This is the purchase of a large quantity of materials when prices are low or when an interruption in supply is anticipated (e.g. an impending strike) to cover production requirements for more than the immediate future.

Speculative purchasing. This refers to the purchase, when prices are low, of more materials than are required for future production in the hope of being able to sell the finished product later at higher prices for a speculative profit—for example, buying woollen cloth when world wool prices are low to be sold later as finished suits. This may involve buying now (e.g. cocoa for chocolate) for future delivery through a commodities exchange.

Contract purchasing. This involves entering into a long-term contract with a vendor to supply materials over a future period at a price fixed in advance or negotiated from time to time. This type of purchasing enables a firm to take advantage of prices that are currently low, to benefit from quantity price discounts (without storing the goods or having to pay for them until delivered), and to be sure of a continuous supply of the materials or parts.

Scheduled purchasing. With this policy, which is often combined with contract purchasing, the supplier is informed of the approximate dates at which the firm will need to purchase more materials. In this way, the supplier can arrange to fill the orders promptly, and thus enable the manufacturing firm to keep its investment in stock to a minimum.

Reciprocal purchasing. This term is used to describe an arrangement whereby a firm agrees to buy goods from firms to which it sells its own goods.

Diversified purchasing. It may be part of a firm's purchasing policy not to become dependent on just a few suppliers. In this way the effect of strikes in supplier plants, price pressure by suppliers, and undue dependence on them can be minimized.

Purchasing Procedure

The principal steps in industrial purchasing are:

Purchase Requisition. The purchasing manager's authority to buy goods is the *purchase requisition*. This is a document, sent to him or her by any person entitled to order, requesting that materials and parts be purchased. Such persons normally include the chief storeskeeper, the production control department, the office manager, and the chief engineer. The purchase requisition shows the materials or parts required; the specifications; the quantity needed; the date by which the goods should be delivered; where they should be delivered; the account to be charged; the signature of the person who is authorizing the purchase; and space for the purchasing department to enter afterwards the supplier's name, price, terms, routing, estimated weight, purchase order number, and promised delivery date.

Request for Quotation. The purchasing manager may, on receipt of the purchase requisition, decide to request information from various suppliers before placing the order. To do this, he or she sends a document called a *request for quotation* to each supplier. This document describes such items as materials required, the delivery date, and requests information as to price, payment terms, time of delivery, and any special conditions or terms.

Purchase Order. On the basis of the quotations received and his or her background knowledge and experience, the purchasing manager will send a purchase order to one of the suppliers. The *purchase order* is a contractual commitment by the purchasing manager's firm to buy the goods from the supplier on the terms stated. A typical five-part purchase order contains, in addition to the information shown on the purchase requisition, instructions as to shipment and inspection. The original and one copy of the purchase order are sent to the supplier, and the copy is returned as evidence of receipt of the order. Of the extra three copies, one goes to the accounting department as authority for payment; another to the follow-up section of the purchasing department; and another to the receiving department to inform it of the nature and expected delivery date of the goods.

Follow-Up of Purchase Order. The follow-up section of the purchasing department, once it has received its copy of the purchase order, is responsible for keeping in touch with the vendor to make sure that the delivery date will be met. If there is an unavoidable delay, early knowledge of this by the follow-up section makes it easier for alternative arrangements to be made.

Receiving Report. Once the materials or parts are delivered to the firm, a receiving clerk will issue a *receiving report*. This document shows exactly what has been received from the vendor. Sometimes a copy of the purchase order, with price and quantity omitted, is given to the receiving department to be checked off against the delivery, and then used as a receiving report. One copy of the receiving report is given to the purchasing department (for comparison with the purchase order), another to the accounting department (to authorize payment), and another to the production head or storeskeeper who made out the purchase requisition (to inform him or her that the goods have arrived). From the receiving department the materials or parts will pass through incoming inspection, and then will be delivered to the stores or to the production department as required.

KEY TERMS

Inventory control	Co-ordinated local purchasing
Working stock	Speculative purchasing
Safety stock	Contract purchasing
Economic ordering quantity	Scheduled purchasing
ABC inventory classification	Reciprocal purchasing
Annual usage value	Diversified purchasing
Storeskeeping	Purchase requisition
Industrial purchasing	Request for quotation
Purchasing manager	Purchase order
Centralized purchasing	Receiving report

REVIEW QUESTIONS

1. What is inventory control?
2. Explain how the rate of usage helps determine the amount of stock to be carried. Why is the rate of usage not the only factor to be considered?
3. Distinguish between working stock and safety stock. What factors help determine the level of safety stock?
4. What is meant by the term "economic ordering quantity"? Explain how it can be determined.
5. What is meant by the ABC system of inventory classification? What is its purpose? What are its limitations?
6. What activities are involved in industrial purchasing?
7. Why is purchasing such an important function in a manufacturing firm? Who is normally responsible for the purchasing function?
8. Compare the merits of centralized and decentralized purchasing. What is co-ordinated local purchasing?
9. Explain the following types of purchasing policy: (a) contract purchasing, (b) scheduled purchasing, and (c) reciprocal purchasing.
10. Describe briefly the principal steps in an industrial purchasing procedure.

CASE PROBLEMS

KING ELECTRIC LTD.
Inventory control in a merchant wholesaling firm

King Electric Ltd. is a Vancouver merchant wholesaling firm which sells electrical supplies, wire, lighting fixtures, and electrical appliances to electrical contractors and retail stores. Its success in the seven years of its life has been built on service to the customer—having the goods available when required and at a competitive price. To provide such service, King Electric Ltd. keeps a warehouse stocked with over a million dollars' worth of different electrical supplies and has a fleet of six trucks for fast delivery. To keep its selling prices low, the firm purchases its electrical supplies in large quantities so as to obtain the most favourable manufacturers' discounts. Purchasing is carried out by three purchasers, each specializing on a certain list of items.

The firm's warehouse building is approximately 10 000 m² in size and is divided as shown in Figure 8.5.

The system of inventory control used by the firm was developed by the warehouse supervisor. For each item of stock, a minimum and maximum balance are agreed upon by the supervisor and the purchaser for the item, based on past experience. The minimum balance is the level at which more stock must be ordered. The maximum balance is the level beyond which the stock should not be allowed to increase. Attached to the shelf below each item of stock are two cards, a white one on top of a green one. Each card contains the catalogue number, name, minimum balance, and maximum balance for the item in stock.

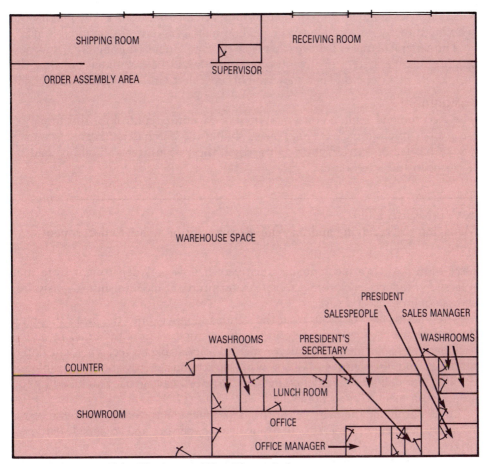

Figure 8.5 Layout of the Warehouse of King Electric Ltd.

Whenever an item is reduced to its minimum balance, one of the warehouse employees removes the white card, fills in the date and the amount of stock remaining, and delivers the card to the warehouse clerk. The clerk in turn delivers the card to one of the firm's three purchasers, who then buys more of the item. When the white card is taken from the shelf, the date is also marked on the green card. Thus the warehouse supervisor can tell, on walking around, which items are on order and when the order was placed. As soon as the replenishment stock is received, the white card with the amount and date of the order is placed over the green one. Access to the warehouse is normally restricted to the warehouse employees, but when business is unusually active, the delivery drivers may help the warehouse employees to assemble orders.

This system has worked fairly well in the past, but recently more and more cards have been lost. This has meant that replacement stock has not been ordered, and customer orders have gone unfilled. Also, the purchasers have not always observed the agreed maximum balances, but have made large purchases at unusually low prices whenever the opportunity has occurred. When the warehouse supervisor has complained that there is no space for all the stock, the purchasers, who are directly responsible to the general manager, have just ignored him.

The general manager believes that with the firm's increasing amount of business a more reliable system of inventory control should be instituted and that the warehouse clerk could play a more important role than is now the case.

Assignment

1. Recommend a more efficient system of inventory control for this firm.
2. What discretionary buying powers should the purchasers have?
3. What factors govern the way in which the various items should be laid out in the warehouse?

SAVE-MORE LTD.
Managing the receiving and marking department of a variety department store

Save-More Ltd. is a medium-size, relatively new variety department store that sells such products as clothing, footwear, furniture, home furnishings, glassware, sports equipment, and toys.

The smooth flow of goods from the various suppliers onto the firm's shopping floors depends in great measure on the efficient operation of the firm's receiving and marking department. This department is responsible for receiving, checking, marking, and distributing all of the firm's merchandise. It is also responsible for packing and delivering free of charge any large or heavy goods purchased by the store's customers to their home addresses.

Linda Farnham, the manager of this department, has working for her a clerk/secretary, a receiver, a marker, an inside delivery person, and an outside delivery-driver.

As soon as goods are received from the supplier's carrier, the receiver checks them to make sure that the shipment is complete and undamaged. Any discrepancies are noted on the delivery slip, a copy of which is given by the receiver to the office clerk. The office clerk, in addition to other duties, works out the unit selling price for each item. The receiver then marks this on the package and carries, pushes, or rolls the item over to the marking area. Copies of the delivery slips are sent daily to the accounting office. Occasionally goods are dropped and damaged by the receiver, who has recently developed back trouble.

The marker prepares and attaches to each item of merchandise a ticket showing the stock control number, the size, and the price. She also packs items for delivery to customers. Each item is placed in a particular place, ready for delivery to the appropriate floor, department, or customer. Sometimes items are placed in the wrong spot with the result that they have to be returned to the receiving and marking department. A receipt is given by each floor department for the merchandise that it receives. Customers are also required to sign for goods received.

The amount of merchandise that passes through the receiving and marking department has been steadily increasing as more and more people are now frequenting the store. This has meant that overtime work is now becoming the rule rather than the exception.

Linda Farnham wishes to hire an additional receiver and an additional marker. Before she does so, she wants to be sure that her department is organized in the most efficient way possible so that the store manager, her immediate boss, cannot legitimately turn down her request.

Sometimes work is held up when one of the staff is absent. Usually, however, the inside delivery person will substitute for the receiver, and vice versa. When the marker is sick, one of the salespeople (who has been given some training in marking) takes her place.

Some discrepancies always seem to occur between the quantity of goods received (as shown by the delivery slips) and the quantity that arrive on the shop floors (as shown by the floor department receipts). When asked about these discrepancies, the staff in the receiving and marking department say either that a mistake must have been made in the records or that some of the floor staff (who have some temporary storage space in the marking and receiving rooms) may be responsible.

Linda Farnham has received occasional visits from business forms salespeople who have suggested that she use a special paper form for her department. Such a form would require:

1. The receiver to fill in: his or her initials, the supplier's name and code number, the carrier's name, the number of the department for which the goods are destined, the number of packages, the receipt number, the delivery date, and the style, quantity, description, and sizes of the items.
2. The office clerk to fill in: his or her initials, the invoice number, the department order number, the unit selling price, and the date.
3. The marker to enter: his or her initials, the type of ticket, and the date.
4. The inside delivery person to fill in: the number of the department to which he delivers the goods, his initials, and the date.

Farnham has always considered the use of a special business form a frivolous waste of money for an operation of this size. Also, she has always felt that the more paper around her office the less efficient the department would be.

The delivery-driver is also a problem for Farnham. Recently Farnham was told confidentially by a friend that the store's driver was making a habit of taking extremely long morning and afternoon coffee breaks at a restaurant on the outskirts of town. When Farnham spoke to the driver about this, the man said that it was untrue and that he always completed all his deliveries quickly and efficiently. When Farnham said that during the last week he had not appeared to have delivered very much, the driver replied that customers often kept him waiting before answering the door, asked him to carry the parcels inside, or insisted on chatting with him. Farnham felt the man was not really earning his wage.

Assignment
1. What should Farnham do?

FINCH COMMERCIAL STATIONERY LTD.
Improving sales order and purchasing procedures

Finch Commercial Stationery Ltd. sells a complete line of office equipment and supplies, including such items as desks, typewriters, filing equipment, adding machines, duplicators, rubber stamps, visible records, cheque protectors, different grades of paper, and pens and pencils.

When a sales order is received from a customer either by telephone or through one of the company's salespeople, it is processed in the following way:

1. The order is typed on a seven-part invoice form.
2. Three copies of the invoice—the shipping copy, the signature copy, and the delivery copy—are then sent to the shipping department. The other four copies are retained in the office.
3. In the shipping department, the shipper makes up the order and indicates on the shipping copy the items being shipped. He then returns the shipping copy to the office.
4. The signature and delivery copies of the invoice are given to the driver who is to deliver the goods.
5. On delivery, the customer's receiver keeps the delivery copy and signs the signature copy, which is then returned by the driver to the Finch shipper. He, in turn, returns it to the office.
6. In the office, the items on the shipping copy are priced by the invoice clerk, and the details are typed on the four copies of the invoice previously retained in the office.
7. Of these four copies, one is mailed to the customer, one is given to the accounts receivable clerk, and the other two are kept as office copies.

Assignment

1. How, if at all, could you improve the efficiency of the sales order procedure?
2. How could provision be made in the sales order procedure for checking the credit of customers?
3. Prepare a purchasing procedure for this firm that will take into account the following factors: obtaining quantity discounts whenever possible; ensuring that a customer who is waiting for an item is notified as soon as it is received; and ensuring that the goods received are those actually ordered.

UNIT 8.4: QUALITY CONTROL

The two characteristics of a product that usually stand out most in the mind of a prospective purchaser are *price* and *quality*. A manufacturer, if he or she wishes to build a good sales image, will try to maintain as high a quality of product as is consistent with the price at which it is sold. This quality is often not the highest possible. Thus, no one today expects a medium-priced car to last more than five or six years whereas most cars built in the 1930s had much longer life spans. However, the consumer will expect a manufacturer to offer the best quality for the price. Thus, if one make of car falls apart after a year or two of use, consumers will soon switch to other makes.

Quality Standards

A manufacturer will decide, as part of its production and sales policy, the quality level of its products. This quality is expressed in the form of standards. A *standard* defines exactly what characteristics a product should have, covering such items as performance, composition, weight, size, and finish. The standards or specifications may be expressed in writing, pictures, or samples, or by some combination of these three.

Most products cannot be so well manufactured that they match the exact specifications. Even if they could, the extra cost incurred to achieve this would not be worthwhile for the manufacturer. Most products are considered satisfactory

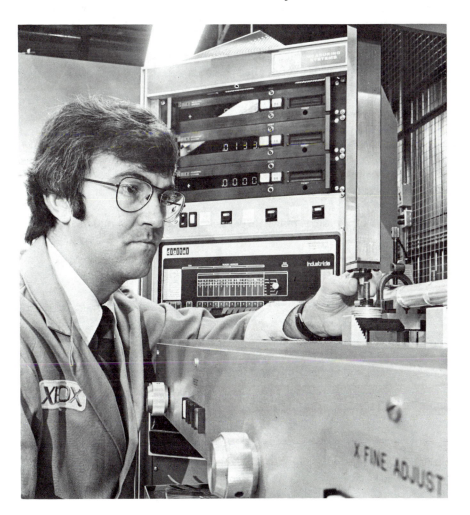

and will pass inspection in the plant if they do not deviate in performance, size, or weight, from the standard or specification by more than a certain amount. This permissible deviation is called the *tolerance*.

To ensure that as few goods as possible are placed on the market with a quality below the acceptable level, a manufacturer can take two steps: prevention and inspection. *Prevention* consists of various measures designed to prevent inferior products from being manufactured. These measures include good product engineering; good machine maintenance; good employee training and supervision; and good quality control of the materials used. *Inspection* is the task of examining materials, parts, sub-assemblies, and finished products to see that they are of the required quality—that is, within the tolerance stipulated.

Quality Circles

Product quality has been improved in many firms by employee involvement through suggestion boxes and other schemes that offer prizes and other recognition for ideas that can improve the quality of the product as well as lower production costs or improve job safety.

One of the best-known schemes for improving product quality is the establishment of small groups of workers called "quality circles" who meet regularly with management to discuss the product, its quality, and ideas for improving it.

Inspection Department

A large manufacturing plant will normally have an inspection department that is responsible directly to the plant manager or superintendent. The inspectors employed by this department will be completely independent of the production supervisors. In this way, an objective assessment of the quality of the output can be made.

The organization of a typical plant inspection department is shown in Figure 8.6.

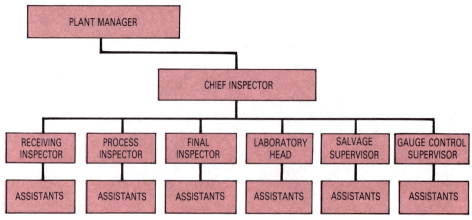

Figure 8.6 Organization of an Inspection Department

The work of the inspection department usually includes: the inspection of materials, parts, supplies, work-in-progress, and finished products; the inspection of tools and machines; the operation of a testing laboratory; the salvaging of below-standard materials and parts; preparation of scrap reports for management; and the choice of inspection devices.

Types of Inspection

The *initial inspection* of all incoming materials, parts, and supplies is essential, and this activity usually takes place in the receiving department before the goods are stored. In some instances, this inspection may be most economically arranged at the supplier's premises just before the goods are shipped to the plant.

Process inspection is the term used to describe the inspection of work-in-process. This may be done either by floor inspection or by centralized inspection.

Floor inspection is inspection carried out at the machines or assembly line by roving, or patrolling, inspectors. This method has the advantages that the handling of materials for inspection purposes is lessened, and poor work may be discovered promptly before any further processing is undertaken. On the other hand, more inspection devices are required, and conditions such as lighting, vibration, and the presence of the worker may not permit careful inspection.

Centralized inspection is the inspection of materials and parts at various crib stations strategically located throughout the plant. Unlike floor inspection, the materials and parts come to the inspector rather than vice versa. This method enables the work of inspection to be carried out economically by teams of inspectors working in relatively good conditions, using specialization of labour, and employing a variety of sophisticated inspection equipment. The main disadvantages are the extra handling of materials and the possible delays caused by materials piling up at inspection points.

Some of the points at which inspection may take place are: after any operation where the possibility of defects is abnormally high (called *key-point inspection*); before assembly operations which could be slowed down by defective parts (also called *key-point inspection*); immediately after a machine has been newly installed or "set up" for a particular manufacturing operation (called *first-piece inspection*); before large-quantity production begins of a product requiring a series of manufacturing or assembly operations (called a *pilot-piece inspection*); at random places along a single fabricating or assembly line; and where one production department's responsibility ceases.

The *final inspection* of the product is the last step in quality control and should be carried out before the goods are placed in storage or shipped out of the plant. This inspection can be visual, or it can involve performance tests (or trial runs) as, for example, in the following illustration.

A balance must be maintained in every plant between the need for inspection and the cost of such inspection. Often, therefore, not all materials, parts, and products are inspected. Instead, samples are used to determine the characteristics of the group from which the samples are taken. This method has proven satisfactory.

In some instances, final inspection is deliberately left to the customer who, if he or she complains, is given a replacement for defective goods.

KEY TERMS

Quality

Standards

Tolerance

Inspection

Initial inspection

Process inspection

Floor inspection

Centralized inspection

Key-point inspection

First-piece inspection

Pilot-piece inspection

Final inspection

REVIEW QUESTIONS

1. What is meant by quality when applied to industrial products?
2. Why do some manufacturers deliberately produce "low-quality" goods?
3. How can a firm ensure that its goods are manufactured according to the standards set?
4. What does the work of a plant inspection department normally consist of?
5. Compare the merits of floor inspection and centralized inspection.
6. How do North American inspection standards for, say, automobiles, differ from foreign ones?

READINGS

There's Money in Boats

Especially for a builder like Doug Rosborough

BY STEPHEN KIMBER

(Stephen Kimber is a freelance journalist based in Halifax.)

Source: *The Financial Post Magazine.* Used by permission of Stephen Kimber.

Doug Rosborough calls himself a vessel designer and constructor but he admits—quite cheerfully—that he spends a fair chunk of each working day just providing ocean going fantasies to land-locked sailors.

"We get more than our fair share of dreamers," he allows as he directs his visitor to "the 10 percent chair" (a chair named for his sales commission). It's the only comfortable seat in his large, littered office and the place reserved for potential customers. The headquarters of Rosborough Boats Ltd., one of the few Canadian firms to specialize in the luxury yacht trade and—even rarer—still dedicated to the dying art of building wooden boats, is in an addition to Rosborough's sprawling home on the outskirts of Halifax. It is a casual, chaotic place strewn with files, plans, boxes of marine equipment and assorted bits of memorabilia. Yet the only hint that it is the launching ramp for a thousand nautical dreams, is the view from Rosborough's corner desk—a local yacht club glimpsed through a maze of telephone wires and across a busy street.

"We get all kinds in that chair," he says as he clears a space for himself at his desk. "College students who want to celebrate their graduation by getting a bunch of friends together and going for a cruise around the world and older people who decide they're fed up with the rat race and want to retire to a last, perfect boat." Rosborough offers the visitor a wry, indulgent smile. "Not much of it ever comes to anything of course."

That's not to suggest that Rosborough doesn't design and build real boats. His 90 completed vessels—ranging from the popular 31-foot, three-masted tern schooners of a type once common in the Atlantic coastal trade to a 65-foot replica of Christopher Columbus' galleon, Santa Maria—are widely regarded as magnificent works of nautical art and, among well-to-do yachting cognoscenti, his boats which range in price from $30,000 to $375,000, are in great demand.

His satisfied customers—mostly Americans—include such diverse types as Richard Blackburn Black, a retired American admiral who hired Rosborough to build him a 45-foot brigantine similar to the one in which he made his first Antarctic voyage as a 20-year-old dogsled driver for Admiral Byrd; and the Young Americans, an inspirational singing group who commissioned the Santa Maria design in 1973. "Rosborough is about the best there is," exults Joseph Lathrop of the Young Americans. Group members were so happy with Rosborough's work, in fact, that they recently asked him to begin work on a second vessel. But business doesn't come his way on style alone.

As Black says: "A year-and-a-half ago I had an appraisal done on my yacht which I paid Rosborough $47,000 to build in 1969. I was told it would cost me $100,000 to replace it today."

Though Rosborough finds it difficult to remember the names of all the celebrities who have sought out his services—people like TV personalities Arthur Godfrey, and Hugh Downs and Reveen the Hypnotist come first to mind—he has almost total recall when it comes to discussing his creations. He explains proudly that six of his vessels, led by the Santa Maria, took part in the small fleet which paraded into New York harbor on July 4, 1976 as part of the American Bicentennial Celebrations. Many of his boats have circumnavigated the globe, others are involved in Caribbean charter work and still another—originally built for pleasure cruising—is now doing well as a supply vessel for an oil exploration company in Canada's far north.

If you have $350,000 available to indulge yourself, Rosborough will gladly build you a water-tight heaven of your own—a luxury cruise ship complete with eight-foot circular bed, crystal chandeliers, fireplace, sunken bathtub, sauna, bidet and even, if it strikes your fancy, a couple of authentic firing cannons to grace the deck. If your dreams outrun your income by a fair bit but you do have 6,000 odd hours to spare and know one end of a hammer from the other, that's all right too. Last year Rosborough unveiled a line of "kit boats"—which include plans, pre-cut pieces and keel-laying to boat-launching instructions—to help you build your own globe-girdling castle. The cost for a 45-foot Privateer ketch is about $6,500 (including material) plus several years of your own sweat. The completed, sail-away model would cost $74,500. Or you can just buy the plans themselves, which for this same Privateer model would cost $650.

But for every thousand would-be yachtsmen who shell out four dollars for his catalogues of boat designs and photographs, only one will actually end up with a Rosborough vessel. The rest? Well, many armchair sailors have the same feeling for their Rosborough catalogues that other men have for *Playboy*. In elite yachting circles it is said that a bottle of rum, a foot-warming fire and a Rosborough catalogue will get even the most sea-hungry landlubber through a winter night. "Some of them," Rosborough says with admiration, "can make just one catalogue last them a whole winter."

Rosborough, 50, doesn't look his role as a fantasy-fulfiller for the very rich. He is a slight, compact man with a weathered but somehow still youthful face, whose style of dress—baggy work pants topped by unfashionable checkered shirt—and close-cropped, slightly greying hair, suggest a man more at home among the rough-hewn craftsmen who build his boats than in the salons of the elite who are his principal customers. He doesn't deny it.

"I regard my clients the same way the French legal system treats accused people," he confesses, "guilty until proven innocent. I consider them all crazy until they prove otherwise."

Doug Rosborough himself is definitely not crazy. The words that spring most quickly to mind when you try to get a fix on him are practical, down-to-earth and rooted. Also busy. Extremely busy.

To build a boat the Rosborough way—using the skills and traditions made famous by Atlantic craftsmen during the Golden Age of Sail around the turn of the 20th century—can take anywhere from six months to a year and, from design to delivery, Rosborough is involved in almost every aspect of the work.

"That's why I call myself a constructor," he explains. "It's really an old-fashioned term for a guy who would design a boat and then roll up the plans under his arm and go to live at the boatyard for the entire time the boat was being built. He would translate the plans into language the boat builders—who weren't very well-educated—could understand and he would supervise all of the construction. When the vessel was completed, he would take it on its sea trials for the owner before going back home to design another one. Things have changed some but that's still essentially the way we operate." At the moment, his firm is building four boats and has deposits on eight more.

Because of his methodical approach and his personal attention to detail, Rosborough allows that, "I don't make as much money as I probably should." In an average year—building five boats—he will gross about half a million dollars and net about 10 percent of that. But to earn this amount, he keeps up an almost frenetic pace. At any one time he may have as many as four different boat yards, spread over 300 miles of Nova Scotia coastline, translating his designs into yachts. Just getting from one to the other to oversee work-in-progress can swallow the better part of a week.

That might not seem quite so impressive until you consider that, prior to this year, the boat building business was technically just a hobby for Rosborough. Until he retired last winter, his regular job was as night supervisor of toll operations (in charge of the special lines used by broadcasters and computer companies) for Maritime Telephone and Telegraph Company Ltd., the private monopoly which provides telephone service for Nova Scotia and Prince Edward Island. After completing his midnight-to-eight a.m. shift at MT&T and catching a few hours' sleep, Rosborough put in a second full day running his boat building business.

"It wasn't so bad," Rosborough now says. "The jobs were so different that when I went from one to the other it was almost relaxing." During 1973, his best year as a boat builder, when he turned out 14 boats, and grossed nearly $1.5 million, he did briefly consider resigning from MT&T "but the company pension plan was noncontributory and if I didn't get in my 30 years I wouldn't have gotten a cent." A practical man with five children to think about, Rosborough took advantage of the plan's 30-year-and-out option, waited until the exact moment he qualified for a pension and managed to retire at 50. Now a few months later, he finally can devote all his time to the boats he loves.

Rosborough can't tell you exactly when he became consumed by the idea of building boats but he suspects it may be as simple as heredity. On one side of his family his ancestors were seafarers (one progenitor, James Heaton Tidmarsh, was an early 19th century Nova Scotia marine captain who eventually lost a government job as Cape Breton's lighthouses commissioner as a result of a quarrel with Samuel Cunard) and, on the other, builders and contractors.

"I'm a mixture of both those traditions," he says, adding with a mischievous smile that although the Rosboroughs were originally Scots, his ancestors spent six centuries in Ireland before eventually emigrating to Nova Scotia in 1828. "I think I picked up a touch of the blarney from that. It comes in handy when you're trying to sell boats."

As a boy, Rosborough passed his summer vacations hanging around the wharves near his family cottage on St. Margaret's Bay just south of Halifax listening as local fishermen shared their casual talk of ships and the sea. He was only 11 when he designed and built his first small rowboat.

But even then, boatbuilding—which had been a tradition in Atlantic coastal villages since the arrival of the first settlers in the 1700s—was already a dying art.

In the fishing industry, big, company-owned trawlers were replacing the handcrafted wooden boats of the local fishermen. And the sturdy wooden schooners which had plied the Atlantic for generations exchanging Maritime cod and timber for West Indian rum and sugar were giving way to steel-hulled freighters which made up in cargo space what they lacked in romance.

Young men like Rosborough—bred with a Depression era sense of the need for security—knew that the future was not in wooden boats. Rosborough picked up an engineering degree in 1949 at Halifax's Dalhousie University, got himself a dependable land-based job at MT&T and settled down to raise a family.

In his spare time, however, he continued to tinker with boats, building the odd small sailboat and converting a few old schooners for pleasure cruising. His hobby won him a local reputation and it was only natural that during the mid-'50s when Sunday sailors from all along the eastern seaboard wanted a refurbished fishing boat they came to Rosborough.

By the late 50's, Rosborough had converted nearly a dozen boats and was making regular pilgrimages to Newfoundland outports in search of a rapidly dwindling supply of boats suitable for conversion. Under the pressures of Premier Joey Smallwood's push for industrialization and faced with declining fish stocks anyway, Newfoundland fishermen were junking their boats for firewood faster than Rosborough could buy them up.

In the early '60s, desperate to fill a growing backlog of orders for old fishing schooners, Rosborough even went so far as to charter a plane to scour the Newfoundland coast for boats. But there were none.

"That was when I first started thinking seriously of trying to design and build my own boats," Rosborough remembers. "The people who wanted the boats were asking me if I could build them one and the people I'd hired to do the actual conversion work were telling me it would be easier to start from scratch than try and resurrect the old ones. So I decided why not and set out to teach myself to design a yacht."

It took him nearly a year-and-a-half of nights and weekends to come up with his first marketable design in 1965:—a 45-foot Privateer ketch which is still the backbone of his business. Rosborough believes the reason the ketch—modelled on turn-of-the-century trading vessels and featuring a large aft-cabin and a transom or sawed-off stern—caught the fancy of yacht buyers is that "it has the flavor of antiquity. It has the same kind of appeal as old pine furniture. There's a sense of history about it." Today, Rosborough offers 17 standard vessel designs and can customize any of them or create an entirely new design in as little as two weeks.

Although the unsettled economic climate has eaten into his business ("Most people buy yachts out of savings," he observes), Rosborough will still gross about $350,000 this year—enough to keep half-a-dozen boatbuilders practising their craft full time and enabling Rosborough to employ his two oldest sons, Bob, 26, and Kevin, 23, in the company as well. Rosborough's 11-year-old son John Patrick (he also has two daughters Kathleen, 27, and Lynda, 24), is already building rafts in the cove near their home and hopes someday to be part of the business.

Although his ships are the plushest of pleasure cruisers, Rosborough's success, ironically, has been based on a return to the traditional values of the old Atlantic boat builders. His creations are not the sleek, wave-slicing racers of Sunday afternoon yachtsmen nor are they made of popular man-made substances like fibreglass, aluminum or steel. They are trusty wooden boats, meant for living and cruising.

"Wood has been used in boats for 2,000 years," Rosborough argues, "and we know everything there is to know about it. How long it will last and what its problems are. On the other hand we're just beginning to learn that fibreglass is affected by the ultraviolet rays of the sun. Salesmen who try to sell people on these new materials make great claims for them but what it comes down to is that boats made out of them are cheaper to build. Our boats cost more but then quality always does."

That clearly is a matter of some dispute in yachting circles. Jack Smith, an associate editor of the U.S.-based *Yachting Magazine*, who writes regularly on vessel design, argues that fibreglass boats are not only more popular but more functional as well. "The simple fact is that they require a lot less maintenance," he says, conceding that, "there are a lot of very knowledgeable and serious yachting people who wouldn't have anything but a wooden boat. They like the feel of it, the smell of it, but that is based more on their own likes and dislikes than on any special functional qualities of the wood."

Erik Hansen, a vice-president at Acadia University in Wolfville, N.S., who is having Rosborough build him a 36-foot schooner, agrees. "I also have a couple of fibreglass boats and they're nice because they don't require a lot of maintenance. But somehow I see fibreglass as a kind of dead material that doesn't excite my soul. Getting a wooden boat ready for the water each year, though it takes a couple of extra weeks, strikes me as part of the foreplay of sailing." Intriguingly, Hansen, as a research chemist for Dominion Rubber in the '50s, was very much involved in the development of fibreglass. "But in my personal tastes," he laughs, "I am still a traditionalist."

Rosborough's other signature design features—like square sails and aft-cabins—are the subject of some debate. Yachting enthusiasts, explains Jack Smith, have very clear ideas about what they like and what they don't like and are happy to argue about their relative merits. Rosborough however defends them on grounds other than simple nostalgia. "When we first started building boats with aft-cabins, we were just about laughed off the ocean. Styles had changed and people forgot what their original purpose was. Yet the aft is the largest and driest place on a boat where you could put a cabin and, if the cabin wasn't there, all you had was wasted space. Now if you look in any yachting magazine, you'll see all the cruising vessels are advertised with aft-cabins. It was the same with square sails. So-called modern sailors would look at them and say, "Those silly old people. They didn't know much.' But the truth is that a square rig is the easiest type to handle."

Rosborough's compromises with the 20th century are almost all below deck. "We put a lot of ballast in the bottom and the design of the keel isn't the same as the old boats," allows Rosborough. "Because our customers aren't usually as hard and tough as the old sailors were. We give them a boat they can enjoy."

The most difficult aspect of his business, says Rosborough, is marrying the dreams of his purchasers to the realities of boat-building and their own financial resources. "When people come in and they say they want this crazy thing and that expensive bit of nonsense, I play the dumb Nova Scotian," he says. "I'll say, 'Fine, fine. Yes, yes, that's what you want now is it?' Then slowly I'll try to focus them in on what they really want."

Perhaps surprisingly, Rosborough's own view is that the best boat is one that is the smallest possible and the least frill-filled and he frankly explains that to potential customers. "Everybody says that 'this is going to be my last boat and I want it to last forever.' And they want everything on it too. But in our experience, most people only keep a boat for an average of three years. Then their interests change or their boating needs change. If they have all kinds of expensive special features on it, the boat becomes that much harder to resell." He pauses and laughs. "You know sometimes I think I spend more time playing psychologist than I do building boats."

Although Rosborough has turned his amateur psychology and professional boat-building skills into a thriving cottage industry, he isn't optimistic about the long-term prospects of keeping his business alive. In the 14 years he has been in business, the costs of building a wooden boat have increased dramatically, since for instance, a boat selling for $50,000 just three years ago now costs $70,000. His boats were once cheaper than similar fibreglass, steel and aluminum-based vessels, but now mass production techniques have finally gotten the better of his boats. "All of the pieces for our boats have to be cut and shaped by craftsmen which takes a lot of time," he complains, "and so about two-thirds of the cost of one of our boats is labor costs.

"Now our builders get about $7 an hour. That's the most we can afford to pay them and stay in business but it's a hell of a lot less than they can get as carpenters in the city where they only have to know how to hammer a nail."

To cut down on labor costs and at the same time tap the growing home handyman-market, Rosborough finally introduced his build-it-yourself boat kits this year. "I had one couple that had been saving for five years for their boat," he notes sadly, "but when they wrote me and told me they were ready to have it built I had to tell them the price had gone up. It went on like that for a couple of years: they'd save some more but it would never be enough. Now I think the kits will make it possible for people like that to get the boat they really want." By mid-year he had already sold seven kits and more than 20 sets of plans to people wanting to build their own vessels.

Rosborough can laugh at the eccentricities of his buyers but there is another side to the man as well. He still gets a special thrill out of making fantasy become reality and given a chance he'll haul out a scrapbook full of clippings sent to him by Rosborough boat owners all over the world. There are stories of his boats surviving sea storm batterings without a scratch; of Founders' Day regattas in small American towns where his vessels were the centre of attention; and of families that have traveled around the world in their Rosborough yacht.

For his own part, Rosborough says he has no unfulfilled fantasies. Just being able to build boats, he says, gives him as much pleasure as other people get from sailing in his creations. Although he has owned eight different boats over the years—all were sold—he confesses that the mere thought of spending more than a couple of hours lazily cruising in one gives him the willies. "I can't just lay around. I have to be doing something."

With that he urges his visitor toward the door. There are piles of letters waiting on his desk: fantasies in need of fulfillment.

Assignment

1. What products does Doug Rosborough sell?
2. What is his market?
3. How does he reach prospective clients?
4. How does he view them?
5. How long does it take to make the product? What are the major steps involved?
6. Where is construction undertaken? How is it controlled?
7. Why is the business located where it is? Why does it remain there? Are boats also built inland in Canada?
8. Are boats a good investment?
9. How would you describe the type of plant layout involved in boat building?
10. Should Rosborough have quit his job at the telephone company earlier to concentrate on building boats? Discuss.
11. How did Rosborough get into the boat-building business?
12. What made him start to build new boats instead of converting old ones?
13. What is his present product line?
14. How profitable is the boat business?
15. Why would people in modern times buy wooden rather than fibreglass boats?
16. What do you think of Rosborough's product strategy?
17. Why is so much psychology involved in selling boats?
18. Why did Rosborough introduce build-it-yourself boat kits?
19. How, in a few words, would you describe Doug Rosborough?

Why John Voortman's Muffins Sell Like Hot Cakes in the US

BY WAYNE LILLEY

Source: *Canadian Business Magazine*. Used by permission of Wayne Lilley.

John Voortman, 54, had a few product development problems when he founded Oakrun Farm Bakery Ltd. in Carluke, Ont., after retiring early from his real estate career. Voortman, who comes from a family of bakers, produced recipes for a complete line of quality goods—and quickly realized a production and marketing truth: he couldn't produce on a scale that would make his products price-competitive with the giants of the industry; and even had he been able to, his sales prospects were dim in Ontario where the conglomerates that control the chains also operate full-line bakeries.

Voortman made two decisions that turned his company around. The first was to winnow his product line down to English muffins, which have a relatively good shelf life as bakery goods go and which he felt he could make better than the competition. More important, he discovered that US chains in large cities close to the Ontario border are local rather than national, as they are in Canada. Using the advantage of his one-product economy and the devalued Canadian dollar, he discovered that the US chains were eager customers. Voortman's exports now account for about 20% of Oakrun's $2.5 million in sales. Mainly on the basis of export growth, he expects 1983 sales to hit $5 million, with exports accounting for 40%.

Currently, Oakrun is cranking out more than 500,000 packages of muffins a week, and US consumers are gobbling up about 100,000 of them. By sticking to a one-product line, Voortman can ensure the quality control that is essential in a business where production is directly linked to orders.

Voortman has extended the principle of efficiency through simplicity to the delivery of his product as well. Oakrun insists on delivering to customers' warehouses. The customer then distributes to the stores in the chain. "It means we only have to deal with one invoice, not 60," says Voortman.

As far as exports are concerned, Voortman is a proponent of having local marketing agents handle Oakrun muffins. But, he says, the agents have to be carefully chosen: "We went through six or seven in New York state before we found one who understood our product and how we wanted to sell it. And in Detroit and Chicago, both big markets, we use food brokers to handle the marketing." Voortman says expansion of US markets also has to be handled carefully and must be co-ordinated with the distribution system to ensure that the product is fresh when it reaches the customer. Although he produces mainly for the consumer market and his muffins are sold through retail outlets, he also sells to Burger King outlets, which have introduced breakfasts in some Canadian markets.

Voortman pays tribute to provincial agriculture ministry officials who helped him participate in food trade shows, as well as industry officials who assisted in laying out the bakery and setting up the accounting system. He has also found that provincially sponsored trade shows are an excellent means of meeting brokers willing to handle his line in the US.

Voortman notes that English muffins were originally made in New England, where they remain popular. He hopes to expand distribution as far south as Boston in the next year to capitalize on that, but he's being careful to keep his costs in line. Most of his start-up financing was done through personal resources, bank loans and a $118,000 Ontario Development Corp. low-interest loan.

Voortman now has the opportunity to show the creativity as a baker that led him into the business in the first place. But he admits he's a little more businesslike about product development. He's currently working on a rusk-like product. "Rusk is made in Europe but nowhere in Canada or the US," he says. "Right now it costs about 12¢ to 15¢ a package to import. We think we can make it just as well and at a competitive price, so we'll be able to take advantage of our distribution network."

Assignment

1. What was John Voortman's initial product development problem? How did he resolve it?
2. What was his marketing strategy?
3. How does Oakrun control the quality of its product?
4. Explain Oakrun's distribution system.
5. What government assistance has Voortman received?
6. How did he finance Oakrun's expansion?
7. Would a "rusk-like" product be a good idea for Oakrun? Discuss.

PART E
MARKETING MANAGEMENT

CHAPTER 9
MARKETING AND THE MARKETING DEPARTMENT

CHAPTER OBJECTIVES

- To explain the basic marketing terms.
- To list and describe the various functions of marketing.
- To discuss the need for marketing.
- To explain how a firm's marketing activities are organized and implemented.
- To describe the basic types of markets for Canadian goods and services.

CHAPTER OUTLINE

9.1   Functions of Marketing
9.2   The Marketing Department
9.3   Types of Markets

UNIT 9.1: FUNCTIONS OF MARKETING

At one time, the term *marketing* was used solely to refer to all the various activities involved in the distribution of goods and services from producer to consumer, such as pricing, advertising, transporting, and selling. In recent years, however, this definition of marketing has been criticized on the grounds that it perpetuates the belief that marketing involves merely the distribution of the goods and services that a firm has produced; in other words, that marketing is something that begins where production leaves off.

The Marketing Concept

The modern view of marketing (known as the *marketing concept*) is that it should be considered more a frame of mind, or outlook, than a set of actitivies. The marketing concept is a philosophy of business action that evaluates the contribution of *every* activity of the firm to the satisfaction of the firm's customers.

Looked at in this way, marketing implies several things: first, that it comprises many different activities all of which help, in varying degree, to both produce and distribute a product; second, that marketing, in striving above all to satisfy customer demand, begins even before a good is produced; third, that a business firm's main goal, and the key to larger profits, is to produce and sell what consumers want, not what the firm has traditionally sold nor what the firm believes consumers *should* want.

The large firm that adopts this *consumer-oriented approach* will often have a president with a marketing background; will have, and pay careful heed to, a marketing department; will use market research to ascertain consumer wants and consumer reaction to new products, new packaging, price changes, and so on; will stress product planning and development; and will constantly try to adjust its products, promotion, pricing, and physical distribution to changes in the marketplace.

The Marketing Mix

If a firm is to achieve a satisfactory volume of sales for each of its products, it must ensure that the various marketing functions are performed in the right intensity and in the correct combination. This is called the *marketing mix*. The better the mix, the larger the volume of profitable sales. An intensive advertising campaign, for example, is of limited use if the product is poorly designed, if the sales force is not ready to take advantage of the campaign, or if additional stocks of the goods have not been delivered to retail outlets to meet the increased demand.

The 4 Ps of Marketing. As shown in Figure 9.1, the marketing mix contains four major ingredients: product, price, place, and promotion. These are sometimes called "the 4 Ps" of marketing and each involves a variety of questions:

1. **Product.** What products to offer to the consumer? Which to discontinue?

Which to modify? This involves such marketing activities as market research, product planning, standardizing and grading, dividing, packaging, and branding.
2. **Price.** How much to charge for the product? What mark-up structure to suggest for wholesalers and retailers? What discounts to allow?
3. **Place.** Where should the goods or services be made available? What channels of distribution to use? How to transport the goods? How to store them on the way to the customer? In the case of importers, wholesalers, and retailers, what goods to buy for resale?
4. **Promotion.** How to persuade consumers to purchase the firm's products? This involves advertising, selling, and other forms of sales promotion. Price, product design, packaging, branding, availability, considered under the three previous headings, will also greatly facilitate or hinder this task.

The various activities involved in marketing a product are listed and explained below under the four basic headings of product, price, place, and promotion.

Product

This involves such activities as marketing research, product planning, standardizing and grading, dividing, packaging, and branding.

Marketing Research. Producers and middlemen must keep themselves constantly informed about the market to which they sell, the channels of distribution, and the various means of sales promotion. This is called *marketing research*. Research about the market alone is known as *market research* and covers such items as price changes, size of market, changes in consumer tastes, conditions of supply, competition, and economic and political changes. Some of the research will be undertaken by the producers and middlemen themselves. Part will be obtained from government agencies—notably, Statistics Canada—from trade papers and from private research firms.

Product Planning and Development. Also known as *product development*, this is the task of deciding, in the case of the manufacturer, what new products or product lines to manufacture and which to discontinue; and, in the case of the middleman, what products to stock and offer for sale. Also involved is the choice of product quality and packaging. Because of the changing pattern of consumer needs and wants, and the activities of competitors, product planning is vital to the success of practically every business. The product planning and development process was discussed in Unit 8.1.

Standardizing and Grading. When a consumer buys a good, he or she expects that it will conform to an agreed *standard*. For example, a can of onion soup should have a taste similar to that of any other can of onion soup

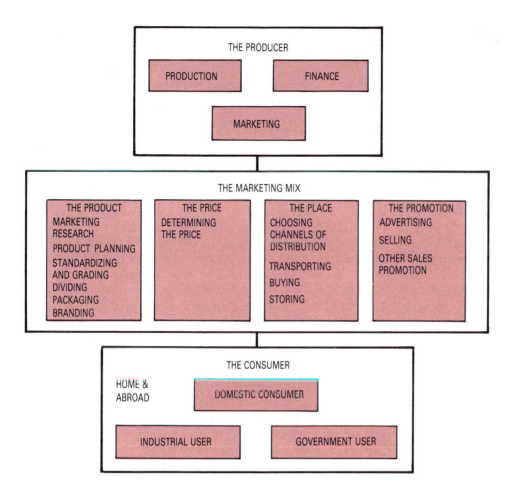

Figure 9.1 The Marketing Mix

from the same manufacturer. If this were not the case, the marketing of many of our goods would come to a halt, for consumers would be justifiably cautious before making a purchase. Certainly, a consumer would hardly dare to order a product without first seeing or tasting it.

Standards are set for colour, size, shape, strength, performance, and taste. Many standards are established by the various industries themselves, as it is in their interest to see that their products are consistently good; otherwise, the image of the products to the buying public would deteriorate. In other cases—for example, the drug industry—standards are set by government legislation.

Grading is the task of sorting products into different classes or grades, so that each grade will consist of goods which conform to the standards set for that grade. Thus, for example, Grade A Extra Large chicken eggs must be over a certain weight. Grading and standardization go hand in hand.

Dividing and Packaging. Goods are not usually produced or sold by the manufacturer or farmer in the quantities most convenient for the consumer. For example, a ton of dried fruit must be divided by the wholesaler into quantities suitable for the retailer, who will in turn divide them into smaller quantities—for example, $\frac{1}{2}$ kg packages—for customers.

Goods must also be packaged to prevent damage or theft on their way from producer to consumer, to prevent deterioration from such factors as exposure to heat and cold, to ensure that they remain hygienic, and to attract the attention of the prospective consumer. The package can also serve as an important means of sales promotion—attracting favourable attention and promoting brand loyalty.

Branding. A *brand* is the name, symbol, and other design, including choice of colours, used to identify the products of a particular manufacturer or middleman. These may be *manufacturer's brands* (also called *national brands* because of the nation-wide distribution of the product) or middlemen's brands, known as *private brands*. The term private brand is used because the identity of the manufacturer is not revealed.

The purpose of a brand is to encourage consumer loyalty to the products of a particular manufacturer or middleman. By advertising, coupled with the offering of a good-quality merchandise, consumers are persuaded that a certain brand of product is better than a rival one, even though the items may in fact be otherwise identical. Consumer loyalty offers several advantages to a manufacturer: it is better able to compete with manufacturers of similar products; it may be able to charge more for its product because of its "uniqueness"; and the firm may use the brand name to help sell new products. However, the creation of brand loyalty is usually an expensive advertising proposition. Nowadays, in contrast to the usual practice, there are also some "no-name products."

Price

Often a manufacturer will set a price so as to obtain a certain average annual percentage return, say 10, 15, or 20 per cent after tax, on his or her investment or a certain dollar amount of after-tax profit.

The actual return chosen may be: a fair and reasonable return, considering the risk involved; the customary rate of return in this line of business; a certain increase over the firm's previous target returns; or a stable level of profits.

All manufacturers set their selling price to the middleman who forms the first link in the channels of distribution for their products. Some manufacturers will also suggest prices that the wholesalers and retailers should charge. This suggested markup is usually a percentage return on sales, for example, 35 per cent of the sales price.

Production and Marketing Costs. Many firms rely wholly or partly on cost as the basis for pricing their products. Thus a manufacturer often sets the factory selling price for his or her product equal to the standard unit cost of production (including a share of overhead) for an expected volume of output

"Whose idea was it to set our price below cost?"

and sales of the product, plus a certain percentage markup for profit. The standard unit cost is determined by dividing the total anticipated costs for the planned output over the next few years by the number of units to be produced. More often, a manufacturer will set the price for the product substantially above cost, charging what he or she thinks the market will bear. However, if the price-elasticity of demand for the product is very great because of the existence of competitive products, the producer will not be able to sell it if the price is more than the going rate. Only if the producer can "differentiate" the product from similar ones by branding can it hope to charge more.

The manufacturer's suggested retail price will allow not only for production costs but also for the marketing costs involved in getting the product to the consumer, plus a reasonable percentage of profit for the various middlemen. If the middleman's markup is not sufficiently attractive, the manufacturer may find it difficult to persuade him or her to handle the product.

If the manufacturer is in a monopoly position, his or her power to charge a high price is very great. This can happen with, for example, a government-appointed marketing board or a manufacturer with the patent for a new product that the public wants. In the case of a new product, such as a movie, the producer may charge a very high price initially to take advantage of that segment of the public that insists on buying it right away. This is called *skim-the-cream pricing*.

Other Pricing Policies. Some firms are willing to set a price, usually for the short term, that will yield little or no profit. The pricing objectives may instead be:
1. *Market introduction*—to help introduce a product to the market.
2. *Market penetration*—to obtain a larger share of the market for a particular type of product.

3. *Market domination*—to obtain control over a market by underpricing competitive products.
4. *Market protection*—to protect an existing market by keeping prices sufficiently low to discourage would-be competitors.
5. *Market image*—to help improve the firm's public image to customers.
6. *Product-line promotion*—to help promote the sale of other products that form part of the same product-line. An example of this is selling razors at a low price to stimulate sales of a certain type of razor blade.
7. *Stable prices*—to try to keep prices stable in the short run even though this may mean a slight reduction in profits as costs increase.
8. *Customer attraction*—supermarkets and other retailers may sell some goods ("loss-leaders") at or below cost to attract shoppers to the store.
9. *Making way for new inventory*—a middleman may sell goods below cost if he or she believes that they will not otherwise sell and if the shelf space is needed for new stock.

Place

The third major group of marketing activities is concerned with getting the products to the right place at the right time so that consumers can buy them when they want to. These activities include choosing the channels of distribution, transporting the goods, and in the case of the middlemen involved, buying and storing the right kinds of products.

Choosing Distribution Channels.
The *channels of distribution* (or *trade channels*) are the paths that a product takes from the producer (farmer, manufacturer, and so on) to the domestic consumer, industrial user, government user, or export market. A firm wishing to market a product must employ one or more of these channels. Which one or ones it uses will depend on such factors as the nature of the product, the ability of the producer to make a profit by personally undertaking all or part of the marketing, the need for after-sales service, the need for aggressive merchandising, the types of consumers for the product, and the location of these consumers. The various types of channels are described in Unit 10.2 of the next chapter.

Transporting.
This function of marketing involves moving goods from where they are produced to where they are consumed. Value is added to a product by making it available where it is wanted (the *place utility* of economics).

The means of transportation include trucks, trains, ships, pipelines, and airplanes. Each of these possesses particular characteristics which make it suitable for the transportation of certain types of goods. Thus ships are suitable for transporting heavy, bulky goods, where speed is relatively unimportant. Airplanes, conversely, are often used for transporting goods that have a high value in relation to bulk and that need to be moved quickly.

Improved means of transportation, such as larger, faster ships, have made it possible for a firm to sell its products farther and farther from the place of production. This extension of the market has, in turn, made it possible for firms to reduce their unit costs of production by longer production runs. Improved means of transportation, such as refrigerated rail cars, have also enabled consumers to purchase goods previously not available at certain seasons of the year.

Buying. This is normally considered the function of the consumer. However, buying must also be considered a marketing function in the sense that many business firms, acting as middlemen in the distribution process, purchase goods not for consumption but for resale. This is the case of wholesalers and retailers. Also, manufacturers buy raw materials and parts to incorporate into a finished good, which will be offered for sale.

Part of the marketing process is, then, the choice by manufacturers and middlemen of goods that they will be able to process or resell and the ordering of them in quantities appropriate to their anticipated volume of business.

If a middleman is going to be able to sell its goods successfully, it must exercise great care in what is purchased. It must take into account such factors as consumer tastes, the prices required, the credit available, how quickly it can obtain a fresh supply, and the manufacturer's advertising and public image. A manufacturer must ensure that the raw materials and parts purchased are of the price and quality required. If it does not do this, the resultant product will be inferior and may result in declining sales.

The function of buying involves: determining the goods required; choosing a supplier; ensuring the suitability of the goods offered (by sample and inspection, or by description); and negotiating the terms of the purchase (quality, price, delivery, and credit). Sometimes the seller will seek the buyer rather than vice versa.

Storing. Goods that are on their way from producer to consumer must be stored at the wholesaler's warehouse or on the retailer's shelves until a sale is actually made. By having the goods available when the consumer needs them, the middleman is adding to their value (*time utility*).

When there is a relatively constant, year-round demand for a product, production can, to a certain extent, be dovetailed with customer demand so that storage of the finished goods by producer or middleman is kept to a minimum.

The storage function becomes more important:
1. *When there are pronounced seasonal variations in consumer demand.* In the case of garden equipment, it may be profitable for the producer to manufacture at a steady rate the whole year round, to accumulate enough stock by spring to meet demand throughout the summer and fall.
2. *When production is seasonal in nature.* Many agricultural products are now frozen or placed in cold storage and sold gradually over the year.

A firm will often rent space from a storage warehouse company to supplement its own storage facilities.

Promotion

This is the fourth and last of the major areas of marketing activity. It includes advertising, selling, and other forms of sales promotion. The combination of advertising, selling, and other promotional activities used by a firm is known as the "promotional mix."

Advertising. This consists of informing consumers by various media (such as radio, television, and newspapers) of the merits of a product or service and attempting to persuade them, openly or subtly, to buy it. Advertising is examined and discussed in Unit 11.2.

Selling. This is the action of the salesperson in encouraging a person or firm to buy a product or service and in completing the transaction. In some cases—for example, real estate salespeople—the work of persuasion can be vital to the sale. In other cases—for example, a drug store—the salesperson may be required to act only as a cashier to complete the transaction; advertising and previous consumer experience with the product will have eliminated the need for further sales persuasion. Selling is considered in some detail in Unit 11.3.

The Need for Marketing

Whereas the need for the production of goods and services is obvious to most people, the need for marketing is not always so apparent. Some of the reasons for it are:
1. The need constantly to stimulate demand in order to absorb all the goods and services that the economy is capable of producing—hence the need for advertising and personal selling.
2. The need to inform consumers about new products as well as old—hence also the need for advertising and personal selling.
3. Producers are rarely located where all their customers are—hence the need for transportation.
4. Producers cannot economically produce goods exactly when they are needed by consumers—hence the need for storage and financing.
5. Producers would be unaware of the consumers' requirements—hence the need for market research.
6. Producers can often reduce their per unit cost of production only by economies of large-scale production—hence the need for sales promotion to increase demand for the product.
7. Producers rarely produce in the quantities suitable for the ultimate consumer—hence the need for dividing.
8. Producers do not always produce a uniform product—hence the need for standardizing and grading to enable consumers to obtain exactly what they order.
9. The need to protect the goods from damage from the time they are produced until they are sold—hence the need for packaging to protect the product from damage or theft.
10. The need to display the goods for consumer selection—hence the need for retailing.

It can be seen from the reasons given that marketing serves a number of useful purposes. This is not to say, however, that its various component activities cannot be performed more efficiently than they often are. But such a criticism applies equally to production, and its validity will depend on the particular activity and the individual firm performing it. Since both production and marketing are carried out by firms in competition with one another, it is reasonable to believe that except for pockets of monopoly, the stimulus for efficiency is present and reasonably effective.

KEY TERMS

Marketing
Marketing concept
Consumer-oriented approach
Marketing mix
4 Ps of marketing
Product
Price
Place
Promotion
Marketing research
Market research
Product planning and development
Standardizing
Grading
Dividing
Packaging

Branding
Brand
Manufacturer's brand
National brand
Private brand
Pricing
Skim-the-cream pricing
Choosing distribution channels
Transporting
Place utility
Buying
Storing
Promotion
Advertising
Selling

REVIEW QUESTIONS

1. Distinguish between the old and modern views of marketing.
2. Give examples of present-day companies that seem to be using the modern approach to marketing.
3. Give examples of present-day companies that seem to be using the old approach to marketing.
4. Marketing is something that begins where production leaves off. Discuss.
5. What is the "marketing concept"? Is it confined to business firms?
6. What might be the characteristics of a firm that uses a consumer-oriented approach?

7. Explain the terms "marketing mix" and the "4 Ps of marketing" and the relationship between them.
8. Explain, with an example, how a poor marketing mix can lead to sales disaster rather than success.
9. What product decisions must be made in the course of a firm's marketing operations?
10. Is pricing a straightforward matter when planning a marketing campaign? Discuss.
11. "Place" is one of the ingredients of the marketing mix. Just what does it involve?
12. What promotional decisions must be made in marketing a new product?
13. Explain, in terms of the marketing mix, the success of Japanese cars in North America.
14. Identify a Canadian product that you believe is being well promoted. Explain the reasons for your choice.
15. Identify a Canadian product that you believe is being badly promoted. Why do you think so?
16. Why is it necessary to spend money on marketing? Give six basic reasons.
17. Distinguish between market research and marketing research. Why is it that some products fare badly in the market place despite intensive prior marketing research?
18. Explain the product planning and development process involved with a new car, book, or other product.
19. Explain the differences between standardizing and grading of products. Are these functions of marketing necessary for all products? Explain with examples.
20. Explain, with examples, the dividing function of marketing.
21. What roles does packaging play in the marketing of a product? Illustrate your answer with examples.
22. What is a brand? Why do firms use them? What are the various types?
23. Are "no-name brands" a good marketing idea? Discuss.
24. What factors are usually involved in the pricing of a new product?
25. Why would a firm set a price for its product that provides little or no profit?
26. What are "channels of distribution"? What factors determine which ones to use in the marketing of a product?
27. The transporting function of marketing provides "place utility." Explain.
28. Improved means of transportation increase the size of the market for a product. Explain with examples.
29. How would the following products most likely be transported to buyers?
    (a) prize bulls from Calgary to Japan
    (b) frozen meat products from Toronto to West Germany
    (c) fresh fish from Boston to Winnipeg
    (d) orange juice from Florida to Ottawa
    (e) newspapers and magazines from Britain to Canada

(f) newsprint from Quebec to France
(g) lumber from British Columbia to Southern Ontario
30. What is meant by the "buying function" of marketing? Is it more critical for some firms than others?
31. The middleman adds time utility to products. Explain.
32. When does the storage function of marketing become particularly important for a product? Explain the relationship between the size of a production run and the need for storage.
33. Advertising and selling should go hand in hand. Explain. Why is it that some products are marketed with little or no advertising?

CASE PROBLEM

WEEKS FARMS LTD.
Marketing your own products

A husband and wife, Fred and Carol Weeks, own a large farm forty-eight kilometres away from a major Canadian city. Vegetables grown by them include carrots, onions, celery, lettuce, radishes, parsnips, beets, and potatoes. The couple also own and operate a poultry farm with a laying flock of 10,000 hens.

Up to the present time, the vegetables and eggs from these farms have been sold at producers' prices to a large produce wholesaler. The couple are now considering marketing their own produce in order to increase their net income.

Assignment

1. Explain, with references to the vegetables and eggs, the marketing functions which the couple will have to perform.
2. What are the channels of distribution that the couple might use for these products? Specify in your answer the different types of industrial and retail outlets. (See Unit 10.2)
3. How would the existence of a marketing board affect your answers to the previous questions?

READINGS

Diners Cheer as a New PEI Industry Flexes Its Mussels

BY JAMES DINGWALL

Source: *Canadian Business Magazine*. Used by permission of James Dingwall.

"Trash!" Until recently, that's the word most Prince Edward Islanders have used to describe the wild blue mussels that populate their inland rivers. They've regarded the shellfish as inedible pests whose sole role in the chain of life is to foul boat bottoms, buoys, fishing lines and docks.

Now, however, they're changing their tune. The reason is that the provincial Department of Fisheries (DOF) and a local entrepreneur have, so to speak, built a better mussel. Ever since it first went on the market last December, it has been drawing glowing testimonials from gourmet chefs in

Montreal and Toronto. The cultured mussel could spawn a new industry worth millions of dollars a year to the island.

That's certainly the hope of Irwin Judson, a director of the DOF's Aquaculture branch and the original mussel builder. Five years ago Judson sampled the wild mussels in PEI's river beds to find out whether they were edible. "We discovered that almost all of the ones we sampled had pearls embedded in the meat," he says. "Fish packers wouldn't touch them. In their opinion, the only people who could make money on PEI mussels were dentists." But he believed that this and other problems could be circumvented if the mussels were raised in a controlled environment. His DOF team set about adapting farming techniques developed by European fishermen. They filled plastic mesh tubes with spats (baby mussels) and suspended them in the rivers far enough below the surface to protect them from the ravages of ice floes during winter, a prime harvest time for mussels. The spats attached themselves to the mesh, which protected them from predators and kept them out of the mud during the 16 to 18 months they took to reach maturity.

In December 1977 Judson harvested his first experimental crop. It was encouraging. The mussels were far plumper and cleaner than their wild brethren. So he gave some of them to an acquaintance, Joe Van Den Bremt, to test-taste. A Belgian by birth, Van Den Bremt had immigrated to Ontario in 1954 and worked on a tobacco farm. In 1969 he moved to PEI and set up his own farm. One thing Van Den Bremt had brought with him from Belgium was a taste for mussels. He was so impressed with the DOF product that in 1978 he decided to gamble $50,000 of his own money to establish the first commercial mussel farm on the Island, PEI Mussel King Inc., in Montague. "We needed someone with drive and ambition to get this going and Joe had both," says Judson. "He got into it in a large enough way to promise some continuity in the market."

Mussel King harvested its first crop last fall, and it now ships 10,000 lb. of mussels a week to major cities in Canada. By the end of next year, Van Den Bremt expects his family business to be shipping more than 1 million lb. a year. At a wholesale price of 50¢ a lb., that would add up to sales of $500,000 in 1981. He is now on the prowl for more efficient harvesting equipment.

Van Den Bremt no longer has the commercial mussel-farming field to himself, however. Judson says that about 18 PEI fishermen planted their own crops of spats last summer, and their crops should reach maturity early next year. He cautiously estimates that mussels could double the amount of money that shellfish, excluding lobsters, pump into the PEI economy—$1.1 million in 1978, the latest year for which figures are available.

In an attempt to make that a reality, PEI's Market Development Centre is helping Mussel King and other farmers come up with off-island marketing strategies. Its aim is to secure as wide a market as possible for the product. But the new mussel has also attracted some private brokers on the cordon bleu circuit. One of them is Michael Vaughan, a Toronto wine critic and marketing consultant. His company, Muscult International Inc., has been demonstrating the virtues of the cultured shellfish at carriage-trade restaurants in Montreal and Toronto. Now Vaughan is selling about 3,000 lb. of them a week to more than a dozen establishments in the two cities, including Toronto's chichi Fenton's and Winston's restaurants. And he's developed his own nifty sales aid, a T-shirt with a message. The inscription? "Muscult Man."

Assignment

1. To what extent has product planning been involved in PEI's mussel success?
2. What marketing strategies are being used or contemplated?
3. Who should get the entrepreneurial credit?

Cartons, Bubbles and Boxes: Just Promotional Tools?

BY EDWARD CLIFFORD

Source: *The Globe and Mail*, Toronto

Consumer activists who see packaging as wasteful of both money and materials have a lot to learn about the role of packaging in preserving and transporting consumer goods, particularly perishables, officials of the Packaging Association of Canada believe.

Lyn Jamison, president of the Packaging Association of Canada, said he has to be patient with people who decry packages as nothing more than fancy promotional tools that waste resources.

In reality, he said, most packages perform important roles in containing, protecting, transporting and storing a product. It is almost incidental that the package is also used as an advertising and marketing medium, he said. Yet uninformed and militant individuals and groups can endanger the industry by their blind approach, Mr. Jamison said.

Retailers find, for example, that one of the greatest wastes of products is that they begin to look "shopworn" by constant handling on the shelves of a store. If it happens often enough, people will not buy the item and it is discarded although otherwise in good condition. Durable packaging can keep a product looking good for its shelf life, however.

Another pet peeve among buyers is that manufacturers put small items into large packages, presumably to encourage buyers to think that the product is much larger than it is in reality.

But the real reason often is that the item, if packaged in its correct size, can be stolen easily. Mounting a small tube of glue on a large piece of cardboard discourages its theft, packagers have found.

Some consumers complain that oversize packaging is also used by manufacturers of loose, dry food products—cereals, for example. These are products that fill their containers when packaged, but settle in subsequent shipping and handling, and manufacturers now print that explantion on their boxes.

Others wonder why a product packaged in a durable container—toothpaste, for example—also needs to be boxed.

The explanation is that toothpaste tubes can be too easily squeezed out of shape on the shelves, and quickly take on that "shopworn" appearance. Even more important, it is very difficult to ship and store toothpaste tubes unless they are put in square containers. And it is almost impossible to stack toothpaste tubes on a store shelf and expect them to stay in place, Mr. Jamison said.

One of the most compelling reasons for manufacturers to avoid waste is the cost of packaging that Mr. Jamison expects will increase substantially in the next decade because of energy costs.

The prospect of such cost increases is spurring the search for new packaging materials and better packaging methods. It has also led to the development of such concepts as flexible vacuum packs and retortable packs in which a meal can be heated before eating.

"Cans will always be around, but the new systems will gain popularity because of their energy-saving features, both at the manufacturer, processor and consumer level."

But adoption by the consumer may be slow at first, because the consumer will have to grow accustomed to some of the interesting new shapes that a change in packaging methods will bring about.

Do not look for any decrease in the amount of plastics used for packaging, however. Out of every 45 gallons of oil used in Canada, only two are used in the manufacture of plastic materials.

Costs of packaging amount to an average of 12.2 per cent of the retail price of consumer products. This can rise to as much as 70 per cent of the price of such products as cosmetics, however.

As the recent Canadian National Packaging Exposition demonstrated, the Canadian industry is in the front ranks of world packagers. Some experts are even on loan to Eastern countries, teaching the packaging science.

J. Keith Russell, who was chairman of the packaging show and is vice-president of Lepage's Ltd. of Toronto, said Canadian technology can help prevent millions in the world from starving.

For example, food wastage in North America is only about 15 per cent of all food produced, thanks largely to efficient storage and transportation which is made possible in part by packaging. In a state such as Mysore, India, however, food wastage can rise to as high as 70 per cent of production.

"Far from being wasteful, modern packaging has the potential for bringing about huge increments in world food supplies quickly, and saving the lives of countless people."

Assignment

1. Product packages are nothing more than fancy promotional tools. Discuss.
2. Why do manufacturers sometimes use oversize packaging?
3. Why do tubes of toothpaste need to be boxed?
4. What developments have taken place in recent years in the packaging of consumer products?
5. How much of the retail price of a product might go to cover the cost of packaging? Which products have the most expensive packaging? Which have the least expensive packaging? Which products have no packaging cost at all?
6. How useful can packaging be? Discuss, with reference to wastage of food and other products.

UNIT 9.2: THE MARKETING DEPARTMENT

This is the department specifically entrusted with the efficient marketing of a firm's products. In the large firm, the marketing department is usually headed by a *vice-president, marketing*, or a *marketing manager*. In the smaller firm, a *sales manager* may be in charge of all selling, advertising, and other marketing activities.

Organization

The organization of a marketing department varies from firm to firm according to various factors:

1. *The firm's marketing philosophy*—The more consumer-oriented the firm, the greater tends to be the marketing manager's jurisdiction. This situation is illustrated by Figure 9.2.

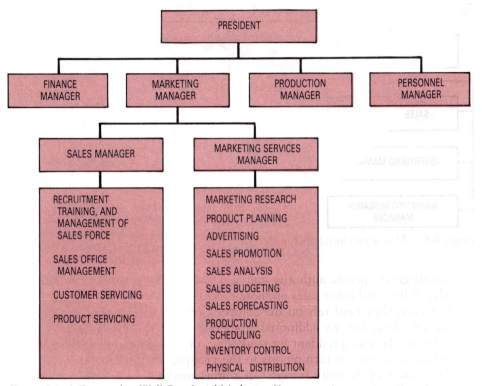

Figure 9.2 A Firm with a Well-Developed Marketing Department

2. *The size of the business*—The larger and more complex the business, the greater the number of levels of authority and the greater the number of staff specialists such as market researchers and public relations people.
3. *The number and variety of products*—If there is a large number of products, or if different types of products require different marketing programs, a firm's marketing department may be organized according to product groups. With the *product division* arrangements (Figure 9.3), the firm's major products are manufactured and marketed by separate divisions. Each division performs the various marketing activities for its own products, and a corporate marketing vice-president at head office co-ordinates marketing activities throughout the firm.

With the *product manager* or *brand manager* arrangement, managers are appointed for each of the major products or brands of the firm. They are

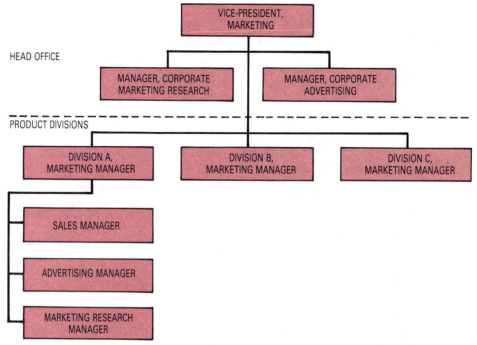

Figure 9.3 A Marketing Organization with Product Divisions

usually given specific authority and responsibility for product planning, advertising, and other sales promotion for their own particular products. However, they must rely on the co-operation of the sales manager and the sales force for any additional promotion. The product managers report either to the vice-president for marketing, or to a general or group product manager who in turn reports to the vice-president for marketing.

4. *The location of the firm's markets*—If a firm's markets are scattered geographically, the marketing activities may be completely decentralized, with a marketing manager and marketing office located in each region. Alternatively, some marketing functions such as advertising and product planning may be performed at head office (usually located in the key market area) and the others performed on a decentralized basis (as shown in Figure 9.4). If a regional market is quite small, a firm may transfer the responsibility for selling, advertising, and physical distribution to wholesalers and other middlemen.

5. *The types of customers*—If a firm has several distinct groups of customers for its products, each with its own particular marketing problems, it may appoint a marketing manager for each customer group. Each manager would then have authority and responsibility for selling, advertising, marketing research, and so on, with regard to his or her own customer group and would be accountable for these functions to the firm's marketing vice-president.

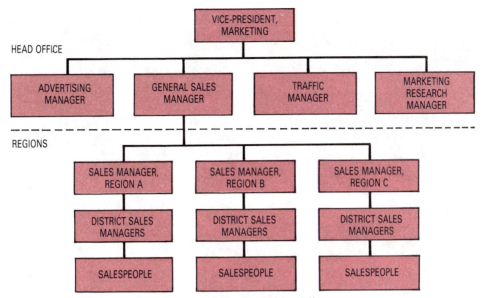

Figure 9.4 A Marketing Organization with Regional Sales Offices

Sales Forecasts

The basis for planning a firm's marketing activities is a realistic *sales forecast* for each brand of the firm's products. This should be in both dollars and units, to satisfy financial as well as production and marketing purposes. Such a forecast can be arrived at by a careful analysis of past sales performance; by a comparison of company sales with industry sales to establish the share of the total market that each brand has previously been able to obtain; and by an intelligent appraisal of new factors (such as changing age of the population or changing habits) that could influence future sales. This analysis should be undertaken for each market segment (for example, clear-cut geographical area or age group). The sales forecast for each product or brand within each market segment then provides the basis for establishing sales targets for each of the firm's sales territories. Most large firms have detailed long-term and short-term marketing plans, as well as historical analyses of past sales and related operations.

Actual methods of sales forecasting range from the "educated guess" by the marketing manager or vice-president to sophisticated statistical and econometric analysis. Usually, the forecast, although originating with the sales or marketing manager, will be thoroughly examined and discussed by a top management committee (often a committee of the board of directors) before it is accepted as a basis for detailed planning.

One popular tool of forecasting is *trend analysis*. This involves plotting the sales data for past years on to a graph, drawing in a trend line and then extending the line into the future. Such a method assumes, of course, that past trends will persist into the future. Since this may be true only to a certain extent, three

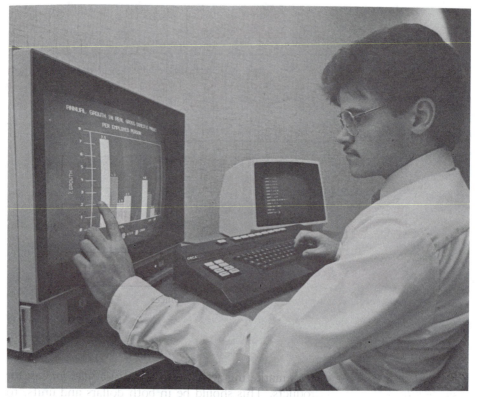

Courtesy The Ontario Ministry of Industry, Trade and Technology

forecasts may be made: one based on the most favourable assumptions, one on the least favourable, and one in between.

Another device used in sales forecasting is *correlation analysis*. This is the identification of a fixed relationship between two different factors—for example, the birth rate and the demand for baby powder, or the total sales of cars and the demand for hub caps. If a definite correlation exists, the future demand for a particular product, part, or material may be forecast on the basis of the estimated change in the factor to which it bears the relationship.

Controllable and Uncontrollable Factors

In planning its marketing policies, a firm has control over the various marketing functions. Thus it can, if it wishes, increase its warehousing facilities, reduce its price, and so on. These functions are sometimes called the *controllable factors* in marketing. However, a firm must also cope, as best it can, with many factors beyond its control. These include: (a) changes in the market—for example, changing tastes; (b) actions of competitors—for example, the introduction of new products; (c) economic changes—for example, a cyclically-induced economic recession; (d) social restrictions—for example, anti-pollution packaging requirements; and (e) political restrictions—for example, an embargo on trade with certain countries. These are called the *uncontrollable factors* in marketing, and the marketing mix must be adjusted accordingly.

Marketing Plan

The plan of action that a firm adopts after careful consideration of the 4 Ps of marketing and the various uncontrollable factors is known as its *marketing plan*. The better the marketing mix, the more likely it is that the firm's marketing plan will achieve its goals—for example, successful introduction of a new product line or successful penetration of a new market.

Market. The first step in drawing up a marketing plan is to analyse carefully the market at which the firm is aiming its product. Usually the market can be divided into a number of segments some of which will suggest themselves, after detailed study, as *target markets* for the product; others as secondary markets; and yet others as markets not worth serious promotional efforts. Once these markets have been clearly defined, using national, regional, and local data obtained from government publications, industry associations, and local chambers of commerce, etc., an attempt can be made to develop a *consumer profile*—that is, a precise, detailed description of the persons who make the buying decision. This is discussed in the next Unit of this book. Also, attention must be paid to the uncontrollable factors mentioned previously: for example, economic and demographic trends; changing technology; cultural and social changes; changes in federal, provincial, and municipal statutes; and changes in distribution channels.

Product. The second major step is to analyse the firm's product to see how it suits customer needs, to determine any modifications that might be worthwhile, and to assess its attractiveness or "competitive edge," if any, over competing products.

A *product*, from the marketing point of view, consists of a certain combination of tangible and intangible characteristics. The tangible characteristics include the quality, design, package, colour, and after-sales service of the product. The intangible characteristics include the purchaser's confidence in the brand, the advertising appeals that are used, and the way in which the product is sold. Each combination of tangible and intangible characteristics creates a product in its own right, and has its own particular ability to satisfy a consumer's wants. Consequently, many products, although similar in many ways, need to be considered individually. For example, canned orange juice sold under one brand name is a different product from that sold under another; coffee sold in bags is a different product from coffee sold in vacuum-packed tins or "brick" packages.

The *product image* is the idea or concept that a consumer holds about a particular product and is affected as much by the intangible characteristics as by the tangible ones.

A *product line* is a group of products, such as metal cookware, plastic toys, or office stationery, which has similar uses and similar physical characteristics. The depth of a product line means the number of types, sizes, qualities, prices, and colours offered of each item.

The *product life* is the number of months or years that a product continues to sell profitably before it is drastically changed or abandoned. Some firms continue to sell well the products they first sold many years ago. Most business firms, however, rarely have the good fortune to manufacture and market products that will continue to sell indefinitely. Many products, in fact, have a very short life. This is sometimes because of incorrect assessment of demand; sometimes because of sudden changes in demand as with fads and fashions; and sometimes because of the actions of competitors in introducing something better in quality or cheaper in price. The concept of the product "life-cycle" is examined a little later in this Unit.

Competition. The third step is to evaluate the competition. What competitive products are there in the marketplace? What market share do they account for? How difficult will it be to dislodge them? What can be done to make the firm's product superior to competing products? How do prices compare? Is the firm's distribution of its products better than that of its competitors? How do competitors advertise and promote their products? How do they use their sales force?

Goals. The fourth step is to consider the firm's marketing goals—for example, a 50 per cent increase over last year in sales of the product; an increase in market share from 20 per cent last year to 40 per cent this year; and an increase in geographical availability of the product, in terms of actual cities and provinces.

Strategies. The final step is to formulate the firm's marketing strategies (product, pricing, channel, advertising, and sales), based on an analysis of all the previous factors.

Product Life-Cycle

Most new products pass through a definite series of earning stages: market introduction, market growth, market maturity, and market decline. Together these stages are called, in marketing terminology, the *product life-cycle*. (See Figure 9.5.) In some cases, the life-cycle can be quite short; in other cases, it can be very long.

Market Introduction. In this stage, the manufacturer must energetically promote the product to the consumers. Such promotion will seek to inform consumers about the existence, uses, and advantages of the product and persuade them to try it. At this stage, the manufacturer's product is unique either because of the nature of the product, such as a new drug, or because advertising has given this manufacturer's product a distinctive image in the consumers' minds. Often, at this stage, promotion costs together with production and other marketing costs exceed sales revenue.

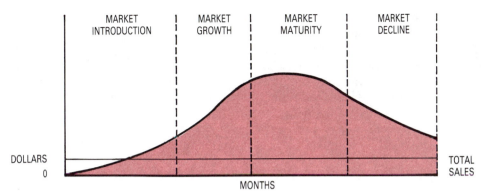

Figure 9.5 A Typical Product Life-Cycle

Market Growth. By this time the consumer has become familiar with the product, and sales increase rapidly. However, other firms will have introduced similar products and will be attempting to capture a share of the market. Advertising, in this stage, is directed more at promoting the advantages of the brand than introducing the product. This period of increasing sales will normally vary from a few months to a few years.

Market Maturity. In this stage, a large number of competitors are now offering similar products. The original innovator begins to get a smaller share of the market, but promotion costs continue to be high because of the level of competition. This stage can last for several years until a new type of product comes to replace the old, such as the replacement of black-and-white television by colour television, or standard typewriters by memory ones.

Market Decline. In this stage, sales by the original innovator are declining as competition from similar products is added to by competition from new types of products. Promotion expenditures are usually reduced in line with the reduction in sales revenue. Eventually, when sales volume has become too small to be profitable, the product will be discontinued. Thus fountain pens, for example, have now largely given way to ball-point pens and may eventually be discontinued.

Implementation

To achieve its sales targets, the firm must choose the most efficient channels of distribution for its products—as discussed in Unit 10.2 of this book. It must then make the brand name and merits of its products well-known to the prospective buyers by a careful advertising campaign (Unit 11.2). Also, it must have a numerically sufficient, well-trained and well-motivated sales force to make the sales (Unit 11.3).

Control and Analysis

The sales achieved by each sales representative must be continuously reported back to the head or regional sales office and compared with the sales targets (or "sales quotas") previously agreed as realistic. Any variances must be quickly reported and the reasons for them examined. Remedial action should then be taken to bring actual sales closer to the forecast. With the availability of modern computer systems, many different types of sales analyses can be undertaken, providing marketing managers with a comprehensive, up-to-date understanding of what is happening in the field. For small and medium-size firms, information of this type can be prepared, on a fee basis, by outside agencies such as Dun & Bradstreet.

KEY TERMS

Marketing department	Product line
Marketing manager	Product life
Product or brand manager	Competition
Planning	Marketing goals
Sales forecast	Product life-cycle
Trend analysis	Market introduction stage
Correlation analysis	Market growth stage
Controllable factors	Market maturity stage
Uncontrollable factors	Market decline stage
Marketing plan	Implementation
Product image	Control and analysis

REVIEW QUESTIONS

1. What factors will affect the organization of a firm's marketing department?
2. How will the marketing department of a large firm differ from that of a small firm?
3. Explain the nature and purpose of the product division arrangement. Give examples of firms that organize their activities in this way.
4. What is a product or brand manager? What types of firms usually have such positions? Why do they use them?
5. Firms which have customers over a wide geographical area usually organize their marketing activities on both a centralized and decentralized basis simultaneously. Explain what is meant by this and the reasons for such an arrangement.
6. How does a firm make provision in the organization of its marketing activities for different types of customers? Give examples as part of your answer.

7. How does a firm go about planning its marketing activities? What types of marketing plans are normally made?
8. What are the various methods of sales forecasting? How reliable are sales forecasts?
9. Distinguish between the controllable and uncontrollable factors in marketing. How can a firm best cope with the uncontrollable factors?
10. What is a firm's "marketing plan"? Is it the same thing as the marketing mix?
11. List and explain some uncontrollable factors that have recently affected the marketing of a particular product.
12. A product image depends on both tangible and intangible factors. Explain, with examples.
13. Give an example of "depth of product line."
14. What is meant by "product life-cycle"?
15. Illustrate, with an example, the different stages involved in the product life-cycle.
16. How does a firm normally attempt to achieve its sales targets? Give a practical example.
17. How does the head of a firm's marketing department know how well or badly his or her sales staff are performing?

CASE PROBLEMS

McCOWAN BAKERIES
Developing a marketing plan

In 1857, John McCowan, a newly arrived immigrant from Glasgow, Scotland, started a small bread bakery in Montreal. The bread that he baked was sold by his wife in the shop at the front of the bakery. As time passed, John McCowan felt that he could increase sales greatly by offering the bread to his customers at their houses. Consequently, he bought a horse and buggy and sent his eldest son out to sell the bread door-to-door.

At this time, John McCowan understandably enough considered his business to be the baking of bread and viewed the success or failure of the bakery in terms of the amount of bread that his wife and eldest son could sell. He spent considerable time, therefore, discussing with them various ways in which to promote sales.

By the 1930s, the McCowan Bakery, still owned by the McCowan family, was selling about one-fifth of the bread consumed in the city. This was distributed by a network of small corner grocery stores and by the use of 25 horse-drawn door-to-door delivery wagons.

By the end of the Second World War, the prosperity of the firm had begun to decline, and this trend continued for a number of years. The decline was caused by the firm's inability to cope with two factors: the revolution in the public's shopping habits and the competition of the very large bread manufacturers.

The shopping revolution consisted of the growth of large suburban grocery supermarkets at the expense of the traditional downtown and suburban corner stores. This growth, made possible by mass car transportation and the shift of the population away from the heart of the city, meant that more and more bread was being bought in the supermarkets and less and less from the corner stores and from the delivery trucks. In terms of price, the McCowan firm was powerless to compete with the supermarkets. Because of large sales volume, the chain supermarkets were able to buy their bread at a relatively low price from the large bread manufacturers who, in turn, because of economies of scale, could produce it more cheaply than the McCowan firm. Also, because of self-service and other features, the chain supermarkets were able to sell their bread with a smaller markup. The McCowan firm, on the other hand, was saddled not only with relatively high production costs but also with an expensive distribution structure. The corner stores were accustomed to receiving high markups and the door-to-door salespeople were only profitable if the bread could be sold at a price considerably higher than that charged by the supermarkets. As it was, with declining door-to-door sales, the bread salespeople were becoming more and more unprofitable every day. The sale of milk, incidentally, was being affected in a similar way.

As if this situation were not bad enough for the McCowan firm, another shopping change, if not a revolution, occurred starting in the 1950s. First, many small grocery stores banded themselves together in voluntary chains such as the Red and White stores. Second, corporate chains of small outlets began to emerge. These types of chain offered their own private label bread which they bought, on a volume contract basis, from one of the large bread manufacturers. This new retailing development reduced even further the McCowan firm's share of bread sales in the city and its suburbs. Now that a purchase offer has been received from a large U.S. bakery firm, the McCowan directors are more than ready to sell out.

Assignment
1. What really is the McCowan firm's business?
2. Summarize the problem that faces the firm.
3. Can the blame be placed solely on factors external to the firm?
4. What might the owners do, instead of selling out?

XYZ CONSUMER PRODUCTS LTD.
Justifying a new product

Assume that you are part of the marketing team of XYZ Consumer Products Ltd. You wish to recommend the addition of a new product to a line of consumer products that the firm already manufactures and markets. The firm's new product procedure requires the marketing team to explain and justify each recommendation to the firm's Vice-President of Marketing.

Assignment
Choose a product. Then prepare a new product proposal covering the following points:
1. Product chosen (e.g., chocolate bar).

2. Product characteristics:
   a) Function (to satisfy appetite)
   b) Physical characteristics (e.g., ingredients, appearance)
   c) Size and/or weight (e.g., 1 gm)
   d) Packaging (e.g., attractive golden paper wrapper)
   e) Proposed name (e.g., Chocolate Delight).
3. Relationship to existing line of products.
4. Competitive products.
5. Size of market (e.g., next 3 years).
6. Market potential for proposed product.
7. Proposed price.
8. Proposed distribution.
9. Projected income statement (e.g., for next 3 years).
   Add any other information you consider relevant to your proposal.

LONG-LIFE ORANGE JUICE
Preparing a marketing plan

Palm Products Inc., a Florida fruit farm, has purchased the right to use a Swedish method of pasteurizing orange juice under aseptic conditions and transferring it to pre-sterilized, air-tight, brick-shaped, one-litre packages. The juice, treated in this way, stays fresh for more than a month without refrigeration. However, once the package is opened, the juice must be kept refrigerated. No metal or glass is used for the package.

Assignment
1. What are the advantages of such a product from the viewpoint of (a) the consumer, (b) the retailer?
2. Prepare a marketing plan for introducing the product in your province.

DUNN PRODUCTS INC.
Preparing a marketing program

The U.S. firm, Dunn Products Inc., of San Diego, California, has developed and holds a patent for a golf shaft made of carbon fibre—a space-age material, only half the weight of steel but considerably stronger. Because of the lighter golf shaft, weight is shifted to the club-head resulting in added club-head speed. The effect, according to the manufacturer, is that up to 20 m can be added to the ordinary golfer's drive. However, according to one expert: "It is only good for people who hit the ball with a wrist-rolling action which was the style in the days of hickory shafts." Also, since the new carbon-fibre shaft has a wide range of flex or whippiness, a player has to find a club with the degree of flex that suits him or her. The retail price of a golf club with a carbon-fibre shaft is about five times the price of a conventional driver. However, with increased sales and output, it is hoped to reduce the price to $100 or less.

Following favourable newspaper reports about the new golf club, Dunn Products, Inc. has been approached by a Vancouver firm that wishes to manufacture and market the clubs in Canada using shafts imported from California.

Assignment

1. How could Dunn Products make a reasonable estimate of the potential market for their shafts and clubs in Canada?
2. Why would Dunn Products consider licensing the manufacture of such clubs in Canada rather than straight export? What other alternative exists?
3. In the case of export, what kind of marketing program might Dunn Products use in Canada for the complete clubs?

READING

Love for Sale

How Harlequin cornered the market on romantic fiction

BY CLAIRE GERUS

Source: *The Financial Post Magazine.* ©Claire Gerus

"It is so refreshing in this world of today to find good clean books with stories that end nicely and leave you feeling good instead of depressed or wondering what the hidden meaning is. I just wanted to let you know there is another Harlequin lover out here."

— An Alberta reader

"For several years I scorned Harlequin paperbacks thinking them a waste of time. Through an ad I became intrigued with the plot line of Beyond the Foothills *by Essie Summers. Upon discovering the setting was New Zealand, a gorgeous locale about which I'd been curious for years, I was hooked! Thank you for a lot of 'great escapes.'"*

— A Maine reader

From British Columbia to the Maritimes, from California to New England, the mail pours in—at a rate of 1,000 letters a month. The object of this avid adoration is not a specific novel or even a particular author, but an entire line of books: Harlequins.

The unprecedented loyalty of readers to a series of paperback romances continues to dazzle Harlequin observers and delight directors at the firm's Toronto headquarters. Today, Harlequin Enterprises Ltd., acknowledged as the world's leading romantic fiction company, boasts a following of 11 million regular North American readers. (Harlequin "addicts" can also pick up the latest titles in France, Israel, Holland, Germany, and England, where the company has operations.) Last year for instance, Harlequin fans around the world handed over $80 million for 109 million paperback romances. Indeed, sales of these slim, pastel-colored pocketbooks have been so successful that the company is now diversifying its interests into full-length feature films and consumer magazines.

What's the secret of Harlequin's success in wooing—and winning—millions of mainly female readers? In a word, escape. With winsome covers sporting forever-young heroines and their handsome beaux, Harlequin books invite readers to escape from the dreary drudgery of reality into a fantasy land of gentle passion and happy endings.

"Discover our world. It's a beautiful place to be," invites the 30-second TV ad which shows a happy, young woman enjoying life on the tennis court, at work and in the city.

Yet, truth be told, behind each of these "romances" lies a well-thought-out, if somewhat pat, plot. And despite minor variations in style, all books *do* stick to a standard format. The setting is usually exotic, transporting the heroine and the reader to a remote destination where the drama can be played out without any intrusion by the workaday world. The heroine is usually young, innocent, hard-working and level-headed. That is, until she meets HIM— the irresistibly attractive but emotionally cold hero. He may even be ruthless, but this is merely a facade because his heart has been wounded in the past. He secretly yearns for a woman worthy of the love he's saved for so long. When they meet, the future lovers usually clash. But after some resistance, they admit to a growing involvement, and ultimately decide to spend the rest of their lives together. The hero, fortunately, is usually wealthy, thus relieving his lady of the burden of fending for herself.

If the plot sounds hackneyed and the prose purple, Harlequin's directors are not perturbed. *They* are buoyed by the company's bottom line, which remains steadfastly black year in and year out. (A perennial moneymaker, in 1975 Harlequin was purchased for $30.3 million by Torstar, the Toronto-based publishing conglomerate, which also owns the *Toronto Star*; it is still the conglomerate's top moneymaker.)

In only seven years, Harlequin has managed to capture 25 percent of Canada's paperback market and over 10 percent of the U.S. market. In 1978, for the eighth consecutive year, Harlequin earnings achieved record levels: total company revenues jumped from $7.7 million in 1970 to nearly $100 million in 1978. Last year, shareholders of Harlequin stock learned that, over the first nine months of 1978 (ending September 30) profits had climbed from 51 cents per share in 1977 to 71 cents per share.

Harlequin Books weren't always the fat cats of the publishing industry. In 1949, Richard and Mary Bonnycastle decided to start a small Winnipeg-based publishing company. To get their new endeavor off the ground, the two young owners struggled to choose potential winners from a pot-pourri of manuscripts. The first 400 titles of this small company called Harlequin covered a variety of subjects and included such authors as Agatha Christie, Jean Plaidy, James Hadley Chase, and even Watergate conspirator Howard Hunt. But the haphazard selections came to an end when Mary Bonnycastle discovered the romantic fiction published by the British firm, Mills and Boon. She convinced her husband to concentrate on these stories "of good taste," and in 1958 the Bonnycastles obtained North American rights to reprint titles from the Mills and Boon backlist. Very quickly, these small romances became Harlequin's mainstay.

After his father's death in 1969, Richard Bonnycastle Jr. decided to increase the firm's business potential by selling stock in the company and moving it to Toronto. Recognizing the need for a skilled management team, he launched a two-year search for the right people. In 1971, his selection was complete, and from this point the Harlequin story begins to assume classic "success" proportions.

Richard Bonnycastle's new teammates were W. Lawrence Heisey, a Harvard Business School graduate with 13 years' marketing experience at Procter and Gamble; Richard Bellringer, a former executive with Coles Bookstores; and William Willson, a management consultant. Within a short time, the trio became co-owners as well. Today, Bonnycastle is chairman of the board, Heisey is president of Harlequin Enterprises Ltd., Willson is vice-president of finance and Bellringer heads up the Harlequin Books division.

One of the first things the new associates decided to do was to purchase the source of the company's income. Mills and Boon was acquired in 1971 for an undisclosed sum and, according to Willson, "the purchase was very friendly." The Boon brothers, Alan and John, were left to continue their successful publishing enterprise without interference from their new owners. One of the terms of the sale gave full editorial control of all Harlequin romances to the Boons and so far, the arrangement has worked out well. Readers enjoy the English flavor of the stories, and with most of Harlequin's writers living in England, it makes sense to keep the company's editorial offices there.

After acquiring a steady source of literary material, the firm's next step was to develop a marketing strategy that would boost Harlequin sales. The trio developed an approach that today impresses some and infuriates others, but indisputably, succeeds.

Applying their combined marketing skills, Heisey, Willson and Bellringer created a packaged product emphasizing a strong, standardized image to make Harlequins easily recognizable. They introduced colorful covers with wholesome couples looking raptly at, or coyly away from each other. In the background are the hills, seaside, African bush, castle, or cottage against which the stories are played out.

"You know when you pick up a Harlequin what you're going to get," says Heisey. "It's almost the same as an author's name. There are between 300 and 400 paperbacks released by all publishers each month in Canada. We've simplified the search for what the reader wants, for those who happen to like our genre."

Today, the romances have also branched out into two main, but not dissimilar, lines. There's the standard 95-cent romance, and the "steamier," more modern Harlequin Presents. The latter may contain more torrid love scenes, with even a scene of a breast being caressed by the hero's hand. This dash of lust will cost you an extra 30 cents, but, smiles England's Alan Boon, "there's nothing that will make Harold Robbins nervous."

Much of Harlequin's success rests on a willingness to try unconventional marketing techniques. "In the past," points out Dave Sanderson, the firm's marketing manager, "there were two *don'ts* of conventional publishing: number one, you can't advertise on TV and number two, you can't sell books in supermarkets."

Undaunted by industry custom, Harlequin executives launched a TV ad campaign in 1974 in 10 selected cities in the U.S. The results were phenomenal. Book sales shot up 79 percent in the areas carrying the commercials, which included Chicago, Dallas, Atlanta and Oklahoma City. In 1977, 398 TV stations ran three, 30-second commercials. Coupled with print ads in 18 women's magazines, an estimated 70 percent of North American women heard about Harlequins and went out to buy them.

At the same time, Harlequin executives decided to market their line in supermarkets. As a result, Harlequin was the first paperback publisher to be accepted in a Canadian supermarket; today the firm's books can be found in such chains as Loblaws, Dominion and Steinberg. Credit for the breakthrough goes to an aggressive sales staff, now numbering about 15.

Eyebrows also went up when Harlequin romances began to be given away as premiums. In 1977, McDonald's restaurants gave customers Harlequins for Mother's Day, and in the fall of 1978, Bio-Ad detergent and Ajax cleanser tucked a sample romance into their boxes. New readers have also been introduced to the books in bridal gift packages, and in Kotex boxes. Avon cosmetics in the U.S. purchased almost 1½ million copies of the novels to give away with their products in 1979.

Although secretive about their future marketing plans, Sanderson did reveal that the company is testing a new promotion technique: cents-off coupons with their books. Research has shown that eight out of 10 Canadian households cash in coupons, so Harlequin may soon offer 25 cents off the next Harlequin purchased. Testing the best method of distributing the coupons ended this month. "There isn't much we do without pretesting," reveals one marketing executive. "And because we test everything, wholesalers trust us when we introduce a new product. It cuts the risk for everyone."

Yet all Harlequin ventures have not been successful. Laser books are a case in point. Launched in 1975, Lasers were Harlequin's bid for the science fiction market. After publishing 53 titles, the series was discontinued one year after its birth. "Our research and testing at that time were far less sophisticated than they are today," Sanderson explains. But Heisey offers another reason for the failure: "I don't think we were consistently good enough editorially to command the loyalty of our readers."

Another Harlequin project that failed to win consumers' hearts was the company's first feature-length film, *Leopard in the Snow*, starring Keir Dullea and Susan Penhaligon, and based on author Anne Mather's romance of the same title. Testing in Manitoba, Saskatchewan, Alberta and the Maritimes last year brought mixed reaction; some critics complained that it's impossible to expect a romantic novel, which focuses on the heroine's thoughts, to translate effectively to the screen. *Leopard* cost $1 million to produce, and Heisey admits, "We're still at the learning stage. We're exploring the reasons for its mixed success and we won't roll out our second film until we learn about the first one." In early December though, the company announced that it would spend $10 million in 1979 on TV and movie romance features. All productions would be based on published Harlequin novels.

The steady sales of Harlequin books, however, goes a long way towards healing any of the company's financial wounds. Heartily encouraged by their books' success in Canada, Harlequin has turned its attention to the affluent neighbor to the south. Unlike many Canadian companies who feel intimidated by American know-how, Harlequin is intrigued by the challenge of conducting business with the Yanks.

Americans are more willing to try a new concept than their northern neighbors, Harlequin's market research reveals, and this willingness has given the company a hefty new source of income. Although exact figures are confidential, Harlequin officials confirm that the U.S. is now their largest market, and provides more than half the company's annual revenues. Romances are distributed in the U.S. by Simon and Schuster's Pocket Books division.

Harlequin consolidated its love affair with the U.S. market last spring when it acquired the Laufer Co. of Hollywood, California, publisher of nine magazines, including such money-makers as the preteen's *Tiger Beat*, *Rona Barrett's Hollywood*, a gossip publication, and a magazine for Blacks called *Right On!* The Laufers exchanged 53 percent of their company's stock for $6.2 million and Harlequin promised to let the firm operate under the former owner Charles Laufer.

Then, four months after the Laufer acquisition, Harlequin took an even deeper plunge into the American magazine market. They hired Carlo Vittorini, former president and publisher of Charter Publishing Co. (*Redbook, Ladies Home Journal, Sport*, etc.) to organize a new magazine division. His task: to acquire any attractive magazines with a broad consumer orientation, such as leisure, home, hobbies, outdoors, or family interests. Anthony Lloyd, director of corporate development, explains the expansion into magazines as "an attractive investment opportunity for Harlequin. We have a real interest in gaining a strong position in the New York publishing scene. We're not interested in fashion or glamor magazines, which have lower profit returns on sales."

In Canada, the company is also keeping a close eye on its newly launched "Historicals" series. ("They're romances in costume, with cavaliers and ladies in long dresses," explains Heisey.) The books, priced at $1.50 each, have been published at the rate of one per month since their introduction in January, 1978.

The firm recently launched yet another new line of books called "Mystiques," taken from the list of Tallendier, a French firm which publishes volumes in many languages. They are slightly different from Harlequin's usual fare (they're romantic mysteries) but hopes are high that readers will accept them. They should. To encourage sales, a budget of $1.3 million has been allocated for promotion.

Having said all this, one must say that this highly visible company with a product of questionable literary merit does have its detractors. Feminists—and even moderate ones—deplore the glamorizing of a weak-kneed heroine who pines for the attention of a callous (though soft-hearted) male chauvinist. One dynamic woman executive says Harlequins encourage "women to accept a second-class citizen attitude, and depend on the generosity of a man who is most probably her inferior as a person."

Canadian writers, too, are unhappy. Despite a steady flow of manuscripts to Harlequin's head office, only two Canadians and one American have burst through the ranks of English authors over the past eight years.

Professor Bernd Baldus, a University of Toronto sociologist who takes Harlequins so seriously that he has offered a course on them for the past few years, says that Harlequins depict and encourage social inequality on both a male-female and an economic basis. "These novels offer a very serious put-down of their female characters. It's a different kind of 'rape.'" Baldus points out that, when it comes to choosing between a career and a man, the career hasn't a chance. But the biggest harm, he finds, is in portraying society as exceedingly static in terms of social change. "If you're born in one position in society—unless you marry or get lucky—these books imply there's little that can be done. And on the basis of what I know, that's utter nonsense."

These concerns hold little sway over the growing number of avid women readers who snatch up Harlequins the way others pop tranquilizers. Why shouldn't they abandon themselves to an exotic tale of romance with a guaranteed happy ending? As one woman says: "I like to flip my brain off for awhile and forget about diapers and bills."

So life goes on at Harlequin, with its own continuing saga of hopes, plans and possibilities. But in the end people there know what they are, and what they can offer.

"We're not champagne," says one executive. "We're Coca-Cola. And we *like* being Coca-Cola."

Assignment
1. How would you characterize the product that Harlequin is marketing?
2. What is the secret of Harlequin's success? Is it luck or careful marketing?
3. How did the business start?
4. What form of business ownership did it assume?
5. How dynamic was the management of this firm? Document your answer with evidence.
6. What was Harlequin's "marketing strategy"? How successful was it?
7. "Much of Harlequin's success rests on a willingness to try unconventional marketing techniques." Explain and discuss.
8. Why have Harlequin movies fizzled at the box office? What other failures has it experienced? Why?
9. Discuss Harlequin's entry into the U.S. market.
10. "Harlequins depict and encourage social inequality on both a male-female and an economic basis." Should such an allegation be of concern to the marketer? Explain and comment.
11. Explain and discuss the statement by one Harlequin executive: "We're not champagne. We're Coca-Cola. And we *like* being Coca-Cola."

UNIT 9.3: TYPES OF MARKETS

There are many different types of markets for a firm's products according to the criteria used, such as buying motives, location, and income level. The most basic classification is into the domestic consumer market, the industrial user market, and the government market. Each of these markets can, in turn, be subdivided. Also, of course, markets can be divided into the home, or Canadian market, and the various foreign markets.

Domestic Consumer Market

This broad market consists of all the individuals in society who buy goods and services for their personal use or on behalf of others.

Consumer Profile. One of the first things that a firm must decide, if it is to be successful in its marketing efforts, is the type of consumer at which it is aiming its product. With its market research it must also try to find out as much about him or her as possible. The term *consumer profile* means a precise, detailed description of the persons who help make the decision to buy the product.

Market Segments. In fact, the buying public can be divided into various groups or segments according to sex, age, income, education, culture, and different combinations of these. Female teenagers are one example of such a group or market.

Target Market. The manufacturer of a product—for example, women's hats—may decide that the market for its product is just one of these groups (sometimes called the *target market*). The manufacturer will then make plans to gain acceptance of its product by that group. Often, a product—for example, historical novels—will have several target markets.

Market Grid. To ensure that no possible market is overlooked, it is common practice to draw up a *market grid* (Figure 9.6), on which all the actual and possible markets are shown.

Low Income	Middle Income	High Income	Age Group
			Teenagers
		Target Market	Young Adults
			Middle-aged Adults
			Old Adults

Figure 9.6 Market Grid for Sports Cars in Canada

Size of Market. Usually a manufacturer is interested in a particular type of consumer and in a particular area. To aid the manufacturer in determining the number of potential customers, census data for each municipality of Canada is available from Statistics Canada. The *Canada Year Book*, the monthly *Canadian Statistical Review* and the *Market Research Handbook*, all published by Statistics Canada, also contain a wealth of statistical information. In addition to this and other *secondary data*, a firm can commission special studies by market research agencies that will involve the collection of *primary data*—that is to say, data collected especially for the purpose of the study. There is also a great deal of useful information available from provincial and local governments and from trade associations and the local Chambers of Commerce.

Location of Customers. The location of prospective consumers can be determined for any area within Canada from the census statistics of population for the various cities, towns, and counties.

A common regional breakdown for marketing purposes divides Canada into the relatively sparsely populated Atlantic provinces of Newfoundland, Nova Scotia, New Brunswick, and Prince Edward Island (now about 2.3 millions); Quebec (6.5 millions); Ontario (8.8 millions); the prairie provinces of Manitoba, Saskatchewan, and Alberta (4.4 millions); and the Pacific province of British Columbia (2.8 millions).

One of the outstanding features of the distribution of the consumer population in Canada is its concentration in a narrow belt approximately 160 km in width and 6400 km long, just north of the Canada-U.S. border.

Particularly important is the interurban complex 80 km wide and 1200 km long, from Windsor, Ontario to Quebec City, that includes what is popularly known as the "Golden Horseshoe."

Age of Consumers. The Canadian population (see Figure 9.7) is quite a youthful one with just over half the population under 30 years of age.

Amount of Income. Estimates of the amount of income that people have to spend can be made using data published by Statistics Canada and Revenue Canada.

Buying Motives. Most human requirements fall into the following groups: food and drink; clothing; shelter; sex; medical care; religion; education; transportation; entertainment; and convenience.

The needs of different consumers are not of course identical, nor do the needs rank in the same order of importance for all individuals.

Age Group	Males	Females	Total	Per Cent of Total
90+	19,610	43,235	62,845	0.26
85-89	44,020	86,920	130,940	0.54
80-84	94,930	161,860	256,790	1.05
75-79	180,480	252,175	432,655	1.78
70-74	281,225	352,190	633,415	2.60
65-69	390,585	453,750	844,330	3.47
60-64	462,385	516,930	979,320	4.02
55-59	568,385	611,530	1,179,915	4.85
50-54	621,660	621,815	1,243,475	5.11
45-49	634,705	620,645	1,255,355	5.16
40-44	674,665	663,240	1,337,905	5.50
35-39	822,295	807,955	1,630,250	6.70
30-34	1,021,480	1,017,100	2,038,575	8.37
25-29	1,084,410	1,093,200	2,177,610	8.95
20-24	1,174,295	1,169,520	2,343,810	9.63
15-19	1,182,015	1,132,875	2,314,885	9.51
10-14	984,740	936,130	1,920,870	7.89
5-9	911,940	864,920	1,776,865	7.30
1-4	728,130	691,525	1,419,655	5.83
Under 1	186,320	177,400	363,720	1.49
	12,068,270	12,274,915	24,343,185	100.00

Figure 9.7 Population of Canada, by Five-Year Age Groups and Sex, 1981
Source: Statistics Canada. Reproduced by permission of the Ministry of Supply and Services Canada.

The actual amount and pattern of consumer spending depend on such factors as:
Sex. Males use after-shave lotion; females use face powder.
Age. Children buy candy; adults buy newspapers.
Income after tax. The high-income person buys such things as oil paintings.
Marital status. The married couple normally buy, furnish, and equip a house.

Culture. Canadians of Mediterranean origin regularly drink wine with their meals; Canadians of English origin are heavy tea drinkers.

Education. Better-educated people spend a larger proportion of their income on insurance, books, and travel.

Social prestige. Other people have something—for example, a new car—so must you.

Leisure time. The more leisure a person has, the more he or she spends on recreational products and services.

The availability of new products. No one could buy a snowmobile or digital watch until it was invented.

Climate. Regional variations in climate affect spending on clothing, shelter, and entertainment.

Fear. Possible illness or accident causes many people to buy life insurance.

Pain. Consumers buy a variety of medical products and services to help alleviate pain and cure illness.

Convenience. Consumers are willing to buy products such as electric carving knives and microwave ovens that enable them to do a job more easily.

Product Preference. Factors which are important in motivating a consumer to choose one make of product rather than another are:

Price. Given the same apparent quality of product, a person will usually buy the cheaper product.

Trust. From past experience the consumer may believe a particular firm's products to be reliable.

Persuasion. Advertising or personal selling may persuade a consumer that one product is better than other, even though there may be no physical difference.

After-sales Service. For some goods, service can be very important. It includes maintenance—of cars, for example—and the privilege of returning a good if dissatisfied—for example, the merchandise of some department stores.

Credit. A consumer may buy one product rather than another because of the retail credit offered.

Appearance. Packaging and colour exercise some influence on the consumer.

Consumer Usage Pattern. To assist a firm in its product planning, four basic questions may be asked: (1) why does the consumer use the product; (2) how does he (or she) use it; (3) where does he use it; and (4) when does he use it? The answers to these questions should give the marketer a good idea of the *consumer usage pattern* for the product.

Industrial User Market

Firms may produce goods for sale to both domestic consumers and industrial users—for example, heating equipment—or to industrial users alone—for example, sheet steel.

Firms engaged in agriculture, the mineral industry, forestry, fishing, manufacturing, transportation, communications, construction, power generation, and the provision of services offer a market for various types of goods and services. These goods and services include capital goods of different types, such as machinery and office equipment; raw materials and parts for use in the manufacturing process; and services such as fire insurance. Statistics as to the number and location of firms in these different industries are shown in the annual *Canada Year Book* compiled by Statistics Canada.

Figures on cost of materials used by individual manufacturing industries are available from Statistics Canada. Information on capital and repair expenditures by manufacturing industries is also available from this source.

An industrial user purchases machinery, equipment, parts, and raw materials for use in the production process. And it will buy these goods in the quantity required to meet its production targets.

What is "necessary" is not always clear-cut. To some extent, the manufacturing process determines material and parts requirements. However, the competition of new processes may render otherwise satisfactory processes obsolete. Newer, more efficient machines may have to be bought to match lower competitors' costs. A new head office may have to be built because the "stature" of the company requires it. A main-frame computer may be bought because it is thought to be a money-saver for the firm, even though this may not prove to be the case.

Generally speaking, industrial users are more rational and less emotional than domestic consumers in their buying decisions. When price, quality, and service are identical among suppliers, however, the salesperson becomes very important, and emotional factors can then be the deciding factor. The factors which the purchasing manager or other industrial buyer will consider are: quality; price; delivery time; service; credit terms; and any reciprocal buying arrangements.

Government Market

The federal, provincial, and municipal governments of Canada together form an important market for goods and services of all types. The construction of roads, schools, hospitals, power plants, waterworks, and sewage systems, and the operation and maintenance of these facilities illustrate the extent of this market.

Figures on federal, provincial, and municipal government spending are available to the public, and a summary of these is presented in the *Canada Year Book*.

It is customary for government agencies, when buying goods or services, to invite offers (or *tenders*) from several different firms. The contract is normally awarded to the bidder who offers the best combination of price and reputation for high-quality products or work. The contract is not necessarily awarded to the lowest bidder. Political patronage is sometimes involved.

Export Market

Canada exports a large volume of products abroad each year, notably motor vehicles and parts, other machinery and equipment, fabricated metals, crude petroleum and natural gas, lumber, woodpulp and newsprint, ores and concentrates, animals and other edible products, and wheat. The largest export market by far is the United States, accounting for well over 70 per cent of the total value of exports, followed way behind by Japan, the United Kingdom, the U.S.S.R., China, and other foreign countries. Successful exporting requires good quality products, competitive prices, careful packing and documentation, and prompt delivery. So long as they are competitive, Canadian firms can overcome the relative smallness of the domestic market by exporting many of their goods abroad.

KEY TERMS

Market segment
Consumer profile
Target market
Market grid
Size of market
Secondary data
Primary data
Location of customers
Age of consumers

Amount of income
Buying motives
Product preference
Consumer usage pattern
Industrial user market
Reciprocity
Government market
Tenders
Export market

REVIEW QUESTIONS

1. What is a "consumer profile"? Choose a product and suggest the consumer profile for it.
2. What are the various segments into which the domestic consumer market can be divided?
3. What is a "target market"? What could be the target market or markets for the following products: athletic shoes; small cars; bookkeeping services; tape decks; electronic games; artificial flowers; and romance novels?
4. Prepare a market grid as part of a marketing plan for a new stick deodorant.
5. What are the basic characteristics of the Canadian population seen from a marketing standpoint?
6. What are the various consumer buying motives? Which ones are involved in the purchase of the following products: hotel accommodation; high-heel shoes; milk shakes; electronic calculators; and jeans?
7. Explain, with examples, how the following factors can affect a person's buying decisions: marital status; culture; education; social prestige; and fear.
   What other factors may affect a person's buying decisions?
8. Why might a person choose one make of product rather than another? Give some personal examples in your answers.
9. How does a firm determine the "consumer usage pattern" for its products?
10. What is the industrial user market? What products does it purchase?

11. Why is buying for the industrial user market considered to be more rational than buying by domestic consumers such as you and me?
12. What factors would the industrial buyer or purchasing manager take into account before making his or her buying decision?
13. What types of buyers are lumped together under the heading "government market"? What products do they buy?
14. How does government buying differ in its motivation and procedure from industrial buying?
15. "When in Rome do as the Romans do." Apply this concept to the marketing of Canadian goods abroad.
16. Which countries are Canada's major foreign customers? What are the principal products sold to them?
17. Why do foreigners buy Canadian goods rather than their own? Why do Canadians buy foreign goods rather than Canadian ones? What factors influence their preference?

PROJECT

1. Using the data shown in Figure 9.7, draw a population pyramid.
2. Then superimpose another pyramid, using the most recent data that you can obtain.
3. Comment on the changes that you observe.

CASE PROBLEM

ECONOMY DIAPER SERVICE LTD.
Assessing the marketing effects of changes in the composition of the population

Economy Diaper Service Ltd. was founded by two sisters, Edna and Jean Macleod. Edna looked after all the cleaning in the laundry plant which they had rented and Jean, in addition to her own customers, was in charge of the eighteen other drivers, each with his or her own separate route.

From the very start, the firm has been quite successful, offering economy-minded young mothers a relatively cheap but excellent diaper service. To ensure that the driver/roundspersons give good service to the customers, the drivers, both men and women, who have been carefully handpicked by the two sisters, are all clean, neat, well-spoken, and reliable, and are paid a reasonably high weekly wage. Business is obtained by advertising in the local weekly newspapers and in the Yellow Pages of the telephone directory.

Upon an initial deposit, a mother is given two large plastic containers and a stock of six dozen prefolded diapers. Then, in exchange for a weekly fee, a driver/roundsperson calls twice a week to pick up the dirty diapers and return, completely sterilized and laundered, the same ones that were picked up on the previous visit.

Until just recently, the firm has steadily increased the number of its customers each month. Lately, however, business has started to drop. Customers who have stopped using the firm's diaper service have given the following reasons: too expensive, especially when compared with disposable diapers featured in sales or available in bulk packages; husband kept sticking the pin in himself or the baby; poor customer relations—had to wait ages on the telephone when trying to change the weekly supply; didn't like the thought of having some other child's diapers.

Recently, also, Jean Macleod saw a newspaper report entitled "Empty Cradles to Stall Marketing Bonanza?" This report made her question in her mind whether the firm would continue to expand as quickly in the future as it had in the past.

According to this report, two apparently contradictory things were happening in Canada: the rate of marriages was rising, but the rate of births was falling. With regard to births, there was no doubt that the rate was falling. These facts were confirmed by a friend who worked at one of the city hospitals and had frequently commented on the large number of vacant maternity beds. The big question was *why* the birth rate was falling. One explanation given by many people was the availability of oral contraceptives, popularly referred to as the Pill. However, the oral contraceptive, although highly effective, was not easily obtained in Canada until three years after the birth rate had started to fall.

Before discussing the matter with her sister and trying to assess the effect of these trends on their business, Jean obtained the statistical information shown in Figure 9.8.

Year	Total Number of Births (000s)	Birth Rate
Av. 1941-45	277	23.5
Av. 1946-50	356	27.4
Av. 1951-55	416	28.0
Av. 1956-60	470	27.6
Av. 1961-65	457	24.1
Av. 1966-70	373	18.0
1971	362	16.9
1972	347	16.0
1973	343	15.6
1974	346	15.5
1975	358	15.9
1976	359	15.7
1977	362	15.6
1978	359	15.3
1979	365	15.5
1980	371	15.5
1981	371	15.3
1982	373	15.2
1983	374	15.1

Figure 9.8 Births in Canada 1941-1983
Source: Statistics Canada

Assignment
1. What has been happening to births in Canada? Why?
2. What effect can the changing population trends have on Economy Diaper Service Ltd.?
3. What other factors may affect the future profitability of this firm?
4. What should the firm do?

CHAPTER 10
DISTRIBUTION

CHAPTER OBJECTIVES

☐ To indicate the different types of products that enter the distribution channels.

☐ To outline the channels that are used to distribute these products to the general public, industrial firms, government agencies, and foreign markets.

☐ To examine the various types of wholesalers and their functions.

☐ To review the different kinds of retailers and the tasks they perform.

CHAPTER OUTLINE

10.1 Types of Goods and Services
10.2 Distribution Channels
10.3 Wholesaling
10.4 Retailing

UNIT 10.1: TYPES OF GOODS AND SERVICES

The goods and services that are distributed in the marketplace are commonly divided into two main groups: consumer goods and industrial goods.

Consumer Goods

These are goods and services intended for use by the general public (or *domestic consumers*) without further commercial processing. They include such items as food, clothing, and furniture. *Durable consumer goods* are goods such as cars and household appliances which have a relatively long life. *Non-durable consumer goods* are goods such as food, gasoline, and certain items of clothing that are

Courtesy *The Financial Post*

used up within a short period of time. Consumer goods are bought by members of the public, normally at retail stores, for personal or family use.

Firms concerned with the marketing of consumer goods find it convenient to classify such goods according to consumer buying habits. Such a classification is into convenience goods, shopping goods, specialty goods, and unsought goods.

Convenience Goods. These are goods for which a consumer's greatest concern is his or her ease (or *convenience*) in obtaining them as soon as they are required. The price and quality of these goods, although by no means unimportant, tend to be secondary factors.

Convenience goods may be subdivided into staple goods, impulse goods, and emergency goods.

Staple goods are items such as bread, milk, cigarettes, soft drinks, and newspapers, which consumers purchase frequently and in small quantities. In marketing such products, a manufacturer or wholesaler will attempt to place them in as many retail outlets as possible, including self-service vending machines. Distribution is also made on a daily door-to-door basis, as with newspapers and milk.

Impulse goods are items, usually small in value, which a consumer purchases on impulse—for example, through seeing or hearing an ice cream vendor—rather than as the result of a previously planned decision—for example, to have a roast on Sunday.

To increase the amount of impulse buying, retailers will display as many of these products as possible in eye-catching positions.

Emergency goods are items which a consumer is forced by emergency, such as a car breakdown or a splitting headache, to purchase. The price of the good or service (in this case, towing and aspirin) is secondary to its availability.

Shopping Goods. These are consumer goods, such as cars, furniture, household appliances, and expensive jewelry, which a person will normally buy only after he or she has compared the price and quality of various makes. The reasons for this "shopping around" are the relatively large sum of money involved in the purchase and the fact that the product will normally be used by the consumer for a number of years. Possible saving on price and greater satisfaction with the quality are considered by the consumer to be worth the time and effort involved in shopping.

Because these goods are not bought frequently by consumers, the number of retail outlets handling them, compared to those selling convenience goods, is quite small. Often these outlets are located near each other in well-established shopping districts. To attract customers, they advertise constantly through the local newspapers, radio, and other media.

Specialty Goods. These are products which possess a unique attraction for the consumer. Thus a person will be willing to wait, travel some distance, search, or pay more in order to obtain such a good. Examples of specialty goods are handmade shoes, specially designed clothes, original paintings, and antique furniture. The development of brand loyalty may make almost any product a specialty good for a particular customer.

Unsought Goods. These are goods which a consumer is unaware of or which he or she does not particularly wish to buy. Examples of the former were products such as electric razors and dishwashing machines in their early days. Examples of goods which the consumer is aware of but does not seek, because he or she does not usually wish to buy, are encyclopaedias and magazine subscriptions. Manufacturers wishing to sell such goods must make a particularly vigorous sales promotion effort.

Consumer Services. A growing portion of the household budget is now spent on consumer services such as health and beauty care; insurance, finance, and legal; sports and other recreation; education and entertainment. All these services are made available to the consumer, either as individuals or as a group, on a direct personal basis. In most cases, the persons providing the services must, for convenience, be located close to the consumer. In certain cases, similar to the shopping or specialty goods mentioned previously, the consumer will be willing to travel some distance if he or she considers the service or person providing it to be unique—for example, a major sports event. In terms of distribution channels, the person or firm providing the service also usually retails it. However, there is considerable variety—for example, in the case of package holidays, these are put together by travel wholesalers who then make use of the services of travel agents to retail them. The hotels, airlines, and car rental companies, as well as making use of booking agents, also handle bookings themselves—the producer-direct-to-consumer channel.

Industrial Goods

These are goods and services, such as iron ore and engineering services, used in the production of other goods or services, such as steel. They may be classified into the following groups: land and buildings; machinery and equipment; raw materials; component parts and materials; supplies; and services.

Land and Buildings. Before production can begin, a firm must lease or purchase land and buildings. Industrial plants, warehouses, office buildings, and retail stores are all examples of this type of industrial good.

Machinery and Equipment. These industrial goods include major equipment such as boilers, presses, furnaces, diesel engines, and computers, and smaller items such as power tools and typewriters.

Raw Materials. These are materials such as cotton, grain, ores, wood, and petroleum, which have undergone a relatively small amount of commercial processing.

Component Parts. These are goods such as tires, carburetors, and spark plugs, which are incorporated into a finished product, such as a truck or car. The same goods may also be considered consumer goods—for example, spark plugs sold to a consumer to replace worn plugs in his or her car.

Fabricated Materials. These are fabricated or processed materials (or semi-manufactured goods) such as industrial chemicals, pig iron, paper, and cement, which are sold for further processing—for example, paper to be made into newspapers and books.

Supplies. These are goods which, although not embodied in the final product, are necessary if production is to be carried on. They include maintenance items such as paint, fluorescent tubes, and cleaning compounds; repair items such as spare parts, screws, and nails; operating supplies such as fuel, lubricating oil, and soap.

Services. A firm may require the services of an accountant, lawyer, or management consultant to give advice. It may also hire outside contractors to undertake general cleaning, window cleaning, security enforcement, painting, or landscaping.

KEY TERMS

Consumer goods

Durable consumer goods

Non-durable consumer goods

Staple goods

Impulse goods

Emergency goods

Shopping goods

Specialty goods

Unsought goods

Consumer services

Industrial goods

Fabricated materials

REVIEW QUESTIONS

1. Distinguish between consumer goods and industrial goods.
2. Explain, from the marketing point of view, the purpose of the distinction between durable and non-durable consumer goods.
3. Give examples of the three basic types of convenience goods, and indicate where they are usually displayed in retail stores.
4. Explain, with examples, the types of consumer goods that fall into the category of "shopping goods." How are such goods marketed?
5. Distinguish between shopping goods and specialty goods. Give examples of each to illustrate the difference.
6. What are "unsought goods"? Give examples of your own. What special problems do they create for the marketer?

7. What are the various types of industrial goods? In what ways does the marketing approach differ for such goods compared with consumer goods?

READING

The Business That Beer Built

How Howard Glossop and Kevin Eccleston made a fortune by putting up their "Dukes"

BY JEREMY FERGUSON

(Jeremy Ferguson is a Toronto freelance writer.)
Source: *The Financial Post Magazine*. By Jeremy Ferguson.

When Howard Glossop issues forth the word "pub," it lingers in the air, exudes a bouquet of enormous warmth and floats to earth with the easy grace of a hot-air balloon. It is, to him, the most precious of words.

"Pub," Howard Glossop says, "is a difficult word, perceived in such different ways. Here it is seen as a big room full of people swilling beer. But that's not a pub; a pub is where the drink is second to things social, where people feel a sense of community, where you walk in and are recognised—and that's worth a million dollars."

To Glossop, Kevin Eccleston and their partners at Triomphe Inc., it is actually worth many millions. For they are the men behind the Dukes, a network of British-style pubs which since 1972, has taken Toronto by storm and is currently punctuating the Ontario map en route to the rest of the country. Unless you live in an igloo, odds are you'll be hearing about the Dukes.

By the end of this year, there'll be 13 pubs with adjoining eateries grossing some $12 million annually in Ontario. By September of 1981, they hope to complete the Ontario base with 24 pubs grossing $20 million, located in such centres as Ottawa, Kingston, London and Windsor. Triomphe Inc. owns the five Toronto locations outright; the rest will be joint ventures under the Triomphe-Cromarty banner.

Beyond Ontario, things will operate still differently and if you are at all intrigued by the pub business, perk up your ears.

"Originally, we planned to own and operate everything ourselves," says Glossop. "Now we're more pragmatic. We don't want to smother the baby." So Dukes in other parts of Canada will be licensed. Triomphe will produce the pub, everything from finished interiors to staff training programs, then hand over the keys. The licensee will foot the construction bill—anywhere from $300,000 to $400,000—pay Triomphe an upfront fee of $50,000 and a royalty of five percent of sales for the first five years and $2^{1}/_{2}$ percent thereafter.

"It's a whole lot different than a franchise," stresses Glossop. "That process has become horrendously cumbersome—too much legality, too much paperwork, too many strings. We'd rather get on with the job of opening more Dukes."

Locations are being scouted from Newfoundland to British Columbia and Glossop, whose corporate specialty is new projects, is eyeing the U.S. It's Triomphe's notion that a pub can survive anywhere there's a sense of community. "And in the U.S. this is reinforced by the energy crises," he says. "The days of driving 40 or 50 miles for a good time are gone. Now people will drive four or five miles."

"It's whimsy at this point," he says, "but on a 10-to-one U.S.-Canada ratio, I can see 480 Dukes south of the border within a decade. The pattern would be a big 'U' running through Colorado, Texas, Florida, New England, Washington." Triomphe has already been approached by interested parties in the U.S., as well as faced inquiries from Australia, South Africa, Japan and blimey, Britain itself.

This burgeoning empire is helmed by six men—principals Glossop and Eccleston, chairman and vice-chairman, respectively, president Philip Hughes and vice-presidents Gerard Gontier, Martin Lilley and Murray Ross. All but Hughes are partners and shareholders. (Pedro Cabezuelo, an original shareholder and vice-president, was with the firm from 1975 to 1978 when his responsibilities increased from designing the menus to promotion and public relations. He left amiably in '78 to become a prime mover behind The Monks restaurant).

Their combined talents run the gamut from interior design through food and beverage to corporate finance. Glossop and Eccleston had been designers before getting into the pub business. Gontier, a seasoned restaurateur and former partner in Toronto's La Bastille, has the restaurant know-how. Lilley is resident expert in corporate management. Ross specializes in funding. And last September, Hughes, formerly a manager with the Bank of Montreal, signed on as president; Triomphe required an administrator with a heavy financial bias, somebody to be responsible for the day-to-day profits and free Glossop and Eccleston to blueprint the global assault.

One problem albeit minor, is inevitable. They are sure to run out of Dukes—the names, that is. Toronto's Dukes are York, Gloucester, Kent, Richmond and Westminster. Glossop has 38 on file, hardly enough to go around, and one of those—the Duke of Buccleuch and Queensbury—is a bit much for a marquee. Yes, he sighs, there will be some duplication.

But there's so much more to the Dukes' incredible momentum than noble nomenclature. What do they hold for Canadians, hitherto unaccustomed to the pub as a social force in their lives?

"Our success is really quite simple," explains Glossop. "Product, people and environment—in that order." The formula is nothing new, but a successful weave seems to have eluded most comers in the past.

Let's begin with product. The Dukes list about three dozen bottled beers, mostly imported, everything from Löwenbrau to Japan's Kirin. But it is the imported draught beers that render the pubs unique. There are six on tap, from Bass Blue Triangle brewed in Burton-on-Trent to Beamish XXX stout from Cork, Ireland. They, plus two domestic draughts—Carlsberg and Labatt's Extra Stock—sell to the tune of 3,000 pints per week per Duke. A lot of suds.

The beers are lovingly chosen by Glossop's principal partner, Kevin Eccleston, a robust Brit acknowledged as a foremost authority on the stuff. He can ramble on forever about how the West Germans are the world champions of beer consumption, about how porter got its name, tell you who's who on the board at Bass and on and on.

Eccleston is particularly aglow when the subject turns to draught. "In Britain, draught is the drink and the breweries concentrate on it. Here it's been a poor relation, associated with ladies-and-escorts and spit-and-sawdust. I'm not trying to sound pompous, but what we've done is make draught respectable. It's a wonderful drink, dating back to ancient Mesopotamia if that means anything."

He is particularly proud of two of the Duke products. One is Stone's Best Bitter. "It's your classic northern English bitter and it's made a huge reputation without spending a cent on advertising," he beams. "It proves that ad hype and marketing strategies aren't everything. If you're volatile enough, you can do it by word-of-mouth."

The other is Beamish XXX stout, black as tar and so thick you suspect a spike might stand aloft in it. "An Irish black beer that keeps the damp out," waxes Eccleston, "very nutritional, too, a meal in itself." Glossop echoes the description with "a very kind sort of drink, well rounded and not as bitter as Guinness, with a creamy head and mysteriously healthy quality."

"We got on to it when things fell through with Guinness—they were switching exports to bottles and cutting back on draught accounts," recalls Eccleston. "Beamish dates back to 1972 and is currently owned by Carling-O'Keefe of Canada. It's the second largest producer of stout in Ireland, but given the predominance of Guinness, has just a tiny share of the market. We sell five kegs per week per Duke—and that's pretty good. Some customers won't drink anything but."

Beer sales are staggering but fate, in the body of the Liquor Licence Board of Ontario, does not smile on unfettered success. Ever vigilant to protect its children from the demon drink, it insists on a dollar in food sales for every buck spent on booze. That may be fine and dandy when you're charging $25 for Chateaubriand, but in a pub situation, it calls for a hell of a lot of steak and kid.

So the pub-makers in Triomphe were thrust into the restaurant business. When the Duke of York first opened in 1976 at a cost of $250,000, a classy continental restaurant, Glossops, was unveiled in the same building. It was a huge success, although it attracted a wholly different clientele than the pub. Toronto reviewers gave the place the nod for such ambitious fare as roast duckling with blueberries and cassis, steak stuffed with paté and rolled in almonds, baby pheasant in chanterelle sauce and lobster in port, brandy, cream and truffles—the gourmet trip with a tab of $60 and up for two.

Glossops remains a one-shot flagship affair. As new Dukes opened, there would be adjoining eateries, each with its own identity but more humbly priced.

The Duke of Gloucester which took $200,000 to start up, came later in 1976. Adjoining was Tramps, a relatively inexpensive—two can dine on very good paté and rack of lamb with a decent plonk for under $25—spot on Yonge St. When the Duke of Richmond was installed in the massive Eaton Centre, it was affixed to The Big Apple, again a cheerful, elegant room offering good food at affordable prices.

Both restaurants are major contenders in the budget gourmet sweeps, but there are problems. The pubs, contrary to expectations, do not automatically promote the restaurants. Neither Yonge St. nor the Eaton Centre superdevelopment are regarded as good restaurant neighborhoods. Evening business can be slow indeed.

In a different class is Simpson's-in-the Strand, the companion restaurant to the Duke of Westminster in the First Canadian Place complex. It came along when Glossop and company had already decided to drop the pub-cum-restaurant format and integrate the two: the shape of Dukes to come.

While Triomphe was building its pub, Olympia & York Developments, the movers behind First Canadian Place, were looking for a big-name, high-profile restaurant. Glossop was en route to London anyhow and he wound up negotiating with the Savoy Hotel Group for rights to the Simpson's name. It was the first time the 150-year-old British dining institution has allowed its banner to hang elsewhere.

Triomphe paid a flat fee plus a continuing royalty of 15 percent on a net-profit basis. In all it's cost them more than $1 million to bring Simpson's to Canada.

What had sold the Savoy group on Triomphe of Toronto was a word and the word was "enthusiasm." It shows in the final product. Triomphe has done somersaults for authenticity. The panelled walls, leather chairs and glittering chandeliers were manufactured in England. Waiters are properly formal. The culinary emphasis is on succulent joints of beef and lamb carved tableside. The cartoon on the menu shows a Simpson's waiter and his customers aghast at words from an impertinent stranger. The caption reads: "The gentleman who asked the carver whether the meat was English or foreign."

Meantime, the company had experimented with a revised format. The Duke of Kent had opened in 1977 with a grill room neatly integrated into the boisterous pub atmosphere. The fare is not exactly haute cuisine, but it's way above pub standards with items like paté, eggs Benedict, lam chops, pepper steak and inevitably, a good English trifle.

But enough of product. People is the ingredient which most fascinates Howard Glossop, an easygoing chap with a conspicuous affection for *homo sapiens*. "Each pub should have a character determined by its locals," he says. "You need a cross-section of age and income groups. A pub should cut through barriers and that's its role in Britain—transcending class structures. I remember one pub near a London railway station. Everybody from porters to top trade union leaders would get together there. It couldn't have happened anywhere else."

The quintessential Triomphe pub is the aforementioned Duke of Kent, located in a north Toronto neighbourhood where a high business traffic makes up the lunchtime trade and cliffdwellers from surrounding highrises pack the place night after night. The conversational din is almost symphonic and after 8 p.m., customers are practically standing on each other's heads.

"It's so community-oriented, we were considering a first anniversary party for the regulars," smiles Glossop. "But they beat us to it and suggested the same thing six months in advance. It fell on a Sunday afternoon, so it had to be a private party. I dropped by to see how things were going and the customers toasted us by cracking open champagne."

A similar sense of community had been evident from the outset at the Duke of York. "Problem was, we were getting lineups and that shouldn't happen at a British pub. It's anti-concept and anti-people. So when we opened the Duke of Gloucester, we hired a bus and offered customers free transportation to the new location. They refused to go—now that's community!"

Not so ideal is the Duke of Westminster, located in the bowels of Toronto's skyscraper district. Its locals are refugees from office towers. "Things bustle until 8 p.m., then drop off because the workers want to get the hell out of the area," says Glossop. "We're trying to counteract that by promoting heavily to the tourist trade and major hotels in the vicinity."

The third plank of the formula is environment: what got Triomphe into the pub business in the first place. Glossop and Eccleston had begun selling British pub interiors to other people, only they emerged as their own best customers.

It began in 1972. Eccleston & Glossop International Ltd. was a graphic design outfit based in Toronto whose clients included the CTV network and Massey-Ferguson and there was a London office doing some business on the other side.

But the two men, who had emigrated from England six years before, were shopping around for tangible, complementary product—real hardware—to sell along with their design expertise. At a "British Week" in Toronto that year, they were introduced to Ayala Sales Ltd., a manufacturer of British pub interiors trying to develop a market in North America.

The liaison was a natural. "Everything Ayala does is real," says Glossop. "It's all solid oak walls, mahogany panelling, plaster mouldings, velvet tufted seating, no veneers and no plastic. We'd be merchandising romance."

Excited, they became North American sales agents for Ayala, mounted an energetic sales campaign and purchased a small percentage of the stock. They also fell flat on their faces. "There was lots of interest, but no sales," says Glossop. "So we decided we needed a working model—you can't ask people to put up $100,000 or more on the basis of pretty pictures."

The working model was the Duke of York and within three days of the opening, it was a runaway success. So much of a success that three months later, Glossop, Eccleston and crew were up against the dazzling reality that they were in the wrong business and by the end of the year had grossed in excess of $1 million. Now they're out of design and wholly into pubs.

The procedure goes like this: the group surveys a given property, works out the practical aspects, designs an interior with a specific theme—Richmond is a British railway station, Westminster a long bar in the financial district—and sends the blueprint off to Ayala. The manufacturer comes back with its modifications, agreements are reached and the pub interior is hammered out. There are no prepackaged parts; everything is customized.

The pub is then shipped across the Atlantic in 20-foot and 40-foot crates. It takes about a month to reconstruct and an Ayala supervisor is on hand to oversee local construction crews.

All of which makes it sound a bit like paint-by-numbers. But that's only the beginning. To come are the more elusive ingredients of beer, friendly people and yes, heart. Where else, we ask you, do the paying customers toast the owners?

Assignment
1. What is a "pub"? Exactly what is a pub operator marketing?
2. Why have Glossop and Eccleston gone into licensing rather than setting up more of their own pubs?
3. What does it cost to obtain a pub licence from Triomphe? How, if at all, does a licence differ from a franchise?
4. How is Triomphe Inc. managed? Who does what?
5. Explain the success of the Triomphe operation. Discuss.
6. What is so special about the product that is sold?
7. How and why did Triomphe get into the restaurant business? How has the drink and food combination gradually changed?
8. Explain the social role of the pub.
9. How did Glossop and Eccleston get into the pub business?
10. How does a pub come into being? Explain the procedure once the licence has been granted.

UNIT 10.2: DISTRIBUTION CHANNELS

The *channel of distribution* (or *trade channel*) is the term used to describe the path that a product takes from the time it leaves the farm or factory until it reaches the consumer's hands. There are in fact many different channels that a firm may use to market its products and, in many cases, more than one will be used for the same product. This may be because of different types of consumers or different locations either within Canada or abroad. Sometimes the firm that manufactures the product will itself undertake the distribution.

Types of Marketing Intermediaries

The *middleman* in marketing is any person or firm, other than the producer, engaged in the distribution of goods to domestic consumers, industrial users, or government users. The two principal types of middlemen are wholesalers and retailers.

The *wholesaler* is a firm which obtains goods from the producer and sells them either to retailers (which in turn resell them to the public), or to industrial or government users (which use them for production or public service). Often a wholesaler will sell in large quantities, but this is not always the case.

The two main kinds of wholesalers are merchant wholesalers and agent middlemen.

Merchant wholesalers are wholesalers who buy goods from a producer to resell to retailers and to industrial or government users. They become owners of the goods and assume the risk of financial loss if they are unable to sell them.

Agent middlemen are wholesalers who act purely as agents for the producer, receiving a commission for their selling services. They do not purchase the goods themselves and therefore risk relatively little financial loss if they are unable to sell the goods. By not having to purchase the goods, they also require relatively little capital to operate. Because of the difference in risk and capital, commission rates for agent middlemen are usually much lower than the average markup on goods sold by merchant wholesalers.

The *retailer* is a middleman who buys goods from a producer or wholesaler and resells them to domestic consumers. *Retailing* is the act of selling goods to the ultimate consumer, irrespective of where the goods come from. Thus a farmer, in selling his goods at a roadside stall, is retailing his products.

Distribution To Domestic Consumers

The four most common channels of distribution from producer to domestic consumer are shown in Figure 10.1.

Direct Distribution. A producer may sell directly to domestic consumers by means of door-to-door salespeople for such products as milk, bread, brushes, vacuum cleaners, and encyclopaedias; by producer-owned retail stores—for example, shoe stores, gasoline service stations, and farmers' roadside stands; and by direct mail—for example, books and records.

There are two main reasons why a producer may use this direct channel of distribution. First the producer may wish to control the manner in which the goods are sold to the public, in order to develop or retain a good public image for the firm and its products—for example, the various gasoline service stations.

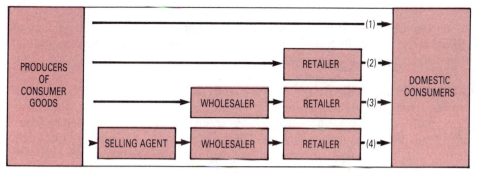

Figure 10.1 Channels of Distribution for Consumer Goods

Second, it may be more profitable. This would be the case where the value of sales is sufficiently large to provide a profit on the producer's own retailing operation.

Use of Retailers. A firm may decide not to retail its own products. It may not wish to venture from manufacturing or farming into retailing, it may not have the capital required, or it may have decided after investigation that retailing would be unprofitable. Instead, the products may be sold to a retailer, who will then resell them to the public.

Many of the goods sold by supermarkets (for example, eggs) and by department stores (for example, costume jewelry) are obtained directly from the producer and illustrate this method of distribution.

Use of Wholesalers. Quite often, producers find it unprofitable to sell to retailers. This occurs when the unit value of the goods is small, when the ultimate consumers are widely scattered, and when the retailer sells a relatively small amount of each particular good. In these circumstances, the order obtained from a small store may not be worth the visit of the manufacturer's salesperson.

Sometimes the producer sells directly only to the large retailers, such as the chain supermarkets, and uses wholesalers to supply the small retailers. The wholesaler will buy the goods from the producer, and the wholesaler's salesperson, in calling on the small retailer, will offer these goods as one of a large variety. The salesperson's visit is made worthwhile by the fact that he or she can take orders for a large number of products at the same time.

A manufacturer can obtain wide geographical distribution of its products by selling to many wholesalers, each in a different area.

Use of Agents. In some instances, as with fruit, grain, and lumber, a producer may find it financially advantageous to sell goods through an agent middleman. This middleman, who does not take title to the goods, receives a commission on the sale. He or she is used by the producer because of specialist knowledge of the market and ability to sell the producer's goods at the best price. The agent middleman sells the goods to wholesalers, who in turn sell the goods to retailers. A livestock auction company is one example of an agency which sells to wholesalers on behalf of the producer. Grain brokers are another example. Selling agents, manufacturers' agents, and commission houses (explained later) all perform this specialist marketing role.

Exclusive Distribution Agreement. Producers who wish to retain some control over the marketing of their products (including some of the marketing profit), without undertaking the wholesaling or retailing themselves, often make an *exclusive distribution agreement* with wholesalers or retailers. This agreement usually comprises both an exclusive dealing arrangement and an exclusive selling arrangement. Under the dealing arrangement, the wholesaler or retailer agrees not to handle competing products. Under the selling agreement (also called a *sales franchise*) the producer agrees not to allow any other wholesaler or retailer to handle the producer's product in a particular area.

Marketing Boards

Many farm products are now marketed in Canada by marketing boards. These are marketing agencies set up by producers for each of a number of major agricultural products. Unlike farmers' marketing co-operatives, which have existed in Canada for many years, marketing boards have compulsory rather than voluntary membership.

The first provincially-authorized marketing board was established in British Columbia over fifty years ago. However, because of the conflict between federal and provincial jurisdiction, marketing boards established under provincial law could only operate within the province concerned. This situation was remedied only in 1949 when the federal Parliament passed an Agricultural Products Marketing Act, which permitted the extension of the powers of provincial marketing boards into interprovincial and export trade. Thereafter, all the provinces gradually passed laws establishing marketing boards for a variety of agricultural products such as eggs, turkeys, milk, potatoes, hogs, various grains, and even honey. These boards differ widely in their authority—some having complete control over production and marketing and others having only full or partial control over marketing alone.

In 1972, in response to producer pressure, a National Farm Products Marketing Council was established to determine which agricultural sectors would benefit from a national marketing organization. So far, as a result, a Canadian Egg Marketing Agency and a Canadian Turkey Marketing Agency have been established. These are additional to the Canadian Wheat Board, established in the 1930s to control the production and marketing of wheat and other grains; and to the Canadian Dairy Commission, established in 1966 to allocate milk production among the provinces on a quota basis and to establish a national milk price support system. Unlike most marketing boards (whose directors are elected by the producers), the directors of the CWB and the CDC are appointed by the federal government.

The justification for such marketing boards is the need for a higher, more stable farm income for agricultural producers, particularly in view of the fact that farming today requires a large capital investment. From the consumers' point of view, marketing boards are usually seen as a means for artificially restricting farm output and forcing up prices.

Distribution To Industrial Users

The channels of distribution for industrial goods are usually much shorter than those for consumer goods. The most common channels are shown in Figure 10.2.

Direct Distribution. Many producers sell industrial goods directly to other producers to be used for production. Where installation and servicing are important, this is the most obvious and profitable way of marketing the goods.

Often a firm will set up its own sales branch staffed with industrial sales representatives to handle the marketing of its goods. Sometimes this branch will be located in or near the market rather than at the plant. The branch will obtain orders from industrial users and these will be relayed to the plant for production and delivery.

Use of Industrial Distributors. If a firm cannot profitably afford to maintain its own sales branch, it may sell goods to an industrial distributor (equivalent to the wholesaler of consumer goods), who will then in turn sell them to industrial users. Because the industrial distributor handles a number of goods, he or she can market the individual producer's goods more economically than the producer could personally. Tools and equipment of various sorts are marketed in this way. Industrial goods sold abroad or imported into Canada are similarly distributed.

Use of Selling Agents. Sometimes a firm will employ an agent on a commission basis to market its goods to industrial users.

Distribution To Government Users

Government users in Canada comprise the federal, provincial, and municipal governments, and the various agencies that have been set up by these governments.

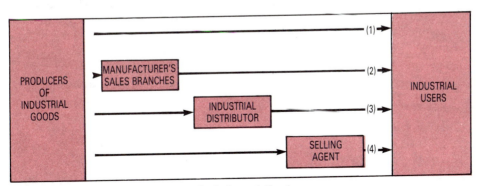

Figure 10.2 Channels of Distribution for Industrial Goods

Producers sell to the government consumers mainly on a direct basis, usually by public tender. Details of the government requirements—for example, aircraft parts—are made known, and offers (or *tenders*) by producers are invited. A purchase contract is usually awarded to the lowest bidder, provided that the reputation of the supplier as to the quality and punctual delivery of the products is sound.

Distribution to Export Markets

A Canadian business firm may export its goods by selling directly to foreign buyers located abroad or it may export them indirectly—by selling them to other firms located in Canada who will in turn ship them abroad. Once the goods have reached the foreign country, they may enter channels of distribution similar to the ones shown previously for consumer, industrial, or government goods.

Direct Export. In this case, the firm will usually need representatives located abroad. These may be:
1. *Company employees*—if the market is sufficiently large; often, one sales representative covers a number of different countries.
2. *Foreign agents*—this is a resident or "national" of the foreign country who agrees to act as agent for the Canadian firm, receiving a commission on goods sold, and sometimes also a basic minimum retainer fee.
3. *Export subsidiary*—if sales are large enough, the Canadian firm may have its own, separate subsidiary company (rather than an export department or section) to purchase its own goods for export.
4. *Export group*—a number of small firms may form an export group to handle foreign sales of their products.

Indirect Export. There are several different ways in which a Canadian firm can export indirectly.
1. *Export merchant*—such a firm will buy another firm's goods outright and assume the risk of being able to sell them abroad at a profit. The export merchant usually specializes in a particular group of products such as chemicals or a particular group of countries such as the South American ones. The export merchant, if large enough, may be known as a trading company or trading house.
2. *Export commission house*—this is a firm which acts as a purchasing agent for foreign companies, receiving as income a commission on the goods that it buys on behalf of its foreign principal or principals.
3. *Resident buyer*—the Canadian producer may be able to sell his or her goods to the representative in Canada of a large foreign firm.
4. *Export agent*—the Canadian producer may retain control over its goods but avoid some of the headaches of exporting by using the services of an export agent. The agent is paid a commission for his or her services.

KEY TERMS

Channels of distribution
Distribution to domestic consumers
Direct distribution
Use of retailers
Use of wholesalers
Use of agents
Exclusive distribution agreement
Sales franchise
Franchisee
Franchisor

Marketing boards
Distribution to industrial users
Direct distribution
Use of industrial distributors
Use of selling agents
Distribution to government users
Tenders
Distribution to export markets
Direct export
Indirect export

REVIEW QUESTIONS

1. What are channels of distribution?
2. What factors will influence a firm's choice of the channels of distribution for its products?
3. What are the four most commonly used channels for selling products from producer to domestic consumer?
4. What are the various types of direct selling? Why would these methods be used?
5. What is pyramid selling? Why has this method of distribution fallen into disrepute?
6. Some products are sold by the producer directly to the retailer who then resells them to the buying public. Give examples of such products. Why would this method of distribution be used?
7. Some firms sell their products to both retailers and wholesalers. Does this make sense? Explain.
8. Why would a manufacturer or other producer use an agent to sell its products rather than sell directly to wholesalers or retailers?
9. An exclusive distribution agreement usually has two key aspects. Explain.
10. What conditions does a franchisor often impose on a sales franchisee?
11. What are the most common channels of distribution for industrial goods?
12. Many industrial goods are sold by the manufacturer directly to the firms that will use them. When is this usually the case? Give some examples.
13. Why might a manufacturer sell its goods to an industrial distributor rather than market them itself?
14. How are industrial goods sold to government departments and agencies? Is the same procedure always followed?

15. There are two basically different ways in which a firm's goods may be exported. Explain.
16. What are the various types of representatives that a firm may have abroad to handle the marketing of its goods?
17. Before a firm appoints a foreign agent to act as its representative, what preliminary steps should it take?
18. What are the pros and cons of having a company employee stationed abroad to handle the marketing of one's goods?
19. What is an export merchant? What services does he or she provide?

CASE PROBLEM

THE SPEE-DEE FIRE EXTINGUISHER
Selecting the channels of distribution for an inexpensive fire extinguisher

One of the hazards to which the Canadian homeowner or tenant is exposed is loss of life or property by fire. Fires are commonly grouped into three basic types: Class A fires, involving ordinary combustibles such as wood, paper, and cloth; Class B fires, involving oils, paints, and inflammable liquids; and Class C fires, involving live electrical equipment, motors, wiring, and appliances.

To combat these fires, manufacturers have developed and marketed a variety of portable fire extinguishers. Until recent years, the most popular type of portable home fire extinguisher for Class A and Class B fires was the vaporizing liquid type. This is a brass canister containing carbon tetrachloride which is released in the form of vapour by means of a pump handle. This type of fire extinguisher has, however, a very serious disadvantage—carbon tetrachloride is highly poisonous.

A portable fire extinguisher used for combating Class B and Class C fires consists of a cylinder filled with liquid carbon dioxide. This extinguisher, which smothers flames with a cold gas mixed with dry-ice snow, is not, however, very effective with Class A fires involving paper, wood, or cloth.

There are also, of course, portable fire extinguishers filled only with water. These are, however, quite heavy and are useful only for Class A fires. One of the most familiar of these extinguishers is the soda-acid type used in school or other public buildings. The water is sprayed by hose when the brass cylinder is turned upside down.

A more modern type of portable fire extinguisher is one that uses dry powder. One of these, suitable for Class B and Class C fires, is a pressurized container holding powdered sodium bicarbonate (household "baking soda"). It is considered to have a fire-fighting effect about five times as great as that of the liquid carbon tetrachloride extinguisher.

The most modern of the powder-type portable extinguishers is one containing monoammonium phosphate. This extinguisher has the great advantage that it is suitable for combating all types of fire: A, B, and C.

The prices of the various portable fire extinguishers approved by the Fire Underwriters Laboratories of Canada are relatively high. Some examples are as follows:

Type of Portable Fire Extinguisher	Approx. retail price
Multi-purpose dry chemical	$40.00
"Standard" dry chemical (B and C class fires only)	$35.00
Carbon dioxide—2½ lbs. capacity (B and C class fires)	$60.00
Soda-acid	$40.00
Pressurized water	$60.00
Hand-operated stirrup pump—2½ gals.	$40.00

A new firm, Canadian Fire Extinguishers Ltd., has recently developed a small aerosol bomb type extinguisher that would be effective against small Class A, B, and C fires and could be sold at a retail price of $15. The firm has already completed a survey of homes in various parts of a Canadian city to determine the potential demand for such a product. The majority of the persons called on have said that they did not have a fire extinguisher at present, and that they would, however, be glad to buy an inexpensive aerosol extinguisher even though it would be effective only against small fires.

The sales manager of Canadian Fire Extinguishers Ltd. is at present trying to determine which channels of distribution to use for the new product. She has already approached several chain supermarkets but has found them unwilling to handle the product unless the manufacturer agrees to undertake an intensive advertising campaign. Canadian Fire Extinguishers Ltd. is financially unable and unwilling to do this.

Assignment

1. What advice would you give the sales manager?

READING

The Hidden Dollars in Distribution

Physical distribution is probably the least glamorous of corporate operations. But it could be your biggest money saver

BY JAMES DINGWALL

Source: *Canadian Business Magazine*. Used by permission of James Dingwall.

A company's loading dock might seem like an unusual place to find members of senior management poking around for new ways to save money. Yet, according to Gordon Ramm of William Neilson Ltd. in Toronto, "The time is over when the top office accepts distribution and transportation expenses as a hefty but unavoidable cost of doing business." These days, in fact, the overhaul of the company's distribution system is beginning to figure in many firms' cost-cutting strategies. It is, for more and more managers, the last real frontier in the relentless pursuit of lower operating figures.

Savings to be found in tight-fisted physical distribution management—which now includes everything from inventory control and warehousing to packaging, shipping, order processing, market forecasting and customer service—can, indeed, be pretty impressive. Those happy heroes who carry the titles of director, general manager or even vice-president of distribution, won't settle for less.

Ernie Barber, director of physical distribution (PD) for Northern Telecom Canada Ltd. in Toronto, is dissatisfied with any effort in his department that does not net the company at least 30% in savings, and this year he expects to slash $19 million from the firm's massive $91-million PD budget.

The reasons why PD can be a gold mine of potential savings are easily explained. Distribution is both capital intensive and energy intensive. The price of oil has more than tripled in the last decade, raising both the cost of fuel and the cost of plastic packaging. Meanwhile, interest rates have risen from single to double digits, boosting inventory carrying costs—for some companies almost 20% annually—to figures that would once have been unimaginable. The effect of those two items alone, says Ron Denham, a physical distribution expert and vice-president of Thorne Stevenson & Kellogg, management consultants, means that distribution and transportation are becoming high cost components in a company's books. "In the manufacturing sector, approximately 25% of the dollar cost to the customer can be attributed to distribution. In the late 1950s, it was just 10%," says Denham.

The new economics of distribution are, not surprisingly, creating a new breed of manager. "There are kids coming out of school today," says Denham, who also lectures at York University in Toronto, "with briefcases full of notes on the subject." Often equipped with an MBA or a science degree, they are changing the old perception of distribution management.

Distribution, in fact, means far more than just getting a product from one place to another. According to Denham, "Distribution management resembles a hi-fi or stereo system. Everything must be in balance." This is achieved through integrated management. There's nothing very mysterious about the process. It simply means that the left hand should know what the right hand is doing, not only within the company, but between supplier, manufacturer, wholesaler and retailer.

In practice, however, even the job of coordinating a company's internal management can be difficult. Denham tells about one client—a record distributor in Ontario—who was persistently at an "out-of-stock" level of 35% despite warehouse inventory levels that were "appallingly" high. So what was the problem? Did the company need a more efficient inventory management system? Better sales forecasting? Better warehousing facilities? Or did the firm need to rationalize its shipping procedures? Superficially, says Denham, the problem was one of inventory controls at the warehouse level. But the real solution was found in devising a better distribution blueprint, based on marketing and retail sales data.

It was found that the company manufactured its records, surface-shipped them by rail to regional warehouses in Ontario and Quebec and then distributed the product from there to its retailers. Denham's group looked at the total system and decided that because the company operated primarily in two provinces, the need for regional warehousing was redundant.

A study of the firm's distribution system indicated that the best way to manage inventories was to shift the transportation load to air freight, bypassing the warehouses and shipping direct to the retailers. While direct air costs added almost $300,000 to the transportation expenses of the company, the savings achieved on inventory and warehousing were found to be close to $500,000. In other words, by switching distribution tactics, the company actually chalked up $200,000 in annual savings. As Denham goes on to point out, a study of just one aspect of distribution often leads to false conclusions. Management must always remember, he says, "that changes made in one division of a company invariably have an impact on all other areas."

In the past, says Denham, corporate structures being what they are, "No one looked across the boundaries of his own division." Consequently, transportation supervisors, inventory managers, marketing people and financial analysts all worked to streamline their own operations but few knew what the others were doing. Taking a look at the big picture is difficult, Denham says, but it is not impossible.

In 1976 and 1977 Northern Telecom decided it wanted to consolidate the company's air freight system. By using Emery Air Freight Corp. of Toronto, the firm reduced inbound goods from its 2,000 US suppliers to 80-90 shipments per day coming into Toronto International Airport. Besides effecting economies of scale, Northern Telecom negotiated one freight rate with Emery, based on the average size and weight of goods being shipped, and applied it to all material transported during the year. At the end of 12 months, the average cost is now adjusted up or down depending on actual shipment experience. In other words, the 50,000 different rate schedules that normally applied to Northern Telecom's inbound transportation were reduced to one. The company's billing system was simplified and accounts payable was centralized in Toronto—a considerable advantage to Emery. In 1981, this consolidated shipping procedure reduced the company's air freight shipping costs by 27%.

The effort, as Barber says, "to make our distribution stream narrow and manageable," works in other areas of the company as well. In 1974, Northern Telecom was using up to 85 different courier services across Canada. Today it has just one service, Purolator Courier Ltd., for intercity delivery and another, Pronto Toronto, for intracity traffic. Last year, says Barber, the company shipped 1,100 pieces between Montreal, Ottawa and Toronto, up from 800 pieces a year earlier. Packages include computer printouts, data sheets, hardcopy communications plus shipments of small components for the next day's delivery to customers. Even with growing shipping demands, Barber says the company is effecting a 30% saving with a "huge" volume discount. "Our guess that small package surface freight could be handled more efficiently by couriers than by our own trucking system proved to be correct."

The growing use of the computer allows integrated distribution management to be put into practice by small and large corporations alike. Such widespread financial burdens as interest carrying costs, cash-flow squeezes and declining sales margins are making the cost of computer applications in the distribution area seem like a bargain today. Says Al Saipe, another consultant with Thorne Stevenson & Kellogg: "A computer can give you information about the rate of inventory turnover, comparative costs of transportation modes and, indeed, data concerning customers who aren't paying their bills within 30 days." Back when interest rates were 6% or less, who cared? Now everyone cares and, he says, "that information from the computer has become pretty valuable."

But the fact is that not everybody within the corporate hierarchy recognizes that saving money is just as important as earning it. Concedes Ernie Barber of Northern Telecom: "Some senior managers still think of us as truck drivers." Barber, like other distribution managers in companies across Canada, sometimes speaks in Rodney Dangerfield tones of "not getting any respect." Granted, says Barber, his division didn't generate a cent of the $2.57 billion in revenue world-wide that Northern Telecom

Ltd. reported in 1981, but as far as he's concerned, his group is worth something in money *not* spent. "On those terms, we estimate that in transportation savings alone we're worth $100 million in sales to the company."

Coordinating the Flow: A Few Things to Ask Before You Go On-line

Properly implemented, a computerized distribution system coordinates the flow of goods and materials and links their movement to the accounting department, the order desk and the head office of the company.

For William Neilson Ltd., the time between taking an order and mailing the invoice is measured in mere hours because of computerization. If Joe Heffernan at Rothmans of Pall Mall Canada Ltd. feels so inclined, while he drinks his morning coffee he can call up the current inventory position of any one of seven regional warehouses in the company's distribution system and keep tabs on their $25 million worth of inventory.

At least one software house, Guardian Computer Systems Inc. (formerly Global Computer Services of Toronto), a subsidiary of TIW Industries Ltd., suggests that its hardware/software system (it ranges in price from $200,000-$500,000) will pay for itself in 30 months or less. On the grounds that 80% of any firm's business is generated by 20% of its products, says John Couse, sales manager for Guardian, "Our system can categorize products as fast-, slow- and really slow-moving items. If a company normally carries $4 million worth of goods, we can reduce the inventory to $3 million by showing management what sells and what doesn't." Ideally, Couse says, "The company that will reap the benefits of our system is usually doing $5 million or more in sales and carrying a minimum of 5,000 SKUs [stockkeeping units]."

Though the Guardian Distribution System (GDS) was designed mainly for auto-part and industrial equipment distributors, it's finding acceptance with other companies such as Distribution Thomcor of Montreal, the exclusive distributor of Parfums Caron, and Thomcor Holdings Ltd., the management group for the duty-free shops at Mirabel and Dorval airports. When the management group of Thomcor Holdings moved the computer from the office of another company in the group to its office in Montreal, it also inherited the GDS, and will be adapting it to the perfume and retail sales segments of the operation. While other software systems might require extensive reprogramming to accommodate the expansion, James Brock, director of operations for Thomcor Holdings, explains that the system can easily deal with its separate operating divisions. "Each new company simply becomes a new warehouse as far as the computer is concerned," he says.

Buying a computer system for your company is not something that can be done overnight, says Al Saipe at Thorne Stevenson & Kellogg. A large company may spend two to three years acquiring and implementing a system. A company's need may be a simple matter of coordinating order entries when customers or regional warehouse managers request products from company warehouses and freight departments, or it might include the handling of invoices for the accounting department. More advanced uses of the computer involve sales forecasting and computer modeling—testing hypothetical situations before implementing them.

However, a computer system that facilitates the flow of goods from you to your customer and relieves your employees of many tedious chores (everything from handling paper—something that happens 22 times for every order, estimates John Couse—to walking from the order desk to the warehouse to check if goods are in stock) is only as good as your ability to define your company's needs.

To do that, says Al Saipe, you need to review your company's current operating procedures. How do you deal with your customers and suppliers? What are your modes of transportation? What are your credit terms? Where are your goods stored? What are your current inventory control procedures? "Develop a picture of the movement of goods through your company and the procedures that support that movement," says Saipe. Next, outline how things are likely to change in the next two to five years. Will your company be expanding into new markets? Will it be developing new products? Clearly, both of these moves will have a direct impact on the kind of distribution system you will need to manage in the future. Possibly more warehousing or new modes of transportation will be required, entailing a more complex distribution system. Knowing where your company is now and where it's going in the future helps you define what you want a computer system to do. Then it's a matter of finding out what's available in the marketplace.

Several companies besides Guardian offer distribution management packages (for a list see *Canadian Business*, "The Software Connection," pp. 23-30, September 1981). Sophisticated systems require at least a minicomputer or a mainframe system, although several packages are available for microcomputers. Systemhouse Ltd. in Ottawa offers three distribution management systems designed for Wang or DEC hardware, including the TOM (The Office Manager), written specifically for Wang hardware. Software from Guardian is designed to work on the Honeywell DPS6 minicomputer. Both companies claim their clients are able to buy the packages "off the shelf" and achieve a high degree of "fit,"

meaning that little change or modification of the company or the computer software is necessary before implementation. According to a product manager for computer distribution systems, the job of customizing software to fit your company might cost as much as $250-$300 a day and the work would probably take at least a week. Therefore, many companies choose to alter their current operating procedures to conform to the computer's way of doing things.

While a fully computerized distribution system seems like a godsend to both managers and employees, it does not, as Saipe stresses, relieve management of its decision-making responsibilities—although it's tempting to try to use it that way. The GDS, for example, can calculate economical order quantities (i.e. weighing volume discounts against what you expect to sell and the cost of carrying it in stock inventory) in such a way that it will tell you how much stock to keep on hand in the warehouse to achieve any level of customer service you want. If you think you can get away with satisfying your customers 75% of the time, then the system will tell you what items and how much inventory to carry.

At best, however, all any computer can do is give you more information about your company. And in some cases, as Ernie Barber at Northern Telecom Canada discovered, it can give you too much.

Four years ago, the company implemented a purchasing, materials and supplies computer system throughout its 29 manufacturing plants across Canada. "It did everything the computer people promised it would do," says Barber. "Unfortunately it generated a horrendous amount of information that no one knew how to use." To rectify the situation, Northern Telecom has had to work closely with various community colleges and its own in-house training people to set up programs designed to raise the computer-consciousness (or the knowledge of how to use the output) of its employees, from loading dock personnel to senior management.

But still, Barber concedes, "While some divisions of the company have some parts of the system, no one division has it all. It's a huge system; it takes time and money to implement. Because all departments don't need every part of the system, they are equipped only with those they need to utilize." And he's also finding that, like so many areas of applied computer technology, "We have to digest what the system can do, one step at a time."

Can You Cut Costs? Here's the Test

Run your eye down this list to see if any of these statements apply to your operation. If you check even one of the boxes, you're paying too much for distribution.

☐ Our trucks are often empty on trips to and from the plant.

☐ There has been no review of the company's truck routes for the past five years.

☐ Charges for demurrage, penalty payments to common carriers waiting at the company dock to unload and minimum-load charges for partial shipments have increased significantly in the past few years.

☐ Our company has the same delivery policy for all of its customers, wherever they're located.

☐ We have never studied the possibility of using public storage facilities in lieu of our own regional warehouses.

☐ We're using the same methods of packing, crating and wrapping as we did a decade ago.

☐ There has not been a recent review of the company's order processing system.

☐ The warehouse staff has not been instructed to locate top-selling items or fast-moving seasonal products for easy storage and retrieval.

How Neilson Sweetens the Margins by Slimming Down Transport Costs

Gordon Ramm, vice-president of transportation at William Neilson Ltd. in Toronto, faces a variety of unusual problems in his job. One is the problem of the chocolate factory itself. It sits squarely in the centre of an old residential section of the city on a narrow street that even unnerves tough truck drivers as they negotiate deliveries and pickups. And those happen frequently, because even though every Jersey Milk or Sweet Marie chocolate bar consumed in Canada and abroad is manufactured here, there is no warehouse space for storage. That lies 30 mi. away in Georgetown.

Not surprisingly, transportation accounts for a significant slice of William Neilson's sales costs. Says Tom Lamont, president of the company, "We figure transportation counts for, on average, six to eight cents of every sales dollar." Every working day the company must ship its finished product from the downtown factory to the outlying warehouse, which doubles as a distribution centre both for finished products and the raw materials needed to make the chocolate bars. That means, says Ramm, that eight to 15 tractor trailers are backing into the loading docks every day, each to pick up 20-25 tons or 300,000-400,000 chocolate bars and then to transport them to Georgetown. From there, the goods are distributed to six regional warehouses across Canada.

For Ramm, the key to reducing costs and saving money in the transshipment of goods is, as he says, "reducing all those empty miles," when a tractor trailer highballs it back to the dispatch yard with nothing but air for cargo. The alternative is to "backhaul"; to make sure the company's transportation fleet does double duty. When the trucks go out with chocolate bars from the downtown factory to the distribution centre, they come back laden with sugar, cocoa and milk.

Backhauling is scarcely new in the transportation business. But where some companies might use the concept as an afterthought, Ramm tries to achieve shipping economies wherever he can. Ramm is a senior executive and, as such, meets regularly with the other vice-presidents of marketing, purchasing, finance and personnel. "It gives me a chance to hear about company operations that go beyond physical distribution," he says.

At one of the monthly management meetings last spring, Ramm discovered that the marketing department was going into Syracuse, NY, to test several brands of chocolate bars. Rather than to simply expedite a shipping order, he was able to point out that the company had a supplier in Syracuse who shipped cereals to the firm by common carrier. Instead of looking at the problem from strictly a marketing standpoint, Ramm examined it from the company's total-cost point of view. The result was that Neilson's trucks delivered the chocolate bars and returned, wherever possible, with raw materials from their Syracuse supplier. "By combining the two efforts," says Ramm, "we figure we're saving 40% on our distribution costs. In this case, the cost of moving the product has dropped to $4 per hundredweight from $7." Such savings are there to be had, continues Ramm. But you have to know where to look.

Future Watch: A Look at What Might Someday Come Down the Pipe

The idea that something other than a liquid might come down a pipeline is by no means new. Ideally, says Gary McLaughlin, acting executive director for the Commodity Pipeline Transport Committee of the Canadian Transport Commission, any large bulk material such as thermal and metallurgical coal, iron ore, sulfur, potash, or even wood chips and grain can be adapted to a slurry pipeline system. Whatever the commodity concerned, it is pulverized and mixed with a liquid such as water—or, more recently considered, methanol—and moved in a suspended state from point A to point B. Currently, attention is being focused on the use of a slurry system to transport coal.

Several years ago, Interprovincial Pipe Line Ltd. studied the feasibility of shipping thermal coal through its existing oil pipeline to markets in the East. More recently, in December 1981, the Alberta government made public a consultant's report it had commissioned to study the feasibility of shipping coal by slurry from Alberta to west coast ports.

There are a few bugs in the slurry concept, however. To begin with, a pipeline built from scratch is a massive capital undertaking, and to make such a system feasible, in terms of costs and benefits, the shipment of a minimum of 10 million tons of coal a year is necessary. The Alberta government report estimated that the capital cost of shipping this amount of coal by slurry would range from $1.6 billion to $1.9 billion during the eight- to 10-year period from concept to operation. Coal pipelines currently being considered in the U.S. would ship 10 million-40 million tons of coal a year at a total capital cost of more than $10 billion. Theoretically, using already-built pipelines seems like the best route to follow, and while gas pipelines are clearly out of the question, oil pipelines would be ideal because they would be able to transport two revenue-producers at the same time. Yet, separating the coal from the oil (or from water) once it arrives at the end of the line is not easy. And besides, the wear and tear on pumping-station valves as the slurry travels through the system would make modifications or even by-passes necessary.

Still, the idea has its adherents, especially in the West, where it is no secret that the existing railroad system—presently the only viable way of shipping coal and other commodities—is under considerable strain. Forecasts suggest that by 1985 it will be incapable of fully handling freight traffic demands.

So, says McLaughlin, bulk slurry systems are "very feasible and could have a major impact on the way we transport goods, possibly within the next 10 to 20 years. The concept is economical now if you have a very high volume, your market is set up, you have an agreement with the mines producing the product and you also have the financing, but a big pipeline will take eight years to set up from concept to operation."

Just as feasible, but looking way down the road, is a "futuristic urban freight pipeline" developed some years ago. The idea is to create a small subterranean or surface pipeline that uses miniature carts to transport packaged goods and materials within a city. Propulsion is provided by pressurized air. "Think of a horizontal pneumatic tube like the ones once used in old department stores and you've got the idea," says McLaughlin. Already, he says, a system of this kind has been proposed for garbage removal in several southern US housing subdivisions.

The real value of such a system, though, would be for use in large urban areas where downtown traffic congestion is making regular small freight deliveries difficult and extremely costly. Shipments to stores could be coded in such a way that optical sensors would be able to identify a box-top code and then route the package to a store's loading dock.

"It's an idea with potentially unique applications," says McLaughlin. "It's analogous to the old use of streetcars in Toronto and then the move to the subways." The technology needed to put such a system to work is already available, but McLaughlin says that the concept is still hypothetical, and he doesn't feel a large-scale delivery system of this kind will be put in place until the 21st century.

Building a Better Freight Train: Invisible Ideas, With Visible Savings

Advances in transportation and distribution seem to occur on two fronts. One is in the realm of the wildly theoretical, the other is in commonplace improvements and advances made to existing systems on a year-to-year basis. According to Cecil Law, a Queen's University professor and head of the Canadian Institute of Guided Ground Transport (the CIGGT is a business- and government-sponsored group based in Kingston, Ont., with a mandate to study questions concerning ground transportation), "The most dramatic changes in the near future will emerge from the continuing number of small developments in existing transportation systems."

Consider the freight train, for example. Credited as the binder twine that brought this country together, rail transportation has steadily improved during the past century. There has, of course, been the historic switch from steam to diesel but, says Pierre Berthiaume, manager of the CN Rail Research Centre in Montreal, other new and improved systems designs are being implemented all the time. Most of these improvements, such as positive traction control (increasing the adhesive friction of locomotive wheels), are almost invisible to the public, but in some cases they will have far-reaching effects on transportation and distribution.

Another such innovation is what Berthiaume calls the radial track system—the wheels of a train tilt when they negotiate a curve. By reducing friction and the necessity of slowing down at every bend, the theory is that average train speeds will increase, fuel consumption will fall and rail and wheel wear will be drastically reduced. There are already 100 radial track system freight cars traveling between Edmonton and Vancouver, and the CN research group is carefully monitoring their performance. On computer-simulated models, in fact, it has already been demonstrated that as much as $1,000 in fuel savings is possible on a 1,250-mi. round trip between the two cities. If this system is used over all of CN's routes, the savings in fuel costs could be considerable.

Recent passenger train developments, however, have not generated the same level of enthusiasm in the freight yards. Trains such as VIA's LRC (for "light, rapid and comfortable") that zip along at 100 mph and more, for example, are unlikely to affect anything but small freight traffic in the near future. "You can't run a high-speed train on a mixed traffic system," says Chris Boon, a researcher at the CIGGT. Although absolute speed is not a problem, traffic coordination problems caused by the different speeds of trains within the system would be considerable.

However, train buffs are allowed to dream, and these days there is news of a magnetic levitation system being researched by the Japanese and the Germans that could whisk both passengers and freight, on cars without wheels, along a track at more than 300 mph. The advantage that freight has in any of these high-speed systems is that it is able to handle turns with more aplomb than passengers, who often suffer from motion sickness.

Best Bets for Savings: Renegotiate, Standardize, and Don't Overservice

Specialists in the field of distribution management, including consultants, academics and, of course, front-line managers responsible for physical distribution, are continually looking for areas within a company where savings or efficiencies (that lead to greater earnings) are possible. As a general rule of thumb, most experts agree that the bigger the costs, the bigger the potential savings. So, it's not surprising that inventory is, as Ron Denham at Thorne Stevenson & Kellogg says, "the major soft spot" for most companies these days.

In fact, reducing inventories, and therefore inventory carrying costs, is a motherhood issue with manufacturers, distributors and retailers. But as most managers realize, if you cut back on stock, you create serious problems in other areas of your business, notably, customer service.

Any manager who sits down to analyze the question of where his company can save money in its distribution system must be aware, however, that there are trade-offs all the way down the line. There is no point, continues Denham, in rationalizing your warehouse capacity to a central depot without also considering the extra cost of transportation. That's why he and others in the field view PD management as a total system, not merely a handful of components.

Here are some of the key areas in the distribution system that a manager can scrutinize for those hidden savings.

Inventory Controls. Any company carrying high-value products and serving a large number of customers, or one having difficulty in forecasting sales, might benefit from a detailed analysis of its inventory management system. In an industrial company you should be alert for a growing number of back orders. In a retail company, you should keep track of the number of "stock-outs."

Clearly, a computer system designed to manage inventories is a plus in determining the items that are selling, and in automatically reordering materials and so on. But handy though it might be, a computer may not be a necessity. Al Saipe of Thorne Stevenson & Kellogg discovered one client who had a real inventory imbalance—40% of the company's inventory was generating just 5% of its sales. Obviously, the company was stocking a number of products over and above sales demand for those items. To correct the imbalance, Saipe worked out a manual reorder and stock replenishing scheme that identified fast-moving items according to region and season. An ordering timetable made allowances for stock in transit. The system worked because of its simplicity.

Order Processing. This is where physical distribution begins for most companies. Handled well, the system affects every aspect of distribution management: shipping orders for transport, inventory levels, invoicing, accounting and customer service. It's not surprising to see an order entry system as the bedrock function of the computer systems available for distribution management. If you bought a system several years ago, it might be a batch system that requires regular data reentry at critical stages of the distribution process. So, orders taken over the phone must be entered at the end of the day or week to readjust inventory levels or to assign a shipping order.

Today, integrated, on-line systems perform all of these functions simultaneously. Even some of the small microcomputer systems that sell for less than $10,000 can handle them. For a small company considering even a simple system, the price is less than one employee's annual salary, and the cost is tax-deductible.

Handling and Packaging. Some companies are investigating the possibility of standardizing packages for all types of goods. The uniform containers stack better, they save space in transit and there is less chance of product breakage.

Customer Service. "Distribution is becoming an important marketing tool," says Ron Denham. "Availability of goods, speed of delivery and reliability are all factors that affect customer satisfaction and are, without a doubt, the responsibility of the distribution manager."

Unfortunately, some companies don't understand what their customers really want. Speedy delivery? Not necessarily, says John Couse at Guardian Computer Systems Inc. When his company was developing its distribution software package, it commissioned the management consulting firm of Woods Gordon to pinpoint what businesses wanted from their suppliers. "Most people seem to want reliable deliveries," says Couse. Companies are willing to accept a longer delivery time if they are sure the goods will get to them as promised.

What usually happens, says Denham, is that a firm often has several customers who require immediate, same-day or overnight delivery. The service is then invariably offered to all of the company's customers, ostensibly as a sales incentive. However, this can lead to costly, partial-load shipments or shipments by air rather than by surface freight. The higher distribution costs will then either come out of the company's coffers or be reflected in higher prices to its customers. In a company with a variety of customers—some big, some small, some in large metropolitan areas, others in small towns—it's costly and inefficient for one service level to apply to all. Stressing reliable delivery instead of same-day or overnight service may mean delaying a shipment for two or three days, but it can also mean the difference between a partial and a full container-load of goods. The bigger a shipment, the lower the cost per hundredweight.

Warehousing. The use of public warehousing is becoming more popular. In St. John's, Nfld., Rothmans of Pall Mall Canada Ltd. uses the public system as its regional warehouse because it is less expensive than its own warehousing would be in that area. Other companies are questioning the need to maintain their own regional warehouses as well. One apparent trend is for companies to ship directly to buyers, using no intermediate storage.

Shipping. Decide to negotiate a new rate with your present haulage company or change modes of transportation. Ernie Barber at Northern Telecom has done both. If your company is generating a steady flow of business, he advises, volume discounts are available. And Northern Telecom now uses couriers to deliver small packages to customers who need parts immediately, piggybacking the shipments with regular inter-company dispatches.

If your business traffic has increased dramatically in recent years and you haven't renegotiated a new freight rate, then you're probably losing money. And if you haven't looked into the possibility of back hauling (perhaps your own raw materials or another company's goods) from a delivery destination, then you're definitely losing money.

Assignment

1. What is "physical distribution management?"
2. Why can PD be a gold mine of potential savings?
3. Why was the record distributor, mentioned in the Reading, persistently at an "out-of-stock" level? How was the firm's distribution system revised?
4. How did Northern Telecom revise its distribution system? And with what result?
5. Why are computers being used more and more in distribution management?
6. How should a company go about computerizing its distribution management?
7. What are some indicators of possibly inefficient distribution management in a company?
8. How did William Neilson Ltd. improve its distribution management?
9. What is the "slurry concept?" How might it help reduce distribution costs for certain products?
10. What new ideas may help to improve rail freight efficiency?
11. What factors might indicate that a firm's inventory control system is inefficient? How can a firm improve its inventory control?
12. How is distribution becoming an important marketing tool?
13. How can public warehousing play an important role in a firm's physical distribution strategy?
14. How can a firm possibly improve its shipping practices?

UNIT 10.3: WHOLESALING

Wholesaling is the process of buying goods from a manufacturer or other producer and reselling them, usually in smaller quantities, to retailers or to industrial or government markets. The two main kinds of *wholesalers* are merchant wholesalers and agent middlemen. The former buy goods for resale; the latter sell them on commission.

Merchant Wholesalers

These may be divided into two main kinds: full-service wholesalers and limited-service wholesalers.

Full-service wholesalers are wholesalers or distributors who provide their clients with a wide range of wholesaling services. These include holding a variety of goods, dividing and assembling goods, giving advice, making deliveries, extending credit, and providing regular visits by their salespeople.

Limited-service wholesalers, as the name implies, provide only limited service to their customers. They may carry only a limited selection of stock, extend no credit, and make no deliveries. Sometimes a limited-service wholesaler will avoid handling and storing goods by accepting only orders for shipment direct from the producer to the consumer.

Full-Service Wholesalers.
These are usually one of three kinds: general merchandise wholesalers, single-line wholesalers, and specialty wholesalers.

General Merchandise Wholesalers carry several different lines of goods, such as groceries, hardware, electrical supplies, plumbing supplies, drugs, and furniture. Their principal customers are general stores, hardware stores, drugstores, and small department stores. Industrial distributors may also be of this type and offer a wide variety of industrial goods.

Single-Line Wholesalers specialize in one or a very few lines of goods, such as groceries, paint, and hardware. These are sold primarily to single- or limited-line stores. In the case of industrial goods, the single-line industrial distributor will attempt to sell a limited range of products to a large number of firms.

Specialty Wholesalers supply a particular type of product rather than a complete line. An example of a specialty wholesaler is a supplier of cheeses.

Limited-Service Wholesalers.
These are merchant wholesalers who perform only a few of the usual wholesaling functions. This group includes: the cash-and-carry wholesaler, the drop shipper (or desk jobber), the truck distributor (or jobber), and the rack jobber (or merchandiser).

The **Cash-and-Carry Wholesaler** provides no delivery service—customers must pick up the goods they require; gives little or no credit to customers; and usually carries only a limited selection of fast-moving goods, mostly staples.

The **Drop Shipper (or Desk Jobber)** is a wholesaler who avoids storage and handling charges by accepting only orders which can be shipped directly from producer to customer. These wholesalers are active in lumber, building materials, farm products, and petroleum, where the products are relatively bulky.

The **Truck Distributor (or Truck Jobber)** carries a particular line of merchandise on the truck and delivers the goods as orders are received from the various retailers on the route. Truck distributors are active in the food field (mayonnaise, potato chips, salted nuts, and candy), in tobacco products, and in bakery goods.

The **Rack Jobber (or Rack Merchandiser)** supplies non-food items such as housewares, patent medicines, books, magazines, stationery, greeting cards, and toiletries to supermarkets and other retail outlets. Unlike most other wholesalers, the rack jobber is paid only for what is actually sold by the retailer. The rack jobber also supplies the display racks and keeps them filled.

Marketing Agents

The marketing agent (or agent middleman), unlike the merchant wholesaler, does not purchase from the producer the goods which he or she sells. Instead, the agent sells on behalf of the producer, receiving a commission on the goods sold.

The most important type of marketing agents are brokers, selling agents, manufacturer's agents, commission merchants, and auction companies.

Brokers. The main function of a broker is to bring together a seller and a buyer. For this service, he or she is paid an agent's commission, either by the buyer or by the seller, whoever is the principal. Brokers are involved in the marketing of farm products, such as grain, fruit, and vegetables; dry groceries, such as flour, sugar, and coffee; and real estate and insurance.

Selling Agents. These are firms which, although independently owned and managed, permanently market all the goods of a producer. In doing so, they have considerable authority over prices and other terms of sale. For this marketing service they receive a commission on sales. Selling agents are used by small- and medium-sized producers to market various types of industrial goods, clothing, and groceries. The goods are sent directly from the producer to the customer.

Manufacturer's Agents. The manufacturer's agent acts as a salesperson for a producer in an area where it would be uneconomical for the producer to have its own salespeople. Such an agent usually represents several non-competing manufacturers simultaneously, selling one or more of their particular products in his or her own individual territory. Unlike the selling agent, the manufacturer's agent handles only part of a manufacturer's output and is normally given little discretion as to the terms of sale. The manufacturer's agent usually carries only samples; orders are shipped directly from the plant. The manufacturer's agent is often used in the marketing of industrial goods, such as farm machinery and industrial equipment; and of consumer goods, such as groceries, dry goods, and clothing.

Commission Merchants. Unlike the selling agent and the manufacturer's agent, the commission merchant (also called commission house) takes possession of the goods which it sells. In addition to finding customers, the commission merchant temporarily stores the goods and delivers them. Sometimes it will also extend credit. Like other agents, the commission merchant receives a commission on sales. Often the cost of handling and storing the goods will be charged to its principal, the producer. Commission merchants are extremely active in the fruit, vegetable, and livestock markets.

Auction Companies. An auction company receives goods from a producer, temporarily stores them, and sells them at auction in its salesrooms to the highest bidder. The company then collects the sales proceeds and remits this amount, less commission, to the producer. The auction itself is conducted by a professional salesperson, the auctioneer, who tries to obtain the highest price for each good by extolling its merits and pitting one buyer against another.

The goods are listed in catalogues, and buyers have an opportunity prior to the sale to inspect the goods or samples of them. The services of auction companies are often used for the sale of furniture, fruit, vegetables, tobacco, and livestock.

Export and Import Agents. Export agents contact prospective buyers in foreign countries. They advise their principal as to how an order should be packaged, labelled, and shipped to the foreign customer, and receive a commission on the value of the sale. Import agents act on behalf of foreign producers or exporters and receive a commission on any goods imported and sold in Canada.

Why Use a Wholesaler?

Many producers prefer to leave the marketing of their products in the hands of middlemen rather than undertake this work themselves.

The two main reasons for this are: first, the producer may not be able, because of lack of time, capital, or "know-how," to carry out the marketing task successfully; and second, the producer may not be able to perform the various marketing functions at as low a cost as the middleman.

Services to Producers. The services which wholesalers provide for producers include:
1. Buying the goods from the producer (merchant wholesaler) or selling them on his or her behalf (agent middleman) so that the producer has funds to finance further production.
2. Informing the producer of the state of the market (for example, trends in demand for individual products, packaging requirements, and competition).
3. Storing the goods on their way to the retailers.
4. Dividing and packaging the goods into more convenient quantities.
5. Advising on and distributing promotional material.
6. Calling regularly on retailers.
7. Delivering the producer's goods relatively promptly to retailers, as and when required.

Services to Retailers. There is nothing to prevent a retailer from buying goods directly from the various producers. In fact, large retailers such as chain stores and department stores, to obtain quantity discounts, do just that. However, most retailers do not have a sufficiently large stock turnover to make it possible for them to order large quantities of each good directly from the manufacturer. These retailers buy their goods from a wholesaler who provides them with the following services:

1. In one visit, the wholesaler's salesperson can take an order for a great variety of goods, thus saving the retailer valuable time.
2. The wholesaler can supply the goods in almost exactly the quantities required, thus removing some of the burden of storage from the retailer.
3. The goods are usually delivered much more promptly from the wholesaler than from the producer.
4. The wholesaler, who has knowledge of the local retailers and funds for trade financing, is usually better able to extend credit to retailers than is the producer.
5. The wholesaler often provides sales promotional aids (for example, brochures and displays) and sales advice to retailers.

Marketing Co-operatives

A special type of marketing intermediary is the co-operative.

A *producers' co-operative* is an association of producers—for example, farmers or fishermen—which has the purpose of marketing the members' products and purchasing their supplies at better than normal prices. Sometimes a producers' co-operative undertakes only one function, marketing or purchasing, but usually both functions are combined.

Service co-operatives provide services rather than supplies to members. Examples of such services are housing, rural electrification, medical insurance, transportation, grazing, custom grinding, seed cleaning, operation of farm machinery, and restaurant operation.

Wholesale co-operatives are federations of local producer and consumer co-operatives which act as marketing and purchasing agents for the member co-operatives.

Advantages of Co-operative Membership.

The most important advantage of membership in a co-operative is the possible financial gain.

The producers' co-operative offers members:
1. The chance of a better price for their products as a result of: a more orderly marketing arrangement—for example, grading of products, storage, and gradual release so as not to saturate the market; co-operative advertising, including promotion of a brand name; and stronger bargaining power as a group.
2. A lower price for supplies such as seed and fertilizer, because of the savings obtained by the co-operative from buying in bulk.
3. Advice and financial assistance.

The service co-operative enables members to save money through lower prices for insurance, fuel, supplies, etc. made possible by bulk buying.

The wholesale co-operative also provides economies to members through the sharing of offices, warehousing, transportation and other buying facilities and by discounts on quantity purchases made on behalf of members.

KEY TERMS

Wholesaling

Merchant wholesaler

Service wholesaler

Limited-service wholesaler

General merchandise wholesaler

Single-line wholesaler

Specialty wholesaler

Cash-and-carry wholesaler

Drop shipper

Truck distributor

Rack jobber

Broker

Selling agent

Manufacturer's agent

Commission merchant

Auction company

Export agent

Import agent

Marketing co-operative

Producers' co-operative

Service co-operative

Wholesale co-operative

REVIEW QUESTIONS

1. What is wholesaling? Why is it necessary? Explain the role of a travel wholesaler.
2. Distinguish between merchant wholesalers and agent middlemen. Give examples.
3. What are the various kinds of service wholesalers? How do they vary from each other?
4. What are the various types of limited-service wholesalers? What services do they provide? What services do they omit?
5. Why is a broker considered to be an agent middleman? Give three examples of brokers, explaining the services provided.
6. What is a manufacturer's agent? What services does he or she provide?
7. Explain, with an example (e.g. livestock, antiques), how an auction company operates and the services provided.
8. Why would a Canadian manufacturer use the services of an export agent in marketing its goods abroad?
9. What are the various services that a wholesaler can provide for a manufacturer or farmer?
10. What services can the wholesaler provide to the retailer?
11. Why do many manufacturers use wholesalers to sell some of their products but sell the rest themselves?
12. What are the various types of marketing co-operatives? Why would an apple-grower, for example, join a co-operative?

CASE PROBLEM

W. HARPER & SON LTD.
Managing a wholesale business firm

W. Harper & Son Ltd. is an old-established rural wholesale firm located in a relatively new warehouse building on the outskirts of a small Canadian town. Recently Alfred Harper, the son of the founder, has assumed management of the firm.

The products handled by the firm include tobacco items such as cigarettes, cigars, pipe tobacco, and plug chewing tobacco; restaurant supplies such as soup, ice-cream cones, chocolate bars, and boxed candy; patent medicines and toiletries such as aspirins, cough medicine, toothpaste, toilet soap, and baby powder; paper products such as paper plates and cups, wrapping paper, meat paper, and stationery; and a variety of other items such as cameras, film, razors, razor blades, and portable radios, many of which are handled in quantity only at Christmas.

The market for the firm's goods consists of retail stores and restaurants in the town itself, and in the surrounding villages within a 45 km radius. There is no other wholesaler servicing this area.

A physical inventory check is made every Friday morning by Alfred Harper. An order is then placed that afternoon for goods that are low in stock. The goods are delivered by truck the following Monday from the city. Payment for orders is usually made within 30 days. Similar credit is extended to the firm's customers.

The firm employs two salespeople and a truck driver. The salespeople go out on a specified route each day and "put up" their orders on their return. The orders are then delivered the next day by the truck driver. The truck driver also helps to put up orders after completing the day's deliveries.

The salespeople, both of whom have been with the firm for many years, have a friendly relationship with the owners of the various stores and restaurants on whom they call. Apart from giving each customer a bottle of whiskey at Christmas and passing on any sales literature received from manufacturers, the salespeople confine their efforts to obtaining orders without, at the same time, overstocking their customers. They do not try to give advice on how the store owners might promote sales because they feel that such advice would be resented.

The area covered by the salespeople is a relatively prosperous farming one. In the summer there is also a small but growing influx of tourists who stay at a new lodge alongside the largest lake in the area. There has been talk of developing the slopes in the area as ski runs, especially as a new all-weather highway now runs close to this part of the province.

Many families in the area are in the habit of purchasing goods from mail order stores.

Assignment
1. Where does Harper & Son Ltd. fit in the distribution channels discussed previously?

2. How can Alfred Harper increase his sales? Indicate any assumptions that you make.
3. Prepare the rough draft of a letter to the owner of the lodge explaining why he should buy his goods from you rather than from manufacturers or from wholesalers further away.

UNIT 10.4: RETAILING

Retailing is the process of selling goods and services to the consumer. The *retailer* is the marketing middleman who buys goods usually from a wholesaler or producer and resells them to the public. Sometimes a producer will retail his or her own goods. Whatever the case, there must be the physical facilities required to store and display the goods at locations convenient for the customer.

Types of Retailers

The various types of retailers are as follows:

General store	Discount house
Convenience store	Supermarket
Single-line store	Combination store
Specialty shop	Mail-order house
Department store	Vending machine
Variety store	Direct salesperson

General Store. The typical general store offers for sale a wide variety of merchandise, including: food; dry goods; notions; hardware; appliances; clothing; shoes; and farm supplies. This type of retail operation was designed to supply as many of the needs of the local community as possible. It flourished at a time when low density population and poor means of transportation made larger or more specialized types of retail operation financially impractical. Today it survives mainly in rural areas.

The retailing services provided by the general store to its customers include: the convenient location of the store; a variety of different lines of goods; personal service; usually the right to return a good if not satisfied; and sometimes, the provision of credit and a delivery service.

Three important disadvantages are: the limited choice within each line of merchandise carried; the fact that prices are often higher than those of the supermarkets; and the frequent inadequacy of parking facilities.

The general store is usually located on the village main street or at a relatively busy crossroads or intersection.

Such a store is almost invariably a family-owned and operated business. Usually it is run as a sole proprietorship, although examples of partnerships and private corporations can be found.

Convenience Store. Usually located in a shopping plaza or at a street corner in older residential districts, (also sometimes called a "corner store") this type of store can be considered a successor to the general store in its attempt to cater to a wide variety of consumer needs. Such stores include chain-style operations but also number many independently-owned and operated establishments. They provide milk and other dairy products; bread and other bakery goods; newspapers and magazines; cards and party goods; soft drinks; gift items; stationery and school supplies; canned and frozen convenience foods; pet foods and supplies; cigarettes and other tobacco goods; and a wide range of candy. Unlike the supermarkets and department stores, they often stay open from early morning until late at night, seven days a week. The term "convenience" stems as much from their opening hours as from the range of products stocked and the location of the store. Prices charged tend to be higher than in the supermarkets.

Single-Line Store. This type of store offers a single line of merchandise, such as food; drugs; furniture; hardware; men's clothing; automobiles; or household appliances. Often relatively small in size, the single-line store attracts business by its specialization, good personal attention (the manager is often the owner), convenient location, credit and free delivery.

The single-line store is found in shopping districts, plazas, and centres—wherever there is enough customer traffic to warrant such specialization.

Specialty Shop. This, as the name suggests, is more specialized in its line of merchandise than is the single-line store. Whereas a men's clothing store is an example of a single-line store, a men's hat shop is an example of a specialty shop. By narrower specialization, the specialty shop can offer greater variety of choice as well as more specialist advice to the customers. Otherwise, the services provided are the same. Specialty shops are usually quite small. Location is the same as for the single-line store.

Department Store. This is a large store comprising a number of different departments, each specializing in a particular line of goods. The goods sold may include: clothing; footwear; furniture; home furnishings; household appliances; television and radio sets; sports equipment; toys; material and parts for home improvements; car accessories; and photographic equipment.

The department store normally offers the following customer services: a wide variety of goods, all conveniently located and well displayed in one building; prices which are the same as or lower than those of single-line stores and specialty shops; usually courteous service; return privileges; free delivery; credit; and parking facilities. Examples of department stores are Eaton's, Simpsons, and the Bay.

Most department stores were originally set up in downtown locations. Like other retail stores, they are now being affected by the movement of the residential population to suburban areas. Inadequate parking facilities, traffic congestion, and long distance have discouraged many people from shopping downtown. However, the department store chains, to avoid losing the suburban customer, are establishing new stores in the suburban areas.

Variety Store. These stores, sometimes quite large, offer a wide variety of goods for sale, such as housewares; small appliances; toys; candy; toiletries; china; hardware; clothing; and stationery.

Compared with the department store, the variety store has a narrower selection of merchandise, sells goods usually of a lower price and quality range, and does not provide such customer services as credit, free delivery, and return privileges. The location of these stores is in busy shopping districts and plazas.

Some of the variety stores belong to corporate chains; that is, each store in a chain is a branch of the same firm, responsible to head office; the firm as a whole is a private or public corporation. Other smaller stores may be independently owned sole proprietorships, partnerships, or private corporations.

Examples of variety store chains are K mart, Woolco, and Zellers.

Discount House. This is a retail store which sells merchandise at a lower price than other retail stores for comparable goods—that is, it sells at a "discount." Some discount houses carry many lines of goods, while others—for example, the discount drug stores—concentrate on one line.

By eliminating many customer services, such as acceptance of telephone orders, credit, delivery, personal service, and expensive furnishings, the discount house is able to offer merchandise at lower prices than conventional stores can. All discount houses try to concentrate on fast-moving items and are usually able to make a profit, even with a small markup, because of the large volume of sales. Discount houses may be found in all types of locations.

Supermarket. This is a large self-service food store in which groceries, meat, fruit and vegetables, dairy products, baked goods, and toiletries are the main items for sale. Other characteristics of this type of store are: a large variety of goods; a clean, bright, roomy shopping area; no credit; usually no delivery; and free parking. The aim of the supermarket was originally to sell a large volume of goods at prices slightly lower than those of traditional grocery and meat stores. Customer services were kept to a minimum—for example, self-service, no credit, and no delivery. The prices today are little different from those of smaller retailers except for customer-attracting "specials."

These stores can be found in the older shopping districts of town and in new shopping centres and plazas.

Combination Store. This is a giant store that sells food, drugs, household products, toiletries, etc. Because of the lower prices offered, the "combos" and "supercombos" are expected to displace many of the present supermarkets. They are usually located on the outskirts of major urban areas where there is good highway access and ample parking.

Mail-Order House. This is a store which originally received most of its orders from customers by mail and delivered most of the goods ordered by the same means. Today, however, a large proportion of its orders are obtained by branch offices known as "order houses," strategically located in cities and towns across the country. Deliveries are now made by mail, the store's own trucks, or by contract delivery service. A well-known example of a mail-order house in Canada is Simpsons-Sears Ltd. This store offers many different lines of products, notably clothing, home furnishings, furniture, china, household appliances, garden implements, camping equipment, boats, and motorcycles. These goods are listed in a catalogue which is mailed to prospective customers, who then order from it. The mail-order service is particularly attractive to people living outside the metropolitan areas.

Since sales are predominantly from the catalogues, the mail-order house has no reason to locate in relatively expensive shopping areas.

Vending Machine. One of the most recent developments in retailing is the spread of the automatic vending machine. In exchange for an inserted coin, these machines serve hot or cold drinks, cigarettes, candy, nuts, and even life insurance policies. Vending machines are to be found in industrial plants, airline terminals, office buildings, schools, and theatres—wherever a market exists.

Direct Salesperson. Certain goods such as vacuum cleaners, encyclopaedias, kitchenware, cosmetics, home insulation services, and even nursery plants are offered for sale by salespeople who call at each house in a neighbourhood or telephone the persons listed in the telephone directory. If the salesperson is successful, he or she may take a down payment on an order to be delivered some days later. Sometimes the person engaged in *direct selling*, as this form of retailing is called, may sell to relatives, neighbours, and friends rather than making "cold calls" on a door-to-door basis. He or she may also invite prospective customers to at-home demonstration parties or attempt to have the products adopted for fund-raising campaigns.

Retail Ownership

Retailers, when considered in terms of ownership, fall into one of four groups: independents, corporate chains, voluntary chains, and co-operatives.

Independents. Most small retail businesses—grocery stores, drugstores, and so on—are independently owned and operated. Usually, because of simplicity and low cost, the form of ownership is a sole proprietorship or partnership. Sometimes, however, the business is incorporated to reduce taxes and/or obtain limited liability.

Merchandise is usually bought from local wholesalers, and sales are made because of such factors as convenient location, prices which are reasonably competitive with the chain stores, personal service, and occasionally delivery and credit. Advertising is undertaken in the local newspaper and by the distribution of handbills. Although there are many efficient small retailers, many of these stores suffer from lack of capital and poor management. Operating costs are frequently high, and when the number of hours which the proprietor and family spend in the store is considered, profits may be low or non-existent.

Corporate Chains. The term *chain*, or *corporate chain*, is used to describe a number of stores all of which are owned and operated by a single corporation. Many supermarkets, variety stores, drugstores, service stations, and restaurants belong to such chains.

The principal characteristics of this type of retail operation are:
1. Buying is done by head office rather than by individual store managers. Because of the large quantities involved, the chain can obtain its merchandise directly from producers, some of which it may own itself, at factory or farm selling prices. It can also obtain carload freight rates in bringing the goods to the chain's warehouses.
2. The sales policy of the chain varies according to the type of operation.
3. Advertising costs are reduced, as a single advertisement (usually prepared at head office) benefits all the stores in the chain.
4. Efforts are concentrated on the promotion of the chain stores' own branded merchandise, on which a larger profit is made.

Voluntary Chains. A *voluntary chain* is a group of independent retailers who agree to do business under a common name and to take part in co-operative buying and advertising.

Voluntary chains have been formed as an attempt by independent retailers to reduce operating costs through bulk buying and co-operative advertising. Sometimes the initiative for such a chain has come from a local wholesaler who acts as the buying agency for the chain and sometimes provides financial assistance and management advice. By joining a voluntary chain, the independent retailer is able to retain his or her independence and at the same time compete more effectively against the corporate chain stores.

Retail Co-operatives. A *retail* or *consumers' co-operative* is an association of private individuals who buy goods from the co-operative and receive a share of the annual profits in proportion to the value of their purchases.

The consumers' co-operative enables members to buy goods such as groceries at a price slightly below normal retail prices. This reduction may be given immediately in the form of lower prices or at the end of the year in the form of patronage dividends—that is, a share of the co-operative's profit for the year. Members sometimes provide labour services.

Perhaps the most commonly used type of consumers' co-operative is the *credit union* which provides a variety of financial services to its members.

Services Provided by Retailers

The retailer is the middleman who sells goods to domestic consumers. His or her continued existence is the result of being able to perform certain essential marketing functions more efficiently than the producer or wholesaler can. These functions are:
1. Choosing goods that the consumer will buy. The retailer must carefully study sales trends, changes in taste and fashion, customers' attitudes, competitors' actions, and so on.

2. Stocking the goods so that they are readily available to consumers in the place where they are required—in local communities rather than at the place of production.
3. Making these goods available in quantities suitable for the customers—for example, individual cans rather than case lots.
4. Packaging the goods, if the manufacturer's package or container is not suitable.
5. Providing personal attention to customers such as greeting them and helping them find what they need.
6. Sometimes extending credit to customers. The retailer may use his or her own funds or those of a finance company.
7. Sometimes delivering goods to customers, free or for a charge.

Suggested Retail Prices

It is common practice in Canada for manufacturers to "suggest" the retail price at which their products should be sold, and for most retailers to accept the suggestion. This price is normally sufficient to cover manufacturing and marketing costs, including the profit. In some cases, where competition is limited, a higher price is charged and a larger profit obtained. The ability of a manufacturer to charge a high price without a substantial reduction in the quantity of goods sold is, of course, dependent on the price-elasticity of demand for the product. Where demand is very inelastic, a higher price may cause no reduction in the amount sold. For some industries, such as the telephone companies, the prices charged are subject to government approval.

The practice of suggesting retail prices is upheld by manufacturers on the grounds that it promotes orderly marketing arrangements. It is condemned by its opponents on the grounds that, if fully observed, it would prevent more efficient retailers from undercutting the prices of the less efficient.

The federal government, by means of the Combines Investigation Act, prohibits suppliers of goods from prescribing and enforcing the prices at which their products are sold. Thus manufacturers are free to suggest retail prices but not to enforce them—for example, by cutting off supplies—except where their products are being used as loss leaders.

High Entry and Dropout Rates

One of the characteristics of retailing is the extremely high entry and dropout rates.

The causes of the high entry rate are the desire of many persons to own their own small business and the ease with which a person may set himself or herself up as a retailer.

Persons wishing to enter retailing, or any small business for that matter, see the following advantages:
1. Independence—the attractiveness of being one's own boss.
2. Financial gain—all the profits belong to the owner.

3. A sense of achievement or pride from owning and operating a successful business.
4. The common belief that retailing requires no special talent, experience, or training.

The desire of many people to own their own retail business is often quite easily translated into practice. This is because of such factors as the small amount of capital necessary and the absence of any legal requirements as to education, training, or experience.

The high dropout rate among retailers is often caused by poor financial results compared with expectations. In some cases, new retailers do not provide themselves with sufficient working capital to tide their business over the initial months. Thus a business may become insolvent and be forced to discontinue, even though with a little more time it could have been financially successful. In other cases, operating results are below expectations because of over-optimistic forecasts of sales revenue and operating expenses. Sales revenue may be low because of: lack of demand in the area; competition by other retailers; and poor salesmanship of the retailer. Costs may be unduly high because of: staff problems, such as too many staff, inefficient, dishonest, or poorly motivated staff; overbuying of stock—many items may later have to be sold at a loss; poor credit policies—many customers may fail to pay; and expensive premises.

Retailing Trends

Competition and technological change have led to various changes in retailing practices. The most important trends are:

Greater variety of goods stocked. The general store, the backbone of retailing in early settlement days, was known for its diversity of goods. With greater population density, specialized stores emerged. Today, the trend has reversed. Supermarkets offer many items other than food, and the term drugstore has become an anachronism.

The growth of self-service retailing. One way of cutting retailing costs has been to let the customer serve himself or herself. The cost of marking merchandise and the loss from theft have been far outweighed by the savings in store labour and the more rapid turnover of stock. With the self-service system, customers tend to buy more and do not have to wait for service, except at the checkout counter.

Improved shopping facilities. To attract customers, many retail stores (notably the department stores and chain supermarkets) are providing clean premises, good lighting, music, attractive displays, and other items calculated to make shopping a pleasure rather than a chore.

The use of novelties. Supermarkets, service stations, and other retailers offer a constantly changing variety of "gimmicks" to attract customers. These include merchandise coupons, cutlery sets, and competitions for money and other prizes.

The spread of discount stores. More and more discount stores are being established to retail goods at below-usual prices. These stores are to be found in such fields as furniture, household appliances, food, and drugs. One of the latest arrivals is the so-called "box store" carrying a limited assortment of items with prices 10 to 15 per cent lower than those of the traditional supermarket. Another is the giant supermarket or "combo."

Greater use of credit. An increasing number of retailers are offering credit terms to attract customers. This is done mainly by membership in credit card plans such as VISA, Mastercharge, American Express, etc. The credit card company undertakes the customer financing in return for a percentage of the retailer's credit sales revenue.

The physical decentralization of retailing. The increased mobility of consumers (with one or two cars in practically every family) has permitted retailers to move away from the traditional main street. Suburban shopping plazas and centres, located among the new residential areas, are now becoming almost commonplace.

The use of electronic data processing equipment to improve operating efficiency. Chain supermarkets are now using electronic computers to keep track of inventory and to analyse sales trends in branch stores. Department stores are using computers to bill customers and keep credit balances up to date.

Sale of no-name products. Supermarkets now offer "no-name" or non-brand name products at lower prices than the brand name ones. Public acceptance has been mixed owing to initial doubts about the quality of the no-name items.

KEY TERMS

Retailing	Direct salesperson
General store	Retail ownership
Single-line store	Independents
Specialty store	Corporate chains
Department store	Voluntary chains
Variety store	Retail co-operatives
Discount house	Services provided by retailers
Supermarket	Retail prices
Mail-order house	High entry and dropout rates
Vending machine	Retailing trends

REVIEW QUESTIONS

1. What is retailing? What are the basic requirements before it can take place? How would retailing in Canada compare with retailing in many underdeveloped countries of the world?
2. What are the principal characteristics of the general store? Why did this type of store flourish more in the past than it does today?
3. Do convenience stores charge high prices? If so, why are they so popular?

4. Explain the success of specialized bakery stores in urban and suburban areas. What other types of single-line stores are flourishing?
5. What is a specialty shop? Give examples of the ones that you occasionally use. What is their attraction?
6. What is a department store? Are they all the same in range of goods and services offered? Why are they still flourishing in Canada?
7. Contrast Woolworths and the Bay or Eaton's in types of goods and services offered to the public.
8. What discount stores exist in your area? What do they sell and what savings do they offer? What disadvantages do they have for you compared with more conventional stores?
9. How are supermarkets changing in the types of goods and services offered to their customers? How will they compete against the "combos"?
10. Give examples of products which are now being successfully marketed by specialty mail-order houses. Discuss the reasons for their success. Contrast it with the decline in popularity of the traditional mail-order houses.
11. Discuss the advantages and disadvantages of vending machines as a means of retailing. List the products and services sold in this way. What possibilities exist for the future?
12. What types of goods are now retailed by direct salespeople? Why are not more goods sold this way? What products are no longer sold in this manner? Do the same arguments apply to home mail delivery?
13. What are the principal characteristics of the corporate chain type of retailing operation?
14. Explain what is meant by a "voluntary chain." What are the reasons for its coming into being?
15. What is a retail co-operative? Why are they relatively few in number compared with other types of retailers?
16. What services do retailers provide for their customers? Are they all necessary? Should others be offered?
17. Retailers are free to set their own prices. Discuss.
18. Why does retailing have high entry and dropout rates?
19. Identify and explain four important present retailing trends. What changes, if any, can you predict for the future?

CASE PROBLEMS

SMITH'S MEAT MARKET
Buying and operating a butcher's store

Smith's Meat Market is the name of a butcher's business started by Fred Smith in 1946 shortly after his demobilization from the R.C.A.F. The form of ownership has always been a sole proprietorship.

The store, which measures 7 m by 17 m, is located on a quiet main street as one of a block of four businesses (Figure 10.3).

The neighbouring area, which is heavily residential, was originally populated by Canadians of English origin. In recent years, however, the population has

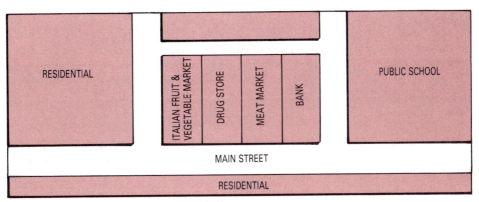

Figure 10.3 Location of Smith's Meat Market

become predominantly Italian and Greek. A bus stop is located outside the Italian fruit and vegetable market. Parking is available on the side streets. A large chain supermarket is located half a kilometre along the road.

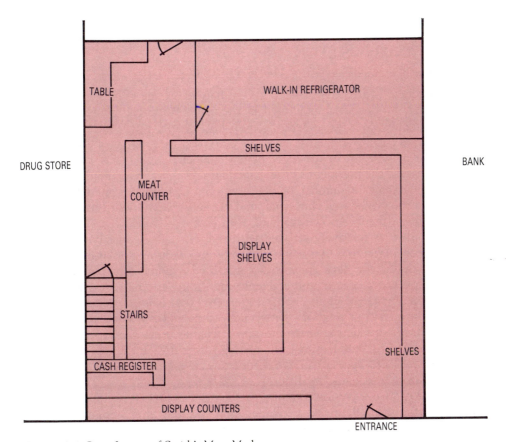

Figure 10.4 Store Layout of Smith's Meat Market

The layout of the meat market is shown in Figure 10.4.

Fred Smith has made a comfortable living over the years with a clientele built up on the basis of good quality meat (he buys only young steers) and friendly, personal service. Customers are attracted to his store partly by word-of-mouth advertising and by a sign outside his door advertising baby beef. No meat is displayed in the shop window where there is an open, uncooled display counter. Advertising is also placed in the local church magazine, and calendars are given to customers.

The Italian fruit and vegetable market, which has been extremely successful since its establishment a few years ago, has recently installed a butcher of its own.

Fred Smith sells, in addition to meat, a selection of dry goods of the type likely to be bought by his English Canadian clientele.

Assignment

1. If you were advising a Greek friend with butchering experience on whether to purchase this business, what additional information would you first require?
2. What steps could your friend take to increase sales if he buys the business?

GEORGE ANDREWS LTD.
Improving the relations between manufacturer and retailers

George Andrews Ltd. is the Canadian subsidiary of a large U.S. sporting goods manufacturer. Products manufactured in the firm's Winnipeg plant include all types of equipment for sports ranging from hockey to tennis. Sales in Canada have increased steadily since the firm was put under new management in 1968, following its acquisition by the U.S. parent company.

Frank Beaton, the president of the Canadian subsidiary, has completed during the last three years, a number of organizational changes designed to tighten control over the production, financial, and marketing activities of the firm. The marketing department is now organized as in Figure 10.5.

The president is relatively satisfied with the job that George Bannoski, the vice-president, marketing, is doing in streamlining the firm's marketing network. This has included the development of centralized regional distribution centres with close inventory control and efficient order-filling and handling methods to replace the multitude of small district warehouses that existed previously. However, Beaton feels that relations between his firm and the small retailers who handle the firm's products are extremely poor. He has, in fact, received evidence of misunderstanding, bad feeling, and even distrust between the retailers and his firm. Their relations appear to have deteriorated even further with the regional centralization of warehouse facilities.

When asked by the president to pinpoint the causes of this poor manufacturer-retailer relationship, Bannoski explained that the following steps were always taken to avoid this situation. First, the salespeople were carefully selected. Second, they were thoroughly indoctrinated with the viewpoint that the retailer and the customer must at all costs be satisfied. Third, a generous markup was

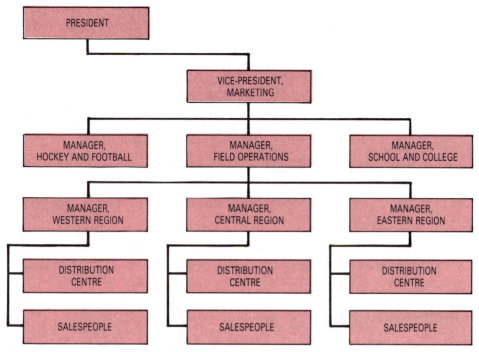

Figure 10.5 Organization of the Marketing Department

given to retailers on the goods sold. Fourth, a variety of promotional aids, including ad mats, layouts, radio and TV copy, window layouts, in-store promotion, and displays were made available to them. He then went on to suggest that there was little else that could be done and that retailers had always been critical of the manufacturer in the past and would probably always be in the future.

Beaton still felt, however, that something should be attempted to remedy the situation. Consequently, on the advice of a good friend who was the president of a large clothing firm, Beaton decided to create a new position in his firm's organization—a director of public relations. The firm's personnel director was given the task of securing and screening applicants for the job. With Beaton's approval, the following advertisement was placed in *The Winnipeg Tribune*.

Director of Public Relations

Large industrial organization, Winnipeg location, requires a director of public relations to promote and maintain good relations between the company and its customers.

The applicant should have a college or university education, several years' experience in public relations work, and will probably be a member of the Canadian Public Relations Society.

Salary open. Please submit complete resume in confidence to:
                              Box 3308

After interviewing several promising candidates, Beaton finally offered the job to John Parsons, the former owner and publisher of *The Rainham Herald*, a weekly newspaper recently purchased by Fairchild Newspapers Ltd., a major international newspaper chain.

John Parsons spent the first weeks at his new job trying to understand fully the public relations problem that faced the company. This involved talking to people at head office and to many people in the field, including salespeople and retailers. After two months, Parsons presented Beaton with a detailed analysis of the situation and recommendations for solving the problems that obviously existed.

The gist of the retailers' complaints was that George Andrews Ltd. was not doing enough to help them. For example, it was frequently mentioned that the change from local warehouses to regional distribution centres had had two bad effects. First, it took longer for the retailer to receive delivery of his or her order. Second, the salespeople were refusing to accept the small orders that the company was at one time only too pleased to get. This, as Parsons pointed out to Beaton, was a good example of how lack of communication bred mistrust and resentment. What no one had bothered to point out to the retailers was that the new warehouse system and minimum order requirements had enabled the company to avoid price increases over the last eighteen months. Also, the larger but less frequent shipments had enabled the company to reduce freight costs—a reduction which had been passed on to the retailer.

To improve permanently manufacturer-retailer relations, John Parsons made the following recommendations:

1. Set up a manufacturer's advisory board consisting of prominent retailers from each province, the president of the company, and the department heads for production, marketing, engineering, and finance. This board would meet at the company's head office in Winnipeg. The members would discuss problems of common interest and would recommend measures that would benefit the retailers, the manufacturer, and the consumers.
2. Give each retailer six weeks' prior notice of each meeting so he or she could send comments, queries or complaints to the retailer representing his or her area for possible discussion at the meeting.
3. Send each retailer a summary of the discussions and recommendations of the advisory board and of the measures that the company had agreed to take.
4. Send each retailer a list of the ways in which he or she can help improve manufacturer-retailer relations, for example, by paying bills more promptly and making better use of co-operative advertising.
5. Have the president visit trade meetings, shows, and conventions to obtain better contact with retailers and learn first-hand how effectively his policies are being implemented by the salespeople and other personnel.
6. Hold regional sales training meetings at which retailers or their leading sales personnel could discuss product lines in detail and the best methods of selling them to the public.

7. Supply better product literature to retailers, illustrating the product, its features, and its benefits to the consumer.
8. Provide more point-of-sale aids and demonstration devices.
9. Sponsor local TV sports shows.

When shown the report by Beaton, Bannoski, the marketing vice-president, condemned it as a waste of money. Also, privately, he was critical of the appointment of a public relations director in the first place.

Assignment

1. Discuss the company's situation and Parson's recommendations for improving it.

READINGS

Crisis of Identity

As specialty shops flourish, department stores must find new ways to profit

BY PATRICIA BEST
Source: *The Financial Post*

Pity the poor department store; its task is to be all things to all people at a time when pop psychology dictates to the consumer that a modern essential—individuality—can be provided only by a specialist. No wonder such stores are suffering an identity crisis.

Faced in recent years with aggressive competition from specialty shops and discount stores, department stores went on a binge of merchandising, marketing and advertising innovations. At the same time, they finally reassessed their operating costs. This self-analysis, industry executives say, has resulted in a rejuvenated, more competitive department store.

Retailing industry analysts do not necessarily agree. During the past two or three years, specialty chains have chipped away at department stores' share of the retail market.

Now the stores are in a quandary. The traditional method of increasing market share is through store expansion, but the era of big expansion programs is over, mainly because of high costs and saturated markets.

Statistics Canada estimates department stores will be able to hold 10%-12% of the retail market into the 1980s, about the same as in the late 1970s.

Mature Industry

"Department stores are a mature industry," Martin Kaufman, an analyst with Nesbitt Thomson Bongard, Montreal, says. "The high cost of living will continue to squeeze take-home pay, so department stores can look for good, consistent growth, but not huge increases."

Another retail analyst comments: "Generally speaking, but particularly in clothing, department stores have to come up with a new formula to stabilize or gain back market share."

Specialty stores stand to gain even more of the retail dollar if they heed the marketing experts—success will depend on how well they fine-tune their image and merchandise to meet the needs of specific customer lifestyles. As one U.S. advertising executive recently told a group of specialty retailers, the "me generation" requires altered marketing strategies.

"It used to be that successful marketing was having the right product at the right price. Now it's having the right product at the right price with the right image."

With a steady erosion of gross margins in recent years, department stores have become more competitive and more promotional in their merchandising. Gross margins have enabled them to stay ahead of rising operating costs—such as wages, which have risen as a percentage of sales—but gross margins are no longer an avenue for increasing profits.

The way to increase margins seems more and more to be in the product mix. The fashion lines yield higher margins and the Bay stores merchandise is now about 50% soft goods. It's a good bet this area will become even more competitive.

"The strategy is to become fairly dominant in apparel but still operate on a full-line basis," according to Albert Guglielmin, the Bay's general manager for department stores. "The emphasis is definitely shifting toward apparel, accessories and shoes. We're looking at a good rate of growth in 1979, and we're optimistic about the 1980s."

But Frank Robertson, senior vice-president of merchandising, Woodwards Stores Ltd., says department stores can't afford to be wrong in this area. "You've got to watch the markups because there's always somebody there to move in under you."

Robertson has to be a hands down winner of the most bullish retailer award. The bright outlook may be because of Woodwards' operating area, Alberta and British Columbia, where retail business is booming.

"I look forward to the 1980s the same way as the 1960s; it was a great decade, and the decade of the 1980s could be the greatest decade Canadians have ever seen."

Analysts expect the rate of department store sales growth to slow from last year's 10.4%; Kaufman puts the rate at 9.5% and, because of inclement spring weather and slower growth, he says the profit picture is not encouraging for department stores.

"If retailers are left with inventory, markdowns will impinge on profits. They have to minimize inventory markdowns without trying to rock the boat, without becoming too competitive."

Growth for department stores into the 1980s will have to come through improved productivity rather than physical expansion. In a recent study of department stores, Statistics Canada notes "suitable and sustained profit margins" are still to come. "Retrenchment, at least over the near term, is a distinct possibility."

All major chains are planning new stores, but there will be fewer of them.

"We will continue to open retail stores, though not as many as in the early 1970s," Richard Sharpe, chairman of Simpsons-Sears Ltd., says. "We'll experiment with smaller stores in smaller cities and satellite stores in big metropolitan centres."

Over the long term, analysts look for a recovery of margins:

"The longer term looks pretty good because of a general economic upturn," one says. "Department stores are more efficient and more conscious of the need to maximize profit; they're more cautious in their buying and they've eliminated those departments that had outlived their usefulness."

Retailers are well aware of the fact shoppers have never been more value-conscious.

"Consumerism has been good for customers: it taught them how to shop," one department store executive says. "It's been good for retailers: it taught them to smarten up. A tough marketplace has made better retailers."

The biggest threat by far to the stores' well-being continues to be the specialty shops, although Fredrik Eaton, president of T. Eaton Co., sees a mutual need.

"For many years people have been calling for the demise of the department store. In spite of all their predictions, it has certainly not come true. You couldn't build a shopping centre without a department store. So it's a strong and vigorous business."

But the era of the big regional shopping centre may be coming to a close. As one retail analyst points out: "The cost to build a regional centre is absolutely phenomenal; they've pretty well saturated the market. The way the department stores are responding to specialty stores, specialty stores will continue to increase market share."

Department store expansion may come full cycle: back to the downtown cores, spurred by recent successes such as Toronto's Eaton Centre.

The department stores' fling with specialty boutiques within their stores appears to be waning.

"The problem is the department stores don't have the expertise of the specialty stores," one retail analyst says. "What a lot of people want is advice, particularly in technical areas. Food, who cares; but it matters when you are buying a hi-fi set."

Although Woodwards operates furniture stores and a book shop chain, Robertson says his company is committed to the concept of a full-line department store.

"I know we can't be everything to everybody, but basically we try to serve as many as we can." It's a sentiment echoed in other department store companies.

Robertson illustrates the difficulty the stores had with "boutiquing."

"It's fine as long as you don't pay lip service to it. You have to have the product and the service. Believability is essential; you've got to do it right."

The Old Ways

Although boutiques within department stores have worked well in fashion lines, the stores found it wasn't just a matter of dividing up the floor space. As a consequence, for many it's back to the old system.

Perhaps the most promising area for department stores, and one in which profit margins can be improved, is nonmerchandising.

The Bay is going for what it calls customer-related service in a big way. Already it provides financial services, dry cleaning, in-home cleaning and car rentals. But, Guglielmin says, it won't stop there.

With references to dental outlets in Sears stores in California and law offices operating in another U.S. department store chain, he adds "These are things we're looking at, although we haven't got anything definite. We're trying to make our major downtown stores a one-stop shopping centre."

The Bay isn't alone.

Assignment

1. "Department stores are a mature industry." Explain and discuss.
2. How have they tried to remain successful? What is their marketing strategy?
3. Explain the relationship between consumerism and the popularity of specialty stores.
4. "The era of the big shopping centre may be coming to a close." Why? Discuss.
5. How should the department stores compete with the specialty stores?
6. Can the department store make a comeback in the downtown area?
7. "Perhaps the most promising area for department stores is non-merchandising." Explain, with examples, and discuss.

The Deli Way

BY GARY WEISS

Source: *The Financial Post.* Used by permission of Gary Weiss.

Shopping centres are where the action is, says fast-food entrepreneur Bruce Druxerman.

He should know. Since plunging into business for himself two and a half years ago as Druxy's Inc., he's created a flourishing chain of eight fast-food outlets with projected sales this year of $3 million.

All the outlets are in major Toronto shopping centres. And in each centre they're in, they lead all similar businesses in sales per square foot. When five more are added this year, including one in the super-chic Holt Renfrew development, Druxy's should hit $6-million in sales next year, Druxerman predicts.

Closet-sized

Surprisingly, this volume is all done from outlets not much larger than the storage closets in most restaurants. Altogether, Druxy's eight units cover only 4,150 square feet, about the size of a single freestanding family restaurant; most are a cupboardsize 500 square feet. But there's nothing small about sales which average $1,000 a square foot per year. Druxy's Famous Deli in Eaton Centre rings up nearly $1,500 a square foot on average sales of only $1.25 each.

The trick is that all Druxy's units are in "food clusters"—groupings of fast-food outlets around a common open area. The retailers supply the food: the landlord supplies the seating and cleaning staff. Fast-food clusters have become popular with Canadian centre developers since the first one, Gourmet Fair, opened in Sherway Gardens, Toronto, in 1971.

As developers see it, fast-food clusters solve the problem of shoppers lingering too long over their meal. Or worse still, coming to a centre just for the food.

For savvy food merchants, the concept opens up the possibility of instant sales with lower fixturing costs than in a conventional restaurant. Furthermore, since major franchise chains avoid food clusters for fear of losing their identity, the field has been open for independents.

For Druxerman, who had been looking for a way to break away from his family business in Winnipeg, shopping centres were a natural. "I was looking for traffic and I didn't want to do a lot of advertising," he says.

Despite a background in restaurants—with his family and later with a Montreal chain—Druxerman says food experience isn't important. "My background is commerce, banking. I consider myself an administrator. In picking new locations, for instance, I need the ability to see the market and the expenses."

Food, he says, isn't really as important as "food concepts." People are always looking for a fast bite. The secret, he says, is catching them with eye appeal. At Druxy's, that means nothing comes out of a chute, prepackaged. All cooking, all sandwichmaking, is done right in front of the customers and all foods are used on the day they're delivered.

The units themselves are spotless—and expensive. Opening costs run up to $160 a square foot, plus shopping centres percentage rents of $6^{1}/_{2}\%$-8% of gross revenues. But the improved turnover and lower staffing costs associated with food clusters more than balance out.

In contrast to most small businesses, financing has probably been the easiest part. Aside from an initial $150,000 in equity, Druxy's has been financed through cash flow and up to $1 million in demand-loan credit, at only $3/4$% over prime.

Why such faith by bankers? Druxerman's eyebrows lift, a friendly finger taps your arm and he confides that his grandmother was the sister of Sam Bronfman. "It opens a lot of doors. It's a good feeling. A secure feeling. It's like insurance."

Assignment

1. What are "fast-food clusters"?
2. For whom do they spell good business? Why?
3. How has Bruce Druxerman taken advantage of this business opportunity? What are his business strengths?
4. Food isn't as important as "food concepts." Explain.
5. Explain and discuss the economics of a fast-food cluster outlet.

Pizza with Pizzazz

Mother's is doing well, marketing atmosphere as well as Italian food

BY DEBORAH DOWLING

Source: *The Financial Post*

While McDonald's, Burger King and Wendy's have been locked in a hamburger battle for the past two years, a skirmish of a different sort has been brewing.

Mother's Pizza Parlours Ltd., the Hamilton, Ont. based chain of 36 "family" restaurants, is doubling its expansion. It plans 14 new stores this year and 18 in 1980 and is also heading into new territories in Manitoba, British Columbia and Washington, D.C.

Also on the growth track is Frank Vetere's Pizzeria & Tavern, another limited-menu Italian food chain of 29 stores owned by Foodex Inc., Toronto. Its ambitious store-opening program, which launched 22 new restaurants last year, calls for a minimum of 15 stores a year in the near term, with possible growth outside Ontario and south of the border.

Different Strokes

Could a pizza war be in the making? Not exactly, says the management of the two non-franchised operations.

"We have different products," says Frank Vetere, executive vice-president of the Foodex group, with restaurant sales (Frank Vetere and Ponderosa Steak House) of $63 million in 1978. "We have a deep-dish pizza, while Mother's is thin like cardboard."

Grey Sisson, the affable president of the privately owned Mother's chain (this year's projected sales, $41 million) agrees, but not with the imagery. "There is a market for the deep-dish pizza, but we are feeling very comfortable with the niche Mother's has carved out for itself."

Although the nine-year-old Mother's chain is the larger of the two, it has generally kept a lower profile.

Over a "grandmother's" pizza and Coke float in the antique "circus room" of a new Brampton, Ont., store, Sisson gestures to typical Mother's customers who may visit the establishment twice a week. Seated around an oil-cloth-covered table beneath a Tiffany lamp is a family of four—the children up to their elbows in pizza while

Mom and Dad eat lasagna and garlic bread, accompanied by a glass of wine and mug of beer.

"Our target market is people aged 18-34 and families with children who we consider to be future pizza customers once they outgrow McDonald's," Sisson says. He doesn't consider Mother's to be a fast-food operation—it takes 12-15 minutes to cook a fresh pizza—but he thinks the concept is the way of the future for the food-away-from-home industry.

"There is a trend among hamburger chains to lessen their dependence on beef, expand their menus and provide more atmosphere," he says. "At the other end of the scale, haute cuisine is trading down in both selection and price. Mother's and operations like Swiss Chalet are right in the middle with a medium-priced, limited menu, alcoholic beverages and pleasant surroundings."

Mother's features an all-you-can-eat salad bar, pizza and pasta dishes and submarines. (Some ingredients are prepared in Hamilton and delivered to Mother's stores two or three times a week.) Because of a growing trade in businessmen's lunches, a meat entree may be introduced this fall.

Mother's was among the first of the new generation of theme restaurants in Ontario. All stores are decorated by Mother's Antique Warehouse, a separately owned business which collects and refinishes antiques. The concept was developed by Sisson, formerly with A & W franchise-holder Controlled Foods Ltd., and two partners: Ken Fowler, a major shareholder in Controlled Foods, and Pat Marra, owner of a take-out-pizza outlet in St. Catharines, Ont.

Key to Success

In 1970, the partners launched two businesses—a self-serve Mother's operation and a take-out pizza business called Pasquales—but in 1971 they decided to concentrate on Mother's. Etcetera Advertising, Niagara-on-the-Lake, helped launch the idea and Vancouver consultant Paul Smith, formerly of Etcetera, still creates Mother's annual marketing and promotion programs which have been credited as keys to Mother's success.

If Mother's had franchised its concept, the operation would probably be a lot larger than it is now and have a greater presence than three stores in the Toronto area. Because policy is to own land wherever possible, new restaurants require a $1-million investment and are expected to be free of debt within two to four years. A partnership program, however, has been instituted to help aid expansion and motivate employees. Mother's has also entered a series of joint ventures with investors in Columbus, Ohio, and Calgary.

In the partnership program, the investment company, Mother's Pizza Parlours Ltd., buys 50% of the shares in each new corporation (equal to 50% or $125,000-$150,000 of the startup costs excluding land) while the partner/manager puts up 20%. In return, the partner receives a salary and dividends are retained until the loan is paid off.

The supervisor of the new store can invest 10% while two partners in other stores are given the opportunity for a cash investment equal to the remaining 10%. As well, veteran partners can contribute a percentage of their earnings to Mother's Realty Corp. which acquires real estate.

Assignment

1. What form of business ownership do Mother's and Frank Vetere's have?
2. What is their target market? How does it differ, if at all, from that of McDonald's?
3. How would you rate the products? Do you agree with Frank Vetere's statement: "We have different products. We have a deep-dish pizza, while Mother's is thin like cardboard."
4. What is a "theme restaurant"? Give examples.
5. Would it have made better business sense to have franchised the Mother's and Frank Vetere's operations, just as McDonald's has done?
6. Explain Mother's "partnership program."
7. What motivation exists for Mother's employees, apart from wages?

CHAPTER 11
SALES PROMOTION

CHAPTER OBJECTIVES

☐ To explain what is meant by sales promotion and how a firm determines its promotional program.

☐ To explain the nature and purpose of advertising.

☐ To explain how advertising media are chosen and how an advertisement is prepared.

☐ To explain what is involved in selling.

CHAPTER OUTLINE

11.1 The Promotional Program
11.2 Advertising
11.3 Selling

UNIT 11.1: THE PROMOTIONAL PROGRAM

Sales promotion is the name given to the marketing activities that a firm undertakes to persuade consumers to buy its goods or services. The most important of these are advertising and selling, discussed in the next two Units, respectively.

Sales promotion also includes any activity—such as the arrangement of sales contests, samples, and premiums—designed to supplement advertising and selling in promoting the sale of goods and services.

Two other terms closely associated with promotion should be mentioned. *Public relations* is the art of cultivating a good public image for a company and for its products. This is achieved partly by advertising, but also by means of community service, good employee practices, good products, and good customer treatment. *Publicity* is the making public of information about the company. Unlike advertising, publicity is not always paid for by the company. An unsolicited newspaper or magazine article may be published which may reflect favourably or unfavourably on the company or its products.

Promotional Blend

In promoting the sale of its products, a company will use a combination of advertising, personal selling, and other sales promotion activities. Thus a firm's promotional program this year might consist of a new company symbol, a 20 per cent increase in its radio and television budget, a 30 per cent increase in the number of its salespeople, and a nation-wide sales contest.

Factors Involved. The promotion blend which a company adopts is an intelligent guess as to the most economical way of achieving a set promotion target—for example, to introduce a new household detergent in a particular area. This guess must take into account the following factors:

1. *The amount of money to be spent.* For example, a small retail store may have to restrict itself to handbills and personal selling in the store, even though it would like to use radio and television and other more expensive forms of sales promotion.
2. *The stage which a product has reached in its life cycle.* In the *introduction* stage, the primary purpose of promotion is to inform consumers about the product. In the *market growth* stage, when competition becomes keen, promotion must be aimed at encouraging brand loyalty. In the *market maturity* stage, product differentiation becomes important. This means creating a belief that a product is different from that of competitors even though it may be the same or almost the same. In the *sales decline* stage, special promotional efforts are required—for example, concentration on the best markets.
3. *The type of consumer, user, or middleman at which the promotion is aimed.* Thus a manufacturer of breakfast cereal (sold predominantly in self-service stores) may concentrate its promotion spending on advertising. Man-

ufacturers wishing to inform wholesalers about their products find they can best achieve this by personal selling.

4. *The nature of the product.* If the product is highly technical, its promotion may have to be of an informational nature. If the product is very similar to others, promotion may concentrate on making it seem different from others—for example, by brand advertising.

Pull and Push Promotional Strategies

On analysis of these factors, a business firm may decide that it should spend most of its money in promoting a demand for the product by consumers, perhaps through radio and television advertising. This demand would then be sufficient to encourage wholesalers and retailers to stock the product. Thus consumer demand would *pull* the product through the distribution channel. The firm may, however, decide that its money would be better spent in promoting the product by personal selling to the wholesalers and other middlemen, who will in time persuade customers to buy it. This is called a *push* strategy. Most promotional programs are usually a combination of both *pull* and *push*.

Other Sales Promotion Activities

Other sales promotion activities include any activity designed to assist personal selling and advertising in promoting the sale of goods and services. The most important of these are the offer of premiums, samples, and cents off; the use of contests and salesperson's aids; and the provision of customer services such as credit, delivery, installation, repair, and replacement.

Credit. Perhaps the single most effective sales promotion tool, after advertising and selling, is the provision of credit. This enables people to buy goods and services on the promise to pay all or part of the price later. Each year in Canada billions of dollars worth of goods and services are bought on credit, involving retail credit cards such as Visa, Master Charge, American Express, and those issued by the major department stores and oil companies, and the 30 days standard credit terms offered by most business firms to their clients. Often, in export contracts, credit is the factor that makes or loses the sale.

Product Warranties. The quality of a product is often difficult to determine, particularly in the case of appliances and other mechanical products such as automobiles. Consequently, the existence of a warranty, the manufacturer's written undertaking to repair or replace the product completely or partly free of charge, can greatly influence a person's decision whether to buy or not.

Special Sales. At the retail level, "sales" are held periodically involving a temporary reduction in the prices of some or all of the goods stocked, to encourage the public to come to the store and buy. In some cases, they are used as a means to clear surplus inventory from the previous season at a substantially reduced gross profit margin for the retailer. In others, involving major retailers, they are passing on to customers part of the cost benefit of bulk purchases. And yet in others, they are genuine reductions, small or large, designed to promote sales in a slow period, to maintain a "go-ahead" image for the firm, or just to keep up with the competition. Occasionally, to the customer's woe, the sale price may be the same or higher than the normal price.

Coupons. Many manufacturers of grocery products now distribute, through marketing agencies, coupons that the public may use at their local supermarket to obtain a reduction in the price of the product. Coupons are used as a means to encourage a person to try a firm's product for the first time as well as to encourage him or her to continue buying it. The coupons are often included in the package, imprinted on the container ready to be cut out, or placed in a newspaper ad. In some areas, they are distributed door-to-door in special coupon envelopes.

Specials. Supermarkets now traditionally offer weekly "specials" to the public. These products are offered for the week at a specially low price in order to encourage a person to do his or her major weekly shopping at the store.

Premiums. A *premium* is something of value which is given as a bonus to the purchaser of a good or service. It may be included in the package, sent to the purchaser in exchange for a box top, wrapper, or label, usually with a certain sum of money; given in the form of a coupon which can be used as part of the purchase price of a specific product; or given in the form of trading stamps, which are collected and exchanged for goods listed in a catalogue.

Premiums can be used to increase the sales of a product and to increase store traffic generally. They can be used for specific market areas or for the market as a whole.

Samples. A *sample* is a product which is given to a prospective customer to try out. The expectation is that the person will be favourably impressed by the sample and will in future buy the product. A slightly different form of sampling is the offer of a product to a customer for a trial period—for example, books which may be bought on a 10-day approval or return basis.

Contests. Contests, with prizes of cash, goods, paid vacations, and so on, are another form of sales promotion. They can be used to encourage personal selling by dealers and salespeople—for example, a Bermuda holiday for two for the year's most successful salesperson—or to stimulate purchases by consumers who may take part in a contest because of a purchase or because of their presence in a store, mall, exhibition, etc.

Sales Aids. Sales manuals, sales portfolios, reprints of advertisements, and information letters all serve to keep the salespeople better informed about the firm's products, the firm's customers, and the firm's competitors. A *sales manual* is a handy reference book containing technical data about the product, and information about the company and its policies. A *sales portfolio* is a collection of illustrations—for example, photos of the product being used in various ways—which the salesperson can show the prospective customer to supplement the oral sales presentation.

Customer Services. Delivery of the item purchased (e.g., furniture) may be made free of charge or for a nominal amount. For goods of a cumbersome, dangerous, or highly technical nature, free installation by the seller often helps to promote sales.

After-Sales Service. Once a sale has been made, an extremely important promotion activity for future sales is to ensure, as much as possible, that the customer remains satisfied with the product. This can take the form of follow-up calls by the salesperson involved in the initial sale, the efficient and courteous handling of complaints and disputes, and help with related problems—e.g., helping the buyer of a new home with advice about service personnel, community facilities, etc. Good after-sales service can mean both repeat business from the same customer and free word-of-mouth advertising to the customer's friends, relatives, and acquaintances.

KEY TERMS

Sales promotion	Sales
Public relations	Coupons
Publicity	Specials
Promotional program	Premiums
Promotion blend	Samples
Product life-cycle	Contests
Pull strategy	Sales aids
Push strategy	Customer services
Credit	After-sales service
Product Warranties	

REVIEW QUESTIONS

1. What are the various forms of sales promotion? What is their purpose? Do they always succeed? If not, why not?
2. Explain the term "public relations." How important is it for a business firm?
3. Explain, with examples, how publicity can be both good and bad for a firm.

4. What factors does a firm take into account in determining its promotional program?
5. Explain the concept of "product life-cycle" and its relevance to a firm's sales promotion efforts.
6. Distinguish, with examples, between pull and push promotional strategies.
7. What other types of sales promotion activity can supplement a firm's advertising and selling efforts?
8. For most business firms, credit can be a "two-edged sword." Explain and comment.
9. "Sales" as a sales promotion device have begun to lose their effectiveness in Canada. Comment.
10. Coupons are considered by most shoppers too time-consuming to be effective as a sales promotion device. Discuss.
11. The salesperson's job finishes once the product has been sold. Discuss.

PROJECT

TROPICAL PRODUCTS LTD.
Promoting the sale of an unfamiliar product

A sales promotion campaign is planned to introduce unfamiliar tropical fruits and vegetables to the Canadian public.

As part of this campaign, the advertising agency for which you work has been asked to prepare an easy-to-read leaflet, for in-store distribution to customers, containing useful information about the product.

The products to be promoted initially are: avocado, papaya, and mango.

Assignment
1. Prepare a suitable leaflet for one of these products.
2. Who would be willing to pay for such a campaign?
3. How should your leaflet be distributed?
4. What else should be done to promote the product?

UNIT 11.2: ADVERTISING

Strictly defined, *advertising* is the paid presentation of ideas, goods, or services to customers in a non-personal way—for example, through newspapers, radio, or television—by an identified sponsor. *Sponsor* is the term used to describe the firm that pays for the advertisement. In practice, particularly for the small business, one of the most rewarding types of advertising can be quite free—namely, word-of-mouth advertising.

Kinds of Advertising

There are many different classifications of advertising. Four of the most meaningful are by type of audience, type of appeal, advertising purpose, and area covered.

Type of Audience. *Consumer advertising* is advertising directed at consumers; *industrial advertising* is advertising directed at industrial buyers; and *trade advertising* is advertising directed at the various middlemen (wholesalers or retailers).

Type of Appeal. A great deal of advertising may be termed *emotional advertising*. This is because the message that the advertisement carries plays on one or more of a person's emotions in order to persuade him or her to buy the product. These emotions include positive ones such as the desire to be personally attractive, pride of ownership, comfort, ease, entertainment, and excitement; and negative ones such as fear, greed, and insecurity. A house ad, for example, may appeal to a person's desire for financial security, comfort, and pride of ownership; a deodorant ad may appeal to a person's desire to be personally attractive and to his or her sense of personal insecurity. Some advertising may be termed *rational advertising* because it appeals to a person's reason rather than emotions. Examples would be advertisements that explain why a particular product is more economical, more healthy, or better value for one. This type of advertising is often used in connection with industrial and government buyers.

Advertising Purpose. *Product advertising* is advertising which attempts to persuade people to buy a product. *Institutional advertising* is advertising which attempts to promote recognition of, and goodwill towards, a firm or industry.

Area Covered. *National advertising* is advertising across the country, both in the advertiser's own community and in areas outside. *Local advertising* is advertising in and around the advertiser's own community.

Other Kinds. The term *informative advertising* is used to describe advertisements that restrict themselves mainly to the provision of information about a product or service or, for example, the uses to which a product may be put or the nature and availability of a government service. *Repetitive advertising* refers to advertisements, often on television, that are repeated over and over again, within a relatively short period of time, to familiarize the public with, or remind them of, a particular brand name. *Celebrity* or *endorsement advertising* refers to advertisements, often on TV, that feature a well-known movie or sports celebrity, using and recommending a product.

Purposes of Advertising

The purposes for which advertising is used are: to introduce a new product or service to consumers; to persuade consumers to buy a product for the first time; to persuade customers to continue to buy a product; or to persuade them to buy more of a product—for example, by using it more frequently or for more purposes; to help salespeople in their personal selling task by familiarizing consumers or users with the name of the company, the name of the product, and the merits of the product; and to promote goodwill for the company among the public and consumers.

Advertising Media

An *advertising medium* is the vehicle which carries an advertising message to its intended audience. The most important media are:

Newspapers
Magazines
Radio
Television
Direct mail
Outdoor advertising
Transportation advertising
Specialty advertising
Point-of-purchase advertising
Package advertising
Word-of-mouth advertising

Newspapers. These are of several kinds: dailies, weeklies, weekend supplements, and shopping news. Also, in Canada there are many foreign language publications directed at the various ethnic groups.

Newspapers, as an advertising medium, have the following characteristics:
1. They are read by a large, relatively varied percentage of the population. Some discrimination as to the type of reader can, however, be made by choosing the type of newspaper and by choosing the position of the advertisement in the newspaper—for example, the sports section.
2. They permit a high degree of geographical selection, since most newspapers are local or regional in circulation.
3. The cost is usually lower than for radio or television advertising, particularly for purely local coverage.
4. The advertisements can be altered quickly and at relatively little expense.
5. Limited use of colour is possible.
6. Flyers or brochures (called inserts) may be delivered within the folds of the newspaper.
7. They can carry a relatively detailed message about product, if desired.

Magazines. The following features are characteristic of magazines as an advertising medium:
1. They are published less frequently then newspapers—for example, weekly or monthly rather than daily.
2. They enable advertisers to direct their message at more specific audiences—for example, to fishermen, hunters, or boating enthusiasts.
3. They are usually national rather than local. Sometimes, however, regional editions permit advertising to be directed at a particular area.
4. They are less flexible than newspapers since advertisements must be submitted several weeks ahead of publication.
5. They remain in use longer than newspapers.
6. They permit the use of colour in the advertisement.
7. They can carry a detailed message that radio and TV cannot.
8. The cost is set per thousand of circulation.
9. The advertiser is given a circulation guarantee: that a minimum number of copies will be printed and distributed.

Radio. This possesses the following characteristics:
1. The advertisement can be heard, but not seen, by the audience.
2. By choosing different times of day and different types of programs in which to insert the advertisements, advertisers can direct their message at specific types of persons—for example, garden fertilizers towards gardeners in Gardening Hour.
3. By choosing different radio stations, advertisers can select the geographical area in which their message can be heard. This can be local, regional, or (through a network hookup) national.
4. Advertisements can be changed on short notice.
5. The cost varies according to the estimated size of the listener audience and the time of the day at which the advertisement is to be broadcast.

Television. This has the following characteristics:
1. It can be both seen and heard by the audience.
2. The advertising message can be directed at specific audiences by choosing the type of program and the time of day.
3. The message can be directed at audiences in particular geographical areas by using local television stations.
4. Television is not as flexible as radio or newspapers, as films take longer to prepare and alter.
5. With the use of colour television, the advertising message can be made more attractive in appearance than is possible with only black and white.
6. The medium is not suitable for detailed messages.
7. Time is sold in units of one minute or less, the cost varying according to station and program popularity and the time of day at which it is to be shown.

Direct Mail. This includes the use of letters, postcards, catalogues, and folders to convey the advertising message to an audience. Mailing lists are made up from such sources as telephone directories, voters' lists, and industry publications.

The chief characterists of direct mail are:
1. A reasonable degree of selectivity as to the type of prospective consumer to which the message is mailed. This depends, of course, on the care with which the mailing list is compiled.
2. Any geographical coverage desired.
3. A high wastage rate—many prospective consumers do not bother to read such mail.
4. The cost includes preparation of the message, the paper, printing, envelopes, and postage. Many advertisers have switched from the post office to private delivery service because of increased postal rates, strikes, and unreliability of service.

Outdoor Advertising. This refers to advertising on poster panels (billboards), on painted displays (usually called bulletins) and on large, electrically lighted displays that are located on well-travelled highways.

The chief characteristics of the outdoor advertising medium are:
1. Outdoor advertising is directed mainly at vehicular traffic but in busy downtown areas pedestrians are also exposed to it.
2. The advertising message must be brief and the graphics bold and quickly visible to the moving motorist.
3. Advertisers may select the markets they wish to cover (there are some 161 poster markets in Canada) and they may select market areas within a city if their products are sold locally in that market, or in close proximity to supermarkets, drug stores, gas stations, etc.
4. Poster showings are generally bought on a monthly basis.
5. Cost is determined according to a special formula that takes into account outdoor reach (i.e., percentage of population exposed to advertisement in a given period of time) and frequency (the number of poster panels carrying the advertisement).

Transportation Advertising. Car cards are used on the interior of subway trains, streetcars, buses, taxis, and railway passenger trains to carry advertisements. Busboards are used on the sides and rear of buses. The audience is restricted to persons who use or see these means of transportation.

Specialty Advertising. This advertising medium consists of such items as calendars, matchbooks, memorandum pads, blotters, and ball-point pens. They carry the name and usually the product or service of the advertiser and are given away free to prospective customers. Because of their frequent use, they constantly remind the customer or prospective customer of the advertiser and its products. These items can be given to any type of prospective customer in the geographical area chosen. They are also useful aids in personal selling.

Point-of-Purchase Display. This advertising consists of window displays, counter displays, wall displays, floor displays, and special door signs. These are located in the store and serve to attract the customer's attention to particular items. Window displays and door signals also help attract the prospective customer into the store. Display material is often provided by the manufacturer of the various products.

Package Advertising. Manufacturers try to make consumer products as eye-catching and eye-appealing as possible by attractive packaging. Also, retailers use shopping bags and boxes to advertise their name and services.

Word-of-Mouth Advertising. This is the recommendation of products or services of a firm by a satisfied customer to relatives and friends. As this is not a paid form of presentation, it does not fall within the customary definition of advertising mentioned earlier. However, word-of-mouth advertising is extremely important for most firms.

Choice of Advertising Media

An advertising campaign requires the use of one or more advertising media to carry the advertising message to its intended audience. The factors which help determine the choice of media are:

1. *The purpose of the advertising campaign.* This might be to announce a sale at a store in a local area; to promote a good public image for a company on a national scale; or to persuade domestic consumers to try a new household detergent.
2. *The size, location, and nature of the intended audience.* The advertising might be aimed at, for example, the young adult male population of Winnipeg, tobacco farmers in Southern Ontario, or house builders in Western Canada.
3. *The money available.* Costs of the different media vary and the best advertising mix for the money must be obtained. For small local advertisers, local newspapers may be the only financially feasible media.
4. *The ability of a medium to reach the intended market audience.* Leather users, for example, can be reached most effectively in a trade journal.
5. *The ability of the medium to reach the intended audience in a particular geographical area.* A local consumer may be reached most effectively by local newspaper of radio.
6. *The cost of each medium in relation to the size of the audience reached.* Television advertising is usually more expensive than radio, for instance.
7. *The ease with which a business can change its advertisement if necessary.* For a firm wishing to keep ahead of competitors, price changes (for example, for supermarket "specials") may be necessary at the last moment.

Circulation

Reliable information as to the circulation of newspapers, magazines, business papers, and farm papers is provided by the Audit Bureau of Circulations. A similar service for radio and television audiences is provided by the Bureau of Broadcast Measurement.

Preparing Advertisements

Most small firms prepare their own newspaper and radio advertisements, sometimes drawing on the assistance of newspaper advertising managers and sometimes using ideas contained in previously published advertisements (by themselves and others). Larger firms may have an advertising specialist or department of their own to prepare advertisements, or they may use the services of an outside advertising specialist, the advertising agency.

An advertisement, to be successful, should contain an objective, a theme, good copy, good illustration, and good layout, and be carried by the correct medium or media.

The *objective* of the advertisement should be specific—for example, "to increase sales through retail outlets by 20 per cent over the next six months," rather than "to promote sales of our product."

The *theme* is the type of appeal, emotional or rational, which is made by the advertisement to its audience. To avoid confusing the audience, the number of themes used in any one advertisement should be limited.

The *copy* is the written or spoken message in an advertisement. To attract the attention of the audience, it should be simple, concise, and clear. To convince the audience to do something—for example, to try a new product—the message should appeal to their reason or desires, should inspire confidence, and should instruct them what to do. The medium to be used for the advertisement will have an important effect on the way in which the copy is written.

The *illustration* is the form of visual presentation to be used. It involves consideration of photography, art work, colour, dramatics, and so on, according to the type of product or service to be advertised and the medium to be employed.

The *layout* is the arrangement of the various parts of the advertisement—headlines, illustrations, colour, and text—into a unified whole. The final advertisement is normally the end result of a series of layouts, each of which is more detailed than the preceding one. The actual layout will depend not only on the type of product being advertised and the market at which it is aimed, but also on the advertising medium being used. The layout of an advertisement for a newspaper can use only words, different types of lettering, simple illustrations, and white space to attract the reader's attention and hold his or her interest. It cannot use sound or animation; and colour is very expensive.

The Advertising Agency

An *advertising agency* is a business firm that specializes in preparing advertisements and placing them in appropriate media for client firms. The services which the agency performs include planning, market research, copy writing, art work, layout creation, choosing media, contracting for media, arranging talent for radio and television advertisements, and verifying the actual showing and accuracy of advertisements.

Organization. An advertising agency is organized either on a departmental basis or on a group basis. In a *departmental type* of organization, the agency has departments for each of the main activities—account management, creative services, media selection, mechanical production, and so on—and these departments serve all the clients of the firm. An example of this type of agency organization is shown in Figure 11.1.

With the *group type* of organization, the agency has for each large account, or for each few accounts, a separate group of employees. Each group consists usually of copy writers, artists, account executives, and traffic people, and specializes in the needs of its particular clients. Available to assist the groups, there are centralized departments such as research, media, radio and television production, and mechanical production. The group type of organization is economically possible only where the advertising agency is very large.

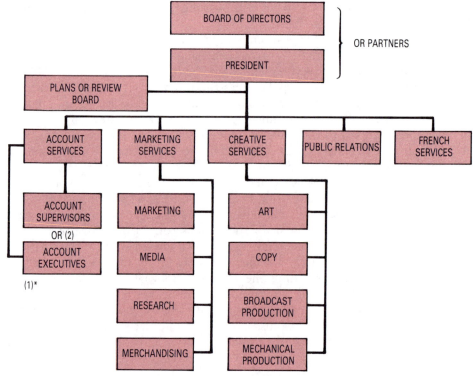

*SOMETIMES THE ACCOUNT EXECUTIVES REPORT DIRECTLY TO THE PRESIDENT

Figure 11.1 Departmental-Type Organization of an Advertising Agency

Staff. This includes among its ranks a variety of specialists.

Account executives are persons appointed to take care of the particular advertising needs of the agency's *clients* (or *accounts*). Unless the client is a major one, an account executive will be responsible for several accounts at the same time. He or she must become intimately acquainted with the products and business philosophy of the advertiser and will draw on the agency's various resources, as required, to help plan, prepare, and carry out the client's advertising program.

Copywriters prepare the text for printed advertisements and for radio and television commercials.

The *artists* prepare visual presentations of the idea or theme underlying the advertisement—for example, a richly furnished room to convey the theme of a high-quality product.

The *layout experts* suggest the most pleasing combination of copy and illustration. Once the layout is approved, the agency's *production department* is responsible for ensuring that production of the advertisement is of the standard required. For a printed advertisement this will mean choosing competent printers and engravers and selecting paper, reproduction processes, type, and inks.

The *media director* (or *space buyer*) gives advice to the agency's clients as to the most appropriate media to employ and arranges to purchase space or time.

Where an agency has its own market research department, *research director* is the title usually given to the person in charge.

The Advertising Department

In a small firm, advertising may be one of the responsibilities of the general manager. In a larger firm, with greater advertising expenditure, the task of arranging suitable advertisements becomes more important. Advertising may then become one of the most important duties or even the full-time duty of one person alone. In very large firms, where many thousands of dollars may be spent on advertising each year, a separate department is made responsible for administering the company's advertising budget. The advertising department may prepare and place the company's advertisements in the various media. More usually, it will employ the services of an advertising agency. The advertising department will also be responsible for preparing exhibits for trade shows and conventions, product catalogues and brochures, and visual sales aids.

KEY TERMS

Advertising	Radio
Consumer advertising	Television
Industrial advertising	Direct mail
Trade advertising	Outdoor advertising
Emotional advertising	Transportation advertising
Rational advertising	Specialty advertising
Product advertising	Point-of-purchase advertising
Institutional advertising	Package advertising
National advertising	Word-of-mouth advertising
Local advertising	Circulation
Informative advertising	Advertising agency
Repetitive advertising	Account executive
Celebrity advertising	Copywriter
Advertising media	Media director
Newspapers	Advertising department
Magazines	

REVIEW QUESTIONS

1. Define advertising.
2. What are the various ways in which advertising may be classified?

3. What are the various purposes of advertising?
4. Do you think advertising is worth the money spent on it?
5. Explain the economic effects of advertising.
6. Discuss the social effects of advertising.
7. How good an advertising medium is a newspaper?
8. From the advertising viewpoint, newspapers are not all the same. Explain.
9. Describe the characteristics of magazines as advertising media. What types of advertisements are carried in them? Why?
10. Compare the characteristics of radio and television as advertising media.
11. Discuss the pros and cons of using direct mail to promote the sale of the following products: plants, cars, and clothing.
12. What types of firms use outdoor advertising? Why? What kinds of messages appear?
13. What factors govern an advertiser's choice of advertising media?
14. Explain the ingredients of a good advertisement. Give an example of a good advertisement and of a bad one.
15. Why use an advertising agency?

CASE PROBLEM

MERCEDES-BENZ
Advertising a top-quality imported car

The West German car-maker Daimler-Benz (the parent company of Mercedes-Benz Canada) began the marketing of its cars in North America in 1962 by granting distribution rights to the U.S. firm, Studebaker. However, this did not work out too well, only 500 cars a year being sold. As a result, the distribution rights were subsequently bought back by Mercedes-Benz. The company then set up, in 1965, a Canadian subsidiary, Mercedes-Benz of Canada Limited (later changed to Mercedes-Benz Canada Inc.) to market the Mercedes-Benz line of cars in Canada. To aid in this task, the new company enlisted the services of Ogilvy and Mather (Canada) Ltd., the Canadian branch of a world-wide advertising agency.

In 1965 when the agency began work for its client, sales of Mercedes-Benz cars in Canada totalled 740 new passenger cars a year. The figure for 1985 sales in Canada is estimated at 3500. Prices for the 1986 cars range from $32,950 to $84,670 (F.o.b. Toronto/Montreal).

In its advertising campaign, the agency always stressed the engineering features of the cars. Unlike its parent company in the U.S., where action shots of the cars had been all the rage, Ogilvy and Mather (Canada) Ltd., featured beauty shots of the cars in most of its advertisements. Also, unlike the U.S. advertising, Ogilvy and Mather (Canada) Ltd. made use of Canada's harsh winter to stress various important features of the cars. With a very limited promotional budget, advertising was confined mainly to one-page, eye-attracting advertisements in leading national newspapers and to participation in international auto shows in

The Mercedes-Benz 300SD and 380SE Sedans offer an intriguing luxury of choice between five-cylinder Turbodiesel and gasoline V-8 performance.

The 1985 Mercedes-Benz 300SD and 380SE: How can two such different sedans be so much alike?

ONE OF THE AUTOMOBILES rushing toward you in the picture above is fitted with the direct descendant of a record-shattering turbodiesel performance engine.

The other is propelled by a lightweight aluminum-block gasoline V-8, cat-quick, turbine-smooth.

The resulting contrast in temperament and personality is vivid–but otherwise, so precise is the similarity that only an expert could easily tell these two sedans apart. Deciding between the 300SD and 380SE thus poses a unique and exquisite quandary.

THE DIESEL THAT REWROTE DIESEL HISTORY

At $52,380,* the 300SD turbodiesel Sedan arguably rules the modern diesel passenger car world.

Its turbocharged five-cylinder engine–a virtual carbon copy of the design of the engine that swept the 314.5-kmh Mercedes-Benz C-111/3 to nine world speed records in a day–revolutionized ideas of diesel performance. Having unleashed the diesel, the 300SD also tames it: its red-blooded power is shrouded in running ease and cruising quiet that vie with gasoline cars.

Yet here is rock-ribbed diesel character to the core, with diesel benefits intact. No spark plugs or electrical components to adjust or replace, for example. The inherent efficiency that burns *one quarter* as much fuel at idle as a gasoline engine of similar size. An aura of iron durability.

PERFORMANCE REDUX

At $59,755,* the 380SE Sedan spearheads a renaissance of driving excitement with a V-8 engine more notable for advanced technology than for sheer brute size.

Overhead camshafts for freer engine breathing. The precision and simplicity of CIS *mechanical* fuel injection. Durability and vibration resistance worthy of a cast-iron block–in a weight-saving cast-aluminum block. Advanced, indeed.

The Editor of *Car and Driver* might well have had the 380SE and this 3.8-litre V-8 in mind when he wrote, "There is nothing like a big Mercedes with V-8 power. Nothing."

PURE MERCEDES-BENZ

Whether the nameplate reads 300SD or 380SE, it exemplifies the engineering integrity that is synonymous with Mercedes-Benz.

As a Mercedes-Benz, it is designed to be a *stable* driving platform free of "luxury" car sponginess. Handling poise is extraordinary. A taut suspension and rigid body structure help take the commotion out of rough-road driving.

Yet riding comfort and passenger accommodation are superb–commending both the 300SD and 380SE for service as corporate flagships. From fine velour carpeting to burled walnut trim to myriad push-button amenities, interior appointments are of presidential caliber.

The company president might well choose to be his own chauffeur. One would almost have to *work* at being uncomfortable in the driver's position. Ergonomic design permits the car to be driven with fluid and almost effortless motions. The seat surrounding you is a 30.8-kg biomechanical support system, shaped and padded to help take the strain out of even 500-kilometre stints behind the wheel. The rear seat is one and a half metres wide–adequate for three passengers.

Beneath it all, the 300SD and 380SE are remarkable exercises in safety engineering. Standard safety equipment is comprehensive. For 1985, Emergency Tensioning Retractors are fitted to both front three-point seat belt mechanisms–meant to instantaneously tighten the belts in the event of a major frontal impact. Additionally, you may order either model with the Mercedes-Benz Supplemental Restraint System,‡ adding a driver's side air bag and other elements to the vital cause of occupant restraint.

THE RESALE FACTOR

To ignore resale value at the time you buy a new automobile is to risk being rudely surprised when you get ready to sell it. You can take reassurance from the remarkable–and remarkably consistent–Mercedes-Benz resale record in Canada, model by model, over the past two decades.

Both cars are backed by a 48-month or 80,000-km limited warranty,‡ a superb parts and service network, and a unique dealer commitment to Signature Service–service worthy of the name Mercedes-Benz.

Engineered like no other car in the world

*Approximate suggested advertised delivered price at port of entry. Dealers may sell for less. ($120 extra for Vancouver delivery.)
†Optional at extra cost. ‡See your dealer for full warranty details.

Mercedes-Benz Advertisement
Courtesy Mercedes-Benz Canada Inc.

Montreal, Toronto, and Vancouver. The company would have liked to use TV also but was too constrained by its advertising budget to do so.

Until 1969, the advertisements placed in newspapers across the country, as well as containing a photo and detailed description of the important features of the car, had a request coupon attached. This coupon could be mailed in by a reader wishing to receive an illustrated brochure describing in more detail the various Mercedes-Benz models. When a coupon was received from a reader, the name and address on it would be sent to the dealer nearest to him.

In 1969, partly as the result of dealers' complaints, the coupon feature was discontinued in Canada even though it was still used in Mercedes-Benz advertisements in the United States. Subsequently, the main advertising thrust in Canada was using newspaper advertisements without the request coupon. However, partly to replace the coupon scheme, the agency often made a direct mailing of the newspaper advertisement to the owners of 3-to-4-year-old high-line Mercedes-Benz cars. The advertisement was accompanied by a covering letter from the head of Mercedes-Benz in Canada and a return card that could be sent in to obtain an illustrated brochure. This scheme, which met with very good results, was based on the theory that the "best fishing is in your own stream."

One of the problems that the agency faced was that the advertising budget remained constant over the years, whereas advertising costs per unit of exposure had risen 50 to 75 per cent. Advertising was confined mainly to quality newspapers. *Time* magazine was used for a while because its profile of readers closely matched that of potential Mercedes-Benz buyers. However, dealers complained that there was no dealer identification and that "customers didn't see the ads." In the United States, however, *Time* magazine was used as a supplemental medium.

Another important form of promotion that began in 1968 and is still used by Mercedes-Benz today is the "hotel salon show." Prospective purchasers are given a personal invitation to inspect the latest Mercedes-Benz cars in the ballroom of a major hotel in their city, with the accompaniment of cocktails and hors d'oeuvres. This event has become so popular, often with an attendance of over 2,000 in an evening, that it is for many something of a "social occasion," with persons asking to be placed on the invitation list.

In 1979, Mercedes-Benz Canada received a larger promotional budget and so took the opportunity to take a second look at the promotional methods used to date. About that time also, a head office decision resulted in the company switching advertising world-wide from the firm of Ogilvy and Mather to a New York firm, McCaffrey and McCall. One important point that emerged from the promotional review was that the target market for Mercedes-Benz cars in Canada had changed. Whereas in the early years, upper middle-income persons could afford to buy the cars, this was no longer the case. Inflation and a stronger West German currency had so affected the price of the cars that its target market had changed from, say, the general medical practitioner to the surgeon or specialist, or, as another illustration, from the vice-president of a business firm to the president. Since the market was now much smaller, comprising only the financially elite group in society, the promotional tactics could switch from the "shotgun" to the "sniper" approach.

Beginning in 1980, this "sniper" approach took the form of a direct mail correspondence campaign, which involved an initial letter and illustrated brochure to each person falling within the elite group, introducing the company and its cars, and offering further information and a demonstration drive. But unlike other direct mail promotions, it was a continuing correspondence, not just a one-shot effort.

In effect, Mercedes-Benz began a dialogue with its prospective clients—hoping by the provision of abundant product information, particularly about the quality of the cars, and by willingness to answer questions about the firm and its products, gradually to make these prospective clients want to own a Mercedes-Benz and become part of the Mercedes-Benz family. This continuing dialogue might involve in the first year as many as five different letters. Included with the letters was a response mechanism—a card that invited the client to send in for additional information or a demonstration drive. Unlike the coupon that had caused some grief among dealers in the early years, this one was not offered indiscriminately but only to the elite group. And so far, the response rate has been excellent. If a client has a question to ask, Mercedes-Benz head office in Toronto answers him or her directly. If it is a request for a demonstration drive, the local dealer is asked to oblige. Also a person showing interest in the cars might be invited to the next salon show.

Advertising was also continued in such newspapers as the *Financial Times*, *Financial Post*, the *Globe and Mail's Report on Business*, and *Le Devoir*, and in professional magazines such as *Canadian Business, Executive, Financial Post Magazine, Time, Canadian Lawyer, Canadian Banker, Canadian Doctor*, and in their Quebec counterparts. An example of an advertisement is shown. Nowadays, "action shots" are preferred by Mercedes-Benz to "stills".

Assignment

1. Why have newspapers and direct mailings been chosen as the advertising media for this product? What role could TV advertising have played in promoting Mercedes-Benz cars?
2. Discuss the advertisement shown from the viewpoint of theme, copy, illustration, and layout. How successful do you think it was? Discuss.
3. How can Mercedes-Benz assess the effectiveness of its advertising and other sales promotion?
4. Why might the use of a return coupon in the newspaper advertisement have been discontinued in Canada?
5. Discuss the suitability of (a) *Time* magazine and (b) *Chatelaine* as advertising media for this product. What types of magazine are used? Why?
6. Explain and discuss the "dialogue by letter" approach.
7. What are the main problems that face the agency in promoting the sale of Mercedes-Benz cars?
8. Discuss the effectiveness of salon shows as a promotional tool.
9. How can the harshness of the Canadian winter be used to make the advertising of Mercedes-Benz cars more effective?

10. Are still shots or action shots better suited for advertisements for this type of car?
11. Contrast, from the viewpoint of advertising effectiveness, the slogans
    (a) "This is the year I will finally own a _____ ."
    (b) "All you really need is a _____ ."
    List five other actual car sales slogans and rate their effectiveness: A, B, or C.
12. What other methods, apart from advertising, direct mail, and salon shows, could Mercedes-Benz Canada use to promote the sale of its cars?

UNIT 11.3: SELLING

Selling (also called *personal selling* to distinguish it from other forms of sales promotion) comprises three major tasks: order getting, order taking, and supporting activities.

Order getting, sometimes called *creative selling*, is the task of seeking out prospective customers and persuading them to buy a product or service. A life-insurance salesperson is an example of an order-getter.

Order taking is the usually routine task, once the customer has been "sold" on the product, of completing the sale by writing up the order and answering any final questions. Once a customer is satisfied with a product, the sales job involved in obtaining new orders may become almost purely one of order taking.

Supporting activities are visits to customers and prospective customers by special salespeople, sometimes called *missionary salespeople*, whose primary purpose is to promote customer goodwill towards the company rather than actively solicit orders, and by technical specialists who provide the customer with technical advice on a problem.

Most salespeople's jobs involve a combination of order getting, order taking, and supporting activities. In some types of selling (for example, door-to-door selling) the major part of the salesperson's time will be taken up with order getting; in others (for example, selling established food lines to grocery stores) order taking may predominate. In selling to industrial users, a salesperson may be very much concerned with what we have termed supporting acitivites—for example, identifying technical problems and trying to help solve them.

Advertising may also be considered an extremely important supporting activity in that it helps to make customers aware of the firm and its products and interested in buying.

The Selling Process

Selling, in the sense of order getting, is an extremely personal matter. Within the same firm, one salesperson will obtain orders through long hours and grim persistence, another will flourish on careful research and gay camaraderie, and another will obtain orders from carefully cultivated social contacts. Furthermore, different products and different customers often require different sales approaches.

There are certain basic steps which must be followed by all salespeople if personal selling is to be effective and sustained. These steps are: preparing oneself; locating prospective customers; arranging to see prospective customers; explaining or demonstrating the value of the product; answering questions and meeting objections; closing the sale; and promoting goodwill after the sale.

Preparing Oneself. A salesperson should have a good appearance and good personal habits. He or she should have enthusiasm for the product or service and tact in dealing with clients.

A salesperson should also have a thorough knowledge of:
1. *The products that he or she is selling*—covering such matters as product use, consumer acceptance, price, delivery, and credit terms.
2. *The customers and prospective customers*—What are their needs? What are their attitudes? What are their past buying habits? Who makes the purchasing decisions?
3. *The market*—Who are the competitors? What are they offering in competition? What other promotion is the salesperson's company undertaking?
4. *The fundamentals of selling*—how to approach a prospective buyer; how to convince him or her of a need for the product; and how to close a sale.

Locating Prospective Customers. Not everyone is a prospective customer. The salesperson's problem is to use the time available most economically by seeing only persons or firms that offer some chance of a sale.

For the retail store salesperson, all persons entering the store are prospective customers. For the wholesaler's salesperson, the list of retailers provided by management represents the basic core of prospective customers. The salesperson may also be encouraged by a commission system to call upon other retailers on the route to see if business can be done with them. The manufacturer's salesperson or agent must determine what type of industrial users or middlemen are interested in the products for sale. There may be a number of established customers from whom not only repeat business, but also some referrals or leads to new customers, can be obtained. The salesperson may also obtain leads by scanning newspapers and other periodicals. For example, a supplier of building material would look for news of construction contracts. Sometimes an advertisement will prompt replies from firms interested in the product. Much new business may come from "cold calls," which are unrequested first visits to prospective customers. These cold calls, although not immediately productive, may bring results if repeated at suitable intervals, and if records are kept of the information obtained at each visit.

Arranging Sales Appointments. Most salespeople encounter little difficulty in seeing a prospective customer, except that they may sometimes be kept waiting. The most common method of seeing prospective customers is to telephone the person, introduce oneself, and make an appointment.

Demonstrating the Product. This part of the selling process can be a brief oral explanation by the salesperson, a demonstration ride (in the case of a car), a visit (in the case of a house purchase), or even a deluxe tour of the manufacturer's plant, especially arranged for the prospective customer.

Answering Questions and Meeting Objections. The salesperson should be willing and able to answer any questions that the prospective customer may have about the product. By preparation, training and experience, the salesperson should be competent both to answer questions and to meet objections.

Closing the Sale. After persuading the prospective customer of the benefit to be obtained from buying the product, the salesperson must bring the customer to a decision. If the prospective customer is allowed to wait too long—for example, "sleep on it," he or she may decide not to buy. A good salesperson should be able to sense the moment to try to bring the customer to a decision and then take appropriate action—for example, by writing up the order and then asking the prospect to sign it.

Promoting Goodwill After the Sale. A substantial part of an established salesperson's business comes from repeat orders by old customers and from "referrals"—orders obtained from new customers referred to the salesperson by old customers. It is, therefore, in the salesperson's interest to keep in touch with his or her customers even though a sale has been completed. This contact can be maintained by such things as regular visits, telephone calls, Christmas cards, and calendars.

Types of Selling Jobs

Selling jobs vary greatly. It is nevertheless helpful to think in terms of four main types of selling jobs, even though there are variations within each type. The four are: manufacturers' salespeople, wholesalers' salespeople, retail salespeople, and service salespeople. Also, of course, the level of complexity will vary (e.g. selling soap versus selling nuclear reactors or professional services).

Factors that vary with each sales job are: the complexity of the good or service being sold; the degree of creative selling involved; and the type of customer or client involved. The more complex the product, the greater the degree of creative selling. Also, the more sophisticated the client, the more demanding is the job and the qualifications required of the salesperson—formal education; technical knowledge and experience; intelligence; personality, appearance, and manners; ease of speech, etc. However, the more demanding the job, the greater usually are the financial rewards. And these can sometimes be very large, particularly when commission is the basic method of payment.

The following is a brief review of four major categories of selling jobs.

Manufacturer's Sales Representatives. These are salespeople employed by a manufacturer to sell its products to middlemen such as wholesalers and retailers, to industrial and government users and, very occasionally, directly to domestic consumers. The term *specialty salesperson* or *sales engineer* is used to describe a manufacturer's salesperson who specializes in the sale of a product which requires considerable technical explanation for installation or use.

Selling jobs in this group may be predominantly order getting—for example, persuading wholesalers to handle a new line of goods—or predominantly order taking—for example, calling on franchised dealers. In all cases, the manufacturer's salesperson is expected to demonstrate a thorough knowledge of product and a willingness to offer advice, where pertinent, on customers' problems.

Wholesaler's Sales Representatives. These sales people call on retailers, offering them a variety of merchandise and checking to ensure that goods are being delivered punctually and in good condition. Once confidence has been established between the salesperson and retailer, the retailer may rely heavily on the salesperson as to the types and quantities of goods to be ordered. Order getting, order taking, and supplementary advice are all important parts of this salesperson's job.

Retail Salespeople. The most numerous type of retail salesperson is the *retail store salesperson*, who is in all retail stores, even self-service stores. Customers are attracted to stores by location, window displays, and advertising. The amount of selling required once they are in the store can vary enormously. Thus a person wanting a loaf of bread requires little or no personal selling, whereas a person wishing to buy a new car usually requires a great deal. The retail store salesperson is primarily an order taker and provider of advice. Such a person should be knowledgeable, helpful, and courteous. The *door-to-door salesperson* is a retail salesperson who actively seeks out customers by calling at their homes. Order getting is his or her most serious concern.

Service Salespeople. In this category, we include persons who sell products such as insurance, banking, stocks and bonds, advertising, accounting, legal, management consulting, market and other research, medical, dental and other services. Often, there is a high degree of creative selling involved. Consequently, the job can be very hard on a person's nerves, with a relatively high "burnout rate" for the profession as a whole. However, successful selling can be financially very rewarding.

The Sales Manager

The sales manager is in charge of the firm's selling activities. This involves planning, organizing, staffing, directing, and controlling, as applied to selling.

Sales Planning. The sales manager must plan how the sales force is to meet the sales targets set by top management. These plans should include targets for each salesperson and should take into account present sales coverage by area and type of customer, the number of salespeople, the type and amount of advertising by the firm, and the actions of competitors.

Sales Organization. In a large firm, the sales manager is responsible to a marketing manager or vice-president, marketing. The marketing manager will also have authority over the heads of the various staff departments—marketing research, advertising, and so on. In a small firm, there may not be a marketing manager. The sales manager may do everything from recruiting sales personnel to carrying out market research.

The sales organization is usually of a line type, with variations caused by geographical coverage, different product lines, and different markets. Three examples of sales organizations are shown in Figures 11.2, 11.3, and 11.4.

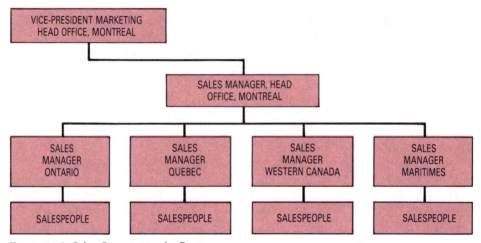

Figure 11.2 Sales Organization by Region

Staffing. The staffing function of the sales manager includes selection, training, and remuneration of salespeople. In large companies, the staffing function may be carried out by a personnel department at head office or in co-operation with the various local sales managers.

Some of the most important characteristics that a firm will look for in a new salesperson are: reasonable intelligence and education (the amount required will vary according to the complexity of the product to be sold and the type of customer to be called upon); good appearance; self-confidence and ability to work on one's own (a "self-starter"); and ambition and determination to succeed.

Selection. The manner in which new salespeople are selected varies from company to company. In some, a written application, including references, and an interview with the sales manager may be all that is required. In others, a written application, a series of interviews (including possibly one for the applicant's spouse), intelligence and aptitude tests, and a high level of academic achievement may be necessary.

Training. The training which a salesperson receives may be one of several alternatives: a "pep" talk from the sales manager, followed by experience acquired on the job; a training program of several weeks duration during which the

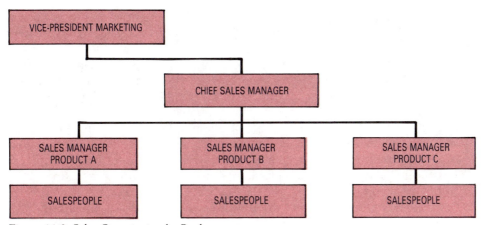

Figure 11.3 Sales Organization by Product

salesperson will become thoroughly familiar with the product and its uses, will be lectured on various sales topics, will practise sales presentations, and will have the opportunity to talk with experienced salespeople; a short indoctrination period, followed by several weeks of training by an established salesperson who will take the newcomer with him or her when making calls; or some combination of these methods.

Remuneration. There are three usual methods of remunerating salespeople for their efforts: straight salary, straight commission, or some combination of both. A salesperson may also receive a bonus for extra achievement and an allowance for expenses.

Straight salary. With this method, the salesperson receives a set monthly salary. He or she is under less nervous pressure to make sales than would be the case under the commission method. But, however successful the salesperson may be, earnings cannot be increased unless performance prompts management to grant a raise in pay.

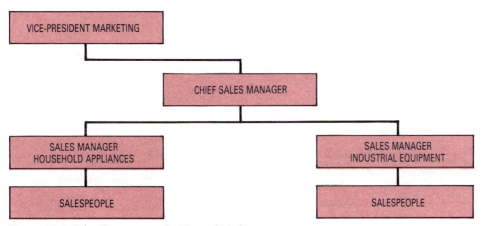

Figure 11.4 Sales Organization by Type of Market

From management's point of view, a set salary has the disadvantages of being an expense that is incurred regardless of the amount of sales, and, in some cases, reducing the salesperson's incentive to sell. For some types of selling—for example, high-class tailors—the payment of a straight salary is considered necessary to ensure that sales personnel give good, unhurried service to customers. Sometimes a firm will pay a salary to a salesperson during the initial training period, after which payment will be on a straight commission basis.

Straight commission. A large number of salespeople (manufacturers' representatives, manufacturers' salespeople, real estate salespersons, and so on) receive only a commission, usually calculated as a percentage of sales (for example, 5 to 10 per cent). This commission provides the salesperson with a strong incentive to work hard, and rewards him or her for success. It can, however, be a deterrent to persons wishing to enter sales work because of the uncertain income and the time necessary to become established. For the firm, it means that payment has to be made only for results.

Salary and commission. To provide their salespeople with some security, yet retain their incentive, a number of firms use a payment plan which combines a basic monthly salary, with a commission on sales.

Bonus. Sometimes a bonus (additional to the salary, commission, or salary and commission) is paid for the achievement of a special sales target—for example, so many new accounts during a year. The bonus may be cash, a paid holiday for the salesperson and spouse, or a new car.

Allowance for expenses. Some firms provide their salespeople with a car and a set monetary allowance for expenses, while others expect their salespeople to cover their selling costs out of their salary and/or commission.

Sales Directing.
This is the task of giving orders. Once a good sales force has been assembled and territories assigned, the need for direction is reduced. As long as sales continue to increase in a satisfactory manner, the sales manager may only hold a monthly or weekly sales meeting at which sales progress is reviewed and problems discussed. Should sales decline, the sales manager may then decide to make changes in the sales force or its methods.

One extrmely important task of the sales manager, sometimes included under direction, is *motivation*. The manager must inspire the salespeople to work harder, to persevere despite lack of success, and to continue even when they may sometimes wish to resign. To motivate the salespeople, the manager may use personal persuasion, a good system of remuneration, and such incentives as sales contests.

Sales Controlling.
Also called supervision, this is the task of ensuring that the activities and results of the sales force are going according to plan and according to any rules which have been set. To help evaluate the performance of the sales force, the sales manager can use sales records and salespeople's reports, as well as information gathered from discussions with members of the sales force.

If a breach of any rule, informal or formal, has occurred, the sales manager must investigate and settle the matter promptly. A frequent source of friction is how the commssion should be split when more than one salesperson is involved in a sale. A commission dispute, if allowed to linger on, can cause bitterness among salespeople and a decline in morale.

KEY TERMS

Selling

Personal selling

Order getting

Order taking

Supporting activities

Selling process

Manufacturer's sales representatives

Wholesaler's sales representatives

Retail salespeople

Service salespeople

Sales manager

Sales planning

Sales organization

Staffing

Directing

Controlling

REVIEW QUESTIONS

1. What is the basic difference between selling and other forms of sales promotion?
2. Selling involves three main tasks. Explain. Which is the most demanding? Why?
3. Why do the formal educational requirements for salespeople vary?
4. What are the basic steps in selling?
5. If you were a residential real estate salesperson, how would you go about finding houses to sell?
6. As a real estate salesperson, how would you go about convincing a client to buy a house?
7. "Salespeople are made, not born." Discuss.
8. In which category of sales job do the following fit: (a) print salesperson, (b) publisher's sales rep, (c) pharmaceutical sales rep, and (d) travel agent?
9. To what extent, if at all, is selling involved today in the practice of (a) medicine and (b) law?
10. What specific tasks does a sales manager perform?
11. Should a sales rep aspire to become a sales manager? Explain the pros and cons.

CASE PROBLEMS

JANE APPLEBY
Selling pharmaceutical products

Jane Appleby, a college graduate in business administration, has accepted an offer to be trained as a sales representative for Mitchell Robbins Ltd., a medium-size Canadian pharmaceutical firm, with head office and manufacturing facilities in Scarborough, Ontario.

In this company, the work of the sales representative or "detail person" is to make periodic calls on all doctors, dentists, and pharmacists in a given geographical area. When calling on doctors and dentists, the sales representative's main goal is to explain the properties of the firm's products and to encourage the doctor or dentist to prescribe or recommend them to his or her patients. When calling on drug stores, the sales representative attempts to persuade the druggist to stock the items so as to be able to fill prescriptions or, in the case of patent medicines, to recommend them to customers.

The sales representatives employed by this firm are of varied background, most with only a high-school education. The result of this lack of higher education is that most doctors and dentists do not feel Mitchell Robbins salespeople are well enough qualified to explain the application of their products. The firm is now trying to improve its image by increasing the percentage of college graduates in its sales force. Very few of the present sales representatives had any medical or pharmaceutical background when they joined the firm.

The sales representatives for Mitchell Robbins Ltd. are paid a monthly salary of $1,000 during their initial two-month training period. This is increased to $1,200 per month for a further 10-month probationary period. Finally, if considered satisfactory, they are paid a salary of $1,500 per month which can increase, with annual reviews, to as much as $25,000 a year in the case of a hospital sales representative.

The firm now employs throughout Canada a total of 171 sales representatives. Each major region of the country has a manager in charge of a regional branch office and warehouse. In the field, and responsible to each regional manager, there are two, three, or four district managers. Each district manager supervises about 10 sales representatives.

Mitchell Robbins Ltd. reinforces the efforts of its sales force by sending a steady stream of advertising literature and drug samples to the doctors on its list. The firm also advertises its drugs in the Canadian medical, dental, hospital, and pharmaceutical journals.

At the company head office in Scarborough, Jane Appleby, together with two other trainees, spent her first month taking part in an indoctrination program designed to give her: an understanding of the company; a working familiarity with the firm's principal drugs, some knowledge of physiology and anatomy; and classroom practice in making sales presentations, using company-prepared written outlines called "structured details" (see page 439). The second month of this training period was spent accompanying experienced sales representatives on their visits to doctors and seeing how sales presentations were actually made in the field.

On completion of the training program, Appleby was placed under the supervision of Mr. Ted Lewis, the district manager for southwestern Ontario. Lewis, whom Appleby had met previously at head office, welcomed Appleby warmly and gave her a list of physicians and dentists on whom she was to call at least once every two months. These doctors had previously been called upon by another salesperson who had left to become a district manager for Miles Laboratories (Canada) Ltd.

> **Dentifresh Structured Detail**
>
> Doctor, our company wants to introduce you and your patients to Dentifresh, a pleasant-tasting, anti-bacterial mouthwash and gargle that has been used in the dental profession for over fifteen years. It is, in fact, becoming one of the most highly regarded mouth washes in North America.
>
> Dentifresh is particularly helpful in relieving any mild discomfort or gingival irritation that a patient may experience after dental instrumentation. A rinse with Dentifresh, full strength, every two or three hours, will give complete relief. Dentifresh can also be used in the rinse cup or in your spray.
>
> Dentifresh contains no antibiotics. Its active ingredient, Dentyl, is a surface-active agent that is highly effective in fighting odour-producing oral bacteria. Dentifresh is also mildly alkaline, which helps to neutralize excess mouth acidity.
>
> Our company can offer you, at an extremely low introductory price, a Dentifresh dispensing unit, containing 4 x 2 L of Dentifresh, a dental dispensing pump, and 44 x 40 mL Dentifresh patient samples. We can offer you this unit, which normally retails at $35, for only $10, prepaid. Will you let me place an order for you now?

During the following three months, Appleby succeeded in visiting all the doctors on her list. In many cases, however, she was forced to wait over an hour before the doctor could see her, and even then, she was often given only a few minutes. According to her instructions at head office, Appleby limited herself in the first visit to introducing herself and the firm and to leaving a few samples.

In each subsequent visit, Appleby concentrated on introducing only two or three of the firm's drugs and spent the rest of the time exchanging pleasantries.

Ted Lewis, Appleby's district manager, met with Appleby once every two weeks to review and discuss the reports which Appleby prepared after each visit.

In his first quarterly report to head office on Appleby's performance, Lewis indicated that Appleby seemed earnest and willing, but that she seemed to be too easily discouraged by the rough treatment that she was getting from some doctors. However, it was too early to judge whether she was going to be a successful sales representative.

During the next six months, Lewis made a point of calling on a number of Appleby's doctors and, after suitable introduction, asking whether they were receiving good service from Appleby. Most doctors interviewed said that she was satisfactory. However, some said that she seemed to be prying into their personal affairs, others said that she didn't know what she was talking about, and one said that she had failed to inform him about the possibly harmful side effects of one of Mitchell Robbins drugs. Several doctors complained of the excessive amount of literature that was being mailed to them by Mitchell Robbins and two specialists complained that they were being sent information in no way related to their specialty. One doctor said that in the past year he had received from all drug companies together 2,753 pieces of mail and 538 samples of different drugs. What worried Lewis more than these remarks by the doctors, however, was the fact that the use of Mitchell Robbins drugs in Appleby's territory, despite a year of visits, was still very small.

In her discussion with Lewis, Appleby has suggested that she could use her time more profitably if some sort of classification were made of the doctors on whom she called. The most important doctors, from the sales point of view, should get more attention. Lewis replied, however, that Appleby could easily call on all her doctors if she did not spend time discussing the weather, sports, and other matters. According to Lewis, Appleby should "not get personally involved with the doctors. Just give them the detail, as it is, and get out."

Appleby believes that she should not stick closely to the structured details, many of which she believes are rather childish. She also believes that it is the personal touch that makes one sales representative stand out from the others. Once she almost told Lewis that if the company wanted educated parrots it should not be trying to hire college graduates.

Assignment
1. Do you consider the firm's sales training program to be a good one? Explain.
2. Why does Appleby appear to be unsuccessful?
3. What action should her supervisor take?

CLIFF REED REAL ESTATE LTD.
Selling real estate

Alfred Bennett, 35, a former car salesman, emigrated with his family from Birmingham, England, to Canada, in the spring of 1975. He was part of the large wave of English immigrants to Canada in that year, brought on to a large degree by the British government's wage freeze and other measures designed to restrict domestic consumption and improve the country's balance of payments. Bennett's livelihood had shrunk rapidly as larger down payments and higher finance charges, together with reduced incomes from unemployment and short-time working in a number of local manufacturing firms, caused a slump in new car buying.

Bennett had decided before leaving England that he would enter the real estate business in Canada and, if successful, perhaps eventually start his own business. In the large Canadian town where he settled, Bennett rented a two-bedroom apartment, and he and his wife began to look for work. Their children, a girl 14, and two boys, 12 and 10, began classes in the neighbouring schools.

One of the newspaper advertisements which attracted Bennett's attention was the following:

REAL ESTATE SALESPERSON

An immediate opening is available for a salesperson in our downtown office. This is an opportunity to become associated with a young, rapidly growing company. A person with Real Estate experience is preferred, but we would be pleased to talk to an inexperienced person with a sales background, who wants to make a career in Real Estate. Training provided. Commission basis. Call Cliff Reed, 259-8231. Cliff Reed Real Estate Ltd.

At the interview which Bennett obtained, Reed explained that, in essence, the job involved first persuading people to use the company's services to sell their houses and then persuading someone else to buy them. He also explained that the commission rate charged by the firm for an exclusive listing was 5 per cent of the selling price of the house. The firm would take half of this in exchange for providing office space, a minimum amount of advertising, telephone service, and a manager's training and advice. He explained furthermore that the local real estate board operated a Photo Multiple Listing Service whereby the particulars of a house listed for sale by a member firm could be distributed to all the other members. This meant that prospective buyers all over the area could be quickly made aware of the listed property. However, the commission rate was higher, 6 per cent instead of 5 per cent. When the salesperson of another firm obtained a buyer for the property, that firm would receive 3 per cent of the price less the listing fee, and the listing broker 3 per cent. Reed also pointed out that there were three different types of listing which a real estate salesperson might obtain. A "listing" means placing a property in the hands of a real estate broker to sell or exchange.

With an *exclusive listing*, the vendor agrees to use only the services of the listing broker. With a *Photo M.L.S. listing*, the services of the listing broker and of all other Real Estate Board members are called upon for the sale of a property through the listing broker. With an *open or general listing*, any real estate broker can sell the property if he or she finds a buyer.

Reed also explained that in order to sell real estate in the province, Bennett would have to obtain a licence from the provincial government. This would be granted only after Bennett had taken and passed a special government-approved Real Estate course, as well as courses approved by the Canadian Real Estate Association. Also, his employer would have to post a surety bond of an approved surety company with the provincial government. The purpose of these measures, Reed explained, was to try to prevent dishonest, "fly-by-night" operators from selling real estate.

Cliff Reed Real Estate Ltd. paid its salespeople on a straight commission basis. However, the firm operated a "draw-plan" whereby a salesperson, to get started, could draw $300 per week to be repaid out of future earnings. The maximum amount that could be owed to the firm at any one time would be $2000. Interest would be payable on the draws at 12 per cent per annum.

Bennett accepted the job and was told, as a start, to study a map of the area, and the manual of the Real Estate Board, particularly the General Instructions for Writing Offers. He was also introduced to the other five salespersons in the office and instructed to accompany one of them the next day, for experience.

In the middle of his second month with the firm, Bennett sold his first house—a two-storey brick semi-detached for $79 000. In the third month, his commission earnings were $2 070, and by the end of his first year his earnings totalled $30 500. Most of his listings had been obtained by choosing a specific residential area and personally calling on everyone there. Before making his calls, he would find out the name of the owner of the property from the tax assessment records at the municipal office.

By now, Bennett had begun to feel more confident of himself as a real estate salesperson. He was also struck by the fact that the more valuable the property, the larger the commission, even though the work involved does not increase proportionately. Following this type of thinking, he approached Cliff Reed with the suggestion that he, Bennett, should attempt to specialize in the sale and leasing of industrial and commercial properties; and that, if this venture proves successful, Bennett could head up an industrial and commercial department for the firm.

Assignment
1. What are the different types of property listings? Explain.
2. What are the various ways in which a real estate salesperson can obtain listings? Explain.
3. How was Bennett trained in his new job? How else could he have been trained?
4. Discuss the importance of personal persuasion by the salesperson in selling residential real estate. How can a prospective buyer be persuaded to sign an Offer to Purchase?
5. Discuss the merits of the "commission with draw-plan" type of remuneration in this firm, from the viewpoint of (a) the owner and (b) the salesperson.
6. Discuss the nature and usefulness of the services of a real estate salesperson to the seller of a house.
7. Distinguish between a real estate salesperson and a real estate broker. What qualifications must a person have to become a real estate broker? (Consult your provincial Real Estate and Business Brokers Act.)
8. How do the selling and leasing of industrial and commercial properties differ from the selling and leasing of residential properties?
9. What personal qualities and qualifications would the manager of an industrial and commercial department in such a firm need?
10. Can local real estate boards insist that their members charge a minimum commission rate to their clients? What are real estate commission rates in your area?

PART F
FINANCIAL MANAGEMENT

For a business firm's marketing and production activities to be worthwhile, revenue must exceed expenses, and the firm must always have sufficient cash to pay its bills.

Financial managers have the important task of advising on the financial implications of marketing and production decisions, ensuring that required funds are available at the lowest cost, monitoring a firm's financial flows, and safeguarding company assets.

In this part of the book, we consider how these important responsibilities are carried out. In the three chapters, we examine financial planning and control, financial solvency, and long-term financing, respectively.

CHAPTER 12
FINANCIAL PLANNING AND CONTROL

CHAPTER OBJECTIVES

☐ To outline the various tasks of financial management in a business firm.

☐ To explain how a firm organizes its financial management activities.

☐ To describe the nature and purpose of financial budgets or plans.

☐ To explain the nature and purpose of an income statement.

☐ To explain and discuss the nature and usefulness of break-even analysis.

☐ To emphasize the importance of return on capital as a criterion for management decisions.

CHAPTER OUTLINE

12.1   Budgeting

12.2   Evaluating Profitability

UNIT 12.1: BUDGETING

Tasks of Financial Management

The first task of financial management is to spell out, as far as possible, how the various management proposals and decisions will affect company profitability and financial solvency. The firm's top policy-makers, whether they be the president or board of directors of a large manufacturing concern or the owner-manager of a drug store, must be advised of the financial implications of various courses of action. In order to make sound decisions, management must know, for example, the cost of setting up and operating a plant, compared to the anticipated revenue from sales; the cost of using a wholesaler to distribute the firm's products, compared to the cost of direct selling to retailers; the cost of installing a computer, compared to the clerical savings and other benefits effected; the cost of extending credit, compared to the revenue from additional sales; or the possible cost, from the income tax point of view, of remaining a sole proprietorship or partnership, rather than incorporating.

The second main task of financial management is to control closely the funds invested in, or loaned to, the business. This is done by establishing, operating, and interpreting a suitable set of accounts; by auditing the accounts; and by carefully selecting and training financial personnel.

The third main task (discussed in the next two chapters) is to ensure the continued financial solvency of the firm by careful cash management and appropriate short, medium, and long-term financing.

The fourth task of financial management is the care of company property. This is usually the responsibility of the treasurer or the company secretary and includes the safeguarding of company cash; the care of securities—for example, shares of other companies; the management of company-owned real estate— for example, leasing of spare office space, rent collection, property maintenance, and payment of municipal property taxes; and the obtaining of adequate insurance coverage—for example, fire insurance for plant and inventory, and life insurance for key executives.

The Finance Department

In the small business, financial management is one of the many functions, such as marketing and production, that the owner-manager must perform. Ability and inclination differ, of course, from one businessperson to another. Thus we frequently find a situation where a business with good sales potential is forced into bankruptcy through lack of good financial management. On the other hand, competent financial management cannot automatically increase sales. The small businessperson can do much to increase his or her financial knowledge and ability—by experience, by reading, and by attending suitable courses. He or she can also, and frequently does, obtain the services of a financial management specialist, an accountant, on a part-time basis. This arrangement may take the form of a monthly visit by the accountant to make sure that the books are being properly kept and bills paid, and to discuss any financial problems that may have arisen. The accountant will also usually prepare the annual income tax return.

The organization of the financial management function in the small business—for example, a hardware store—is extremely simple (Figure 12.1). However, the organization and staffing of the financial management function in a large business can be quite complex.

At the top is the *vice-president, finance*, who is responsible to the president of the corporation. This person's duties include, first, the provision of financial advice as to the profitability and feasibility of measures proposed by top management. As a member of the top management team, he or she must be able to work easily with colleagues and provide clear logical advice on a variety of key problems. Second, the vice-president, finance, is responsible for the planning, initiation, and execution of measures designed to improve the profitability of the firm, such as improved accounting systems and procedures and better financial control of subsidiaries. By virtue of the position, this person will have a large area of discretionary authority. A third duty of the vice-president, finance, is the control and safeguarding of company funds and other assets. Fourth, he or she is responsible for the preparation of suitable financial records covering income and expenditures; money owed to and by the company; the cost of doing business; and changes in the assets and ownership of the company. A fifth duty of the vice-president, finance, is the supervision of the work, training, promotion, and welfare of his or her subordinates.

Not all large firms use the title vice-president, finance. Some use the term *controller or comptroller*. Then again, in the very large companies, both a vice-president, finance, and a controller may be employed, with the latter the subordinate position.

Some companies, particularly in the medium-size range, give their chief financial officer the title of *secretary-treasurer*. This position combines the duties of company secretary and company treasurer. The *company secretary* has the responsibility for the formal records of the company: the letters patent; the corporate seal; the company bylaws; and the minutes of shareholder and director meetings.

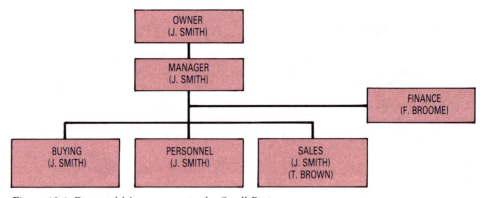

Figure 12.1 Financial Management in the Small Business

He or she also makes the arrangements for these meetings and, where necessary, represents the company in court of law and in any dealings with government. The company secretary acts, furthermore, as the signing officer in company contracts. The company treasurer's work is the same as that described for the controller. The two positions are frequently combined because of the usually sporadic nature of the company secretary's duties.

The actual responsibilities involved and the personal qualities demanded in these top financial management positions naturally vary with the size and nature of the firm.

The next level of financial management in the larger firm is the heads of the various financial departments or sections: general accounting; cost accounting; tax accounting; auditing; budgeting; and credit and collections. In some firms, sections for data processing, and systems and procedures, will also form part of the finance department. In some large companies, an assistant controller, assistant treasurer, or chief accountant will act as the overall head for several of these departments. Whatever the case, the heads of these departments will be qualified, experienced financial personnel.

The staffs of the various financial departments comprise assistant heads, secretaries, clerks, and management trainees, many of whom will be enrolled in professional accounting courses.

An example of the organization chart of the finance department of a large firm is shown in Figure 12.2.

The Operating Budget

For purposes of financial planning and control, business firms usually construct two main types of financial plans or "budgets": the operating budget (or "profit plan") and the capital budget.

The *operating budget* is a statement of the anticipated revenue, planned operating expenses, and net income for the budgetary period. For a small business, a monthly operating budget (and actual results) might be as shown in Figure 12.3.

For a manufacturing firm, the preparation of an operating budget is somewhat more complex, as the cost of manufacturing the goods also has to be estimated.

The Budgetary Process. The process of drawing up an operating budget involves a number of distinct steps. First, management must agree on a figure for estimated future sales. Such forecasts are based on past sales experience and an intelligent appraisal of present and anticipated future market conditions and trends. In large firms, the sales forecast may be initiated by the sales or marketing manager, but is usually thoroughly discussed by a special budget committee of top management before being approved by the board of directors. On this forecast of anticipated sales hinge all the planned operating expenditures of the firm for the budget period.

Once the annual or six-months' forecast is adopted, a *master budget* is drawn up, showing for the firm as a whole: estimated sales, product by product and month by month; and estimated expenses, department by department, to permit

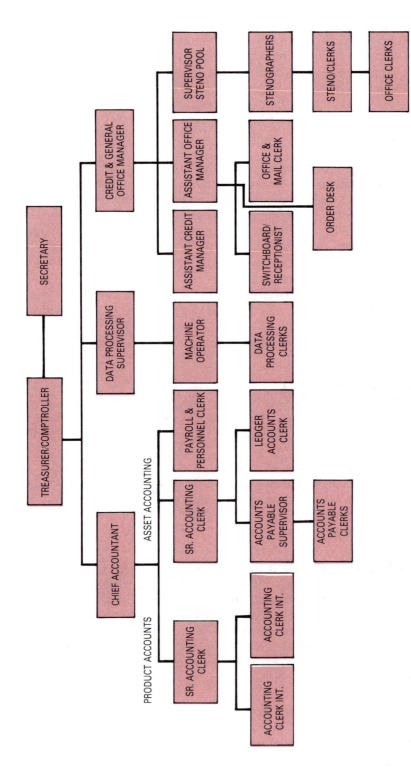

Figure 12.2 Finance Department of a Large Firm

Income and Expenses	Budgeted		Actual		Variance
Sales	$6 000		$5 000		$1 000
Cost of Goods Sold	$4 800		$4 000		$800
Gross Profit	$1 200		$1 000		$200
Operating Expenses:					
Rent		$400		$400	
Wages		750		800	
Advertising		225		200	
Miscellaneous		125		150	
	$1 500		$1 550		$50
Net Operating Income	−$300		−$550		−$250

Figure 12.3 Budgeted Income Statement for a Small Business for November, 198—

this volume of sales. Each department or division (production, sales, advertising, office, materials, research, and so on) will have its own budget, based on the master budget. For example, the production division will have to draw up a *production schedule* (that is, an estimate of the quantities of the different products it must manufacture each month to keep up with the anticipated sales). From this, it will calculate a *production division budget* which will indicate in detail the various plant operating costs (wages, materials and supplies, and overhead) that will be incurred in meeting the production schedule. This divisional budget will then be broken down into department or shop budgets, often on a weekly basis.

Purposes of Operating Budgets. The master budget and the subsidiary budgets serve several different purposes. First, they serve as a financial planning tool to help management foresee how the firm's future revenue will exceed expenditure—the "profit plan" approach. Second, they serve as a guidance or leadership tool, giving employees a greater sense of direction and purpose through the establishment of overall and departmental targets for sales, production, and expenses. The budgets should, however, be flexible enough to take into account new circumstances affecting the firm—for example, changing economic conditions. Third, budgets serve as a financial control tool, whereby management can check actual performance against intelligently predetermined standards and obtain reasons for variances.

The Capital Budget

The operating budgets make no allowance for the fact that a firm must replace old or obsolete equipment, acquire new plant, or sometimes invest money in special long-term research. They are concerned with the immediate future. The longer-term spending needs are provided for separately in a *capital budget*. This budget shows: the amount of funds required at various dates in the future for plant and equipment; the amount of funds available to finance these capital expenditures from within the firm—for example, from retained earnings; and the amount that will have to be raised from outside the business—for example, by bond or stock issues or a mortgage loan.

Zero-base Budgeting

More and more public institutions, and to a lesser extent, business firms, are turning to what is called zero-base budgeting as a means of controlling expenditures. With normal institutional budgeting, each department starts with the previous year's spending up to the budgeted amount and then considers proposed increases. As a result, there is an incentive during the previous year to spend the full amount budgeted even though savings could be made. This is because the actual spending rather than the budgeted amount for the past year is usually taken as the starting point for the new year. However, with zero-base budgeting, each department starts from zero and has to justify each and every proposed expenditure in its new budget. This means that the reasons for each proposed expenditure must be carefully reviewed each year. Also, the department concerned is usually required to rank each expenditure in order of priority so that, if an overall budgetary ceiling is imposed, the lowest priority items are the ones that are first eliminated.

KEY TERMS

Financial management
Finance department
Vice-president finance
Controller
Comptroller
Secretary-treasurer
Company secretary
Budget
Operating budget

Budgeting process
Budget committee
Sales forecast
Master budget
Production budget
Purpose of operating budgets
Capital budget
Zero-base budgeting

REVIEW QUESTIONS

1. What are the principal aims of financial management?
2. How can the manager of a small business improve the firm's financial management?
3. Explain the duties of: (a) a vice-president, finance; (b) a comptroller; and (c) a treasurer.
4. What are the duties of the company secretary? Why is this position frequently combined with that of the treasurer?
5. How does management use budgets?
6. Distinguish between an operating budget and a capital budget.
7. Describe how an operating budget is prepared for a manufacturing firm.

8. What is zero-base budgeting? Why has it become so popular as a financial planning technique? What are its strengths and weaknesses?
9. Are all business decisions made purely on financial grounds? Discuss, with examples.
10. Financial planning is unnecessary in the small business. Discuss.

READING

Zero Base Budgeting Technique Seems Certain to Spread

BY TIMOTHY PRITCHARD
Source: *The Globe and Mail,* Toronto

Zero base budgeting is time-consuming and sometimes unsettling. But a few Canadian companies and institutions are applying it with what they believe are good results, so the technique seems certain to spread.

The idea, basically, is to examine each area of spending every year to see whether new or existing programs are worthwhile. Conventional budgets are often set by adding the cost of new activities to existing ones (with the usual allowances for expansion and inflation).

The formal evaluation system in zero base requires that activities be isolated in "decision packages". These must contain enough information to determine the merits of a task and to compare and rank it with competing proposals.

Managers must identify alternative methods of performing the minimum level of an activity and following that selection, prepare "incremental decision packages" to indicate the costs and benefits of successive increases in effort.

Westinghouse Canada Ltd. in Hamilton used it to cut 10 per cent from $17-million of projected head office spending this year. McMaster University, also in Hamilton, overcame a crisis with zero base three years ago and has stuck with it.

Canadian Broadcasting Corp. has for the past three years used what David Lint, director of planning in Toronto, described as a modified zero base system for its administration activities.

"There is as much benefit in the process as in the end result," J.H. Goar, director of corporate development at Westinghouse, told Report on Business. "It sharpened our awareness of what outputs we say we're producing and how much they cost."

Zero base budgeting is not new. Texas Instruments Inc. of Dallas, Tex., used it in 1970; U.S. President Jimmy Carter introduced it when he was governor of Georgia and other states have followed. In earlier days, operational audits provided a similar approach.

The textbook *Zero Base Budgeting* by Peter Pyhrr, who once worked at Texas Instruments, was published in 1973. Some managers have applied his concept wholly; others have used modified versions. But either way, it is a technique for the times.

This is mainly because inflation—reflected in fast-rising wage, material and other costs—is a problem that requires discipline. Zero base is disciplined but, also important, it involves top and middle management in the decision-making process.

McMaster University tried zero base in its 1975-76 fiscal year to see what could be done to trim costs that threatened to outrun $40-million of revenue by $2-million to $4 million, said John MacFarlane, assistant vice-president of administration.

A big jump in wage costs posed the major threat. Support staff at the university wanted parity with those working at the teaching hospital on campus. The hospital staff had been given healthy increases to match other hospitals in Southern Ontario.

What happened that first year was basically a cost-cutting exercise, Mr. MacFarlane said. "Our concern was that if we were going to make cuts, would we make them wisely?" Everyone feared cutbacks that would suggest that academic standards were suffering.

Faced with the potential deficit, McMaster might have done the usual thing and made across-the-board cuts of 6 to 10 per cent in every departmental budget. But it was recognized that some activities should be trimmed, while others would still need to be expanded.

The first year of the process was the most traumatic. One department and about 65 jobs were cut. In the second year, staff levels were held about even and in the third year there has been a slight growth in employment.

The second-year process was used to check whether any big mistakes had been made a year earlier, and this year's budget is being considered against university-wide priorities. "It's time-consuming but well worth doing," Mr. MacFarlane said. "We're learning a tremendous amount."

He said the budget process had initially been rough on some managers. "They had to review their operations in a tough way and some were sensitive about how visible these had become. It was uptight time."

The most valuable part of the exercise is that managers have to think about alternatives and state them, he added. This is an opportunity for those with new ideas. For those who like the status quo it is an incentive to get ideas from subordinates.

At Westinghouse the zero base concept had been considered for more than a year before being adopted for the head office in mid-1976, Mr. Goar said. Production divisions, such as the Power Systems Group, may also use it now on a voluntary basis.

There are four head office divisions each headed by a vice-president—finance and administration, personnel, secretarial and legal, and marketing and technology. After two months to prepare decision packages in each group, the review process began.

D.C. Marrs, president, appointed task forces to review the decision packages for the four head office divisions. Each task force was headed by the vice-president of an operating division—"they are the consumers of the service," Mr. Goar noted—but, significantly, the task forces were asked to report back to the relevant head office vice-president not to Mr. Marrs.

"There were some pretty brutal challenges against the decision packages being presented—it wasn't a patsy type of operation," Mr. Goar said. "But the task forces were not going to rush off to the president. There was a good spirit of co-operation."

Mr. Goar, who had laid out the program, acted as secretary for each of the task forces. Management consultants from Woods, Gordon and Co. in Toronto sat in as observers.

Cuts in the head office budget amounted to roughly 10 per cent of earlier projections but only about half of that represented a real saving. Some jobs were simply shifted to other divisions in the belief they could be done there more efficiently.

About 20 jobs were eliminated in the process, although many of these people found jobs elsewhere in the company. One group in charge of a central salvage operation was disbanded, accounting for the largest single staff cut.

In that case, management concluded that salvaging unneeded equipment and materials should not be done centrally, but could be done as well by fewer people in the various operating divisions. That decision saved $100,000 a year.

The budget studies also led to a decision to do more key punching of computer information in field operations and less in Hamilton. Other decisions reduced the number of names handled manually on the executive payroll, and eliminated head office screening of expense accounts that already had been approved.

In future years, Westinghouse will probably want to look more closely at the cost of advances on expenses (considering the extensive use of credit cards), and the cost of collecting payments for Canada Savings Bonds, Mr. Goar said.

Some of the company's activities that rated low in decision package ratings were not automatically cut because it was recognized that they also had some public and employee relations value. These decisions were referred to the president.

Although some big cuts are possible, the general experience has been that savings come from a lot of little things. But these can add up. At McMaster it was discovered that there were not one or two internal delivery systems, but seven of them to be rationalized.

In Mr. Goar's view, zero base budgeting is simply a disciplined method of assessing activities and costs. "It doesn't make decisions for you but it produces a data base to make decisions more objective, more informed. The decisions still have to be made by managers."

It is especially valuable for head office overhead activities that cannot be measured for efficiency on the bottom line of a profit and loss statement. It helps to come to grips with questions like: "How much auditing should you do? How much is enough?"

Those who have tried it are not sure how often zero base must be practiced. Once every five years is one suggestion. Mr. Lint, who believes it works best in crisis situations, is nonetheless considering a modified ongoing program for CBC.

It would embody many of the principles of Management by Objectives and Zero Base Budgeting. The regional management of divisions would work with a central auditing unit, headed by the national director, only once every two or three years.

The experience of those who have started the program is that managers need a lot of help in preparing their decision packages. The first year is the most demanding but some handholding continues from year to year.

Because of time and cost, zero base may turn out to be a fad or an infrequent exercise. It may also stimulate more basic thinking about the way businesses operate. There is no time in the budget process to think about changes in relationships, Mr. Goar said, but a fresh approach helps to isolate the things that need longer term study.

Assignment

1. How does zero-base budgeting differ from traditional budgeting techniques?
2. What are the advantages of zero-base budgeting?
3. How can it best be implemented, if considered suitable?
4. What is the relationship between zero-base budgeting and "management by objectives"?

UNIT 12.2: EVALUATING PROFITABILITY

The Income Statement

The most important tool that management uses to watch over the profitability of the enterprise is the income statement. This is a summary of the income, expenses, and net profit or loss of the business for a given period of time. The length of time, known as the *accounting period*, may be one month, three months, six months, or a year. Frequent statements are required by management, but a year is the usual period for the owners. The year chosen is called the *fiscal year*, which need not coincide with the calendar year. A firm with heavy Christmas sales, for example, may end its year on March 31st.

To illustrate the income statement, let us consider the example of a small hardware store. This is an example of a merchandising operation organized as a sole proprietorship. The owner started the business, but was forced to close down after a year's operation. He had overestimated potential sales, had started with insufficient capital to carry him over the initial starting period, and had been unable to obtain sufficient short-term financing from a chartered bank or other lender. The following is an income statement for the most recent month:

Sales	$55,000
Cost of Goods Sold	44,000
Gross Profit on Sales	11,000
Expenses	13,270
Deficit	$ 2,270

This income statement shows that the *revenue from sales* was $55,000. The *cost of goods sold*, which is the beginning inventory plus purchases less closing inventory, was $44,000. The *gross profit* (or *gross margin*), which is the profit made from the sale of goods before expenses are deducted, was $11,000. Net income (or *net profit*), obtained by subtracting expenses from the gross profit, was negative—a deficit of $2,270. *Expenses*, which are the costs of transacting business, include such items as rent, wages, and provision for taxes, and totalled $13,270. These are often separated, in a larger company, into administrative expenses and selling expenses.

Administrative expenses consist of rent, salaries of office staff, accounting fees, electricity, and so on—costs that are associated with the administration of the enterprise. *Selling expenses* comprise salespeople's salaries and commissions, travelling expenses, advertising, and other costs associated with the purely selling function.

Break-even Analysis

An important tool that financial management can employ to evaluate a particular course of action, such as making and marketing a new product or opening a new branch store, is *break-even analysis*. This involves a comparison of the total anticipated revenue from the sale of a product, at different possible levels of sales, with the total anticipated expenses. The purpose of such a comparison is to determine what volume of sales is necessary for revenue to cover expenses. Unless this point, called the *break-even point*, can be reached, there will be no profit. And if it takes too long to reach it, there will be a large accumulated loss to recover before the venture can be said to be profitable.

Once a firm's break-even analysis reveals, however tentatively, the volume of sales required to break even, an attempt can be made through market research to determine how quickly, if at all, the firm can achieve this level of sales. If the firm concludes that it would take too long, or that it might never be achieved, then it can decide to refrain from production without having invested any money in the venture—apart from the time and effort involved in the break-even analysis. The firm can then turn its attention to other possibly more worthwhile projects.

An example of a break-even analysis is shown below. The break-even point, where total revenue of $40,000 equals total expenses, is 4,000 units.

Volume of Sales (Units)	Total Anticipated Revenue (@ $10.00 per unit)	Total Anticipated Costs	Anticipated Profit (or Loss)
1 000	$ 10 000	$ 25 000	$ (15 000)
2 000	20 000	30 000	(10 000)
3 000	30 000	35 000	(5 000)
4 000	40 000	40 000	—
5 000	50 000	45 000	5 000
6 000	60 000	50 000	10 000
7 000	70 000	55 000	15 000
8 000	80 000	60 000	20 000
9 000	90 000	65 000	25 000
10 000	100 000	70 000	30 000

Figure 12.4 Example of a Break-Even Analysis

It should be noted that total costs consist of both fixed costs and variable costs. *Fixed costs*, also called "overhead," are costs that remain unchanged whatever the level of production. That is why, in Figure 12.5, the fixed cost line is a horizontal one, extending from left to right, starting at zero units sold. Such costs include depreciation of plant, equipment, and vehicles; certain fixed labour costs; insurance; property taxes; and other costs that do not vary with the level of production or sales. As more units are produced and sold, the fixed cost per unit declines.

Variable costs are costs that vary with the number of units produced. They include the costs of the labour, materials, and other variable expenses involved in the production of each unit of the product. In our example, it costs $5.00 to produce each extra unit, in addition to the fixed costs. In Figure 12.5, total variable costs are represented by the line sloping upwards to the right from the zero cost level on the vertical axis on the left.

The line that starts at the $20,000 fixed cost level, and slopes upward to the right, represents total costs—the fixed costs plus the variable costs—at each particular volume of sales. Thus the total cost of producing 2,000 units is $30,000, consisting of $20,000 of fixed costs and $10,000 of variable costs (2,000 x $5.00). At 6,000 units, total cost is $50,000, made up of $20,000 of fixed cost and $30,000 of variable cost (6,000 x $5.00). It can be seen in the chart (Figure 12.5) that the total revenue and total cost lines intersect when the volume of sales is 4,000 units. This is the break-even point where revenue and expenses both equal $40,000 and corresponds with the data shown in the previous table.

Before the break-even point is reached, each unit sells for less than it costs to produce. Beyond the break-even point, the opposite occurs—each unit sells for more than it costs to produce. In our example, for $10.00 less the variable cost of $5.00, for a profit of $5.00 per unit. The concept of break-even analysis

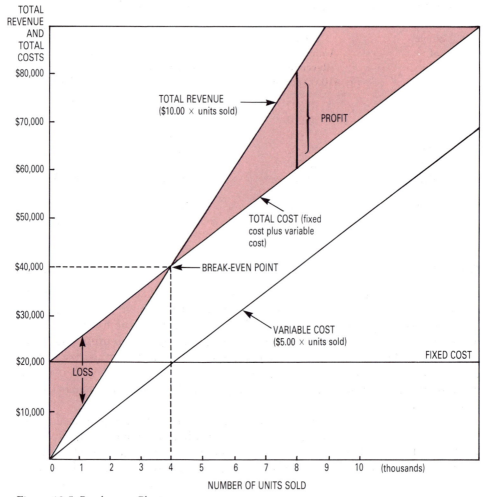

Figure 12.5 Break-even Chart

is most effectively demonstrated by the type of table and chart just shown. In practice, however, the break-even point, shown either as the volume of sales or the value of sales, can be determined much more quickly by use of algebraic equations.

Break-even analysis is a popular business tool. However, one should keep in mind the basic underlying assumptions: a constant price at which the product is sold and a constant variable cost in making it, whatever the volume of sales. Should these not remain constant, the break-even analysis must be modified accordingly. One should also note that some costs are fixed only over a certain

---

Calculating the Break-even Point

Break-even point: the number of units that a firm must sell of its product for total revenue to cover total costs.

Formula for calculating the unit break-even point:

$$\text{Unit B.E.P.} = \frac{\text{Total Fixed Costs}}{\text{Fixed Cost Contribution Per Unit Sold}}$$

$$\text{or } \frac{\text{TFC}}{\text{FCC Per Unit Sold}}$$

where FCC = Selling Price *minus* Variable Cost Per Unit

Situation A: ABC Publishing Company has spent $80,000 to publish 10,000 copies of a famous politician's autobiography which it plans to sell to retail bookstores for a net price of $15.00 each. How many books would it need to sell to break even?
Answer: Here there are no variable costs; only fixed costs. Therefore, the number of books that must be sold is:

$$\frac{80,000}{15} = 5,333$$

Situation B: (i) A manufacturer of power microscopes, priced to sell at $50.00 each net, has fixed costs of $150,000 per month and a variable cost of $30.00 per unit. How many microscopes must the manufacturer sell each month to break even?
Answer: In Situation A, the total costs were all fixed costs. In this example, there are both fixed and variable costs and the latter will vary according to the number of units sold. Therefore, using the formula, the number of microscopes that must be sold is:

$$\frac{150,000}{50 - 30} = \frac{150,000}{20} = 7,500 \text{ units per month}$$

(ii) Suppose the manufacturer wishes to know the dollar break-even point instead of the unit one. One way is to calculate the unit B.E.P., then multiply the number of units by the price. In our example, it would be:

$$7,500 \times \$50 = \$375,000$$

However, the following equation can also be used.

$$\text{Dollar B.E.P.} = \frac{\text{TFC}}{1 - \dfrac{\text{Variable Cost Per Unit}}{\text{Selling Price Per Unit}}}$$

Therefore,
$$\frac{\text{TFC}}{1 - 30/50}$$

$$= \frac{\$150,000}{20/50}$$

$$= \frac{\$150,000 \times 50}{20}$$

$$= \$375,000$$

(iii) How many microscopes must be sold per month to make a 10% profit on the investment?

Solution: The investment was the total cost of $375,000 (7,500 units × $50.00). Therefore, the profit required would be $37,500. We then use the previous equation, but divide the Profit Figure (instead of Total Fixed Costs) by the Fixed Cost Contribution Per Unit, in order to determine the additional units of output that must be sold. The profit required may be thought of as an additional fixed cost.

$$\text{Extra units required} = \frac{\text{Profit (or additional Fixed Cost)}}{\text{Fixed Cost Contribution Per Unit}}$$

$$= \frac{37,500}{20}$$

$$= 1,875$$

Therefore, the total number of power microscopes that must be sold per month to give a 10% profit on the investment = 7,500 + 1,875 = 9,375.

range of production. Beyond this, they will increase because, for example, of the increased cost of opening a new production line. Consequently, allowance must be made in the analysis for any of these "semi-variable" costs. Another consideration is that break-even analysis is best suited to a single product. When there is more than one product involved in the analysis, there must be a constant product mix if a single break-even analysis is to be used. Otherwise there must be a break-even analysis for each product with a separate allocation of shared costs.

Return on Capital

It is not sufficient for a business merely to break even. If the venture is to be worthwhile, whether it be a new store or plant or a new product line, it must also earn a satisfactory return on the capital invested by the owner or owners. The rate of return is obtained by dividing the net profit of the venture by the owner's equity capital.

What is a satisfactory rate of return will depend on current interest rates. If a business can earn, say, 8 per cent a year by investing its money in term deposits at a bank, then it must expect to earn considerably more than that by investing it in the business. One reason for expecting a higher rate of return is that the money in the bank is highly liquid—it can be withdrawn as and when required; whereas the money invested in the business will remain tied up in materials, equipment, and other plant assets. A second and very important reason for expecting a higher rate of return is that there is little risk involved in lending money to a major bank; whereas money invested in the business may all be lost or the rate of return be negligible if the investment turns out to be a poor one—often through no fault of the business. The higher the risk involved in the investment, the higher must be the expected rate of return—otherwise the investment in the business is not justified. Thus, far from just breaking even on a new venture, a business must plan to do much better than that. The break-even point can only be the goal if the business has included among its costs its desired profit.

Suppose, in our previous example, that the capital investment required is $100,000 and that the money could earn ten per cent a year, or $10,000, on deposit at the bank. Then, assuming that the time period for our break-even analysis is also one year, the business would need to sell 6,000 units to earn a similar rate of return. If it wants to earn 25 per cent, it must be able to sell 9,000 units. (See Figure 12.4 on page 455.)

Payback Period

Another method used in evaluating an investment is called the *payback period*. This is the number of years required for the investor to recover his or her money. In calculating return on capital, the net profit figure that we used was arrived at by subtracting from revenue all expenses including depreciation. However, depreciation is a non-cash expense—the cash required to pay for the asset having previously been paid. Consequently, for payback purposes, we recalculate net income by adding to it the depreciation charge—which thereby gives a truer picture of the actual flow of cash into the business. Also, if the company is planning to borrow to cover part of the cost of the investment, the interest cost of such borrowing should be subtracted from the net income. The adjusted net income is then in effect the *cash flow* of the business venture.

Suppose that the projected cash flow of the business venture, determined in this way, is $20,000 per annum. Then if the equity investment required is $100,000, the payback period is five years. In considering alternative investment opportunities, a company may well choose the one with the shortest payback period. Also, a company may, as part of its investment policy, have a definite rule as to the maximum payback period that it will contemplate.

Non-Monetary Factors

It should be mentioned, in conclusion, that management decisions are not always made on a financial basis. Thus a small business owner—for example, the publisher of a country newspaper or the owner of a convenience store—may continue to operate, even though the return on his or her capital is negligible. He or she may not be aware of his or her actual position; may know no other way of life; may hang on for sentimental reasons; or may not be able to find a buyer willing to pay a reasonable price for the business. Also, as another example, the owner of a business may train his or her son or daughter to succeed him or her even though perhaps more capable business managers could be hired.

KEY TERMS

Income Statement	Variable costs
Break-even analysis	Return on capital
Break-even chart	Payback period
Break-even point	Cash flow
Fixed costs ("overhead")	Non-monetary factors

REVIEW QUESTIONS

1. What is an income statement? What does it summarize?
2. What is break-even analysis? What are its purposes? Does it take place before or after the event?
3. What is a break-even chart? How is it constructed? What do the lines indicate?
4. What is the break-even point? How is this shown on a break-even chart?
5. If you anticipate that a new business venture will break even within a reasonable period of time, should you proceed with it? What other information do you require, if any? Discuss.
6. If a business earns less revenue than its expenses, should it shut down? Discuss.
7. The break-even point can be shown either in dollars or units. Explain.
8. "A business needs to do better than just break even." How much better?
9. What is the "payback method" of evaluating an investment? What are its merits?
10. What non-monetary factors may influence a business decision?

CASE PROBLEMS

ACE RECORD COMPANY INC.
Producing a new record

Martha Goreski is a talented folk-singer as well as a business student. As a professional musician she receives royalties of 5 per cent of the list price of each album of her songs. One of her albums is listed at $5.89 and two others at $6.29 each. Albums of some better-known folk and rock stars sell for as much as $9 or $10 each. Last year, the company for whom she records sold 1,895 copies of her lower-priced album and 3,773 copies of the other two combined.

Recently, Martha Goreski has been toying with the idea of recording and distributing her own songs, with financial help from relatives and friends. As she does not have her own pressing plant, she will have to spend about 60 cents per album (10% of the proposed list price of $5.89) for making the master disc and cutting the purchasable record copies from it. Another 40 cents per album is to be set aside for administration, including bookkeeping. Packaging is estimated to cost 50 cents per album—this figure is based on the fact that the cost of a record jacket varies from 15 cents to one dollar, depending on how elaborate it is. Advertising would require another 50 cents per album.

The records would be distributed through a wholesaler who would in turn sell them to retailers. The retailer expects to obtain at least 40 per cent of the list price as his or her markup—to cover store operating expenses and to provide a profit. The wholesaler expects in turn to make a gross profit of 10 per cent of the list price by buying the albums for $2.90 each from the record company and reselling them to the retailer for $3.50.

Assignment

1. How much capital would Goreski require to produce and advertise 2,000 copies of her own new album? This is the minimum economic production quantity.
2. How many copies would she need to sell to break even?
3. What would be the rate of return on her capital if she sold all the 2,000 copies?
4. How much gross profit would the wholesaler and the retailer make on the sale of 2,000 copies? Why is the wholesaler willing to operate on a smaller gross profit margin than the retailer?
5. How much better off is Goreski by producing and selling her own records? If she sells (a) 1,000 albums only, (b) 3,000 albums, and (c) 5,000?
6. What intangible factors should also be considered?

BLAKE UNIFORM RENTAL COMPANY LTD. (1)
Making a break-even analysis

Malcolm Blake, 28, is at present employed as a men's clothing salesman in one of Canada's leading department stores. His wife, Sandra, is a public school teacher for the local school board. Together they have accumulated $10,000 for investment in a business and can borrow a further $5,000 from relatives and $10,000 from the bank.

The business that they intend to establish is a uniform rental company. Coveralls, shopcoats, counter coats, pants, and shirts would be rented to mechanics, miners, and service station attendants in their town in exchange for a fee that also covers weekly cleaning. The rates to be charged indicate an average rental fee of $20 per month per customer, that would cover one or two items each.

The Blakes must decide within a week whether to go ahead with their plan, as a small dry cleaning plant has now come on the market at a rental of $800 per month. The plant contains dry cleaning equipment, pressing and sewing equipment, a cash register and a typewriter—all in reasonably good condition.

The cost to the firm of buying the garments to be rented is as follows: coveralls $15 each, shopcoats $12 each, counter coats $8 each, pants $8 each, and shirts $6 each. An initial stock of 300 of each garment would be bought with further purchases as business increases. A second-hand truck for collection and delivery can be purchased for approximately $5,000.

The staff would consist of Malcolm as manager/cleaner/salesman/driver receiving $1,500 per month and two sewer/pressers, receiving $700 each. Malcolm's wife would continue at her present job.

Other fixed expenses are estimated on a monthly basis as follows: electricity and gas $350, advertising and promotion $600, truck operation $220, truck depreciation $100, uniform depreciation $500, and miscellaneous (including loan interest) $300. There will also be a variable cost—cleaning supplies, estimated at $50 per month for every 50 customers. The maximum capacity for the plant is 800 customers, after which cleaning will have to be sent out or a larger plant obtained.

Assignment

1. Prepare a table showing, in vertical columns, total monthly revenue, total monthly expenses, and the monthly profit or loss, at various numbers of customers (100, 150, and so on up to 500).
2. Construct a break-even chart for the proposed business venture based on the previous table.
3. How many customers would be required for the venture to break even?
4. How many customers would be required for a return of 2 per cent per month on the Blakes' $10,000 equity capital?
5. At 600 customers, indicate: (a) the rate of return on the Blakes' $10,000 equity capital; and (b) the rate of return on an equity capital of $5,000 if the Blakes borrow an additional $5,000 from their relatives at 12 per cent per annum and reduce their equity capital from $10,000 to $5,000. How has the rate of return on equity capital changed? Why? What financial principle does this question illustrate?

READING

Attic's at the Top

Al Mair and Tom Williams have made it Canada's most successful independent record company

BY ANDREW WEINER

Source: *The Financial Post Magazine.* Used by permission of Andrew Weiner.

Simpsons department store, Yonge Street, Toronto, sixth floor. The corporate vice-president is on an undercover mission to see how well his product is stocked, displayed and priced.

"Rovers front-racked, two pockets, $5.98. Good."

He scribbles in his notebook. He carries no briefcase on these expeditions. He prefers to, as he puts it, "sleaze around," draw as little attention as possible.

The corporate vice-president is dressed, much as usual, in jeans, a leather jacket and shades. His hair is long, frizzy and slightly greying. His name is Tom Williams, he is 36 years old and he is vice-president and co-founder of Toronto's Attic Records, one of Canada's most successful independent record labels.

Satisfied that the Rovers are getting a fair shake, Williams turns his attention to another major Attic product, vibraphonist Hagood Hardy, finally locating him under "Instrumental." The first album in the Hardy section is an old item recorded for another record company. Deftly, Williams pulls it out and shuffles it to the back.

Last year Attic sales were up 74 percent over 1979, at a time when overall industry sales plunged 20 to 25 percent. This year the company will gross close to $4 million. And still, it all adds up. Williams observes that no music is playing in Simpsons' record section. "If they were playing the Rovers now, they'd probably sell four copies. It drives me crazy."

Everyday life in the record business. In appearance Williams may be every teenager's fantasy of a rock 'n' roll record company executive. But the realities of the business—reshuffling Hagood Hardy albums in Simpsons—are often rather less glamorous.

On this cold February day, Williams will spend another four hours trekking up and down the Yonge Street strip, in and out of record stores, checking the racking of Attic products. The following week Williams will be in Vancouver, to meet with local record salesmen, visit radio stations to promote Attic artists, hold discussions with promoters about forthcoming tours... and to check out more record stores. In some ways, he says, that will be the most important part of the trip.

Al (Alexander) Mair, the 40-year-old president and co-founder of Attic Records, is poring over his appointment calendar from the Cannes MIDEM (Marché International de Disques et de l'Edition Musicale) international music festival in January 1981—the seventh in a row he has attended—trying to decode his own left-handed scrawl. "At 3:30 I met with an English record company, then at 5:30 with a German record company and at six with another English company..."

"And those," he says, "were just the formal appointments." Mair was staying at the Carlton, "the key hotel in Cannes—no one registered under the rank of vice-president," and the huge lobby was constantly swarming with circulating music industry types. "You could spend a whole day in the lobby just going from table to table."

At the Carlton one is constantly squinting at name tags, making connections that may not pay off until a much later date. "This is a business of connections," Mair says. "Some people I may see 10 times before we do any business."

In a business of connections, Mair is clearly very well-connected. "The respect with which Al is held on the international scene," says music journalist and recent MIDEM attendee Richard Flohil, "is quite remarkable." Or as Tony Tobias, president of the Pangaea Music House in Toronto says, "When you go over to MIDEM, Attic is the Canadian company they talk about."

Connections run both ways. On one hand, Attic now earns about 20 percent of its total revenues through foreign record sales and royalties. This year at Cannes, for example, Mair firmed up a South African distribution deal for the label. At the same time, Attic is building a substantial business as a Canadian outlet for overseas acts. Belgian rock artist Plastic Bertrand, for example, sells records in the hundreds of thousands in Quebec on Attic. And then there is the music publishing arm, Attic Publishing Group, which—again through Mair's connections—represents lucrative song catalogues, like that of the Swedish superstars Abba, in Canada. In other words, every time an Abba record plays on the radio, a cash register rings for Attic.

If his partner Tom Williams looks exactly as you might have expected a record company executive to look, Al Mair is harder to pin down. His office style is weekend suburban laid-back: slacks, sweater, open-necked shirt, shortish hair, neat moustache. And Mair lives, along with his wife and two young children, in the exclusive Baby Point area of Toronto's west end, while his bachelor partner prefers to own a home downtown.

Mair's idea of relaxation is playing with his kids or reading a book. Footloose Williams still gets to make the rounds of the music clubs, night after night, checking out current and potential Attic talent. Mair is quiet, serious and, in the words of one acquaintance, "sometimes a little humorless": all qualities that served him well in his years of guiding the business affairs of superstar Gordon Lightfoot prior to setting up Attic. Williams is fast-talking, wise-cracking, outgoing: qualities that served him well in his pre-Attic career as national promotion manager for WEA Records in Canada.

Outsiders tend to stereotype them: Williams as the front man, the salesman, the good-time guy, the shaper of Attic's style; Mair as the backroom brains, the man who watches the till, the real substance of the operation. But it really isn't that simple. While Mair handles music publishing, international contacts and contract negotiations, Williams is responsible for day-to-day running of the domestic operation. Both must co-sign the cheques. And, Williams says, "We can both read a balance sheet. We're different people and we tend to hold each other in check... I use Al as an excuse when people want more money."

Originally from Dunnville, Ont., Tom Williams came to Toronto with his family in 1957 and discovered CHUM—Canada's first nonstop Top 40 pop station.

Although he never played music, Williams was always involved with it, from MC-ing his high school dances to promoting concerts at Massey Hall while still studying at Toronto's Ryerson Polytechnical Institute. After a stint with a Hamilton TV station, he returned to Toronto to run the all-night show on CKFH radio. It was then he first encountered Al Mair, then a promotion man for Compo Records. In fact it was Mair who recommended Williams for his next job in the promotion department of the Canadian operation of the U.S.-based multinational WEA Records in 1969.

As a promotion man Williams visited radio stations, organized press parties and devised such strange stunts as dressing up an employee as a rooster to promote WEA artists Atomic Rooster. He was particularly well-regarded for his literate and witty press releases, a tradition he has continued with the Attic newsletter *Under the Eaves*. Toronto *Star* rock critic Peter Goddard recalls him as "a terrific promotion man, one of the best, and the most charming of the bunch."

One of the artists Williams promoted during this period was Gordon Lightfoot, then being managed by his friend Al Mair. Born in Toronto's west end, Mair had lived a similarly music-fixated adolescence as Williams. He began collecting records at 12 and working part-time in record stores at 14. While still in high school he was making $100 a night deejaying and running high school dances.

When Mair left high school, he first worked as a clerk at Massey Ferguson. But he soon moved on to Capitol Records, initially as an accountancy trainee, then in sales. After a series of similar jobs in and out of the record industry, he joined Compo (now MCA Records) in 1964, becoming director of national promotion in 1966.

Among the artists Mair promoted was Gordon Lightfoot, then under contract to a U.S.-based manager and dissatisfied with the handling of his affairs. In 1968 Lightfoot hired Mair as a salaried employee, while continuing to pay the percentage of his earnings demanded by his contract to his U.S. manager. Mair worked for Lightfoot until 1974, the period during which he was solidifying his status as an international superstar. Outsiders believe that Mair played a critical part in this process. "A lot of the things that Al did for Lightfoot," says Tony Tobias, "he has never been credited for."

As Lightfoot's business manager Mair was involved in high-level negotiations with international lawyers and record company executives—developing experience and contacts that he would later put to good use with Attic. But during this entire period he remained a salaried employee—albeit a very highly paid one—even after the expiration of Lightfoot's U.S. management contract.

Mair is reluctant to talk about his time with Lightfoot, but he will say that "I had not left Compo to be an employee but to be an independent businessman in partnership with someone else... He [Lightfoot] offered me a partnership, basically. But in his mind he couldn't have a partner." Originally they had planned to develop new artists together under the wings of Lightfoot's Early Morning Productions. But Lightfoot's enthusiasm cooled rapidly. He didn't want to take on the responsibility of helping new acts establish themselves. And he wanted Mair's undivided attention.

Frustrated with Lightfoot, Mair began to talk seriously about setting up an independent record company with his friend Tom Williams, who was becoming equally frustrated with WEA. In 1970 the CRTC had passed its famous "Canadian content" rule, requiring radio stations to devote 30 percent of their air time to Canadian music. There was a tremendous demand for suitable Canadian music for these radio stations to play, and the U.S.-owned multinationals had been slow to meet it. "I didn't feel that WEA was doing all it could in signing native talent," Williams recalls. "I felt that on two levels: both the nationalist level and the fact that there was money to be made." (Both Williams and Mair are genuine, if extremely pragmatic, in their nationalism.) In November 1973, Williams quit his job to begin working full-time on setting up Attic.

The Canadian content rule had already sparked a rush to form independent record labels. Most, however, were poorly planned, poorly financed and would stumble on towards bankruptcy in the years ahead. Mair and Williams wanted a properly financed company able to present a full range of artists rather than just specializing in folk or jazz or rock. Their dream was an "Asylum of the North," modelled after a U.S. independent that handled a small and select roster of artists including Linda Ronstadt and the Eagles. With this dream, they began to approach possible investors.

During this start-up phase, Williams and one employee were working in a converted kitchen, the back room of Gordon Lightfoot's Toronto headquarters. Mair was in the next room, still dividing his time between Lightfoot's affairs and his new venture. Even at this point, Mair was tempted by the idea of inviting Lightfoot in as an investor and partner and perhaps, eventually, as a recording artist as well. It would have speeded up the growth of the company tremendously. And Lightfoot was not completely uninterested in the idea. But in the end Mair and Williams decided that the idea was unworkable. As Mair puts it, "You can't get headstrong, creative people in a business atmosphere to work together."

Ultimately, through loans and sales of shares, they were able to raise $300,000 to finance their first three years of operation: enough, Williams says, "to survive even if we didn't have any hits—and we were pretty accurate on that score." Some of the money was their own, with Mair slightly the larger investor ("That's why he's president," Williams says), enough to give them the controlling equity interest in the company. Some came from their bank. Some came from a consortium of investors, including several members of the Irish Rovers. But perhaps the decisive contribution—about one-third of the total—came from the Canadian Enterprise Development Corp., a Montreal-based venture capital outfit.

Why would a venture capital firm that usually invests in more conventional industrial enterprises invest in an exotic—for it— notion such as an independent record company? Derek Mather, CED executive vice-president, explains that in venture capital "people are almost always the most important single factor. We don't usually control companies in which we invest, so the biggest question is—who does? And how good are they?"

Mather knew nothing about the record industry. After reviewing Mair's credentials his question was, "Who is Gordon Lightfoot?" But he was tremendously impressed with Mair and Williams and with the track records his investigations revealed. "They're definitely music people, but they're also very sound, sensible corporation builders. They have many of the attributes you find in any successful business person: good lifestyle, character, integrity, honesty... I was so convinced they were going to do well that I didn't look at it as a risk, but as a fantastic investment opportunity."

So Attic was in business, incorporating officially in June 1974, and Williams turned his considerable promotional abilities to putting Attic on the map. Take the first annual meeting, for instance. While CBS Records threw a $500,000 sales convention, Mair, Williams and their single employee adjourned to a local tavern for beer, potato chips and speeches. Several photographs of the event ran a full page in the music trade press. Total budget: $12.30.

The company itself could hardly be described as an overnight success. The first three major signings, singer/songwriters Ron

Negrini, Ken Tobias and Shirley Eikhard, were all acquired relatively cheaply: Attic advanced recording costs of about $35,000 per album, but only Tobias also got a small cash advance. All three turned out "turntable hits," which means they garnered airplay in the heavy CanCon atmosphere of the time, but failed to sell in great numbers. All three have since parted company with Attic.

The failure with Eikhard was especially puzzling, says Goddard, since her talent was so evident; "It Takes Time," a song she wrote, had been a major hit for Anne Murray long before Eikhard joined Attic. "I'm sure Attic tried," adds Goddard, "but the spark was missing." Eikhard herself claims no bitterness about the experience, though she says that she's quite disappointed "they only pressed a few thousand copies of my last album—they didn't seem to have enough belief in me to press more."

Tony Tobias, manager and brother of Ken Tobias, suggests that Mair and Williams were simply spread too thin in the early years: They had few resources to draw on, they were under tremendous psychological pressure and, in a sense, "they were competing with themselves. While they were promoting themselves corporately and trying to get the company off the ground, it was also difficult to promote new acts and give them the career development and artistic direction they needed."

Additionally, Tobias suggests, Attic was having problems getting its records into the stores. At that time, distribution was handled by London Records of Canada, a company that lacked the retail strength of the majors. Moreover, soon after Attic began, the majors finally began to sign and heavily promote Canadian talent. "Attic just didn't have the resources to compete with that kind of machine," says Tobias. "And, all in all, both the artists and the company were the victims of circumstance."

Looking back on this, Williams says "I think we gave them [the artists] all a good shot. The bottom line is that they didn't sell enough records." At the same time, he points to a "lack of management support" for these artists. When Mair and Williams started Attic they made a deliberate decision not to become involved with management. Yet they found that there were very few good managers out there to do the job. Many of the best music managers in Canada were already running their own independent record companies, which featured only their own clients—men like Bernie Finkelstein and Bernie Fiedler at True North (Murray McLauchlan and Bruce Cockburn) or Vic Wilson and Ray Danniels at Anthem (Rush, Max Webster). Because of this Mair and Williams have often found themselves doing the work of managers by default at no charge to the artists. Both Williams and Mair concede that they made a lot of mistakes in the early years. For all their expertise, they had a great deal more to learn. And financially, these were extremely lean times. In the first year Attic grossed $36,000 and ran at a loss of $100,000. Not until the third year did they break even.

Three things saved the two. The first was the fact that they had budgeted for hard times. "They had a habit of meeting their budgets," says Derek Mather. " And that's rare in risk capital. You almost always run into a few bumps in the life of an investment."

Then there was the cash flow from music publishing: the air-play royalties from their own artists and from the foreign publishing deals made possible by Mair's overseas connections from the Lightfoot years—including, at this time, representing the Beatles catalogue in Canada. Today about 20 percent of Attic's revenue comes from music publishing.

Finally, and perhaps crucially, there was Hagood Hardy. Hardy had written a tea company jingle that the advertising agency kept getting requests for, even though he had no recording deal at the time. So Hardy recorded the jingle (renamed "The Homecoming") on his own label and picked up some radio play. Hardy and Mair met at MIDEM in 1975 and Attic signed him up. After some heavy promotion, "The Homecoming" single went gold (75,000 sales) and gave Attic its first platinum album (100,000 sales) and its first double-platinum album (200,000 sales).

"Without that hit," Williams says, "we probably wouldn't have been able to survive." With it they were able to establish Hardy as a steady seller of albums and to move on to new glories.

The next great leap forward came with Triumph, a Toronto-based rock trio, which impressed Mair and Williams as hardworking, intelligent and extremely marketable. Attic spent $50,000 in promoting the then unknown band's first album in 1976, an expenditure which they did not expect to recoup in immediate sales, but instead through the group's long-term growth potential.

That judgment proved correct. With each new Triumph album and tour, sales of its previous albums have taken another jump, and it has now racked up a series of gold and platinum albums in Canada. Even then, Williams says, the time and money invested in promoting Triumph—or indeed, any Attic act—can rarely be recovered through Canadian sales alone. "But we're building acts that will sell in the rest of the world." In Triumph's case, this is already happening in the U.S., where Attic has negotiated a lucrative deal with RCA to release the band's albums. On a typical U.S. deal, says Williams, Attic receives between 75 cents and $1.20 per album sold, and that money is divided up between Attic and the recording artist.

Success with Hardy and Triumph gave Attic the leverage it needed to negotiate a new distribution deal with powerful CBS Records, in January 1979. (Attic's previous distributor, London Records of Canada Ltd., has since gone out of business, hurting many smaller independents that lacked Attic's clout to get a better deal.) And CBS's superior distribution network opened the way for major growth in 1980.

Some of that growth was due to the development of a third major Attic artist, U.S. blues musician George Thorogood. Recording for a small American independent, Thorogood had become dissatisfied with his Canadian distribution deal and sought out Attic. Williams caught Thorogood's act live in Toronto and a deal was made for a small advance soon afterwards. Since then Attic has given Thorogood his first (and still only) gold album anywhere and his first platinum album.

But the biggest coup of all came with the Irish Rovers. The Vancouver-based group gave sell-out concerts around the country, but its record sales had plummeted in the years since the million-selling "The Unicorn" of 1968. Radio stations were so reluctant to play "Irish" music that even the band's hardcore fans were unaware that it was still making records.

Several members of the Irish Rovers had been investors in Attic from the beginning, but not until 1979 did the band and the company agree that it was time to make an album together. Veteran rock producer Jack Richardson was brought in to give the group a more contemporary sound, and the Rovers themselves found a novelty drinking song called "Wasn't That A Party" as an obvious single release.

The problem that remained was to get the album and the single played on the radio. And so Williams persuaded a rather reluctant band to drop the word "Irish" from its name.

As a result, radio stations began to play the album by this "new" band called the Rovers; they also played the single. And to the astonishment of all, both the album and single soared up the Canadian charts and are now repeating the same trick in the U.S. through its distributor, Cleveland International.

For an independent record company to compete with the majors, observes Earl Rosen, executive secretary of the Canadian Independent Record Production Association (CIRPA), it must go where the majors are not prepared to go, take risks the majors are not prepared to take, "find the niches in the market, the kind of music the majors are turning down."

Actually, beating out the majors may not be as difficult as it sounds. In the first place, as Richard Flohil points out, "most record companies are run by accountants" and tend to the unimaginative. And then, decision-making by Canadian outlets of the U.S. multinationals can be desperately slow, often requiring final approval from head office. "By the time a major can decide what to do about a signing, Attic has done it three times over," says Flohil. Recently Attic beat out its own distributor, CBS, to sign Hamilton rock band Teenage Head, not so much by out-bidding, Mair says, as by "out-hustling." Result: another gold record.

Of course, beating out the majors is only worthwhile if the product is going to sell. But though, as Flohil says, "Attic has put out some turkeys," in recent times its successes have far out-weighed its failures. "Tom and Al have incredible ears as to what might work. CBS would never have signed the Rovers. So they look at Attic and say, 'My God, how did they do that?' CBS would not have bothered with a George Thorogood... But now it has him at second-hand, and he's selling."

For all its recent success, Attic remains a small company. Apart from its foreign artists it has a roster of about a dozen Canadian pop artists and has no desire to expand further at this time. The goal, Mair says, is still "to try to maintain personal relationships with our artists, which is not possible in the bigger companies."

These days, Mair and Williams and their 10 employees occupy the top floor of a renovated office building on Queen Street in Toronto's trendy lower east side district, one floor above True North ("I look up to them all the time," says Bernie Finkelstein). Walls and surfaces are cluttered with gold and platinum albums, Juno awards and stacks of demonstration tapes from potential new acts—Williams estimates that they listen to about 2,000 a year. The gold and platinum albums are awarded on the basis of sales certified by the Canadian Recording Industry Association. "I've got a basement full of them," Williams says, "so my relatives can see I'm not such a ne'er-do-well as I seem."

Last year Attic paid off its remaining loans. This year Mair hopes to announce the first dividend for shareholders: "As a substantial shareholder, I'm very much in favor of dividends."

Equally impressive is the almost universal respect which Mair and Williams have won over the past seven years. "They're two very astute businessmen and at the same time two very good record people," says CBS Senior Vice-President Stan Kulin. "That's a very unusual combination and it's the key to their success." Or as lawyer Stephen Stohn says, "They've done something very successful—opened a record company without going broke."

Even Tony Tobias, who might perhaps be expected to nurse some resentment following Attic's failure with his brother Ken, calls Mair "very much a teacher for me...

someone I've observed and learned from and have aspired to equal."

In fact, just about the only criticism that might be raised against Mair and Williams is that they have been too concerned with commercial success. "They're involved in the music *business*, underlining the word 'business'," says Peter Goddard, "and they're much better at that than anyone else." Goddard also sees Attic as different from a label such as True North, where "the focus is much more on the artists" and where the company owners "have to be committed to what the artists are doing."

By pursuing commercial criteria, Goddard says, Mair and Williams have built a successful yet "rather amorphous" label—a bewildering mixture of styles from folk to pop to punk-rock, which has yet to establish a firm corporate identity. "They made very good moves, but I don't think it added up to anything. What Attic is missing is at least one major centrepiece."

Mair and Williams, for their part, will insist that they always intended to present a full range of sounds: a kind of mini-major, rather than the typical highly specialized independent. And Williams (though not Mair) will further insist that he personally likes *everything* released by Attic.

In one sense, Mair and Williams are fortunate men. They have translated a teenage obsession into a successful and still growing business. But they are under no illusions as to the fact that what they do is *work*, and very hard work at that. Though both try to keep regular office hours, Williams spends many nights a week monitoring the bar scene and at least 12 weeks a year on the road overseeing domestic operations. Mair travels out of the country at least eight weeks a year, not counting frequent day trips to New York.

Both are also heavily involved in music industry organization. "I'd rather not leave my future up to anyone else," Mair says, explaining his involvement.

When Mair and Williams listen to music these days—and they listen to it almost constantly—it is usually for business rather than pleasure. Mair monitors patterns of radio air-play, checks out demo tapes on the cassette player of his Mercury Zephyr, but rarely plays his home stereo system. And Williams even conceded to occasional battle fatigue: "When you're going to the Nickelodeon [a Toronto rock club] for the 400th time, when you're working 18-hour days, when you're going out west in the summer for two weeks when you could be lying around at the cottage… it's work."

Today, Williams finds that "most of my friends aren't involved in music. They've never heard of Gruppo Sportivo [a recent Attic signing from Holland]." Yet he claims not to often feel any generation gap between himself and the typical rock fan.

Mair and Williams are only just beginning to reap the fruits of success, and they have had to run very hard to attain it. Presumably they will have to keep on running hard in the future. In the record business, as in the movies, you are only as good as your last hit. And as Mair says, "Attic Records means nothing. Nobody buys an Attic record because it's an Attic record. The important thing is the artist on the label."

With the artists currently on the label, and with those currently being lined up for signing, Attic looks set to keep on churning out the hits.

"Attic," says Derek Mather, "still has its greatest growth ahead of it. It's done very well to get as far as it has in a difficult industry at a difficult time. I'm hopeful that there will be glorious profits in the future."

So You Want to Start A Record Company

Theoretically, says Earl Rosen, executive secretary of the Canadian Independent Record Production Association, you could start a record company for $1,000: record a single for $500 and press a few thousand copies for another $500. "There's no way you could start a shoe manufacturing plant for that kind of money." But your problems would only be beginning. In order to get your record into the stores, you would need to be able to conclude a deal for distribution with one of the major record companies or an independent distributor.

There are two routes an independent can go to get its products to market. One is simply to *license* the master tape of the recording to a major company and let it do the work of manufacturing, distributing and promoting it: This is how one of Canada's most successful independents, True North, does business. The other, the route taken by Attic, is to make a *buy-sell* arrangement in which, Tom Williams explains, "We are responsible for signing the act, recording the act, pressing the album, designing the record jacket, printing the jacket, printing point-of-sale posters, for everything except getting the records from the warehouse to the store and collecting on the accounts." The advantage of such a deal is that it is potentially more lucrative than a licensing arrangement. The disadvantage is that it involves more work and more risk.

In either case, you will need a viable product in order to entice the major company into a distribution deal. And realistically, a single produced for $500 is not going to attract much interest. The big money these days is in albums, not singles. And to record an album these days will usually cost at least $30,000 and typically $50,000. The record company advances the cost of recording to the artist. If the record is successful, this debt is paid off from out of the artist's royalties on album sales (typically eight to nine percent of the album's list price). But perhaps only one album in two does well enough even to recover its recording costs.

On a buy-sell arrangement, Tom Williams says, the independent might expect a return of about $1.50 an album after paying all royalties and manufacturing costs. On an album that costs $50,000 to produce, you might expect to break even after selling about 33,000 copies. And yet to sell that many copies you will have to put an additional $25,000 to $50,000 into promotion. That promotion money has to come out of your $1.50, as does your office overhead. According to lawyer Stephen Stohn, "To make any sort of profit in the Canadian market, you have to sell at least 50,000 albums, which is gold." To make really big money, you have to crack the international market as well.

"If I make a $50,000 album and it sells 100 copies," Williams says, "the kid who pays $6.98 for it is holding a $500 record." And yet there is always the chance of the really big score. The best-selling album of all time, *Saturday Night Fever*, grossed over $200 million worldwide. "It's a crap-shoot," Williams says.

Given the high-risk nature of the business, it is not surprising that the great majority of Canadian independents remain enfeebled and woefully undercapitalized. Recently, the independents have been lobbying the government to introduce a record tax shelter, modelled after the movie tax shelter, to attract investment. Although Attic no longer needs that sort of help, it would no doubt benefit from it. "The difference between a movie and a record," Williams says, "is that you don't need $5 million to make a record. You can make 100 records and have 100 shots at it." Given that sort of investment incentive, he says, the Canadian independents could work wonders worldwide. "If Abba can bring more money into Sweden than Volvo, then Attic can bring more into Canada than the potash industry."

Assignment

1. What functions does Tom Williams perform in Attic Records? Which are managerial?
2. What is Al Mair's role in the company?
3. "This is a business of connections." Explain. What is so different about this industry?
4. "Connections run both ways." Explain, with examples.
5. What was Williams' background as a promotion man?
6. What was Mair's business background?
7. What made the two set up their own business together?
8. How did they finance their new business?
9. Why did their first major signings flop? Whose fault was it?
10. What happened to the company financially in the early years? What kept it afloat?
11. How did Attic move out of the financial basement? What was the most important single reason for the improvement in its fortunes?
12. Attic may be said to epitomize the virtues of the small business versus the large. Explain, with examples.
13. Where is Attic located? What factors seem to have governed the choice?
14. What kind of record company does Attic seem to be?
15. How hard do its owners work?
16. "In the record business, as in the movies, you are only as good as your last hit." Why?
17. How much capital do you need to start a record company?
18. How could you get your product to market? Distinguish between licensing and a buy-sell arrangement.
19. Explain how break-even analysis applies to the record business. What is the break-even point for a record album?
20. What is a record tax shelter? How would it work? What might it achieve? What objection might there be to such a proposal?

CHAPTER 13
FINANCIAL SOLVENCY

CHAPTER OBJECTIVES

☐ To emphasize the importance of cash flow to a business and to explain how it is monitored.

☐ To show how a firm forecasts its future cash inflows, outflows, and surpluses or deficits by means of a cash budget.

☐ To indicate how a firm can assess its liquidity.

☐ To explain how a firm monitors its overall financial stability.

☐ To explain why a firm needs to borrow short-term capital and how it goes about it.

☐ To outline the nature, purpose, and sources of medium-term financing for business.

☐ To explain how and why a firm takes out insurance.

CHAPTER OUTLINE

13.1   Cash Management
13.2   Short-Term Financing
13.3   Medium-Term Financing
13.4   Business Insurance

UNIT 13.1: CASH MANAGEMENT

Importance of Monitoring the Cash Flow

Of great concern to every firm, large or small, is the flow of cash into and out of the business. If there is not enough cash to pay the bills falling due, suppliers will be reluctant to extend further credit. They will insist on prior cash payment, cash on delivery, or settlement of outstanding debts before further materials and parts and other supplies are provided. The utilities may be cut off or the premises seized and padlocked by the landlord. The firm may even be put out of business by irate creditors.

Even if the firm is basically solvent, further short-term borrowing to cover a cash deficit can mean a heavy additional interest expense. Conversely, wise cash management can prevent embarrassing calls from creditors, including the bank manager. It can also enable the business to reduce its normal amount of seasonal bank borrowing and so reduce the interest cost. In some cases, temporary surpluses of funds may enable a firm to earn interest income from short-term investments, perhaps in bank term deposits.

The Bank Statement

The most fundamental record of a firm's cash flow is its *bank statement* (Figure 13.1). So long as all the firm's receipts and disbursements are processed through the firm's bank account, this provides an accurate monthly record of all the firm's cash transactions and the firm's opening and closing cash balances. For many small business owners, the bank statement is a much more vital document than the income statement. This is because it reveals, on a much more frequent basis, financial solvency—a more immediate and pressing need than profitability. In the long run, a firm may be very profitable on paper but because of overly generous credit to customers or heavy investment in inventory, equipment, and other assets, be extremely short of cash, with possibly dire consequences.

The Cash-Flow Statement

Because of its vital importance to owners and managers, a firm's cash flow is usually monitored on a daily, weekly, or monthly basis. The statement that is drawn up, summarizing all the various inflows and outflows of cash that have taken place, is known as a *cash-flow statement*. Many small businesses are content to let their bank statement serve also as their cash-flow statement, endeavouring to make sure that all financial transactions, including petty cash items, are routed through their bank account. Usually, however, a running statement, based on the monthly bank statement, but updated on a daily, weekly or other basis, is prepared by the business, to keep the owner or manager really up-to-date on the firm's cash position. Compared with the income statement, the cash-flow statement includes *all* financial transactions, not just revenue and expense ones. Thus, for example, a bank loan and its gradual repayment will appear in the cash-flow

13.1 CASH MANAGEMENT

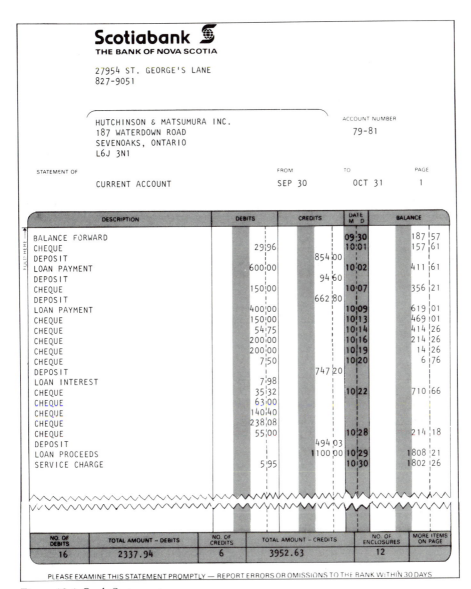

Figure 13.1 Bank Statement

statement but not in the income statement. Conversely, depreciation will appear in the income statement but not in the cash-flow statement, because no current outflow of cash is involved.

The Cash Budget

Perhaps the most useful tool that a firm can employ to help ensure financial solvency is the *cash budget*. This is a forecast, usually on a weekly or monthly basis, of all the funds that will be received and disbursed by the firm, and the resulting surplus or deficit. In estimating the cash flow, financial management takes into account not only the firm's operating and capital budgets, but also the ratio of cash sales to credit sales and the paying habits of its customers, including the likely percentage of bad debts. To estimate the cash outflow, it also considers the promptness with which the firm usually pays for materials and merchandise. In preparing or revising its cash budget, a firm will also pay careful attention to its past cash flows. By making a cash budget, financial management can, to some extent, foresee how much cash will be needed to operate the business each week, when the firm will need additional short-term funds, and when it will have surplus funds to invest. This information can enable the firm to time its capital expenditures more appropriately; to accelerate collection of accounts receivable (if possible without losing customers) to ward off a cash shortage; to plan its short-term borrowing well in advance; and perhaps even to invest a temporary surplus.

An example of a cash budget is shown in Figure 13.2.

Item	July	Aug.	Sept.	Oct.	Nov.	Dec.
A. Receipts	$1 000	$2 000	$3 000	$5 000	$6 000	$8 000
B. Payments:						
Purchases	500	1 500	2 000	4 500	6 500	4 000
Rent	400	400	400	400	400	400
Wages	750	750	750	750	750	750
Advertising	225	225	225	225	225	225
Miscellaneous	125	125	125	125	125	125
Total Payments	$2 000	$3 000	$3 500	$6 000	$8 000	$5 500
C. Cash Flow from Operations Surplus (or Deficit) (C = A − B)	($1 000)	($1 000)	($ 500)	($1 000)	($2 000)	$2 500
D. Cash Balance:						
Cash at Start	$4 000	$3 000	$2 000	$1 500	$1 000	$1 000
Cash Flow from Operations	($1 000)	($1 000)	($ 500)	($1 000)	($2 000)	$2 500
Bank Loan (L) or Repayment (R)	—	—	—	$ 500L	$2 000L	$2 500R
E. Cash at End	$3 000	$2 000	$1 500	$1 000	$1 000	$1 000

Notes 1. Minimum cash balance required by the bank as a condition for granting a line of credit is $1 000.
2. Where sales are made on credit, instead of cash, a schedule of estimated receipts can be drawn up. This would show, for example, that the money for $1 000 sales in July would be received, say, 20 per cent in July, 70 per cent in August, and 10 per cent in September.

Figure 13.2 Example of a Cash Budget

Liquidity Ratios

These are indicators of a firm's *liquidity*—that is, ability to convert its assets into cash without substantial loss in their value. They are obtained by comparing a firm's current assets with its current liabilities. *Current assets* include cash, accounts receivable, inventories of finished goods, materials and supplies, and securities—in other words, cash and assets that can be reasonably quickly converted into cash. *Current liabilities* include loans payable, accounts payable, taxes owing, and amounts due to shareholders—in other words, debts that must be paid in the near future. The larger the amount of current assets compared with current liabilities, the more "liquid" the firm is. Two liquidity ratios commonly used in business are the current ratio and the quick-asset or acid-test ratio.

Current Ratio. This ratio is found by dividing total current assets by total current liabilities. Thus, for a firm whose current assets increased over a year from $37,000 to $45,000 and whose current liabilities increased from $12,000 to $19,000, the current ratio would have declined from 3.1 to 2.4.

$$\frac{37{,}000}{12{,}000} = 3.1 \qquad \frac{45{,}000}{19{,}000} = 2.4$$

To be meaningful, the current ratio must be compared with the ratio at previous dates. Thus a firm's current ratio, although in itself apparently high, may be much lower than last year's. Also attention must paid to the type of business. In some firms, it may be that inventory, although a current asset, can be turned into cash quickly only at a substantial loss—for example, by auction or by cut-price sale. For some businesses, such as furniture stores, where sales may vary considerably from month to month, the desirable current ratio may be higher than that for businesses such as food stores where business is steady.

Quick-Asset Ratio. The *quick-asset or acid-test ratio* is another test of a firm's liquidity. It is found by dividing the total of cash and accounts receivable by total current liabilities.

The quick-asset ratio takes into account the fact that inventory is not as easily convertible into cash as are other assets such as accounts receivable. It is thus a more cautious assessment of a firm's ability to pay its debts.

KEY TERMS

Cash flow

Cash management

Bank statement

Cash-flow analysis

Cash budget

Liquidity

Current assets

Current liabilities

Current ratio

Quick-asset ratio

REVIEW QUESTIONS

1. For many businesses, the bank statement is a more important financial document than the income statement. Explain and discuss.
2. What are the consequences for a business of a cash deficit? How can it be temporarily resolved?
3. What is a cash-flow statement? What is its purpose?
4. How does a cash-flow statement differ from an income statement?
5. What is a cash budget? How is it constructed? What is its purpose?
6. Explain the difference between the current ratio and the quick-asset ratio. What do these ratios reveal? What size ratio should a firm aim for?

CASE PROBLEMS

ABC ENTERPRISES INC.
Preparing a cash budget

1. Using the format shown in Figure 13.2, prepare a cash budget for ABC Enterprises Inc., for the next six months, with the following estimated monthly data:

   Rent: $500
   Wages: $1,000
   Equipment depreciation: $250
   Advertising: $250
   Miscellaneous: $500
   Bank loan repayment: $500
   The opening cash balance is $5,000.

   Receipts: Month   1. $5,000   2. $6,000   3. $7,500
                       4. $8,500   5. $9,000   6. $10,000
   Purchases: Month   1. $2,500   2. $3,000   3. $4,000
                       4. $5,000   5. $5,500   6. $6,000

2. What conclusions do you draw from your results?
3. What would happen if the five shareholders insisted on a quarterly dividend payment of $1,000 each?

BLAKE UNIFORM RENTAL COMPANY LTD. (2)
Preparing a cash budget

Malcolm and Sandra Blake have decided to proceed with their plans to set up a uniform rental business.

The branch manager of the bank from which they have requested a $10,000 loan has asked, among other things, for a cash budget for the first twelve months of operation. This would help him to see how the business would be able to maintain a minimum balance of $500 in the firm's account at the bank and to repay the loan in monthly instalments of $1,000 commencing in the third month of the firm's operation.

The anticipated growth in the numbers of customers (each paying an average of $20 per month) is as follows:

Month	Estimated Customers
1	100
2	200
3	250
4	300
5	350
6	400
7	450
8	500
9	500
10	550
11	600
12	600

The estimated expenses (except for the loan repayment) are as indicated in Blake Uniform (1). Initial capital would be $25,000, from which must come the cost of the uniforms and the truck and the money to cover possible losses in the early months.

Assignment
1. Prepare a cash budget for the first twelve months of the firm's operation.
2. Will the firm have sufficient working capital? If not, what should the Blakes do?
3. As branch manager of the bank, assess the plausibility of the estimated revenues and expenses.

WILLIAM SPENCER LTD.
Exercising financial control over a dealer network

William Spencer Ltd. is one of North America's largest manufacturers of farm machinery. Its Canadian subsidiary, with headquarters in Hamilton, Ontario, had sales last year of $105 million, out of a total Canadian farm-equipment market of about $600 million.

To help sell its equipment, William Spencer Ltd. has a network of 565 dealers spread right across Canada, with the major concentration in the prairie provinces. Sales have rapidly increased over the last few years as farmers have felt the financial benefit of rising world food prices. However, individual dealer sales performance, even within the same province, varies greatly. John Hall, president of the Canadian company, feels strongly that the "good times" will eventually end and the firm's dealer network should be tightened now before business deteriorates.

Already, Frank Hodgson, the marketing vice-president, holds meetings every six months with the dealers in each region to discuss their problems, to provide product news, and generally to boost morale. However, at the suggestion of the finance department, he now plans to introduce a uniform dealer accounting system. This will require each dealer to record sales and cost data in a special book called a Management Review and enable him to compare his own performance with company-set standards. If a dealer falls short in any way, the territory manager (a company official) can step in and advise on corrective action. Company goals include: (a) turning working capital six to eight times a year; (b) turning used equipment three to four times per year; (c) turning spare parts two to three times per year; (d) maintaining an asset/liability ratio of 1.3 to one; (e) maintaining a quick-asset ratio of one to one; and (f) generating a return on total assets of 12 per cent.

Assignment

1. Explain each of the company goals. What other goals might be included?
2. What purpose will the new accounting system achieve? Should it be compulsory?

READING

Entrepreneur Blames Investment Community for Company's Misfortune

BY MARTIN DEWEY

Source: *The Globe and Mail*, Toronto

The way C. Richard Gerald figures it, he has three months left—three months to rescue a promising business before he must throw in the towel and accept financial ruin.

Mr. Gerald is a software man, as they say in computer circles. As head of his own company, System Selections Ltd. of Toronto, he made an excellent living selling computer programs and systems designed in the United States.

Then for two years he went into hiding to design a system of his own—one that could be exported southward, for a change. The result, unveiled last spring, was an accounting system for credit unions and other near-banks that was built around the first minicomputer of International Business Machines Corp. of Armonk, N.Y., the Series 1. The new system was called Credits.

Mr. Gerald was satisfied that SSL had built a better mousetrap. Credits was, in fact, the best credit union accounting system yet devised for the Series 1. As IBM pushed ahead with the marketing of its minicomputer, he could confidently expect many Canadian and U.S. buyers to beat a path to his door for the software.

But it never happened that way. Today, Mr. Gerald is worse than broke; he has run out of private funds, he owes $40,000 to suppliers and his bank has just been awarded judgment against his personal assets for repayment of a $58,000 loan. If he cannot find fresh capital—fast—he and his company are finished.

The fortunes of business? Not at all, growls Mr. Gerald. He feels there is a villain in the piece: an investment community so concerned for security, so faint-hearted and short-sighted, that small- and medium-scale entrepreneurship has become virtually impossible in Canada.

Only a year ago everything seemed to be going swimmingly for SSL. True, the company had made only two sales, both to credit unions in Ontario, and it had spent a lot of money on development—$150,000 of its own and $50,000 of the bank's. But there was a lot of money to be made, and the bank appeared to agree. According to Mr. Gerald, it had verbally assured him that his line of credit could be extended to $125,000 when he needed it. The period of preparation was over; it was time to cash in.

The nightmare—for that is what Mr. Gerald calls it—started last January when the bank had second thoughts about the extra money, probably because SSL was running "a couple of months behind the projections." His line of credit was abruptly frozen a month later and he found himself with no money to follow up the inquiries that were beginning to come in from credit unions on both sides of the border.

Selling the product suddenly seemed unimportant; what mattered was saving the company. A shaken Mr. Gerald went looking for money, armed with what seemed to him an impeccable set of business credentials and an unassailable list of reasons for backing SSL.

At age 53, he was able to point out, he had been working with computers and office systems for 28 years, 12 of them with IBM itself. His Credits system had proved itself to be the best available fit to the IBM Series 1 minicomputer in credit union operations. (Mr. Gerald said he is now negotiating with IBM to have Credits adopted as the system used in its sales demonstrations world-wide—an assertion ever-discreet IBM will neither confirm nor deny.)

And the market certainly seemed to be there. Mr. Gerald's research indicated that there are more than 31,000 credit unions and savings and loan companies in North America and 19,000 that could be regarded as potential Credits users. He told prospective backers that Credits was already under consideration by about 60 U.S. and Canadian credit unions.

If he had the resources to follow up all those prospects, he argued, he could be selling systems at the rate of one a month, rising gradually to as many as five a month. What he needed was money enough to assemble a proper sales force and to keep refining and expanding his system.

He said he did get offers: "I talked to the Alberta Opportunity Fund; that's an agency that draws on the Heritage Fund. They were really enthusiastic about going ahead. But they could only put up a third of the new money. They insisted that I get the Federal Business Development Fund and some private investor to put up the rest."

In other words, they would help him once he no longer needed help. Another problem was that the fund wanted the Credits system applied to the specific needs of Alberta and would have required the company to set up a separate division for the province. "I decided I couldn't set up a second organization in the midst of trying to rescue the first."

There were also some venture capitalists willing to put up $40,000, he said. For this money they wanted 50 per cent ownership of the company plus voting control.

"I would have been happy to have a couple of good fellows join me. But I wasn't going to give them control for a quarter of the money we had already spent.

"At one point I approached what was ostensibly Arab money. The guy who was ready to co-ordinate it wanted $3,000 up front before I could even talk to them. He said he could get me a line of credit worth

$300,000 if I signed away every personal asset I had and guaranteed them 25 per cent of every sale I ever made. That was in addition to debt interest."

Mr. Gerald shrugged. What can you say about terms like that?

"When it comes to so-called venture capitalists in this country, they are really non-existent. It's so easy for these people to get secured investments of all kinds. They're simply not attracted to risks, even with high potential." As for banks, he learned that he was an untouchable because he had been sued by a bank. "Besides," he said, "banks will deal with secured lenders only; that's all there is to it. At all times they want security worth two and three times what they're lending."

He found that some private investors he approached were unprepared to talk about computer software; there had been too many failures by small, inexperienced operators. Others lost interest when they learned about his debts. With still others he ran into an unexpected obstacle: his venture was too small to interest them.

"The clock was running out," Mr. Gerald said. It was the low point in his fortunes, and not a good moment to read in the newspapers that Prime Minister Joe Clark had ticked off Canadian businessmen for lacking entrepreneurial energy and being afraid to risk new projects.

Angry and frustrated, he wrote a letter to the editor describing himself as "a private businessman who has an excellent chance of getting the worst kind of reward for taking significant risks—financial disaster."

The story may yet have a happy ending, however. Because government help takes time, and time was what he had little of, Mr. Gerald had not thought of asking for federal funds. But finally, in desperation, he made an application to the Federal Business Development Bank, an agency of last resort.

"I asked for $100,000 to $150,000 and got a very favourable response. If they go for it, they would be prepared to lend me the money on an equity basis, which is fine. It will take two or three months. But if we don't get assistance of this magnitude, we're done for."

With a third sale now in the bag to help eke out the wait, Mr. Gerald is beginning to think he may make it after all—thanks to the federal Government and no thanks at all to Canada's private investment community.

Assignment
1. What kind of business does C. Richard Gerald have?
2. What was his new product? What did it cost to develop?
3. Was Gerald's optimism about his product justified by the market's reaction?
4. What was Gerald's "nightmare"? How can a profitable company become insolvent?
5. How helpful was the government?
6. Why did he not accept the help of venture capitalists? What is his opinion of them? How justified is it?
7. What may be his salvation?

UNIT 13.2: SHORT-TERM FINANCING

Working Capital versus Fixed Capital

When a business is established, some of the funds invested are used to purchase fixed assets, such as tools, machinery, furniture, land, and buildings. The rest is used to provide a pool of *working capital*, consisting of cash and other assets—such as inventories and accounts receivable—which will soon be converted into cash. The funds invested in working capital follow a circular flow. The money is used to buy stocks of materials and merchandise and to pay for employee services; the finished product is then sold either for cash or on credit; and finally, money flows back into the firm. During the course of the business year, this cycle may be completed several times.

Net Working Capital. The term "working capital" is also sometimes used in a narrower sense to mean the surplus of current assets over current liabilities or, in other words, that portion of current assets which is financed from long-term or permanent sources. For this more restricted concept, the term *net working capital* is sometimes used.

Working Capital Needs

Here, financial management is in a delicate situation. If it keeps the surplus of current assets over current liabilities excessively high, it unnecessarily ties up funds that could be invested either in plant expansion or in short-term investments—for example, interest-bearing bank deposit certificates. On the other hand, if it lets the surplus of current assets over current liabilities get too low, it risks making the firm *insolvent*—that is, unable to pay its debts as they fall due.

The amount of working capital necessary is not always easy to determine. It will vary greatly according to the type of firm and type of industry. If, for example, a business is subject to unexpected sales fluctuations or slow payment of accounts receivable, management should keep current assets well in excess of current liabilities. A current ratio of 2:1 might be appropriate for such a firm. If, on the other hand, there is a steady relationship between the inflow and outflow of cash, a current ratio of 1.5:1 or even 1:1 may be adequate.

In relation to total assets, working capital for manufacturing firms amounts to over 50 per cent. For retailing firms, particularly those with leased premises, the percentage is much higher due to larger investment in inventories. Size of the firm, type of production, type of retail business, buying and selling terms, cyclical and seasonal variations in business all affect the amount of working capital required.

Seasonal Needs. The most important business need for short-term funds is to finance inventories on a seasonal basis. The cash crop farmer, for example, must plant, cultivate, and harvest, before he can sell; he needs money most in the spring and summer, but receives it, from the sale of the crop, in the fall. Another example is the department store, which needs money in the fall to build up inventories of goods for sale near Christmas. Manufacturing businesses can sometimes avoid this seasonal financing problem by dovetailing production of winter and summer lines—for example, winter ski wear with summer casuals. The vast majority of businesses, however, must resort to short-term financing. Such loans are usually *self-liquidating*—that is, the goods whose production is financed with the borrowed funds provide the money, when sold, to repay the loan.

Growth. As a business grows in size, more and more working capital is required to meet payroll and other expenses. Some of this extra working capital may come from profits ploughed back into the business. Additional equity capital investment may also be forthcoming—for example, by taking in a partner or by turning "public" and selling shares—but such funds are not usually immediately available.

Cyclical Needs. Upswings and downswings of business activity are characteristic of our economic system. The upswings, which are not easily predictable, accelerate the growth of a business and create an additional need for working capital that may have to be met by short-term financing. Downswings, conversely, may bring about a surplus of funds within the business.

Unexpected Events. Occasionally a business will be faced with an unexpected event that will necessitate short-term financing. For example, a labour dispute may hold up production and sales and thereby slow down the flow of funds into the business. The outward flow of funds—for example, for payment of materials—may be slowed much less, thereby creating a cash shortage. Other events that might place a financial strain on a business are: unexpectedly poor sales—for example, in starting up a business; weather catastrophes—for example, flooding; unexpected competition—for example, loss of a vital sales contract; loss of a key manager; theft; and arson. Risk is more inherent in some businesses—for example, men's or women's clothing—than in others—for example, telephone service. Even if a risk is covered partly by insurance (for example, fire or key-personnel insurance) it may take some time before the firm receives its money.

Trade Credit

An important source of short-term financing for a business, particularly a small business, is the firm from which it buys its raw materials, merchandise, and services. This type of short-term financing is called *trade credit*. Unlike the other types, it involves no transfer of funds. Instead, the buyer is given a period of time in which to pay for the goods purchased and received. This is, of course, the equivalent of borrowing from a bank or elsewhere to pay cash to the vendor at the time of purchase.

Most businesses extend trade credit, not because they enjoy lending money free of charge, but because it is expected of them. Non-conformity means lost customers, as credit terms are usually available elsewhere.

Many firms in the retail phase of business extend credit (the exchange of goods or services for a promise to pay at a later date) as a means of obtaining additional sales. In manufacturing and wholesaling, trade credit of 30 days, and sometimes more, is traditional practice. By not requiring the buyer to pay for the goods immediately upon purchase, the seller faces, of course, the risk of not being paid at all.

Trade credit is one of a firm's important sales weapons. However, by extending trade credit, the vendor must wait 30 days, 60 days, or even longer for the money to be paid. To encourage buyers to pay more promptly, many vendors offer a 2 per cent discount on the sum owing if payment is made within 10 days of billing. Alternatively, they may impose an interest charge of say, $1\frac{1}{2}$ per cent, or 2 per cent per month on accounts that are not paid within 30 days.

Open-Book Accounts. One common instrument of trade-credit is the open-book account. This means that the vendor merely records in its accounts receivable ledger that the customer has bought goods or services on credit.

A business will naturally take precautions before extending credit. It will require bank and business references and, in many cases, a satisfactory mercantile credit agency report—for example, from Dun & Bradstreet. Often a business will limit the amount of credit allowed new customers until the customer has proven to be a satisfactory credit risk.

Credit Terms. These vary, depending upon such factors as the relationship between seller and buyer, the buyer's credit position, the state of business in general, and the position of the buyer in the manufacturing or distribution process. For example, manufacturers usually get a relatively long period in which to pay for raw materials, because it takes them much longer to manufacture, sell, and collect the cash for their efforts than it does for a retailer to buy goods from a wholesaler and resell them to the public. Usually, however, credit terms are granted for 30, 60, or 90 days. Occasionally the device of *dating* will be used as a means of offering the buyer more advantageous credit terms. Thus, as the credit period begins with the date shown on the sales invoice, more generous credit terms can be given to a special customer by dating the invoice later than the date of shipment. In this way, a firm can ostensibly adhere to its traditional credit policy, yet remain flexible in the face of competition.

The open-book method of short-term financing is popular because it is so simple. It has, however, a serious disadvantage. The vendor faces a harder task in obtaining a court judgment against a purchaser and securing payment if the purchaser eventually refuses to pay than if some written acknowledgement of the debt (in addition to signature on a delivery slip) had been made. Trust, then, is vital to the use of open-book financing.

Payment Methods. When payment is due, the purchaser of the goods sends the money to the vendor by means of a cheque, bank draft, or bank money order.

A *cheque* is a written order by the purchaser to the bank instructing it to pay

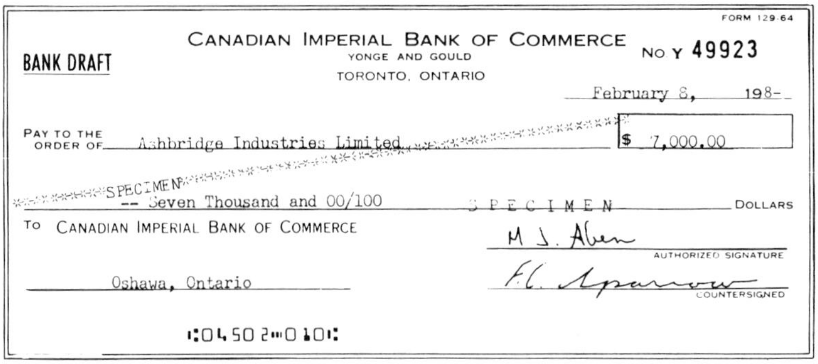

FORM 129-64

BANK DRAFT

CANADIAN IMPERIAL BANK OF COMMERCE
YONGE AND GOULD
TORONTO, ONTARIO

NO Y 49923

February 8, 198-

PAY TO THE ORDER OF Ashbridge Industries Limited $ 7,000.00

SPECIMEN

-- Seven Thousand and 00/100 SPECIMEN DOLLARS

TO CANADIAN IMPERIAL BANK OF COMMERCE

Oshawa, Ontario

AUTHORIZED SIGNATURE

COUNTERSIGNED

⑆04502⑈010⑆

Figure 13.3 Bank Draft for $7,000

Courtesy Canadian Imperial Bank of Commerce

on demand to the person or firm on the cheque the sum of money stated. With a *certified cheque* the bank deducts the amount of money stated on the cheque from the drawer's account and stamps "certified" across the face of the cheque. The bank then becomes legally responsible for payment of the sum indicated. Cheques have the disadvantage, compared with bank drafts, that collection charges are payable if remittance is over long distances.

A *bank draft* (Figure 13.3) is a written order by a bank, on behalf of a customer, instructing another branch of the same bank to pay a stated sum of money to a person or firm upon satisfactory identification. Bank drafts are used when money is to be paid to a vendor at some distant location. A *bank money order* is similar to a bank draft except that it is restricted to a certain maximum amount.

Consignment Terms. Goods may sometimes be bought by a retail store or other business *on consignment*. This means that the seller remains the owner of the goods until such time as they are resold to the public. Since the *consignee*, the firm to which the goods have been consigned, does not buy the goods, the short-term financing involved is borne by the original seller, the *consignor*. Since no sales risk is incurred by the consignee, the profit margin on such sales is smaller than usual.

Time Drafts. Suppose a firm sells goods or services on credit but does not wish to rely too heavily on the good faith of the purchaser, or does not wish to wait until the end of the credit period for its funds. Then it may employ the trade acceptance form of the bill of exchange (Figure 13.4). The *trade acceptance* (also called a *time draft* or a *term draft*) is a written promise by the purchaser to pay the vendor a certain sum of money on or before a given future date in exchange for value received. The firm selling the goods on credit (the *drawer*) prepares the draft and sends it, along with the sales invoice, to the buyer (the *drawee*) for *acceptance*. The buyer's signature is legally sufficient for acceptance, but the usual practice is to write or stamp the word "accepted" in one corner or across the face of the bill, followed by the date of acceptance, the place of payment, and then the signature.

When the vendor trusts the purchaser, the vendor may ship the goods directly to him or her, attaching the time draft to the bill of lading, sales invoice, insurance certificate, and so on. If the purchaser is satisfied with the goods, the buyer will then sign and return the draft. With the accepted time draft, the vendor now possesses written evidence of the money owed. As the draft is negotiable, the vendor may *discount* it at its bank to obtain immediate funds. *Discounting* is the term used to describe the selling of the draft at less than its face value.

If the vendor feels the need for self-protection, it can arrange for the draft to be accepted before the goods are actually handed over to the buyer. It does this by obtaining from the shipper—for example, the CNR—a receipt for the goods, known as an *order bill of lading*. The shipper, having conveyed the goods to their place of destination, will hand them over to the buyer only on receipt of the original copy of the order bill of lading. The vendor, or its bank, will give this original copy to the buyer only when the buyer *accepts* the time draft for the amount owed.

Banker's Acceptance. In some instances, particularly in foreign trade, where the purchaser's credit standing may be less certain, the vendor may require a *banker's acceptance*. This means that the purchaser must arrange for its bank to accept the bill and thereby guarantee payment when due. The vendor is notified of the bank's intention by a *letter of credit*. The vendor's bank usually handles the presentation of the draft, or bill, for acceptance and later collects the money due.

Sight Draft. Although the trade acceptance can be used as an instrument of short-term financing, the same is not true of another type of commercial draft, the *sight draft*. This is just a collection device, and no credit is involved. The vendor in this case sends a sight draft (a written order to pay the amount indicated) along with the bill of lading to the purchaser's bank. The bank will then hand over the bill of lading to the purchaser (which will enable it to get

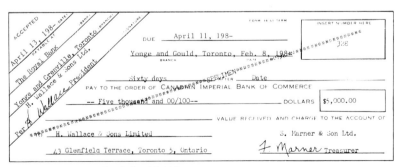

Figure 13.4 Term Draft for $5,000
Courtesy Canadian Imperial Bank of Commerce

the goods from the shipper) on acceptance of the sight draft. The purchaser will have to provide the required cash after the statutory three days of grace.

Promissory Notes. This is a written promise by the purchaser to pay the vendor the sum owing at a specified future date, usually 30, 60, or 90 days hence. It differs from a time draft only in that it need not originate with the vendor; the purchaser may draw up the promissory note personally. Like the time draft, it provides the creditor with written acknowledgement of the debt and, being negotiable, may be discounted for cash.

Bank Loans

Another major source of borrowed funds for a business firm's working capital needs are the chartered banks, which in Canada combine the functions of a savings bank and a commercial bank. Of these banks, the major ones have a network of branches spread across the country. Each branch manager has the right to make business loans up to the limit for each loan set for his or her branch. Requests for larger loans are referred to head office for study and approval. Generally speaking, the chartered banks make only short-term loans, for periods of up to one year. Some loans may, however, be for two years or even longer, depending on the standing of the borrower and the security offered. Also, it should be remembered, many short-term loans are renewed almost automatically.

Contrary to popular belief, a business does not borrow only when it is in financial trouble. Usually, short-term borrowing by a business is a deliberate feature of its financial policy and is planned well in advance. The main reason for this deliberate borrowing is that the required level of current assets often varies considerably throughout the year. As a result, it is normally more efficient for the owner to borrow at short-term, as and when required, rather than to have extra cash of his or her own tied up in the business, as additional net working capital, idle for a considerable part of the year. Bank loans are the traditional major means of such short-term business financing.

Demand Loan. A demand loan, with a "line of credit" arrangement, is the usual type of short-term business financing provided by a chartered bank. A *demand loan*, as the name implies, is a loan whose repayment the bank may demand at any time—for example, if it loses confidence in the borrower's financial stability. The borrower's promise to repay the money at any time is evidenced by a *demand note* (Figure 13.5).

The *line of credit* is an arrangement whereby the bank allows the business to borrow up to a fixed maximum amount during an agreed period of time—for example, six months. The line of credit is useful to the business because it need not borrow and pay interest on a sum larger than its actual requirements in any month. This is particularly important where working capital requirements vary considerably throughout the year, as in the case of a Christmas card manufacturer. Interest is generally calculated monthly on the outstanding daily balance of the loan. With a line of credit, a charge of $^1/_2$ of 1 per cent per annum is usually made by the bank on the amount unused.

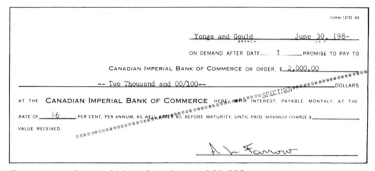

Figure 13.5 Demand Note for a Loan of $2,000
Courtesy Canadian Imperial Bank of Commerce

An *overdraft* occurs when a business issues cheques for a total amount greater than the balance in the firm's bank account. This can happen with or without the prior consent of the bank manager. The policy of the chartered banks in recent years has been to discourage overdrafts and to require instead that a businessperson takes out a demand loan covered by a promissory note.

Three C's of Credit. In deciding whether to grant a loan, the branch manager of a chartered bank examines carefully what are termed the three C's of credit: the character, capacity, and capital of the applicant.

Character refers to the willingness of the applicant to meet obligations and is a personal judgment by the manager, based on such things as an interview, past borrowing records, and personal references. *Capacity*, or the applicant's ability to repay the loan, is determined by an analysis of the firm's plans (as shown by the pro forma financial statements and cash budget) and a judgment as to the ability of management to carry out these plans. The age and past financial record of the business are important indications of its future ability. *Capital* refers to the owner's equity capital in the business. The larger this amount, the greater will be the protection for the bank should the borrower fail to repay the loan.

Collateral. In many instances, the bank will require that the borrower pledge some part of the business assets—for example, accounts receivable—as security (or collateral) for repayment of the loan. When this is done, the loan is known as a *secured loan*. When only the general credit standing or reputation of the borrower is relied upon, the loan is called an *unsecured loan*. In some instances, the bank may require as additional security that a businessperson give his and/or someone else's *personal guarantee* to the lender to make payment. This promise or *personal covenant* means that the businessperson, who may be a partner or a director, would be required to sell his or her own personal assets to repay the loan if the money is not forthcoming from the business. The spouse may also be asked to sign a personal guarantee.

Other Loans. Under special circumstances—for example, a well-established relationship between bank and client—a bank may grant a business loan on conditions different from those of a demand loan. For example, the interest charged may be relatively low (the *prime rate*); repayment may be set for a fixed date in the future, rather than on demand; or the repayment schedule may be made more flexible.

Discounting. One type of short-term financing which a bank provides to a limited extent is the discounting of time drafts and promissory notes obtained by customers in the course of their business. In purchasing them at a *discount*, that is, at less than face value, the bank assumes the short-term financing originally extended by the trade creditor. The latter has obtained his or her money from the bank (rather than waiting for the customer to pay), less a discount to cover interest charges and collection expenses. The bank now has to wait for reimbursement of the money paid to the trade creditor until the date when the time draft or promissory note falls due.

Finance Company Loans

Another source of short-term business financing is the finance company, variously called a commercial credit, discount, acceptance, instalment, or sales finance company.

Loans. One method of short-term financing used by these lending companies (also used by the banks) is a loan made against the security of manufacturers' or wholesalers' accounts or notes receivable. Loans are also made on the security of inventories of goods or materials as evidenced by warehouse receipts. Sometimes short-term loans are also made to finance the purchase of equipment, with the equipment itself serving as security for repayment. Sales finance companies play an important role in financing automobile dealers' inventories. Retailers' inventories of other durable goods are usually financed by the manufacturers.

Discounting. A method of short-term financing widely used by sales finance companies is the discounting of time drafts, promissory notes, and conditional sales contracts.

A *conditional sales contract* is a written agreement between a buyer and a seller, specifying amongst other things, how the balance of the purchase price of a good will be paid—for example, in monthly instalments over a period of three years—and the fact that ownership of the good is to remain with the seller until full payment has been completed. A conditional sales contract is used when a business can pay only part of the purchase price of the machine required, usually a minimum of one third. Instalment equipment financing, as this type of trade credit is called, extends to the purchase of such items as plant equipment, hotel and restaurant fixtures, equipment for beauty and barber shops, and medical equipment. Conditional sales contracts are also made between retailer and consumer—for example, for the purchase of cars, furniture, and appliances.

To attract business, finance companies offer to manufacturers, wholesalers, and retailers who bring them instalment sales contracts, a share of the total finance charge paid by the customer—varying from 10 per cent to 20 per cent. They also share the risk of default by agreeing to locate the goods if the buyer has disappeared, to repossess them, and to deliver them to the dealer, who then has to repurchase its sales contract from the company. However, there are some "full recourse" agreements which leave the full liability with the dealer. The finance companies also provide a credit investigation service.

Factor Companies

When a business pledges its accounts receivable as security for repayment of a loan, the collection of the money owing on the accounts remains the responsibility of the firm. This is true even when the proceeds are earmarked for direct payment to the bank. It is possible, however, for a business to sell its accounts receivable rather than just pledge them. In this way, the business, for a fee, relieves itself of the problems of extending credit, making collections, and running the risk of some debts not being paid. This can reduce costs and release working capital for other purposes. A company which specializes in buying accounts receivable, usually from 30 to 90 days, without recourse, is called a *factor* (or *factoring*) company. The services of such firms are being used more and more widely in Canada.

Short-Term Money Market

Occasionally a large commercial or industrial firm of good reputation, sometimes by means of a financial subsidiary, will borrow funds for 90 days or less (often 30 days) by issuing promissory notes at a discount. These promissory notes, usually for $25,000 or more each, are then sold by investment dealers acting as agent for the borrower, to business corporations and to financial intermediaries such as mutual funds, insurance companies, and trust companies. Often, the terms of the loan are subject to negotiation between borrower and lender.

On a regular basis, finance companies, such as Industrial Acceptance Corporation Ltd., borrow money in the short-term money market for periods ranging from 30 to 360 days by the sale, usually through investment dealers, of promissory notes at a discount.

The advantages to a business of this method of raising short-term funds are that the rate of interest charged is slightly lower than that charged by a chartered bank; and that no minimum balance need be kept in the borrower's accounts as is often required with a bank loan.

Loans from Directors, Shareholders, and Employees

Sometimes a private business corporation will borrow money from its directors, shareholders, or even employees.

KEY TERMS

Working capital
Net working capital
Borrowing needs
Seasonal needs
Growth
Cyclical needs
Unexpected events
Trade credit
Discount
Open-book account
Cheque
Certified cheque
Bank draft
Bank money order
Consignment terms
Time draft
Discounting
Order bill of lading

Banker's acceptance
Letter of credit
Sight draft
Promissory note
Bank loans
Demand loan
Line of credit
Overdraft
3 C's of credit
Secured loan
Unsecured loan
Personal covenant
Sales finance companies
Conditional sales contract
Factor company
Short-term money market
Shareholder loans

REVIEW QUESTIONS

1. Distinguish between working capital and net working capital. What is the purpose of the distinction?
2. Why does a firm deliberately resort to borrowing to finance part of its working capital needs?
3. Explain and illustrate how seasonal needs affect working capital requirements.
4. What unexpected events can increase the working capital needs of a business?
5. What is trade credit? Why is it used so much in business?
6. Explain the advantages and disadvantages of the open-book method of trade credit.
7. What is meant by "selling goods on consignment?"
8. Explain the nature and purpose of a time draft. How does a sight draft differ?
9. What is a promissory note? How does it differ from a trade acceptance?

10. What is meant by a "demand loan, with a line of credit arrangement"?
11. Distinguish between a bank loan and an overdraft.
12. What are the three C's of credit? Are these criteria reasonable?
13. Most loans are secured. Explain.
14. A bank may require a borrower's personal covenant. Explain.
15. What is a bank's "prime rate?" Who gets it?
16. What is meant by the discounting of drafts? What is its purpose?
17. What is a conditional sales contract? How and why is this used as an instrument of short-term financing?
18. What is a factor company? Why would a business use its services?
19. Who uses the short-term money market and why?
20. Why would a company borrow money from its directors, shareholders, or employees? Why would they lend it?

CASE PROBLEM

J. FOX & SON LTD.
Arranging short-term financing

J. Fox & Son Ltd. is a small- to medium-sized Canadian manufacturing firm, producing a variety of paints, varnishes, and lacquers. Sales are made to painting contractors, manufacturing firms, government institutions, and paint and hardware stores. The credit terms given are 1/10, net 30, and relatively few accounts remain unpaid after 30 days. In its purchases of raw materials, the firm takes advantage of the 1 or 2 per cent discount available for payment within 10 days.

Because of the seasonal nature of most exterior and interior painting, sales usually drop considerably in the late fall and do not pick up again until the following spring. During the winter, when sales and cash inflow are low, the firm must, however, continue to manufacture so that stocks will be sufficient to meet peak demand in the summer. These circumstances create a seasonal need for short-term financing for the period January to May inclusive.

Until last year, the firm had a large cash fund built up from retained earnings. Most of this money, about $40,000, would be used to finance purchases of raw materials and the payment of other operating expenses during the winter. During the summer and fall, the money would be invested in short-term securities.

Last year, two things happened. First, the company purchased new and larger premises. This meant that, after the sale of their former plant, about $20,000 of their seasonal cash fund was required to help meet the equity payment on the new plant. Second, with all the strain and excitement of moving, Mr. Fox Senior, well into his 60s, suffered a heart attack and died. Mrs. Fox, his widow, and now the majority shareholder of this private corporation, was then faced with the problem of raising enough cash to pay estate taxes and other expenses. Part of the money was available from the proceeds of a life insurance policy, and part was obtained by selling some of her shares to a senior employee. To raise the remaining cash, other than by selling more shares (which would have meant loss of voting control of the company), Mrs. Fox arranged with the other directors of the firm that a $25,000 loan be made to her from the company funds. As a result, the firm's seasonal cash fund of $50,000 has been reduced to $5,000.

Mr. Robbins, the firm's secretary-treasurer, is now faced with the problem of obtaining short-term financing for the winter. As the firm has relied on its own financial resources in the past, it has no established reputation as a reliable borrower.

Assignment
1. From what sources might Mr. Robbins obtain short-term financing?
2. What preparations should Mr. Robbins make for his loan application?
3. If Mr. Robbins is unable to obtain the financing required, what action should he take to prevent the firm from becoming insolvent?

UNIT 13.3: MEDIUM-TERM FINANCING

Occasionally, a business will need to borrow funds or obtain credit for periods longer than a year. When this period does not exceed 10 years, the financing involved is customarily defined as *medium-* (or *intermediate-*) *term financing*. Sometimes the name is also used to include loans for up to fifteen years.

The basic purposes of medium-term financing are to enable a business: to acquire extra working capital that can be repaid gradually over a period of years; and to purchase assets such as machinery, equipment, and vehicles, the cost of which is usually too large to be paid off within a year.

The Chartered Banks

The chartered banks, through specialized subsidiary companies, provide medium-term financing to business. The type of loan given is called a *term loan*. Its key characteristics are: it is for a period of one to fifteen years; periodic repayment of the principal is required; and the terms of the loan are tailored, through direct negotiation between borrower and lenders, to the firm's particular needs. Because of the longer period during which its money is loaned out, a bank, in addition to requiring collateral, may also place restrictions on the operation of the borrowing firm. It may require, for example, that no change in ownership or management be made without its approval; that no additional borrowing be undertaken; that salaries and other deductible expenses be restricted; that current assets not be allowed to drop below a certain level; that dividends be restricted to a percentage of future earnings after repayment of principal; that audited annual statements and unaudited interim financial statements be filed with the lender; and that periodic certification by a senior officer of the borrowing firm be made to the effect that all the conditions of the loan have been complied with. The loan is usually repaid out of the retained profits of the business.

Other Private Sources

Other private sources of medium-term financing, either for term loans or discounting facilities, are the sales finance companies, mortgage corporations, insurance companies, and trust companies. There are also firms specifically established to make medium-term loans and to advance equity funds. Often the loan is arranged in such a way that it can be converted into an equity investment.

Small Businesses Loans Act

In 1960, to help the owners of small businesses obtain loans more easily, the federal parliament passed a Small Businesses Loans Act. Under the terms of this Act, loans (called Business Improvement Loans) may be made by designated lenders to any small business with a gross revenue of less than $1,500,000 in the current fiscal year. However, such a business firm must be engaged in manufacturing, wholesale or retail trade, service, transportation, construction, or communications. Business firms not eligible for financing under the Act include those engaged in finance, real estate, insurance, or the professions. Non-profit organizations, charitable and religious, are also excluded.

The lenders under the Act, called "banks," include chartered banks, credit unions, *caisses populaires* or other co-operative societies, trust companies, loan companies, insurance companies, and Province of Alberta Treasury Branches. Repayment of the loan, in the event of the borrower's default, is guaranteed by the federal government. However, "banks" are expected to make such loans with the same care that they normally take in the conduct of their ordinary business. Nevertheless, the existence of the government guarantee makes it much more likely that the small businessperson will get a loan and get it at a reasonable rate of interest.

Types of Loans. The types of business improvement loans that may be made under the Act are: (a) fixed equipment loans—for the purchase of equipment of a kind usually affixed to real or immoveable property, for the cost of installation of such fixed equipment, and for the renovation, improvement, or modernization of equipment where this is appropriate; (b) moveable equipment loans—for purchase, renovation, etc. of equipment of a kind not usually affixed to real or immoveable property; (c) premises loans—for the purchase, construction, renovation, improvements, or modernization of the premises in which the business is carried on, excluding the land; and (d) loans for purchase of the land necessary for the operation of the business enterprise. Loans may not be made, however, for the refinancing of existing debts or for working-capital requirements.

Terms and Conditions. The borrower and the lender work out between them the detailed terms and conditions of any loan. However, in establishing the loan terms, the lender may take into account the type of business in which the loan applicant is engaged, the purpose for which the loan is to be made, and the borrower's ability to repay. The only restrictions are that: (a) the business should not, at any time, have more than $50,000 outstanding under the Small Businesses Loans Act; (b) the loan is used to finance not more than 80 per cent of the cost, including installation of fixed or moveable equipment; or not more than 90 per cent of the cost of renovations or improvements of premises or of the purchase price, or the cost of construction of premises; (c) the term of the loan is not more than 10 years, with at least annual repayment instalments; and

(d) there is security for repayment of the loan—a first charge on equipment or a mortgage on premises, as well as a promissory note signed by the borrower.

Federal Business Development Bank (FBDB)

The FBDB, a crown corporation, was established in 1975 as a successor to the Industrial Development Bank.

Its main purpose is to encourage the establishment and development of business enterprises in Canada by providing them with financial and management services. It supplements such services available from others and it pays particular attention to the needs of smaller enterprises.

FBDB financing is available by means of loans, loan guarantees, equity financing, or leasing, or by any combination of these methods, in whatever manner best suits the particular needs of the business. Loans are made at interest rates in line with those generally available to businesses.

Many of the bank's customers use FBDB funds to acquire land, buildings, or equipment. Others use them to strengthen the working capital of their business, to establish new businesses, and for other purposes.

FBDB financing ranges in size from a few thousand dollars upwards. The amount that can be borrowed for a specific purpose depends upon the borrower's ability to satisfy the general requirements of the bank. Businesses may obtain FBDB assistance on more than one occasion if they meet its requirements.

FBDB loans are usually repaid by way of monthly instalments of principal and interest. However, where the particular needs of the business would make it appropriate, other arrangements may be considered. Most FBDB loans must be repaid within ten years.

The FBDB can extend financial assistance to new or existing businesses of almost every type in Canada which do not have other sources of financing available to them on reasonable terms and conditions.

The qualifications for FBDB financing are:
(a) that the amount and character of investment in such a business by persons other than FBDB may reasonably be expected to ensure the continuing commitment of these persons to the business, and
(b) that the business may reasonably be expected to prove successful.

Collateral for Medium-Term Loans

Collateral is the term used to describe the various types of assets which borrowers can *assign* (that is, transfer) to lenders as security for repayment of their short or medium-term loans. These assets include: accounts receivable; inventories; other moveable assets such as furniture, equipment, and vehicles; fixed assets such as land and buildings; stocks and bonds; and life insurance policies with cash surrender values.

Accounts Receivable. The money owed to a firm by its customers is recorded in its accounts receivable ledger. These accounts receivable may be of the open-book type or may have been formally acknowledged by the customer's acceptance of a time draft or by the signing of a promissory note. All these accounts receivable may be used as collateral for a loan.

The assignment of open-book accounts to the lender is made under a formal agreement. This agreement specifies: the accounts assigned; the ratio that must be kept between the total value of these accounts and the amount of the loan (for example, the loan may not exceed 75 per cent of the total value of the specified accounts receivable); the rights and duties of lender and borrower; and the way in which the loan may be drawn on and repaid.

Any money paid by the firm's customers in settlement of their outstanding accounts is usually earmarked for repayment of the loan. There are two ways in which this is done. Under the *notification plan*, the customer is requested to send his or her payment directly to the lender. This method is always used when the accounts receivable are sold to a factor company. Under the *non-notification plan*, the customer pays the creditor firm, which then pays the lender. In the latter case, the firm's customer remains unaware that the account has been pledged as security for a loan.

When an account receivable has been formally acknowledged by the customer, the time draft or promissory note can be assigned by the creditor as security for a bank loan. This is done by the borrower's *endorsement* of the note—that is, by the borrower's signing his or her name to a statement stamped on the note that the note is being transferred to the lender as security for a loan. This endorsement changes the note from a *one-name paper* to a *two-name paper*. In other words, the note has become the obligation not only of the original maker but also of the payee who has endorsed it.

Lenders, in accepting accounts receivable as collateral for a loan, will try to ensure that such accounts are current and that the debtors are responsible business firms likely to meet their obligations.

Inventories. Inventories of goods may be used as collateral for a loan in two different ways. By the first method, the raw materials or finished goods are placed by the borrower in a bonded public warehouse, and the *warehouse receipt* (the written evidence of ownership) is endorsed by the borrower in favour of the lender. If the borrower fails to pay the loan when due, the lender retains possession of the warehouse receipt and uses it to obtain possession of the goods for eventual sale.

The second way of using inventory as collateral is by the use of a *trust receipt*. In this case, the borrower holds the goods—for example, raw materials to be manufactured into a finished product—while the lender, under the terms of the trust, legally owns them. Such a loan is usually self-liquidating; once the finished product has been manufactured and sold, the money which helped make this possible can be repaid.

Equipment. Other types of moveable property (besides raw materials and finished products) that may be used as collateral for a loan are furniture, machinery, equipment, and vehicles. The normal procedure is for the borrower to sign a *chattel mortgage*, whereby ownership of the chattel (as the mortgaged property is called) is transferred to the lender if the borrower defaults on the loan.

Land and Buildings. Fixed assets, such as land and buildings, are normally used as security for long-term loans. A mortgage on the property is given as a condition of the loan. Occasionally fixed assets are used to secure short-term loans.

Stocks and Bonds. Assets such as shares and bonds of other companies, government bonds, and the cash surrender value of life insurance policies are also used as collateral for short-term loans.

KEY TERMS

Medium-term financing	Notification plan
Chartered banks	Non-notification
Term loan	Endorsement
Small Businesses Loans Act	One-name paper
Approved lenders	Two-name paper
Fixed equipment loans	Inventories
Moveable equipment loans	Warehouse receipt
Premises loans	Trust receipt
Federal Business Development Bank	Chattel mortgage
Collateral	Fixed assets
Accounts receivable	Stocks and bonds

REVIEW QUESTIONS

1. What is "medium-term financing?"
2. Explain the purposes of medium-term financing.
3. What is a term loan? What restrictions are usually placed on the borrower?
4. What are the various private sources of medium-term financing?
5. What is the Small Businesses Loans Act? What are its chief features? What restrictions are placed on the borrower?
6. What is the Federal Business Development Bank? What types of loans does it make available? To whom? And under what conditions? What qualifications must a potential borrower have?
7. What is meant by "collateral?" What are the most readily acceptable types?

8. What arrangements are often made when open-book accounts are assigned to a lender?
9. What is meant by a notification plan?
10. What is meant by a "one-name" paper and a "two-name" paper?
11. What is the purpose of a warehouse receipt? Does it always provide security for a lender?
12. Explain the nature and purpose of a chattel mortgage.
13. What types of security are required for long-term loans?

UNIT 13.4: BUSINESS INSURANCE

Every business firm is faced with *business risk*, that is to say, the possibility of a financial loss. There are two main types of risk. First, there is the risk of losing all or part of the firm's assets through, for example, fire or theft. Second, there is the risk of a reduction in the firm's earning power through, for example, the loss of a key executive or the outbreak of a labour strike.

The existence of business risk is one of the inevitable characteristics of our private-enterprise system. The private business firm, in competition with others, is given the chief responsibility for anticipating consumer demand and producing and marketing the goods and services that the consumer wants. If the firm is successful in its task, its revenue will exceed its expenses and it will make a profit. However, if it is unsuccessful (as is often the case), it will make a loss and may even be forced to close down.

There is no way that a business firm can protect itself completely from the possibility of financial loss. For, as consumer demand changes, as new laws are enacted and as new competitors emerge, a firm's revenue and expenses are invariably affected, either for better or for worse. Nevertheless, business risk can to some extent be reduced by diversification of investments, better market analysis, larger reserves of working capital, more thorough plant safety precautions, and various other measures. It can also be reduced by the use of business insurance, the topic of this chapter.

The Nature of Insurance

It is impossible to prevent the occurrence of fire, theft, personal injury, and other hazards that may threaten a business firm with financial loss. However, it is possible to spread this loss, when it occurs, over many firms rather than make it the burden of just one. This is done by means of business insurance, whereby a firm, in return for a periodic payment to an insurance company, has all or most of any loss met by that company.

An insurance company can afford to offer this kind of service to other business firms because of the *law of large numbers* (or *law of averages*). Although it is impossible to predict the losses that a particular firm will incur from an insurable risk during a given period of time, it is possible to predict with a reasonable degree of accuracy the losses that business firms as a whole will incur. Thus, for example, an insurance company may predict, on the basis of past experience, that out of every thousand firms in a certain area, four will, on an average, suffer fire losses during the coming year totalling $100,000. The larger the number of similar risks included in the group, the greater the certainty that the actual losses will be the same as those predicted.

As we have already noted, not all business risks are insurable. The essential requirements for insurability are: (a) the loss must be entirely accidental; (b) the loss must be measurable; (c) the loss will be incurred by only a small percentage of the group at any one time; and (d) there will be a relatively large number of firms seeking insurance for the same type of risk. It is true that Lloyds of London is willing to insure practically any type of business risk. However, an extremely high premium must be paid for what is normally considered a non-insurable risk.

Principal Elements of an Insurance Policy

The principal elements of an insurance policy, or contract, are the names of the insurer, the insured, and the beneficiary; the type of risk covered; the amount of money for which the risk is insured; the time period involved; the amount of the premium; and the various exemptions and other limitations of coverage. The *insurer* is the insurance company, the *insured* is the person or firm that has contracted for insurance protection, and the *beneficiary* is the person to whom any reimbursement for loss is to be paid. The *premium* is the amount paid either periodically or as a lump sum to the insurance company for the insurance protection.

In drawing up a contract, an insurance company will usually make use of its standard form policy. However, if the insured requires more extensive coverage, the insurer will add to the contract an attachment called a *rider*. Should the insurer and insured wish to alter the existing terms of the policy in any way, they can do this by means of an *endorsement*. If a loss occurs, a person known as an *insurance adjuster*, who specializes in the appraisal of property losses, will visit you to determine the extent of the loss and to advise the insurance company of its liability under the policy involved.

There are many different forms of business insurance (Figure 13.6), each designed to provide protection against a particular type of risk. Let us now consider some of these.

Fire Insurance

When a business firm acquires a building, it must make sure, even before ownership is transferred, that there is adequate fire insurance. Fire damage to property is, in fact, one of the most common business risks that face a business firm. Fortunately, any financial loss can be reduced by fire insurance of the building. The amount for which the building is insured should be periodically raised, as inflation continues, to conform with current replacement costs, minus an allowance for depreciation. Thus, if a ten-year-old building would now cost $800,000 to replace, then (assuming depreciation of 2 per cent a year) it should be insured for $640,000. The amount relates, of course, only to the building, as the land on which it stands cannot be damaged by fire. Also, the building should not be over-insured, as the insurance company will not pay more than the present value of the building.

TYPE OF RISK	FORM OF INSURANCE
Loss of Property	
Damage or destruction	Fire
	Plate-glass
	Boiler and machinery
	Power interruption
	Water leakage
	Marine
	Automobile
	Aircraft
Theft	Burglary, theft
	Forgery
Infidelity	Fidelity bonding
Failure of others	Surety bonding
	Credit
Legal liability	General (or public) liability
	Employers' liability
	Automobile liability
	Elevator
	Aircraft
	Product
	Sports
	Physicians
Loss of Earning Power	
	Key-personnel
	Partnership
	Business interruption

Figure 13.6 Business Insurance

As very few buildings are completely destroyed by fire, business firms have a natural tendency to under-insure their property. To discourage this practice, fire insurance companies usually insert a *co-insurance clause* in their contracts. Such a clause requires the business firm to insure a property for at least 80 per cent of its current market value (if the firm is to be fully reimbursed for its loss). Thus a building worth $1,000,000 must be insured for at least $800,000. If a business firm carries less insurance than required under a co-insurance clause, its indemnification for loss is adjusted accordingly. Suppose, in our previous example, only $600,000 of fire insurance were carried, instead of the required $800,000. Then, if there was a fire loss of $400,000, the insurance company would pay only

$300,000 (three-quarters of the loss). This figure is calculated as follows: ($600,000 ÷ $800,000) × $400,000. Co-insurance clauses, incidentally, are not usually included in fire insurance policies for residential buildings. The simple formula involved is as follows:

$$\frac{\text{Did}}{\text{Should}} \times \text{Loss} = \text{Amount of claim payable}$$

$$\frac{\$600{,}000}{\$800{,}000} \times \$400{,}000 = \$300{,}000$$

If a building is damaged by fire, a business firm may also suffer loss of rental income (if all or part has been rented to other firms or persons); loss of output in the case of a manufacturing plant; loss of sales in the case of a retail establishment; or additional expenses from renting alternative accommodation. These losses, called *consequential losses*, are not normally included in the standard fire insurance policy. However, a consequential-loss clause can usually be included for an additional premium.

The actual cost of fire insurance varies according to the type of construction (concrete, brick, or wood) of the building, its location in the municipality (with particular reference to fire hydrants), the history of fire losses in the area, and the types of neighbouring buildings. The cost, or *premium*, is then quoted at so many cents per $100 of insurance, on an annual basis.

Marine Insurance

A business firm involved in shipping goods from one part of Canada to another or to foreign countries faces the risk of financial loss from damage to these goods in transit. To protect itself from this danger, it can purchase marine insurance.

Inland marine insurance covers goods that are shipped within a country by land, lake, river, coastal waters, or air. The protection provided is usually against loss from fire, theft, lightning, wind, hail, flood, and collision.

Ocean marine insurance covers goods shipped by sea (and the vessel in which they are shipped), while in port, and on the high seas. The hazards covered include sinking, capsizing, stranding, collision, and theft. The insurance coverage, which is tailored to the individual firm's requirements, may be for a single voyage or for a given period of time.

Theft Insurance

Every business firm faces the danger of financial loss from burglary, robbery, and theft. *Burglary* is forced entry into premises for purposes of stealing. *Robbery* is the taking of property from another person by actual or threatened violence. *Theft* is the act of stealing.

There are many different policies covering these risks—for example, a combined burglary and robbery policy for small retail stores. Hazards that may be covered under the various types of policies include burglary of safes and inventory;

burglary damage to money, securities, merchandise, furniture and equipment; and robbery inside and outside the premises.

Fidelity Bonding

Another source of possible financial loss to a firm is the dishonest employee. This is particularly true of firms such as banks, finance and trust companies, and retail stores, whose employees may have access to large amounts of cash. To reduce the risk of this type of financial loss, a business firm will usually arrange with a bonding company for a *fidelity bond* covering some (for example, bank tellers and supermarket cashiers) or all of its employees. In the latter case, the term *schedule bond* is sometimes used. In return for a periodic payment, the business firm receives reimbursement for any money misappropriated by its employees.

Surety Bonding

A firm may also suffer financial loss if a third party fails to meet its obligations—for example, the failure of a building contractor to complete a factory or office building on time. To guard against such a loss, a firm can take out a *surety bond*. The surety company will then assume responsibility for any loss and for ensuring completion of the contract.

Credit Insurance

Whenever a firm extends credit to its customers, there is bound to be some percentage of bad debts. It is not possible for a firm to protect itself completely against this type of financial loss other than by charging a higher price for goods sold to its customers. However, manufacturers, wholesalers, and some retailers can obtain credit insurance to cover abnormal losses.

Liability Insurance

Business firms, through ownership of property and various business activities, are in constant contact with the general public. Consequently, a business firm is liable to be sued for any personal injury or property damage to a third party caused by the firm's *negligence*—that is to say, failure to exercise due caution or prudence when involving others. Examples of such negligence are: a druggist's error in preparing prescriptions; food poisoning in a restaurant; medical malpractice; and personal injury caused by a slippery shop floor. To protect itself from any financial loss from this source, a business firm will usually purchase a *comprehensive general liability policy*.

Key-Personnel Insurance

Many business firms take out insurance policies on the lives of their managers and other key personnel. Consequently, if a manager dies, the firm receives a substantial sum of cash to cover any loss that may be incurred in the operation of the business.

The type of life insurance purchased is *term insurance*. As with automobile insurance, the firm pays only for protection against loss. It pays the premium and is the beneficiary. There is no savings and investment element as there is with other types of life insurance policies such as straight-life or endowment.

Partnership Insurance

If one of the partners in a business dies, the firm may have to be sold if the persons inheriting the estate of the deceased partner wish to receive cash rather than a share of the business. To avoid being forced into this situation, many partnership firms have a buy-sell agreement providing for the purchase of a deceased partner's share of the business by the surviving partners. The firm will also have a term insurance policy on the life of each partner, with the partnership as the beneficiary. In the event of the death of a partner, sufficient cash is thereby made available to finance the purchase of the deceased partner's share of the business.

Buy-Sell Agreement. Such an agreement usually covers the following main points: (a) how the ownership of the business is divided among the partners, (b) the agreement of the surviving partners to buy the deceased partner's share of the business, (c) the agreement of each partner that his or her share of the business be sold upon death, (d) the way in which the price for the deceased partner's share is to be determined and provision for review of the price arrived at in this way, at the request of the surviving partners or the executors of the deceased partner's estate, (e) the insurance policies to be held to provide funds for the purchase of the deceased partner's share of the business, (f) the business to own the policies and pay the premiums, (g) how any surplus funds are to be distributed, and (h) the duration of the buy-sell agreement.

In the case of a sole proprietorship, life insurance can also play a useful role. If the business is to be discontinued, stock may have to be sold at a loss, outstanding debts paid, and some accounts receivable written off. Certainly there will be a need for ready cash. If the business is to be sold, there may be considerable delay before any funds are received, even if the price is a reasonable one. If the business is to be continued (for example, by a member of the deceased person's family) there may be some delay before this person can be freed from other obligations. Also, when the successor does take over, it will probably be some time before profits regain their previous level, if at all. As with a partnership, there can be a buy-sell agreement between the present owner and the person who would like to buy the business after the owner's death (for example, a relative, employee, or supplier who wishes to control a key outlet). In all these circumstances, *sole proprietorship insurance* can provide ready cash in time of need.

Business Interruption Insurance

If a fire or other insured peril occurs, the small business owner should, with adequate fire insurance, receive enough money to rebuild the premises and buy new equipment and furnishings. However, the owner would not receive compensation for the loss of revenue and profit while the firm's normal business activities are interrupted. Also, the owner would be faced with the problem of paying fixed expenses such as salaries and wages of essential employees, interest on bank and other loans, taxes, and rent.

With a *business interruption* insurance policy, a small business owner receives full compensation for such trading losses as (a) net income lost because of lost sales, (b) continuing fixed expenses, or "overhead," and (c) extra expenses incurred in trying to keep the business operating after interruption by an insured peril. If records of accounts receivable are destroyed, the policy may also cover losses from additional bad debt caused thereby. If desired, all payroll (not just that of essential employees) may be insured. The cost of business-interruption insurance varies according to the gross earnings of a business. Compensation commences as soon as damage from an insured peril has interrupted normal business operations and continues until the premises are repaired or rebuilt or profits restored. Sometimes, as with fire insurance, a mandatory co-insurance clause requires the insured to maintain the business interruption insurance at at least 50 per cent of gross earnings. This figure may be 80 per cent if, for example, more than one location is covered.

Business Automobile Insurance

There is no special automobile insurance policy for cars or other vehicles owned or used by a business. It is the standard automobile policy used by the public in general. As such, it provides coverage (often for as much as $500,000) for claims from third parties, for mandatory "no fault" accident benefits, and for loss of or damage to the insured automobile.

However, many different endorsements can be purchased at extra charge. One example is the case of a firm whose employees (for example, sales representatives) use their own cars and receive a mileage allowance for doing so. If a third party is injured in an accident, the claim may be against the firm as well as against the employee. This is because the sales representative was probably engaged in the firm's business when the accident occured. To protect itself, the firm can have an endorsement to its automobile insurance policy to cover the excess of any claim above the limit of liability coverage taken out by its employee. Then if the court awards $350,000 to the injured person, and the employee only has coverage of $200,000, the firm will be reimbursed for the $150,000 that will have to come from its own pocket.

Another example is the car-rental business. Here the firm would need an endorsement for cars that are leased by it to others. Other endorsements are available for automobile dealers, garages and service stations, vehicle repairers, and parking lots.

If a business owns more than five vehicles, it can obtain a "fleet discount" on its insurance premium.

KEY TERMS

Business risk	Burglary
Insurance	Robbery
Insurability	Theft insurance
Law of averages	Fidelity bond
Insurer	Schedule bond
Insured	Surety bond
Beneficiary	Credit insurance
Premium	General liability insurance
Rider	Key personnel insurance
Endorsement	Term insurance
Insurance adjuster	Partnership insurance
Fire insurance	Buy-sell agreement
Co-insurance clause	Sole proprietorship insurance
Consequential clause	Business interruption insurance
Consequential loss	Business automobile insurance
Marine insurance	

REVIEW QUESTIONS

1. What are the two main types of business risk?
2. How, and to what extent, can business risk be reduced?
3. Explain the basic nature of insurance. What is the significance of the law of large numbers?
4. What are the essential requirements for a business risk to be insurable?
5. What are the principal elements of an insurance policy?
6. How should the amount of fire insurance that a firm requires be determined?
7. Explain the nature and purpose of a co-insurance clause. What is a consequential-loss clause?
8. What are the two basic types of marine insurance? What coverage do they provide?
9. How can a business reduce the risk of financial loss by theft?
10. Distinguish between fidelity bonding and surety bonding.
11. How can a firm reduce the risk of financial loss from bad debt?
12. What is general liability insurance? What does it cover?

13. Key personnel insurance is prudent business practice. Explain.
14. What is partnership insurance? Why is it necessary?
15. Explain the nature and purpose of a buy-sell agreement.
16. Explain the nature and purposes of sole proprietorship insurance.
17. What is business interruption insurance? What financial protection does it provide?
18. What insurance is available for a firm's automobiles?

CHAPTER 14
LONG-TERM FINANCING

CHAPTER OBJECTIVES

☐ To explain the difference between the working capital needs and the fixed capital needs of a business firm.

☐ To distinguish between equity financing and debt financing as a source of long-term funds.

☐ To show how a balance sheet summarizes a firm's assets, liabilities, and owner's equity at any particular date.

☐ To illustrate how financial leverage can help a business secure a better return on its investment.

☐ To indicate how and where a business obtains long-term funds.

☐ To review the different types of capital stock that a firm may issue to raise equity funds.

☐ To indicate the different types of bonds that a firm may issue to raise long-term borrowed funds.

CHAPTER OUTLINE

14.1 Equity, Debt, and Financial Leverage
14.2 Equity Financing
14.3 Debt Financing
14.4 The Canadian Securities Market

UNIT 14.1: EQUITY, DEBT, AND FINANCIAL LEVERAGE

A business needs cash to provide it with a pool of working capital to pay wages and salaries, purchase materials and parts, meet other operating expenses, and provide credit to its customers. It also needs cash to pay for its fixed capital—land, buildings, furniture, machinery, and equipment. In the previous chapter, it was explained that short-term financing from trade creditors, banks, and other lenders helps provide for a part of a firm's working capital needs, particularly seasonal variations. The remainder of the working capital—net working capital—is provided by medium- and long-term funds. The fixed capital needs are provided, to a limited extent, by medium-term financing and, to a very large extent, by equity financing and debt financing.

Equity versus Debt Financing

Equity financing is money provided by the owners of a business which remains permanently within the firm. It includes the owners' original investment, retained earnings, new ownership capital, and depreciation allowances (the amount by which profits have been understated by the inclusion of an allowance for depreciation of equipment among current expenses, even though no cash outflow may currently be involved).

Debt financing is money provided by lenders which must eventually be repaid. An important distinction between the two types of capital is that the equity capital is rarely repaid whereas the debt (or long-term borrowed capital) must be repaid at a specific future date. Also, interest must be paid on debt capital, whereas dividends are paid on equity capital only when a corporation's board of directors considers it appropriate to do so. In times of economic recession, the cash burden of heavy interest payments can often spell financial doom for a business corporation that has a large amount of borrowed capital.

Equity-Debt Ratio

The relationship between the amount of equity capital and the amount of debt capital that a firm has, is called the *equity-debt ratio*. If, for example, a firm has $100,000 of equity capital and $200,000 of debt, the ratio is 0.5. The higher the ratio, the more financially sound the company is. Separate ratios may be calculated for equity capital versus long-term debt and equity capital versus total debt.

There is no generally accepted rule as to the ratio that a firm should maintain between its equity capital and its debt capital. For many years it was considered sound business practice to rely on equity capital as much as possible for a company's capital needs. The greater the proportion of equity capital, the lower the risk of financial insolvency. However, more and more, business firms are now balancing financial strength against the possibly higher rate of return on the owner's equity capital that judicious long-term borrowing can bring.

The Balance Sheet

The assets, liabilities, and owner's investment in a business on any particular day are summarized in a *balance sheet*. The owners' *equity* or *net worth* is always equal to the total assets of the business minus the total liabilities. The following is a brief description of the balance sheet.

Assets. The assets of a business are usually classified in the balance sheet into current assets, sundry assets, and fixed assets. Another classification is into current and non-current. The basis of this classification is *liquidity*, that is, the ease with which assets can be converted into cash without substantial loss.

Current Assets. These consist of cash and other assets which can be turned into cash within a period of a year. They include, in order of liquidity: cash; marketable securities; accounts receivable; notes receivable; inventories; and short-term pre-paid expenses. Accounts receivable are considered current assets because, after allowance for bad debt, they can be expected to be paid in the near future. Prepaid expenses such as rent are included because, if these expenses were not already paid, the firm would have to find cash to pay them.

Sundry Assets. These are the assets which are neither current nor fixed. They include: land held for development; long-term investments in securities; investment in subsidiary or associated businesses; and funds set aside for plant expansion, bond repayment, or pension fund payments.

Fixed Assets. These are assets of a permanent or relatively permanent nature that are intended for use in the business rather than for sale. They include, in order of greatest use-life, such items as: land; buildings; machinery and equipment, furniture and fixtures; office equipment; and delivery vehicles. Also included in fixed assets, though under a separate sub-heading, are *intangible assets*. These comprise: patents, franchises, and trademarks; leaseholds; copyrights; and goodwill.

Liabilities. The liabilities of a business are divided into current liabilities and long-term liabilities, based on how soon these liabilities fall due.

Current Liabilities. These are obligations of the business that are payable on demand or, at the most, within the business year. Current liabilities include: accounts payable; notes payable; dividends payable; accrued taxes, wages and salaries, and interest; contingency reserves; revenue collected in advance; and long-term debt due within a year.

Long-Term Liabilities. These are liabilities which become payable more than a year after the date of the balance sheet. They consist of term loans payable, mortgage loans payable, bonds payable, and long-term liability reserves.

Owner's Equity. The owner's equity, or net worth, in a sole proprietorship is shown by the capital account in the balance sheet. The initial capital plus retained earnings equal the assets of the business minus the liabilities. However, because of the owner's unlimited liability by law, the strength of the business from, say, a lender's viewpoint would also encompass the owner's personal assets.

The value of the business as a going concern should also take into account the owner's business ability and the rate of expected earnings.

Partnership. The investment of each of the various partners is usually shown separately in the capital account of a partnership balance sheet. As with the sole proprietorship, the real value of the business as a going concern extends beyond the balance sheet.

The Corporation. The owners' equity in a corporation is shown in the balance sheet by the amount of capital stock plus retained earnings. The capital stock itself is usually divided into common and sometimes preferred shares. *Retained earnings* are past net profits, after tax, that have been retained in the corporation rather than paid out as dividends. Frequently, a separate statement of retained earnings is prepared, showing in detail the various additions to, and subtractions from, retained earnings during the fiscal year. An example of the balance sheet for a small business is shown in Figure 14.1.

Assets

Current Assets			
Cash on hand and in the bank		$ 500	
Accounts receivable		—	
Inventory		12 430	
Prepaid rent		—	
Total Current Assets			$12 930
Fixed Assets			
Sign		900	
Counters and display cases		2 900	
Land and buildings		—	
Total Fixed Assets			$ 3 800
Total Assets			$16 730

Liabilities, Owners' Equity, and Deficit

Current Liabilities			
Accounts payable		2 000	
Bank loan		1 500	
Total current liabilities			3 500
Long-Term Liabilities			—
Total Liabilities			$ 3 500
Owners' Equity and Deficit			
Capital		20 000	
Less: Deficit	$2 270		
Owner's drawings	4 500		
		$ 6 770	$13 230
Total Liabilities, Owners' Equity, and Deficit			$16 730

Figure 14.1 Balance Sheet for ABC Co. as at Jan. 1, 198–

Financial Leverage

By the use of borrowed capital, a business can sometimes substantially raise the rate of return on its equity capital. If, for example, a business can borrow money at 18 per cent per annum and make it earn, as part of the total capital of the enterprise, 24 per cent per annum, then the 6 per cent difference goes to increase the rate of return on the equity capital. This simple, but very effective, principle is called *financial leverage* or "trading on the equity."

Let us suppose that a small business now earns a net profit before tax of 24 per cent per annum on an equity capital of $25,000. Then, as can be seen in Figure 14.2, the rate of return can be raised to 28 per cent, if the owner puts in only $15,000 of his or her own money and borrows the rest at 18 per cent per annum. The lower the cost of the borrowed funds, the better the rate of return.

	Per Month	Per Annum
Sales	$10 000	$120 000
Net Profit	$500	$6 000
Rate of Return on $25 000 Equity Capital		24%
Cost of Borrowing $10 000 at 18 Per Cent per Annum	$150	$1 800
Net profit minus the cost of borrowing	$350	$4 200
Rate of return on $15 000 equity capital		28%

Figure 14.2 Return on Capital in a Small Business. The difference between 24 per cent and 28 per cent is "leverage."

Another example of how financial leverage can increase the rate of return on the equity capital is shown in Figure 14.3.

	(1)	(2)	(3)
Equity Capital	$100 000	$50 000	$25 000
Debt Capital	—	50 000	75 000
Total Capital Invested	100 000	100 000	100 000
Rate of Return	20%	20%	20%
Interest Paid (at 15% per annum)	—	7 500	11 250
Net Profit	20 000	12 500	8 750
Return on Equity	20%	25%	35%

Figure 14.3 Example of the Effects of Financial Leverage on the Return of Equity Capital

Financial leverage should, of course, be used with caution. If sales drop, the fixed burden of interest payments might well become more than the business can afford. Also, the cost of borrowing may exceed the rate of the return on the borrowed money, when used in the business. This means that financial leverage is operating in reverse, forcing down the rate of return on the equity capital rather than raising it!

Effects of the Form of Ownership

Unincorporated Firms. Sole proprietorships rely heavily for their long-term financing on the savings of the individual owner and on internally-generated funds. If these are insufficient, other persons may have to be brought into the business and a general or limited partnership formed. As with the sole proprietorship, the long-term financing for a partnership is available mainly from the partners' savings and from reinvested profits. Unlike a public business corporation, the partnership cannot solicit funds from the general public by selling shares or bonds. Additional long-term funds can, however, be arranged by mortgaging fixed assets. The need for long-term funds can be substantially reduced by leasing buildings, equipment, and vehicles, rather than buying them.

Incorporated Firms. A corporation can raise long-term funds by selling shares of capital stock to the limit authorized in its charter. It can also secure a long-term loan by issuing a bond.

A private business corporation is relatively handicapped, compared to a public business corporation, in its ability to raise long-term funds. It may not advertise the sale of its shares to the general public; and the ownership of the shares is not easily transferred once they have been sold—the approval of the board of directors must be obtained, and, usually, existing shareholders must be given first right to purchase the shares. Private business corporations tend, consequently, to rely heavily on reinvested profits for their capital expansion.

The public business corporation, on the other hand, can publicize the sale of its shares through advertisements and stock exchange listings; can sell them to any number of persons; and does not usually require that transfer of their ownership receive the approval of the corporation's board of directors.

The Investment Dealer

When a firm needs professional advice about raising money from the public, it will usually call upon the services of an *investment dealer*. This is a firm which underwrites new issues of government and corporate bonds and corporate stocks. *Underwriting*, in this sense, means buying all or part of a new issue in the hope of being able to sell it afterwards at a profit to the various long-term investors such as insurance companies and mutual funds. The investment dealer thus acts as a financial intermediary in the Canadian capital market, channelling funds from investors into investment opportunities. The dealer makes its profit (or loss, if the issue will not sell) by buying stocks or bonds at one price from the issuing corporation and selling them at a higher price to investors. Often, to share the risk, several investment dealers will combine into a syndicate to underwrite a new issue. In Canada, there are many investment dealers, concentrated mainly in Montreal and Toronto. In addition, some stockbroker firms do underwriting.

Not all corporate stock or bond issues are marketed by the investment dealers, stockbrokers, or broker-dealers (firms which specialize in distributing speculative issues to the public). Some large corporations, with the advice of their own financial staff, decide what types of issue to make and sell them directly to investors. This is called *private placement*.

Sources of Long-Term Funds

Long-term funds for business come both from within the business itself (retained earnings and depreciation allowances) and from outside sources. In Canada, depreciation reserves and undistributed profits have been estimated to provide almost half the total financing required for business expansion. For businesses that are not incorporated, internal sources are usually more important because of the difficulty of obtaining long-term loans. These are described more fully in the next Unit.

The most important external sources of long-term funds are life insurance companies; trust companies (including pension plans); mortgage loan companies; investment companies; and government agencies.

Government Agencies. Most provincial governments have development funds of one sort or another (the Development Fund of Manitoba, Industrial Estates Limited of Nova Scotia, and the Ontario Development Corporation) that provide medium- or long-term loans to business firms—so long as such firms meet location, employment, and other requirements.

At the federal level, the Department of Regional Industrial Expansion makes grants and long-term loans to firms establishing or expanding in slow-growth areas of Canada. Also, the federally-owned Canada Development Corporation, with shareholdings in private venture capital firms, hopes to increase the supply of equity capital available to Canadian businesses.

Reducing Fixed Capital Needs

A firm can reduce its capital needs by leasing fixed assets rather than buying them. Renting a store or leasing cars and trucks are typical examples. Nowadays, even ships and airplanes are leased. In the case of real estate, a firm wishing to have a new office building, manufacturing plant, or warehouse can often find investors willing to build it to the firm's specifications. In return, the firm must agree to lease the building for a considerable number of years at a rent that will provide the investors with a reasonable return on their money. Disposal of the building at the end of the lease period will form part of the rental agreement. Such an agreement is called a *finance-lease agreement*.

There are other firms that have already tied up funds in the form of real estate. These firms can unlock this fixed capital by entering into a *purchase leaseback* (or *sale and leaseback*) *agreement*. The procedure is for the firm to sell its land and buildings to an investor on the agreement that the property will be leased back to them at a fixed rent for a certain period of time. The firm gains by releasing some of its capital, yet retains the use of its buildings. The investor gains by obtaining a good long-term investment.

KEY TERMS

Equity financing
Debt financing
Equity-debt ratio
Balance sheet
Net worth
Liquidity
Current assets
Sundry assets
Fixed assets
Intangible assets

Current liabilities
Long-term liabilities
Owner's equity
Retained earnings
Financial leverage
Investment dealer
Underwriting
Private placement
Finance-lease agreement
Purchase leaseback agreement

REVIEW QUESTIONS

1. What is meant by equity financing? For what purpose is it used?
2. Distinguish between equity capital and debt capital.
3. What ratio should a firm maintain between the amount of its equity capital and the amount of its borrowed capital?
4. Explain how a firm's equity-debt ratio is calculated. Should a firm try to keep the ratio as high or as low as possible?
5. What does a firm's balance sheet reveal?
6. What is meant by financial leverage? Explain, with an example, how it can benefit a firm.
7. Financial leverage can sometimes bankrupt a firm. Explain and discuss.
8. How does the form of business ownership affect a firm's ability to arrange equity financing and long-term debt financing?
9. Explain the role of the investment dealer.
10. Explain the terms: (a) underwriting and (b) private placement.
11. What are the various private sources of long-term funds?
12. What are the various government sources of long-term funds?
13. How can a firm reduce its fixed capital needs?
14. What is meant by a finance-lease agreement?
15. What is a purchase leaseback agreement? Explain how it can benefit both parties.

CASE PROBLEMS

EXCELSIOR PRODUCTS LTD.
Raising funds by "going public"

Excelsior Products Ltd. is a small, private business corporation established in

1953, specializing in the production of artificial Christmas trees and coloured sets of lights. The trees are made in either of two colours, with a choice of number of branches and texture of needles—either soft and randomly twisted or smooth-barked and regular. Also, as an optional extra, the branches can be pre-sprayed with aerosol pine scent. Because of the rising cost of natural trees in the big Canadian cities and a growing awareness of the fire hazard involved, Excelsior has found a rapidly growing market for its artificial trees. Furthermore, the negotiation of a sales agreement with a large national retail discount chain in 1978 caused sales to show an average growth rate of almost 15 per cent during the next five years.

To manufacture its coloured Christmas lights (its other main product), Excelsior has over four million dollars' worth of highly sophisticated machinery. This machinery molds sockets on the wire (produced by Excelsior's own modern cable- and wire-drawing subsidiary), then cuts and packages strings of indoor and outdoor Christmas lights. These are sold under Excelsior's own name and by several other larger firms under their own brand names. Sales have shown a good steady annual rate of increase—just over 12 per cent per annum in the last decade. The only cloud on the horizon, as far as future sales are concerned, is the possibility of government restrictions to conserve electricity.

Because of the firm's relatively rapid expansion, Mr. Frank Krickler, president (and majority shareholder) of Excelsior, has always found it difficult to pay his creditors on time. Just as soon as the cash from sales has come in, it has to be paid out again in wages, rent, material payments, finance payments on the equipment, and so on. Also, Mr. Krickler has wanted for some time to take some cash out of the business to build and furnish a new home and to buy a yacht. As his wife has said: "You should enjoy some of it now, before it is too late—you have worked hard enough for it over the years!" Mr. Krickler's top executives have pointed out that many other companies offer stock options as a performance incentive above the regular salary. Mr. Krickler also appreciates that his future plans to enlarge his business by the takeover of several other smaller, related firms might be helped if he were to turn his private business corporation into a public one.

After consultation with both his vice-president and the firm's lawyer, Mr. Krickler finally decided to approach Steinmetz, Kline, and Paquet, a prominent firm of investment dealers, about a possible underwriting. A week later, a team of technical and financial analysts arrived to undertake an exhaustive examination of Excelsior's plants, inventory, books, and earnings prospects. This was followed by a "letter of intent" in which the investment dealer offered to buy 260,000 common shares at a net price to Mr. Krickler of $8.00 each. Eventually, agreement was reached at a price of $8.15—which represented an earnings multiple similar to that of many other companies that had recently gone public.

The hard work now began: to turn what was previously a private, provincially incorporated business corporation into a public one. Much to Mr. Krickler's dismay, he was required in subsequent weeks to spend hour after hour with lawyers, accountants, a consultant, and underwriters, helping to draft, correct, debate, redraft, scrutinize, recorrect, sign, and proofread a collection of fifty-eight legally phrased documents. Even more painful to Mr. Krickler was the cost of going public: $130,000 to Steinmetz, Kline, and Paquet for the underwriting discount, $85,000 for legal and accounting fees, $13,000 for the printing of the prospectus by a specialist firm, $5,000 for production of the stock certificates, and $300 apiece for listing the shares on the Toronto and Montreal stock exchanges.

Listed in April of last year, the stock traded for several months just below its issue price of $8.65. This led to a certain embarrassment for Mr. Krickler, who had recommended the stock to relatives and friends on the assurance of the investment dealer that the stock would trade at a modest premium.

Perhaps the greatest change in Mr. Krickler's life (apart from receiving a cheque on behalf of the company for over two million dollars) was the invasion of his privacy. Now, as the president of a public business corporation, he has to spend considerable time talking to journalists, financial analysts, and disgruntled shareholders.

Assignment
1. Why would a growing and profitable business find itself short of cash?
2. How has Mr. Krickler been able to provide more cash for his business? What other methods might he have employed?
3. How can he obtain more cash for his personal use?
4. Outline the steps involved in "going public."
5. What is the usual basis for setting the issue price of a stock?
6. How did the market react to the stock? Why?
7. "As president of a public business corporation, Mr. Krickler must now spend his time looking after the capital stock rather than the business." Explain and comment.

MASKOW ENTERPRISES LTD.
Analysing a firm's financial results

Maskow Enterprises Ltd. is a firm that is involved in four main areas of business activity: food, beverages, engineering, and communications. Its consolidated financial results for the last five years are shown in Figure 14.4.

Assignment
1. Analyse the company's financial results from the viewpoint of: (a) a major shareholder; (b) a major bondholder; and (c) top management.

Earnings Statistics	Year 5	Year 4	Year 3	Year 2	Year 1
Revenues	$32 542 237	20 945 938	14 388 899	4 889 355	2 884 621
Depreciation	647 896	484 614	315 527	58 782	43 273
Pre-tax Earnings	3 258 395	2 392 547	758 361	247 022	194 919
Current Taxes	533 177	275 389	139 851	2 217	12 764
Deferred Taxes	978 528	824 776	93 133	131 008	78 029
Net Earnings	1 746 690	1 292 382	525 377	140 797	104 126
Cash Flow	3 373 114	2 601 772	933 901	337 325	225 428
Dividends Paid	150 493	97 204	nil	51 638	41 565

Balance Sheet Statistics	Year 5	Year 4	Year 3	Year 2	Year 1
Current Assets	$11 184 643	7 076 106	3 462 991	1 189 655	739 623
Current Liabilities	8 265 418	6 279 055	3 895 026	819 778	447 821
Working Capital	2 919 225	797 051	(432 035)	369 877	291 802
Fixed Assets	12 752 947	8 177 940	5 165 317	2 940 064	810 745
Long-Term Debt	10 032 670	3 993 232	2 839 583	1 565 532	302 200
Shareholders Equity	7 529 954	5 459 833	3 105 092	2 020 998	691 914
Common Share Statistics					
Earnings per Share	$1.05	.83	.36	.12	.12
Cash Flow per Share	2.03	1.68	.64	.27	.27
Dividends per Share	.09	.06	nil	.05	.05
Equity per Share	4.50	3.37	2.10	1.65	.78
Other Statistics					
Average Shares Outstanding	1 664 541	1 548 570	1 449 040	1 229 090	831 296
Number of Shareholders	1 600	1 550	1 450	1 100	650

Figure 14.4 Consolidated Financial Data for Maskow Enterprises

UNIT 14.2: EQUITY FINANCING

Capital Stock

A corporation is authorized by the letters patent, articles of incorporation, or memorandum of association that brings it into being, to issue a certain number of shares of capital stock. These shares are known as the authorized capital stock, and they usually far exceed a company's immediate requirements. However, as more equity financing is required, more shares are issued. The funds obtained from the sales of these shares are locked permanently within the company in the various forms of assets.

The *capital stock* of a corporation represents the owners' equity (or ownership) and consists of common shares and also, in the majority of cases, of preferred shares. A person owning shares of a corporation is called a *shareholder* or *stockholder*. Stockholders can sell their shares only by transferring them to new owners; they cannot get their money back from the corporation unless the firm is wound up (that is, voluntarily terminated) and its assets sold.

Share Values

Most corporations now issue their shares at no-par value. The term *par value* means that a corporation has attached a definite price to the share, usually stated on the *stock certificate* (the written evidence of ownership), at the time of issuance. *No-par value*, or *without par value*, means that no price is stated (Figure 14.5). The actual price or value of any share is what it will fetch in the stock market. This is known as the *market price* or *market value*.

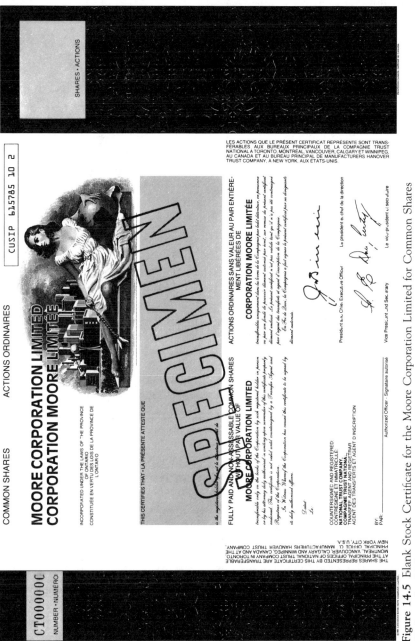

Figure 14.5 Blank Stock Certificate for the Moore Corporation Limited for Common Shares Without Par Value.

Courtesy Canadian Bank Note Company, Limited

The *book value* of a share is the value, as shown in the company books, or financial accounts, of each share's portion of the corporation's assets. It is calculated by dividing the net worth of the corporation (total assets minus total liabilities) by the number of shares issued. It should be noted that the value of the assets, as shown in the books of account, may be more or less than their market value.

Common Shares

Each common share of a corporation's capital stock entitles the owner to certain benefits: to vote at shareholders meetings; to share in the profits of the corporation; and to share in the assets of the corporation on liquidation.

Voting Rights. Normally, each common share entitles the owner to one vote at the shareholders meetings. In some companies, two classes of common stock, A and B, are issued, with the class A carrying the voting rights. Any person or group owning a majority of the voting common shares can appoint the board of directors and thereby control the management of the corporation. In raising additional long-term capital by selling more common shares, the directors must therefore take into account how these new shares may affect voting control.

Sharing Profits. The common shareholders of a corporation have the right to any profits that remain after preferred shareholders have received their fixed rate of dividend. This right does not mean, however, that the profits have to be paid out to them. *Dividends* are that part of the corporation's profits which the board of directors decides to pay to the shareholders. One of the duties of the corporation's board of directors is to decide how much of the profits should be distributed to shareholders in the form of dividends, and how much should be kept in the business as a contingency reserve or to finance business expansion. If the dividend policy is unsatisfactory, the shareholders can change it only by changing the board of directors. One of the most important reasons why directors retain earnings in the business is to provide additional long-term equity capital. From the shareholder's point of view, a conservative dividend policy is not entirely unfavourable. In the first place, the corporation will be in a financially stronger position, and this should be reflected in increased earnings. Secondly, the extra assets usually cause the market price of the shares to rise in anticipation of a future increase in dividends. When the shares are sold, this can result in a capital gain for the seller.

Dividends, when paid, may be in cash or in the form of stock dividends. *Stock dividends* are fully paid-up shares of stock which are given to shareholders instead of cash dividends. Since the net worth of the company is now divided among a larger number of shares, the asset value of each share is reduced. The shareholder will benefit if the decline in market value of the shares is not as great as the reduction in asset value, and by having lower-priced, and possibly more marketable, shares. The corporation itself has benefited by distributing stock rather than cash, which it can retain for company use.

Another device, somewhat similar to a stock dividend, is a *stock split*. In this case, a company does not issue new stock backed by retained earnings; it merely splits existing shares into a larger number of shares. Each new share now has a smaller amount of company assets behind it. For example, a four-for-one split reduces the assets behind each share to a quarter of its previous amount. A stock split is often made when the market price of the present shares is too high—for example, $500 each— to make them easily marketable. Often, when the stock is split, the market price of each new share may be more than the exact proportion of the old. This is because of the greater attractiveness to the investor of a relatively lower-priced share.

A corporation may give its shareholders the opportunity to buy new stock, at less than the current market price, before the stock is offered to the general public. These privileges, which lapse within a short period of time, are called *rights*, and are usually in proportion to the amount of stock at present owned. The number of rights granted to a shareholder is stated on a certificate called a *warrant*. These rights can be traded in the securities market. The term warrant is also used to describe a certificate giving the holder an option to buy shares of a company over a relatively long period of time, often several years, at prices which are gradually increased throughout the period. Such a warrant is sometimes attached to bonds and preferred shares as a promotional feature. Like a right, a warrant may be traded.

Sharing Assets. Usually the least important benefit to a shareholder is the right to share in the assets of the corporation on its liquidation. Normally a corporation is wound up because it is unprofitable; as a result there tends to be little money left for shareholders from the sale of the company's assets, once the various tax collectors, bondholders, and other creditors have been paid. This is especially true when the corporation is forced into bankruptcy by its creditors.

Preferred Shares

The capital stock of a corporation may consist of preferred shares as well as common shares. Where this is the case, the preferred shares, as the name implies, enjoy a favoured or "preferred" position with regard to profits and assets.

Voting Rights. The right to vote is normally withheld from preferred shares in exchange for the preferences given. However, the right to vote for the directors may become effective if preferred dividends have not been paid for a certain number of months or years. In this way, the preferred shareholders are given the opportunity to influence management, usually by having a representative on the board of directors.

Sharing Profits. Preferred shareholders are entitled to receive, from the profits of the corporation, a fixed dividend on their shares before anything is distributed to the common shareholders. This fixed annual rate of dividend is set as a percentage of the par value of the share or as a specific amount per share.

The right to a preference in receiving profits applies, it should be noted, only to profits that are distributed. There is no contractual obligation for a company to pay a preferred dividend each year; the profits may be retained as additional long-term capital. However, preferred shares are normally *cumulative*, unless otherwise specifically stated. This means that any dividend withheld in one year must be paid in subsequent years, before any dividend may be paid on the common shares. Where a preferred share does not have this right, it is described as *non-cumulative*.

Some corporations give a preference in dividends to one preferred share over another. Where this is done, the different types of preferred shares are ranked Preferred A, Preferred B, and so on.

Sharing Assets. Should the assets of the corporation be sold—for example, on voluntary liquidation—preferred shareholders rank before common shareholders in their claim to a share of the proceeds. They may receive, however, only the sum stated on the preferred share certificate. The common shareholders are entitled to receive all the remainder.

Other Features. Preferred shares, in addition to their other characteristics, may also be *callable* (or *redeemable*). By making the preferred shares callable, management gives itself the option of repaying this type of equity capital at a pre-set price whenever it finds it advisable—for example, to replace an issue carrying a high dividend rate with one carrying a lower rate. The holder of the share must, however, be given due notice and be paid a prescribed premium.

Another feature sometimes added to a preferred share is that of convertibility. A *convertible* preferred share is one that may be exchanged, or "converted," at the option of the owner into common stock at a fixed price or at a set ratio—for example, one preferred share for every two common shares. This option is given either for a fixed number of years, or for as long as the shares are outstanding. The purpose of making preferred shares convertible into common shares is to add a speculative element to them. Thus, if the corporation prospers and the market price of the common shares rises, the preferred shareholder can make a capital gain by converting the preferred shares into common shares. This speculative element, or "sweetener," helps the corporation to sell these shares and thereby raise long-term capital.

A preferred share may also be *participating*. This means that once the preferred shares have received their fixed dividend, and once the common shares have received a stated amount—for example, $1 per share in any one year—the preferred shares are entitled to receive a predetermined part of the remaining profits.

Prospectus

Before a public business corporation may sell shares to members of the public, it must file a prospectus with a government-appointed securities commission and send a copy to each prospective shareholder. A *prospectus* is a written, detailed description of the company. Its purpose is to provide the investing public with

enough information about a company to enable them to make an intelligent, well-informed investment decision and to prevent them from being defrauded. The information that must typically be included in a prospectus is as follows:
1. The date of incorporation and the head office address;
2. Particulars of the directors, proposed directors, chief executive officers, and auditors;
3. The general nature of the business;
4. Particulars of the share capital;
5. Particulars of loan securities;
6. Earnings of the company;
7. Property purchased; and
8. Director's interests in property acquired or to be acquired.

Retained Earnings

Another important source of long-term equity financing is the profits (or earnings) that are retained in the business rather than paid out as dividends. These internally-generated funds may be used to increase working and fixed capital and to retire debt and preferred shares.

The advantages of financing by these means are: the absence of any obligation to repay the money (as would be the case with debt financing); freedom from restrictions in the use of the money (as are often placed on the firm by lenders); and an improvement in the financial strength of the corporation by having an increase in the ratio of equity capital to borrowed capital.

Depreciation Allowances

It is customary for a firm to include among its annual expenses an allowance for depreciation of its plant and equipment. This allowance is not an expense in the normal sense. No money is paid out to others or set aside in a special fund. This expense represents the allocation or share, for the current year, of the large cost incurred at some time in the past when the plant or equipment was bought.

The actual profit of a firm in any year is the surplus of its revenue over its *actual* expenses. This surplus is represented by an increase in the firm's total assets over the year.

The inclusion of depreciation allowances—which are an artificial expense—in the firm's income statement causes the profit shown on the statement to be less than the actual level. As the firm can distribute to its shareholders only an amount equivalent to the profits (after tax) shown on the statement, that part of the surplus revenue over expenses equivalent to the depreciation allowance remains locked within the company. In this sense, depreciation allowances represent a source of long-term financing.

Depreciation, it should be noted, is an allowable expense for business income tax purposes. Thus a firm does not, as is the case with retained earnings, have to earn almost two dollars before tax (at a 46 per cent corporate income tax rate) to provide one dollar, after tax, for reinvestment. In other words, for every dollar allowed for depreciation by Revenue Canada, a dollar's worth of assets remains in the firm; whereas for every dollar of profit, 46 cents' worth of assets is paid to the government and 54 cents' worth either paid to the firm's shareholders or left in the firm.

KEY TERMS

Capital stock	Rights
Shareholder	Warrant
Par value	Preferred share
Stock certificate	Cumulative preferred
Market value	Callable (or redeemable)
Book value	Convertible
Common share	Participating
Dividends	Prospectus
Stock dividends	Retained earnings
Stock split	Depreciation allowances

REVIEW QUESTIONS

1. What is capital stock? What forms does it take?
2. Distinguish between a shareholder and a stockholder.
3. Can a stockholder recover his or her investment by selling the shares owned back to the company?
4. Distinguish between the par value, the market value, and the book value of a share of capital stock.
5. What voting rights belong to the holder of common shares?
6. What are dividends? Who decides if and when they should be paid? Are they an expense of the business?
7. What are stock dividends? How do they benefit (a) the company and (b) the shareholder who receives them?
8. Explain the nature and purpose of a "stock split."
9. Distinguish between "rights" and "warrants."
10. What is a common shareholder's entitlement, if any, if the company has to be "wound up"?
11. Distinguish between common and preferred shares.
12. What voting rights does a preferred shareholder enjoy?
13. Distinguish between cumulative and non-cumulative preferred shares.
14. How is the preferred shareholder's dividend calculated? Does it vary in the same way as that of the common shareholder?
15. Why do some investors buy common shares and other preferred shares?

16. What right to share assets do preferred shareholders have if the company has to be dissolved?
17. What is a callable preferred share? Why are they issued? Why would anyone buy them?
18. A convertible preferred share gives an investor the best of two worlds. Explain and discuss.
19. Another feature that a preferred share may possess is "participation." Explain.
20. What is a prospectus? Who requires it? What must it contain? Who benefits from it?
21. Explain how retained earnings are a source of equity financing.
22. What are depreciation allowances? Why are they considered to be an important internal source of equity financing?

CASE PROBLEM

MITCHELL ELECTRICAL INDUSTRIES LIMITED
Arranging long-term financing

Mitchell Electrical Industries Limited is a major Canadian manufacturer of electrical goods. Its products include large apparatus such as high-voltage power transformers, hydraulic power generators, and circuit breakers for power utilities and heavy industry; light apparatus such as visual landing aids for aircraft pilots, and electric heating units for high-rise apartment buildings; and consumer goods such as air conditioners and dishwashers.

Over the last few years, the company's sales in the Canadian market and overseas, particularly in Britain and the Caribbean, have increased substantially. As a result, the company is now planning to expand its production facilities. This expansion will include, among other projects, a transformer plant in Montreal and a switchgear and circuit breaker plant in Vancouver. To help finance the expansion scheduled for next year, the company will need to raise $3.2 million in the capital market. The board of directors have asked the Toronto investment dealer firm, J.P. Fenner and Sons Ltd., to prepare a report on the most suitable method of raising this money.

The company's financial statements for last year are shown in Figures 14.6 and 14.7.

Assignment
1. Discuss the present financial solvency of this company. Calculate the current ratio, the equity-debt ratio, and the return on capital as part of your answer.
2. List and explain the factors which will help decide the method of financing to be used.
3. What are the possible advantages and disadvantages for this company of raising the money by an issue of additional common stock?

4. By an issue of 11½ per cent cumulative preferred stock?
5. By an issue of 9 per cent debenture bonds?
6. What other sources of long-term financing does the company have apart from the capital market?

ASSETS

	Last Year ($000's)	Previous Year ($000's)
Current Assets		
Cash, including time deposits	$ 268	$ 424
Accounts receivable	29 367	24 733
Inventories valued at the lower of cost or market	28 542	27 617
Prepaid taxes, insurance and rentals	538	669
	$58 715	$53 443
Fixed Assets		
Land, buildings, and equipment at cost	57 921	54 537
Less accumulated depreciation	36 837	35 848
	21 084	18 689
Other Assets	117	397
	$79 916	$72 529

LIABILITIES

	Last Year	Previous Year
Current Liabilities		
Bank and other short-term indebtedness	359	3 519
Accounts payable and accrued liabilities	13 587	11 236
Income and other taxes payable	3 135	2 012
	17 081	16 767
Funded Debt		
5% sinking fund debentures due April 15, 198–		
Authorized—$14 000 000		
Issued	13 639	10 271
Shareholders' Equity		
Capital stock		
Authorized—500 000 shares of no par value		
Issued—330 238 shares	12 288	11 787
Earned surplus	36 908	33 704
	49 196	45 491
	$79 916	$72 529

Figure 14.6 Mitchell Electrical Industries Limited: consolidated balance sheet as at June 30, last year (with comparative figures for previous year)

INCOME

	Last Year ($000's)	Previous Year ($000's)
Sales	$158 058	$138 827
Operating costs and expenses including depreciation	151 137	136 239
Income from operations	6 921	2 588
Other Income:		
Profit on disposal of fixed assets	28	53
Investment income	138	97
	7 087	2 738
Interest on Debentures	510	498
Income Before Income Taxes	6 577	2 240
Income Taxes	3 123	1 112
Net Income for the Year	$ 3 424	$ 1 128

EARNED SURPLUS

	Last Year	Previous Year
Balance at Beginning of Year	$33 704	$32 576
Net Income for Year	3 454	1 128
	37 158	33 704
Dividends Declared	250	
Balance at the End of Year	$36 908	$33 704

Figure 14.7 Mitchell Electrical Industries Limited: statement of consolidated income and earned surplus for the Year Ended June 30, last year (with comparative figures for previous year)

UNIT 14.3: DEBT FINANCING

When a corporation borrows money, it usually makes a written promise to repay this money at a certain future date. These written promises may be either promissory notes or bonds. A promissory note is normally used when the period of the loan is less than 5 years. A bond is used for longer periods, often for as much as 20 or 30 years and usually for at least 10.

A *bond* is a written acknowledgement by a corporation, made under seal, that it owes a certain sum of money. The terms of this contractual obligation are set out in detail in a document called the *bond indenture*. The indenture specifies not only the sum owed (the *principal*); but also the fixed annual rate of interest; the date on which the principal has to be repaid (the *maturity date*); the particular assets, if any, which are pledged by the corporation as security for repayment of the loan (for example, buildings); and the persons appointed to look after the bondholders' interests (the *bond trustees*), who usually consist of a trust company and a private individual.

Under the terms of the bond indenture, a large number of individual bond certificates are sold. These certificates outline the principal features of the bond issue and are usually for amounts (*denominations*) of $1,000 each (Figure 14.8). When a bond sells for less than face value, it is said to sell *at a discount*; when it sells for more than its face value, it is said to sell *at a premium*.

Secured Bonds

Bonds are either secured or unsecured. A *secured bond* is one in which management has pledged the title to certain of the corporation's assets—for example, land and buildings—as security for repayment of the loan. There are two main kinds of bond security: a real estate mortgage and a chattel mortgage.

Real Estate Mortgage. This is a form of deed whereby the borrower (the mortgagor) transfers ownership of a property to the lender (the mortgagee) as security for repayment of the loan. In some provinces, because of a different method of land registration (the Torrens system), ownership remains with the borrower but a charge is created in favour of the lender.

The mortgage contract provides that ownership returns to the borrower if all the terms of the bond are met. These terms include: the amount, time, and method of payment of interest; maintenance of the property in good condition; payment of insurance and taxes on it; and repayment of the principal in the manner and at the time stated. The property is said to be *redeemed* when the loan has been fully repaid (and the debt *retired*). Should the corporation fail to make the interest or principal payments when due (that is, *default* on its obligation) the bondholders, represented by the bond trustees, may start *foreclosure* proceedings. This is a court action whereby the judge permits the bondholders to take possession of the mortgaged property. Once the property has been sold, the bondholders may deduct from the proceeds the money owing to them plus expenses. The remainder, if any, must be returned to the borrower.

A corporate mortgage bond itself has several variations according to priority of claim on the property, the nature of the security, and the right to raise more money using the same property as security. Thus we have, as one variation, *first mortgage* bonds and *second mortgage* bonds whereby the bondholders of the former issue must, on default by the borrower, have all their claims settled before the second mortgage bondholders can. These are also called *senior* and *junior* mortgage bonds. *Closed mortgage* bonds forbid the corporation to make further first mortgage bond issues. *Open mortgage* bonds allow additional bonds of equal rank to be issued, but usually only against newly acquired assets.

Chattel Mortgage. The second type of bond security is a *chattel mortgage*. This is similar to a real estate mortgage, except that moveable property (chattels) is involved, and that ownership is always transferred to the lender until the loan is repaid. A chattel mortgage is used for *equipment trust certificates*. These are bonds for which moveable property such as railway rolling stock or plant ma-

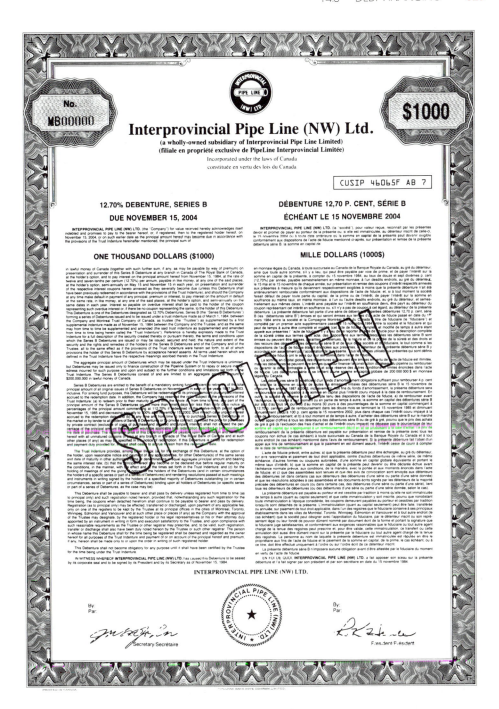

Figure 14.8 Debenture Certificate for One Thousand Dollars of Interprovincial Pipe Line (NW) Ltd.

Courtesy Canadian Bank Note Company, Limited

chinery is used as security. A *collateral trust bond* is another bond of this type. Here, the stocks or bonds owned by the borrowing company are placed with a trust company as security for repayment of the loan.

Unsecured Bonds

Bonds that have no specific assets pledged as security for repayment of the loan are called *debenture bonds*, or merely *debentures*. Often when a debenture is issued, the issuing company formally agrees that no mortgage bond may be subsequently issued. This is called a *negative pledge*. Should the corporation default on its obligations, the debenture bondholders must rely for settlement of their claims on the money remaining from the sale of the corporation's assets after secured bondholders have been paid. Debentures are therefore a riskier form of investment than secured bonds. Sometimes, however, debentures are secured by a floating charge on a company's assets. Also, sometimes they may be partly secured by a charge upon some of the firm's assets. When the latter is the case, the bond is known as a *secured debenture*.

Special Features in Bonds

In order to attract money from different types of lenders or to retain flexibility for the corporation, management may include in a bond various other features in addition to security.

Redeemability. Management may provide for a bond to be *redeemable*, or *callable*. This means that the corporation reserves the right to repay the principal before maturity at a price (the *call* price) stated in advance. However, this right can be exercised normally only after a fixed initial period of time. Redeemable bonds thus enable management to repay borrowed long-term funds as soon as they are no longer required or as soon as they can be replaced by cheaper ones.

Convertibility. To attract investors who would like the possibility of a speculative gain in addition to the usual safety of a bond, management may make a bond *convertible*. Such a feature allows the bondholder to exchange his or her bonds for stocks during all or part of the lifetime of the bond. This right, being an optional one, gives the bondholder the opportunity to convert into common shares if their market price rises considerably, or stay with his or her bonds if the corporation fails to prosper.

Repayment. One of the financial problems that face a corporation is the need to have sufficient funds available to repay long-term loans when they mature. One answer to this problem is to issue bonds which mature in different years. Bonds with varying maturity dates that are part of one bond issue are known as *serial bonds*. Another answer is to set aside a certain sum each year, so that when the bond matures, enough money will be available to repay it. When this annual sum is deposited with the bond trustee and made a feature of the bond, the result is a *sinking-fund bond*.

Other Features. Other features to be found in bonds are: *participation*, whereby bondholders (as an investment incentive) are allowed a share in earnings in addition to their fixed interest; *income*, whereby management—to help ensure financial solvency—pays bond interest only if it has been earned that year; *guarantee*, whereby repayment of the bond principal is guaranteed by a corporation other than the borrower; *registration*, whereby the name of the owner is shown on the bond certificate and recorded by the corporation, the interest being sent to the named bondholder; and *coupon*, or *bearer*, whereby the bond certificate does not indicate the name of the owner, and the interest is paid only to the person presenting the dated interest coupons.

KEY TERMS

Bond	First mortgage bond
Bond indenture	Second mortgage bond
Bond principal	Chattel mortgage
Maturity date	Debenture bond
Bond trustees	Negative pledge
Secured bond	Redeemable bonds
Real estate mortgage	Convertible bonds
Default on payment	Serial bonds
Foreclosure	Sinking-fund bond
Corporate mortgage bond	Coupon (or bearer) bond

REVIEW QUESTIONS

1. What is a bond? When is a promissory note more usual?
2. Explain the terms: (a) bond indenture, (b) bond principal, and (c) bond trustees.
3. Sometimes a bond sells at a discount; at other times at a premium. Explain.
4. Explain how a real estate mortgage is used in connection with a bond.
5. What are foreclosure proceedings? When do they take place?
6. Distinguish between: (a) first mortgage bonds and second mortgage bonds and (b) closed mortgage bonds and open mortgage bonds.
7. What other kind of bond security exists?
8. What is a debenture?
9. Explain the difference between a redeemable bond and a convertible bond.
10. Distinguish between a serial bond and a sinking-fund bond.
11. Explain the following bond features: (a) participation (b) income (c) guarantee (d) registration, and (e) coupon.

CASE PROBLEM

BROWN MANUFACTURING INDUSTRIES LIMITED
Analysing a company's financial statements

One of your tasks as the financial analyst for Edward and Townsend, investment dealers, is to examine and interpret the financial statements of companies wishing to issue shares or sell bonds.

One such company is Brown Manufacturing Industries Limited, a firm specializing in the manufacture of motor vehicle parts. This firm would like to borrow an additional two million dollars at long-term to expand its plant to take advantage of excellent sales opportunities. These opportunities have arisen because of the Brown firm's well-established position as supplier to a firm specializing in the manufacture of small cars, which are expected to show substantial sales increases in the years ahead.

See the following pages for the Financial Statements of Brown Manufacturing Industries Ltd.

Assignment

1. Do you feel that the firm could handle an additional loan of this magnitude? Justify your answer.
2. Would you recommend an alternative means of raising the money? Justify your answer.
3. Would you recommend that a client invest in this company as a lender or as a shareholder?

BROWN MANUFACTURING INDUSTRIES LIMITED
(Incorporated under the laws of Ontario)
and subsidiaries

CONSOLIDATED BALANCE SHEET—DECEMBER 31, LAST YEAR
(with comparative figures for previous year)

ASSETS

	Last Year	Previous Year
Current Assets		
Cash	$ 8 724	$ 33 725
Accounts receivable	2 093 936	1 701 861
Income taxes recoverable	50 117	238 079
Inventories, at the lower of cost and net realizable value	2 536 893	1 562 271
Prepaid expenses	56 865	57 063
	4 746 535	3 592 999

	Last Year	Previous Year
Fixed Assets		
Land, buildings and equipment, at cost	4 433 660	4 446 052
Less accumulated depreciation	1 507 255	1 188 862
	2 926 405	3 257 190
Other Assets		
Excess of cost over book value at dates of acquiring shares of subsidiaries	379 322	379 322
Patents, at cost less amortization	73 612	76 492
Other	58 816	152 662
	511 750	608 476

Approved by the Board
    S.T. McGregor, Director
    M.P. Saracini, Director

	$8 184 690	$7 458 665

LIABILITIES

	Last Year	Previous Year
Current Liabilities		
Bank loan, secured by general assignment of book debts	$1 245 000	$1 115 000
Accounts payable and accrued liabilities	2 576 341	1 665 911
Income taxes payable	73 678	
Principal due within one year on long-term debt	306 928	317 816
	4 201 947	3 089 727
Long Term Debt	1 642 607	1 645 432
Deferred Income Taxes	250	296 896
Interest of Minority Shareholders in Subsidiary	11 189	6 888

SHAREHOLDER'S EQUITY

	Last Year	Previous Year
Capital Stock		
Authorized—600 000 common shares without par value		
Issued —351 400 common shares	1 069 731	1 069 731
Retained Earnings	1 258 966	1 340 991
	2 328 697	2 410 722
	$8 184 690	$7 458 665

STATEMENT OF CONSOLIDATED RETAINED EARNINGS

Year Ended December 31, Last Year
(with comparative figures for previous year)

	Last Year	Previous Year
Balance at beginning of year	$1 340 991	$1 416 090
Loss for the year	82 025	75 099
Balance at end of year	$1 258 966	$1 340 991

STATEMENT OF CONSOLIDATED EARNINGS

Year Ended December 31, Last Year
(with comparative figures for previous year)

	Last Year	Previous Year
Sale	$14 313 668	$12 431 102
Expenses		
Cost of sales and expenses other than the undernoted	11 991 878	10 541 672
Depreciation	367 329	345 169
Amortization	2 880	2 880
Interest		
Long-term debt	121 596	133 790
Other	134 664	124 125
Selling and administrative expenses	1 806 134	1 486 776
	14 424 481	12 634 412
Loss before undernoted item	110 813	203 310
Write-off of development expenditures	177 893	
Loss before income taxes and minority interest	288 706	203 310
Income taxes		
Current (recoverable)	85 664	(229 702)
Deferred (reduction)	(296 646)	109 817
	(210 982)	(119 885)
Loss before minority interest	77 724	83 425
Interest of minority shareholders in earnings (loss) of subsidiary	4 301	(8 326)
Loss for the year	$ 82 025	$ 75 099
Loss per share	$ .23	$ .21

Figure 14.9 Financial Data for Brown Manufacturing Industries Limited

UNIT 14.4: THE SECURITIES MARKET

The term *securities* is used broadly to mean common and preferred shares (also called stocks) and various types of debt instruments. The latter, also known as "financial instruments," include promissory notes, bills, and bonds issued either by private firms or by governments and their agencies. These are also known as "financial instruments."

Securities Market. This term refers to the network of firms and institutions that exists for the sale and purchase of such securities. Notable among these are the stock exchanges, the stockbrokers, the investment dealers, and the bond houses.

Trading of Securities

The trading of common and preferred shares is carried out by stock brokerage firms (or *stockbrokers*) who buy and sell stocks, usually as agents for their clients, receiving a commission for their services. Trading in bonds, once the initial, or primary, distribution has taken place, is carried out in Canada by investment dealers and bond houses—buying and selling on their own account. This is sometimes called the "secondary bond market."

Trading in stocks takes place in specially designed and equipped buildings known as *stock exchanges* or "over-the-counter" by stockbrokers contacting each other directly, either in person or by telephone or telex. Over-the-counter trading involves only "unlisted" stocks, i.e. ones which have not been approved for trading in the stock exchange. Bonds are traded in some stock exchanges, but not in the Toronto one. Most bond trading is conducted "over-the-counter." Whatever the facilities used, the price of the security is determined by competitive bidding by prospective buyers on the one hand, and competitive offering by prospective sellers on the other.

Stock Exchanges

There are five stock exchanges in Canada: one each in Toronto, Montreal, Vancouver, Winnipeg, and Calgary. However, the Toronto Stock Exchange accounts for about 77% of the total dollar value of shares traded in Canada followed by Montreal (about 13%) and Vancouver (about 10%). Each stock exchange has a limited number of "seats" or memberships all of which are owned by various stock brokerage firms and which may be bought and sold at a price determined by prevailing supply and demand. Each seat permits the member plus a small number of persons called *floor traders* (or *attorneys* in Montreal) to transact business on the floor of the stock exchange.

Management. The operation of each stock exchange and the conduct of its members are governed by provincial statute; by the stock exchange's bylaws (which are made effective through a majority vote of the members); and by the rulings of its Board of Governors, which meets regularly each week. A president, assisted by a small staff, is in charge of day-to-day operations.

Purpose. The purpose of a stock exchange is to provide an organized marketplace, including the requisite facilities, particularly communications equipment, for the efficient buying and selling of listed stocks by its members. In a broader sense, a stock exchange satisfies an investor's need to be able to sell securities quickly if the need for cash arises. Because of this ease of liquidity, persons and institutions are encouraged to invest money in stocks and thereby help provide long-term funds for business expansion. The stock exchange also enables prices of stocks to be established by the interaction of demand and supply.

Income. A stock exchange is a non-profit organization, its cost of operation being met by an annual levy on members; by attorney fees; clerk fees; telephone booth fees; and transaction charges. The largest sources of revenue are the fees charged to corporations for listing their securities on the exchange and the transaction charges imposed on member brokers for transactions made on the floor of the exchange.

Securities Traded. In the case of the Toronto Stock Exchange, the facilities are available to members only for the trading of listed stocks (of which there are over 800). Bonds are not bought or sold. A *listed stock* is one that has been approved for trading by the stock exchange.

Approval for listing on the exchange is normally granted to corporations that meet minimum financial standards set by the exchange and can provide the exchange with evidence of good management.

Reasons for Listing. The reasons why a public business corporation may decide to have its stock listed on a stock exchange include:
1. Increased prestige, since investors realize the company must have met, and must maintain, certain minimum financial standards.
2. Greater shareholder goodwill as the buying and selling of the stock becomes easier.
3. Easier access to short-term credit as the market value of the corporation is more easily recognizable.
4. Easier access to debt financing through a public issue of shares.
5. Listed stocks can be accepted as collateral for a loan.
6. More information is available on listed companies than on unlisted or private companies.
7. The financial press carries full trading details of listed companies, allowing shareholders to follow closely the latest market activity, thereby increasing the overall marketability of the stock.

Trading Facilities. The trading floor of the exchange (see photo) has a number of *trading posts*, around which the buying and selling of stocks takes place. Each offer to buy or sell must be shouted out for all traders to hear. Around

Trading Floor of the Toronto Stock Exchange
Courtesy the Toronto Stock Exchange

the floor of the exchange are telephone booths where each member has a telephone clerk to receive orders and relay them to the member's floor traders. At each trading post computer screens display the latest bid and ask prices of the listed stocks, to keep traders up-to-date on the marketplace.

Stock Quotations. The transactions which take place in the stock exchange are published daily in the newspapers. A partial list of such *stock quotations* is shown in Figure 14.10.

The information given for a particular day, reading from left to right, is the highest and lowest price paid for the stock during the last 52 weeks; the abbreviated name of the stock; the dividend paid in the current year; the highest price per share paid that day; the lowest price per share paid that day; the last (or closing) price paid that day; the net change or difference between the closing price that day compared with the previous day; and the total number of shares traded on that day. The prices quoted are in dollars and fractions of dollars ranging from $1/8$ to $7/8$. The use of a "z" next to the volume means "less than board lot."

Weekly summaries of trading (as for example, in the *Financial Post*) usually include such additional information as the indicated dividend rate, earnings per share for the last two years, and the latest price/earnings ratio.

52-week								
High	Low	Stock	Div.	High	Low	Close	Ch'ge	Vol.
23 1/4	17 1/2	C Marconi	.28	$22 1/2	22 1/4	22 1/2	+ 1/4	3650
45	15	Cdn Nat Res		22	22	22	+3	6200
32	24 1/4	C Ocdental	.64	$26 3/4	26 1/2	26 5/8	+ 1/8	15364
21 3/4	15 5/8	CP Ltd	.48	$17 1/2	17 1/4	17 1/2	+ 1/4	156786
6 1/8	405	Cdn Roxy		$ 5 5/8	5 3/8	5 3/8	− 2/8	23348
7 3/8	325	Cancom		$ 6 3/8	6 3/8	6 3/8	+ 3/8	410
16 1/2	11	Cdn Tire	.20	$12 1/2	12 3/8	12 1/2		1000
11	8 1/8	CTire A	.20	$ 9 1/8	9	9		47180
19	16	CUtil A	1.28	$19	18 3/4	19		301164
19	16 1/4	CUtil B	1.28	$19	18 3/4	19	+ 1/4	1978

Figure 14.10 Stock Quotations
Courtesy *The Globe and Mail*

Stock Trading Process

A person can establish an account with a stockbroker by completing a "know-your-client" form that will provide particulars of age, occupation, net worth, investments, bank branch, etc. and providing a satisfactory bank reference. He or she will normally deal with an employee of the firm known as an *account executive* (stockbroker, or *registered representative* or *RR*). The account executive will, if requested, provide advice about stocks to buy, taking into consideration the prospective customer's financial circumstances and wishes. Once the customer's credit standing has been satisfactorily established, arrangements may be made for stock purchases to be partly financed by the stockbroker. When a customer uses credit, he or she is said to be *buying on margin*. Usually the maximum credit permissible is 50 per cent of the market price of the stock. However, rates vary depending on the value of the stocks purchased. The stock itself is held as security for repayment of the loan.

Once the customer has given a firm order (either in person or by telephone, mail, or telegraph), the account executive records the details on a stock ticket. He or she then arranges for the order to be sent to the firm's order clerk, located in the firm's booth on the edge of the trading floor of the exchange. The clerk will then call over one of the firm's floor traders, who will take the order to the appropriate trading post and shout it out. The order may be to buy or sell a stock at a definite price or *at market*, that is, at the best price obtainable.

Once the trader has found another trader willing to do business at an agreeable price, the transaction is made and recorded on a three copy floor ticket. Both traders initial the floor ticket and keep one copy each. The third copy is handed in at the nearest trading post where a Stock Exchange input operator, working at the post, time stamps it and records the sale on a keyboard connected with the Exchange computer. The details contained in the floor ticket, which provides a permanent record of the transaction, are then sent out by the exchange to all parts of the country on electronic tickers. On the floor itself, the trader informs the firm's order clerk that the transaction has been completed; the clerk relays this information back to the stockbroker's office; and the account executive then telephones the customer that the stock has been bought or sold. An official confirmation is mailed the same day. Payment for the shares plus commission, in the case of a purchase, must be made within five business days of the transaction. The rate of commission charged by the stockbroker varies with the value of the order and with the number of shares purchased. Also, it may vary from one brokerage firm to another. The stock certificate, issued by the transfer agent of the corporation whose shares have been bought, is usually made out in the name of the stockbroker who has made the purchase. This is because most persons buying stocks prefer that the stock certificates be held by their stockbroker, either as collateral when buying on credit or to facilitate further trading. If an investor wishes to have the stock certificate made out in his or her own name, the stockbroker should be advised accordingly. It might then take from 6 to 12 weeks before the investor receives the stock certificate from the transfer agent.

Stockbroker's Office

A typical stock brokerage firm is likely to comprise many partners, including possibly a senior partner, a managing partner, and partners in charge of each of the different business departments. These departments usually include a retail sales department, an institutional sales department, a managed accounts department; an unlisted department and wire room; an underwriting department; and a research department. Some firms also have a money department, a bond department, and a commodities department. In addition to the partners, there are account executives, bond traders, research staff, accountants, floor traders, and clerical and secretarial staff.

To supplement the activities of the account executive or "registered rep," in his or her dealings with clients, the research department will often provide weekly or monthly reports on market trends and on the record and prospects of individual stocks.

There is also a variety of communications equipment in the stockbroker's office to bring market news immediately to staff and customers. This equipment includes a long, narrow screen, along which moves the electronic ticker. The *electronic ticker* is a running report of the transactions which have just taken place on the floor of the stock exchange and of the latest bid and ask quotations. An example is shown in Figure 14.11.

Sales are reported in the following way:
1. A symbol is first printed on the top line of the tape to indicate the name of the firm—for example, BNS for Bank of Nova Scotia.

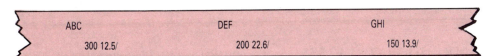

Figure 14.11 Example of Electronic Ticker

2. The number of shares traded is shown on the bottom line of the tape. If, however, the transaction is for 100 shares, the last two digits are dropped and only the number "1" is shown. Similarly, 300 shares is represented by the number 3, and 3,000 shares by the number 30. For quantities of shares other than multiples of 100, the exact number is shown, followed by the letter s. Thus 4 s. means 4 shares sold.
3. The price at which the shares were sold is shown on the bottom line of the tape immediately following the number of shares. Prices are shown either in terms of dollars and one-eighth fractions of a dollar or in terms of cents and one-eighth fractions of a cent. Thus $25\frac{7}{8}$ can mean 25 dollars and $87\frac{1}{2}$ cents ($\frac{1}{8}$ of a dollar = $12\frac{1}{2}$ cents) or $25\frac{7}{8}$ cents. The price is shown in cents as well as dollars for all stocks under $5.00. Prices shown on the electronic ticker are shown to the nearest decimal point. Thus, for example, $12\frac{1}{2}$ is shown as 12.5; $22\frac{5}{8}$ as 22.6; and $13\frac{7}{8}$ as 13.9.

Bid and ask prices for stocks are also shown on the ticker. The symbol for the firm is shown on the top line of the ticker, followed, on the bottom line, by the bid price and the offering price—for example, CGE 62b65, which means $62 per share bid Canadian General Electric and $65 per share the offering price per board lot (100 shares). If there is no offering, only the bid is shown. If there is no bid, this is indicated by a zero (OB) followed by the offering price. A bid or offering for an odd lot is denoted by an asterisk on the bottom line.

Sometimes, when the volume of trading on the Exchange floor is extremely heavy—for example, because of a rumoured mining "strike"—the information may be minutes behind the time when the transaction actually took place. This is called *late tape*.

An account executive can use *Candat*, a communications system which provides instant access by remote terminal (in, for example, a stockbroker's office) to the stock exchange data computer. Enquiries about stock prices, trading volumes, and a wide range of other stock market data are immediately answered.

Over-the-Counter Market

The first part of the securities market that we discussed was the stock exchanges; the second part is the *over-the-counter market*. This refers to the large volume of trading, in bonds as well as stocks, that is carried on (predominantly over the telephone) by stockbrokers, investment dealers, bond houses, banks, trust companies, mutual funds and insurance companies. Unlike the stock exchange, where bid and ask prices are automatically posted for all to see, the trader in the over-the-counter market must constantly telephone other traders to inform them of his or her requirements and availabilities. Lists of stocks and bonds, with latest prices, are also published in the newspapers. All the stocks traded in this market are unlisted ones.

Bond Trading Process. The trading department of an investment dealer contains a number of *trading desks* or *turrets*. Each trader has a telephone and a number of *key boxes*, so that by merely pulling a key above a certain label, he or she can get into touch immediately with the trading desk of another firm.

A typical trade would be as follows:

Trader A: "How are you on Canadian Breweries 5 to 88?"
Trader B: "92 to 4."
Trader A: "Sold you 5 and I've got 10 to go."
Trader B: "I'll take the other 10 and I'm still bidding."

In this transaction, trader A has asked trader B for his or her buying and selling prices for a 5 per cent bond issued by Canadian Breweries and due for repayment in 1988.

Trader B has indicated that he or she is willing to buy these bonds at $92 per $100 face value, or sell them at $94 per $100 face value. (This bid or offer applies to a minimum of five bonds of $1,000 each—known as a *board lot*.)

Trader A, accepting trader B's offer to buy at $92, has sold him or her $15,000 par value for $13,800. Each of the two traders would note the transaction on a slip, which would then be sent to their respective accounting departments.

Securities Legislation

Each province has a Securities Act, as well as a number of other laws affecting in various ways the raising of funds for business purposes from the general public. Most of the Securities Acts closely resemble each other and provide for a Securities Commission to regulate industry in various ways: by the approval and registration of practically every person in any way connected with security issuing or trading; by the investigation of individuals' or companies' books and affairs generally; by the right to give or deny consent to the operation of a stock exchange; by the right to accept or reject prospectuses (setting out the company's background, capital, provisional directors, purposes, and so on), which must be approved before funds may be solicited from the public; and by requiring that a corporation make "full, true and plain disclosure" of all relevant facts before the distribution of its shares to the public.

As a further safeguard of the public interest, certain rules are enforced by the various stock exchanges, by the Investment Dealers' Association in Canada, and by the local Broker-Dealer Association, to ensure an ethical standard of conduct by their members.

However, despite all these precautions, it is still possible for the public to be hoodwinked by a fraudulent promoter.

Buying Stocks and Bonds

A person buying securities normally has one or more of the following motives: to build capital for future spending (e.g. retirement or children's education); to protect savings from the effects of inflation; or to supplement current income. Also, a person will usually want to have the investment in as liquid a form as possible — that is, easily convertible into cash, without a substantial loss in the principal sum. Common shares, preferred shares, bonds, and all their variations— for example, convertible preferred—offer the investor different attractions.

Safety of Principal. If an investor's foremost concern is the desire to preserve savings, then he or she should first consider bonds. On the maturity date, say 20 years hence, the investor will get from the firm or government that has issued the bond the exact amount of principal stated on the bond certificate. He or she will also receive each year a reasonably high, fixed rate of interest on the investment. This is the reasoning behind government legislation that encourages insurance companies and trust companies to invest a large proportion of their funds in this type of security. However, in the period before maturity, bond prices can vary as a result of fluctuations in general interest rates.

Unfortunately, the steady rise in prices, or inflation that occurs over the years, means that $1,000 in the future will buy less than $1,000 today. To preserve savings, therefore, an investor must receive back more than the present $1,000. One way to do this is to buy common shares, since their prices usually keep pace with most other prices. However, buying common shares involves a much greater risk because their market price can greatly fluctuate. The answer then, for many people, is to invest in selected *blue chip* stocks (stock of financially strong and stable companies with proven records of steady earnings and dividends) or in a diversified selection of common stocks—for example, by purchasing shares of a mutual fund. Also, a person may adopt an investment strategy known as *dollar-cost averaging*. This is to invest a fixed sum of money in one stock, irrespective of price movements, at fixed intervals over a long period of time. The weakness of this method is that the price of the stock may be gradually declining.

High Return. The desire to obtain a high return is another motive for investing. In recent years, bonds have offered a rate of interest usually higher than the yield (the dividend paid as a percentage of the price of the stock) of common and preferred stocks. However, one important advantage of common stock is that its market price may rise considerably, even over a short period of time. In other words, an investor may buy shares at one price and soon be able to resell at a higher price. Thus, in addition to any dividends received, the common stock investor may also make a capital gain. And (unlike dividends from shares and interest received from bonds), only half of this gain is subject to personal income tax. The possibility of capital gain makes common stock a particularly attractive investment for the person whose main concern is a good return on the money, as well as protection from the effects of inflation.

The reasons for the rapid price changes in common stock lie in the nature of the demand for and supply of these securities. The people who own stock and the people who wish to buy stock can be greatly influenced by such factors as political events, economic recessions, and rumours. People often wish to buy or sell stock, not because of any rise or fall in the earnings and assets of the companies concerned, but because of what they believe will happen to the price of these stocks in the future. Obviously, in trying to forecast the future, there is ample room for error and difference of opinion. Also, when a wave of buying or selling begins, many people, however irrationally, will join in. When prices are increasing, the market is termed a *bull market*. When they are decreasing, it is termed a *bear market*.

Some people—professional and amateur speculators—attempt to make money by concentrating their attention on short-term changes in stock prices. One method of speculation is to buy stock when prices are low (perhaps after a change in government) and sell soon afterwards when and if they are higher. Another method, called *selling short*, is to make an arrangement to sell particular stocks to someone at an agreed price at a certain future date. Implicit in this transaction is the speculator's belief that he or she can buy these shares between the time of the agreement and the delivery date at a price lower than that which he or she will receive. If market prices rise rather than fall, the speculator will have to buy the shares for more than they can be sold for and will thus suffer a loss. To sell short, the speculator must possess the stocks which he or she is agreeing to sell at a future date. What the speculator does is borrow them, for a fee, from the stockbroker and return them when similar stock is bought at a later date.

Liquidity. The third motive that an investor may have in buying stocks or bonds is a desire for liquidity. The existence of the stock exchanges for trading in listed stocks, and the over-the-counter market for other stocks and for bonds, makes it easy for a person to sell shares at short notice. However, when the investment is in stocks, selling at short notice may mean a substantial loss in the principal sum, depending on the level of stock prices at the time. With bonds there is less risk of a loss in principal, though many bond investors have in fact seen the market value of their investments substantially decline in the past decade as inflation and other factors have caused interest rates to rise.

KEY TERMS

Stockbroker	Board lot
Stock exchange	Odd lot
Floor trader	Late tape
Listed stock	Over-the-counter market
Trading post	Blue chip stocks
Stock quotation	Averaging
Account executive	Bull market
Buying on margin	Bear market
Electronic ticker	Selling short

REVIEW QUESTIONS

1. Distinguish between the primary and secondary distribution of stocks and bonds.
2. Explain the nature and purpose of a stock exchange.

3. Describe the stock trading facilities of: (a) a stockbroker and (b) a stock exchange.
4. Describe the process by which a stock brokerage firm handles the sale of a listed stock.
5. What is the nature and purpose of the over-the-counter market?
6. Explain the trading process for unlisted stocks.
7. What, if anything, helps prevent the investing public from buying worthless stock?
8. Explain the motives that underlie the purchase of stocks and bonds.
9. Why would the market value of a bond decline as the general level of interest rates rises?

READING

The Little Pizza That Could

How three men from Moncton turned two decrepit pizza stands into a national empire

BY STEPHEN KIMBER

(Stephen Kimber is a Halifax-based freelance writer and editor.)

Source: *The Financial Post Magazine*

Moncton, New Brunswick is a city from which ambitious young men take their leave. And why not? The years have played Moncton cruelly like a yo-yo. Up and down, boom and bust—mostly down and mostly bust. Large employers like the Eaton's Catalogue Centre and Swift's Canadian have locked their Moncton doors and even those companies that remain are anxiously squeezing back on their work force.

Moncton is a city where enterprises end, not begin.

Bernard Cyr pays absolutely no heed to such depressing notions and has even less time for another bit of conventional wisdom about this city—that if life here is generally tough, it is that much worse if you happen to be an Acadian. Thirty-five percent of the city's 60,000 residents are French-speaking and their traditional role has been as hewers of wood and drawers of water for *les maudits Anglais*.

Bernard Cyr could tell you what it's been like in Moncton for Acadians. Back in 1968, he was a member of a delegation from the University of Moncton which tried to convince the city's controversial Mayor Leonard Jones—he has since disappeared to Ottawa as an MP—to do the decent thing and recognize French as an official language of city business. Instead, the mayor gave the students the back of his hand and touched off an ugly confrontation that lasted for more than a year.

Bernard Cyr could recite the story, chapter and verse, but this morning he's too busy. He is now the president of Pizza Delight Corp., a fast food chain which is not only based in Moncton and owned by francophones but which is also now spreading itself across the map of Canada and beyond. There is far too much work to be done to muddle back in time to the "one side-tracked mind of Leonard Jones and all the dumb things he did."

Cyr apologizes that we can't use his office for the interview. It's being renovated. Again. The company's head offices, on the second floor of a modern brick building on the city's outskirts, have been redesigned so many times in the past two years that the carpenters have begun to seem like regular employees.

The renovations are necessary because business is so good. In the last year alone, the number of employees has quadrupled to more than 80—not counting franchisees or their employees—and new franchises are opening up so fast, it takes an internal newsletter just to keep track.

The official count this morning is 215 outlets, Cyr says as he opens the door to the company boardroom, his makeshift office. By the end of this year, he expects to be presiding over an empire of 300 stores and when the expansion program ends—if it ever does—there will be Pizza Delight stands all over the world. When that happens, he adds with a smile, the company will have lived up to the boast of its founders that it would become the Kentucky Fried Chicken of the pizza trade.

Bernard Cyr doesn't look in the least like Colonel Sanders. He is, at 30, only now escaping boyishness, and with his droopy mustache, modishly long hair, gold wire-rimmed glasses and dark, pinstriped, three-piece suit, he looks more like a young lawyer or the program director for a rock music radio station than a company president.

He is, in fact, the guts of the operation, the no-nonsense, mean-pencilled, dollars-and-cents guy whose addiction to cost efficiencies perfectly balances the driving, expansionist dreams of his partner, Bernard Imbeault, the 32-year-old soul and chief executive officer of Pizza Delight. Meshing their personal strengths into a single will, they have transformed the company from a pile of debts and two lonely pizza stands—retail sales, $48,000—10 years ago into Canada's largest pizza peddler (and 15th largest restaurant chain). Last year, Pizza Delight sold $40 million worth of its spicy pies from Canada's east coast to Japan.

Japan! Cyr says it as calmly as if he were ordering pizza with the works to go, as if it were every day that a company with its head office in Moncton, N.B., of all places, was pushing pizzas in Japan.

The story of Pizza Delight begins in Moncton's turbulent 60s when Leonard Jones was still the mayor and the University of Moncton was struggling to shuck off the traditional French Catholic goals of producing teachers and scholars and to become, instead, a greenhouse for a new species of tough-minded francophone businessmen.

In 1964, Bernard Cyr, Bernard Imbeault and a third friend, Roger Duchesne, were wide-eyed freshmen at the university, all anxious to carve out their own pedigrees in that new breed. What cemented their friendship was a shared passion for the business world and a strong, but unspoken urge to prove to the Leonard Jones's of the world that Francophones could occupy important places in the economy.

They became inseparable; hanging around on campus together, going on dates together, demonstrating against Leonard Jones together and, most of all, dreaming career dreams together.

In their second year, they formed a private club with a dozen other students and would rent a motel room every week to share a few beers and debate business, religion or politics with a guest lecturer.

But more than any subject, what made their mental juices flow was business. In their final year, they went so far as to rent a downtown office for $100 a month. "We had no idea what we were going to do but we ended up in this office with desks and everything and we told everybody we knew that we were in business," Duchesne says now.

"Then we looked at each other and said, 'What do we do now?'"

What they did first was to wangle a Renault car dealership for the campus and then, somehow, to convince K.C. Irving to lease them a service station near the campus for the princely sum of one dollar for the school term. By the time classes ended in the spring of 1967, they had sold 40 cars to graduating students at $100 down and at $100 a month and—with a razzle-dazzle assortment of promotional gimmicks, including hiring mini-skirted co-eds to clean car windows—managed to pump more gas than any other Irving station in the city.

Despite solemn vows that they would work together, graduation scattered them. Cyr landed a job with Canadian General Electric, Imbeault wound down the service station business while finalizing plans to go to Paris for further studies in economics and Duchesne headed for Montreal to sell insurance.

"I sold insurance for three months and then I just decided that I would never again work for anyone but myself," Duchesne remembers. "I was married by then and I told my wife I was going to Moncton for the week-end. When I got there, I talked to Imbeault and I told him that I would see what I could find for us to do in Moncton together while he was studying. I came back to Montreal and told my wife that I had rented an apartment in Moncton and we were moving back there."

Duchesne soon found the opportunity he was looking for—a pizza business.

Franchising had been one of the many schemes Duchesne, Cyr and Imbeault had toyed with during their endless bull sessions. Franchising, they knew, was booming, and they had gone so far as to narrow their focus to fast foods. Winnowing still further, they had eliminated hamburgers and fried chicken as markets already too crowded and competitive, and had settled finally on pizza as the fast food in need of an entrepreneur.

The two decrepit pizza stands and the name Pizza Delight discovered by Duchesne were real. The deal he was offered was far from generous. The owners were willing to let him run the stands for a year with an option to purchase the whole thing for $150,000. But in order to make any money for himself under the terms of the agreement, he had to sell new franchises.

Duchesne jumped at the chance.

He spent his weeks throwing pizzas in his main outlet and on Friday nights, he hopped the bus for such exotic places as Chatham, N.B., and Greenwood, N.S., trying to cajole local entrepreneurs into parting with $5,000 for a Pizza Delight franchise.

Within six months, he was ready to exercise the option to purchase and he called Imbeault in Paris. "The owner was very surprised when we came to him," Duchesne recalls.

While Bernard Cyr watched his friends anxiously and hopefully from his more comfortable perch on the way up the corporate ladder at CGE, Imbeault and Duchesne redoubled the effort to sell franchises. Above their main outlet—the site of the present head office—they set up a small factory to produce pizza dough and a "secret" sauce mix.

By the end of 1968, they had sold 14 franchises, but it was a sweaty and tense struggle to remain solvent. For the first year, they didn't even make enough money to pay themselves a salary and had to depend for their survival on the incomes of their working wives.

The next few years were also a continual teetering on the edge of calamity. Every year they would force another 50,000 miles on their protesting cars as they moved across the Maritimes, pizza stand by pizza stand.

Often, however, it took the $5,000 they made from each franchise sale just to meet their growing payroll. There was little left over to put into helping new franchise owners.

The problem was simple—both Imbeault and Duchesne were buccaneers who, while they were driven by the excitement of opening up new territory, were hopelessly bored by the administrative detail of making the company run. They needed a bloody-minded accountant.

Finally, in mid-1972, they turned to their old friend, Bernard Cyr, who was now the Montreal-based supervisor of customer relations for CGE. Despite his promising corporate career, Cyr was itching for an opportunity to strike out on his own. He quickly agreed to a $4,000 cut in salary to return to Moncton and oversee the company administration.

There were now 30 pizza stores in the chain and they had also bought up a successful Montreal muffler shop with plans to parlay that into a second franchising operation. Duchesne moved to Montreal to oversee the muffler business and to spearhead Pizza Delight's Quebec expansion.

The first Pizza Delight stand in Montreal opened and closed within six months after losing $50,000. There are rumors, which none of the principals will discuss, that they were squeezed out of business by mobsters who would not tolerate competition from a company that refused to buy supplies from mob-controlled wholesalers. But there was also another important problem—Duchesne had by this time become more interested in the muffler business.

"The fact of the matter was that Bernard Imbeault and I were just too much alike," Duchesne says now. "We were both the type of people who needed to be in control."

They split amicably a short time later with Duchesne taking over the muffler business as his own separate company. Today, his Minute Muffler operation has 148 franchises and recently diversified into brake shops as well.

Imbeault took Cyr in as his new partner and, with some vicious cost cutting and financial controls imposed by Cyr, Pizza Delight turned its first profit the next year, 1973. Plowing every penny of profit back into the business and maintaining modest personal lifestyles, they began to elbow their way from province to province. They bought a cheese plant in Quebec, a string of small pizza and fries stands in the Maritimes and finally, last year, cemented their hold on the Canadian market with the acquisition of Pizza Patio Management Ltd., a Vancouver-based outfit that had developed a large chunk of the western Canadian pizza market and had even established some outlets in Japan.

Today, a Pizza Delight franchise costs two to three times as much as it did in 1968 and, to get one, a would-be franchisee has to have a lot more capital behind him than the meager $600 with which Imbeault and Duchesne started. There are now three categories of franchise, ranging from the traditional take-out pizza operation (requiring an investment in equipment, inventory, leasehold improvements and working capital of about $35,000, plus a $10,000 franchise fee) to full-service, licensed restaurants with seating for 100 people or more that would cost the franchisee $100,000, including a $15,000 franchise fee.

"These days," says Cyr with a wry chuckle for the bad old days, "a person gets every penny they pay out back in help. When a store opens now, we have spent all of that $15,000 and more just to make sure everything works out all right."

The company is still not in the same league as such industry giants as McDonald's whose annual sales per outlet average more than $1 million. Prospective franchisees in the Pizza Delight chain are told that they can expect to make pre-tax profits of 15 percent to 18 percent (slightly above McDonald's) but sales average only about $400,000 for a full-service restaurant down to about $120,000 for a take-out unit. And franchisees must also turn over five percent of gross annual sales to the company.

Again unlike McDonald's, the franchisee usually owns or leases his own location rather than having it chosen and owned by the franchisor. That is beginning to change, however, following the acquisition of Pizza Patio which owned four of its 20 outlets and Cyr says that the trend will be to more company-owned stores. There are now 14.

Bernard Cyr thinks there is room for 600 Pizza Delight franchises in Canada alone, but the company's plans are much grander. "We're no longer preoccupied with Canada," he says. "Our outlook is now strictly international. We expect to move into the American market with a couple of stores this year and we are seriously looking at expansion in Europe and the Middle East. The Middle East, now there's an untapped market."

Expansion has already sparked big changes. Several of the company's divisions, including public relations and marketing, have been moved to Toronto and more than 80 percent of its business is now outside New Brunswick. And Cyr and Imbeault are paying a price for that: they are often on the road more than they are at home. "Moncton is not the easiest place to fly in and out of," sighs Cyr. Developing the business from this city has necessitated exhausting 15-hour days, working weekends and few vacations. Cyr went for four years without a break until last year and, even then, after only a two-week vacation, he hurried back to the office.

"People look at us and the hours and they think we're crazy," admits Cyr, "but this is what we like to do. It's what we wanted and now that we have the business going well, we just want to keep at it."

And the two men seem determined to make it work from Moncton. They continue to make the key decisions there and say they have no intention of moving the head office anywhere else.

To begin with, the city's reputation as hostile territory for Acadians is out of date, says Cyr. "This is a very nice city, a very nice place to live and bring up a family." And indeed, most people would argue that things have improved dramatically for Francophones since Leonard Jones went to Ottawa. But it's also true that the local English Speaking Association (a pressure group opposed to bilingualism and generally hostile to the Acadians) can hold a meeting in the dark of a winter's night and still attract a couple of hundred people. And even a matter as picayune as having a French-language commemorative plaque at City Hall arouses such passion that, when the deed was done recently, it took place in the middle of the night. Just in case.

Perhaps more important, however, Bernard Imbeault argues that the city's other reputation as stony ground for entrepreneurs is now irrelevant. "Look at Kentucky Fried Chicken," he says. "Their head office is in Louisville. You don't have to be in New York or Toronto to make a go of fast food. In fact, when we start getting involved in the American market, Moncton will be very convenient to the east coast markets there."

Making it in the U.S. will not be easy. There, Cyr and Imbeault will be going up against the world's largest chain, Pizza Hut, which has more than 2,700 outlets. And because they don't hold the American rights to the name, Pizza Delight, they will be slowly converting the entire operation to the name Pizza Patio over the next five years.

Clearly, it's a game for the young and

energetic. And, on that score, Pizza Delight would seem to have the right kind of personnel. Almost all its top executives, says Cyr proudly, are under 35.

"We're a young company in more ways than one and the thing that pleases me most is that there is so much room to grow still."

A worldwide empire ruled from Moncton?

It is, he says, exactly what they have in mind.

A Slice of The Action

"Hey mister," the kid with the freckles persists, "can I have a T-shirt *and* a free Coke? Please mister, please?" The 216th Pizza Delight franchise, on St. Laurent Boulevard in downtown Ottawa, is now officially open for business.

Several dozen customers jostle one another in the confined spaces to get near John Grieco, a slight man with a wispy moustache and salt and pepper hair, who is busy taking orders, sorting out prizes, distributing pizza and avoiding small children. He looks more harried than elated by the excitement.

"Hey John, feast your knockers on this, will you!" Len Goldsmith, the staff supervisor, shouts over the din as he thrusts a piece of cash register tape through the crowd. Grieco glances briefly at the numbers on the piece of paper, manages a fleeting smile, tucks it into his pocket and asks of no one in particular, "Have you been served yet?"

"It was fantastic, an incredible, incredible day," he says later. "We had a sales target for opening day and very early on we exceeded that target so I'm very, very pleased."

Grieco, 43, had meandered through close to a half a dozen different jobs since 1959 when he was graduated with a degree in electrical engineering from Queen's University, Kingston, Ont. Most of the jobs he'd held were solid, responsible and respectable. But he was always working for someone else.

He had just passed 40 when he began to wonder if there might not be a better future on his own. But the road to a Pizza Delight franchise actually began more recently while he was helping his older brother look for a new job. It was much the same road followed by Pizza Delight's principals.

"I was struck by the number of franchising opportunities in the classifieds every day," he says. "The more I saw the more intrigued I became. I decided to do a little research for myself and pretty soon, I guess I was looking more for myself than my brother."

John Grieco is a diligent, cautious man, and what appealed to him about franchising was that it gave him the security of not having to start a business from ground zero, but, at the same time, allowed him to be pretty independent. He took about six months to narrow his interest to the fast food business. "The fast food market in Canada is about five years behind the United States and it became clear to me that the growth in Canada during the next 10 years is going to be phenomenal. Then I began to look at pizza and I discovered that there was a swing to eating pizza." A recent survey conducted by *Scholastic Magazine* in the U.S. and quoted in Pizza Delight's internal newsletter indicates that pizza has taken over from hamburgers as the preferred fast food for American teenagers.

Grieco eventually settled on a Pizza Delight franchise because "the company allowed me the most room to grow on my own."

That's not to say Pizza Delight is perfect. Grieco does have some complaints. He says he found that the actual investment required was slightly higher than the $60,000 maximum predicted by company officials and he found the staff training program "too much theory and not enough practical." As well, he says that the rapid expansion resulted in the district offices being staffed by inexperienced people. "For a while there they were spreading themselves too thin but that seems to be changing now and the operation is becoming more professional."

Like many franchisees, he was a little surprised at first to discover the company head office was in Moncton, but it hasn't caused him any serious problems. "Most of my day-to-day dealings are with the regional office in Toronto anyway."

And on balance, Grieco seems pretty happy with his choice. He has a multi-franchise deal with Pizza Delight, and not long after our conversation, he opened a second outlet in Ottawa. He is already busy scouting for other sites all over the Ottawa Valley.

Assignment
1. How did Cyr, Duchesne, and Imbeault start out their business careers?
2. How did they become involved with Pizza Delight? What was their motivation?
3. Why would someone like John Grieco become a Pizza Delight franchisee?
4. What was his experience?
5. Did the three friends make good business partners?
6. How long did it take to make Pizza Delight a profitable operation? How was it achieved?
7. What does a Pizza Delight franchise cost? What earnings can be expected?
8. Who owns the franchisee's premises? Explain.
9. How suitable does Moncton seem to be for the head office of a national pizza franchise firm? Discuss.
10. Should Pizza Delight go international?

PART G
HUMAN RESOURCES

One of the most important problems that faces a business firm today is the efficient management of its work force, together with the maintenance of harmonious labour-management relations. If employee morale is poor, there will inevitably be work stoppages and shoddy work; and the reputation and profits of the firm will suffer.

In this part of the book, we consider, first of all, the nature of personnel management and the roles of the personnel manager and of the *personnel department* — the staff department entrusted with the specialized task of helping the various line departments to fulfil their personnel management function. Then, in the same chapter, we look at wage and salary administration. Next, in Chapter 16, entitled Labour Relations, we look first at labour unions and collective bargaining and, second, at labour legislation.

CHAPTER 15
PERSONNEL MANAGEMENT

CHAPTER OBJECTIVES

☐ To indicate the nature and importance of personnel management in a business firm.

☐ To explain how a firm forecasts its personnel needs and recruits, trains, and promotes people to fill these needs.

☐ To indicate the role of a firm's personnel manager and personnel department.

☐ To explain how a firm remunerates its employees with both wages and fringe benefits.

CHAPTER OUTLINE

15.1   Functions of Personnel Management
15.2   Wage and Salary Administration

UNIT 15.1: FUNCTIONS OF PERSONNEL MANAGEMENT

Management, as we discussed earlier in this book, involves the planning, organizing, staffing, directing, and controlling of human and other resources. However, *personnel management* (or *personnel administration*) is concerned with the management of human resources only. By careful recruitment, induction, training, motivation, and other means, a firm can ensure a highly productive work force. At the same time, by attending to their mental, physical, and financial well-being, a firm can give its employees maximum personal benefit.

The task of personnel management is carried on by every manager throughout the firm, from the president down to the supervisor or section leader. It is essential in every functional area—marketing, production, finance, and so on—wherever human resources are employed.

Personnel Policy

The attitude that a firm adopts in the treatment of its employees is known as its *personnel policy*. This policy is much more enlightened today than it was only a few decades ago. The employee is now usually treated as a human being with aspirations of his or her own, rather than as a mere tool of production. Also, the female employee is given much greater equality of opportunity and remuneration.

At one extreme, a firm can treat its employees as a group of lazy good-for-nothings who should be driven as hard as possible and paid the minimum permissible wage. At the other extreme, a firm can treat its employees with respect, try to make their work as interesting and pleasant as possible, give them maximum job security, and provide above-average wages and fringe benefits. The effectiveness of a firm's personnel policy can be measured in terms of productivity, absenteeism, employee turnover, time lost in strikes and other work stoppages, and employee attitude towards orders and supervision.

A good personnel policy should include at least the following: (a) adequate pay and fringe benefits; (b) reasonable job security for satisfactory workers; (c) opportunity for employee advancement; (d) fair treatment in work allocation and disputes; (e) respect for subordinates by superiors; and (f) a reasonable amount of information as to what is going on in the firm. Obviously, to be a leader in pay and working conditions, a firm must be reasonably prosperous. However, as the example of many firms suggests, good employee treatment and high labour productivity often go hand in hand.

Quite often, a firm will find that its personnel policy is not for it alone to decide. Nowadays, a labour union will help determine, at the bargaining table, just what treatment a firm's employees are to receive. Many firms that in the past believed themselves to practise enlightened personnel management have found themselves rudely shocked by labour union demands, and perhaps even more by the concessions they have been persuaded or forced to make. As a result, they have adopted a new, hard-line attitude of giving their employees only what

"There's a newspaper reporter asking whether there's any progress in the labour dispute …."

is actually spelled out in the labour agreement. Although the disappearance of the benevolent employer is to be deplored, most workers believe that express, legal commitments of good treatment are preferable to good intentions. Finally, as we shall see, a firm's personnel policy is also partly dictated by government labour legislation.

Most large firms will make use of a specialized *personnel department* to assist in implementing their personnel policy and in carrying out the various personnel management functions.

The functions of personnel management include: employment planning; job analysis; recruitment of employees; induction, training, and follow-up; promotions, transfers, layoffs, and dismissals; services such as health, recreation, and safety; employee records and statistics; wage and salary administration; and labour-management relations.

Employment Planning

This involves (a) forecasting a firm's employment needs, and (b) planning how these needs are to be met.

The forecasting of the firm's employment requirements involves several steps. First, a careful study must be made of the existing use of a firm's human resources to determine whether it can be improved. Second, a forecast must be made of the firm's future work volume. Third, a detailed estimate must be made for each of the next few years of the numbers and types of employees that this expected work volume will require. One method of doing this is by *ratio-trend forecasting*, whereby the future expected work volume, based on past trends, is multiplied by the present ratio between the amount of work and the number of persons required to perform it. Another, more sophisticated method is to base the future expected work volume, not just on past trends, but on a careful analysis of the firm's long-range plans, which, in turn, are based on careful market research and product development forecasts. After estimating how the size and nature of each of the firm's major activities will change, management can make a detailed forecast of each department's future employment needs. Whatever method is used, a firm will have a forecast of its future employment needs for each of a number of occupations, often for as much as five years ahead. This forecast will be revised as each year goes by.

The second major aspect of employment planning is to plan how to meet the firm's expected future demand for employees. This involves, first, an analysis of how the firm's present labour force will change over the years as a result of normal turnover from retirements, promotions, and other causes. To aid this task, many firms maintain an *employment inventory*. This is a detailed analysis of the present labour force, according to age, sex, occupation, length of service, employment location, and other characteristics. Once the expected contribution of the present labour force to future employment needs is known, management can move on to the second step: planning for the recruitment of sufficient new employees to fill the expected employment gap.

Recruitment

One of the first tasks in personnel management is to develop sources of supply of the various types of employees that the firm will constantly need to recruit.

Job Analysis. To do a satisfactory job of screening applicants and selecting new employees, management must first have a clear understanding of what each job involves. It must know the different tasks to be performed and the abilities required to carry them out. The process of obtaining this information, called *job analysis*, involves the observation of the tasks performed and interviews with workers and supervisors.

The information collected in the job analysis is then used as the basis for a *job description*. This is a detailed written description of the job, containing such information as: the title of the job; its location in the plant; the duties and responsibilities involved; the tools and equipment to be used; the materials and supplies required; the working conditions; the rate of pay; the training, if any, provided; and the opportunities for promotion. From the job description, a job specification is prepared.

Courtesy *The Financial Post*

The *job specification* is a written summary of the duties of the job, and a detailed description of the personal qualifications necessary for a person to perform it satisfactorily. These qualifications include such things as: health, education, experience, skills, intelligence, and appearance. The job specification serves as a guide for recruiting the right person.

Some firms combine the job description and the job specification into one document.

Sources of Employees. For the small firm, an appeal for suitable applicants is often made by a telephone call to the local Canada Employment Centre or by an advertisement in the classified section of the local newspaper. For many firms, particularly the large ones, these two sources will not suffice. At different times and for different types of employees, these firms may also make use of the following sources: schools, colleges, and universities; employment agencies, personnel consultants, or "executive search" agencies; the offices of union locals; professional associations; employment applications on file with the firm; recommendations of past and present employees; and personnel within the firm itself.

Recruitment Procedure. This will vary from one firm to another, even for the same type of position. Some firms tend to be extremely cautious when hiring new employees; others make snap judgments; most are somewhere in between. The steps which may be included in a "typical" employment procedure are:

1. The Completion of an Application Form. This will show personal particulars, previous employment, education, and personal references. This form provides the firm with its first impression of an applicant and should therefore be filled out with care. The information about previous employment is important because it not only indicates experience and earnings, but also reveals whether an applicant has a tendency to switch jobs frequently.

2. A Preliminary Interview. This takes place at the personnel office or, in the case of university and college recruitment, on campus. The interview is designed to obtain additional information about the candidate—for example, personal attitudes, appearance, ambition, and ability to think and to communicate. The interview also serves to provide the candidate with information about position openings and what the company provides in salary, working conditions, promotion possibilities, location, fringe benefits, training and so on.

Sometimes, particularly for senior appointments, a firm will conduct group interviews, whereby the applicants are brought together at a hotel and their behaviour is observed in solving group problems and participating in social functions.

3. The Completion of Various Tests. For example: intelligence tests; aptitude tests; interest tests; skill tests; and personality tests. These must, however, be used with caution.

4. Investigation of the Candidate's Background. For example, checking references, contacting previous employers or teachers, and obtaining a credit report.

5. A Medical Examination. This is usually performed by the company doctor and is designed to reveal whether the candidate is physically capable of performing the job.

6. An Interview with the Prospective Superior. In the case of management positions, a series of interviews, each with a different manager, may be required to form the basis for a combined decision on the applicant. Alternatively, the candidate may be interviewed by a panel of managers.

At any of the different steps of the recruitment procedure, the job applicant may be rejected.

Induction, Training, and Follow-Up

Once employed, a person may find that he or she has moved out of the spotlight into the shadow. Some firms, after using a careful and elaborate recruitment procedure, fail to introduce the new employee properly to the place of employment, to provide thorough training, or to follow the new employee's progress. There are many firms, conversely, that do a thorough job of induction, training, and follow-up. In the case of senior employees, a written contract of employment may be prepared and signed. In the case of employees who automatically become members of a labour union, the labour agreement in force will cover them.

Induction. The term *induction* describes the process of introducing a new employee to his or her job, to colleagues and superiors, and to the firm as a whole. Some firms have a classroom program designed to acquaint new employees with the history of the firm, its products, its position in the industry, its formal organization, the names of the department heads, company policies, and the mechanics of the individual jobs. These induction programs are often handled by the personnel department. After the initial phase of the induction (the "indoctrination" phase) is completed, a personnel representative will often accompany the new employee to the job to introduce him or her to the supervisor. At this point, the supervisor usually takes over. Sometimes the induction will include a tour of the plant, a movie about the firm, and a visit to the cafeteria. In other firms, the new employee may go straight to the job and be given, after introduction to colleagues, a series of pamphlets containing information about company policies on a variety of matters affecting employees. Working conditions, safety and health regulations, discipline, education, training, pay, promotion, fringe benefits, recreational facilities, holidays, and vacations are matters that may be covered in this way. Other detailed information on such matters as methods of reporting absence, date of payment of wages and salaries, cafeteria facilities, and locker facilities may be given verbally.

Training. Training of new and old employees goes on continuously in every firm, either formally or informally. New employees must become familiar with the firm and learn the skills and techniques required for their jobs. Old employees must keep up with changes, learn new jobs, and train for higher positions. This training can be informal —for example, by the employee's watching and asking colleagues or by the sporadic coaching of his or her immediate boss. Often more formal methods of training are used:

Training on the Job. This happens when a person learns a job while actually doing it. This usually takes place under the supervision of a supervisor or senior employee. A salesperson in a retail store is often trained this way. Such a method is possible only when mistakes by the inexperienced employee cannot cause serious loss to the firm.

Training for the Job. When a firm cannot afford to let its new employees learn from their mistakes, it may use one of several types of pre-job training. These are:
1. *Classroom* (or *vestibule*) *training.* A new employee is sent to a company school for training, by demonstration and practice, before being allowed to start actual work.
2. *Apprenticeship training.* Young people sometimes enter into contracts of apprenticeship. In return for a thorough training in a craft, for time off to attend trade school, and for the opportunity of obtaining a tradesperson's certificate, an apprentice agrees to work for a firm for a fixed number of years at relatively modest wages. In the manufacturing industry, with its

mechanization and extreme division of labour, training by the apprenticeship system is nowadays unusual. This is because the employee needs to learn only a very specialized skill—for example, operating one type of machine which can be taught in a number of days rather than years. However, apprenticeship training is still required, for example, for electricians, plumbers, and tool and die makers.
3. *Supervisory training.* Employees who stand out in ability, education, leadership, or experience may be selected for supervisory training. Such courses of training emphasize the need for technical proficiency, combined with the ability to motivate others by example and persuasion rather than by bullying.

    Many firms have in-house courses on technical subjects, company procedures, and the handling of labour problems. These courses often combine short lectures with group discussions, projects, and other forms of participatory learning. Many firms also encourage their supervisory staff to attend outside courses at various colleges and universities.
4. *Retraining.* Mechanization and automation have displaced some workers from their jobs. This has happened, for example, in insurance companies and banks with the introduction of electronic computers. Many firms, rather than dismiss these employees, have retrained them for new jobs.

A good training program can yield many benefits to a firm. These include: an improvement in employee morale; increased productivity; the introduction of new work methods; the provision of qualified replacement personnel; a reduction in the amount of work supervision required; better use of equipment; a reduction in material wastage; and a better quality product.

Follow-Up. In the small firm, the new employee is constantly in management's view. If he or she does not adapt to the job or fit in with colleagues, this fact soon becomes known. In the large company, however, the first indication that something is wrong may be the failure of the employee to show up for work or the arrival of a letter of resignation. To resolve this problem, some companies have instructed their personnel departments to make a periodic follow-up on new employees. The first check usually takes place a few days after the employee has started work. Other visits then follow periodically, often at intervals of six months or a year. The purpose of the follow-up is: to identify employees who have proven unsuitable for their jobs, so that they may be helped, transferred, or dismissed; and to identify employees who have demonstrated good ability, so that they may be rewarded by bonuses or promotion. Other firms rely solely on the immediate superior to watch over and report on the new employee's progress.

Transfers, Promotions, Layoffs, and Dismissals

Not all employees will remain with their first firm. Some will leave voluntarily, others will be dismissed. Of those who stay, some will be promoted, some transferred, and some will continue in the same job until retirement.

Transfers. The term *transfer* is used to describe the moving of an employee from one job to another, without any increase in duties, responsibilities, or wages. A transfer may be required for one of several reasons: because the employee has been placed in an unsuitable job; because the employee cannot get along with colleagues; because the work of the department has decreased; to look after the needs of older or disabled workers; to provide training in a variety of jobs; to rotate employees in unpleasant or dangerous jobs; and to take account of the changing interests, experience, and skills of employees. Most firms have rules to ensure that such proposed transfers are in the best interests of the firm and the employee. Whenever possible, the employee should be told the reasons for the transfer and whether it is temporary or permanent. Unexplained transfers are a certain source of employee discontent.

Promotions. A *promotion* is the advancement of an employee to a more responsible and financially more rewarding position in the firm's organization. Promotions occur because jobs become vacant at higher levels through: retirement because of age or health; the growth of the company; the promotion of persons in these higher levels; dismissals; and voluntary resignations.

In filling a vacant position, a firm will usually try to *promote from within*, rather than look outside the firm for a suitable candidate. Such a policy, by rewarding employees who are already working for the company, is conducive to good employee morale. Strict adherence to a policy of promotion from within may, however, sometimes be against the company's best interest. A suitable person may not be available in the firm, especially for technical or senior management positions. This would most likely be the case if the firm does not have any clear program of management development or advanced technical training. Occasionally, when promotion from within takes place, the resentment aroused among employees who are rejected as unsuitable may be more damaging to morale than recruitment of an outsider. Certainly, if employees are to feel satisfied with a firm's promotion policy, all vacancies should be advertised; existing employees should have an opportunity to apply and know that their application will receive fair consideration; and an employee with the necessary abilities should know that there is a chance to rise, if he or she wishes, to the middle or top management of the firm.

The promotion of an employee may be made on the grounds of merit or seniority. Sometimes, but much less commonly, nepotism (that is, family connections) and favouritism will play a part.

Merit is the ability of the employee, as demonstrated in the past, to perform jobs efficiently. Intelligence, knowledge, experience, responsibility, personality, skills, and ability to communicate will be involved to a greater or lesser degree, depending on the job. The periodic formal evaluation of a person's performance, which is usually done by an immediate superior, is called a *merit rating*. This is done for purposes of promotion, salary increases, and bonuses. To help ensure sound, unbiased judgment on the part of the superior, a carefully designed rating form is often used. For evaluating non-supervisory employees, this form may include quality of work, amount of work, knowledge of work, initiative, attitude

"Shame about Crenshaw. The only one in the department who's completely loyal, punctual, and <u>never</u> takes a day off ... but incredibly incompetent."

towards work, and attitude towards others. Often the evaluation is discussed with the employee. Sometimes employees are invited to fill out an evaluation form about themselves and to discuss it with their superiors. For supervisory personnel, the rating may include ability to get a large amount of good quality work done by others; ability to maintain high morale among subordinates; skill and effectiveness in training employees; personal co-operativeness; and ability to turn out a satisfactory amount of good quality work.

Seniority is another important ground on which promotions are made. This is the employee's status in terms of length of service with the company. Promotion on the basis of seniority means giving preference to the candidate who has worked the longest time for the firm. There are certain advantages and disadvantages to using seniority as the basis for promotion. One advantage is that it is considered by many employees to be a fair way of rewarding long service, thus helping morale. Another advantage is that it is often the only reasonable way to decide among candidates of equal merit. The major disadvantage is that this method will often prevent the most able candidate from obtaining the vacant position. Experience comes with long service, but the experience may be all of a limited scope and may not suit the needs of the new position. A second disadvantage of promotion by seniority alone is that the more able and ambitious of the newer employees will leave the company to work for firms where their merit is more quickly rewarded.

In most businesses, management promotions take place mainly on the basis of merit. Length of service with the firm will be considered as part of the candidate's background. Occasionally, seniority may be used as an impartial method of deciding among a few candidates already selected on the grounds of merit.

Promotions for non-management jobs are often based on a mixture of merit and seniority. If the firm is unionized, the labour contract often specifies that promotion of rank-and-file employees be based on seniority—in line with the union's demand for security for the worker and the desire to eliminate any possibility of favouritism in promotions.

Layoffs. At one time or another, a firm may find it necessary to lay off some of its employees. A *layoff* is the temporary withdrawal of work from an employee. When the reasons for the layoff have disappeared, the employee will normally be re-employed. Layoffs occur mainly because of a fall in the demand for a firm's products as a result of economic recession or seasonal changes. Other reasons for layoffs include interruptions in the supply of parts and materials, perhaps because of a trucking strike or a strike in a supplying plant; and interruptions in work owing to the need for a changeover in the production line. If the reduction in work is not large, management, rather than lay off any workers, may reduce the number of hours worked by all.

When a layoff is considered necessary, management usually lets go first the employees with the lowest efficiency or the shortest length of service. The latter

Courtesy The Ontario Ministry of Industry, Trade and Technology

is the application of the seniority principle to layoffs. This principle is usually one of the provisions of a labour union contract. Rehiring takes place also on this basis, those with the greatest length of service being taken back first.

A labour union contract may also provide for *bumping*. This means that if a number of people are to be laid off in a certain department, they can apply to work in a different department where there are employees with shorter service. The latter employees would then be the ones to be laid off. For such a transfer to take place, the more senior employee must be capable of doing the work of the employee replaced. Bumping, although providing greater security for the longer-service employee, often creates inefficiency because of rapid labour turnover and the need for training each new member in the ways of his or her new department. It also means that high-priced labour is being used for work that could otherwise be done at lower cost.

Dismissals. This is the permanent withdrawal from an employee of his or her job with the firm. This may occur because the job is redundant — perhaps as a result of mechanization or automation; because of a merger with, or takeover by, another firm; because of the closing down of certain product lines; or because of a frantic effort in times of economic and business recession to cut production or marketing costs.

Dismissal may also occur because the employee is no longer considered suitable for the job because of incompetence, laziness, moonlighting, personality conflict, or other reasons. However, discharge for reasons of unsuitability is considered by many employers to be a last resort. Except on such grounds as dishonesty, immorality, extreme incompetence, or wilful disobedience, management will normally attempt to correct the cause of the trouble.

The decision whether to transfer, promote, layoff, or dismiss an employee is the responsibility of line management. However, the personnel department may be asked for assistance on these and other matters, such as recommending merit-rating policies and handling a transfer once it has been decided upon.

If, as often happens, an employee resigns from a job, the personnel department should try to find out the real reasons for this action. In this way, the good employee may be persuaded to stay, perhaps with a transfer to another department. But even if the employee does leave, the reasons for the departure may enable the personnel department to uncover the source of the trouble—for example, unduly heavy work demands or an unreasonable supervisor.

Personnel Services

Many employers believe that their responsibility to their employees extends beyond the provision of satisfactory pay and a safe place in which to work. Those who do not feel this way are compelled to some degree by labour legislation and, in some cases, by labour unions to provide additional benefits. These benefits may include all or some of the following:
1. Paid public holidays and vacations;
2. Unemployment insurance contributions;

3. Worker's Compensation premiums;
4. Group health, accident, and life insurance plans for which the firm may pay part or all of the premium;
5. A health clinic with a doctor or nurse in attendance;
6. A company retirement pension plan for which the firm pays all or part of the employee's contribution;
7. Special discounts on the purchase of goods and services produced by the company;
8. The provision of meals and snacks at subsidized rates;
9. Rest and recreational facilities;
10. Legal advice and assistance; and
11. Credit union facilities.

All of these employee services cost the firm money, in the form of either direct subsidy or company time taken by members of the personnel or other departments to organize and administer them. To some extent, this may be offset by more efficient production and reduced labour turnover as a result of improved employee morale.

Health and Safety

Most provinces now have an Industrial Health and Safety Act to help protect the health and safety of workers in factories and other workplaces. Matters covered include sanitation, heating, lighting, ventilation, and the guarding of dangerous machinery. Under, for example, Ontario's Occupational Health and Safety Act, joint labour-management health and safety committees must also be established at most workplaces in which there are twenty or more employees, or in which there is exposure to a toxic substance or physical agent regulated by a government order. Very often, it is the personnel department of a firm that is involved in the establishment and operation of such a committee.

Employee Records and Statistics

Another personnel management function is the keeping of records and statistics about employees. Personnel records contain such details as the identification and personal particulars, education, experience, medical history, and leisure interests of each employee. The personnel records will also contain important information about the employee's career to date, courses and assignments completed, assessments by superiors, and career potential. This information is useful for such purposes as promotions and employment planning. The personnel department may also provide references for past employees. It will also compile statistical information such as accident rates, absenteeism, and labour turnover, for use by management.

The Personnel Manager

The *personnel manager* (or *director of personnel* in the large firm) is the person entrusted by the medium- or large-size business firm with specialist responsibility for efficient management of the firm's human resources. Since the firm's personnel are scattered thoughout the organization, with each employee owing allegiance to a particular department head, the personnel manager's role is mainly an advisory one. Unless authority for certain personnel matters (such as education, medical examinations, and canteen facilities) has been delegated to the personnel manager, his or her line authority is limited to the employees in the personnel department. However, as an advisor with specialist knowledge, the personnel manager can have great influence throughout the firm. For, unlike the line department heads, the personnel manager's field of activity is the whole firm, not just one part of it. Also, since the personnel manager is usually responsible directly to the company president or executive vice-president, there is the opportunity to influence the company's policies. Whether this opportunity is taken will depend on the personality of the person who fills the job.

The qualities required in a personnel manager include the usual attributes of any good manager, such as intelligence, good character, fairness, and ability to communicate. But they also include a specialized knowledge of personnel management, particularly labour relations, and, ideally, actual management experience in a line department. Furthermore, because of the advisory nature of the position, the qualities of tact, patience, and tolerance are also sought.

Not every firm, we should emphasize, has a personnel manager. In the smaller firm, these duties will be performed by the office manager, the treasurer, or the company president. In the large firm, however, he or she will be the head of a substantial personnel department, aided by a corps of bright, university- and college-trained personnel assistants.

The Personnel Department

This is the staff department set up to help the line managers carry out their personnel management duties more efficiently. Not every firm has a personnel department. In the small firm, the manager, perhaps with the aid of a secretary, looks after all personnel work in addition to other tasks. Other firms have one person, possibly the office manager, who relieves the general manager of part of this work. Only when the number of employees is large will a separate personnel department be economically justified.

Although a firm may have a personnel department, there is no guarantee that enlightened personnel policies will be applied throughout the firm. Even when such recommendations are approved by top management as company policy, their translation into practice will depend on each individual line manager. A function of the personnel department, if there is to be good personnel management in the firm, is to help train and inspire the line managers. This can be done by arranging personnel seminars for them, distributing useful reading material, and arranging for their participation in outside courses. The example set by top management will often be the key to the type of personnel management practised throughout the firm.

Organization. The organization of the personnel department will vary from firm to firm depending on the activities that it performs. One example is shown in Figure 15.1.

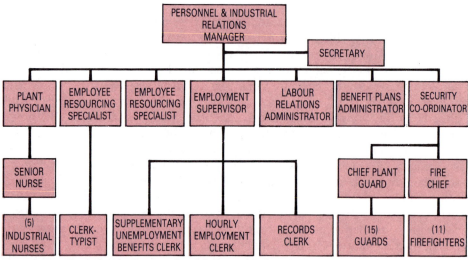

Figure 15.1 Example of a Personnel and Industrial Relations Department

KEY TERMS

Personnel management

Personnel policy

Functions of personnel management

Employment planning

Ratio-trend forecasting

Employment inventory

Job analysis

Job description

Job specification

Recruitment of employees

Sources of employees

Recruitment procedure

Induction

Indoctrination phase

Training

Supervisory training

Retraining

Follow-up

Transfer

Promotion

Promotion from within

Merit

Merit rating

Seniority

Layoff

Bumping

Dismissal

Personnel services

Employee records and statistics

Personnel manager

Classroom training
Apprenticeship training
Personnel department

REVIEW QUESTIONS

1. What is personnel management? What is its purpose? Whose responsibility is it in the business firm?
2. How can a firm forecast its manpower needs?
3. Explain job analysis.
4. Distinguish between a job description and a job specification.
5. What are the various sources of supply of employees available to a business?
6. Explain a typical employment procedure.
7. What are group interviews? What is their purpose?
8. What is job induction? How important is it?
9. Why do senior employees often have a written contract of employment?
10. What are the various methods of job training?
11. How does a firm benefit from an efficient training program?
12. Explain the nature and purpose of employee follow-up.
13. What is a job transfer? Why does it take place?
14. What are the various factors that determine job promotion?
15. What are the characteristics of a good promotion policy?
16. What is merit rating? What purposes does it serve?
17. Distinguish between a job layoff and a discharge. Why do layoffs occur?
18. What is "bumping?" Why is it favoured by labour unions?
19. Explain the different types of personnel services that a business firm may provide.
20. What personal records should a firm keep about each of its employees? What purpose do these records serve?
21. What is the role of the personnel manager of a business?
22. What are the functions of a personnel department?

CASE PROBLEMS

JONES FURNITURE CO. LTD. (2)
Role of a personnel manager

One of the functions performed by David Jones, the owner and president of the Jones Furniture Co. Ltd., has been the hiring, training, and promotion of all the staff for his main store, and of the managers for his branch stores. Unfortunately, he has not been happy with the performance of the salespeople he has chosen. Their increased volume of sales has been accompanied by complaints from customers that they are being talked into buying items they do not want. The switch from a straight salary to a straight commission system of remuneration a few years ago has caused many of the salespeople to overlook the store's motto: "A Satisfied Buyer—A Satisfied Seller."

David Jones partly blames himself for the present situation because he has been able to devote only a small part of his time in recent years to personnel matters. He now hopes to rectify this mistake by hiring a personnel manager.

The staff at the main store now consists of Jones as owner/president, an accountant/credit manager, 21 salespeople, a secretary-typist, a delivery driver and a driver's helper. The staff at each of the five branch stores consists of a branch manager, eight salespeople, and, on a part-time basis, a typist, a driver, and a driver's helper.

Assignment
1. What do you consider to be the functions of a personnel manager in a firm of this size?
2. What part, if any, should Jones continue to play in the hiring, promotion, and dismissal of personnel?
3. What should be the relationship of the personnel department to the rest of the organization?
4. What is the best method of remunerating the store salespeople?
5. What measures would you suggest that Jones and the personnel manager take to improve customer relations?
6. How can Jones, as president, evaluate the efficiency of his personnel manager?

THE SECURITY FINANCE COMPANY LTD.
Recruiting management personnel

Nancy Parsons, the personnel manager of the newly formed Security Finance Company Ltd., has drawn up the following procedure for hiring management personnel for the company's proposed new branches:
1. The applicant completes a detailed employment application form.
2. The assistant personnel manager interviews the applicant.
3. The assistant personnel manager checks, by telephone and letter, the information provided by the applicant.
4. The personnel manager reviews the verified information and then interviews the applicant.
5. The personnel manager and the assistant personnel manager together discuss the applicant, and the personnel manager decides whether to recommend hiring him or her.
6. The recommendation is then given to the general manager for approval. The first three parts of the application form are as follows:

APPLICATION FOR EMPLOYMENT

Name _____ Date _____
      Last   First   Middle

Address _____ Telephone _____

1. PERSONAL PARTICULARS

Birth date _____ Sex _____ Height _____ _____Weight
Marital status _____ Number, age, and sex of children _____
Father's occupation _____ Brother(s) occupation_____
Participation in community activities _____
_____
Chronic health conditions (hay fever, asthma, ulcers, etc.) _____
Physical handicaps (hernia, varicose veins, flat feet, etc.) _____
Is applicant willing to move? _____
Is applicant's spouse willing to move? _____
Is spouse agreeable to applicant's keeping irregular hours if necessary? _____
Why does applicant wish to work for this company? _____
_____

2. EDUCATIONAL RECORD

	Name	From	To	Course	Diplomas, Degrees
High school					
College					
University					

Scholarships, bursaries, etc.: _____
School activities, offices held: _____
Other interests, including recreational activities: _____

3. EMPLOYMENT RECORD

	Company	Address	From	To	Pay
Last					

Duties _____
Reason for leaving _____
Next previous _____
Duties _____
Reason for leaving _____
Next previous _____
Duties _____
Reason for leaving _____
Next previous _____
Duties _____
Reason for leaving _____
What job was enjoyed the most? _____ Why? _____
Where was applicant most successful? _____

To aid the personnel manager and her assistant in evaluating an applicant, the personnel manager has prepared the following list of questions.

Review of Applicant's Qualifications

1. Does the applicant have a suitable manner and appearance?	Yes	No	Perhaps
2. Does he/she express him/herself well (voice, clarity, self-confidence)?	Yes	No	Perhaps
3. Does he/she have the right attitude?	Yes	No	Perhaps
4. Is his/her educational record satisfactory?	Yes	No	Perhaps
5. Is his/her employment record satisfactory?	Yes	No	Perhaps
6. Do reasons for leaving previous jobs appear logical?	Yes	No	Perhaps
7. Is applicant's background free from the following "Danger Signals:"			
(a) Too many changes in jobs?	Yes	No	Perhaps
(b) Unexplained gaps in employment?	Yes	No	Perhaps
(c) Failed in business for self?	Yes	No	Perhaps
(d) Previous income too high?	Yes	No	Perhaps
(e) Excessive personal indebtedness?	Yes	No	Perhaps
(f) Recently separated or divorced?	Yes	No	Perhaps
8. Does he/she appear to be adaptable and trainable?	Yes	No	Perhaps
9. Are reference checks satisfactory (both business and personal)?	Yes	No	Perhaps
10. Is the starting salary in line with the applicant's financial obligations?	Yes	No	Perhaps
11. Are his/her business interests and ambitions in line with company opportunities?	Yes	No	Perhaps
12. Does he/she seem to be able to work on his/her own without close supervision?	Yes	No	Perhaps
13. Is he/she willing to travel or move at company request?	Yes	No	Perhaps
14. Is applicant's spouse agreeable to applicant's keeping irregular hours if necessary?	Yes	No	Perhaps
15. Does applicant have a history of good health?	Yes	No	Perhaps

Assignment

1. Prepare a Financial Record section for inclusion in the Application For Employment.
2. Should any other question be included in the Application for Employment? Any deleted?
3. In the Review of Applicant's Qualifications, what do you consider to be "the right attitude?" What other questions, if any, should be included in the Review?
4. Explain and discuss the usefulness of aptitude tests as a means of selecting job applicants for this firm.
5. Discuss the need for both the personnel manager and her assistant to interview job applicants.
6. Should the same application form and hiring procedure be used for secretarial staff for this firm?
7. Write a job description and job specification for the position of branch manager.
8. Does the Application for Employment comply with the provisions of your provincial Human Rights Code? Explain.

READING

Our Human Resources Plan Works

Financial Post digest of remarks made to the 65th annual convention of the Ontario Chamber of Commerce

BY E.S. JACKSON, President of ManuLife
Source: *The Financial Post*

Human-resources development has to be real, and it has to flow from the top. It should be buried deep in the corporate psyche, enshrined in its philosophy, and put in the charge of someone with a business background and some exposure to a relevant discipline, such as sociology, psychology or adult education.

It's a noble thing to develop human potential, but it should also serve the ends of the corporation. It will, providing it is a well-conceived and professional enterprise.

Attractive salaries are no longer the most seductive inducement for people with prospects and talent to join a company—or even to stay with it indefinitely. There isn't enough money to compensate them for boredom, enervation, frustration, a lack of opportunity and a lack of definition about their role in the corporation.

A human-resources development program attempts to engender self-esteem and job satisfaction by preparing to grow into more challenging jobs and creating an appropriate environment. People want to work, if they can find it, and if it offers some kind of dignity and promise. Most of all, people want to feel satisfaction in their work, to feel motivated, and to have a sense of direction within the corporation.

ManuLife's human-resources division was established about five years ago. The 85 people in the division at our head office in Toronto handle recruitment, compensation, counselling, development programs, a weekly in-house newspaper, an audiovisual and learning-resources centre, space planning and office design, arranging meetings and travel services for staff, and training head-office staff.

The greatest impact has been on opening up communication within the company. How did we do it? We literally knocked down walls that separated people. You can't post a memo instructing your staff to feel free to communicate and expect them to do it—if that's the only sign of management's intention to do the same. An appropriate environment must be created, and so the first thing we did was to tear down the walls to virtually drive the managers out of their closed offices into the midst of the staff.

It's called office landscaping, and I can tell you it works.

Our head-office building was transformed from institutional drab, with banks of offices and rows of desks, to a wide-open, contemporary office landscape setting. We kept a few private offices for conferences, but apart from that, everybody's office, including mine, is defined by screens and plants. It took some getting used to—but I can't imagine anyone now wanting to return to the old, closed system.

The project took two years to complete, at a cost of more than $1 million. From a cost-benefit standpoint, it was worthwhile. You can't expect miracles from a human-resources development program if your offices are dehumanizing. A pleasant office environment has become an indispensable element in the recruitment of staff, the length of their stay, and the level of their performance. There is, of course, more to freeing up communication than making people more accessible to one another. There has to be a channel for open communication—a newspaper, for example. We have a weekly tabloid newspaper—definitely not a mouthpiece for management and completely free to criticize anything it wants. Nobody, myself included, has ever instructed the newspaper to tone down its criticism, even obliquely. The paper is a forum for managers and staff to express their displeasure or their delight, in guest editorials or letters to the editor. On a personal level, I try to keep my channels of communication open. I often eat lunch with staff in our cafeteria, and once a month I have lunch with 12 different staff members in the company's dining room. I always come away with many useful ideas and suggestions, which are incorporated into our general approach to open communications.

Our human-resources division staff includes a psychologist, a sociologist, adult education and library-science specialists, former teachers, and others who have insight, judgment, experience and an instinct for helping others.

The main focus of the division's effort is to provide expert advice to management to achieve specific goals within an overall corporate context. Improved managerial competence, effective utilization of women, helping employees understand and cope with the dynamics of change, and improved communication and information flow within and between management levels, are among these specific goals.

We are vitally concerned with teaching new skills, and we are also interested in feedback. "ManuLine" at head office is a telephone line to a senior staff member in the division, over which we get calls from staff and managers. The use of that line has dwindled progressively as the level of trust has risen, and it has been supplanted to a great extent by more direct communication.

ManuLife has a range of job-evaluation, job-posting and performance-appraisal systems. That whole process is to make sure that everyone in the organization knows which jobs are open, and that at least once or twice a year the nature of their job and their performance is assessed. The human-resources division is a guarantee that our staff has access to more challenging jobs and salaries commensurate with their performance.

Corporate reorganization was conceived and later implemented by an internal project team. We have continued to use that approach to deal with a number of important issues. It is one of the most valuable of our human-resources development techniques. It is in this mode that development of individual learning and contributing on the project team is fully integrated with the work of the corporation.

ManuLife has examined the whole question of equal opportunity for women, again by project-team approach. The task force of 12 management and staff people made a number of recommendations to ensure equal opportunity for women in the company, including recruitment, job evaluation, performance appraisal, compensation, equal access to training and skill building programs, acquainting managers and staff about women's issues, and career counselling. Management has endorsed every recommendation.

On balance, human-resources development is working well for us. Morale and productivity are high, middle-management jobs are filled quickly from within, which means our own people are ready and eager to move up, and there is enough scope for it within our organization.

Assignment

1. Explain the nature and purpose of ManuLife's human-resources development program.
2. Explain the pros and cons of office landscaping from the viewpoint of (a) the manager and (b) the clerical employee.
3. How does the president of ManuLife try to keep in personal touch with his subordinates? What would you do in his place?
4. What is the composition and role of the human-resources division?
5. What are your views on equal opportunity for women?

UNIT 15.2: WAGE AND SALARY ADMINISTRATION

The employees of a business are rewarded for their services by the payment of a wage or salary, plus various fringe benefits. The term *wage* is normally used for weekly payments to manual, semi-skilled, and skilled workers employed in manufacturing plants and elsewhere; the term *salary* for biweekly or monthly payments to managerial, professional, and sometimes, clerical staff. Often the distinction in terms is made more for purposes of prestige than logic.

Reasons for Differences in Pay

A business firm, when hiring a new employee, will usually pay the "going rate" for the quality of person that it needs. This rate will depend on the demand by employers for that type of employee and the available supply. This interplay of demand and supply largely determines the variations in wages and salaries that exist among different employees in the same firm. Thus the president of the corporation may earn ten times as much as a copy-typist because of the relative scarcity of the former.

A business firm's demand for different types of employees depends on the size and nature of the firm. And the size of the firm itself depends on the demand for its products or services and the production technology involved. As long as a firm believes it can profit from hiring more employees, it will hire more. This is the marginal productivity concept of economics. In deciding how much labour to employ at prevailing wage rates, a firm will also take into account the possibility of using machines instead of labour. Until recently, mechanization and automation replaced mainly manual tasks, with a consequent reduction in demand for plant and office workers. The advent of electronic data processing has resulted, however, in many middle management tasks, as well as purely clerical tasks, being taken over by machines.

The supply of the different types of employee is affected by the following factors: varying degrees of intelligence, ambition, and other personal qualities; differences in education, training, and experience; restrictions on entry into certain types of work by professional associations and labour unions; and unwillingness or inability to move from one geographical area to another or from one firm to another.

Competition among employers seeking employees and among employees seeking employers tends to result in a common wage or salary emerging for a certain type of employee. Of course, differences from the "average" rate will occur.

Purpose of a Firm's Pay Policy

A firm's pay policy is designed (a) to attract and keep enough employees of the required quality to enable the firm to meet its objectives; and (b) to keep them highly motivated and content.

This means, first, paying wages and salaries that are competitive with those of other firms in the same field; and, second, providing a system of regular pay increases to offset changes in the cost of living and to reward length of service and demonstrated merit. If a labour union is present, the remuneration will be determined by management-labour negotiation. One important task of a firm's personnel department is to help determine the most appropriate wage and salary structure for the firm.

Job Evaluation

One of the problems that a firm faces in its wage and salary administration is deciding how much one employee should be paid compared with another. The task of measuring in a systematic way the relative value and importance of the various jobs in a firm is known as *job evaluation*. Very often, both labour and management participate in this task, usually by joint committees. There are five common methods of job evaluation: job ranking, job classification, factor comparison, the points system, and the job group concept.

Job Ranking. With this method, the name of each job and a simple description of it are written on a card. The cards are then arranged (or "ranked") from high to low in order of the relative importance of the jobs, as judged by a senior manager or a labour-management committee. Wage and salary rates are set, based on this order of importance. This method is quite simple to use and is particularly suitable for smaller business firms where the person or committee doing the ranking is reasonably familiar with all the jobs.

Job Classification. Here, a number of different categories of work are established on the basis of increasing job difficulty or value. These categories might range from beginners on probation to skilled, experienced tradespeople. Each job is then examined and placed in one of the categories. The pay rate for the job will then depend on the job's classification.

Factor Comparison. With this method of job evaluation, various factors such as education, experience, physical demand, mental demand, responsibility for equipment, and working conditions are chosen as the basis for a comparison of the various jobs in a plant. Next, a number of easily recognized jobs, called *key jobs*, are selected, each representing a different wage level. Then the pay for each job is allocated among the various factors present in the job. Thus, of an hourly rate of $6.50, fifty cents may be allocated to "hazards." Other jobs are then studied and values established for them, according to the degree to which the various factors are present in each job.

Points System. This is a widely used method of job evaluation in large manufacturing firms. It consists of breaking each job down into its various factors (education, experience, and so on), assigning a number of points to each factor according to its relative importance, and then totalling the number of points for the job. The job with a larger number of points receives a higher wage. Thus, jobs with points totalling less than 100 may be in Class I, paid at the lowest rate per hour; jobs with points totalling from 100 to 149 may be in Class II with a higher rate per hour; and jobs with 150 points or over in Class III, with the highest rate per hour. Often the number of wage classes is very large.

Job Group. With this system, the worth of one job, as compared with others, is ranked within a related and generic group of jobs on the basis of the various factors such as the education and experience required for efficient performance.

Reasons for Job Evaluation. Most firms undertake job evaluation, by one method or another, because: (a) it establishes a systematic outline of the relative worth of different jobs, which is the necessary basis for any fair system of wages and salaries; and (b) the job description evolved can also be used in the recruitment, promotion, and transfer of employees.

Job Evaluation Manuals. Professionally prepared job-evaluation manuals, with a factor breakdown of various jobs, are now available for different industries. The factors usually taken into account in each job are (a) *skill*—comprising education, experience, honesty, dexterity, and initiative; (b) *effort*—physical, mental, and visual; (c) *responsibility*—for other workers, equipment, finished goods, parts, and materials; and (d) *working conditions*—physical environment, unavoidable hazards, and monotony.

Different Methods of Employee Remuneration

There are many different ways of remunerating employees: time wages, piece wages, salary, commission, bonus, or some combination of these methods.

Time Wages. Most non-office workers are paid so much per hour for their services, the rate varying according to the job. Often, a standard work week of 40 hours is set, and any worker required to work beyond this (that is, to work *overtime*) is paid at a higher rate—for example, time-and-a-half on weekdays and Saturdays, and double time on Sundays. The amount of time worked is usually strictly controlled, either by the person in charge, or by time clocks which stamp on the employee's time card the time of arrival and departure. How the employee spends his or her time while at the plant is controlled by the supervisor.

Time wages are commonly used throughout industry as a method of remuneration. One reason for this is that the work that an employee performs cannot always be easily measured. Thus it becomes difficult to pay an employee on the basis of results. Another reason is that many employers believe that time wages (rather than piece wages) result in better quality work and in a more contented labour force. A third reason is that labour unions favour this method and, wherever possible, make it a part of the labour contract. The main disadvantage is that time wages provide no incentive for an employee to work hard. Therefore, to obtain the best results from its employees under this system, a firm must usually provide close supervision and perhaps add some bonus system for overall, departmental, or individual results.

Piece Wages. With this method, an employee is paid so many cents per unit or piece of work produced. Often a unit is a particular operation in a complete manufacturing process.

The main advantage for the employer of this payment method is that it provides the employee with an incentive to work hard. The employee knows that the greater is the output, the greater will be the earnings. The employer knows, too, that he or she need pay only for work done. The principal disadvantage for the employer is that a worker is under constant pressure to produce as fast as possible. This may result in a fall in quality and an increase in spoilage and waste, which can be checked only by careful supervision and inspection; and such a close control is, of course, expensive. Another disadvantage is that the primary purpose of this method of remuneration—to increase output per worker—is often defeated by the employees' fear that if they work too hard the rate of payment per unit or piece will be reduced.

Salary. Most office workers—clerical, research, managerial—are paid so many dollars per week, month, or year. The rate of pay is linked only very indirectly to the number of hours worked. As a result, time off for personal reasons is often permitted without reduction in salary; conversely, overtime (at home or at the office) is often required with little or no additional pay. The payment of a salary is accompanied by a paid annual vacation and, more and more frequently, by a certain number of days of paid sick leave.

The output of an office employee, particularly a manager, is extremely difficult to measure. Except in sales, the "straight" salary plan is therefore the most logical to use. Unfortunately, it has the same strengths and weaknesses as the time wages mentioned earlier, notably, the failure to provide incentive. This deficiency is overcome in most firms by supervision and the threat of replacement; and on the more positive side, by leadership, motivation, and the chance of salary increases, promotion, and bonuses.

Commission. Persons employed in selling are often paid a straight commission. This means that their earnings depend solely on the value of the sales made. The commission may be either a fixed sum per unit sold or a percentage of its value. A real estate salesperson, for example, may receive $2\frac{1}{2}$ per cent of the value of each house sold and the employing broker another $2\frac{1}{2}$ per cent, depending on the type of property listing and on the salesperson's terms of employment. Some real estate brokers will give their salespeople more than half the total commission.

Since it normally takes time for a salesperson or sales representative to develop a clientele, many firms—for example, insurance companies—pay their new salespeople a fixed monthly salary during an initial training period. After this period has elapsed, the salesperson may be allowed a weekly "draw." This draw represents a loan by the company to be repaid out of the salesperson's future earnings. A limit is set beyond which a salesperson may not allow his or her loan balance with the firm to rise. Interest is sometimes charged by the firm on the outstanding balance.

The commission method of remuneration is in many ways identical to the piece-rate system mentioned previously. Its main advantage to the employer is that it motivates the salesperson to work hard. Also, the employer need pay only for results. From the salesperson's point of view, it allows him or her to relate personal earnings to some extent to personal efforts. Whether he or she will earn much or little will depend on: the type of product or service that is being sold; the competition; the commission rates paid by the firm; and his or her ability to sell.

Salary Plus Commission. Some firms pay their salespeople a basic salary, plus a commission that varies according to their sales. This method of remuneration provides the salesperson with a certain amount of security—he or she knows that there will be the basic pay every month as long as he or she makes a reasonable effort and continues to be employed. It also provides the salesperson with the incentive to "get out and sell," but only as long as the basic pay is not unduly large. When a basic wage is paid, commission rates tend to be lower than when commission only is paid.

Different Types of Fringe Benefits

A *fringe benefit* is any payment in money or kind that is made to an employee over and above the regular wage. These benefits will vary from firm to firm. Some are the result of the employer's initiative, others of labour legislation, and others of labour union action. Together with the wage, they comprise the cost to a firm of employing a worker. Fringe benefits may easily add 10 per cent or more to a firm's labour costs.

Profit-Sharing Plans. A number of firms set aside a certain amount of each year's net profit to be shared out among the employees. The amount of the *bonus* that each employee receives will depend on his or her importance to the firm. The method of measuring this contribution is usually the employee's salary or wage: the larger the wage, the larger the bonus.

Profit-sharing plans may be of the cash type, deferred distribution type, or a combination of both. With the cash type, the employee receives all the bonus right away in the form of cash. With the deferred payment type, the money is put into a special fund from which the employee's share is paid on retirement or, in some cases, for particular purposes such as buying a house. Profit-sharing plans have become increasingly popular in Canada in recent years. This is because they help motivate employees to work harder; reduce labour turnover; and offer significant income tax benefits to an employee when set up in a "deferred" form.

Productivity Bonus. Some firms pay a weekly, monthly, or annual monetary bonus to their employees if they succeed in improving plant productivity. One type of bonus plan is the *Scanlon plan*, which uses the ratio of total labour cost over total sales value of output as the criterion of efficiency. Any reduction in the ratio is considered to signify an increase in efficiency and a bonus is paid accordingly.

Courtesy *Oakville Beaver*

Stock Bonus. Many firms give their top managers stock bonuses as an extra reward for a good performance and as a means of attracting and keeping key personnel. For many years, the most usual type of bonus was a *stock option*. This is a right to buy so many shares of the company at a price below the market price. It means, therefore, the opportunity for a manager to obtain a substantial capital gain by selling the shares at a higher market price. The better the company performs, the higher should be the selling price of its shares and the greater the size of the possible capital gain.

In recent years, stock-option plans have become less popular. One reason is that half of any capital gain from the sale of the stock must now be added to the manager's taxable income and incur personal income tax at the marginal rate. Another reason is that executives, having seen their stock become worthless in time of stock market slump, prefer a more predictable form of incentive plan.

Other popular incentive plans are: (a) *cash incentive plans*—whereby a cash bonus is paid for good management performance; (b) *performance shares*—whereby a top manager, as a reward for good performance, is given company stock free of charge; and (c) *stock-purchase arrangements*—whereby a company pays an agreed portion (for example, one-third or one-half) of the total cost of purchases of company stock or bonds by its managers and sometimes by other employees.

Flexible Working Hours. Instead of requiring all their employees to start and stop their working day at the same time, a number of firms are offering flexible working hours. This means that an employee has the right to choose, within broad limits, when to work the required 40 or less hours per week. Thus, a person may start the day later or earlier than the usual starting time of eight or nine o'clock. Also, if desired, he or she can work a longer day and take a half-day off every week or a full day off every two weeks. Other firms have offered their employees a compressed work-week—for example, four 10-hour days instead of five 8-hour days.

The advantages to the employee of such schemes include: the avoidance of congested peak travel-times; the opportunity of recreation, shopping, and other pursuits during less crowded weekdays; and the adjustment of working hours to a person's tastes—for example, getting out of bed early or late.

Pension Plans. By law, an employer must match the employee's contribution to the Canada Pension Plan. The plan provides retirement pensions, disability pensions, death benefits, widows' and orphans' pensions.

Some employers also have their own private pension plans for their employees. Contributions are usually made jointly by employer and employee.

Insurance Plans. Often a firm will arrange for an insurance plan for its employees whereby coverage for life, accident, medical care, dental care, and hospitalization is available at group rates. Sometimes the premiums are paid wholly or partly by the employer. In some provinces, hospitalization and/or medical insurance is mandatory, and an employer must contribute half or more of the premium.

Unemployment insurance, administered by a federally appointed Commission, also requires contributions from employers as well as from employees.

Workers' Compensation, which provides disability pensions and widows' benefits for persons disabled or killed in the course of their employment, is financed by contributions from employers alone. The Board that administers this insurance plan in each province is appointed by, and is responsible to, the provincial government.

Shorter Workweek. Another fringe benefit is the reduction in the length of the working week. In the last century, 60 hours per week was considered by many to be the standard. Later this was reduced to 48 hours and then to 40 hours. Nowadays a $37\frac{1}{2}$ hour workweek is common in Canada and some employees have obtained a workweek even shorter than this.

Time Off. Many employers give their employees time off during the day without any reduction in wages. This time off may include a ten-minute coffee break in the morning and afternoon, a half-hour lunch break, a five-minute wash-up time at the end of the day, and time off for personal reasons (particularly among office staff).

Sick Leave. More and more firms are allowing their employees a certain number of days' paid sick leave per year. To discourage employees from taking days off when they are not sick, some firms have a system of checks, including personal visits and medical inspections. Others pay their employees a cash bonus for each day's sick leave that is unused.

Maternity Leave. Some firms give their female employees a certain number of weeks off for maternity reasons. During this time, they may be given full or partial pay—sometimes the difference between the unemployment benefit received and their regular wage. Their job is held open until they are able to return to work.

Other Fringe Benefits. These include free or reduced rate travel for transportation employees; discounts on purchases for retail store employees; payment of education fees; payment of social club memberships; use of the firm's car for pleasure as well as business; turkeys at Christmas; and so on.

A number of other benefits, now taken for granted, are those prescribed by federal or provincial law. These include minimum wage rates, a weekly rest day, limited working hours, annual paid vacations, paid general holidays, and notice of dismissal. They are discussed in Unit 16.2.

KEY TERMS

Job evaluation

Job ranking

Fringe benefit

Profit-sharing

Job classification	Productivity bonus
Factor comparison	Stock bonus
Points system	Stock option
Job group	Flexible working hours
Time wages	Pension plans
Overtime	Insurance plans
Piece wages	Shorter workweek
Salary	Time off
Commission	Sick leave
Salary plus commission	Maternity leave

REVIEW QUESTIONS

1. Why does the president of a corporation earn more than a clerk?
2. What factors affect the demand for different types of labour?
3. What factors affect the supply of different types of labour?
4. Explain briefly the various possible methods of employee remuneration.
5. Why are time wages the most common method of employee remuneration?
6. Explain the advantages and disadvantages of the commission method of remuneration.
7. What are the main types of profit-sharing plans? How can profit sharing benefit the owners of a business firm?
8. What is a fringe benefit? Give five examples. What new fringe benefits are employees now seeking?

READING

Distinctions Between Capitalist, Worker Blurred at Trent Rubber Services

BY MARTIN DEWEY
Source: *The Globe and Mail*, Toronto

Nothing is quite as it seems at Trent Rubber Services Ltd. in Lindsay.

The factory buildings date from the First World War and look as if they had been on the losing side. Yet the ancient red bricks enclose a highly efficient plant that turns out a third of all the rubber inner tubes produced in Canada and contains some of the most up-to-date rubber-mixing equipment in the world.

Inside, the plant is a topsy-turvy place where textbook distinctions between capitalist and worker have been blurred beyond recognition. Of the 132 men and women who work there, 85 per cent are part-owners of the operation, some of them convinced they are pioneering a new kind of industrial democracy. Karl Marx would have had an attack of vertigo within a mile of the place.

There was nothing extraordinary about the company when it first set up shop 80 miles northeast of Toronto in what had once been a shellcasing factory. Eighty per cent of the shares were owned by Polysar Ltd. of Sarnia, the giant Crown corporation, and the rest by the company founders, chairman of the board George Plummer and president David Hay.

At the time there were seven major tire manufacturers in Canada but only four of them made inner tubes; the rest had to buy from their competitors. Stepping into the gap, Trent was soon supplying the needs of the tubeless three and doing a brisk business on the side in rubber compounds mixed to order for manufacturers of non-tire goods.

Trouble struck in 1974 when a takeover in the tire industry cost Trent an important customer. Then came a lengthy strike, which closed down Canada's major tire makers and produced a pile-up of tubes in stockrooms across the country.

"In the summer of 1975 we didn't get a single order for tubes," Mr. Hay said.

But matters soon began to improve. Of the four original tube makers, B.F. Goodrich Canada Ltd. had already started buying from Trent. Then the company won the Uniroyal Ltd. account. Only Goodyear Canada Inc. and Firestone Canada Inc. remained in full production. Then, just as everything was looking so good, the roof fell in.

"In April, 1978," Mr. Hay said, "I went down to a board meeting in Toronto. When I got there Polysar had two things to tell me. The first was that I was getting a big, fat raise. The second was that they had received an offer to buy Trent Rubber Services. They were in the midst of negotiations.

"We were thunderstruck and told them they were out of their skulls to sell us. But if they wanted to sell, we wanted to buy."

After much begging and pleading from Trent's management, Polysar agreed in the next month to let it have the company if it could match the outside bid within 10 working days. The price: slightly more than $2-million.

"Ten days in May. That's what we called it," Mr. Hay recalled. "We mortgaged our souls and got large loans from the bank, a commercial lending corporation and two of our customers—both interest-free. But on day seven we were still short by $100,000."

That might have been the end of it but for the special talents of George Plummer. After retiring as president of Dunlop Rubber Canada Ltd. in 1970, he put together a much-publicized deal in which pulp workers in Temiscaming, Que., prevented a shutdown of the local mill by buying it in a joint venture with management and the provincial Government.

That partnership worked well, reasoned Mr. Plummer; why not try to save Trent in much the same way by asking the employees to put up the shortfall? Hastily knocking together a joint purchase proposal, he and Mr. Hay laid it before their staff in a series of round-the-clock meetings between shifts. Time was short, they said; they needed answers within 24 hours. Twenty-four hours later, the employees had oversubscribed with commitments of $140,000. Trent was saved.

"I worked out the purchase program so that management investors would take most of the risks," Mr. Plummer said. "I believe that the less an employee understands of the complexities of running a business, the greater should be his security."

The employees took roughly half the available class A preferred shares, which were participating and callable. Management took the other half as well as all the

B shares (6 per cent non-cumulative) and all the common shares.

Today, the employees' share of equity is roughly 20 per cent, which is a long way from giving them control over their workplace. But it has been enough to make a dramatic change in management-employee relations.

The key to the arrangement is that three members of the nine-member board of directors are elected from the factory floor, giving employees access to the company books and to the decision-making process. The result, according to Mr. Hay, has been a heightened sense of involvement on the factory floor that is reflected in increased productivity, little absenteeism, little turnover and a great readiness to accept change. Management does its part by holding sales and administration costs down to 5 per cent of operating costs. Said Mr. Plummer: "It's a helluva good way to run a business. I have no doubt that the next generation of capitalism will involve employee participation. If you want people to be responsible, you must give them ownership."

For the arrangement to work, Trent must of course sell a lot of inner tubes and mix a lot of rubber. At the moment, everyone is confident.

A company press release says that "in the year and a half since the employees took over, every production figure has been met, productivity has increased and sales have skyrocketed—to a record $1-million level in October alone."

Does Mr. Hay think Polysar made a mistake in bailing out when it did?

"I'd say so," he said.

Shop Talk is Unusual at What Employee-Owners Call "Our Plant"

In the machine shop at Trent Rubber Services Ltd. in Lindsay some of the boys were chatting beside a lathe.

There was Fred Coffey, whose lathe it was. A round, white-haired cherub with the face of Charles Laughton, and some of the accent too, he was wearing a half-unzipped parka that revealed a sweatshirt of machinist's grey.

Terry Downer had come over from the rubber-mixing area where everything, especially the people who work there, is coated with a soot-like substance called carbon black. The only clear spot on Mr. Downer was his glasses.

A third man leaning against the wall obviously hailed from the inner-tube assembly area. There, where the air is filled with talcum powder, everything is as white as the mixing area is black. (Talc keeps heated rubber surfaces from sticking together. The men have been told that it, like carbon black, is an inert substance that does no harm to human lungs.)

The three were talking shop, but not in the usual way of factory workers. These were part-owners of the enterprise, capitalists all.

"The average in the plant, I'd say, is 10 shares each," said the man against the wall, explaining that a share is $100. Of course, everyone knew of the maintenance man who had responded to the company's original share offer by buying 150 of them.

Mr. Coffey, besides being a worker and a shareholder, is also one of the three non-management representatives on the board of directors. And if that is not enough he is chairman of the plant committee, which is as close as Trent has ever come to having a union steward. Sometimes he must have to feel his head to find out what hat he has on.

"On the board, we talk over everything," Mr. Coffey said. "At the end of the last fiscal year we had to decide how much of a dividend to give on employees' preferred class A shares over and above the 7 per cent that's guaranteed. We added another 8 per cent. That came to $15 a share, which is not bad."

In addition, he said, there is a profit-sharing plan that has been in place since before the employees bought into the company. Profits are distributed in fixed shares that have nothing to do with salary levels and are paid to all employees, not just shareholders. Last year everyone received slightly less than $1,000.

"Nothing goes on in the company that the employees don't know about," Mr. Coffey said. "When the German purchase came up, we talked about it in the plant before any decision was made. On the board, I voted for it."

The "German purchase" had been no trifling matter. A management team flew to Munich, West Germany, last September and in a single day of negotiation bought all the tube-making equipment of Metzeler Kautschuk AG for $625,000—equipment that Trent feels would have cost $4-million new. Once installed, it will broaden the company's range of products to include tubes for large tractors and off-road equipment, and will increase over-all tube-making capacity by 60 per cent. One day, the company hopes, it will be selling tubes to the very people who sold them the equipment.

Asked if his different jobs did not sometimes get in the way of each other, Mr. Coffey replied "not at all. When I'm on the board it's company business. When I'm on the plant committee it's employee business. On the plant committee we have six employees and five people from management. That's where we bargain for wages, benefits and better working conditions. Last year we got 75 per cent of what we bargained for." Did they get all the wages they asked for?

Mr. Coffey produced a grease-smudged notebook filled with neatly printed figures. "Last time we got 9 per cent. Of course, we don't get the highest wages in Lindsay. We're No. 3."

He said the leader was a local branch of a large multi-national corporation and that there was no way Trent could compete. But then, he added, he would not like to work for that company.

"There, they say, 'We are the boss, you are the worker.' Here, we have a say, too."

Mr. Downer added that "we don't have to call anyone mister. We're on a first-name basis with management all down the line. You know, there's a plant here in town where you have to punch out to go to the washroom. Seriously. Here, we don't even have punch cards; we just sign in and out. And if we want a coffee we just go and get one."

That is not to say the employees are loafers, he said. "Most people have a real interest in the job. In slack times, a guy might pick up a broom. And if someone is goofing off all the time, one of us—not one of the bosses—would tap him on the shoulder."

"You see," Mr. Coffey said, "this is our plant. Nobody can come and say they're closing it down or moving it somewhere else. This is a Lindsay plant, owned and operated by Lindsay people."

He said it with the air of a man who had said it before but felt it worth repeating.

Assignment

1. What does Trent Rubber Services produce?
2. What are the firm's origins?
3. What happened in 1974? How was the crisis overcome?
4. What made the roof fall in four years later?

5. Who were the new owners? Discuss the division of shares between management investors on the one hand and employees on the other.
6. How did management of the firm change after the new owners took control?
8. What effects has the new ownership had within the plant?
9. What was the "German purchase?" Why was it good for the firm? Who made the decision?
10. What are Coffey's two different roles in the firm? How does he reconcile them?
11. How are wage rates, etc. determined in this firm?
12. How does the work environment differ in this firm from that in other local firms? How does it affect productivity?
13. Can employee stock-ownership ensure job security? Discuss.
14. List the pros and cons of employee stock-ownership plans.

CHAPTER 16
LABOUR RELATIONS

CHAPTER OBJECTIVES

☐ To review the role of labour unions in the modern workplace.

☐ To review the different federal and provincial labour statutes that set minimum employment standards in Canada.

CHAPTER OUTLINE

16.1   Labour Unions and Collective Bargaining
16.2   Labour Legislation

UNIT 16.1: LABOUR UNIONS AND COLLECTIVE BARGAINING

All provinces now have labour relations statutes which aim to strengthen the bargaining position of the worker, promote more harmonious relations between employers and employees, and to facilitate the settlement of industrial disputes by means of a collective bargaining procedure. A key feature of these statutes is the recognition of the right of most employees to be represented, for bargaining purposes with the employer, by a labour union. A second feature is the compulsory requirement for employers to negotiate in good faith with the labour union once it has been certified as the collective bargaining agent for the employees concerned. A third key feature is the requirement to use the services of a government-appointed conciliation officer to try to bring about a collective labour agreement by peaceful persuasion before any lockout or strike takes place.

Courtesy *The Financial Post*

Labour Union Defined

A *labour union* (also called a *trade union*) is an association of workers practising a similar trade or employed in the same industry whose purpose is to improve the economic and social welfare of its members through collective, rather than individual, bargaining with employers. Most unions call themselves unions, but some use the terms association, brotherhood, or guild.

Types of Labour Unions

Labour unions differ according to whether they are craft unions or industrial unions. Another distinction is whether they are international, national, or local.

Craft Unions and Industrial Unions.
Labour unions began in Canada in the nineteenth century as associations of workers who practised a similar skill or trade—hence its name *craft union*. However, in the early twentieth century, the growing number of unskilled and semi-skilled workers employed in the new mass production industries required a collective voice. As these workers were not eligible for membership in the existing craft unions, they eventually established their own unions—to be known as *industrial unions*.

A *craft union* is a labour union whose members carry on the same craft or trade. Examples are the Painters and Decorators of America; the United Brotherhood of Carpenters and Joiners of America; and the Amalgamated Meat Cutters and Butcher Workmen of North America.

An *industrial union* is one whose members include all workers eligible for union membership in a particular industry irrespective of their jobs. Examples are the United Automobile, Aerospace and Agricultural Implement Workers of America; the United Steelworkers of America; and the Canadian Food and Allied Workers.

International, National, and Local Unions.
As can be seen from Figure 16.1, about 40 per cent of all union members in Canada belong to *international unions* (unions that charter locals in the United States and Canada) with their head offices in the U.S.A. Prominent international unions (which include both craft unions and industrial unions) are the International Brotherhood of Teamsters, Warehousemen and Helpers of America and the International Brotherhood of Electrical Workers.

National unions are unions that charter locals in Canada only. About half of all union members in Canada now belong to them. Examples are the Canadian Air Line Pilots' Association and the Canadian Brotherhood of Railway, Transport and General Workers.

Independent local organizations, as the name indicates, belong neither to an international union nor to a national union. Two examples of such local unions are the Kingston Independent Nylon Workers' Union and the Eaton's Employees' Association (Victoria) of British Columbia. These are local organizations and not formally connected or affiliated with any other labour organization.

Type of Affiliation	No. of Unions	Membership Number	Membership Per Cent
International Unions	71	1 461 693	40.0
AFL-CIO/CLC	44	848 232	23.2
AFL-CIO/CFL	10	217 697	6.0
CLC only	4	134 897	3.7
AFL-CIO only	7	157 540	4.3
Unaffiliated unions	6	103 327	2.8
National Unions	151	2 049 756	56.1
CLC	27	1 058 371	29.0
CNTU	9	209 493	5.7
CSD	3	21 785	0.6
CCU	21	40 622	1.1
Unaffiliated unions	91	719 485	19.7
Directly Chartered Unions	374	41 769	1.1
CLC	66	8 178	0.2
CNTU	5	591	0.0
CSD	303	33 000	0.9
Independent Local Organizations	203	97 286	2.7
Total	799	3 650 504	100.0

Figure 16.1 Union Membership by Type of Union and Affiliation, 1984
Source: Labour Data Branch, Labour Canada, *Directory of Labour Organizations in Canada*, 1984, Reproduced by permission of the Minister of Supply and Services Canada.

Directly chartered local unions are locals organized by, and receiving their charter from, a central labour congress. They also are not part of an international or national union.

Union Membership

Union membership, as a percentage of the working force, has been relatively stable in Canada in recent years, as shown in Figure 16.2.

The sixteen largest unions, in terms of Canadian membership, are shown in Figure 16.3.

Aims of Labour Unions

The purpose of a labour union is to improve the economic and social welfare of its members. It does this by negotiating with employers for such things as higher wages, a shorter standard workweek, higher overtime pay, longer vacations, the recognition of seniority rights in layoffs, a just procedure for settling employee grievances, and recognition of the right of the union to represent the employees.

Year	Union Membership (Thousands)	Total Non-Agricultural Paid Workers (Thousands)	Union Membership as Percentage of Civilian Labour Force	Union Membership as Percentage of Non-Agricultural Paid Workers
1955	1268	3767	23.6	33.7
1960	1459	4522	23.5	32.3
1961	1447	4578	22.6	31.6
1962	1423	4705	22.2	30.2
1963	1449	4867	22.3	29.8
1964	1493	5074	22.3	29.4
1965	1589	5343	23.2	29.7
1966	1736	5658	24.5	30.7
1967	1921	5953	26.1	32.3
1968	2010	6068	26.6	33.1
1969	2075	6380	26.3	32.5
1970	2173	6465	27.2	33.6
1971	2231	6637	26.8	33.6
1972	2388	6893	27.8	34.6
1973	2591	7181	29.2	36.1
1974	2732	7637	29.4	35.8
1975	2884	7817	29.8	36.9
1976	3042	8158	30.6	37.3
1977	3149	8243	31.0	38.2
1978	3278	8413	31.3	39.0
1980	3397	9027	30.5	37.6
1981	3487	9330	30.6	37.4
1982	3617	9264	31.4	39.0
1983	3563	8901	30.6	40.0
1984	3651	9220	30.6	39.6

Note: The method of reporting was changed in 1980. Thus statistics for 1955 through 1978 are for Dec. 31 of each year. But statistics for 1980 are for Jan. 1 (i.e.,—equivalent to Dec. 31, 1979). This explains the absence in the table above of 1979 figures.

Figure 16.2 Union Membership in Canada, 1955-1984
Source: Labour Data Branch, Labour Canada, *Directory of Labour Organizations in Canada, 1984*, Reproduced by permission of the Minister of Supply and Services Canada.

The labour unions also exert pressure in federal, provincial, and local politics by offering support to political parties willing to help promote union aims and by direct representations to the federal and provincial governments.

Why Workers Join a Labour Union

One of the foremost reasons why workers join unions is to secure improved pay

Union	Membership
1. Canadian Union of Public Employees	293 709
2. National Union of Provincial Government Employees	242 286
3. Public Service Alliance of Canada	181 192
4. United Steelworkers of America	148 000
5. United Food and Commercial Workers	140 000
6. International Union, United Automobile, Aerospace and Agricultural Implement Workers of America	110 000
7. Fédération des affaires sociales	93 000
8. International Brotherhood of Teamsters, Chauffeurs, Warehousemen and Helpers of America	91 500
9. Centrale de l'enseignement du Québec	86 200
10. United Brotherhood of Carpenters and Joiners of America	78 000
11. International Brotherhood of Electrical Workers	72 927
12. International Association of Machinists and Aerospace Workers	66 558
13. Service Employees International Union of Canada	65 000
14. Canadian Paperworkers' Union	63 180
15. Labourers' International Union of North America	59 310
16. International Woodworkers of America	55 781

Figure 16.3 Sixteen Largest Unions in Canada, 1984
Source: Labour Data Branch, Labour Canada, *Directory of Labour Organizations in Canada, 1984*, Reproduced by permission of the Minister of Supply and Services Canada.

and fringe benefits and better working conditions. Another equally important reason is to obtain the sense of security that comes from belonging to such a group. No longer does the worker feel weak and alone in his or her dealings with management. The worker now belongs to an organization whose representatives can talk and bargain as competently as management. An additional reason is compulsion: to obtain or keep a job, a worker must often become a member of the union in his or her firm. Some workers, however, resent being forced to join a labour union.

Organization of a Labour Union

The Local. The basic unit of organization of the labour union is the *local*. In the case of an industrial union, a local may consist of either the employees of several small firms in a given area or the employees of one large firm. In the case of a craft union, the membership consists of persons practising a common skill—for example, bricklaying—in a given area.

The internal organization of a typical local is shown in Figure 16.4.

The union local draws up its own bylaws governing the conduct of its officers and members and has authority for such matters as: obtaining new members, handling grievances, collective bargaining, and recreational activities. Power is usually exercised by an executive committee, comprising the president, vice-

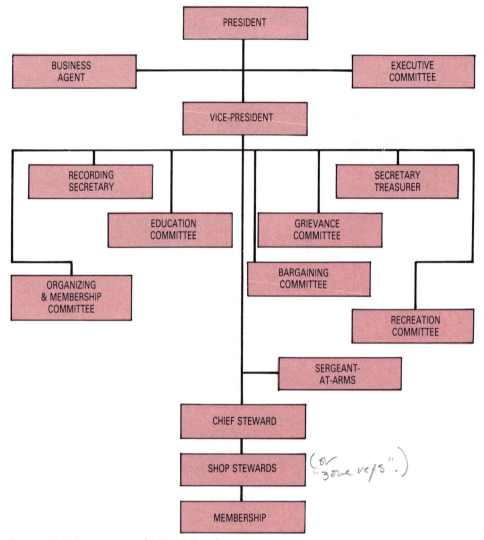

Figure 16.4 Organization of a Union Local

president, and business agent. Part of this authority is delegated to the various other committees: the grievance committee (which represents the union in grievance proceedings); the organizing committee (which studies methods of raising membership); the recreation committee (which looks after dances, parties, excursions, and so on); and the education committee (which disseminates information about union aims and activities to members).

In the plant itself, other union officials, the *shop stewards* or *zone representatives*, look after the grievances submitted to them by union members. In charge of the shop stewards for a particular area or division is a *chief steward*.

In the smaller locals, all the various positions are held on a voluntary part-time basis by working members. These persons are elected by the members of the local every two years. Only in the larger locals is there a full-time business agent whose salary is paid either by the local itself or by head office. The part-time officials are reimbursed for time taken from work for union business. Where there is a business agent, he or she will handle much of the work of the union, particularly the enrolment of new members and the representation of the union in grievance complaints or in contract negotiations.

The power of the union local can vary considerably according to the union of which it is a part. Generally speaking, the locals of craft unions have more autonomy than those of the industrial unions. Thus the craft union locals usually negotiate their own collective agreements, whereas in the industrial unions, the headquarters' officers and regional representatives handle most of the collective bargaining.

The Head Office. In all unions, the head office wields great power by virtue of its control over union funds. In many cases, union dues are remitted directly to union head office by the employer. The local's share is then sent from head office. Also, the union's welfare and strike funds are managed by head office.

Most union headquarters retain the right to veto collective agreements or strikes proposed by their locals. Some head offices exercise close control over the organization and operation of their locals and have the constitutional right to dismiss regional, district, or local officers, and place the units concerned under "trusteeship."

Any local dissatisfaction with head office can be expressed in the way the local delegates vote at the annual union conventions, and, in more extreme cases, by refusal to obey head office orders—for example, by engaging in "wildcat," or unofficial, strikes.

Labour Councils (city or district)

In Canada, the locals of many labour unions are affiliated with a labour council established by charter of the Canadian Labour Congress for their particular city or district. The delegates from the various locals elect the council's officers, who are responsible for furthering the interests of the labour union movement at the community level—for example, by lobbying municipal governments or by organizing strike aid. These district councils are sometimes called joint boards or conference boards.

In industries organized along craft lines (such as painting and decorating), unions or union locals in a particular area may form a special council to coordinate members' activities and resolve jurisdictional problems. Such a council is sometimes called an *Allied Trades Federation*.

Labour Federations (provincial)

Most provinces have a federation of labour, chartered by the Canadian Labour Congress, which acts as the central organization for the labour union movement in the province. The federation holds annual conventions where delegates from the affiliated locals vote on policy matters and elect officers. The purpose of the federation is to represent labour's interest at the provincial level, particularly in the establishment or amendment of labour legislation by the provincial government.

Canadian Labour Congress (Canada)

The major central organization for labour unions in Canada is the Canadian Labour Congress, with headquarters in Ottawa and regional offices in most of the provinces. National and international unions, locals, labour councils, and federations are all directly affiliated with the CLC and send delegates to its biennial conventions. The purpose of the CLC is primarily a political one: to act as the common spokesman, particularly in Ottawa, for organized labour throughout Canada. It is also active in helping to settle jurisdictional disputes among the affiliated unions.

Certification of a Labour Union

An employer may voluntarily recognize a union as the bargaining agent for its employees. If voluntary recognition is not forthcoming, the union can appeal to the provincial Labour Relations Board to have the union certified as the bargaining agent. If certification is granted, the employer is required by law to negotiate a labour contract with the union.

The usual procedure for certification is as follows:
1. The labour union applies to the Board for certification as the bargaining agent of the employees in a unit that the union claims to be appropriate for collective bargaining—for example, the employees of a particular plant.
2. The Board then determines the unit that is appropriate, the number of employees at the time of the application, and the number of employees who have already become members of the union making the application.
3. If the Board is satisfied that not less then 35 per cent and not more than 65 per cent of all the employees in the bargaining unit are members of the labour union, the Board will order a representation vote to be held at the firm. If more than 50 per cent of *all* employees eligible to vote (not 50 per cent of those who vote) cast their votes in favour of the union, the Board will certify the labour union as the bargaining agent. Both union and management can be prosecuted if they use coercion on employees to influence their votes.
4. If, in other cases, the Board is satisfied that more than 65 per cent of the employees in the bargaining unit are members of the labour union, it may certify the labour union as the employees' bargaining agent, or it may first order a representation vote.

Collective Bargaining

Once a labour union has been certified as the bargaining agent for a group of employees, it must give the employer written notice of its desire to negotiate a collective labour agreement. The employer and labour union must then, according to the Labour Relations Act, meet within a specified period of time (e.g., two weeks) or longer if mutually agreed. At the meetings they are expected to bargain in good faith and make every effort to arrive at a collective agreement, covering terms of employment, job security, etc.

Conciliation

Another provision of most labour relations statutes is the requirement of compulsory conciliation in labour contract negotiations. This means that before a strike or lockout may legally take place, the conciliation procedure set out in the Acts must be followed. This procedure provides for a conciliation officer of the provincial government to intervene in the dispute to help bring about agreement between the two parties.

The conciliation officer, it should be noted, has no power to impose a settlement on the disputing parties; and can only make suggestions. In many cases, his or her only achievement has been to provide a "cooling-off" period before a strike actually takes place. This function, as well as that of being an impartial go-between, is considered useful by many. Others, however, criticize compulsory conciliation as being a futile and time-wasting delay. If conciliation fails, the trade union may legally call a strike, or the employer lock out the employees.

When the public interest is threatened, the government may intervene directly to settle a labour dispute. However, the federal and provincial governments intervene only as a last resort and even then very rarely.

Union Finances

Each union member is required to pay monthly what are termed *union dues*. This sum (say $20 per month) is normally deducted from the employee's pay by the employer and remitted to the union under the terms of the labour contract. This is known as the *check off*. Depending on the agreement, the money is paid to the local union or to the head office. Thus, out of a $20 monthly due, the local might retain $8 and remit the balance to head office. From the balance of $12 per person, $7 might go for head office expenses and $5 for the Union's Strike Insurance Fund.

The money received by the union is used by head office for rent, salaries, travelling expenses, and various benefit programs for all members, such as health insurance, and for maintaining a strike-fund; and by the local union for general expenses, such as hall rent, supplies, reimbursement for time lost on union business, donations, affiliation fees, legal services, local union publications, cost of elections, and, in some cases, for funds for education, citizenship, recreation, and retirement.

Union Security

A labour union will try to ensure that all eligible employees are dues-paying union members. The union considers it unjust that workers who are not union members should be "free riders"—that is, obtain the benefits of union activity without sharing the cost. Some workers feel equally strongly, however, that they should not be forced to join a union. Ivan C. Rand, former Chief Justice of the Supreme Court of Canada, suggested as a compromise that labour agreements might require all employees to pay normal union dues but give them the choice of becoming union members or not. This is known as the *Rand Formula* and has gained some acceptance among employers and labour unions. Most union security provisions are of the following types:

Closed Shop. This exists when a firm agrees to employ only union members. Thus a person who wishes to work for the firm must first obtain union membership and must remain a member in good standing. Since a closed shop virtually transfers control of hiring from management to the union, this type of arrangement has been strongly opposed by employers. A closed shop is legal in Canada; however, provincial legislation usually states that the obligation to become a union member applies only to employees hired *after* the labour agreement is made.

Union Shop. Under this agreement, management may hire non-union labour. However, after an initial probationary period, new employees must become dues-paying members of the union if they are to continue to be employed.

Open Shop. In this situation, employees are free to choose whether or not to join the union. Nowadays such an arrangement is rare because of labour union hostility.

Grievances

To provide for the settlement of disputes that may arise between management and labour during the life of a collective agreement, each labour agreement contains a grievance procedure. A *grievance is an alleged violation of the labour contract or of customary practice in the firm*. The *grievance procedure* specifies the steps which must be followed in settling such an alleged violation. These steps vary according to the particular labour contract, but are normally as follows:
1. The employee will ask the foreman's help in settling the complaint.
2. If no satisfactory solution is found, the employee will report the grievance to the *shop steward*, who is the unpaid union representative in each shop, or section, of the plant. The shop steward, who is permitted time off from his or her job in the shop to handle grievances, will take all the particulars in writing and then attempt to settle the grievance with the shop foreman. Most grievances—for example, overtime still unpaid—are settled at this stage or at the previous one.
3. If the foreman's decision is not acceptable to the employee, the chief steward for the plant may take the matter up with the department superintendent.
4. If the grievance is still not resolved to the employee's satisfaction, the

union may ask for a meeting of the firm's Industrial Relations Manager and the Union's Grievance Committee at which, hopefully, the matter will be resolved. If this meeting fails to achieve a decision acceptable to both sides, arrangements are made for an arbitrator or an arbitration board to settle the matter.

Arbitration

An arbitrator is an outside person (often a retired judge or a professor), acceptable to both labour and management, who will listen to the viewpoints of management and the union, ask questions, and finally make a decision. Arbitration is the making of a decision which is legally binding on both parties. The provincial Labour Relations Acts make compulsory the inclusion of an arbitration provision in all labour contracts. The cost of the arbitrator is usually shared equally by management and the union. While the collective agreement is in force, a strike or lockout is illegal. However, illegal or "wildcat" strikes do sometimes occur, with or without the tacit support of the union.

Labour's Methods

A *strike* is the temporary refusal of a firm's employees to continue working. Usually the employees leave the plant (hence the term *walkout*). In other cases, the workers remain at their jobs but refuse to work (the *sitdown strike*), or continue to work but at a much slower pace (the *go-slow strike*). A slow-down is sometimes achieved when the employees observe many of the detailed rules governing their work which they had previously ignored. This is called a *work-to-rule movement*. A *wildcat strike* takes place when the workers go on strike without the official consent of the union. A *jurisdictional strike* backs up a union's attempts to force management to recognize it instead of another union as the representative of the employees.

In some provinces, certain types of employees, such as police officers, firefighters, and hospital workers, are forbidden the right to strike, because of the essential nature of their work.

The purpose of a strike is to halt or slow down production, thereby causing the employer financial loss. This loss is caused by the failure of the firm to produce and sell sufficient goods to cover its fixed costs of production (rent, office staff, interest charges, and so on). Also, as long as production is halted, the employer is losing the opportunity to earn a profit.

For a strike to be successful, the labour union must be able to stop production. Sometimes the union may fail to do this. As a result, the union continues to weaken itself financially by paying strike pay to its members, without moving any closer to a favourable settlement of the dispute. And the individual members receive only strike pay, usually on a very limited basis, instead of their regular, much higher wages.

The employer is sometimes able to continue production by using newly hired workers and non-union personnel within the firm—for example, office staff—to perform the jobs vacated by the striking employees. The union, to prevent this,

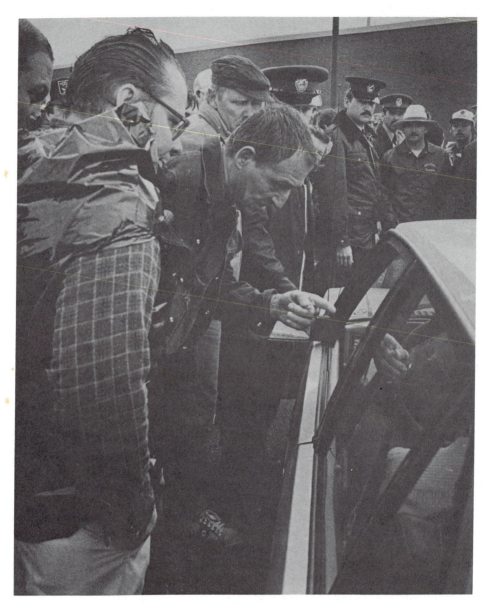

Courtesy *Oakville Beaver*

can *picket* the firm. This means placing union members at the entrances to the firm with signs to indicate to the public why they are on strike and to discourage persons (the so-called "scabs") from taking employment there. Pickets are not allowed physically to obstruct workers entering and leaving the plant; if they do so, they can be charged with assault by the police.

When on strike, a labour union may also be able to strengthen its position by enlisting the support of other unions. This help may take various forms: financial assistance; manpower assistance—for example, organizers, pickets, and canvassers; the refusal of other unions to handle materials and goods going to, or coming from, the struck firm; and the arrangement of *sympathy strikes*, whereby the unions in neighbouring or related firms bring their members out on strike in sympathy with the existing strikers. Another labour weapon, although illegal, is *sabotage*. This is the malicious destruction of the employer's property. Such action is open to criminal as well as civil charges.

Sometimes a union will try to establish a *boycott*. This is the refusal by union members, and any other persons who can be persuaded, to buy the goods of the firm whose employees are on strike. This is not a very effective weapon, since demand is usually widespread.

Management's Methods

Management may use various means to prevent a union from becoming the certified bargaining agent of its employees or to oppose its power once it has become certified.

To prevent the "unionization" of a plant, many firms offer better pay and other conditions of employment than prevail in neighbouring union firms. This is, to some extent, a hollow victory, since labour costs have been increased to keep the union out. Management may also dismiss or transfer workers who are known members or sympathizers of the union. This and other actions, called *unfair labour practices*, are illegal under the Labour Relations Act once the union has applied for certification. Also, employers may keep an informal *blacklist* of such persons to prevent them from gaining employment.

A more drastic measure used by management is to lock out its workers. In a *lockout*, the employer refuses to allow the workers to enter the plant to do their jobs. An extreme example of this is displayed when the owner of a plant closes a plant permanently rather than allow it to be unionized. A lockout, whether temporary or permanent, means, of course, considerable financial loss to the owner.

Another weapon that management may use is the *injunction*. This is a court order forbidding the persons to whom it is directed from carrying on a certain activity. Formerly, court orders were used to forbid a wide variety of union activities. Nowadays their use appears to be restricted to persons damaging the employer's property, committing acts of violence, trespassing, and engaging in acts of intimidation—for example, mass picketing. An injunction may be granted if the court is convinced that damage will otherwise be done to the employer's property and that this damage could not be compensated for by a monetary award. An injunction can also be used against any conspiracy to commit personal injury, to induce a breach of contract, or to interfere with contractual relations. The injunction carries the weight of the law behind it.

The use of the injunction has been strongly criticized by labour unions on the grounds that by limiting pickets, for example, a strike is made ineffective. In other words, they consider that the use of the injunction confers an unfair bargaining advantage on the employer.

KEY TERMS

Labour union
Craft union
Industrial union
International union
National union
Independent local organization
Directly chartered local union
Union local
Shop steward
Labour council
Labour federation
Canadian Labour Congress
Certification
Collective bargaining
Collective agreement
Conciliation
Union finances
Union security

Rand formula
Closed shop
Union shop
Open shop
Grievance
Grievance procedure
Arbitration
Strike
Jurisdictional strike
Wildcat strike
Picketing
Sympathy strike
Sabotage
Boycott
Unfair labour practices
Blacklist
Lockout
Injunction

REVIEW QUESTIONS

1. Distinguish between a craft union and an industrial union. Explain the reason for the existence of these two types of union.
2. What is (a) a local union, (b) a national union, and (c) an international union?
3. Discuss how and why union membership has grown in Canada.
4. Explain the influence of British and U.S. labour unions in the development of the labour union movement in Canada.
5. Explain and discuss the reasons why workers join unions.
6. Explain how a typical union local might be organized.
7. Explain the role of (a) a labour council, (b) a labour federation, and (c) the Canadian Labour Congress.
8. Discuss the finances of a union local from the viewpoint of (a) revenue and (b) expenditures.

9. With regard to union security, distinguish between (a) a closed shop, (b) a union shop, and (c) an open shop.
10. "Unions are no longer necessary." Discuss.
11. Explain the procedure by which a union becomes certified as the bargaining agent for a group of workers.
12. What is meant by collective bargaining? Why is this desirable, from the employee's point of view?
13. What is a grievance? Outline a typical grievance procedure in a manufacturing firm.
14. What methods can labour use to achieve its aims, such as better pay and better working conditions?
15. How can management prevent its workers from becoming unionized?
16. What methods can management use to enforce its own point of view in its dealings with labour unions?

CASE PROBLEM

FROST ELECTRICAL CO. LTD.
Handling employee grievances

The Frost Electrical Co. Ltd. is a small- to medium-size manufacturing firm, with 133 plant workers producing stove switches, oven controls, pilot lights, convenience outlets, and electronic switches.

The production of electronic switches involves several different assembly operations, after which the finished switch is inspected to make sure that it meets the required engineering specifications. The different operations, including inspection, are performed by female employees, each of whom has the same grade of job classification.

Mrs. Evelyn Jones, one of the employees doing the inspection work, has complained for some time that her job demands greater mental concentration and personal reliability than any of the assembly operations and that it should therefore be more highly paid.

Dave Brampton, her shop steward, has suggested that she apply, as a grievance, to have the job reclassified to a higher grade.

The grievance procedure set out in the union contract is as follows:

ARTICLE XV

GRIEVANCE PROCEDURE

1. It is the mutual desire of the parties hereto that complaints of employees shall be adjusted as quickly as possible. If an employee has a complaint, he shall submit it to his Foreman within five (5) full working days after the circumstances giving rise to the complaint have occurred. He may do this personally, with or without his Zone Representative present, or he may request the Zone Representative to do it for him. The employee will be present when the matter is discussed by the Zone Representative and the Foreman, if either party so requests. The Foreman's verbal decision shall be given within three (3) working days from the day the complaint was first presented to him.

It is understood that an employee has no grievance until he has first given the Foreman the opportunity of adjusting his complaint. If the employee's complaint is not settled and arises from a dispute over the interpretation, application, administration, or alleged violation of this Agreement, it may be taken up as a grievance within three (3) full working days after receiving the Foreman's decision, in the following manner and sequences:

Step No. 1—The employee, who may request the assistance of his Zone Representative, will present his grievance in writing to his Foreman. The grievance shall be signed by the employee and shall set out the nature of the grievance, the remedy sought and the section or sections of the Agreement allegedly violated. The decision of the Foreman shall be rendered in writing within three (3) full working days following presentation of the written grievance.

Failing settlement, then:

Step No. 2—Within three (3) full working days following the decision under Step No. 1, the Zone Representative shall present the written grievance to the employee's General Foreman (or the person in the equivalent position). A meeting will then be held within three (3) full working days following the presentation of the grievance in this step between the employee, the Zone Representative, the employee's General Foreman, or the person in the equivalent position and the Industrial Relations Manager. The decision of the General Foreman shall be given in writing within three (3) full working days following such meeting.

Failing settlement, then:

Step No. 3—The written grievance shall be submitted by the Zone Representative to the Union Grievance Committee which shall within five (5) full working days following the decision under Step No. 2, submit it to the Factory Manager (or his designated representative) and a meeting shall be held within five (5) full working days after his receipt of the written grievance, between the Grievance Committee and the Factory Manager and/or any other person(s) designated by him. An International Representative of the Union may be present at such meeting. The decision of the Factory Manager shall be given in writing within five (5) full working days following such meeting.

2. Failing settlement under Step No. 3 of any grievance arising from the interpretation, application, administration, or alleged violation of this Agreement, including any question as to whether a matter is arbitrable, such grievance may be taken to Arbitration by either party by delivering to the other party, within ten (10) full working days after the final decision under Step No. 3, a written request for Arbitration which shall name a nominee.

The conciliation procedure was set in motion to settle the dispute. But at each step management argued that the job was already fairly evaluated and correctly classified.

The part of the labour contract relating to job evaluation was as follows:

ARTICLE XXII
JOB EVALUATION AND CLASSIFICATION

1. The responsibility for the evaluation of any work will continue to be vested in the Company and made on the basis of the Company job evaluation plan. It is the purpose of the job evaluation plan to determine classifications relative to wage structure. This is accomplished by careful analysis of each job based on various factors which are usually present to some degree in every job.

2. It is the responsibility of the Company to see that each new job is evaluated and classified. The Union will be given a copy of the evaluation upon its being placed into effect. If the Union disagrees with the new evaluation, the matter may be referred to Step No. 2 of the Grievance Procedure within ten (10) working days.

3. In the case of requests for re-evaluation of existing jobs which have changed since the date of

this Agreement, the request may be made by an employee working on such a job by signing a "Request for Analysis Form" and delivering it to his Foreman.

4. (a) When an employee regularly performs work in jobs of different labour grades during the normal course of his work, he will be classified in the job having the highest labour grade, providing the work performed on the job meets the requirements as described by the evaluation and providing that he has spent fifty (50) per cent or more of his time during the preceding three (3) months on the highest paid job.

Where full-time occupation of another job classification is clearly of short duration (three months or less) re-classification will not be made.

(b) In the case of a new employee who completes his probationary period, the Company shall pay the job rate provided the employee is satisfactorily performing the full requirements of the job. However, an employee hired for a labour Grade XI job but started at the labour Grade XII rate shall, after completion of his probationary period, be paid the job low for labour Grade XII for sixty (60) working days or less before receiving the rate for the job.

As no agreement could be reached between management and union at any one of the steps in the grievance procedure, the dispute was eventually referred to arbitration according to Article XVI of the labour contract.

ARTICLE XVI
ARBITRATION

1. When either party requests that a grievance be submitted to Arbitration as provided in Article XV Grievance Procedure, the party receiving such a timely request, which nominates an arbitrator, shall within five (5) days thereafter, also nominate an arbitrator; provided, however, that if such party fails to nominate an arbitrator as herein required, the Minister of Labour for the Province of Ontario shall have power to make such appointment upon the application thereto by the party invoking the Arbitration Procedure. The two arbitrators so nominated shall promptly confer and attempt to settle the grievance. Failing settlement they shall within five (5) days after such conference attempt to settle by agreement a chairman of the Arbitration Board. If they are unable to agree upon such a Chairman within such period, they shall then request the Minister of Labour for the Province of Ontario to select an impartial chairman, provided that the chairman shall be selected from other than the Civil Service and shall be chosen having regard to his impartiality, his qualifications in interpreting collective bargaining agreements and his familiarity with the industry. If the case involves job evaluation, the Chairman shall be experienced in the relevant techniques. In such cases the Arbitration Board shall be limited to a determination of whether or not the evaluation in dispute was arrived at by a consistent application of the Plan. It shall not then have the power to establish a new evaluation. If it determines that this has been done, the matter shall be referred to the Company for appropriate action. No person may be appointed as an arbitrator who has, prior to his appointment, been involved in an attempt to settle the grievance.

2. No matter may be submitted to arbitration which has not been properly carried through the required steps of the Grievance Procedure.

3. The Arbitration Board shall not have jurisdiction to amend or add to any of the provisions of this agreement, nor to substitute any new provisions in lieu thereof, nor to give any decision inconsistent with the terms and provisions of this Agreement.

4. The proceedings of the Arbitration Board will be expedited by the parties hereto and the decision of the majority of such Board will be final and binding upon the parties thereto.

5. Each of the parties hereto will bear the expenses of the Arbitrator appointed by it, and the parties will jointly bear the expenses of the Chairman of the Arbitration Board.

Assignment
1. What is job evaluation? How is it carried out? What purpose does it serve?
2. Summarize the grievance procedure for this firm. What is the purpose of this procedure?
3. How is the arbitration board selected? What facts should it consider in making its award? What award would you make?

UNIT 16.2: LABOUR LEGISLATION

Historically, labour has proven to be the weaker party when dealing with management. Only in recent years, with the growth of labour unions and professional associations, has labour reached more equal terms. To protect labour in its relations with management, the federal and provincial governments have passed various Acts to supplement the common law duties of the employer.

Common Law Duties of the Employer

Under Common Law, the traditional system of law brought from England, the employer has a number of duties. These include the duty to:
1. honour any contract entered into with the employee or with the union that represents him or her;
2. provide a safe place in which the employee can work;
3. employ reasonably competent and careful fellow employees;
4. give an employee reasonable notice of dismissal or wages in lieu thereof—unless dismissal is for dishonesty, wilful disobedience, incompetence, or permanent disability or illness; and
5. pay, in the absence of an express contract of employment, the wages customary for the job in that area. (This common law obligation has now been replaced by the statute law requirement to pay the minimum wage decreed for a particular occupation in a particular area.)

Common Law Duties of the Employee

The employee, in turn, has various duties towards his or her employer. Thus he or she must: obey lawful orders; exercise care and skill in the job; show good faith and avoid any conflict of interest; account to the employer for any monies, materials, or other valuables involved in the job; and safeguard any confidential information.

Labour Jurisdiction

The Constitution Act, 1867, which allocated legislative power between the federal parliament of Canada and the provincial legislatures, gave to the provinces the right to enact laws with regard to "property and civil rights" and, with some exceptions, "local works and undertakings." As a result, most labour legislation in Canada is provincial. The federal government has authority only over: (a) industries under its jurisdiction; (b) works declared by parliament to be for the general advantage of Canada or of two or more provinces; (c) workers employed under federal government works contracts and on works partly financed by federal government funds; and (d) matters handed over to it by the provincial governments, such as unemployment insurance and pensions.

Canada Labour Code (Federal.)

In July 1971 a comprehensive federal labour statute, the *Canada Labour Code*, came into force, replacing various individual labour statutes.

The Code applies to all employees in:
(a) air transport, aircraft and airports;
(b) radio and television broadcasting;
(c) banks;
(d) federal Crown Corporations (e.g., the St. Lawrence Seaway Authority);
(e) all extra-provincial shipping and services connected thereto (such as longshoring and stevedoring);
(f) works or undertakings connecting one province with another or with another country, such as rail, bus, or truck services, ferries, tunnels, bridges, canals, pipelines, telegraph, telephone and cable systems; and
(g) defined operations of specific works that have been declared to be for the general advantage of Canada or of two or more provinces, such as flour, feed and seed cleaning mills, feed warehouses, grain elevators, and uranium mining and processing.

The Canada Labour Code as originally enacted consisted of five parts, dealing in turn with: fair employment practices; female employees' equal pay; labour standards; safety of employees; and industrial relations. However, on March 1, 1978, Parts 1 and 2 were repealed and replaced by the relevant provisions of the Canadian Human Rights Act.

Labour Standards. The Code requires that employers: (a) limit the hours of work of employees to a standard maximum of 8 per day and 40 per week; (b) pay one and one-half times the regular rate of wages for any hours worked in excess of the standard ones, such overtime work to be permitted only with special Ministry of Labour authorization and only up to a maximum of 8 per week; (c) pay a government-specified minimum hourly wage for persons aged 17 and over, and another government-specified minimum hourly wage for persons under 17; (d) provide each employee with a minimum of two weeks vacation with vacation pay (4 per cent of the employee's annual wages) after every completed year of employment or, should the employee leave before the year is over, pay him or her the vacation pay for the completed portion of the year of employment; and (e) provide each employee a holiday with pay on each of the general holidays (New Year's Day, Good Friday, Victoria Day, Dominion Day, Labour Day, Thanksgiving Day, Remembrance Day, Christmas Day and Boxing Day) falling within his or her period of employment.

Safety of Employees. The Code tries to ensure safe working conditions for all employees in industries and undertakings under federal jurisdiction by: (a) specifying all the elements of a complete industrial safety program and the general obligation of employers and employees to perform their duties in a safe manner; (b) authorizing regulations to deal with problems of occupational safety; (c) authorizing the use of advisory committees and special task forces to assist in developing the industrial safety program, to be accompanied by continuous consultation among federal and provincial government departments, industry, and organized labour; (d) providing for research into causes and prevention of accidents; (e) authorizing an extended program of safety education; and (f) providing for regional safety officers and federally authorized provincial inspectors to enforce the Code.

Industrial Relations. The Canada Labour Code regulates industrial relations in industries under federal jurisdiction. The Code recognizes the right of employees to organize and bargain collectively through trade unions. However, both employers and employees are required to bargain in good faith and to include in the labour contract a provision for the arbitration of disputes. The Code prohibits unfair labour practices (such as discrimination and coercion) by employers and employees, and provides for govenment conciliation officers or boards to help mediate differences between the two parties in contract negotiations. The administration of Part Five of the code is the responsibility of the Federal Minister of Labour. Part of the minister's authority—for example, the provisions covering the certification of bargaining agents—has been delegated to the Canada Labour Relations Board.

Industries Under Federal Contract

Fair Wages Policy. Under the Fair Wages and Hours of Labour Act, the wages paid to persons employed on federal construction contracts must be those current in the area for the type of work, and certainly no less than those prescribed in Part Three of the Canada Labour Code. Also, the standard work hours are stipulated at 8 per day and 40 per week. Any hours worked in excess of these must be with the agreement of the employee and be paid at one and one-half times the normal rate.

By Order-in-Council PC 1954-2029, wages and hours of work of suppliers of equipment and materials under federal contract are controlled as follows: wages must be current, or fair and reasonable, but in no event less than the minimum wage set by the provincial government for that province; and the hours of work must be those customary, or fair and reasonable, in the area. The Order-in-Council also prohibits such firms from refusing employment to a person because of race, nationality, colour, or religion.

Unemployment Insurance

By the terms of the Unemployment Insurance Act, all regular members of the labour force in Canada are compulsorily insured against loss of wages or salaries through unemployment. The main exceptions are the self-employed, workers over 65 years of age, and some part-time workers. Both employers and employees pay contributions, with the employer rate being somewhat larger than the employee rate. The government also makes a contribution. There is no fund and contributions are adjusted yearly. Coverage, contributions, and benefit entitlement cease at age 65. The plan is administered by the Canada Employment and Immigration Commission (CEIC).

Under the Act, a person can draw unemployment benefits up to a maximum number of weeks, as long as he or she has made the required contributions and meets certain conditions of being available, capable, and searching for work. Persons who have made contributions for a longer period of time or more weeks can claim a wider range of benefits including: prepayment of three weeks of regular benefit for work-shortage layoffs; benefit payments when the interruption of earnings was caused by illness or pregnancy; and three weeks retirement benefit for older workers.

Canada Pension Plan

Every province except Quebec, which has its own comparable pension plan, participates in a federally run pension plan. This plan, the Canada Pension Plan, came into effect in 1965 and covers, on a compulsory basis, practically every employee between the ages of 18 and 70, whatever his or her occupation. It is financed by equal contributions from employee and employer. A person is eligible for a pension at age 65.

The plan provides the following benefits: a retirement pension; a disability pension; benefits for the children of disabled employees; a widow's pension; benefits for the children of a deceased employee; benefits for disabled widowers; and a lump sum payment to a deceased employee's estate.

These benefits are portable. This means that if a person changes his or her job or place of residence, the pension rights remain the same. With a private plan, an employee would frequently lose all or part of an employer's contribution if he or she left the job.

Provincial Labour Legislation

By virtue of their constitutional power, the provincial legislatures have enacted a large number of labour laws, many of which are frequently being revised.[1] The most important of these provincial labour laws are as follows:

Minimum Wage Rates. All the provinces have legislation under which a provincial government board sets minimum wage rates, usually for both sexes, for industries in the province. In Ontario, for example, the statute that sets minimum standards in this and other areas is the *Employment Standards Act*. Such legislation is intended to ensure that a minimum standard of living is enjoyed

---

[1] For detailed current information, see *Labour Standards in Canada*, published annually by the Canada Department of Labour.

by all employees and their families. For a few types of industrial employment, a higher minimum wage may be set under industrial standards laws. Provincially set minimum wage rates now cover almost all employment. Exceptions include farm labour and domestic service in certain provinces.

Weekly Rest-Day. Six provinces (Alberta, British Columbia, Manitoba, New Brunswick, Quebec, and Saskatchewan) provide for a weekly rest-day, if possible Sunday, for most employees. In the other provinces, similar legislation is directed at specific groups of employees.

Limited Working Hours. The number of hours of work which an employer may demand from an employee are limited by provincial statute in most provinces. Many employees do, however, work more than this on a voluntary basis. In all provinces, they must be paid at one and one-half times the regular or minimum hourly rate. In many provinces, hours of work and wage rates in particular industries are regulated under the various Industrial Standards Acts or, in Quebec, under the Quebec Collective Agreement Act. These Acts encourage conferences of employers and employees to discuss and recommend minimum wages and maximum hours of work for employees in their industries.

Annual Vacations With Pay. All the provinces have legislation providing for compulsory paid vacations for employees in most industries. Employees not covered include farm workers in all provinces except Newfoundland and domestic servants in all except Newfoundland, Saskatchewan, and Prince Edward Island. Vacation pay stamps are used in some provinces. Vacation requirements after a year of service are usually two weeks. In Saskatchewan, three weeks paid vacation is required, with four weeks after five years of service.

Minimum Age for Employment. Every province has a set minimum age below which a person may not be employed. In Ontario, for example, this limit is fifteen for factory work, eighteen for mining below ground, and fourteen for work in shops or restaurants. Persons under sixteen may not, however, work in Ontario during school hours (8 a.m. to 5 p.m.) unless they have been granted special permission or they are on school holidays.

Fair Employment Practices. All provinces prohibit any discrimination by employer and labour union against new employees and members by reason of race, colour, nationality, or religion. Certain provinces also prohibit discrimination on the grounds of age and sex. The Human Rights Acts expressly prohibit the publication of advertisements, use of application forms, and the making of inquiries in connection with the hiring of an employee which express or imply discrimination on any of the forbidden grounds.

Equal Pay. Provincial legislation throughout Canada tries to ensure equal pay for men and women. British Columbia, New Brunswick, Nova Scotia, Ontario, and Prince Edward Island prohibit any discrimination as to rates of pay between men and women doing the same work. In Alberta and Manitoba the statutes refer to identical or substantially identical work in the same establishment. The Saskatchewan Act refers to work of comparable character.

Apprenticeship. Some provinces require that certain tradesmen—for example, plumbers, carpenters, electricians, and barbers—undergo a period of apprenticeship training and pass a test before being allowed to offer their services as qualified craftsmen.

Notice of Dismissal. In most provinces an employer is required by law to give written notice of termination of employment in cases of individual dismissal. In some provinces, notice is also required for group dismissal. In Quebec, notice must also be given in case of mass lay-off.

Health and Safety. Most provinces have a Factory or Industrial Safety Act to help protect the health and safety of workers in factories and other workplaces. Matters covered include sanitation, heating, lighting, ventilation, and the guarding of dangerous machinery. There are also provincial laws regulating the design, construction, installation, and operation of mechanical equipment such as boilers and pressure vessels, elevators and lifts, and electrical installations; the use of gas and oil-burning equipment and radiation-producing equipment, such as laser sources; and the standards of qualification for workers who install, operate, or service such equipment. In Ontario, as one provincial example, the *Occupational Health and Safety Act* strictly regulates the health and safety of employees in the workplace.

Workers' Compensation. In every province, a Workers' Compensation Act provides for the establishment of a fund, financed solely by employers, to pay compensation to an employee for industrial injury or disablement. An employee does not have to prove negligence on the part of his or her employer to obtain compensation. On the other hand, compensation may be withheld if the accident arose from the employee's gross misconduct. If an employee is disabled, he or she may receive all necessary medical care and hospitalization, cash payments to compensate for loss of wages, a life pension for permanent disability, and rehabilitation services. If an employee dies as the result of an industrial accident or disease, the spouse will receive a monthly pension, a special lump payment, an allowance for funeral expenses, and a monthly allowance for each child below a certain age limit.

General Holidays. Alberta, British Columbia, Manitoba, Nova Scotia, Ontario, and Saskatchewan have legislation governing paid general holidays. In these provinces, an employee must receive regular pay even though he or she does not work; if he or she does work, special overtime rates must be paid. The number of holidays named varies from seven to nine. The provisions for payment also vary slightly between provinces. In Ontario, the seven public holidays are New Year's Day, Good Friday, Victoria Day, Dominion Day, Labour Day,

Thanksgiving Day, and Christmas Day. The two additional holidays in, for example, Saskatchewan are Remembrance Day and Saskatchewan Day.

KEY TERMS

Common law rights	Weekly rest-day
Labour jurisdiction	Limited working hours
Canada Labour Code	Annual vacation with pay
Labour standards	Minimum age
Safety of employees	Fair employment practices
Industrial relations	Equal pay
Industries under federal contract	Apprenticeship
Unemployment insurance	Notice of dismissal
Canada Pension Plan	Accident prevention
Provincial labour legislation	Workers' Compensation
Minimum wage rates	General holidays

REVIEW QUESTIONS

1. What are the common law rights of an employee?
2. Explain how and why responsibility for labour legislation in Canada is divided between the federal and provincial governments.
3. What is the Canada Labour Code?
4. Explain how Canada's unemployment insurance plan operates. Evaluate its effectiveness.
5. Describe briefly the nature and purpose of the Canada Pension Plan.
6. Describe three provincial labour laws.
7. What is Workers' Compensation?

PART H
SMALL BUSINESS

In this part of the book, we consider the possibility of owning and operating a small business as a full-time or part-time source of income and employment.

CHAPTER 17
STARTING A SMALL BUSINESS

CHAPTER OBJECTIVES

☐ To indicate what is involved in starting and operating a small business.

☐ To explain how to prepare a small business plan for management and financing purposes.

☐ To outline the various sources of government and private assistance.

☐ To review the various "books" and other financial records required in a small business.

CHAPTER OUTLINE

17.1 Basic Requirements
17.2 Preparing a Business Plan
17.3 Government Assistance
17.4 Basic Business Records

UNIT 17.1: BASIC REQUIREMENTS

The vast majority of business firms in Canada are quite small in size, whatever the criterion used—number of employees, value of assets, amount of business income, or management by owner. These small business firms (organized as sole proprietorships, partnerships, or private business corporations) are particularly widespread in the farming, wholesaling, retailing, and service industries. They now number over one million and employ over 40 per cent of the labour force.

In fact, an increasingly large percentage of the civilian labour force is becoming employed in the service industries, where the benefits of large-scale production and marketing are not so evident as in manufacturing, mining, or electrical power production and where the small business firm can consequently continue to flourish. Examples of such businesses include retail stores, hair stylists, beauty parlours, lawyers, doctors, accountants, service stations, funeral parlours, laundromats, housebuilders, electricians, plumbers, advertising agencies, architects, and engineering consultants.

The continued prosperity of the small business firm is considered essential for Canada's economy. This is because such firms provide: (a) important services to consumers, business firms, and governments; (b) a great deal of employment and income in every community, large and small; and (c) the starting point and training ground for enterprising businesspersons (or "entrepreneurs") who will later expand their small firms into large businesses.

Pros and Cons of Small Business Ownership

Frank Addison, a former assistant purchasing manager with Levy Home Furnishings Ltd. of Winnipeg, resigned his job two years ago to open his own furniture store in a new suburban shopping centre and, despite the long hours and large initial investment, has never looked back.

Donald Nelson, the former owner of an East Toronto hamburger franchise, bemoans not only the fact that he and his wife lost money from the day they opened up, but also (just as important to him) the sheer monotony of his experience of cooking and serving hamburgers day after endless day.

Assuming that a person has the right personal attributes (intelligence, determination, etc.) and the necessary business knowledge, should he or she attempt to establish and operate a small business?

The *advantages of small-business ownership* include: (a) personal challenge—the success or failure of the business depends mainly on the owner's efforts; (b) job satisfaction—you can see the results of your efforts; (c) independence, or the freedom of being one's own boss; (d) relatively high economic security, especially with a well-established business—you are not likely to fire yourself; (e) community status—you play an important and recognized role in the local community; and (f) the chance of an excellent income, if your business is successful.

The *disadvantages of small-business ownership* include: (a) the burden of responsibility for ensuring that the business continues to operate at a profit; (b) the constant need for solving problems and making decisions; (c) the irregularity of income in many small businesses; (d) the long hours of employment, particularly in the early stages; (e) the capital investment required; and (f) the risk of financial loss.

The decision to start one's own small business is obviously a personal one. It must take into account the previous factors but also a number of other ones that will vary from person to person. For example, whether a person has had sufficient experience in that line of business. Whether a person feels confident enough to be an owner. Whether a person has had any previous managerial experience. Whether a person wants to invest his or her savings in such a business. Whether a person has the financial and moral support of spouse or other family. Whether a person has another source of income that can be relied upon, if necessary, during the "teething" period of the new business. Whether a person has sufficient "drive" and desire to succeed that will carry him or her through the difficulties that will inevitably arise. And whether a person is really prepared to change his or her current lifestyle.

Small Business Opportunities

Consumers Distributing Ltd., recognizing that the old-time discount stores had moved up over the years into the ranks of the high-overhead retailers, set about giving what many customers wanted: a low-price, no-frills, wholesale-cum-retail service. Now, like many other former small businesses, it has grown right across Canada and become big business.

What Mr. and Mrs. Andrews overlooked when they purchased the motel last year was that a major new highway would soon divert holiday traffic away from the area.

The first step in establishing a successful small business is to identify a definite consumer need for goods or services and one that is not being satisfied by someone else. Thus, for example, to start a flower shop in a district that already has several good florists is to stack the odds against small-business success. Conversely, to start the only flower shop permitted in a new suburban shopping centre is to ensure a relatively large number of customers and a reasonable gross revenue. The problem may then be one of earning sufficient revenue to offset the relatively high shop rent. Usually, however, the monopoly location is worth the higher rent.

The need to ascertain the size of the potential market is crucial for any type of small business, whether it be retailing, services, manufacturing, exporting, or importing. And the inadequacy of the market is a major cause of small-business failures. Ability to anticipate a market (for example, for health foods or package tours) can, on the other hand, bring great success. Indeed, the small-businessperson's chief asset is often the ability to assess a business situation in a particular area and take advantage of it. As one example, Roy Thomson (later Lord Thomson) started his spectacular career as a radio and newspaper magnate in Canada and abroad by setting up a small radio station in Northern Ontario in the 1930s when he found that no one would buy the radios that he was trying to sell, for the simple reason that there was nothing to listen to.

It is not easy to determine the extent of the market for a new small business. There is inevitably a high degree of uncertainty—even though the size of the permanent and commuter population, pedestrian traffic patterns, amount of competition, prices charged by competitors, and other factors are investigated. However, it is foolish to open a new business interest without undertaking such an investigation, however sketchy the results, as undue optimism can lead to much headache and grief, including the loss of thousands of dollars. Often a person's keen desire to open a particular type of business (for example, a dress shop) will tend to blind him or her to the fact that market opportunities in a particular location are better suited to a different type of enterprise.

Business Knowledge

We have already suggested some of the most important personal attributes of the successful small-business owner. However, such attributes must be bolstered by

Courtesy *Oakville Beaver*

sound business knowledge which may often be acquired as one goes along. Ideally, the small business owner should have an understanding and appreciation of the management of all the facets (marketing, production, and finance) of the chosen line of business, as well as a knowledge of general management practice. However, a person who is strong in one key aspect (for example, marketing) can get competent full- or part-time help in the other aspects of this business, either on a partnership, employee, or fee basis. An example is the use by the small-business owner of an accountant or lawyer, on a part-time basis, perhaps to advise on tax planning or incorporation.

Business management tools that can be of use to the small-business owner include the following:

1. *Break-even analysis.* This is an estimate (see Unit 12.2) of the required volume of sales for a business to cover its fixed and operating costs.
2. *Cash-flow analysis.* This is a forecast (see Unit 13.1) of the expected flow of cash into and out of a business to reveal the expected weekly or monthly cash balance and the adequacy of available funds.
3. *Ratio analysis.* This is an analysis (see Unit 13.1) of the relationship between major variables of a business such as sales, inventory, profit, capital, and assets, to reveal profitability and liquidity. The most commonly used profitability ratios are percentage growth in sales, return on total capital, return on equity capital, gross and net profit margin on sales, and inventory turnover. The most popular liquidity ratios are the current ratio, the quick asset ratio, and the debt ratio. All together, they provide useful yardsticks against which the small-business owner can measure the efficiency of his or her operations.

Possibly the soundest way of acquiring the necessary knowledge to run a small business successfully is: (a) to work in that line of business as an employee and learn as much as possible about all its problems; and (b) study management and other business techniques from business books and courses and from practising businesspeople. Nowadays, since most aspiring businesspersons usually seek a college or university education first (often as a form of personal career insurance), the chance to acquire actual business experience is delayed until their early twenties. There is nothing, however, to prevent a person beginning his or her small-business career directly after high school or while working at a full-time job.

A New Business Versus An Established One

One of the first major decisions that the prospective small-business owner must make is whether to (a) start a new business or (b) buy an established one.

The *possible advantages of starting a new business* include: (a) a smaller capital investment—since no goodwill (that is, the firm's established reputation) has to be purchased; (b) greater freedom to choose one's location, employees, store or plant layout, type of goods, equipment and production, marketing, and other techniques; and (c) the large financial reward that comes from providing a product or service which was not supplied previously, or was not available in the quality required. The *possible disadvantages* include: (a) the lack of an established clientele and the possibly overoptimistic assessment of potential sales; (b) the lack of experienced staff; (c) lack of properly equipped premises; and (d) lack of established suppliers and sources of financing.

The *possible advantages of buying an established business* include: (a) a proven earnings record, reflecting good location, good products or services, and other factors; (b) less financial risk because of the already established clientele; and (c) avoidance of the headaches involved in starting a business from scratch. The *possible disadvantages* include: (a) the larger investment involved through purchase of goodwill that would otherwise have to be gradually built up in a new business; (b) the risk of buying a business whose earnings capacity may suffer a decline—for example, because of the departure of the former owner, new competition, or changing shopping habits; (c) the risk of paying more than the business is actually worth; (d) the possible inheritance of inefficient equipment, methods, or staff, or of outdated stock.

Obviously, there is no pat answer as to the relative merits of starting a new business or buying an established one. Like many other decisions, it is one that the prospective small-business owner must make in the light of actual circumstances.

If the decision is made to buy an existing business, the person is then faced with the problem of finding one that is for sale at a realistic price. Here he or she can refer to the Business Opportunities section of the classified newspaper advertisements, to commercial real estate advertisements, or to word-of-mouth news within the community.

It is not easy to assess the market value of a going business. A person may need the professional help of a business realtor, accountant, or lawyer. Past financial statements should be checked for several years. The actual and potential profitability of the business should be critically reviewed not only by examining sales records, etc., but also by talking with knowledgeable local persons, including customers of the business. Any buildings and equipment should be professionally appraised. The sale price should bear a realistic relationship to the net physical assets and the projected net income stream. Also a vital factor affecting a purchase decision would be the proposed terms of payment. Finally, it is always useful to know, if possible, the real reason why the business is being sold.

Franchises

Since World War II, many persons have begun their small-business careers by entering into a franchise agreement. *Franchising* is a system of retailing goods and services whereby small independently owned businesses (the *franchisees*) are given the right by a large national or multinational firm (the *franchisor*) to use the franchisor's name and the other symbols (including design of building) that characterize its operations.

The individual businessperson, or group of businesspeople, wishing to acquire a sales franchise must, of course, be willing to pay for this privilege. This involves: (a) payment of an initial fee, often amounting to many thousands of dollars, depending on how valuable, in terms of earning power, the franchise is considered to be; (b) payment of a continuing franchise fee, usually calculated as a percentage of gross sales; (c) agreement to purchase materials, supplies, and merchandise only from the franchisor or from suppliers specified by him or her; (d) agreement to maintain certain minimum standards of business performance, for example, store cleanliness; and (e) agreement to observe common operating procedures, for example, a uniform accounting system, and to make books available for inspection.

In return for these payments the franchisee receives: (a) the sole right to use the franchisor's name and symbols in a specified geographical area; (b) professional training and guidance in operating such a business—for example, McDonald's new franchisees receive a three-week training course at McDonald's "Hamburger University"; (c) head office advertising, including promotional campaigns; and (d) financial assistance, in certain companies.

Some franchise firms (for example, Canadian Tire, McDonald's, and Kentucky Fried Chicken) have been very successful in terms of sales and profits. As a result, the franchise fees are high and the list of applicants long. Other franchise operations (for example, in fish and chips and Mexican foods) have been spectacularly unsuccessful. In some cases, franchise operations have been used fraudulently to part the unwary, would-be small-businessperson from his or her hard-earned savings.

Guidelines for Small Business Success

There is quite a high casualty rate among small business firms—for hard work, by itself, is no guarantee of success. However, awareness of the principal causes of small business failure—whether it be the termination of the business or its continued operation at a very low rate of return on the money invested—can be of great value. To be forewarned is to be forearmed!

Good Prospects. In starting a business or purchasing an existing one, it is very easy for a person to let sentiment cloud his or her judgment. Often the aspiring small-business owner has such a strong desire to run his or her own business that impatience encourages the purchase of the first business that can be afforded, irrespective of whether its potential earning power is modest or even on the decline. Alternatively, the desire to run a particular type of business—for example, a florist, pet shop, or small grocery store—may blind an individual to the fact that competition from existing stores may be too fierce.

The only sound basis for starting a business is, in fact, a cool-headed appraisal of the demand for the product and the anticipated revenue of the business in relation to the investment of the businessperson's time and money. This appraisal must pay particular attention to the various factors (such as location) that will influence revenue in the years to come and to the various factors (such as labour and material requirements) that will influence expenses. Break-even analysis, however rudimentary, may avert disaster.

Sufficient Cash. Although a small business venture may eventually be highly profitable, it usually takes months (and in some cases even years) for the owner to build up a good clientele. If there is insufficient cash available in the business to pay for wages, materials, and supplies during this interim period before the firm breaks even, the owner may find that creditors will force him or her into bankruptcy. Even when the owner has started out with adequate cash, he or she may (through unwise financial policy) tie up far too much of it in fixed assets and slow-moving goods for resale. The owner's bank may or may not help out. A careful cash-flow analysis is essential, therefore, for the average small-businessperson—for only cash will pay the bills!

Careful Planning and Control. Some small-businesspersons still operate on a hit-or-miss basis: failing to plan ahead as to products to be stocked, goods to be made, or advertising to be done. They also fail to control carefully what is happening in their businesses, whether it be excessive wastage, theft, poor purchasing, or bad debt. The need to plan ahead is particularly important in an industry subject to rapid change—for example, electronics production. Unless new products are developed, existing sources of revenue may easily dry up. If control is lax, the profitability of the business will decline. At the worst, funds may be embezzled or the business may be forced to close down.

Decentralization of Authority. When a person starts a small business, he (or she) must in the early months and years make all the decisions. Consideration should, however, be given at a relatively early stage as to how the business will be managed if the owner is taken ill, wishes to go on vacation, or wishes to retire. This means that a person must consciously delegate authority while still active; for if the owner acts like a dictator within the firm, good subordinates will eventually leave, and the remaining employees will become overly dependent. As a result, when the owner is absent the business may well grind to a halt.

Canadian Federation of Independent Business (CFIB)

In August 1971, a political action group called the Canadian Federation of Independent Business was established in Canada to represent the interests of small and medium-sized Canadian businesses. Membership includes manufacturers, wholesalers, retailers, farmers, and professional persons. Head office is in Toronto with branch offices in other major Canadian cities.

The basic objectives of the CFIB are: (a) to promote and protect a system of free competitive enterprise in Canada and (b) to give the independent businessperson a greater voice in the formulation and alteration of laws governing business and the nation.

To achieve these objectives, the CFIB:

1. Researches and distributes the "Mandate," a monthly presentation of current national and provincial issues, to keep members informed of Federation action and legislative proposals, and through the Mandate ballot enables members to

express their opinion on legislation and public issues to their federal MPs and provincial government;

2. Maintains contact with all levels of government in order to influence legislation and government action affecting free enterprise;

3. Carries out a national publicity program through forums, speaking engagements, and the media promoting the views of members as expressed through the Mandate;

4. Carries out an education program in schools and colleges in order to acquaint students and teachers with the importance of independent Canadian enterprises in a free society;

5. Acts as a "watchdog" to prevent abuse of power by government agencies, public service monopolies, giant corporations, and trade unions.

6. Initiates debate on public issues such as social policy and industrial policy so that independent business is not cast in the negative role of reacting to or opposing government initiatives.

7. Conducts surveys of members in order to keep abreast of current problems affecting the free enterprise community.

KEY TERMS

Small business

Franchises

CFIB

REVIEW QUESTIONS

1. How would you define a small business firm? What is the nature and importance of small business in Canada?
2. What personal attributes are desirable for success as a small-business owner?
3. What are the possible advantages of small-business ownership?
4. What are the possible disadvantages of small-business ownership?
5. Why is salaried employment the goal of most college and university graduates?
6. What do you consider to be the most important initial steps in establishing a new small business?
7. What business knowledge do you consider to be necessary for the owner of a small business?
8. Why is it sometimes better to buy an established business than to start a new one?
9. What are the possible drawbacks of buying an established small business?
10. What are the advantages and disadvantages of a sales franchise as a means of starting one's own business?
11. Explain the role of the CFIB.

CASE PROBLEMS

JACK STODDART
Starting a small business

Jack Stoddart, the assistant manager of a branch furniture store, has been saving part of his salary and annual bonus for some years with a view to going into business for himself. Now, at age 28, he has accumulated $10,000 and believes that he can borrow a similar sum from his bank if his business venture appears sound. Although his retailing experience since leaving high school has been mainly in furniture, he feels that there is too much competition and too much capital involved in this line of business.

His fiancée, Mary, has suggested that, with his interest in animals, he might do well in starting up a pet shop, which could become the forerunner of a complete chain. However, his father, a long-time municipal government employee, has thrown cold water on the whole idea of his son's going into business for himself. "These days," his father has said, "the cards are stacked against you. Even if you can get satisfactory help, and your customers don't steal your goods, and you can afford to pay the rent for an indoor shopping-centre location, the government will take most of your profit. You'll end up working all hours for peanuts and Mary will end up having to get a job to support you and the kids." Naturally, this kind of advice didn't please Jack.

Assignment
1. How much capital would be required to open up a pet shop? Prepare an itemized list. How could capital needs be reduced?
2. What potential does a pet shop have for later expansion into a centrally owned chain-style operation?
3. How could a pet shop be developed into a franchise operation? What might would-be applicants obtain in exchange for a franchise fee?
4. What factors should Jack take into account in deciding whether to buy an existing pet shop or to start one from scratch?
5. What steps should Jack take before starting his own pet shop?
6. How valid, in your opinion, are the father's comments? What is the other side of the story?

THE LOG CABIN LTD.
Purchasing a sales franchise

Three friends (a doctor, a lawyer, and a former restaurant manager) have decided to invest time and money in establishing a franchise fast-food restaurant business. This business, incorporated as The Log Cabin Ltd., would be based on a simple and not unknown idea: to prepare a small range of popular foods on an assembly-line basis and to pass on part of the savings to customers in the form of lower prices. What would give this franchise food business a distinctive character would be the use of a cedar log building to house each food outlet. These buildings, which could be erected relatively cheaply, would, it is hoped, appeal to people who yearn subconsciously for the rustic life. Over each building would be a large red illuminated sign with the name The Log Cabin. Inside, these buildings, although traditionally decorated, would contain the most modern cooking and counter equipment.

As a customer-attracting special, the Log Cabin would feature an attractively priced, hot "Settler's Meat Pie" containing good-quality minced beef and liberally sprinkled, at the customer's discretion, with a specially formulated sauce. The menu would also include beefburger, cheeseburger, eggburger, hot dogs; grilled cheese, bacon and other sandwiches; french fries, onion rings; milk shake (3 flavours); coffee, tea, and milk; coke, root beer, and orange.

If the first pilot food outlet proved successful, The Log Cabin Ltd. would sell Log Cabin franchises for $20,000 each. The franchise holder would receive in return for his or her $20,000: the right to rent from The Log Cabin Ltd. for twenty-five years a building and land valued at approximately $100,000; the exclusive right to use the Log Cabin name and trade marks in a given area; an initial period of training at the pilot Log Cabin; food formulas; the management by Log Cabin Ltd. of all bookkeeping and advertising; periodic inspections; audit service; volume purchasing participation; and expert help in organization, purchasing, production control, and inventory control. Under the recommended system of inventory control, every food item is to be counted daily to reveal shortages, waste, or theft. The amount of labour used each day is also to be strictly controlled.

The franchise holder is required to deposit with the franchisor $5,000 as lease security. He or she must also purchase the equipment for the outlet from The Log Cabin Ltd. The individual can make a down payment of $10,000 and pay off a further $10,000 over ten years. He or she is also required to purchase the $6,000 sign with $1,000 down and the balance over five years, and he or she must pay a royalty equivalent to 5 per cent of the gross sales. To enable The Log Cabin Ltd. to control royalties, the franchisee agrees in the franchise agreement to submit weekly sales reports and monthly income statements to the firm. The franchise holder must also pay an advertising contribution equivalent to 1 per cent of gross sales. Working capital required at the start is $10,000.

The gross profit for each outlet on estimated sales for the first year of $100,000 is forecast at $50,000. This figure is obtained by subtracting from the sales revenue of $100,000 the cost of the food sold ($45,000) and of paper used, etc. ($5,000).

From the gross profit of $50,000 must come anticipated operating expenses, including royalty, advertising, interest and rent payments, of $20,000 and administrative expenses of $10,000, leaving a net profit before tax and before equipment and sign payments of $20,000.

Assignment
1. What would be a franchise holder's initial investment? After five years? After ten years?
2. What is the equity capital, borrowed capital, and total capital at the start of the business?

3. What would be the percentage rate of return on a franchisee's investment in the first year before and after income tax at, say, a flat 25% rate?
4. What would be the percentage rate of return on the total capital in the first year, before and after tax?
5. What would be the cash flow from this business in the first year?
6. Assuming that the cash flow remains the same, what would be the payback period?
7. What precautions would you take before investing your money? Have any major expenses been omitted?
8. Why would anyone in his or her right mind pay $20,000 for a Log Cabin franchise? What factors might cause the business to prove unsuccessful?
9. What financial commitments would you still have in such a case?

PROJECT

Choosing a Business

Clip a selection of current "business opportunities" from the appropriate page of a major newspaper.

Assume that you have sufficient funds to enter the business of your choice.

Assignment

1. Choose three business opportunities that you would like to investigate. Write down the reasons for your choice.
2. Prepare a list of questions that you would like answered about each of your chosen business opportunities before you invest any of your money and time.
3. What are the main problems that you foresee in operating your own business? How can you overcome them?

READINGS

Where There's Paint There's Profit for Students—and College Pro

Source: *The Financial Post*

"This is the bible," says Greig Clark, plunking down a dog-eared copy of *The Making of McDonald's*.

With a tightly tuned franchising system, Clark believes he can revolutionize the residential painting business as Ray Kroc did the restaurant business.

At 26, Clark is president and founder of College Pro Painters Ltd., which operates a network of franchises for individual students who set up their own College Pro painting outlets in their own home towns.

This summer, he expects 35 College Pro outlets in Ontario will paint 2,800-3,500 houses, for total sales of about $1.5 million.

And if Clark's five-year, pro forma statements are on target, by 1982 he will have 115 outlets operating in the U.S. and Canada, grossing $5 million. Longer term, he's penciled in expectations of $40 million-$50 million.

Which may sound like so much pie-in-the-sky, until you analyze Clark's recipe.

Look at it this way: most residential

painting is done during the summer. Clark himself started painting houses in his home town, Thunder Bay, Ont., in 1971, the summer of his first year at the University of Western Ontario. House painting has been a traditional source of employment for students, but Clark was quick to recognize that their amateur status has given student painters a poor reputation as fly-by-night quick-buck artists. On the other hand, professional painting firms charge a pretty penny for assured quality. Clark saw a gaping niche for "professional" student painters who could guarantee top-quality work at affordable student wages.

World Trip

Clark painted his way through a bachelor's degree in business administration, employing 14 painters in his third summer and earning more than $10,000. After graduation, his brother continued running the business while Greig took a trip around the world before joining the marketing staff at General Foods Ltd. in 1975.

Two years there gave Clark a rigorous schooling in business systems and in August, 1977, he left GF—taking with him about $50,000 accumulated from reinvested earnings and savings—to run College Pro Painters full time, opening 20 franchises in 1978.

Clark claims his company does work as good or better than any professional company, at 25%-30% less than prevailing rates. Customers receive a written, two-year guarantee on the job, and Clark's franchisees must agree to honor all outstanding guarantees in their areas.

Clark advertises on university campuses in the fall, and selects all managers by Dec. 1. By Christmas, successful applicants are given a 200-page manual that covers all facets of a successful painting business, including marketing, estimating, selling, production, personnel and accounting. Managers must attend two weekend training courses.

Once the franchise is ready to begin business in the spring, Clark provides $500-$1,000 start-up cash. College Pro head office helps the student manager to rent a van, hire student employees, do central record keeping for taxes and insurance, and to provide training aids to student painters, including Clark's own Super 8 training films on professional painting techniques.

College Pro takes $1.25 per labor hour in royalties, leaving the franchisee with $2.75 per hour. After overhead costs, the average student manager takes home $7,000-$8,000 for his summer's labors.

Paint is supplied to the customer at cost. Painting crews are paid an average of $4.50 per hour (workers $4, and foreman $5), and priced to the customer at $9 per hour. This compares to the $11-$12 per hour non-union professional painters command, and the $18 per hour charged by union contractors.

Apart from the occasional extravagance—such as his top-of-the-line BMW car—Clark says he leaves most of the profits in the business. Clark won't say what the company's current net worth is—only that he's doing "substantially better" than his $25,000 parting salary at General Foods. Within five years, he expects College Pro earnings to touch the $1-million mark.

"It's worth that now, if you measure it by a price/earnings multiple," he says.

In 1978, with 20 outlets, College Pro's central office would have pulled in roughly $100,000 in royalties. Out of this would come $15,000-$20,000 Clark advances to his franchises for initial start-up costs, including advertising; in addition, there would be salaries for a secretary and his vice-president Richard Wearing, and overhead for his three room suite of offices in midtown Toronto. Clark took out a bank loan to see him through a cash squeeze to finance this year's expansion, but he says his ratio of debt to cash in the business is less than 1:1.

Clark will test marketing areas in Western Canada and New York this year, and plans to test market regions in Quebec, Pennsylvania and Ohio in 1981.

"While 100,000 population is ideal," he says, "College Pro has shown an ability to capture at least 5% of any market it goes into because of the strength of its advertising and product."

Small business provides a secondary target group for College Pro. The company logged 10 contracts last year, ranging $5,000-$25,000 each.

Further down the road, Clark has identified several other services College Pro could provide home owners—window washing, pool painting and lawn care are only a few he sees students able to provide during the summer months.

Clark says he has ideas for a couple of other franchise businesses after College Pro is firmly established. And later, he says, he might go back to teach at university.

Politics? "Oh no," he says. "I'd burn myself out in five minutes. I'd take every criticism too seriously and personally."

But then, Greig Clark taking his houses "personally and seriously" is just what has, more than anything, accounted for College Pro Painters' success.

Assignment

1. What was the business opportunity that Greig Clark recognized?
2. How did he get started?
3. How does he operate his business?
4. Why has he franchised the business?
5. What is the target market for this business?
6. How successful has it been in penetrating the market and competing with other painting firms?
7. What directions may the firm take in the future? Would such a move make good business sense?

Franchises Attracting Growing Numbers of Would-be Private Businessmen

BY MARTIN DEWEY

Source: *The Globe and Mail*, Toronto

What does McDonald's Restaurants of Canada Ltd. have in common with St. Clair Paint and Wallpaper Ltd., Sheraton Ltd., Budget Rent-a-Car of Canada Ltd. and H. and R. Block?

They are all franchise operations, representatives of a U.S. mode of business that swept into Canada in earnest about 15 years ago and is now gaining ground almost as fast as Mr. Submarine can slap together a salami with tomato and lettuce.

"Franchise operations have grown 60 per cent in the past five years alone," according to Raj Dargan, new president of the Association of Canadian Franchisors. He is also director of marketing and franchising for Becker Milk Co. of Toronto, which operates 167 franchised convenience stores in Ontario.

He said there are at least 350 franchising companies in Canada with an estimated 17,000 outlets operating under such varied trade names as Holiday Inns, Shoppers Drug Mart, Dairy Queen, IGA, Century 21 and Manpower Temporary Services. He estimates that up to two-thirds are U.S. companies or branch operations of U.S. companies.

"Last year, franchising accounted for about $25-billion in retail sales, which was almost a third of total retail sales in Canada," he said.

"Food is the biggest growth area now. With more women coming into the work force, they don't have time to cook. There was a tremendous growth in pizza outlets and donut shops last year; I'd say it was 50 per cent. A year ago, we even started selling sandwiches and coffee in our own (Becker's) stores."

There are two basic types of franchise, Mr. Dargan said. The traditional type, which accounts for perhaps 60 per cent of the total, includes car dealerships, service stations, bottling plants and other businesses in which the franchisee is licenced to sell the franchisor's products, but often possesses a large measure of independence and also may handle other goods.

However, the major growth in recent years has been in the second type, called "business format franchises." These are turnkey operations in which the outlet is operated in a uniform manner set down by the franchising company.

"The franchisee takes over an operation already in place and he must rigidly adhere to standards of operation. Some companies don't franchise an outlet until the company itself has operated it for a few years and got rid of any problems. It's very bad for a franchisor if a dealer should fail."

That does not happen very often with established franchise companies, according to Mr. Dargan. "Because of the recession, the failure rate for new businesses in the United States was practically 80 per cent last year; for franchise operations it was a little over 1 per cent. In Canada it would be much the same."

For the privilege of running a relatively low-risk operation under an established trade name, an applicant must be prepared to pay royalties—with Becker's, it averages 3 per cent on gross sales—in addition to a franchise fee ranging from a few thousand dollars for a rug cleaning service to possibly millions of dollars for a hotel franchise.

Fees are rising fast, Mr. Dargan said. "Five years ago, you could get into a Becker's store for as little as $30,000. Now it's a minimum of at least $60,000."

Peter Bigalke, director of franchises for McDonald's, said the cost of taking over one of the about 40 McDonald's outlets that open each year was about $300,000 in 1977 and now is $400,000.

"To get a McDonald's franchise, an applicant must have at least $190,000 in cash," Mr. Bigalke said. "This is usually raised through liquidating personal assets like property or other investments. The rest is usually financed by a bank or other financial institution over five or seven years. Today, anyone with a McDonald's franchise finds it pretty easy to get financing."

Strictly speaking, operators of Canadian Tire Corp. Ltd. outlets are dealers rather than franchisees, but they operate much like business format franchisees and they, too, need a hefty cash outlay at the start.

"We have a minimum requirement of $40,000 unencumbered," said Mary MacMillan, supervisor of dealer selection. "This is the dealer's equity. We don't charge royalties; Canadian Tire makes its money through wholesaling.

"Applicants must also be able to support themselves through a six-month training period in which they work in seven or eight stores, followed by five weeks of intensive classroom training."

But while a franchise-style operation may offer lowered risks, it is no guarantee of easy profit. Few Canadians would envy the operator of a convenience store that stays open from morning to night seven days a week, 52 weeks a year—for the kind of return that even Mr. Dargan would not call lavish.

"A Becker's dealer doing $250,000 worth of business a year—that would be the average—will come out with around $20,000 net income before taxes. That will be after paying his help," he said.

Could it be that some high-effort, low-return franchise outlets are old-style sweatshops in new clothing?

"Not at all, not at all," said Mr. Dargan. "If people work hard, it is because they choose to do so. This is the way they can increase their return."

Hard work or not, Canadians are lining up for franchises, with some of the better-known companies reporting waiting lists of 18 months. Increasingly, Mr. Dargan said, applicants tend to be professional people—accountants, engineers and so forth, either freshly retired or who want out of the professional rat race.

And as the numbers of applicants expand, so do the opportunities as franchising moves into new areas.

"Nowadays, people want to extend the lives of their cars, and car maintenance is one of the emerging growth areas of the franchising industry," Mr. Dargan said. "Others are plumbing, career counselling and guidance, word processing service bureaus, discos, roller skating, nut and dried fruit stands, specialty stores selling single products like knives, that sort of thing.

"There's even a franchising operation that started in California selling those wooden tubs people bathe in. Then there are those suntan places—you know, just a room with lights where people can go instead of going to Florida. They say the tan is very natural."

According to Mr. Dargan, franchising has something for everyone. For the franchising company, it offers a way of expanding and earning royalties without having to raise vast amounts of new capital. For the franchisee, it offers the chance of being a private businessman without the perils of starting afresh.

"That's why it's growing so fast," he said, "faster here than in the United States. Franchising is also taking hold in Japan, Australia, New Zealand, Mexico and many other countries."

It may not be entrepreneurship in the old, free-wheeling style, but franchising clearly meets the needs of growing numbers of investors around the world.

Assignment
1. Make a list, with examples, of industries in which franchising now exists.
2. What industries are untouched by franchising? Why?
3. How important is franchising in Canada?
4. Why is food the biggest growth area?
5. What are the two basic types of franchise? How do they differ?
6. Why is the failure rate for non-franchised new businesses much higher than for franchised ones?
7. What does it cost to become a franchisee? Give examples.
8. Is it always worth the cost?
9. What types of persons become franchisees? Why?

UNIT 17.2 PREPARING A BUSINESS PLAN

If a person needs to borrow money from a bank or other financial institution to start a business venture, he or she will need to prepare a written *business plan*. The same thing will be required if other persons are to be invited to become partners in the business.

Obviously any lender or investor will want to know what is involved. Also, such a business plan is good discipline for the person planning to start the business. It forces him or her to think through the venture in a logical, scientific way before committing funds, rather than riding on emotion or flying by the "seat of the pants."

Essentials of a Business Plan

There is no standard format for a business plan. Nevertheless, all such plans should cover certain essentials, as suggested below:
1. Borrower's personal background
2. Description of proposed business
3. Physical facilities required
4. Profitability analysis
5. Cash-flow forecast
6. Borrowing proposal
7. Miscellaneous documents

Personal Background. This should include the person's name, address, residence, education, and business or other work experience. It should also include a statement of *personal net worth* (personal assets minus personal liabilities) and current income, by source.

Proposed Business. This part should explain the nature of the business operation (manufacturing, retail, or other service) and the *market analysis* that has been done, covering product need, special product features, potential customers, price, distribution, market size, competition, etc.

Physical Facilities. This should be a summary of the amount and type of physical space required, the proposed location of the business, whether it is proposed to lease or purchase the building, and the types and cost of equipment required.

Profitability. There is no sense in starting a business unless there is a good chance of making a profit, after allowing in the expenses for reasonable reimbursement for the owner's time. To estimate whether the business will be profitable involves two steps: first, estimate the break-even point and, second, do some market research to determine, as much as possible, how long it will take to reach and surpass the break-even point. How to make a break-even analysis is explained in Unit 12.2.

Suppose the business would need to sell, say, 3,000 units per month to break even in order to cover its total operating costs. And suppose, from market research, it seems unlikely that sales would ever exceed 3,500 units. The conclusion may be that the rate of profit would be insufficient to justify the risk.

In the case of a new business, a bank or other lender would be pleased to receive *pro forma financial statements*—that is, a projection of what the firm's balance sheet might look like in a year's time and a projection of what the first year's income statement (revenue, expenses, and net income) might be. In the case of an existing business that wishes to expand or undertake a new venture, the lender would also wish to see the financial statements for the past few years.

Cash-Flow Forecast. For any new business, a very real concern is whether it will have sufficient funds to continue operating while it is building up its clientele. In fact one of the objectives of any market research would be to determine just how long it might take the business to break even. In practice, it often takes months or even years from the actual start-up date. Until break even is reached some time in the future, the business will be operating at a loss—that is, expenses exceeding revenue. This means that working capital will be gradually drained from the business to cover the ongoing loss. The situation will be worse if the owner misapplies the funds that are generated—for example, tying too much of the money up in fixed or semi-fixed assets.

In determining what amount of funds will be required for the business, both initially and on an ongoing basis, a person will have to assess both fixed capital and working capital needs. *Fixed capital needs* are funds required to pay for buildings, equipment, etc. *Working capital needs* are funds required to pay for materials, goods for resale, wages, rent, utilities, taxes, etc. The business plan will help a person to ensure that the allocation of the funds between those two different purposes is appropriate. One way to reduce fixed capital needs is by leasing rather than purchasing equipment and buildings. Obviously, working capital needs must take priority. This is because insufficient funds, as the business struggles to grow, can force it into receivership and eventual bankruptcy.

For purposes of the Business Plan, a person should prepare a cash budget which will attempt to forecast, as realistically as possible, the cash receipts and disbursements of the business and resultant cash surplus or deficit each month over the next, say, twelve, eighteen, or twenty-four months. An estimate can then be made of the *cash break-even point*—that is, the number of units that must be sold each month, etc. to provide enough cash to cover disbursements. This break-even point is normally different from the one for sales.

The actual format of the cash budget is set out in Unit 13.1. This cash budget can be used to indicate the total amount of funds required from the owner and lenders for working capital needs until the business can generate sufficient funds to be *self-financing*. By combining the working capital needs with the fixed capital requirements, a person will have a good estimate of the total capital required.

Borrowing Proposal. Here the person should set out (a) the total amount of funds required for the business venture—say $100,000; (b) the proposed use of these funds; (c) the amount of funds that the owner plans to invest; (d) the amount of funds that the owner wishes to borrow; and (e) the way in which the person plans to repay the borrowed money—for example, twelve monthly instalments of principal and interest.

Miscellaneous Documents. A prospective lender may wish to see various documents: a partnership agreement or articles of incorporation; a list of partners or shareholders; a summary of the qualifications of the borrower and other key people, such as the manager; copies of leases and other important contracts; and copies of patents, trademarks, etc. Also, as previously mentioned, actual and/or pro forma financial statements should be supplied.

KEY TERMS

Business plan	Cash-flow analysis
Personal net worth	Fixed capital
Market analysis	Working capital
Break-even point	Cash budget
Break-even analysis	Cash break-even point
Pro-forma financial statements	Borrowing proposal

REVIEW QUESTIONS

1. Why should a prospective small business owner prepare a "business plan"?
2. What basic points should be covered by such a business plan?
3. What is meant by personal net worth? How is it calculated?
4. What items should be covered in a market analysis for a new business venture?
5. What is "break-even analysis"? How can it be useful to the prospective small business owner?
6. What is "cash-flow analysis"? What is its purpose?
7. What can happen to a small business if it takes longer than expected to break even?
8. How can a business reduce its needs for funds?
9. Distinguish between the fixed capital and working capital needs of a small business.
10. Explain the nature and purpose of a cash budget.
11. Distinguish between the sales break-even point and the cash break-even point.
12. What items should be included in a borrowing proposal for a new small business venture?

UNIT 17.3 GOVERNMENT ASSISTANCE

Because of its vital importance to the economy, the small business sector receives various forms of government assistance.

Federal Business Development Bank (FBDB)

Financing. If a small business cannot obtain short or medium-term financing from a privately-owned bank on reasonable terms, it can apply to the Federal Business Development Bank for a loan. Such loans range in size from a few to many thousands of dollars and can be used to increase the working capital of the business or to acquire land, buildings, or equipment. The rate of interest charged is usually two percentage points above the prime rate. Most FBDB loans must be repaid within ten years in the form of monthly instalments of principal and interest. More information about FBDB financing is contained in Unit 13.3.

Counselling. The Federal Business Development Bank provides, at a nominal fee, a management counselling service known as CASE (Counselling Assistance to Small Enterprises). It is designed to assist small businesses in Canada in improving their methods of doing business and in overcoming specific business problems. This program makes available the experience of retired business persons and of other counsellors as required.

Management Training. The FBDB also provides a management training service designed to improve managerial performance in small Canadian businesses. This service is provided in various ways. First, the bank conducts management training seminars, at a nominal registration fee, in smaller cities and towns across Canada. These seminars are planned to meet the needs of owners and managers of small businesses. Second, the FBDB sponsors and supports conferences to promote good management practices. And, third, it develops and co-ordinates the distribution of management training courses for implementation by provincial education authorities.

Information. The FBDB has an information service to provide competent advice on the availability of programs of federal assistance to small businesses. Where possible, this may be extended to provincial and other assistance programs.

The FBDB also publishes booklets on a wide range of topics pertaining to the management of small business in Canada. It distributes a bulletin featuring business developments. And, at its branch offices, it maintains reference libraries with a variety of publications on small business management which can be obtained free or at a low cost from their publishers.

Criticisms. In the early 1980s, as a result of operating losses, the FBDB cut its staff and reduced the number of its branch offices to 88. It also tended to concentrate its lending on medium rather than small-size businesses. Some critics argue that its mandate should be terminated or at least revised.

Small Businesses Loans Act (SBLA)

Under this statute, passed in 1961, the federal government provides a guarantee of repayment to the private banks and other approved lenders who make what are termed "business improvement loans" to eligible small businesses. Such loans may be used for the purchase of fixed equipment, moveable equipment, premises, or land. The loans can be for as much as $100,000 and at the prime rate of interest plus one per cent. If the borrower cannot repay the loan, the federal government covers 85 per cent of the loss. More details of such medium-term financing are contained in Unit 13.3.

Enterprise Development Program (EDP)

This is a federal government program of financial and technical assistance to business administered by the Department of Regional Industrial Expansion through central and regional Enterprise Development Boards. The program, aimed particularly at smaller and medium-sized businesses, has the overall objective of enhancing the growth of the manufacturing and processing sectors of the Canadian economy. It hopes to do this by providing financial and other assistance to firms willing to undertake relatively high-risk projects of innovation and adjustment that are economically sound and promise attractive rates of return on total investment. Such projects should help the firm to become more viable and internationally competitive.

Forms of EDP assistance include:
a. *grants* to develop proposals for projects eligible for assistance; to study market feasibility; to study productivity improvement measures; for industrial design; and for innovation projects.
b. *loans* or *loan-insurance* to facilitate restructuring or rationalization of manufacturing and processing firms in Canada by providing last-resort financial assistance.

Firms eligible for EDP assistance are small and medium-sized incorporated businesses engaged in manufacturing or processing.

Income Tax Relief

The owner of an unincorporated business must include business income in his or her personal income tax return. If the marginal rate of personal income tax is high, the small business owner may reduce the income tax payable by incorporating the business.

Small Business Deduction. Normally, a business corporation pays a combined federal and provincial flat rate of corporate income tax of about 46 per cent. However, if the business corporation is Canadian-owned and the annual business income is less than a certain amount, the incorporated business may be eligible for the "small business deduction" that can reduce the flat rate of corporate income tax to about 25 per cent, depending on the province in which it is located. This rate may be reduced even more if the firm also qualifies for the "manufacturing and processing deduction."

Other Federal Government Assistance

Financial assistance is available to specialized groups in Canada under various statutes and programs.

Agriculture. Under the *Farm Improvement Loans Act*, repayment of term loans to farmers by banks and other approved lenders is guaranteed by the federal government. The loans may be used for the purchase of agricultural implements, livestock, agricultural equipment, construction, repair, or alteration of farm buildings, additional land, drainage, irrigation projects, etc. Loans, up to a maximum amount per borrower, must be secured. The maximum period of repayment, ranging from 3 to 15 years, depends on the purpose of the loan. Other statutes involving government financial assistance to farmers include the *Prairie Grain Advance Payments Act*, *The Farm Credit Act*, and *The Farm Syndicate Credit Act*.

Fisheries. Under the *Fisheries Improvement Loans Act*, repayment of term loans to commercial fishing businesses by banks and other approved lenders is guaranteed by the federal government. The loans may be made for purchase or construction of a fishing vessel or fishing equipment, major repair or overhaul of a fishing vessel, purchase or construction of shore installations, or development or improvement of a primary fishing enterprise. Loans must be secured (usually by a chattel mortgage) and there is a maximum amount per borrower.

Provincial Ministries

One or more provincial government ministries usually have special programs of financial, counselling, and other assistance to small business.

Ministry of Industry, Trade, and Technology. In Ontario, for example, the Ministry of Industry, Trade, and Technology through a network of offices throughout the province, provides counselling services for persons interested in starting a small business and to inventors. It also provides consulting services with regard to management, marketing, financing, manufacturing technology, and industrial development. From head office in Toronto, specialists advise small businesses in such matters as marketing, business development, finance, promotion, productivity, energy management, technology, computerized business planning, physical distribution, and starting a new business. The Ministry also provides a Small Business Management Development Program to help existing small businesses improve their operations, and it funds a Small Business Consulting Service provided by the business schools of most Ontario universities.

Provincial Development Corporations

Most provincial governments now have their own Development Corporations that provide comprehensive financial and advisory services to small businesses. In Ontario, there are: the Ontario Development Corporation (ODC), the Northern Ontario Development Corporation (NODC), and the Eastern Ontario Development Corporation (EODC). Financial assistance is tailored to the applicant's needs and consists of one or more of the following:

a. consulting help in approaching private lenders or government funding sources
b. guarantees to encourage private lenders to provide financing
c. direct loans with a variety of terms and conditions of repayment
d. special incentives, if a proposal has the potential for significant economic benefit to the province, and there is a demonstrated need for such incentives.

KEY TERMS

FBOB

SBLA

EDP

MITT

REVIEW QUESTIONS

1. What types of financial assistance are available from the FBDB?
2. Explain the counselling role of the FBDB.
3. What management training does the FBDB provide?
4. What information is available from the FBDB?
5. What is the Small Businesses Loans Act? What assistance does it provide?
6. What is the Enterprise Development Program? What assistance does it provide? To whom?
7. What particular assistance does the federal government provide to firms involved in agriculture?
8. How is Canada's fishing industry helped by the federal government?
9. What income tax concessions are made to small businesses?
10. What provincial ministry assists small business in your province? What assistance does it provide?
11. What role do provincial development corporations play in assisting small business?

UNIT 17:4: BASIC BUSINESS RECORDS

Every business needs to keep certain basic financial records so that the owners, managers, lenders, and government (Revenue Canada) can obtain an accurate picture of what is going on.

Balance Sheet

The first type of information required is a summary of the assets, liabilities, and capital of the business at any particular time. This is called a *balance sheet*. It shows, first, of all, what *assets* the business owns—cash, materials, goods for resale, accounts receivable, buildings, equipment, and anything else of value. It shows, second, what *liabilities* the business has—that is, the amount of money owed to other persons—for example, accounts payable for materials and goods purchased on credit, taxes payable, rent payable, and so on. It shows, third, the owner's *capital*—the money originally invested by the owner or owners plus the profit that has been made and retained in the business or minus any loss. Liabilities can be thought of as a claim by creditors against the assets of the business, and capital as a claim by the owners. The total of these claims (liabilities plus owner's capital) is always equal to the total of the assets. And the portion of the assets that is not owed to creditors belongs, by definition, to the owner. The owner's capital is also the same as the *net worth* of the business—for the business is worth the total of its assets minus its liabilities. The balance sheet is explained in more detail in Unit 14:1.

Income Statement

The other critical piece of information required by the owner, etc. is a summary of the revenue, expenses, and net income (profit or loss) of the business for a given period of time. This is called an *income statement* or *profit-and-loss statement*. It shows, first, what *revenue* the business has received from the sale of its goods or services during a given period of time. It shows, second, the various *expenses* that have been incurred in operating the business—for example, material purchases, wages, rent, and utilities. And it shows, third, the *net income* of the business—that is, the revenue minus expenses for the month, quarter, year, or other period of time.

Ledger Accounts

In order to make possible the preparation of the balance sheet and income statement, a business must first keep a record of the balance of each item that appears in these financial statements. Thus each item has its own written record called an *account*, which is kept together with all the others in a book called a *ledger*. Each ledger account, with its own name and number, has several columns: one for the date, one for a brief description of the entry, one for the posting reference (the journal from which it was posted) and two columns for dollar amounts. The balance of each item is taken, when required, for inclusion in its proper place in the balance sheet or income statement. By having the ledger accounts up-to-date, and in the order in which they are placed in the financial statements, the owner of a business can look through the ledger and obtain a good idea of how the business is faring. Also, preliminary financial statements can be drawn up just as quickly as the ledger account balances can be copied from the ledger.

Debit and Credit Entries

Every business transaction has two sides. Take, for example, a cheque received from a customer to whom the business has sold goods on, say, 30 days credit. On the one hand, the bank balance of the business is increased whereas, on the other hand, the amount owed to the business by the customer is decreased. Therefore, for every transaction, the business must make two entries in its ledger accounts—hence the name "double-entry bookkeeping." One of these entries (e.g. the increase in the "cash in bank" account) is called a *debit* entry and the other (e.g. the decrease in the "accounts receivable") is called a *credit* entry. Debit entries are made in the first of the two dollar columns in each ledger account. Credit entries are made in the second dollar column. If the books are to balance, the bookkeeper must ensure that each debit entry is offset by an equal credit entry. Normally, before preparing the financial statements, the bookkeeper will prepare a "trial balance" to check that the total of the debit balances from the ledger equals the total of the credit balances. If they are unequal, the bookkeeper must search out and correct one or more mistakes in entry somewhere in the ledger accounts before the financial statements can be prepared. Otherwise, they will not balance.

Certain ledger accounts normally have a debit balance and others a credit balance. Asset and expense accounts normally have a debit balance. Liability, capital, and revenue accounts normally have a credit balance (as shown in Figure 17.1). To increase the balance of an account will, depending on the type of account, require a debit or credit entry. Similarly, to decrease the balance of an account will, again depending on the type of account, require a debit or credit entry. Thus for an asset account, which normally has a debit balance, a debit entry will increase the balance of the account and a credit entry will decrease it.

Journals

Usually, there are too many transactions to make it practical for the bookkeeper to record them directly in the ledger accounts. Instead they are first recorded in a book called a "journal," also known as a "book of original entry." This may be a single "general journal" in which details of each transaction are recorded: date, brief details, dollar amount, and type of ledger accounts involved. Usually,

Type of Account	Usual Balance	To increase the balance, enter item as a:	To decrease the balance, enter item as a:
Asset	debit	debit	credit
Liability	credit	credit	debit
Capital	credit	credit	debit
Revenue	credit	credit	debit
Expenses	debit	debit	credit

Figure 17.1 Ledger Accounts and Their Balances

however, several specialized journals are used so that similar transactions can be grouped together. The most common of such journals are the sales journal, the cash receipts journal, the cash disbursements journal, the purchases journal and the expenses journal. Then, at the end of the day, week, or month, the amounts in the journals are totalled and transferred or "posted" to the appropriate ledger accounts. To ensure that no transaction is overlooked, the owner of the business should insist that each transaction has some supporting document—for example a purchase order, sales slip, invoice, or cheque stub.

Usually a specialized bookkeeper is employed on a full or part-time basis to keep the books. An accountant may be used to set up the system; to "close off" the books at the end of the business's financial year, with appropriate "adjusting" and "closing" entries; to prepare the annual financial statements; and, if the business is incorporated, to complete the federal and provincial corporate income tax returns.

Statement Analysis

The financial statements prepared in this way can be used by owners, lenders, etc. to draw conclusions about the performance of the business (e.g. return on investment) and its financial solvency (e.g. current assets versus current liabilities). The financial ratios most commonly used in this type of analysis are reviewed in Units 12.2 and 13.1. The financial statements can be even more informative when compared with those of previous years. In fact, accountants often present last year's figures alongside the current year's when drawing up the statements.

KEY TERMS

Balance sheet	Debit entry
Assets	Credit entry
Liabilities	Double-entry bookkeeping
Capital	Trial balance
Net worth	Debit balance
Income statement	Credit balance
Account	Journal
Ledger	Statement analysis

REVIEW QUESTIONS

1. What would a balance sheet for a small business reveal to a prospective lender?
2. What is meant by the "net worth" of a business? How is it calculated?
3. What is an income statement? What does it show?

4. What is a ledger account? What purpose does it serve?
5. What is meant by the term "double-entry bookkeeping"?
6. Explain the nature and purpose of a "trial-balance."
7. Which ledger accounts normally have a debit balance?
8. Which ledger accounts normally have a credit balance?
9. What is a "journal"? What is its purpose?
10. Why do firms often use more than one journal? What are these various journals?
11. What is meant by "statement analysis"? What information would a person seek?

PART I
INTERNATIONAL BUSINESS

If Canada is to provide job opportunities for its young people and provide the average citizen with a good standard of living, its business firms must increase their sales to foreign markets.

CHAPTER 18
EXPORTING

CHAPTER OBJECTIVES

☐ To review Canada's international trade, emphasizing the need for more Canadian exports.

☐ To distinguish between direct and indirect exporting.

☐ To review such aspects of exporting as organization, research, pricing, and promotion.

☐ To identify the various foreign barriers to Canadian exports.

☐ To explain how Canadian exporters make sure of getting paid for the goods they ship abroad.

CHAPTER OUTLINE

18.1   Canada's International Trade
18.2   Export Marketing
18.3   Export Financing

UNIT 18.1: CANADA'S INTERNATIONAL TRADE

Many Canadian business firms, in both the primary and secondary industries, now sell their goods abroad as well as at home. In fact, for some firms, exports account for the major portion of their sales revenue. Altogether, exports now generate 30 per cent of Canada's national income and provide employment for one out of every five Canadians. The biggest foreign market by far is the United States, which now takes about 76 per cent of the total value of Canadian exports.

Why Firms Export

There are many good reasons why Canadian firms sell their goods abroad:
a. good sales and profit opportunities;
b. growth possibilities for a firm that has already reached its sales peak in Canada (a relatively small market);
c. lower per unit production costs as a result of longer production runs when export sales are added to domestic sales (This is the logic behind the occasional decision by a U.S. multinational to grant its Canadian subsidiary a "world product mandate" whereby it produces a particular item—e.g. computer keyboard—for sale in all the multinational's markets around the world);
d. better use of production facilities if seasonal "slack" at home can be counterbalanced by seasonal demand abroad;
e. protection, through diversification, against falling sales at home caused by economic slowdown or increased competition; and
f. various forms of government export assistance.

Reasons for Predominance of U.S. Market

The predominance of the U.S. market is explained by such factors as:
a. *size*—a population of about 265 million persons;
b. *wealth*—the largest Gross National Product (or GNP) in the world and one of the highest average per capita incomes;
c. *closeness*—many key East Coast U.S. markets are closer to Ontario and Quebec than Western Canada; also West Coast U.S. markets are closer to Alberta and B.C. than is Eastern Canada;
d. *communications*—communication between Canadian exporters and actual and prospective customers in the U.S. by telephone, mail, etc. is efficient;
e. *transportation facilities*—road, rail, and air facilities are excellent;
f. *culture*—the language and culture are similar;
g. *multinationals*—many U.S. multinationals ship parts and finished goods to the U.S. from branch plants in Canada;
h. *trade arrangements*—special trade arrangements such as the automotive agreement (or "auto pact") encourage a two-way flow of trade across the Canada – U.S. border; and

i. *cheaper Canadian dollar*—the weakness in the foreign exchange rate of the Canadian dollar has made Canadian goods cheaper in terms of U.S. dollars.

Principal Exports

The types of products that Canada sells most successfully abroad are listed in Figure 18.1. Most of them are resource-based products rather than manufactured goods (although it is the latter which offer better employment and income opportunities). One important exception is motor vehicles, engines and parts, which account for about 26 per cent of Canada's export earnings. These have grown substantially since 1956 when the "auto pact" between Canada and the U.S. came into force. However, there has also been a tremendous increase in Canadian imports of motor vehicles and parts from the U.S., although not sufficient to eliminate a current net benefit for Canada under the auto pact.

Item	$ Millions	Percent
Motor vehicles, engines and parts	29,401	26.1
Newsprint paper	4,772	4.2
Wheat	4,611	4.1
Crude petroleum	4,481	4.0
Lumber	4,284	3.8
Natural gas	3,966	3.5
Woodpulp	3,895	3.5
Petroleum and coal products	3,199	2.8
Chemicals, inorganic and organic	2,621	2.3
Fabricated iron and steel	2,254	2.0
Aircraft, engines and parts	1,973	1.8
Aluminum and alloys	1,909	1.7
Precious metals	1,570	1.4
Fertilizers and fertilizer materials	1,530	1.4
Iron ores and concentrates	1,207	1.1
Other	40,838	36.3
Total	112,511	100.0

Figure 18.1 Canada's Principal Exports, 1984
Source: Statistics Canada, *Quarterly Estimates of the Canadian Balance of International Payments*, cat. 67-001. Reproduced by permission of the Minister of Supply and Services Canada.

Principal Export Markets

The U.S. is Canada's major foreign customer (see Figure 18.2). Other key countries are Japan, the United Kingdom, other EEC countries, the U.S.S.R., and the People's Republic of China.

Country	$ Millions	Percent
United States	85,865	76.3
Japan	5,535	4.9
United Kingdom	2,496	2.2
Other EEC	4,483	4.0
Other countries	14,132	12.6
Total	112,511	100.0

Figure 18.2 Canada's Principal Export Markets, 1984

Source: Statistics Canada, *Quarterly Estimates of the Canadian Balance of International Payments*, cat. 67-001. Reproduced by the permission of the Minister of Supply and Services Canada.

Current Account Deficit

Usually, Canada exports more goods than it imports. In other words, it has a "trade surplus"—earning more abroad from export sales than it spends on imports. However, in Canada's balance of international payments (Figure 18.3), the *current account* consists of payments not just for "goods" but also for "services." And the surplus that Canada records in trade in goods (the "merchandise trade" or "visible trade") is usually more than offset by the deficit in services (the "non-merchandise trade" or "invisible trade") as clearly shown in Figure 18.4. The main causes of the large services deficit are: the payments made by Canada for interest on money borrowed from abroad; dividends on foreign equity capital invested in Canada; and spending by Canadians on tourism abroad.

Canada's Need for More Exports

In the past, Canada's large current account deficit has been counterbalanced by a capital account surplus. This surplus has resulted from substantial long- and short-term borrowing abroad by Canadian governments and business corporations and by heavy foreign investment in Canada. However, the continuation of this situation in the future is probably neither possible nor desirable. Therefore, it is essential for Canada to improve its current account situation. One important way of doing this is by exporting more products—both goods and services. Failure to do so can mean a drop in Canada's international monetary reserves and a continued decline in the foreign exchange rate of the Canadian dollar, compared with the U.S. dollar.

A second critical reason for increasing Canada's exports is the extremely high unemployment level in Canada (now over 2 million persons). Much of this unemployment, by the way, has resulted from Canadian inability to compete in the home market with many goods (for example, consumer electronics, clothing, and footwear), produced more cheaply abroad.

A third reason for boosting Canadian exports is to increase income. Only if Canada's GNP continues to grow can Canadians maintain, let alone increase, their present relatively high material standard of living. In fact, many Canadians are already on the welfare rolls, often because of lack of job opportunities.

Year	Merchandise exports	Merchandise imports	Merchandise trade balance	Service receipts	Service payments	Balance on goods and services	Net transfers	Balance on current account	Net capital movements inflows and outflows (—)		Special Drawing Rights allocations	Net official monetary movements[2]
									Long-term	Short-term[1]		
						(Millions of dollars)						
1950	3,139	3,132	7	1,034	1,405	−364	45	−319	610	431	—	722
1955	4,332	4,543	−211	1,405	1,847	−653	−34	−687	414	229	—	−44
1960	5,392	5,540	−148	1,590	2,549	−1,107	−126	−1,233	929	265	—	−39
1965	8,745	8,627	118	2,437	3,714	−1,159	29	−1,130	833	455	—	158
1970	16,921	13,869	3,052	4,246	6,345	953	153	1,106	1,007	−583	133	1,663
1971	17,877	15,314	2,563	4,304	6,702	165	266	431	664	−318	119	896
1972	20,129	18,272	1,857	4,451	6,978	−670	284	−386	1,588	−983	117	336
1973	25,461	22,726	2,735	5,257	8,228	−236	344	108	628	−1,203	—	−467
1974	32,591	30,902	1,689	6,401	10,107	−2,017	557	−1,460	1,041	443	—	24
1975	33,511	33,962	−451	6,941	11,627	−5,137	380	−4,757	3,935	417	—	−405
1976	38,166	36,607	1,559	7,624	13,822	−4,639	530	−4,109	8,022	−3,390	—	522
1977	44,498	41,523	2,975	8,312	16,034	−4,747	413	−4,334	4,284	−1,371	—	−1,421
1978	53,362	49,047	4,315	9,945	19,227	−4,967	50	−4,917	3,221	−1,604	—	−3,299
1979	65,582	61,157	4,425	11,950	21,881	−5,506	666	−4,840	2,111	4,419	219	1,908
1980	76,681	67,903	8,778	14,350	25,443	−2,315	1,201	−1,114	1,112	−1,495	217	−1,280
1981	84,468	77,140	7,328	16,227	31,131	−7,577	1,513	−6,065	154	7,128	210	1,426
1982	84,539	66,726	17,814	17,201	33,722	1,294	1,372	2,665	8,085	−11,443	0	−694
1983	90,825	73,120	17,705	17,343	34,143	904	780	1,686	2,310	−3,448	0	549
1984	112,510	91,679	20,831	19,357	39,028	1,159	796	1,955	3,352	−6,396	0	−1,088

[1] Includes net errors and omissions.
[2] Net official monetary movements include transactions in official international reserves and official monetary liabilities.

Figure 18.3 Canada's Balance of International Payments, 1950-1984

Source: Statistics Canada, *Quarterly Estimates of the Canadian Balance of International Payments*, cat. 67-001. Reproduced by permission of the Minister of Supply and Services Canada.

	Average 1971-1980	1981	1982	1983	1984
Balance of trade	3.0	7.3	17.8	17.7	20.8
Balance on services	−6.1	−14.9	−16.5	−16.8	−19.7
Balance on goods and services	−3.0	−7.6	1.3	0.9	1.2
Net transfers	0.5	1.5	1.4	0.8	0.8
Balance on current account	−2.5	−5.8	2.7	1.7	2.0

Figure 18.4 Summary of Canada's Current Account Balance, 1981-1984, in billions of dollars
Source: Statistics Canada, *Summary of External Trade*, cat. 65-001. Reproduced by permission of the Minister of Supply and Services Canada.

Principal Imports

The goods that Canada buys from abroad, although including food and raw materials, are predominantly manufactured goods—for both consumer and industrial use. As Figure 18.5 shows, motor vehicles, engines and parts, communication equipment, computers and office equipment, chemicals, and crude petroleum are the leading items that Canada imports.

Item	$ Millions	Percent
Motor vehicles, engines and parts	25,709	28.0
Communication equipment	4,673	5.1
Electronic computers and office equipment	4,365	4.8
Chemicals and related materials	3,773	4.1
Crude petroleum	3,382	3.7
Aircraft, engines and parts	2,283	2.5
Agricultural machinery	1,769	1.9
Apparel and apparel accessories	1,729	1.9
Fabricated iron and steel	1,642	1.8
Coal	1,095	1.2
Precious metals	545	0.6
Other	40,714	44.4
Total	91,679	100.0

Figure 18.5 Canada's Principal Imports, 1984
Source: Statistics Canada, *Quarterly Estimates of the Canadian Balance of International Payments*, cat. 67-001. Reproduced by permission of the Minister of Supply and Services Canada.

Principal Foreign Suppliers

The United States, as well as being Canada's main export market, is Canada's principal supplier, providing 72 per cent of the value of Canada's imports. Far behind (see Figure 18.6) come, in order of importance: Japan; the United Kingdom; other EEC countries such as Germany, France, and Italy; Venezuela; and other countries such as Brazil.

Country	$ Millions	Percent
United States	66,008	72.0
Japan	5,478	6.0
United Kingdom	2,305	2.5
Other EEC	5,841	6.4
Venezuela	1,207	1.3
Other countries	10,843	11.8
Total	91,679	100.0

Figure 18.6 Canada's Principal Suppliers, 1984
Source: Statistics Canada, *Quarterly Estimates of the Canadian Balance of International Payments*, cat. 67-001. Reproduced by permission of the Minister of Supply and Services Canada.

Pattern of Goods Traded

An analysis of Canada's international trade reveals that, with the exception of vehicles and parts, Canada exports predominantly resource-based products and imports predominantly manufactured goods. In fact, Canada has an enormous trade deficit in manufactured goods (see Figure 18.7). This means, in terms of employment and income, that Canada's trade surplus is not as favourable as might at first be supposed. This is because manufactured goods provide more employment and income for the firms that produce them than do other kinds of exports. Therefore, Canada must aim to increase not only the total of its exports but also the proportion of manufactured goods.

	Average 1973-1980	1981	1982	1983	1984
Agricultural products	1.8	4.4	5.3	5.5	4.9
Crude materials	3.5	3.0	6.2	7.2	9.6
Fabricated materials	8.4	16.7	16.0	16.3	18.9
Manufacturing	−11.0	−18.8	−11.0	−12.8	−15.5
Motor vehicles and parts	−1.5	−2.3	2.2	2.7	3.7
Miscellaneous	0.6	2.0	1.3	1.4	3.0
Total	3.3	7.3	17.8	17.7	20.8

Figure 18.7 Canada's Trade Balance by Commodity Group, 1981-1984, in billions of dollars
Source: Statistics Canada, *Summary of External Trade*, cat. 65-001. Reproduced by permission of the Minister of Supply and Services Canada.

Geographically (see Figure 18.8), the bulk of Canada's trade surplus is with the United States, which makes Canadian industry and agriculture highly vulnerable to any protectionist U.S. trade measures.

	Average 1973-1980	1981	1982	1983	1984
United States	1.1	3.7	11.3	14.1	19.9
United Kingdom	0.7	1.0	0.8	0.8	0.2
Other EEC	0.6	1.4	1.0	0.1	−1.4
Japan	1.0	0.3	1.0	0.3	0.1
Other OECD	0.0	0.4	−0.1	−0.4	−0.3
Other countries	−0.1	0.5	4.0	2.9	2.3
Total	3.3	7.3	17.8	17.7	20.8

Figure 18.8 Canada's Trade Balance by Geographical Region, 1981-1984, in billions of dollars
Source: Statistics Canada, *Summary of External Trade*, cat. 65-001. Reproduced by permission of the Minister of Supply and Services Canada.

KEY TERMS

Exports

World product mandate

Auto pact

Export market

Trade surplus

Current account

Capital account

Visible trade

Invisible trade

REVIEW QUESTIONS

1. Why might a Canadian firm decide to start selling its goods abroad?
2. What is a "world product mandate"? Why is it granted?
3. Why is the United States usually the preferred export market for Canadian firms?
4. What are Canada's principal exports? Why?
5. Which countries are Canada's principal export markets? Why?
6. What is a "trade surplus"? Does Canada have one? Why?
7. What is Canada's "current account"? Is it usually in surplus, deficit, or in balance? Why?
8. Explain the term "invisible trade." What is Canada's experience?
9. Why does Canada need more exports?
10. What are Canada's principal imports? Why?
11. From which foreign countries does Canada purchase most of its imports? Why?
12. What is the pattern, if any, of goods traded between Canada and foreign countries (e.g. Canada and Japan)? What accounts for it?

READINGS

Aloro Foods

They pine for our pizza in Saudi
Go bananas for our blueberries in Japan
From bubble gum to Cheddar cheese
From Moosehead beer to Christmas trees
The world is waiting for our exports

BY SARAH LAWLEY AND
DOUG SCANLON

Source: Reprinted from *Canadian Living Magazine*, November 5, 1984 issue.

Canada has started a revolution in Saudi Arabia—a revolution in eating habits. We've introduced the Saudis to a fast food so tasty and exotic that it's taking a bite out of the traditional falafel market. What's causing all the fuss? Pizza! What's more, it's 100-per-cent Canadian.

Granted, it's not quite the same as the bacon-and-double-cheese concoction we pick up at the local pizza parlor, but then it has to comply with Moslem dietary requirements, which prohibit pork and pork products. "We use all-beef pepperoni, and cheese with no pork rennet," says Don Dalgleish, president of Aloro Foods Inc. of Mississauga, Ont. The company also supplies certificates to show that all the pizzas are *halal*, which is the Moslem equivalent of kosher. But despite these variations, the Saudis love our pizza, and Aloro Foods expects them to munch their way through $1 million worth this year.

Pizza is just one of a multitude of products Canada makes for export. In 1983 we sold $90.6 billion worth of goods to countries from the Soviet Union to Singapore, with the United States buying about 75 percent of all our exports. The figures show we have the imagination and ability to compete with the best in the world: although we have only one-half of one percent of the world's population, we hold a 3.7 percent share of international trade. To further promote foreign trade, this October has been declared Canada Export Trade Month. The event, organized by External Affairs Canada, is to be repeated next year and possibly in following years.

Metals, minerals, motor vehicle parts, and farm, fish, forestry and energy-resource products account for about two-thirds of our exports. We sell everything from aged Cheddar, kippered snacks and bubble gum to wild rice, clover honey and lobster; from armoured cars, space technology and airplanes to chickens, crumpets, and milk.

And that's just the tip of the iceberg—or perhaps we should say ice cubes, since we've even discovered that the citizens of Haines, Alaska, itself nestled between glaciers, love to cool their cocktails with imported Canadian ice.

Here, we present a sampling of just a few of the wild and wonderful products that the rest of the world wants from Canada.

Many of our exports are rather down-to-earth—potatoes, for instance. Because these starchy tubers grow best in sandy soil, it shouldn't be surprising that Algeria, with its corner of the Sahara Desert, is interested in growing them. To start things off, McCain Produce is supplying the north African country with more than $8 million worth of seed potatoes from Prince Edward Island and New Brunswick, whose splendid spuds are world renowned.

Another popular export from the Maritimes is Moosehead Canadian Lager Beer, produced by the family-owned Moosehead Breweries in Saint John, N.B. Moosehead, with a picture of the said head on its label, is the fastest-growing imported beer in the United States. In 1980, only two years after its introduction to the U.S. market, it ranked seventh among the 225 imported brands sold there. Today it's in fourth place, and closing in on third. The brew that made Saint John famous is enjoyed by Americans in every state.

Then there are our wonderful wild blueberries, about which the Japanese are absolutely bananas. They buy about 2,000 to 3,000 tonnes from us each year to use in everything from pie and ice cream to bubble gum. Canadian blueberries are also extremely popular in Europe, but the Japanese are definitely our most enthusiastic buyers. "They appreciate the superior quality of our berries," says Lad Javorek of Cobi Foods in Berwick, N.S. "Quality gives us the edge over our Scandinavian and eastern European competitors." In 1983 we exported 70 percent of our wild blueberry crop.

The Japanese are also developing a taste for Canadian cherries. This is indeed an honour, considering that the Japanese attribute almost mystical qualities to cherries, cherry blossoms, and anything remotely related. They grow plenty of their own, but ours have a slightly different flavour. We managed to break into this exclusive market because our West Coast cherries, unlike those of many other countries, are able to meet the rigid quality standards demanded by the Japanese for their legendary fruit.

We wouldn't expect Japan to be interested in Canadian cars, because Hondas, Toyotas, and their cousins continue to dominate the North American auto market. But there's one innovative Canuck who's making a dent—albeit a small one—in the Japanese market. George Fejer of the Super Seven Sports Car Company in Newmarket, Ont., says he can't produce enough of his handsome handmade sports cars to meet Japanese demand. He's just set up a dealership in West Germany to make inroads in the western European market.

There are few things more typically Canadian than maple syrup. The very mention of it evokes vivid images of sleigh rides through a sugar bush and that first sweet taste of syrup-covered snow. And it seems that much of the rest of the world shares our love affair with the maple's sap. Slightly more than half our maple syrup and maple sugar exports go to the United States, and the rest goes to western Europe, Japan, Australia, and New Zealand. Before the Second World War, most maple products were used for industrial purposes, such as flavouring tobacco. This is still the case in some countries—in Scandinavia, for instance. But most industries have since substituted cheaper artificial flavours for the real thing, so maple products are now used chiefly in the home.

Canola, which used to bear the more prosaic name of rapeseed, is another big seller for Canada, bringing in more than $525 million last year. An herb of the mustard family, it's grown primarily in the Prairies, and its uses are similar to those of soybeans. In 1983 we sold almost 1.3 million tonnes of unprocessed seeds (mainly to Japan), plus 171,000 tonnes of canola meal and 93,000 tonnes of canola oil to South Korea, the United States, India, and dozens of other countries. While canola exports continue to increase, no one can say for certain whether the name change is responsible for its booming popularity.

Speaking of things Canadian, we cannot ignore (much as we might like to) ice and snow, with which many of our exports are intimately associated. Perhaps we're most famous for the hockey players we've shipped to the United States, such as Brian Trottier. But our contributions to skating don't stop there. Phoenix Fashions of Toronto expects to export more than 100,000 competitive figure-skating outfits to the United States this year, and, already having impressed buyers in West Germany and Finland, it hopes soon to cut a swath through the entire European market.

And let us not forget that wonder of climatic adaptation: the snowshoe. Surprisingly, it's big business. Magline of Canada, a company in Renfrew, Ont., that regularly supplies snowshoes to U.S. and NATO forces, was awarded a $2-million contract in July to provide the U.S. Defense Department with snowshoes for the infantry and for emergency use by flyers. Although made with nylon webbing and magnesium frames instead of the usual animal gut and wood, the snowshoes are still hand-strung by Algonquin Indians from Golden Lake, Ont., and Wakefield, Que.

Also in great demand is Canadian fur. Because this country was founded on the fur trade, it makes sense that we supply the world with some of its best furs, such as beaver, muskrat, mink and wolverine. Scandinavians, who suffer no shortage of fine furry creatures themselves, actually prefer Canadian furs, says Ken Sunquist, director of Canada Export Trade Month. "Canadian furs are considered to be in a class by themselves," he says. "They're highly recognized for style, quality, and reliability." But it's not only the cool-weather countries that buy our furs. Last year The Arctic Trading Co. of Churchill, Man., sold eight thick polar bear hides to Saudi Arabian customers—presumably a triumph of fashion over function in that scorchingly hot country. The same company also supplied a New York museum with 10 muskox hides to be used in the creation of a lifelike mastodon.

In a rather old-fashioned way, Arctic Trading has brought a new dimension to the growing export market for native art, by encouraging mail-order shopping. The company still conducts business out of its trading post in Churchill, but Bob Reeve, Arctic Trading's chief factor, says, "To most people that's about two miles north of nowhere, so four years ago we decided to get into the mail-order business."

Their award-winning catalogue offers everything from handmade moccasins and coats to works of art by some of the most esteemed Inuit and Indian artists. Though Arctic Trading sells a few articles to customers in the Middle East and Europe, most of its export goods are bought by Americans.

Canada excels in the field of high tech, too. Much has already been said about Canadarm, the brave little mechanical arm that made it to outer space, but there are countless other Canadian technological exports, ranging from light armoured cars to tethering systems for recovering seaborne helicopters, and from earth satellite stations to the technological expertise needed to operate these wonders.

Finally, with Christmas coming soon, our booming Christmas tree business is worth a mention. Every year, Quebec, Ontario, New Brunswick, and Nova Scotia export between eight million and ten million trees all over the world, but mostly to our American neighbours. A few trees even make their way to Nassau, where they mingle with the palms in the balmy Bahamian breezes. So if you plan to go south for the Christmas holidays, chances are the tree you'll decorate will be a fir or Scotch pine from home.

Assignment

1. Why do the Saudis love Canadian pizza?
2. Why are the Japanese wild about Canadian blueberries and cherries?

3. What is "canola"? Why is it one of Canada's best sellers abroad?
4. What "high-tech" products does Canada export?
5. Give some examples of your own of successful Canadian exports.

Electronics Put Small Nova Scotia Town on the Map

BY VALERIE BACHYNSKY, DRIE, NOVA SCOTIA

Source: *Canada Commerce*

Saulnierville, Nova Scotia, a small town between Digby and Yarmouth, is not well known in Canada. Yet, companies in Britain and the Far East recognize it as a major source of Canadian electronic equipment.

"In Korea, they don't know how small or isolated we are; they just think Canada," explains Hugh Roddis, president of Orion Electronics Limited, a Saulnierville electronics firm that is making inroads into export markets. "In fact, in Korea they think Saulnierville must be somewhere near Montreal."

Orion Electronics manufactures special radio equipment, VHF receivers and transmitters and oil spill markers and trackers.

Easier to Sell Abroad

For Roddis, who has experienced some difficulty selling to Ottawa, it sometimes seems as if it's easier to sell his products abroad than to central Canada. If the entertainment world is any indicator of what happens in electronics, central Canadians will soon pay more attention because Orion has begun to capture international attention and markets.

Roddis is an engineer turned businessman and, he says, the process of transformation is still going on. Exploring foreign markets is something he does himself. That's necessary for a small business, he explains, because someone is needed with technical knowledge who can also make decisions.

Orion's involvement in the export market has been gradual. "We knew all along we'd have to export," says Roddis, "because there's no market here. However, at first, all export sales were handled by the Nova Scotia Research Foundation (NSRF)."

Over time, the company felt that there were too many levels between it and its customers and began to explore markets on its own. NSRF introduced Orion to agents and, with help from the federal Program for Export Market Development (PEMD), the company started to attend trade shows.

Value of Trade Shows

One of the real values of the trade shows is that they provide the opportunity to meet people and learn about their unique requirements. "It's useful to learn about people's problems; they might lead to ideas," says Roddis, for whom trade shows are one more way to stimulate his creative process.

Exporting provides a lot of stimulation. Roddis visited South Korea, Singapore, The Philippines and Malaysia in 1983 and he describes it as "an eye-opener."

"The trip opened my eyes to the competition over there. It's very much where the future lies. The market potential is tremendous but you have to be very competitive. We re-designed our product as a result of that trip."

The trip to Korea resulted partly by chance. The company realized there might be a market there when the Koreans bought some of Orion's tracking equipment. Company officials didn't know why since they hadn't sought out Korean contacts.

On doing some research, the company found that the Korean scientists had been trained in Canada under a Canadian International Development Agency (CIDA) program. Their exposure to the Canadian market proved an excellent way to sell Canadian equipment.

Not Much Difference

In the Far East, one might naturally expect some culture shock and radically different ways of doing business. Yet, according to Roddis, "there isn't much difference these days: they're so used to dealing with Westeners." However, he was shocked by Singapore. "You expect to be in an underdeveloped country and you're not! I counted 58 freighters in the harbour."

The export trade business is competitive, fast-paced and high pressured. "In the Far East, it seems that everyone is a wheeler-dealer," says Roddis.

He found that he had to keep himself firmly focused on what he intended to achieve. "You can get excited about a lot of things that might not turn out. It's hard to pick and choose the real opportunities and not make promises you can't fulfil."

In that atmosphere, the Canadian Embassy serves as a useful "home base" for weary, uncertain exporters. The embassy staff can provide introductions and give an unbiased view of the country. "Most important, embassy staff are not complete strangers; you can bounce ideas off them."

One of the most difficult things about the export business, according to Roddis, is to find the right agent and to make sure he stays the right agent. "Agents rise and fall. It's something that you have to keep track of. You can't just sign a contract with someone and forget it."

Basic Advice

For business people who are considering trying to enter the export market, Roddis has two basic pieces of advice—know your market and know your competition.

"The competition is very good and you have to make the effort to compete. Canadians sometimes have the feeling that their products are great and that's enough—but you also have to make the effort."

However, Canadians do enjoy one immense advantage in much of the world. They, and many of their products, have people's trust and confidence. Countries need the security of not buying from a "fly-by-night" outfit and will sometimes sacrifice price for reliability.

If Canadians can combine the advantage of a good reputation with more competitive marketing skills, who knows what might be achieved.

Assignment

1. Who is Orion?
2. How did it get into the export market?
3. What help did it get from the Canadian government?
4. What is the advice that Hugh Roddis gives to would-be Canadian exporters?
5. What big advantage do Canadian firms enjoy in the export market?

UNIT 18.2: EXPORT MARKETING

Direct versus Indirect Exporting

A Canadian business firm may export its products by selling them directly to foreign buyers located abroad or it may export them indirectly—by selling them to other firms located in Canada (known generally as export trading houses) who will in turn ship them abroad. Sometimes, Canadian manufacturers will engage in direct exporting for one type of product or market (e.g. the U.S.) and indirect exporting for other products or other markets (e.g. overseas).

Export Organization

Normally, a Canadian firm will make use of its present organization to handle export sales, either the marketing or the sales department. Sometimes, a suitable employee may be designated as export sales manager and supplied with a competent secretary. Obviously, selling to the U.S. is a lot simpler, because of common language, good communications, and geographic proximity, than selling overseas and the organizational requirements usually reflect this. Once export sales become a major source of revenue, a special export section or department is justified. Such a department may include, in addition to a manager and secretary, export sales "reps," a traffic manager (responsible for routing shipments), export clerks, perhaps a code clerk, and typist-translators. In the case of the small or even medium-sized business, the services of an outside firm, called a *freight forwarder*, may be used on a fee basis to handle shipping, documentation, and insurance.

The company that sells directly to customers in foreign countries will require some form of representation abroad. Usually, this is a foreign agent who is paid on a commission basis for his or her services, which are set out in an agency agreement. Such a person may be selected with the assistance of one of Canada's *trade commissioners*—Department of External Affairs employees stationed at Canadian embassies abroad, with the primary task of assisting Canadian exporters. If the export sales warrant it, a Canadian firm may station one of its own employees abroad (in a city such as Paris) to represent it on a regional basis. Often, a Canadian manufacturer will use its own sales force to sell in the U.S., but appoint foreign agents for sales overseas.

Export Research

Some firms get into exporting as the result of a foreign trip, perhaps a government-sponsored trade mission, or a private visit with financial assistance from the federal or provincial governments. Others start with a chance inquiry from a foreign firm that has heard about the firm's products. But most firms enter exporting in a more systematic way. This usually involves various types of export research.

Product Research. First of all, a firm should critically review its products to determine, as far as possible, their potential sales appeal abroad, and also what after-sales service, if any, would be necessary.

Market Research. Next, the Canadian firm should determine which countries to sell to. For most firms, this question only becomes a problem after the firm is already selling successfully in the U.S. market and is planning to expand its export sales overseas. The scope of the market research might include estimated demand for the product; competitive products; necessary product modifications; price abroad; import regulations in the foreign country; tariff and non-tariff trade barriers; packaging requirements; promotion materials; patent and trade mark registrations.

Distribution Research. Once the foreign market has been selected, the Canadian exporter must consider how its products are to be distributed there. Sometimes, the channels of distribution are quite different from those in Canada. The Canadian exporter must also decide which particular distributor to use, perhaps on the advice of the foreign agent, or the Canadian embassy.

Operations Research. Also, once exporting, the Canadian firm must monitor its program to see how the export operations can be improved and what new markets to tackle or what new products to introduce.

Sources of Export Information and Advice. There is a wealth of information available about foreign markets and export opportunities. It includes publications and/or advice from all the following:
a. *Federal government departments and agencies*—for example, the Department of External Affairs (DEA); the Department of Regional Industrial Expansion (DRIE); Statistics Canada; the Export Development Corporation (EDC); and the Federal Business Development Bank (FBDB).
b. *Provincial government departments and agencies*—for example, Ontario's Ministry of Industry, Trade and Technology (MITT), and the provincial development corporations.
c. *Chartered banks*—for example, their regional trade centres or international departments.
d. *Freight forwarders*—firms that specialize in routing shipments abroad but also provide other related services, including export advice.
e. *Private associations*—for example, the Canadian Export Association (CEA); the Canadian Manufacturers Association (CMA); the local Chambers of Commerce; the bilateral Chambers of Commerce (e.g. Canada-West Germany); and the World Trade Centres.

Foreign Visits. A well-planned foreign visit can give the Canadian exporter a good "feel" for the foreign market, including an opportunity to meet prospective agents and even customers. Such a visit may be as part of a federal or provincial "trade mission" or it may be a private visit, perhaps with part of the cost financed by the federal government under its Program for Export Market Development (PEMDE) or by a provincial government (e.g. Ontario's Export Success Fund).

Pre-Testing. Many firms send samples to prospective foreign customers. Another way of obtaining foreign feedback is to display the Canadian product at a foreign trade fair, perhaps with federal or provincial government help.

Trade Commissioner Service. The Canadian firm can also request that the Commercial Division of the Canadian Embassy in the foreign country of interest assign one of the Trade Commissioners to prepare a preliminary market report about the firm's product. However, such a request should be accompanied be detailed information about the firm, its products, and present sales.

Export Pricing

The Canadian firm must consider carefully what price it will charge for its product. For example, an F.O.B. ("Free on Board") Vancouver price would normally take into account all costs incurred up to the time the goods are loaded aboard ship in the Canadian port, including: factory cost; export packing, labelling, and marking; manufacturer's profit; inland freight; financing; documentation; and incidentals. A C.and F. price quotation would include all the above, plus the cost of ocean freight to the named port of destination (e.g. Buenos Aires). And a C.I.F. price quotation would be all the above (i.e., C. & F.), plus the cost of marine insurance. If the price is quoted in a foreign currency (e.g. U.S. dollars), an exchange conversion cost would also have to be included.

Sometimes, to make its export pricing more competitive, a firm will not include in the selling price the normal contribution to "overhead" (fixed factory costs) that each unit of domestic sales is expected to make.

Export Barriers

The Canadian firm will find, in doing its market research, that foreign countries have erected a variety of barriers to goods from Canada and elsewhere. (Canada also restricts imports in various odd ways.) The first type of export barrier is the *tariff* (also called customs duty or import duty). This is an import tax levied *ad valorem* (that is, a percentage of the value of the goods), *specific* (that is, so much money per unit), or a combination of the two. Sometimes the tariff is so high that the price of the Canadian good, if imported into the foreign country, would no longer be competitive. However, since Canada is a member of GATT (The General Agreement on Tariffs and Trade), reciprocal tariff reductions have been negotiated with many countries of the world. So tariffs are not usually an insurmountable barrier.

Special import duties may sometimes be imposed on particular products. Thus an "anti-dumping duty" may be imposed if it can be shown that the Canadian exporter is selling its product abroad at a lower price than at home. Also, a "countervailing duty" may be imposed if it can be shown that the export price of the Canadian product is being subsidized by the government authorities in Canada.

Non-Tariff Barriers. In addition to import duties, the Canadian product may face one or more "non-tariff barriers." The possibilities include:

a. *Import quotas*—the foreign government may permit only limited imports of a particular product.
b. *Exchange controls*—the foreign government, usually through its central bank, may ration the amount of scarce foreign exchange that may be spent on certain types of imports, particularly so-called "luxury goods." Without the foreign exchange permit, the would-be importer cannot obtain the necessary import licence.
c. *Prior deposits*—sometimes, to discourage imports, the foreign government may require that the importer place all or part of the purchase price on interest-free deposit with the country's central bank for several months before the import may take place.
d. *Customs delays*—sometimes, the Canadian firm may encounter unreasonable difficulties in having its goods cleared through foreign customs, perhaps as the result of foreign government policy to slow imports. Canada has itself used this tactic in the past in slowing the import of Japanese cars through the port of Vancouver.
e. *Government purchasing policies*—government departments and agencies abroad may follow a deliberate policy of purchasing their equipment and other needs from local firms.
f. *Technical barriers*—there are reasonable or unreasonable (phoney) technical standards or conditions that must be complied with if the product is to be sold in the foreign country (e.g. special-size containers or special testing).

Export Promotion

In promoting the export of its products, the Canadian firm will have to decide upon an appropriate "blend" of advertising, selling, and other sales promotion acitivities. Factors that will have to be considered before a decision can be made include:

a. the *promotion budget*—how much money is available;
b. the *nature of the product*—for example, is it a consumer or industrial good? What are its key features?
c. the *type of consumer*—who will buy the product?

Usually, consumer goods require a bigger percentage of the promotion budget (say 50 per cent) spent on advertising than on selling. Industrial goods, on the other hand, require most of the budget (say 60 per cent) spent on selling.

If the Canadian firm has appointed a foreign agent, it should work closely with that firm or person in developing a promotional strategy—perhaps using the services of a local advertising agency or the foreign branch of one of the well-known U.S. ones. If the Canadian firm is using its own export sales force (e.g. in the U.S. market), it will probably rely upon its own advertising de-

"No, there's nothing wrong with Canadian tuna; we've been eating it ourselves for years ...."

partment or agency in Canada to prepare the promotional campaign. The Canadian exporter should also make sure that its name and products are included in the *Exporter's Directory* that is compiled by the Department of External Affairs, and used as a reference book by Canada's Trade Commissioners abroad when sourcing Canadian goods for prospective foreign customers.

Selling

If the Canadian exporter is using a foreign agent, it should proceed cautiously in selecting such a person, perhaps with the help of a Canadian Trade Commissioner or, at the provincial level, with the help of, for example, one of Ontario's "International Offices" located in strategic cities around the world. It is easy to rush in and appoint an agent who then proves worthless. Also, the relationship between each foreign agent and the Canadian exporter, including rights and duties of both, should be set out in detail in an agency agreement.

One of the most effective selling techniques in international trade is to participate directly in a *trade fair*, either at home or abroad. This is a privately-organized exhibition, held in a major city, of a specialized range of goods (e.g. packaging machinery). Here the Canadian exporter can meet prospective customers, agents, and distributors and also see what competitors have to offer. Government financial assistance, federal or provincial, is available to help the

Canadian exporter take part in an appropriate foreign trade fair, perhaps as part of a government-sponsored Canadian or provincial pavilion. Another excellent selling technique is for the Canadian exporter to participate in a government-organized, specialized trade mission to various foreign countries. Alternatively, he or she may make a private visit, with a business itinerary including meetings with prospective foreign distributors, planned well-ahead—perhaps with the help of the Canadian Embassy in the foreign country.

KEY TERMS

Direct exporting

Indirect exporting

Export organization

Freight forwarder

Export research

F.O.B. price

C. & F. price

C.I.F. price

Tariff

G.A.T.T.

Anti-dumping duty

Countervailing duty

Import quota

Exchange control

Prior deposit

Customs delays

Government purchasing policies

Technical barriers

Export promotion

Promotion blend

Agency agreement

Trade fair

Trade mission

REVIEW QUESTIONS

1. Distinguish between direct and indirect exporting.
2. What organizational changes in a business firm might export sales require?
3. What export activities might be contracted out?
4. What representation would an exporter need abroad? What is the usual practice?
5. What types of export research should a prospective Canadian exporter undertake?
6. What are the various Canadian sources of export information and advice?
7. How can a firm, planning to export, pre-test its products abroad? Discuss the pros and cons of each method.
8. What is a Trade Commissioner? How can he or she help the Canadian exporter?
9. What items should a firm take into account in setting its export price? Distinguish between F.O.B., C. & F., and C.I.F. prices.
10. How and why might normal contributions to "overhead" be ignored in export pricing?

11. What is a tariff? What are the various types? Why are they levied?
12. What is an "anti-dumping duty"? When is it sometimes imposed? Why?
13. What is a "countervailing duty"? When and why is it sometimes levied on imported goods?
14. Explain the nature and purpose of import quotas.
15. What are exchange controls? Why are they sometimes applied? What is their effect?
16. Explain the term "prior deposit." Why is it considered to be a form of non-tariff barrier?
17. How can foreign customs delay the importation of a Canadian product?
18. How could Canadian exporters be harmed by foreign government purchasing policies?
19. What are examples of foreign technical barriers that hinder Canadian exports?
20. What factors should the Canadian exporter take into account in planning its promotional strategy? How would the strategy for consumer goods vary from that for industrial goods?
21. How would the Canadian exporter go about advertising its products abroad?
22. How should the Canadian exporter select an agent abroad? What key points should be covered by an agency agreement?
23. What is a "trade fair"? What possible benefits can it offer the Canadian exporter?
24. What is a "trade mission"? Why would a Canadian exporter want to participate?

CASE PROBLEM

T. JONES & CO. LTD.
Entering into an export agency agreement

T. Jones & Company recently exhibited their product, a line of industrial machine tools, at a trade show held in Toronto. At the show, they demonstrated their products to a number of foreign visitors, many of whom took the technical literature available and asked a variety of questions, including the possibility of exclusive representation in their countries. Yesterday, a letter and a draft agency agreement arrived from one of the foreign firms (see Figure 18.9) that had shown interest.

Assignment
1. Should the Canadian firm sign the agreement? If not, why not?
2. How should T. Jones & Co. Ltd. go about selecting an agent for Venezuela?
3. Does the Canadian firm need a foreign agent? What are the alternatives?
4. What would have been the purposes of the trade show held in Toronto, from the export point of view?

Venex, P.O. Box 6823 – Caracas, Venezuela

Importers – Distributors – Exclusive Agents
Manufacturers' Export Managers
Bankers: Banco Industrial de Venezuela, Caracas
Cable: Venexpo
Code: Bentley's Complete Phrase
Phone: (02) 572-9523
TELEX: 21124

T. Jones & Co. Ltd.
347 Yonge Street
Toronto
Ontario / CANADA
M5B 2X1

Your Ref   /   Our Ref   04/SP/tv   Caracas   19th March 198-

Dear Sirs,

<u>TORONTO EXHIBITION 1986-</u>

We confirm the visit of our director, Mr. Osvaldo Herrera, at your stand during the above exhibition, as well the various discussions held during this same visit for co-operation.

Presently, you are kindly requested to give an immediate follow-up to these discussions, sending to us the requested offers urgently, and quoting us your most reasonable prices on both ways Ex-Factory C.3% and CIF/La Guaira C.3% through the most competitive way available.

We will appreciate therefore, to receive your most complete offers the soonest possible, along with few basic samples for evaluation and demonstration.

We please you, to give to us the maximum possible of details concerning these offers, in order to allow us to save time and place our orders as soon as possible without any delay.

Further, we are most pleased to inform you, that we could accept to act in Venezuela as your exclusive agents on a commission basis of 3%, and in accordance with the form agreement herewith attached.

In this end, we please you to send to us a supply of Catalogues and Price-Lists, which will allow us to contact several Importers/Wholesalers at the same time.

Looking forward to your early comments, we remain, with best regards,

Sincerely yours

Exclusive Agencies

Department

TRIAL EXCLUSIVE AGENCY AGREEMENT FOR VENEZUELA

BETWEEN: VENEX C.A., Torre Viasa, Sur 24 Plaza Morelos,
P.O. Box 6823, Caracas, Venezuela

and: _____

_____

It is agreed that:

1) The Factory grants to Venex the exclusive Agency for all Venezuela, the complete line of their products.
2) The Agent will be working on a commission basis of 3%, booking orders from Importers, Dealers, etc. in Venezuela, and is authorized to import also on his own account, receiving always 3% commission on the net amount of the invoices.
3) The Factory agrees to quote always the best possible and lowest prices, including 3% commission for the Agents.
4) The Factory will not make any delivery to the territory of Venezuela, without having the agreement of Venex, and without crediting his account with the commission of 3%. All inquiries from Venezuela will be forwarded to Venex.
5) The Agent agrees to do his utmost with regard to booking orders for the Factory. Venex and his customers will have to pay their purchases against confirmed and irrevocable letters of credit, or other legal tender in accordance with the Factory.
6) This agreement should be considered trial, valid for a period of 12 months. After this first year, the annual turnover will be discussed in common agreement, on the base of the achieved results.
7) The Factory agrees to send from time to time to Venex, reasonable quantities of catalogues, prospectus, labels, informations, and other advertising material at no charge, as well as price lists signed, sealed, and recently dated, including always the Agent's commission of 3%, and eventually few basic samples.
8) This agreement will be effective from   1 NOV. 198-
9) The commission of point 2) must be deducted directly from every invoice, and paid to the Agent in bolivars by the buyer in Venezuela.

FOR THE FACTORY: FOR THE AGENT, VENEX:

_____   _____

Figure 18.9 Letter and Draft Agency Agreement

READING

Champion Launches Sales Offensive

BY HARVEY ENCHIN

Source: *The Globe and Mail*, Toronto.

The tip of a huge road grader blade delicately pushes in the tabs on the top of a can of Pepsi. "We sell a quality can opener," jokes Bill Metcalfe, advertising director at Champion Road Machinery Ltd. of Goderich, Ont.

Marketing techniques like the videotaped Pepsi demonstration, illustrating the degree of operator control in Champion's road graders, are part of a strategy to capture a bigger share of a declining world market.

There are too many players in the industry and not enough business, according to Mark Sully, 33, the family-owned company's marketing vice-president. The slowing pace of road construction activity, particularly in developing countries, will weed out uncompetitive manufacturers and poor merchandisers, he said.

The company, which relies on exports for 70 percent of its business, is enduring a difficult transition from being a manufacturing-driven operation to a marketing-driven one to ensure that it is not among them, he said.

"We're changing. We're beginning to do things that have been shown to be successful in other industries."

Those things include audiovisual methods in sales, training and employee communications, computer-aided design and manufacturing, system sales, worker involvement in quality control (quality circles), active pursuit of government aid programs and heavy participation in trade missions and shows.

Located in a picturesque community of 7,500 people on the shores of Lake Huron about 220 kilometres west of Toronto, Champion is not exactly on the main street of road grader manufacturing.

Nevertheless, the company has prospered there since 1945 when Mr. Sully's grandfather bought the near-bankrupt Dominion Road Machinery Co. It had begun corporate life in 1886 as Good Roads Co. in Ohio.

The company made a wide range of products—hoists, conveyors, cranes and crushers among them—until Bruce Sully, the company president and Mark Sully's father, began phasing out product lines in the 1950s. By 1968, Champion made road graders exclusively.

Exports were, at first, a way to overcome the seasonality of road grader sales. Now they are the company's life blood because Canada's market of roughly 400 machines a year, half of prerecession levels, is not sufficient to sustain the company since it must share that market with competitors.

From a 1980 peak of 1,300, Champion's payroll has been cut to 900 at its operations in Goderich and in Columbia, S.C. Of these, 50 work solely on export sales. According to Mr. Sully, it is one of the largest export groups in Canada.

Their work is cut out for them. The industry includes some of the toughest competitors in the world: Caterpillar Tractor Co. of Peoria, Ill., Deere and Co. of Moline, Ill., Aveling Barford International Ltd. of Britain, Orenstein and Koppel AG and Faun Fritch Baumaschinen, both of West Germany, Fiat-Allis Construction Machinery Inc. of Deerfield, Ill., part of the Fiat group of Italy, Galion Manufacturing, a division of Dresser Industries Inc. of Dallas, Komatsu Ltd. of Japan, Terex Corp. of Ohio and Volvo AB of Sweden.

The industry is highly secretive. Neither the companies nor their trade organizations, such as the Construction Industry Machinery Association in Illinois, would disclose sales or market share figures.

"We like to think we're No. 2," Mr. Sully said, conceding first place to Caterpillar. "We build more graders than anyone in North America."

However, a brand awareness study conducted last year by Construction Equipment Magazine of Des Plaines, Ill., suggests Champion has a long way to go. The survey showed Caterpillar with a whopping 69.2 percent, Deere 10.1 percent, Galion 7.5 percent, Fiat-Allis 1.9 percent and Champion 1.4 percent.

U.S. shipments of road graders totalled 2,559 machines worth $216.2-million (U.S.) in the first nine months of 1983, according to figures compiled by the U.S. Department of Commerce.

The value of shipments of graders, scrapers, rollers and off-highway trucks shows a decline last year of 18 percent from 1982, said Martin Fleming, a Boston-based economist, but 1984 will be 46 percent above 1983.

The industry received a boost from rebounding U.S. housing starts and a 5-cent-a-gallon gasoline tax to fund road and bridge construction and maintenance.

Mr. Sully, however, is not so optimistic. "I don't see why it would come back," he said. "There's no money to refuel spending after the recession."

Champion has equipment running in 85 countries, a record he attributes to top-notch distributors who, he said, are all successful entrepreneurs.

But the company was prevented from manufacturing road graders under its own flag in New Zealand and South Africa, where it had done business for many years, because competitors established manufacturing operations first.

"We were reactive in South Africa and New Zealand," Mr. Sully said. "We have to be proactive."

So far, the company has also been blocked out of Indonesia because it cannot get import licences. It is targeting its major export effort toward Southeast Asia.

Protectionism looms as a major factor in export business, Mr. Sully said. "You have to believe in free trade. But most countries are broke."

Nevertheless, Champion is making inroads in new export markets. Mr. Sully said the company has signed agreements in China where road graders will be made using Champion design and technology.

The company has been negotiating with manufacturers in Thailand to set up a 50-50 joint venture there and talks are also under way with two large trading houses from South Korea.

Champion landed a 100-machine order worth roughly $10-million in Canadian funds in Egypt for the U.S. military late last year, and Turkey will be in the market for 500 graders in the next 18 months, he said. Champion "didn't get a stick" of a 1,800-machine order from the U.S. armed forces last year; that went to Caterpillar.

But Mr. Sully said he prefers to avoid the massive volume contracts and make normal commercial transactions Champion's bread and butter.

The 300,000-square-foot plant is already cramped despite the modern computer-controlled machine tools, and the 180,000-square-foot plant in Columbia is running at capacity.

With 40 to 50 percent of its business dependent on offshore sales, Champion cannot afford to lose. Although success is far from certain, even Champion's competitors admire its feistiness. "Wherever we compete head to head, they are a strong competitor," said Steven Newhouse, a spokesman for Caterpillar.

Assignment
1. Who is Champion?
2. What has been its product strategy?
3. How did Champion become a Canadian exporter?
4. What problems does Champion face in the export market?
5. What has been Champion's track record in exporting?

UNIT 18.3: EXPORT FINANCING

It makes no sense for a Canadian firm to export its goods if it does not get paid for them. Therefore, in sending a price quotation to a prospective foreign buyer, the Canadian exporter should stipulate the method of payment.

Methods of Payment

Even in sales transactions within Canada, sellers are usually unwilling to ship goods without assurance of payment. Therefore the usual practice is to run a credit check on a new customer and to limit credit sales per customer to a certain amount. The payment problem becomes much more acute when selling goods to a foreign country where a different political and legal jurisdiction, together with problems of distance and language, make chasing a bad debt correspondingly more difficult. Ideally, the Canadian exporter would like to be paid partly or fully in advance of shipment. But to insist on this would probably mean receiving no purchase orders at all—unless it is for a good that needs to be custom-made, costs an extremely large sum of money, or cannot be purchased from anyone else.

Open Account

If the Canadian firm trusts the foreign buyer, it may ship the goods, send an invoice, and expect to be paid by cheque, or bank draft, on or before the due date. When the order is filled, the foreign buyer's account is debited. When payment is received, the account is credited and the balance owing eliminated. This method of payment is usual when the Canadian branch of a foreign multinational exports parts or finished goods to the parent company, usually in the U.S., or to other branches around the world. It is also quite usual when Canadian firms ship goods to trusted customers in the U.S., Europe and other countries even further afield.

Documentary Drafts

If the amount of trust between the Canadian exporter and the foreign buyer is not very great, a method called "documents on payment" (or D.O.P.) can be used. With this method, the Canadian firm, after shipping the goods against an order, hands over to its bank a complete set of shipping documents. The bank then sends these documents to its branch or, if it does not have one, to its "correspondent bank" in the foreign country. The latter would be a trusted foreign bank that acts on the Canadian bank's behalf. The bank in the foreign country then presents to the foreign importer a *sight draft*—which is an instruction, prepared by the Canadian exporter, to the foreign buyer to pay the sum of money owing for the goods to the Canadian exporter's authorized agent: the bank. Alternatively, if the Canadian exporter is providing credit, the bank abroad will require the foreign buyer to sign a document called a *time draft* (or "bill of exchange"). This draft, which is also previously prepared by the Canadian exporter, is a written promise by the foreign buyer to pay a stated sum of money "for value received" on or before a stipulated future date. Once payment has been made against the *sight draft*, or once the *time draft* has been signed thereby acknowledging the debt, the bank hands over the shipping documents to the foreign buyer. These documents (see Figure 18.10) include the ocean *bill of lading* which is both (a) the written contract between the exporter and the shipping company for shipping the goods to the foreign port and (b) the document of ownership of the goods. Possession of the bill of lading gives the foreign importer or its agent the right to remove the goods from the customs warehouse in the foreign port. Other documents that may be required from the Canadian exporter, depending on the type of goods shipped and the country of destination, include: a marine insurance certificate; a certificate of origin of the goods; a consular invoice (a special invoice approved and stamped by the consul in Canada of the foreign country); a commercial invoice; a certificate of quality; a packing list; and a health certificate (in the case of live animals, etc.).

Discounting

If the Canadian exporter has given credit terms to the foreign buyer, the bank in the foreign country, acting on the exporter's behalf, will have released the documents in return for the accepted "time draft." This time draft will contain the importer's promise to pay so much for the goods at a specified future date. And the bank may hold this draft, on the exporter's behalf, for the 60, 90, 180 days, or whatever, that is specified, and then present it to the importer for payment. However, the Canadian exporter, if it wishes to obtain funds sooner, may request that the draft be returned to Canada. Then the exporter can arrange to "discount" the draft at its bank. The bank purchases the draft from the exporter for less than its face value (the "discount") and takes over the financing and subsequent collection. The exporter, on its part, has most of the cash owed to it for its goods now rather than later, although the bank may come back to it ("recourse") should the foreign importer later fail to pay the bank.

Letters of Credit

The Canadian exporter may believe, quite rightly, that it cannot be certain of payment despite using the "documents on payment" procedure just outlined.

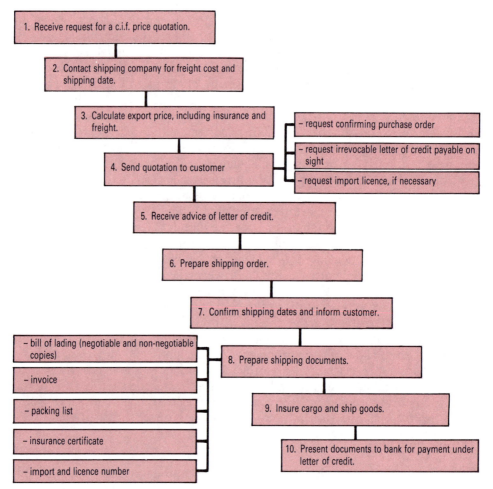

Figure 18.10 Export Transaction Procedure

This is because the foreign buyer may change its mind about the transaction, (perhaps because of discovery of a cheaper source of supply, loss of a customer, or financial difficulties) and refuse to pay for the goods or "accept" a time draft. The Canadian exporter would then have its goods sitting in a foreign port, waiting to be otherwise disposed of. This can mean financial loss, despite the Canadian exporter's right to sue the foreign buyer for breach of contract. It can also mean extra headaches. Therefore, many Canadian exporters will only ship goods abroad against a *letter of credit*. This is a document issued by the foreign importer's bank at the request of the foreign importer. In it, the foreign bank agrees to pay against a sight draft or, if credit is involved, accept time drafts drawn upon it by the seller (the Canadian exporter) so long as the conditions set out in the letter of credit (e.g. latest shipping date, no partial shipments, etc.) are complied with. It should be noted that the letter of credit does not replace the draft. Both are required.

Irrevocable or Revocable. The Canadian exporter should stipulate that the letter of credit be "irrevocable." Otherwise, the foreign bank, on direction of the foreign buyer, could cancel it at any time. If irrevocable, the letter of credit will expire only on the date stipulated in it. This expiry date should be sufficiently far in the future to enable the Canadian exporter to make the shipment. If too close, the exporter should ask the foreign buyer to have the letter of credit amended on this point before accepting the order. An irrevocable letter of credit can be altered (or *amended*) at any time, so long as both exporter and importer agree.

Confirmed vs. Unconfirmed. Although fine-sounding, the irrevocable letter of credit is still not a cast-iron guarantee of payment for the exported goods. Occasionally, a foreign bank, for one reason or another, will not honour its own financial commitment. Sometimes also, the sudden imposition or alteration of foreign exchange controls in the importing country may prevent payment even though the foreign bank wishes, and has the local currency, to fulfil its obligation. Consequently, if the Canadian exporter is unsure about the foreign bank's reliability or the foreign country's foreign exchange situation, it should insist not just on an irrevocable letter of credit but also on a "confirmed" one.

With a confirmed, irrevocable letter of credit, a Canadian bank undertakes to pay for the export shipment if the foreign bank fails to do so. However, the Canadian bank may be reluctant to confirm a letter of credit if it has any doubt about the trustworthiness of the foreign bank or fears that foreign exchange controls may prevent payment in Canadian or U.S. funds. In such a case, it may refuse confirmation unless the full amount of the funds involved is transferred to it right away from the foreign country.

By stipulating that the foreign importer arrange for an irrevocable letter of credit, the Canadian exporter knows that if it ships the goods as agreed, it will have the foreign bank's assurance of payment. And if the letter of credit is "confirmed," the exporter will have a Canadian bank's assurance also. The Canadian exporter need not rely on the good faith of the foreign importer alone.

EDC Insurance

Normally, when shipping on a C.I.F. price basis, the Canadian exporter will arrange for marine insurance to protect itself from financial loss should the export shipment be lost or damaged in transit to the foreign destination, from "perils of the sea" and other specified risks. However, such insurance does not provide protection against failure of the foreign buyer to pay for the goods as agreed, perhaps because of insolvency or state of war. To cover this risk, a federal Crown Corporation, the *Export Development Corporation* (or *EDC*), provides short-term global insurance to Canadian exporters. The risks covered are both commercial (insolvency or bankruptcy of the buyer, or repudiation of the goods by the buyer) and political (blockage of funds, war or revolution, or cancellation of the import permit). To obtain coverage, the Canadian exporter must supply the EDC with adequate evidence of buyer credit worthiness; make monthly declarations of shipments and/or contracts signed; pay a monthly premium; provide details of accounts overdue 90 days or more; and participate in recovery of bad debts. The EDC also provides long-term financing and other export services.

KEY TERMS

Open account

Documents on payment

Correspondent bank

Sight draft

Time draft

Bill of lading

Consular invoice

Discounting

Letter of credit

Irrevocable letter of credit

Confirmed letter of credit

EDC

REVIEW QUESTIONS

1. Why are credit sales abroad riskier than credit sales at home?
2. What is selling "on open account"? What precautions are required? When is this practice usual in international trade?
3. What is meant by the term "documents on payment"? What are the documents referred to?
4. What is a "correspondent bank"? What functions does it perform as such?
5. What is a "sight draft"? What purpose does it serve?
6. What is a "time draft"? How does it differ from a sight draft?
7. What is a "bill of lading"? Why is it such an important document?
8. What other documents may be required for an export shipment?
9. What is "discounting"? Who does it? What are its advantages and disadvantages for the Canadian exporter?
10. What is a "letter of credit"? Why is it used?
11. What is an "irrevocable" letter of credit?
12. Why may the Canadian exporter require that a letter of credit also be "confirmed"? By whom? And why?
13. What is the EDC? How can it help protect the Canadian exporter in its export transactions abroad?

PART J
ELECTRONIC DATA PROCESSING

CHAPTER 19
COMPUTERS IN BUSINESS

CHAPTER OBJECTIVES

☐ To describe the basic equipment or "hardware" components of a business computer system.

☐ To explain the electronic data processing cycle.

☐ To review the main input and output devices.

☐ To indicate how a computer program is prepared.

☐ To review various business applications of computers.

CHAPTER OUTLINE

19.1 Computer Hardware
19.2 Business Software

Unit 19.1: COMPUTER HARDWARE

Electronic Data Processing (or EDP) is the processing of data by means of an electronic computer system.

Characteristics of a Computer System

An electronic computer system has the following main characteristics:
1. It can process data, without human intervention, according to a pre-arranged sequence of instructions.
2. These instructions (the *program*), as well as facts, can be stored for use as required in the computer's memory unit or in auxiliary storage devices. This information is never forgotten and can be recalled for use almost instantly.
3. Calculations are performed electronically at incredibly high speeds.
4. All the various pieces of equipment in the system are automatically controlled by a central processing unit (CPU); however, direct human control is possible through a keyboard.
5. Data and instructions can be stored on a variety of devices—such as magnetic disks, magnetic tape, etc.—for fast entry into the computer system.
6. Unlike people, a computer does not make mistakes in carrying out the data-processing instructions given to it. However, the instructions have to be correct and the data accurate.
7. A computer, because it is a machine (even though a highly sophisticated one), is subject to occasional breakdown—with sometimes disastrous consequences. Also, of course, it needs a constant supply of electricity. And programs and data can be accidentally erased by the operator.

Basic Types of Computers

Computers now available consist of the following basic types:
1. *Supercomputers*—these are the most powerful types of computers and are used, because of their tremendous "number-crunching" abilities, for special purposes such as scientific research.
2. *Mainframes*—these are very powerful computers and are used by large and medium-sized business firms, academic institutions, government departments, etc., for centralized data processing.
3. *Minicomputers*—these are small but quite powerful computers that are used by small and medium-sized business firms and other organizations as their primary computer system and by some larger firms for specified functions as a supplement to their mainframe system. They are distinguished from a microcomputer by the fact that (a) they are more powerful and (b) more than one computer terminal is connected to the CPU.
4. *Microcomputers*—these are the smallest types of computers used in business (as well as in the home) for a variety of data processing applications. Although small, they have the memory and data processing capabilities to

execute a variety of tasks, including word-processing, invoicing, record-keeping, mailing, and production control. A small business may have one such machine whereas a large business may have several hundred, as individual work stations that can be used in the office, in the employee's home, or, with a portable model, "on the road". Several microcomputers may be linked together in a *network* that can simultaneously access computer programs and data banks.

Benefits of Computerization

The main reasons why more and more business firms are using computers are:
1. *Cost-savings*—it is usually cheaper to perform many data-processing tasks this way, because of the labour savings to be achieved.
2. *Accuracy*—the data processing is performed more accurately, so long as the program is appropriate and the data are entered correctly.
3. *Speed*—a computer can perform a data-processing task (e.g. payroll preparation in a large firm) much faster than can people.
4. *Storage capacity*—vast amounts of data can be stored in the computer or on magnetic disks, tapes, etc., in a fraction of the space otherwise required. Also, this data can be accessed almost instantly.
5. *Management information*—the computer can assist management decision-making by providing essential data in usable form and by facilitating "what if" calculations.
6. *Opportunities*—the computer can manipulate data so quickly that it makes feasible many new data applications—for example, computerized air traffic control, computer-aided design and manufacturing (CAD/CAM), and computerized cash registers.

Computer Hardware

The basic equipment, or *hardware*, in a business computer system (Figure 19.1) consists of:
1. A *central processing unit (or CPU)*, divided into:
   (a) A *primary storage unit*, or memory—for storage of facts and instructions;
   (b) An *arithmetic-logic unit (or ALU)*—for performing the basic arithmetic functions and for making logical comparisons as directed by the control unit;
   (c) A *control unit*—for selecting, interpreting, and executing the instructions stored in memory, and for controlling, by means of electronic circuits, the correct performance of operations by the arithmetic-logic unit.
2. A *keyboard with video display*, for permitting a human operator to give directions to the computer system as required—such as starting a program—and to see what is taking place. In some models, there is an electronic "light pen," mouse, touchscreen, etc. for communication between the operator and the system.
3. *Peripherals*, divided into:
   (a) *Input devices*—such as keyboard terminals, magnetic disk drives, magnetic

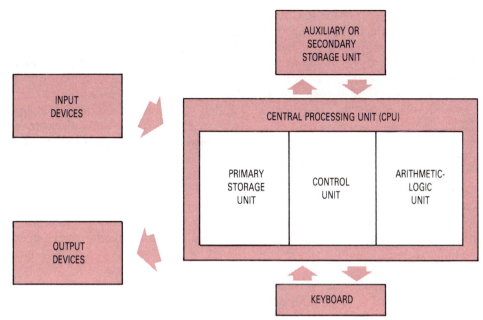

Figure 19.1 The Basic Components of a Computer System

tape drives, and diskette drives—for feeding facts and instructions into the storage unit of the CPU;
(b) *Output devices*—such as printers, cathode ray tubes, magnetic tape drives, and plotters—for obtaining processed data from the CPU;
(c) *Auxiliary storage devices*—such as magnetic disk drives, magnetic tape drives, or diskette drives—for storing information until it is required for use.

Computer systems vary, of course, in size and data-processing capability. For the large firm, a mainframe system may be necessary. It may be a multiple station computer system that permits authorized persons at many different company locations to have direct, daily interaction with the computer—to inquire, for example, about the latest inventory balance of an item. With the appropriate software, it can handle such tasks as accounts receivable, invoicing, materials planning, statistics, production planning, purchasing, credit control, inventory control, sales analysis and payroll. To a declining extent, some firms find it more efficient to undertake *time-sharing*, whereby many firms, using telephone lines to access a common CPU, share the use of a computer system owned by someone else and pay only for the time used. For the smaller firm, one or more minicomputers may be more suitable.

Computer Operation

The data processing cycle used in a computer system has four main phases: input, storage, calculation, and output.

Input. Facts to be processed, and instructions as to the nature and sequence of operations, are fed into the storage unit of the central processing unit by means of one or more input devices. As the computer can distinguish only between two possible states — for example, an open or a closed relay—all data to be processed must first be converted from decimal or alphabetic form into a form intelligible to the computer. This "machine language," called *binary code*, uses only the binary digits (or *bits*) of 0 and 1. Thus, as can be seen in Figure 19.2, a decimal 2 is represented by a binary 10. A code often used with business computers is a variation of the binary system and is known as Binary Coded Decimal.

Calculation. Once a complete set of instructions and the necessary factual data have been fed into the storage unit, a human operator can use the keyboard to instruct the control unit to proceed with the first instruction. From that point on, the computer will continue on its own until all the instructions have been completed.

Output. The data, once processed, are stored temporarily in the storage unit and then fed out of the central processing unit by means of one of the various output devices.

Central Processing Unit

In this section we examine the component units of the central processing unit, or CPU, in a little more detail.

Decimal			Binary			
(× 10)			(× 2)			
100	10	1	8	4	2	1
0	0	0	0	0	0	0
0	0	1	0	0	0	1
0	0	2	0	0	1	0
0	0	3	0	0	1	1
0	0	4	0	1	0	0
0	0	5	0	1	0	1
0	0	6	0	1	1	0
0	0	7	0	1	1	1
0	0	8	1	0	0	0
0	0	9	1	0	0	1
0	1	0	1	0	1	0
0	1	1	1	0	1	1

Figure 19.2 Binary Representation of Decimal Values

1. Storage Unit. Data fed into a computer system have to be stored temporarily in the primary storage unit to await processing. Data that have undergone processing may also have to be temporarily stored to await further processing either in the main storage unit or auxiliary ones.

Nowadays, the usual storage device is an integrated circuit on a tiny *silicon chip*. Because of this invention, storage units are now much faster in operation, much more compact in size, and cheaper.

Also, a storage management technique, called *virtual storage*, makes possible much better use of main storage capacity. This is done, during the processing of data, by retaining in main storage only the active sections of each program. The inactive sections are temporarily stored on slower and less costly disk auxiliary storage units and recalled to main storage as and when required. Consequently, a computer with virtual memory can appear to process many large programs simultaneously. In the future, other types of storage devices are anticipated such as *bubble memory*—magnetic "bubbles" or spots on a thin layer of magnetic film.

2. Arithmetic-Logic Unit. The arithmetic-logic unit of the CPU is able to perform two main functions: add, subtract, multiply and divide data; and tell, by comparison, whether two numbers are equal or unequal, whether one number is greater than another, or whether a number is positive, negative, or zero.

3. Control Unit. The control unit is the hub of the central processing unit. It mechanically supervises the operation of the storage unit, the arithmetic-logic unit, and the input and output devices, to ensure that the instructions fed into the computer are correctly carried out.

Keyboard with Video Display

An operator can exercise manual control over the computer system either by a control panel on the central processing unit or by a keyboard with a video display. The keyboard can be used: to start and stop the computer; to enter program commands; and (in the case of a microcomputer) to enter data for immediate processing and/or storage.

Input Devices

As a preliminary stage, employees may use what is called a *key to storage unit* to key data from source documents (e.g. purchase orders) onto magnetic tape, disk, diskette, cassete, paper tape, or punched cards (although less and less frequently). The data can then be transferred later, in chunk-size portions, to the computer's central processing unit by means of an input device for what is called *batch processing*. The input devices used, once the data have been entered on the input medium, include: magnetic tape drives, hard disk drives, floppy disk drives, and punched card readers. The data input devices may be located at the same place as the CPU or they may be at a remote location and linked to the CPU by telephone line, microwave station, or satellite transmission.

1. Magnetic Tape Drive. This is a device that is able, at high speed, to read data from magnetic tape to the CPU and to write data from the CPU to magnetic tape. The magnetic tape commonly used is one-half inch wide, made of plastic, and coated on one side with metallic oxide. The oxide side contains either nine or seven tracks running the length of the tape. On these tracks, spots are magnetized in one direction or another to represent numbers and letters.

As an input medium, magnetic tape has the advantages of being cheaper per unit of data stored than some other media (e.g. disks); extremely fast to read; able to store data for long periods of time; quite durable; very compact; and capable of reuse. A disadvantage for some users is that it is a sequential medium, so that particular data cannot be obtained without first passing many feet of tape—a relatively slow process—before arriving at the required data. At one time, data first had to be punched on cards before it could be transferred to tape. However, key-to-tape methods are now widely used.

2. Hard Disk Drive. These are of two types. First, a single rigid "Winchester" type disk for a microcomputer. And, second, a direct access storage device (or DASD) for a mainframe computer. The latter is a device that contains a large number of special magnetic disks (similar to long-play records) mounted on a vertical shaft. Data is stored on these disks in the form of magnetized spots on the circular tracks on each surface. The data is placed on the disk or taken from it by means of read-write heads. These heads are mounted on arms which move horizontally in the spaces between the various disk surfaces. The disks are constantly spinning as the vertical shaft revolves.

The magnetic disk has the advantage, compared with magnetic tape, of permitting faster access to the information required. This is because there is direct access to the data, and no sequential searching need be done until the required data is located. Disks are, however, a more expensive medium than magnetic tape.

3. Floppy Disk Drive. This device converts into electrical impulses the data stored on oxide-coated plastic *floppy disks:* (or *diskettes*) and sends them to the CPU. It is the basic input device used with a microcomputer. Often, two disk drives, A and B, or left and right, will be used with one micro to facilitate the storage of information.

4. Punched Card Reader. This is the oldest type of input device. Today, however, punched cards are not greatly used in business. The punched card system requires that data to be processed first be recorded on special cards in the form of holes punched at certain positions. The system used is called the Hollerith code, named after its inventor, Dr. Herman Hollerith, a statistician with the U.S. Census Bureau. For many years, the punched card contained 80 vertical columns, each of which could be punched to represent a different letter, number, or special character. There is also now a 96-column card—about one-third the size of the standard 80-column card and with 20 per cent more capacity. One of a few remaining uses for punched cards in business is for billing the

"This is our latest model. The crystal ball is a new feature that can be used for sales forecasting, employment planning, production control, and so on."

customers of telephone, gas, electric, oil, and credit card companies. The punched cards are referred to as "turnaround documents" because they come out of the computer system and, when returned by the customer with payment, are fed back in.

Another type of card used in electronic data processing is the *mark-sense card*. These are used for such purposes as recording the answers to questions in door-to-door surveys (a form of multiple-choice question). The information marked on these cards can be mechanically read and punched into punched cards or fed directly into the computer, ready for processing.

5. Direct Operator Entry Devices.

Instead of entering data via an input medium such as magnetic tape, disk, or diskette, a person may enter data directly into the computer by means of a keyboard terminal, light pen, mouse, etc.

(a) Keyboard Terminal. Here a person types or *keys* the data into the computer system, using a keyboard. There is also usually a CRT (cathode ray tube) screen for displaying the data being transmitted and for receiving responses or queries from the CPU. An example would be a keyboard on a microcomputer or computer terminal. On a mainframe computer, a console typewriter is used to preserve a hard copy of all operator instructions and messages.

(b) Light Pen. Data may be entered on a CRT screen by means of a *light pen* which uses a laser beam to transmit signals to the CPU. The operator may be required to write on the screen (e.g. enter name) or point to a desired function (e.g. display inventory balance). The light pen can also be used to prepare or modify a design or layout (e.g. a machine component or a production line).

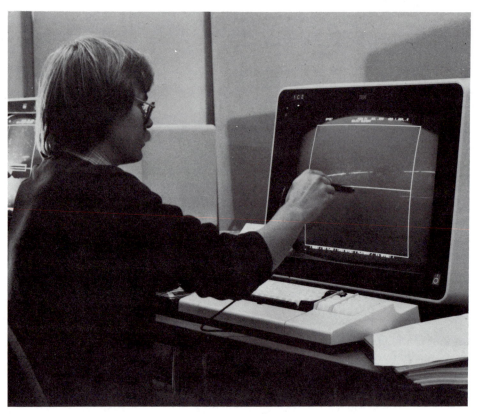

Courtesy The Ontario Ministry of Industry, Trade and Technology

(c) Mouse. This is a device, used mainly with a microcomputer system, to move a cursor on the CRT screen to choose a specific function (such as opening a new file).

(d) Touch-Sensitive Screen. Here, a person may indicate a choice or transmit a command merely by touching the screen in the appropriate place.

(e) Voice Recognition Unit. This input device interprets the operator's spoken word, transmitting the corresponding electronic signals to the CPU. Usually, the message is first verified, before onward transmission, by the device repeating the message back to the operator. Such units are still relatively new.

(f) Touch-Tone Telephone and/or Portable Keying Device. Here, for example, a bank teller or customer may access a particular bank account by keying in the appropriate code on a touch-tone telephone. A portable keying device is also available that enables a person to enter data using any standard telephone.

(g) Automatic Teller Machine (ATM). This is a data entry terminal, located at bank branches and elsewhere, that enables customers to make deposits and withdrawals, usually over a 24-hour period. To access an account, the customer must first insert a plastic bank identification card in the machine and then key in a personal identification number that only the customer is supposed to know.

6. Direct Machine Entry Devices. These input devices, called optical scanners, can "read" data directly from a source document, thereby eliminating the need for keying data. The data, once read, is stored on a magnetic tape or disk to await future batch processing. The "reading" of the source document is done by a laser or photoelectric device that converts the characters or codes (e.g. a bank account number) into electronic signals.

(a) Optical Character Recognition Device. Such a device can read data that has been typed or even handwritten on a source document. However, the equipment is quite expensive (thereby requiring intensive use for it to be cost effective) and prone to error. The latter disadvantage can be reduced by ensuring that the data to be read conforms to certain basic rules of legibility (e.g. making letters big, using block letters, not linking characters, fully completing each character, etc.). On a smaller scale, hand-held *wand readers* are now being used in libraries and many other institutions to read optical characters containing inventory data.

(b) Bar Code Reader. This device scans the bar code on an item and transmits the corresponding data to the CPU. It is widely used in supermarkets for totalling customer purchases, recording sales, and supplying inventory data. The bar code reader is also used in warehouses, assembly plants, or wherever inventory control is a major activity. Compared with optical character readers, bar code readers are much cheaper and more accurate. However, they can only read bar codes.

(c) Optical Mark Reader. Also called a mark-sense reader, this device can detect the presence of pencil marks on a predetermined grid (such as a computer-scored test card). Although widely used for educational testing purposes, the device also has a number of business applications, e.g. utility meter readings.

(d) Magnetic Ink Character Reader (MICR). This is a specialized banking input unit. Each bank cheque, when supplied to the customer, contains the bank number, the account number, and the cheque number encoded at the bottom. Subsequently, when the cheque is used by the customer, the dollar amount for which it is written is also encoded at the bottom of the cheque, by the bank in which it is deposited or sometimes by the company to which it is paid. The MICR then reads all the magnetic ink digits on each cheque and, after sorting the data, transmits it to the CPU, which then adjusts the bank accounts accordingly. Also, the cheques are sorted by bank and customer account number so that, depending on the type of chequing account, they can be returned to the customer with the monthly bank statement.

(e) Personal Banking Machine. This is a machine designed for use in a retail store, that reads the MICR line on a customer's cheque and authorizes it for acceptance at the store's checkout area for any amount up to an established store limit. The machine also disburses cash in up to five different currency denom-

Courtesy IBM Canada Ltd.

inations and four different coin denominations, to customers wishing to obtain cash.

Output Devices

The output devices most commonly used with computer systems include: printers, cathode ray tubes, graphic display terminals, audio response units, and computer output microfilm units.

1. Printer. This is used to provide data in the form of printed reports, still the most widely-used type of computer output medium. There are three basic types of printer: serial, line, and page.

(a) Serial Printer. This type of printer includes: (a) the *dot-matrix* printer which forms the characters by pressing a specific pattern of pins against a carbon ribbon; and (b) the *daisy-wheel* printer, with interchangeable print wheels, which prints fully-formed characters. Most of the serial printers are of the impact type whereby a hammer strikes a key. However, there are now also non-impact type printers that use thermal or ink-jet devices to form the characters. Serial printers, particularly the dot-matrix type, are used as "hard-copy" terminals to provide immediate answers to queries and to print reports at remote locations. They are also used as printers for microcomputers—for which their relatively low cost offsets their relatively slow speed.

(b) Line Printer. This type of printer prints one line of output at a time, rather than just one character. Because of its fast speed, it is used with mini and mainframe computers.

The most commonly used type of line printer uses a flexible stainless steel print band. Other types use a moveable chain or cylindrical steel drum. Most line printers are impact printers, with speeds varying from 100 to 2000 or more lines per minute.

(c) Page Printer. This is a non-impact printer that prints a page at a time, using a laser beam directed onto a drum. Printing speed is at least 60,000 lines per minute. However, the cost of the printer is still very high, although dropping. Another type of page printer, although much less popular, is the xerographic type that prints in a manner similar to that of a photo-copy machine.

2. Cathode Ray Tube (CRT). This output device displays information from the computer on a TV-like video screen. The CRT is useful for supplying information at remote locations, when printed data is unnecessary. As such, they are used, for example, for displaying flight information at airports, the latest quotations from the stock exchange in stockbroker offices, and inventory balances in warehouses and service counters.

3. Graphics Display Terminal. This is a CRT unit that can display on its screen, often in colour, various types of graphic, pictorial, and even animated data. Such data can then be printed by a hard-copy plotter or graphics printer.

Courtesy IBM Canada Ltd.

4. Audio Response Unit. This is an output device that gives the user a verbal rather than a printed or displayed response—for example, about the status of a person's bank account, confirmation of the placement of a purchase order, or the inventory balance of a particular item. Often, communication with the audio response unit is by telephone.

5. Computer Output Microfilm (COM) Unit. This unit, when linked to a CPU, can prepare, at a high rate of speed, microfilms or microfiches containing the computer-supplied output data. In this way, large quantities of data (hospital records, for example) can be stored in a fraction of the normal space. The data can then be retrieved, as the need arises, by means of a computer terminal which can read and locate the address assigned to each document. The document required can then be viewed with a microfilm reader.

Auxiliary Storage

Information can be stored outside the main computer system on auxiliary (or secondary) storage devices. The most popular storage media are magnetic tape and magnetic disk. This is because both media can store large quantities of data in a relatively small space and permit extremely fast retrieval of the data whenever it is required.

Any comprehensive collection of data relating to a particular entity (for example, a product) is called a *masterfile*. A collection of data relating to a business transaction (for example, a sales transaction) is called a *transaction file*. Each file is, in turn, subdivided into *records* (one record per product, for example). Each record is subdivided into *fields* (such as product number, description, price, etc.). The auxiliary storage devices can be permanently linked to the primary storage unit in the computer system so that information can be brought to the CPU in a matter of seconds.

Electronic Workstations

More and more large firms are establishing what are known as *workstations* for their managerial, professional, and technical personnel. These are small work areas designed around a microcomputer or a computer terminal which is linked to a large computer in the same building or elsewhere. The micro or terminal is used to: (a) send and receive messages; (b) access various central data banks; (c) help schedule meetings; (d) word process reports, memos, etc.; (e) process data (calculating costs, or preparing a sales forecast); and (f) file data.

KEY TERMS

EDP

Program

CPU

Mouse

Touch-sensitive screen

Voice recognition unit

Mainframes
Minicomputers
Microcomputers
Network
Hardware
Peripherals
Software
Time sharing
Binary code
Silicon chip
Virtual storage
Batch processing
Magnetic tape drive
Hard disk drive
Floppy disk drive
Punched card reader
Mark-sense card
Keyboard terminal
Light pen

Touch-tone telephone
Automatic teller machine
Optical scanner
Wand reader
Bar code reader
Optical mark reader
MICR
Personal banking machine
Serial printer
Line printer
Page printer
CRT
COM
Auxiliary storage
Masterfile
Transaction file
Record
Field
Electronic workstation

Review Questions

1. What are the main characteristics of an electronic computer system? To what extent is a computer system infallible?
2. What are the basic types of computer systems?
3. Why might a firm decide to purchase a computer?
4. Explain the nature and purpose of the central processing unit in an electronic computer system. What are the basic components of the CPU?
5. What are the various peripheral devices? What are their purposes?
6. Explain briefly the data processing cycle in an electronic computer system.
7. Explain the difference between the decimal and the binary numbering systems.
8. How is data stored in a computer system?
9. What are the purposes of the arithmetic-logic unit and the control unit? What is the relationship between these two units?
10. Compare the merits of magnetic tape and magnetic disk as input media.

11. How is data fed into a microcomputer? Why do many people use two drives rather than one?
12. What is a punched card? For what business purposes can it be used?
13. What are the various kinds of direct operator entry devices?
14. What are the different types of optical scanner?
15. What specialized computer input units exist in banking?
16. List and compare the basic kinds of computer printers.
17. For what purposes are CRT units used?
18. What is a COM unit? For what purposes is it used?
19. What is "auxiliary storage"?
20. Explain how data is filed in computer storage.
21. What is an electronic workstation?

Unit 19.2: BUSINESS SOFTWARE

Computer Programs

A *program* is a set of instructions for the computer, detailing the sequence of steps to be followed in performing a data processing operation. Computer programs are of two basic kinds: (a) *operating system programs*—programs that help the computer to run more efficiently; and (b) *application programs*—programs designed to help perform a specialized task such as a business firm's bookkeeping, direct mailing, or inventory control.

Program Preparation

The preparation of a program consists of: (a) *analysing*—which is the systematic summarizing of the input, output, and logic to be handled by the computer; (b) *programming* (also known as *coding*)—which is the preparation of detailed instructions for the computer; (c) *debugging* and *testing*—checking the program for errors, making corrections, and testing the finished program (often, depending on the firm, a systems analyst will perform the analysing, and a programmer the programming, debugging and testing); and (d) *documenting*—making a written record of the program for future reference. Computer programs in general are called "software." The term "programming" is also sometimes used in a broad sense to mean the whole problem-solving procedure involved in computerizing a business or other task.

At one time, programmers used a highly individualistic approach in their programming. Nowadays, to reduce the cost of developing and maintaining programs, programming is done in a more standardized way—called "structured programming."

Analysing. In analysing an operation, a systems analyst will first examine user needs and then make use of a *systems flow chart* to set out the various steps performed in the operation and the relationship between them. The analyst will, by questioning, attempt to clarify any step or relationship not clearly spelled out.

He or she will attempt to determine not only the steps involved in processing a normal transaction, but also the steps for each abnormal or exceptional one. The key personnel for the systems analyst to talk to are: (a) the clerical staff that input the data and (b) the clerical and management staff that use the output from the computer.

Programming. The programmer's plans for processing the data by computer are set out in the form of a *programming flow chart* (see Figure 19.3). This chart shows where *branching* (choosing between two alternative instructions) has to be done. Instead of a flow chart, the programmer may prefer *pseudocode*. This is the use of "plain English" rather than strict programming English (or *real code*) to indicate the sequence of steps required (e.g. read an input record, write a line, or stop). Another programming tool is a *HIPO chart* (which stands for Hierarchical Input-Process-Output). Such a chart requires the programmer to focus on the main procedures before the subsidiary ones (hence the term, "hierarchy") and to focus on the input, processing, and output elements of a structured design.

Once the program logic has been determined, using either a flowchart, pseudocode, or a HIPO chart, the programmer must write the instructions in one of the symbolic languages used by the computer. Two well-known symbolic languages are COBOL (Common Business-Oriented Language) and FORTRAN (Formula Translator). Each symbolic language possesses merits for different purposes. The instructions once written (or "coded") are keyed into the computer, with each keyed line containing a separate instruction. The complete set of instructions, after being checked for accuracy, is then converted into the *machine language* of the computer to be used.

Debugging and Testing. The computer program is then checked and tested with all imaginable types of actual, or "live," data which has also been processed manually. Finally, often after some adjustments, the program is ready for use.

Documenting. A necessary last step in computer programming is to make a written record, or documentation package, of the program.

Networks

Programs are now available to link large numbers of computers into a data processing network so that users can draw on programs in any computer in the network.

Business Applications

Some of the many business uses for computer systems are: word processing; accounting; inventory control; sales records and analysis; accounts receivable; purchasing; production control; industrial design; mailing lists; appointment

686 CHAPTER 19 COMPUTERS IN BUSINESS

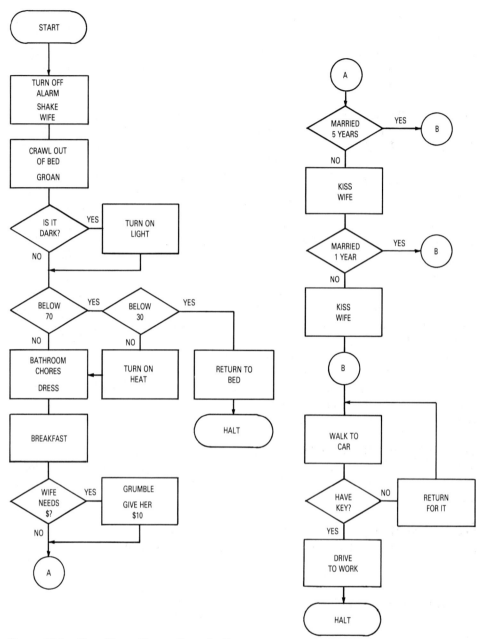

Figure 19.3 Flow Chart: How to Start the Day

scheduling; customer records and mailing lists. In the following pages, we review some of the most popular uses of computers in business.

Word Processing. One of the characteristics of the computerized (or automated) office is the use of word processors. This may be a *dedicated word processor*—that is, a machine that can only do word processing; or it may be a *microcomputer* (or a terminal linked to a mini or mainframe computer) that performs word processing as only one of several different possible functions. The word processor consists of a keyboard, computer, and video screen which together permit the user to compose letters, reports, memos, etc. on the screen and then, when ready, print them out on a printer. Not only can words be inserted and deleted as required, but whole paragraphs can be switched around. Also, standard paragraphs can be stored and retrieved as required—for example, in a lawyer's office for standard documents such as wills, deeds, or partnership agreements. Similarly, standard letters can be combined with a mailing list to produce personalized direct mail letters. Spelling can be automatically checked with the use of a spelling program.

Electronic Filing. In the computerized office, the storage and retrieval of data are no longer done manually. Instead, the information is stored electronically on magnetic tape, magnetic disk, microfilm, or microfiche. The electronic *data base*, as it is called, consists of a large number of individual *files*—data grouped together because of common characteristics (for example, sales records). Each of these files is *cross-referenced* to the others, so that information from any of the files can be quickly accessed.

Electronic Mail. Although the telephone is quick for transmitting messages, the sender often finds that the intended receiver is not available. Similarly, although internal and external mail are reasonably fast, there are often delays. Therefore, the modern computerized office uses an *electronic mail/message system* (or *Emms*) to send, store, and deliver messages.

One type of electronic mail system, called *computer message switching*, permits messages to be sent from one person's computer terminal to another where they appear on the video screen. If the intended receiver is not there, the terminal stores the message until it is picked up. Alternatively, there may be a centralized computer "post office," in which each person has an *electronic mailbox* that he or she periodically checks for messages. A second type of electronic mail system, called *facsimile*, permits documents to be transmitted over the telephone from one place to another by telephone line or satellite signal. A third type of system is the *voice store and forward system* (or VSF) whereby a caller's spoken message is electronically stored, then retrieved and reconstructed when the receiver is ready to receive it.

Electronic Conferencing. A great deal of time is spent by business executives travelling between different cities and different parts of Canada and the United States to attend sales and other meetings. One way of avoiding that is to participate in a "computer conference." Each conference participant, after having attached his or her telephone to a desktop computer, can key in messages that are then displayed on the computer screens of the other conference members. Such a conference can last for a number of hours, with questions being asked and answered and information sent to and fro. Unlike a telephone conference, participants can leave their desks periodically and receive and respond to messages on their return. All the messages are then stored in a computer file which can be printed out as a transcript of the proceedings.

Another type of electronic conferencing is known as *teleconferencing*. This may take the form of an *audio conference* in which the participants, who are connected to each other simultaneously by telephone, can talk and listen to each other. Alternatively, it may be an *audiovisual conference* in which the participants, who must sit in specially equipped rooms at each location, can see each other as well as talk and listen to each other. In both cases, documents may be transmitted by the facsimile method, to supplement the proceedings.

Electronic Spreadsheets. Software packages, such as Lotus 1-2-3, VisiCalc, Calcstar, and SuperCalc, permit a variety of data to be displayed on the microcomputer screen in columns and rows. The user can change any particular item and see, almost instantaneously, the effect of the change on all the other items. Such software has proven extremely useful for accounting and other "what if" applications such as cost projections and sales forecasts.

Database Programs. Such programs enable the user to establish a data base (for example, of items stocked in a store), access it as required, and draw data from it, summarized and sorted at will.

Integrated Software. Newer software programs, such as Jazz, Symphony, and Framework, combine in one package the spreadsheet, word processing, and data base management features offered separately in other software packages.

Computer Monitoring. Nowadays more and more firms are using computers to monitor the job performance of their employees. Such electronic surveillance is to be found in, for example, the telephone industry, hotels, clerical offices (e.g. insurance), supermarkets, and mail-sorting centres. Thus the cleaners in a hotel may now be required to tap a code number into the bedside push-button telephone when they start and finish the cleaning of a room so that the hotel computer can record their work time and compare it with company-set standards.

KEY TERMS

Program

Analysing

Networks

Word processing

Programming	Electronic filing
Structured programming	Data base
Systems flow chart	Electronic mail
Programming flow chart	Facsimile
Branching	Electronic conferencing
Pseudocode	Teleconferencing
Real code	Electronic spreadsheets
HIPO chart	Database programs
COBOL	Integrated software
FORTRAN	

Review Questions

1. What is a computer "program"? What are the two basic types?
2. List and briefly explain the various steps involved in preparing a computer program.
3. Distinguish between a systems flow chart and a programming flow chart.
4. What is "pseudocode"? Why is it used? By whom?
5. What is a HIPO chart?
6. What features do modern word processing programs contain? How are they used in business?
7. How does elecronic filing differ from the traditional method?
8. What is electronic mail? Why is it becoming popular in the modern office?
9. Explain the various types of electronic conferencing. How are they useful?
10. What is an electronic spreadsheet? For what business purposes could it be used?
11. What is a Database program? For what business purposes can it be used?
12. What is meant by "integrated software"?
13. What is computer monitoring? Why is it a controversial development? In your answer, explain the viewpoint of both the employer and the employee.

CASE PROBLEM

RAYBURN INDUSTRIES LTD.
Problems in using a computer for inventory control

To the Shareholders:
Since introducing computer facilities into the Northview Division in the middle of last year, we have had difficulty determining monthly profits realistically for this division. This is because reports always showed inventory amounts higher

than actually turned out to be the case when year-end physical inventories were counted. We have not encountered these problems in our other operating divisions where inventories have always been, and still are, controlled manually. Nor did we have these problems in Northview before introducing the computer.

Not once since the installation of the computer have Northview's records been correct in its inventories without a physical count. The records have always shown a higher amount of inventory than actual. It is obvious that this type of problem causes misinformation and leads to inefficient operations. For this reason we are disposing of the computer and going back to a manual system.

Physical inventories were counted as of June 30, of this year, and revealed an overstatement of inventories in the records of some $250,000 at Northview. This overstatement has been adjusted in the records at June 30, to agree with the results of the physical count at that date. Henceforth, inventory will be counted at the end of every quarter in each division of the company prior to the issue of quarterly reports until we are satisfied that book records are under control and properly reflect the actual inventory on hand.

Although results for the first half of this year are disappointing, they are an improvement over last year. We expect to continue this improvement in the second half of this year provided the economy holds up.

August 26, 198–

A.B. Smith
President

Assignment
1. Why would a firm wish to use a computer to keep count of its inventories?
2. What information would the computer require? How could it receive this information?
3. What might have gone wrong in this firm?

INDEX OF CASE PROBLEMS

ABC Enterprises Inc. 478
Ace Record Company Inc. 460
Alford and Wells, T.V. Repairs 76
Anderson Lumber Co. Ltd. 292
Bentley Shoes Ltd. 248
Blake Uniform Rental Company Ltd. (1) 461
Blake Uniform Rental Company Ltd. (2) 478
Bolton's Photo Studio 77
Britanis, S.S. 36
Brock Machine Works 277
Brown Manufacturing Industries Limited 532
Campbell Stores Ltd. 183
Choosing a Business 623
Cliff Reed Real Estate Ltd. 440
Complaints About a New Car 46
Cooper Metal Co. Ltd. 45
Dunn Products Inc. 343
Economy Diaper Service Ltd. 355
Excelsior Products Ltd. 515
Fairview Stores Ltd. 142
Finch Commercial Stationery Ltd. 304
Fox, J., & Son Ltd. 493
Frost Electrical Co. Ltd. 601
George Andrews Ltd. 402
George Sharpe & Company Ltd. 151
Hastings Lodge 116
Harper W., & Son Ltd. 391
Jack Stoddart 621
Jane Appleby 437
John Pieters, Builder 101
Jones Furniture Co. Ltd. (1) 128
Jones Furniture Co. Ltd. (2) 567
Jones T., & Co. Ltd. 659
King Electric Ltd. 300
Landing Rights 35
Log Cabin, The 621
Long-Life Orange Juice 343
Mallory Soups 284
Maskow Enterprises Ltd. 517
McCowan Bakeries 341
Mercedes-Benz 426
Miller Drugs Inc. 182
Mitchell Electrical Industries Limited 525
Motor Specialty Manufacturers (Ont.) Ltd. 33
Pohlmann Equipment Co. Ltd. 197
Rayburn Industries Ltd. 689
Redirack Industries Limited 35
Save-More Ltd. 302
Security Finance Company Ltd., The 568
Sherbluk Manufacturing Industries Ltd. 47
Smith's Meat Market 400
Snow White Ltd. 34
Spee-Dee Fire Extinguisher, The 374
Swansea Steel Products Ltd. 277
Toy Shop, The 76
Tropical Products Ltd. 417
Vetch Office Furniture and Supplies 57
Weeks Farms Ltd. 329
Whitby Chemicals Inc. 90
William Spencer Ltd. 479
XYZ Consumer Products Ltd. 342

INDEX OF READINGS

Aesthetic Entrepreneur, The 90
Aloro Foods 648
Attic's At the Top 463
Business That Beer Built, The 363
Cartons, Bubbles and Boxes: Just Promotional Tools? 331
Champion Launches Sales Offensive 662
Crisis of Identity 405
David Confronts Goliath in Attempt to Win Piece of Glass Fibre Market 249
Deli Way, The 408
Diners Cheer as a New P.E.I. Industry Flexes Its Mussels 329
Distinctions Between Capitalist, Worker Blurred at Trent Rubber Services 581
Electronics Put Small Nova Scotia Town on the Map 651
Entrepreneur Blames Investment Community for Company's Misfortune 480
Everything's Coming Up Blueberries 262
Fast Footwork Wins Big Bouts for Jimmy Pattison 111
Franchises Attracting Growing Numbers of Would-be Private Businessmen 625
From Wrecks to Riches 12
Hidden Dollars in Distribution, The 375
Iron Will of Harry Steele, The 211
Japanese Fix, The 225
King of the Real Estate Jungle 199
Little Pizza That Could, The 544
Lord of the Rinks 130
Love for Sale 344
Newfoundland's Helicopter King 58
Our Human Resources Plan Works 571
Pizza with Pizzazz 409
Popcorn Explosion 143
Rewards of Running Your Own Show, The 154
Supermarket Socialism 117
Swallowed Alive 107
There's Money in Boats 308
Turfed Out? Why Not Try Nelson Adam's Fast-Growing Product: Instant Grass 285
Where There's Paint There's Profit for Students — and College Pro 623
Why John Voortman's Muffins Sell Like Hot Cakes in the U.S. 315
Women: The Best Entrepreneurs 78
Zero-Base Budgeting Technique Seems Certain to Spread 451

SUBJECT INDEX

ABC inventory classification, 295
Accident prevention, 41, 609
Accountability, 192
Account executive, 424, 538
Accounting period, 454
Accounts receivable, 496-97
Acid-test ratio, 477
Active partner, 64
Administration, 127
Advertising, 326, 417-25
   kinds of, 417-18
   preparation of, 422-23
   purposes of, 418
   quality of, 21-22
Advertising agency, 423-25
Advertising budget, 139
Advertising department, 425
Advertising media, 419-21
   choosing, 422
Administration, defined, 127
Administrative expenses, 454
After-sales service, 416
Agent middlemen, 368, 387-88
   use of by producers, 369-70
Agriculture, 633
Analysing, 684-85
Analytical process, 240
Anti-dumping duty, 655
Appraisal of managers, 170
Apprenticeship training, 558-59, 609
Arbitration, 597
Arithmetic-logic unit, 672, 675
Assembly process, 240
Assets, 510
Auction companies, 388
Audio conference, 688
Audio response unit, 682
Audiovisual conference, 688
Auditing, 88
Auditor, 88
Auditor's report, 87
Authority, 192
Automated assembly, 245

Automatic teller machine, 679
Automation, 243
Automobile insurance, 505
Auxiliary storage, 673, 682
Averaging, 542

Babbage, Charles, 208
Backward integration, 103
Balance sheet, 510-11, 634-35
Bank draft, 486
Bank loans, 488-90
Bank money order, 486
Bank Rate, 43
Bank statement, 474
Banker's acceptance, 487
Bar code reader, 679
Batch manufacturing, 240
Batch processing, 675
Bear market, 542
Bearer bond, 531
Big business, reasons for growth of, 102-104
Bill of exchange, 665
Bill of lading, 487, 665
Bill of materials, 289
Binary code, 674
Blacklist, 599
Blue chip stocks, 542
Blueprints, 289
Board lot, 541
Board of directors, 146
Bond certificate, 528, 529
Bond indenture, 527, 528
Bonds:
   buying, 541-43
   defined, 527
   secured, 528, 530
   unsecured, 530
Bond trading process, 540-41
Bond trustees, 527
Book value of share, 520
Borrowing proposal, 629-30
Boycott, 599

Branching, 685
Brand, 7, 322
Break-even analysis, 454-58, 616
Break-even chart, 456
Break-even point, 455, 456, 457-58, 628, 629
Brokers, 387
Bubble memory, 675
Budget, 139
Budgetary process, 447, 449
Bull market, 542
Bumping, 563
Business corporation, 82
Business Corporations Acts, 42
Business ethics, 30-31
Business insurance, 499-505
Business interruption insurance, 504-505
Business management, 122-71
  defined, 123
  levels of, 124-25
Business organization, 172-99
Business plan, 628-30
Business Practices Act, 40
Business records, 634-37
Business risk, 499
Buying, 325
  on margin, 538
Buying motives, 351-52
Buy-sell agreement, 504
Bylaws, 86

CAD/CAM, 245
Callable (or redeemable) shares, 522
Call price, 530
Canada Business Corporations Act, 84-85
Canada Development Corporation, 514
Canada Labour Code, 605-606
Canada Pension Plan, 41, 607
Canadian Federation of Independent Business (CFIB), 619-20
Canadian Labour Congress (CLC), 593, 594
Candat, 540
Capital account, 643

Capital budget, 139, 449
Capital stock, 518
Cartels, 106
CASE, 631
Cash-and-carry wholesaler, 386
Cash budget, 139, 162, 475-76
Cash flow, 459, 474, 616
Cash-flow forecast, 629
Cash-flow statement, 474-75
Cash management, 474-77
Cathode ray tube (CRT), 681
Celebrity advertising, 418
Centralization, 193
Centralized management, 193-94
Centralized purchasing, 296
Central processing unit (CPU), 671, 672, 674-75
Certification, of a union, 594
Certified cheque, 486
CFIB, 619-20
Channels of distribution, 324, 367-72
Chartered banks, 494. See also entries beginning with: "Bank".
Chattel mortgage, 528, 530
Check off, of union dues, 595
Cheque, 485-86
Circulation, 422
Closed shop, 596
COBOL, 685
Co-insurance clause, 501-502
Collateral, 489, 496-98
Collateral relationships, 187
Collateral trust bond, 530
Colleague relationships, 187
Collective bargaining, 594-95
COM, 682
Combination store, 394
Combines Investigation Act, 19, 20, 38, 397
Commission, 576-77
Commission merchants, 387-88
Committee system, 174
Committees, use of, 188-89
Common law duties, of employer and employee, 604
Common shares, 520-21

Community protection, 41
Competition, 5-8, 338
Composite sales estimate, 137
Computer hardware, 672-82
Computer integrated manufacturing, 245
Computer monitoring, 688
Computers:
   basic types of, 671-72
   benefits of, 672
   business applications of, 685, 687-88
   operation of, 673-74
   software for, 684-89
Computer systems:
   business applications of, 399, 685, 687-88
   characteristics of, 671
Conciliation, 595
Conditional sales contract, 490
Conditioning process, 240
Conglomerate, 104, 195
Consignment, 486
Consular invoice, 665
Consumer advertising, 418
Consumer goods, 359-61
Consumer-oriented approach, 319
Consumer Packaging and Labelling Act, 39
Consumer profile, 337, 349
Consumer protection, 37-40
Consumer Protection Act, 40
Consumer Reporting Act, 40
Consumer, responsibilities of firm to, 19-22
Consumers' co-operative, 114, 396
Consumer services, 361
Consumer's freedom of choice, 9-10
Consumer usage pattern, 352
Contests, 415
Continuous-flow manufacturing, 242
Continuous-line layout, 252-53, 254
Continuous-line manufacturing, 242
Contract purchasing, 298
Controllable factors, 336
Controller, 446
Controlling, 162-65

Control unit, 675
Convenience goods, 360
Convenience store, 393
Convertibility, 522, 530
Convertible preferred share, 522
Co-operative membership, advantages of, 389-90
Co-operatives, 114-15
Co-ordinated local purchasing, 296-97
Co-ordination, 150
   principles of, 150
Copywriters, 424
Corporate chain in retailing, 396
Corporate form of ownership:
   advantages of, 97-99
   disadvantages of, 99-100
Corporate mortgage bond, 528
Corporation, *See also* Incorporation.
   long-term financing for, 513
   owner's equity in, 511
Correlation analysis, 336
Correspondent bank, 665
Cost accounting, 162
Cost ratios, 162-63
Coupon bond, 531
Coupons, 415
CPU, 671
Craft union, 588
Credit, 399, 414
Credit insurance, 503
Credit terms, 485
Credit union, 396
Criminal Code, 39
Critical path, 165
CRT, 681
Cumulative shares, 522
Current account, 643, 644
Current assets, 477, 510
Current liabilities, 477, 510
Current ratio, 477
Custom manufacturing, 240, 243
Customer services, 416
Customs delays, 656

Daisy-wheel printer, 680
Data base, 687

Database programs, 688
Dating, 485
Debentures, 530
Debt financing, 509, 527-31
Debugging, 684, 685
Decentralization:
    of authority, 194, 619
    of retailing, 399
Decentralized management, 194-96
Decentralized purchasing, 296
Dedicated word processor, 687
Delegation of authority, 193
Demand loan, 488-89
Demand note, 488, 489
Departmentation, 175-76
Department of Regional Industries
    Expansion (DRIE), 514
Department store, 393
Depreciation allowances, 523-24
Deviations, 164-65
Direct distribution, 368-69, 371
Direct export, 372, 653
Directing, 145-50
Direction, principles of, 145-46
Directly chartered local unions, 589
Direct mail, 420
Directors of a corporation, 85-87
    powers of, 86
Direct selling, 395
Discipline, 147-48
Discount house, 394, 398-99
Discounting, 490-91, 665
Dismissals, 563
Dispatching, 287, 290, 291
Dissolution, of a sole proprietorship, 53
Distribution channels, 324, 367-72
Distribution research, 654
Diversified purchasing, 298
Dividends, 520
Dividing, 322
Documentary drafts, 664-65
Documenting, 685
Documents on payment, 664-65
Domestic consumer market, 349-52
Donoghue v. Stevenson, 40
Dot-matrix printer, 680

Drop shipper, 386
Drucker, Peter, 210
Durable consumer goods, 359

Ease of expansion, 260
Economic-lot quantity, 287
Economic ordering quantity
    (E.O.Q.), 295
Economies of scale, 103
Education, 29
EDP, 399, 670-89
Electric power, 243-44, 259-60
Electronic conferencing, 687-88
Electronic filing, 687
Electronic mail, 687
Electronic spreadsheets, 688
Electronic ticker, 539-40
Electronic workstation, 682
Emergency goods, 360
Emotional advertising, 418
Employees:
    records and statistics on, 564
    social responsibilities of, 27-28
    sources of, 556
Employment inventory, 555
Employment planning, 554-56
Employment policy, 43
Employment Standards Act (Ontario),
    41, 607
Endorsement advertising, 418
Endorsement, in insurance, 500
Enterprise Development Program
    (EDP), 632
Entertainment, and business, 29
Entrepreneurship, 126-27
Environment, 30
Equal opportunity, 27
Equal pay, 608-609
Equipment trust certificates, 528, 530
Equity (or net worth), 510-11
Equity-debt ratio, 509
Equity financing, 509, 518-27
Ethics, in business, 30-31
Exchange controls, 656
Exclusive distribution agreement, 370
Executive vice-president, 124

Export agent, 372, 388
Export barriers, 655-56
Export commission house, 372
Export Development Corporation (EDC), 667-68
Exporter's Directory, 657
Export financing, 664-68
Exporting, 640-68
Export marketing, 653-58
Export markets, 353-54, 642-43
  distribution to, 372
Export merchant, 372
Export organization, 653
Export promotion, 656-57
Export research, 653-55
Exports, principal, 642
Extraction process, 239

Facsimile, 686
Factor companies, 491
Factor comparison, 574-75
Factors of production, 123
Fair employment practices, 608
Fair price, 19-20
Fair rate of return, 4-5
Fair wages policy, 23, 606
False advertising, 39
Farm Improvement Loans Act, 633
Fayol, Henri, 207-208
Federal Business Development Bank (FBDB), 496, 631
Feed-back, in automation, 243
Fidelity bond, 503
Field, 682
Finance company loans, 490-91
Finance department, 281, 283, 445-47
  organization of, 446-47, 448
Finance-lease agreement, 514
Financial co-operatives, 115
Financial instruments, 535
Financial leverage, 512
Financial management, tasks of, 445
Fire insurance, 500-502
First-line management, 125
Fiscal policy, 43
Fiscal year, 454

Fisheries Improvement Loans Act, 633
Fixed assets, 510
  as collateral, 498
Fixed capital, 629
Fixed costs, 455
Fixtures, 259
Flexibility in building design, 260
Flexible working hours, 579
Floor traders, 535
Floppy disk drive, 676
Flow chart, 685, 686
Flow diagram, 258
Follow-up, of new employee, 559
Follow-up, in production control, 287, 290, 291
Foreclosure proceedings, 528
Foreign suppliers, 645-46
Foreign visits, 654-55
FORTRAN, 685
Forward integration, 103
Four Ps of marketing, 319-20
Franchises, 617-18
Freedom of choice, 9-10
Freight forwarder, 653
Fringe benefits, 23, 577
Full-service wholesalers, 386
Functional authority, 188
Functional plan of organization, 188, 189
Fundamentals of selling, 431

Gantt, Henry L., 209
GATT, 655
General merchandise wholesalers, 386
General partnership, 64
General-purpose machines, 259
General store, 392
Gentlemen's agreements, 106
Gilbreth, Frank and Lillian, 209
Goodwill, after the sale, 432
Go-slow strike, 597
Government agencies, as sources of long-term funds, 514
Government assistance to small business, 631-34
Government intervention, 36-43
Government market, 353

Government purchasing policies, 656
Government users, distribution to, 371-72
Grading, of products, 321
Graphics display terminal, 681
Grievance procedure, 596-97
Group dynamics, 168-69, 222
Group leader, 222

Hard disk drive, 676
Hardware, 672-82
Hawthorne experiments, 219
Health and safety, 564, 609
Health and social welfare, 29
Heating, 260
Hierarchy of needs, 220
HIPO chart, 685
Holding company, 104
Holidays, 609-610
Hollerith Code, 676
Horizontal merger, 104
Hours of work, 608
Human relations approach to management, 218-23
Human Rights Code (Ont.), 41

Imperfect competition, 7
Import agents, 388
Import quotas, 656
Imports, 645
Impulse goods, 360
In-basket exercise, 169
Income statement, 454, 635
Income tax, 632-33
Incorporation:
    advantages of, 97-99
    disadvantages of, 99-100
    requirements for, 83
    systems of, 82, 83
Independent local organizations, 588
Independents, in retailing, 395
Indirect export, 372, 653
Induction, 557, 558
Industrial advertising, 418
Industrial channels, 371
Industrial distributors, use of, 371

Industrial goods, 361-62
Industrial purchasing, 296
Industrial relations, 606
Industrial union, 588
Industrial user market, 352-53
Informal organization, 178
Informative advertising, 418
Injunction, 599
Input devices, 672-73, 674, 675-80
Inspection department, 306-307
Inspection forms, 290
Inspection, types, of, 307-308
Institutional advertising, 418
Insurance adjuster, 500
Insurance co-operatives, 115
Insurance plans, 579-80
Insurance policy, 500
Integrated software, 688
Inter-group behaviour, 222-23
International trade, 641-47
International unions, 588
Inventories, as collateral, 497
Inventory control, 293-95
Inventory turnover ratio, 163-64
Investment dealer, 513
Invisible trade, 643

Jigs, 259
Job:
    analysis, 555
    classification, 574
    description, 555
    evaluation, 574-75
    ranking, 574
    satisfaction, 26-27
    security, 24-25
    specification, 556
Job-order manufacturing, 243
Joint and several liability, 73
Journals of business, 636-37
Jurisdictional strike, 597

Keyboard terminal, 672, 675, 677
Key boxes, 541
Key-personnel insurance, 503-504
Key to storage unit, 675

SUBJECT INDEX 699

Labour defined, 8
Labour councils, 593
Labour federations, 593-94
Labour jurisdiction, 604-605
Labour legislation, 41, 604-610
Labour relations, 586-610
Labour Relations Act (Ont.), 41
Labour-saving equipment, 25-26
Labour standards, 605
Labour unions, 588-96
    aims of, 589-96
    certifications of, 594
    finances, 595
    membership, 589, 590
    organization of, 591-93
    security, 595-96
    types of, 588-89
Laissez-faire, 36
Land, defined, 8
Late tape, 540
Layoffs, 25, 562-63
Layout, 423
Leadership, 148-49
Ledger accounts, 635-36
Letter of credit, 665-67
Letters patent, 83
Liabilities, 510
Liability insurance, 503
Light pen, 678
Limited liability, 98
Limited partnership, 64
Limited-service wholesalers, 386-87
Line- and staff organization, 174, 186-88
Line of credit, 488
Line organization, 174, 185-86
Line personnel, 186
Line printer, 680-81
Liquidation, sharing assets on, 521, 522
Liquidity, 510, 543
Liquidity ratios, 477
Listed stock, 536
Local advertising, 418
Local, of labour union, 591-93
Lockout, 599
Long-range plan, 138
Long-term financing, 508-543

Long-term funds, 514
Long-term liability, 510
Loss-leaders, 324

Machine-data cards, 258
Magazines, 419
Magnetic disk, 676
Magnetic tape drive, 676
Mail-order house, 394-95
Mainframes, 671
Management:
    by exception, 165
    by objectives, 210
    functions of, 125
    information systems, 165, 672
    theories of, 205-35
    trainee, 167-68
    training techniques, 168-69
Managerial method, 125
Manufacturer's agents, 387
Manufacturer's brand, 322
Manufacturing:
    defined, 239
    types of, 239-47
Manufacturing order, 290
Manufacturing processes, 239-40
Marine insurance, 502
Market grid, 350
Market research, 320, 654
Market segments, 349
Market share, 136-37
Market value, of share, 518
Marketing, 319
    agents, 368, 369-70, 387-88
    boards, 370-71
    concept, 319
    co-operatives, 114, 389-90
    department, 281, 282, 332-40
    intermediaries, 368
    manager, 332
    mix, 319-20
    need for, 326-27
    plan, 337-38
    policy, 139-40
Markets, types of, 349-54
Mark-sense card, 677

Maslow, A. H., 220
Mass production, 240, 242
Masterfile, 682
Materials handling equipment, 259
Materials requisition form, 290
Maternity leave, 580
Matrix organization, 189-90, 191
Mayo, Elton, 219-20
McClelland, David C., 220-21
McGregor, Douglas, 223
Mechanization, 243
Media director, 424
Medium-term financing, 494-98
Memorandum of association, 82
Merchant wholesalers, 368, 386-87
Merger, 37, 104
Merit, 560
Merit rating, 560-61
Methods analysis, 267
Microcomputers, 671-72, 687
Micromotion analysis, 271
Middle management, 125
Middleman, 368
Minicomputers, 671
Minimum age for employment, 608
Minimum wage rates, 607-608
Ministry of Industry, Trade, and Technology (Ontario), 633
Misleading advertising, 21-22, 39
Missionary salespeople, 430
Monetary policy, 43
Monopolistic competition, 7
Monopoly, 5, 7, 37
Mortgage, 528, 530
Motion economy, principles of, 272-73
Motion study, 209, 267, 269-72
Motivation, 146-47
Mouse, 678
Move orders, 290
MTM (Methods-Time Measurement), 276
Multinational corporations, 104-105
Multiple-activity analysis, 271

National advertising, 418
National unions, 588

Net working capital, 483
Networks, 672, 685
Net worth of business, 635
Newspapers, 419
Newsprint production, 241
Non-cumulative shares, 522
Non-durable consumer goods, 359-60
No-name products, 322, 399
Non-monetary factors in management, 460
Non-price competition, 7-8
Non-tariff barriers, 656
No-par value, 518
Notice of dismissal, 609
Notification plan, 497

Objectives of a business firm, 135-37
Occupational Health and Safety Act (Ontario), 41, 609
Odiorne, George S., 210
Oligopoly, 7, 105-106
Open-book accounts, 485, 664
Open shop, 596
Operating budget, 139, 162, 447
    purposes of, 449
Operation analysis, 271-72
Operations research, 654
Operator-machine analysis, 271
Optical character recognition device, 679
Optical mark reader, 679
Optical scanner, 679
Order-getting, 430
Order-taking, 430
Organization:
    basic types of, 185-90
    principles of effective, 179-80
Organizational design, 178-79
Organization chart, 176, 177, 178
Organization manual, 176, 178
Organization structure, 176
Outdoor advertising, 420-21
Output devices, 673, 680-82
Overdraft, 489
Over-the-counter market, 540-41
Overtime, 575
Owner's equity, 510-11

Package advertising, 421
Packaging, 322
Page printer, 681
Participating preferred share, 522
Participation rate, 43
Partners, types of, 64-65
Partnership, 64-74
   advantages of, 71-72
   agreement, 68, 70-71
   balance sheet, 511
   disadvantages of, 72-74
   dissolution of, 69
   formation of, 64
   insurance, 504
   long-term financing for, 513
   name, 65
Par value, of share, 518
Payback period, 459
Pay policy, 574
Pension plans, 579
Peripherals, 672-73
Personal banking machine, 679-80
Personal covenant, 489
Personal guarantee, 489
Personal selling, 430
Personnel department, 554, 565-566
Personnel management, defined, 553
Personnel manager, 564-65
Personnel policy, 140, 553-54
Personnel services, 563-64
P.E.R.T., 165
Pickets, 597-98
Piece wages, 576
Place utility, 324
Planning, 135-41
   defined, 135
Plans of a company, 138-40
Plant buildings, 260-61
Plant closures, 26
Plant equipment, 259-60
Plant layout:
   aids in, 258-59
   factors influencing, 256, 258
   purposes of, 252
   types of, 252-56
Point-of-purchase advertising, 421

Points system, 575
Policies, of a company, 139-40
Predatory pricing, 38
Predetermined time standards, 275-76
Preferred shares, 521-22
Premiums, 415, 500
President, 124
Pre-testing, 655
Price, 322-24, 397
   competition in, 5
   discrimination in, 37-38
   for export, 655
   fixing of, 37
   misrepresentation in, 38
   suggested retail prices, 397
Primary data, 137, 350
Primary industries, 239
Prime rate of interest, 490
Printers for computer systems, 680-81
Prior deposits, 656
Private brands, 322
Private business corporations, 82
Private enterprise, 3
Private ownership, 4
Private placement, in financing, 514
Procedures, 140
Process analysis, 267-69
Process charts, 258, 267, 268, 269
Producers' co-operative, 389
Product:
   advertising, 418
   defined, 337
   design, 283-84
   development, 103
   differentiation, 7
   division, 333, 334
   image, 337
   quality, 20-21
   research, 654
Production control, 286-91
   purpose of, 286
Production control department, 288
Production department, 280-81, 283
Production equipment, 259
Production policy, 140
Production run, size of, 240, 242

Production study, 274-75
Productivity, 245-47
  factors affecting, 246-47
Productivity bonus, 578
Product life, 338
Product life-cycle, 338-39
Product line, 337-38
Product planning and development (PPD), 280-84, 320
Product policy, 139, 280
Product preference, 352
Product warranties, 414
Profit, 4-5
Profitability, evaluating, 454-60
Profitability ratios, 163
Profit centre, 195
Profit motive, 5
Profit-sharing plans, 577-78
Pro forma financial statements, 629
Program, 671, 684-85
Programming, 685
Programming flow chart, 685, 686
Projected sales, 162
Project management, 190
Promissory notes, 488
Promotion, 169-70, 325-26, 560-62
Promotion blend, 413-14
Promotional program, 413-17
Prospectus, 522-23
Provincial Development Corporations, 633-34
Provincial labour legislation, 41, 607-610
Proxy, 84
Pseudocode, 685
Public business corporations, 82
Publicity, 413
Public relations, 413
Pull or push promotional strategies, 414
Punched card reader, 676-77
Purchase leaseback agreement, 514
Purchase order, 298-99
Purchase requisition, 298
Purchasing:
  department, 296
  manager, 296
  policies, 297-98
  policy, 140
  procedure, 298-99

Quality circles, 267, 306
Quality control, 304-308
Quality of product, 20-21
Quality standards, 305-306
Quick-asset ratio, 163, 477

Rack jobber, 387
Radio 420
Rand formula, 596
Rational advertising, 418
Ratios, financial, 162-63, 616
Real code, 685
Real estate mortgage, 528
Receiving report, 299
Reciprocal purchasing, 298
Recruitment:
  of employees, 556-57
  of managers, 166
  program, 166-67
Redeemability, 522, 530
Registration, of partnership, 65-67
Registration system, 82-83
Repetitive advertising, 418
Request for quotation, 298
Resale price maintenance, 38
Resident buyer, 372
Responsibility, 192. *See also* Social responsibilities.
Restrictive trade practices, 37-38
Right to choose one's job, 8-9
Right to employ productive resources, 8
Retail co-operatives, 396
Retailer, 368
  services provided by, 396-97
  types of, 392-95
  use of, by producers, 369
Retailing, 368, 392-99
  high entry and dropout rates, 397-98
  trends, 398-99
Retail ownership, 395-96
Retail prices, 397
Retained earnings, 523
Retraining, 559

Return on capital, 458-59
Return on investment, 136
Rider, 500
Rights:
    of individuals and firms, 8-10
    shareholders', 521
Robotics, 245
Route sheet, 289
Routing, 287, 289, 290
Rules, 140

Sabotage, 599
Safety of employees, 605-606
Safety Standards Act, 39
Safety stock, 295
Salary, 576
Sale of Goods Act, 40
Sales:
    aids, 415-16
    forecast, 137, 335-36
    franchise, 370
    manager, 332, 433-37
    organization, 434
    promotion, 412-37
    ratios, 163
    special, 414-15
Samples, 415
Scale-model layouts, 258-59
Scanlon plan, 578
Scheduled purchasing, 298
Scheduling, in production, 287, 289-90, 290-91
Scientific management, 208-10
Secondary data, 137, 350
Secondary industries, 239
Secretary-treasurer, 124-25, 446-47
Secret partner, 65
Secured bonds, 528, 530
Secured loan, 489
Securities market, 535-43
Securities legislation, 541
Self-service retailing, 398
Selling, 326, 430-37
    exports, 657-58
Selling agents, 371, 387

Selling expenses, 454
Selling jobs, 432-33
Selling process, 430-32
Selling short, 543
Seniority, 561-62
Serial bonds, 530
Serial printer, 680
Service co-operatives, 115, 389
Service equipment, 259-60
Several liability, 73
Shareholder, 518
    rights of, 84-85
Shareholder protection, 41-42
Shareholder loans, 491
Share value, 518, 520
Sharing assets on liquidation, 521, 522
Sharing profits, 520-21, 521-22
Shop layout, 253, 255
Shopping goods, 360
Shop steward, 592
Short-range plan, 138
Short-term financing, 483-92
Short-term money market, 491
Sick-leave, 580
Sight draft, 487-88, 665
Silicon chip, 675
Simo chart, 271
Single-line store, 393
Single-line wholesalers, 386
Single-storey buildings, 260-61
Single-use plans, 140
Sinking-fund bond, 530
Sitdown strike, 597
Skim-the-cream pricing, 323
Sleeping partner, 65
Small business, 612-37
    government assistance to, 631-34
    guidelines for success in, 618-19
    importance of, 613
    opportunities in, 614-15
Small business tax deduction, 632-33
Small Businesses Loans Act, 495-96, 632
Small-business ownership: pros and cons of, 613-14
Smith, Adam, 36, 208
Socially acquired motives, 220-21

Social responsibilities:
   of the business firm, 18-31
   of employees, 27-28
Sociogram, 222
Software, 684-89
Sole proprietorship, 51-55
   advantages of, 51-53
   disadvantages of, 53-55
   long-term financing for, 513
Solvency ratios, 163
Span of control, optimum, 179
Specialization in manufacturing, 244
Special-purpose machines, 259
Specials, in retailing, 415
Specialty advertising, 421
Specialty goods, 360-61
Specialty shop, 393
Specialty wholesalers, 386
Specifications, 289
Speculative purchasing, 297-98
Sponsor, 417
Staffing, 166-70
Staff personnel, 187
Staff specialists, 174
Standard costs, 162
Standardization, 244, 320-21
Standard manufacturing, 243
Standing plans, 139
Staple goods, 360
Stationary product layout, 255-56
Stock bonus, 579
Stockbrokers, 535
Stockbroker's office, 539-40
Stock certificate, 519
Stock dividends, 520
Stock exchanges, 535-37
   Toronto Stock Exchange, 535, 536-37
Stockholder, 518
Stock option, 579
Stock quotations, 537, 538
Stock ratios, 163
Stocks, 535
   buying, 541-43
Stock split, 521
Stock-trading process, 538-39
Storage unit, 675

Storing, 325
Strike, 597-99
Sub-system, 223
Suggested retail prices, 397
Sundry assets, 510
Supercomputers, 671
Supermarket, 394
Supervisors, behaviour of, 222
Supervisory management, 125
Supervisory training, 559
Surety bond, 503
Sympathy strikes, 599
Synchronization in manufacturing, 244
Synthetic process, 240
System, 223
Systems approach, 223-24

Takeover, 104
Target market, 337, 349-50
Tariff, 655
Taylor, Frederick W., 208-209
Technical barriers to exports, 656
Technology, 8, 244-45
Teleconferencing, 688
Television, 420
Template layouts, 258
Term insurance, 504
Term loan, 494
Tertiary industries, 239
Textile Labelling Act, 39
Theft insurance, 502-503
Theory X and Theory Y, 223
Therbligs, 271-72
Three Cs of credit, 489
Time drafts, 486-87, 665
Time off, 580
Time sharing, 673
Time standards, 273
   predetermined, 275-76
Time study, 273-76
Time tickets, 290
Time utility, 325
Time wages, 575-76
Tolerance, 306
Tool analysis, 289
Tool requisition, 290

Top management, 124-25
Touch-sensitive screen, 678
Touch-tone telephone, 678
Trade:
    acceptance, 486-87
    advertising, 418
    channels, 324, 367-72
    commissioners, 653, 655
    credit, 484-88
    fair, 657-58
    mission, 658
    policy, 43
    surplus, 643
    unions, *see* Labour unions.
Trading desks, 540
Trading posts, 536, 537
Training, 558-59
    for the job, 558-59
    of managers, 168-69
    on the job, 558
Transaction file, 682
Transfers, 170, 560
Transportation advertising, 421
Transporting, 325-25
Trend analysis, 335-36
Truck distributor, 387
Trust receipt, 497
Trusts, 106
Turnaround documents, 677

Uncontrollable factors, 336-37
Underwriting, 513
Unemployment insurance, 606-607
Unfair labour practices, 599
Unions, *see* Labour unions.
Union shop, 596
Unity of command principle, 179
Unlimited personal liability, 53-54, 72-73
Unsecured bonds, 530
Unsecured loan, 489
Unsought goods, 361
U.S. market, importance for Canada, 641-42

Vacations with pay, 608
Variable costs, 455
Variety store, 394
Vending machine, 395
Vertical integration, 103
Vertical merger, 104
Vice-president, finance, 446
Virtual storage, 675
Visible trade, 643
Voice recognition unit, 678
Voice store and forward system, 687
Voluntary chains, 396
Voting rights, 520, 521

Wage and salary administration, 573-80
Wages, 22-23
Walkout, 597
Wand reader, 679
Warehouse receipt, 497
Warrant, 521
Warranties, 414
Weekly rest-day, 608
Wholesale co-operatives, 389, 390
Wholesaler, 368
    main kinds of, 386
    services to producers, 388
    services to retailers, 388-89
    use of by producers, 369, 388-89
Wholesaling, 386-90
Wildcat strike, 597
Word-of-mouth advertising, 421
Word processing, 687
Work groups, 221-22
Working capital, 483-84, 629
Working stock, 295
Workers' Compensation, 41, 580, 609
Work-to-rule movement, 597
Workweek, 580
World product mandate, 641

Zero-base budgeting, 450

INDUSTRY'S 500

Rankings 51-100

Rank by sales 1984	1983	Sales or operating revenue $'000	Company (head office)	Rank by assets	Assets $'000	Rank by net income
51	60	1,900,766 [1]	Inco Ltd. (Toronto)	19	4,111,041	423
52	48	1,875,550	F.W. Woolworth Co. (Toronto) Jan./85	120	644,147	78
53	50	1,817,064	Mitsui & Co. (Canada) (Toronto) Mar./85	n.a.	n.a.	294
54	78	1,656,620	Cargill Grain Co. (Winnipeg) May/84	189	332,061	173
55	55	1,646,187	Amoco Canada Petroleum Co. (Calgary)	46	2,077,762	20
56	62	1,622,984	Consolidated-Bathurst Inc. (Montreal)	60	1,675,913	41
57	54	1,613,000	British Columbia Hydro & Power Authority (Vancouver) Mar./84	5	9,593,000	59
58	49	1,610,339	Atco Ltd. (Calgary) Mar./84	29	2,882,057	144
59	57	1,575,400	Suncor Inc. (Toronto)	37	2,385,500	31
60	64	1,570,829	Mobil Oil Canada Ltd. (Toronto)	56	1,716,853	19
61	66	1,522,044 [2]	Alberta Wheat Pool (Calgary) July/84	134	486,215	89
62	56	1,511,537	James Richardson & Sons Ltd. (Winnipeg)	68	1,303,496	398
63	61	1,508,398	Groupe des Epiciers Unis, Métro-Richelieu Inc. (Montreal) Sept./84	238	211,246	326
64	58	1,492,408	Anglo-Canadian Telephone Co. (Montreal)	26	3,284,739	51
65	59	1,490,893	Molson Cos. (Montreal) Mar./84	92	986,689	58
66	53	1,482,640	Alberta & Southern Gas Co. (Calgary)	119	649,430	286
67	63	1,417,708	Canadian General Electric Co. (Toronto)	89	1,017,045	77
68	70	1,412,446	Ultramar Canada Inc. (Toronto)	77	1,188,842	394
69	76	1,367,511	Union Gas Ltd. (Chatham, Ont.) Mar./84	65	1,399,241	53
70	65	1,359,372	Federated Co-operatives Ltd. (Saskatoon) Oct./84	159	406,276	101
71	68	1,283,458	Mitsubishi Canada Ltd. (Vancouver) Mar./84	324	111,950	311
72	71	1,279,965 [2]	United Grain Growers Ltd. (Winnipeg) July/84	168	388,537	202
73	69	1,269,583	Dow Chemical Canada Ltd. (Sarnia, Ont.)	57	1,703,479	304
74	101	1,193,935	Ivaco Inc. (Montreal)	84	1,117,329	95
75	77	1,176,025	CIL Inc. (Toronto)	81	1,156,308	81
76	75	1,170,597	Du Pont Canada Inc. (Montreal)	115	666,866	74
77	79	1,156,877	Co-operative fédérée de Québec (Montreal) Oct./84	221	240,048	178
78	80	1,152,120	Westburne International Industries Ltd. (Calgary) Mar./84	123	630,831	222
79	73	1,147,807	Westcoast Transmission Co. (Vancouver)	55	1,751,781	50
80	97	1,141,774	Rio Algom Ltd. (Toronto)	58	1,697,497	40
81	67	1,140,000	Burns Foods Ltd. (Calgary)	n.a.	n.a.	n.a.
82	85	1,101,171	Great Atlantic & Pacific Co. of Canada (Toronto) Feb./84	241	203,387	163
83	74	1,091,161	Woodward Stores Ltd. (Vancouver) Jan./85	126	577,965	318
84	89	1,084,329	Southam Inc. (Toronto)	109	716,532	67
85	91	1,060,300	British Columbia Resources Investment Corp. (Vancouver)	38	2,359,500	364
86	84	1,029,532	Canfor Corp. (Vancouver)	95	893,975	416
87	88	1,026,654	Consumers Distributing Co. (Toronto) Feb./85	n.a.	n.a.	n.a.
88	98	1,022,985	Jim Pattison Group (Vancouver)	124	604,198	n.a.
89	87	1,014,726	British Columbia Forest Products Ltd. (Vancouver)	76	1,217,173	216
90	83	993,909	K-Mart Canada Ltd. (Brampton, Ont.) Jan./85	133	492,079	189
91	90	978,843	Alberta Government Telephones (Edmonton)	39	2,323,523	191
92	127	961,631	International Harvester Canada Ltd. (Hamilton) Oct./84	184	344,396	352
93	114	940,821	Inter-City Gas Corp. (Winnipeg)	59	1,690,778	111
94	94	938,915	Procter & Gamble Inc. (Toronto) June/84	113	669,455	49
95	86	938,487	Nabisco Brands Ltd. (Toronto)	137	483,059	69
96	96	926,676	Dylex Ltd. (Toronto) Jan./85	145	445,719	73
97	120	902,656	Maclean Hunter Ltd. (Toronto)	100	814,685	62
98	149	886,896	Daon Development Corp. (Vancouver) Oct./84	70	1,292,806	61
99	111	880,446	McDonald's Restaurants of Canada Ltd. (Toronto)	179	370,177	70
100	99	878,966	Rothmans of Pall Mall Canada Ltd. (Toronto) Mar./84	111	675,387	65

[1] All figures converted from US$.

[2] Sales include grain purchases for the account and delivered to the Canadian Wheat Board; assets include grain held for the account of CWB.